Market-Led Strategic Change

Transforming the Process of Going to Market

Second edition

Nigel Piercy

BUTTERWORTH
HEINEMANN

To My wife Nikala and my son Niall

Butterworth-Heinemann
Linacre House, Jordan Hill, Oxford OX2 8DP
A division of Reed Educational and Professional Publishing Ltd

℞ A member of the Reed Elsevier plc group

OXFORD BOSTON JOHANNESBURG
MELBOURNE NEW DELHI SINGAPORE

First published by HarperCollins Publishers Ltd 1991
First published as a paperback edition by
Butterworth-Heinemann 1992
Second edition 1997

British Library Cataloguing in Publication Data
A catalogue record for this book is
available from the British Library
ISBN 0 7506 3285 2

Composition by Genesis Typesetting, Rochester, Kent
Printed and bound in Great Britain by
Biddles Limited, Guildford and King's Lynn

Market-Led Strategic Change

The Marketing Series is one of the most comprehensive collection of books in marketing and sales available from the UK today.

Published by Butterworth-Heinemann on behalf of the Chartered Institute of Marketing, the series is divided into three distinct groups: *Student* (fulfilling the needs of those taking the Institute's certificate and diploma qualifications); *Professional Development* for those on formal or self-study vocational training programmes); and *Practitioner* (presented in a more informal, motivating and highly practical manner for a busy marketer).

Formed in 1911, the Chartered Institute of Marketing is now the largest professional marketing management body in Europe with over 24,000 members and 28,000 students located worldwide. Its primary objectives are focused on the development of awareness and understanding of marketing throughout UK industry and commerce and on the raising of standards of professionalism in the education, training and practice of this key business discipline.

Books in the series

Contents

PART III THE *REAL* ISSUES TO MANAGE IN GOING TO MARKET

PART IV MAKING MARKET STRATEGY HAPPEN

About the author

Nigel Piercy BA, MA, PhD is the Sir Julian Hodge Professor of Marketing and Strategy at Cardiff Business School in the University of Wales, Cardiff. He has also been visiting professor at Texas Christian University, and at the University of California, Berkeley. He has managerial experience in retailing and was in business planning with Amersham International plc. His mother worries that he has not got a 'proper' job yet. He has extensive experience as a consultant and management workshop speaker and facilitator with many organizations throughout the world, specializing in the issues of market strategy planning and implementation. Recent client companies have included: British Telecom, Allied Dunbar, Ford Cellular, AT&T, Honeywell, AIB Group, ICL, Yellow Pages, and other smaller companies. He has worked with managers and management students in the UK, Europe, the USA, the Far East, and South Africa. Professor Piercy has written eight books and some 200 articles and papers published in the management literature throughout the world. Among other awards and prizes, he was the UK Marketing Author of the Year for three years, and has published papers in the *Journal of Marketing*, the *Journal of Advertising*, and the *Journal of Business Research*, as well as writing on management and marketing issues in the *Sunday Times* and the *Independent*.

Preface to the second edition

So, now it is time for *Son of Market-Led Strategic Change* – the new, revitalized and improved product – *Market-Led Strategic Change II* is unleashed on an unsuspecting world! Well, some things have changed and some have not. In the Preface to the first edition of *Market-Led Strategic Change*, I wrote the following:

'The goal of this book is to provide managers with a number of practical new tools for evaluating the marketing performance of their organizations and, as a result of that evaluation, for identifying how best to improve marketing performance.

This goal comes directly from an absolute belief in a number of fundamentals which we should deal with right at the start:

- every organization of every kind has *customers* – even if it is difficult in some cases to decide who they are, that is no excuse for not doing so;
- for all organizations the only thing that really matters at the end of the day is not the technology, or company policies, or computer systems, or products, or even the management and employee development programmes, but *the long-term satisfaction of customers* – this is the only reason for the existence of any organization and the only way it can survive – whether that survival requires volume and profit in the commercial sector, or a different kind of achievement in the 'not-for-profit' sector;
- this means that every organization relies on a *marketing process* to achieve its purposes, but the most important and strategic marketing tasks may be those carried out by chief executives, production executives, accountants, service engineers, human

resource managers, and front-line operatives, rather than by specialist marketing and sales executives;

- the process of marketing goods and services of any kind is incredibly simple in concept or principle, but again and again we have proved, beyond doubt, in organizations, that putting it into practical effect and achieving what we want is excessively difficult;

- the most common reasons why marketing fails in practice are not because of a lack of sophisticated models and analytical techniques, because these are available in plentiful supply – they are to do with muddled and confused management decisions about strategic marketing issues and a lack of real commitment, where it counts most, to make marketing work;

- there is an urgent need to go back to basics and to clarify the important issues to be addressed in how we want people in our organizations to understand the customer and the role of marketing, and the fundamental changes in our organizations, which all too often are urgently required to make it actually happen.'

I stand by those fundamentals for the second edition of this book, which is also aimed at the manager and the teacher, not the academic audience. I made this point about target audience in the first edition. Notwithstanding this statement of positioning, the first edition of the book (and its author!) has been subjected to some considerable vilification and abuse from some business school academics, who appear to feel threatened by the pragmatic stance taken here. Indeed, this has amounted to a form of 'academic stalking' by some individuals, tripping over their beards to leap out from their hiding places to launch further attacks! However, the response from managers and management students has been very positive, and I remain unrepentant for upsetting academics who teach theory which has no practical value to managers.

Changes in the second edition

The revisions made in the second edition of *Market-Led Strategic Change* are first, to reflect changes in thinking and practice since the first edition; and secondly, to respond to feedback from managers and management trainers who have used the book in their companies and development programmes.

The focus of the book has changed from 'marketing' in the conventional sense to an emphasis on the 'process of going to market', partly to reflect the changes in major organizations from Business Process Re-engineering, but more fundamentally to underline the point that customers and how we perform in the market is an issue for *everyone* in the organization, not the concern of the marketing department (if there still is one). The book is aimed at managers, and the goal is to provide them with tools for achieving superior performance in the marketplace.

There is a new chapter concerned with sales management, reflecting the issue of how market strategies can be managed through to the field sales operation. In addition, the emergence of relationship marketing as a useful strategic approach has been adopted in a number of places in the text. The rapid developments in information technology and direct marketing methods have also been incorporated in a number of chapters to reflect changes in these issues. Lastly, the chapter concerned with organization for marketing has been expanded to address the development of new organizational forms and alliances for market strategy, and the growing importance of interfunctional integration in companies.

Also in response to managerial reader feedback, the following things have been changed: the coverage of market strategy has been substantially extended to offer more practical tools for in-company use in identifying a 'Strategic Pathway' in the process of going to market; the coverage of the implementation issue and strategic internal marketing has been integrated into a single chapter; and the somewhat flippant writing in places has been toned down, since it seriously irritated some readers (I admit that I have only partly succeeded on that last point!).

Many readers suggested that case studies would be a useful way for the individual reader to understand better the points being made in the text, and to establish practical benchmarks for working on the important issues in their own companies. Also, for management development and training programmes and business education courses, cases provide a useful device for discussion and analysis. Twelve new and previously unpublished cases have been prepared for the second edition of the book, as follows: *Avis Europe Ltd* – prepared by Lesley Colyer, Vice President – Personnel, Avis Ltd; *CIGNA Employee Benefits*; *Ford Cellular Systems*, prepared by Ian Irving, Ian Irving Associates, Lynda Irvine and myself; *Allied Dunbar*; *IBM (UK)*, prepared by Garry Veale, IBM plc, and Neil Morgan, University of Cambridge; *Virgin*; *Daewoo Cars*; *Trolley Wars*; *British Airways*; The Opus Partnership: *Otis plc* and *Nokia Mobile Phones*, prepared by Noel Austin, OPUS Group; and *Swallows Stores Ltd*, prepared by Lloyd C. Harris, Cardiff Business School.

I am extremely grateful to the individuals who provided this support, both to those who wrote cases themselves and those who contributed insights to the cases I wrote (who are acknowledged at the beginning of each case), and fully acknowledge their substantial contribution to the new book.

Acknowledgements

Many colleagues, industrial contacts, research collaborators, students and others have played a part in shaping the *Market-Led Strategic Change* book, and no attempt can be made to list them all here. I would, however, like to express my continuing gratitude to my friend, Mr William Giles. William taught me much about market planning, and we collaborated in a variety of consultancy projects and article writing. Sadly, William died in 1992. He is greatly and frequently missed for numerous reasons, both personal and professional. I would also like to express my appreciation to David W. Cravens of Texas Christian University, from whom I have learned a great deal in the last several years.

It is also fitting to acknowledge my debt to my friend and mentor, Professor Roger Mansfield, Director of Cardiff Business School. He is the one who managed the growth of Cardiff Business School to its current top ten position in British university business schools, and the development of many careers in the process.

I would like to express gratitude also to Sir Julian Hodge and the Jane Hodge Foundation for the endowment that supports my Chair and my research at Cardiff Business School.

The efforts of my secretary, Kathryn Holman, in sorting out the manuscript for this second edition also deserve many thanks. The proof-reading efforts of Lloyd C. Harris, Ahmad Jamal and Carolyn Strong at Cardiff Business School were greatly valued also.

Lastly, on a personal note, I would like to thank my wife, Nikala, and my son, Niall, for their support and encouragement in my work, and the book is dedicated to them.

Naturally, the shortcomings and limitations of this book, and any errors contained therein, remain the responsibility of the author (until such time as he can find someone else to blame, as he usually does, or so say Nikala and Niall, but what do they know?*).

Nigel Piercy, Cardiff Business School, April 1997

---

* Nikala: More than you think, Champ!

What readers said about Market-Led Strategic Change

'Much is known about good marketing practice, but little is known about how to transform a company into a first-rate marketing company. Nigel Piercy has provided the best guide I've seen to creating a market-led company – replete with worksheets, diagnostics, and many convincing illustrative cases . . . a very useful and readable book that will make a contribution to many companies that manage to read it and act on it.'

Professor Philip Kotler
S. C. Johnson & Son Distinguished Professor of International Marketing, Northwestern University, Evanston, Ill., USA

'Professor Piercy lives up to his promise to provide management with a number of tools and techniques to help implement marketing effectively in their own companies so that customer considerations and satisfaction are put at the top of the management agenda. A very practical manual, full of good useful advice . . . I enjoyed reading it.'

Professor John O'Shaughnessy
Professor of Business, Columbia University, New York, USA

'It is not just the chapter titles which are provocative. The more closely one reads the contents of the individual chapters, it becomes apparent that they constitute a healthy mix of foundation material (informative), well-reasoned questioning of certain heretofore unchallenged assumptions and practices (provocative), and clear directions to managers as to how the content of the individual chapters can be put to use in organizations (instructive) . . . I was looking for new insights, needless to say I was not disappointed . . . an outstanding contribution.'

Professor P. Rajan Varadarajan
Foley's Professor of Marketing, Texas A & M University, College Station, Texas, USA

'I think it's fantastic! It's well-written . . . and talks about what needs to be talked about, which is marketing-as-done, rather than marketing-as-conceived. It will make a big impact on the manager, who can actually use it.'

Professor Thomas V. Bonoma
Professor of Business Administration, Harvard Business School, USA, President and CEO, Benckiser Consumer Products Inc., Germany

'This book is aimed at the reflective practitioner who wants to get things done. It is a management perspective on marketing, where marketing is not just the Marketing and Sales Department but a way of life that permeates every corner of the company. *Market-Led Strategic Change* demonstrates the author's ability to combine systematic analysis with practical advice for action. The book is rich in practical examples from the author's own experience and research.'

Professor Evert Gummesson
Professor of Marketing, University of Stockholm, Sweden

'By now everyone knows (or should know) what marketing *is* and what benefits will accrue to the marketing-oriented organization. The problem is not *WHAT* but *HOW.* Virtually all the recent work on competitiveness and competitive success . . . confirms that "it ain't what you do, it's the way that you do it". In his new pragmatic and practitioner-oriented book Nigel Piercy provides usable insights and advice on *how* to establish, develop, deliver and sustain long-term customer satisfaction which can be the only guaranteed road to survival and success. I will use the book myself both as an educator and a senior manager/company director.'

Professor Michael J. Baker
Professor of Marketing, University of Strathclyde, Scotland, UK

'Once in a while comes a book that is clearly a classic. Nigel Piercy writes for managers responsible for designing and implementing profit-effective strategies – that is, *all* managers. The key is a practical obsession with serving customers, with the creation of long-term customer satisfaction. The ideal of customer-oriented management has long been preached by theoreticians. But in this remarkable book it is now made realistic and actionable. No marketing manager can afford to be without this book. Nor can any non-marketing manager.'

Professor Gordon R. Foxall
Professor of Consumer Policy, Birmingham Business School, UK

'I have always enjoyed reading what Nigel Piercy has to say about marketing, because he always has something interesting and useful to say. This book is no exception. It is creative, original, punchy, practical, challenging, thought-provoking, actionable, and a very enjoyable read to boot. I shall definitely be recommending it to as many people as possible. It will make an enormous contribution to marketing practice.'

Professor Malcolm McDonald
Professor of Marketing Planning, Cranfield School of Management, UK

'British business has been in search of the customer-driven organization for three decades. This book is an important step forward in the pursuit of this elusive goal . . . There are no quick-fixes in the world of market-led change. This practical book helps lay out a way forward for the manager caught up in the politics of delivering success to his organization.'

David M. Battye
Associate Director, Harbridge House Consulting Group, London, UK.

'There are too many books on marketing theory and too few on how to change the culture of a company to make it market responsive. Nigel Piercy's book is pragmatic and has the whiff of battle and the real world about it.'

Sir John Harvey-Jones
Formerly Chairman, ICI plc, UK

'Essentially management is about change and, for a commercial undertaking, very much about the change necessary to secure and grow markets. Professor Piercy's book *Market-Led Strategic Change* both teaches and reminds us what it takes to develop and deliver that business essential, the marketing plan . . . I very much enjoyed reading the book and I am happy to admit that I learned from it.'

Sir Graham Day
Formerly Chairman, British Aerospace, UK

PART I

The Customer Imperative

CHAPTER 1

Whatever happened to marketing?

It sort of went away into a corner and sulked

Introduction

Without doubt, many people – managers, marketing trainers and business school academics – will suggest that the last thing the world needs right now is yet *another* book about marketing. That is fine. This is a book about the process of going to market, not marketing – the difference is explained shortly. It also sets out to be controversial, not conventional. Partly this is because the book is grounded in work with managers in companies, not in traditional marketing theory – it is sad that these should be such different things, but they are. On these questions there is really quite a lot left to be *said* and even more to be *done*.

'This is a book about the process of going to market, not marketing'

This book is not yet another restatement of the prevailing wisdom, but the fact that there is a 'prevailing wisdom' about marketing is quite clear, and will probably be familiar to executives who have received some conventional business education or training, or have read the standard books, or done any of the other things managers are supposed to do.

There is a small problem with the conventional marketing view of how companies take their products and services to a customer – it assumes and relies on the existence of a world which is alien

3

and unrecognizable to executives who actually have to *manage* such things for real. It rests on implicit assumptions such as the formalization and integration of 'marketing' in an organization, not to mention explicit assumptions that market strategies are specifically formulated and directly lead to related marketing programmes. It assumes that the whole market problem is solved by marketing research to fully understand customers and markets. All these assumptions come from the page of the idealistic, ivory-tower, prescriptive textbook, not the reality as it is perceived, experienced and faced by line executives who have the real problem of managing.

However, perhaps it follows that this present volume is *not* necessarily the first book about the market that the manager should read. Perhaps it is the second. Possibly the manager's approach should be first, to gain an understanding of our conventional knowledge of the marketing variables which are available, and which have to be managed (sketchy though this is in places). This can be gleaned from such classic, conventional works on marketing management as those in the USA by Philip Kotler[1], and John O'Shaughnessy[2], or the fine works published in the UK by Michael Baker[3] or Tom Cannon[4] or Gordon Foxall[5] or David Jobber[6] or David Mercer[7] or Peter Doyle[8], as well as attempts to bridge the gap between US and European approaches to marketing[9]. Then begins the quest for something to make the conventional approach to marketing more realistic and actionable.

The managerial reaction to conventional marketing can be summarized by one executive's remarks to me at a Director's Workshop which I ran for a particular company. After my predictably masterly exposition on the tools of strategic auditing and market strategy models, this particularly ungrateful individual said something like this:

> That is great. I have no quarrel with what you say, there are some things I have learned. But you have told us *what* marketing plans and strategies are, and *what* the tools and techniques are, but not *how* to do it in practice, and definitely not *how* to make it happen in *this* company!

At the time I disagreed. Now I do not. He was right, and this book is an attempt to build a systematic attack on precisely the problems he foresaw – the problems of making the things that matter in the market happen in a company. Such are the seedy origins of what follows.

In fact, this is 'son-of' *Market-Led Strategic Change*, and there have been some significant developments since the first edition in

1991. The main issues raised in the first edition were important at the time, but using the material in working with companies has suggested to me that we were becoming too concerned with marketing plans and organization and marketing information systems and barriers to marketing implementation – in fact, too concerned with marketing. These things may all be important – but only if there is a market strategy to drive them.

The core of this new book is the Strategic Pathway in Part II. This leads us through the stages of developing a market strategy: strategizing instead of planning; making critical market choices; developing a value proposition to our customers based on our differentiating capabilities; untangling the key relationships that we have to manage because the market strategy depends on them. The organizational context is important only as a route to market-led strategic change. The real key is a customer-focused market strategy based on offering value that we are good at delivering to a customer who wants it.

Some readers may still wonder why I have dropped the use of the word 'marketing' in many places in the book and in my work with executives:

- 'going to market' instead of 'marketing';
- 'market strategy' instead of 'marketing strategy';
- 'market-led' instead of 'marketing-led', and so on.

The reason is simple. It is not a ploy to save paper and ink (unless you are a green marketing fan – in which case, that's really what it is). It is simply because markets are more important than marketing, and we should say so. It is also because markets and customers are the responsibility of *every* manager in a company, not the 'property' of marketing specialists.

'basically traditional marketing is dead in the water'

There is another reason also – basically traditional marketing is dead in the water.

The days of the large corporate marketing department, with its market research surveys and brand managers and obsession with advertising, have gone – if indeed they ever existed for most companies. In a prize-winning paper in 1995, Antony Brown of IBM observes:

'There are now two types of corporation: those with a marketing department and those with a marketing soul. Even a cursory glance at the latest Fortune 500 shows that the latter are the top performing companies, while the former, steeped in the business traditions of the past, are fast disappearing' [10].

Instead, he says, new marketing will be a corporate philosophy driven by clusters of teams building alliances inside and outside the organization, based around customers and supported by IT.

'"going to market"' is a process owned by everyone in the organization – the "part-time marketers"'

My view of this is that if 'marketing' is what traditional marketing departments do (or did), then 'going to market' is what companies do (and always will). 'Marketing' belonged to marketing specialists, but 'going to market' is a process owned by *everyone* in the organization – the 'part-time marketers' [11], the chief executive [12], cross-functional teams [13] – and that is how we have to learn to manage it.

The process of going to market

The important differences in managing the process of going to market, instead of just 'marketing' are:

- we base our strategies on our customers and markets – we are market-led or market-driven [14];
- our internal programmes of change and our external actions in the marketplace are driven by that strategy;
- we concentrate on getting our act together around the things that matter to delivering our customer-focused strategy into the market – the 'ownership' of activities by functional departments, the existence of 'specialists' in professional disciplines, and conventional organizational structures are all secondary to this;
- boundaries between traditional functional departments, and even between organizations, are crossed by teams focusing on the creation of value for customers;
- new types of relationships – with customers, collaborators, competitors and co-workers – are more fundamental than contracts and transactions; and
- new ways of doing business are underpinned by information technology, as the infrastructure supporting complex relationships inside and outside the organization.

Now that is a pleasingly pompous set of platitudes, is it not? Actually, the perspective of the process of going to market instead of traditional marketing has very practical implications.

Certainly, this viewpoint does not sit happily with many conventional views of how things should be done. But who cares about conventional views when they are demonstrably out-of-date?

In fact, I would go still further. If you look at the many cases of market success studied in this book, in almost no case can you put the success down to structured marketing programmes with great planning, and the application of advanced theories of market behaviour by traditional marketing departments and executives. They are more often about managers with a sense of what will go with a particular type of customer, putting together a deal that will attract that customer and driving that strategy through the internal and external obstacles.

That is really the difference between managing marketing and managing the process of going to market. Of course, marketing activities – new product development, branding, pricing, distribution, marketing communications, and so on – are a part of the process of going to market, and often a vital part. The difference is that the context for marketing should be the process of going to market, not the marketing department.

It is also why most of what follows comes out of what companies and consultants are *having* to learn to achieve superior market performance, not out of academic theories about marketing.

In fact, I would go yet further – if you look at the companies that *achieve* superior performance in the market and *sustain* that superior performance, the route they take is by managing better how they go to market, not by excellence in conventional marketing terms. Peter Doyle[15] summarizes this as the difference between companies with a robust growth strategy, as opposed to those with a radical or rational growth strategy – see Table 1.1. Doyle underlines the success characteristics of the robust growth companies by noting that these are the companies where the market strategy requires management:

> to reject the notion of 'quick-fixes', whether these be rationalisation, acquisition or marketing gimmicks. Sustained growth depends upon hard work and continuous investment in strategy, systems and staff over a long period. World class competitiveness depends upon delivering products and services which offer better value over rivals in the market.[15]

In short, superior performance comes from going to market better than competitors, not from marketing departments and publicity. The focus of going to market is choosing and managing a strategic pathway involving appropriate market choices, a robust and sustainable value proposition to customers, and a set of key relationships that underpin the value proposition.

Table 1.1 Robust growth strategies*

Radical growth strategies	Rational growth strategies	Robust growth strategies
Achieve extraordinary growth in sales and profits, but are short-lived because they do not build superior products or services	Achieve high performance by creating new products which are significantly superior or cheaper than traditional competitors	Achieve steady performance over very long periods of time by creating superior customer value and long-term customer relationships
Characteristics of these strategies are: ● *Acquisition-based growth* – e.g. Ratners, WPP, Blue Arrow ● *Marketing department-based growth* – high levels of advertising and proliferating product line extensions ● *Public relations-based growth* – media hype attracts new customers, e.g. Saatchi & Saatchi	Characteristics of these strategies are innovations in technology, marketing methods or distribution channels, which may be radical and re-invent the business, and which create superior customer value, e.g. Amstrad, Direct Line, Sock Shop, Polly Peck	Characteristics of this strategy are: ● focus on providing superior customer value, but recognize that no innovation offers a sustainable advantage ● make long-term investments in relationships with suppliers, distributors, employees and customers ● strategy is built around 100% satisfied customers based on the capabilities and motivation of their people ● build effective supply chains and IT to deliver superior operating performance Examples include Marks & Spencer, 3M, Johnson & Johnson, Toyota
The weakness is that they do not build customer value – they build size, not quality. They do not build long-term shareholder value	The weakness is that they do not build barriers to competitive entry (e.g. Direct Line's telephone marketing was quickly imitated by other insurers), and they do not build long-term customer relationships. They do not build long-term shareholder value	The strength is a clear strategy built upon continuous learning and innovation. They build long-term shareholder value

* Source: Adapted from Doyle [15]

So, what do managers need to know?

We have said that this is a book about the process of going to market. This leaves the question of who it is for.

The content of this book is chosen with two very simple questions in mind. Those questions may be simple, but they seem to have been somewhat neglected recently. The guiding questions are:

- What does a manager really need to know to improve the company's process of going to market, to change the way things are done, and to attain superior performance in the marketplace?
- What does a marketing executive need to see when she/he stands back from day-to-day operations to see the big picture of going to market, to do it better?

> *'What does a manager really need to know to improve the company's process of going to market'*

The things a manager really needs to get a handle on, in the process of going to market, are:

- *Customers* – understanding customers and focusing on the market offering we make to them and what it produces in customer value, satisfaction and loyalty;
- *Market strategy* – choosing market targets and a strong market position based on differentiating capabilities to create a robust and sustainable value proposition to customers and networks of critical relationships;
- *Implementation* – driving the things that matter through the corporate environment to the marketplace.

We are pretty short on technical details – pricing theories, new product development programmes, market research techniques, advertising theory, buyer behaviour models, and so on. There is a reason for this. Managers do not need to get involved in technical detail. We can underline this point.

What managers do not need to know

I sincerely believe that managers should focus on the process of going to market and they (probably) do not need to know much about:

- *Market orientation* – In recent years, academics have been obsessed with market orientation because someone finally figured out a way to measure it [16, 17, 18, 19] – seeing what it relates to, who has it and who doesn't*, and so on. The pioneer of market orientation studies, Bernie Jaworski, says this stuff is past its sell-by date. I agree. Also it is very, very boring and of little practical significance to anyone except academics who write papers about it. This book is for managers, not academics, so we will talk about customers instead.
- *Marketing programmes* – Surely we need to know all about product policy and pricing and advertising and promotion, and all that stuff? Maybe – but really that is a job for marketing executives and agencies, not managers (and you can get chapter and verse on these topics in the conventional textbooks to which I referred earlier, p. 4). We need a market strategy first, or none of the technical marketing expertise makes sense. The harsh truth is – customers could not care less about impeccably planned and structured marketing programmes. They are only concerned with the value of what we offer them, so that's where we start.
- *Consumer behaviour theory* – Why don't we just let the psychologists have fun doing their laboratory experiments and studies on rats and students?† They have been doing this quite happily for decades and have yet to produce anything of practical significance that was not blindingly obvious in the first place. If the situation changes, I will let you know.‡
- *Market research techniques* – Managers need to know how to understand customers and markets better, not how to design questionnaires, develop sampling frames, collect data, analyse and model data, and all the rest of it. The manager needs to be better at market 'sensing' or market understanding, not running surveys and building databases – that is a job for technicians or research agencies.

---

* . . . how much it weighs, what colour it is, what it smells like, and so on – you get the picture?

† And sometimes you have to use students in experiments, because some people like rats and are concerned for their well-being.

‡ There is nothing personal in this. I have friends who write about consumer behaviour. They are great people to have a beer with. They just can't seem to tell me the relevance of what they do to what we have to sort out in companies.

- *Postmodernism in marketing* – Conventions of decency in language and the laws of libel preclude me from making any comment whatsoever about the practical contributions of postmodernism to marketing.*

That should make life easier?

Admittedly, the things managers do not need to know listed above knock out about 95 per cent of most conventional training and education courses in marketing. However, all we are doing is putting the *easy* stuff on hold, to focus on the *difficult* things that really matter: customer focus, market strategy, and effective implementation in the process of going to market. These are the tough issues, and the ones we cannot afford to run away from. This has just made life a lot harder. Sorry.

Market-led strategic change?

This brings me to the question of the possibly somewhat pretentious title of this book. The label 'market-led strategic change' (MLSC) is one we have applied to the research into market strategy implementation, which we have done over the past several years, together with the associated consultancy and in-company development work. The MLSC approach makes the following assumptions and assertions:

- that ultimately *all* organizations are forced to follow the dictates of the market (i.e. the paying customer), or go out of business when someone else *does*;
- in this sense we can pursue organizational effectiveness by being 'market-led' and focusing on the customer's needs, wants and demands;
- most of the barriers to doing this do not come from ignorance of customer characteristics, lack of information, inflexible technology, competitive threats, and so on, they come from the way we run our organizations;
- being 'market-led' may require substantial and painful upheaval in the way our organizations are structured, the way decisions are made, the key values we communicate to employees and managers, how we all do our jobs, and how we look at the outside world;

---

* However, if you are intrigued by this topic, at least Stephen Brown makes it funny [20].

● this amounts to a programme of deep-seated, fundamental strategic change in organizations, not just hiring a marketing executive or doing more advertising or any other short-term tactical ploy.

The key to all this strategic change is quite simply that we put the pursuit of customer satisfaction (and thus our organization's goals and survival) back where it should be – at the top of *everyone's* list of priorities.

Strangely, the point that seems to trouble people here is not the importance of strategic change, but that of being 'market-led'. This is one point in which I am prepared to get quite tough.

For example, Robert Heller writes that '*market-led* and *customer-led* have become clichés. Instead of making things happen, the market-led company is reacting' [21]. This is exactly wrong. Being market-led is simply about putting the customer at the

'Being market-led is simply about putting the customer at the top of the management agenda'

top of the management agenda and the list of priorities. It is about focus on the customer, specialising in the customer, finding better ways of doing what the customer values, educating and informing the customer, commitment and care. This is the only thing we have that genuinely makes sense of our business operations. It is certainly not altruistic or submissive, let alone reactive. It is about the most proactive thing we can be.

The point is that the harsh reality is that as soon as the customer can get a better deal (in his/her terms, not ours) elsewhere, that customer will toss us aside without a care in the world. This is even less surprising, of course, if our whole approach is to take 'hostages' instead of satisfying customers [22]. If all we do in our marketing and selling is make our customers feel like a necessary inconvenience to the seller, then why should we be surprised if the customer ceases to inconvenience us the first chance he or she gets?

The sad truth is that none of us have any right to prosper unless we provide the fickle, disloyal, but *paying* customers with what they value most, and we keep on doing that (or pay the consequences). We come to the market-led strategic model not in a spirit of altruism, but one of survival in the harsh reality of the customer marketplace.

But why upset the applecart?

. . . because if you don't, someone else will. The more you think about your company's process of going to market, instead of conventional marketing, the more likely you are to become aware of two quite frightening things:

- customers and markets have changed – radically and for ever;
- the manager's job has changed – radically and for ever.

Consider the following examples of the challenges we face in responding to new markets in new ways.

The new challenges in going to market

Few companies today could deny that what they see happening in their markets includes:

- new customer demands and expectations;
- new competitors, often unconventional ones;
- new types of organization being established; and
- whole new ways of doing business being developed.

New customers

One of the paradoxes we face is that as we get better at focusing on customers, improving quality, upgrading service level, and so on, we fuel further and higher *customer expectations* for more of the same: 'Expectations spiral as our customers gain experience with world-class service' [23]. It does not matter whether you are selling to consumers or business – you will (unfairly) be compared with the best around, and if you do not line up against these standards, you will have problems.

For example, a recent study of market leadership [24] raises questions here:

- Why is it that Federal Express can 'absolutely, positively' deliver a package overnight, but most airlines have trouble keeping your bags on the plane? Do they think you don't care?
- Why is it that it takes only a few minutes, and no paperwork, to drop off a rental car at Hertz, but twice that time and an annoying name/address form to check into a Hilton hotel. Are they afraid you'll steal the room?
- Why is it that Swatch can produce an inexpensive watch that will run accurately for years, but Rolex can't or won't do the same for a hundred times the money? Doesn't Rolex understand that the standards have changed?

The point is, you no longer get tested by customers against your immediate competitors – they compare you to the best and ask questions like those above.

One driver of increasing customer expectations is giving *customer sophistication*: they know what we are doing and demand transparency. Increasingly, consumers are marketing-literate – they talk about brands, and market leadership, and market position; they see through promotional objectives; then refuse to be patronized and to do things the way we want to do them. For example, look at what business customers are demanding from sellers (pp. 496–99) in terms of explicit added value and openness in dealing with us.

We have problems with sophisticated customers in traditional marketing – it is much easier to run neat marketing programmes

'We have problems with sophisticated customers in traditional marketing – it is much easier to run neat marketing programmes if customers are compliant, deferential and easily satisfied'

if customers are compliant, deferential and easily satisfied, the trouble is, those days have gone [25]. Alan Mitchell has recently laid down the challenge summarized in the model in Figure 1.1. This identifies the following situations:

- *IV: Unsophisticated customers, low loyalty.* The traditional marketing response in this situation has been low-quality, shoddy products backed by excessive advertising and promotion, and the complaining customer is treated as the enemy.
- *III: Unsophisticated customers, high loyalty.* In protected markets or industries dominated by a few companies, customers have to be thankful for what they get, and they are loyal because they have no choice or they don't know any better. This is the environment in which many British brands grew up – marketing stresses image to

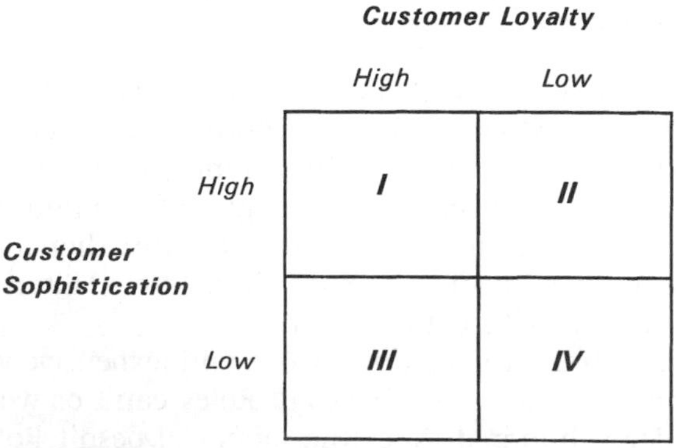

Figure 1.1 Sophisticated customers and loyalty

avoid sharper value-based comparisons, there is no incentive to improve real performance, and complaining customers are bought off, e.g. with free products.

- *II: More sophisticated customers, low loyalty.* Customers begin to see through the bad deals on offer. This is the era of the own-label and Virgin-style challenges to the conventional companies (see pp. 312–20). Marketing responses are customer satisfaction surveys and loyalty schemes and customer complaint response systems.
- *I: Sophisticated customers, high loyalty.* The emphasis on 'loyalty' and 'customer retention' moves to 'openness' and 'transparency', and the 'picky, fault-finding, hard-nosed, sophisticated customer' [25] forces you to learn and try continuous improvement in the things that matter to customers.

This is an intriguing model. What is worrying is that much of the conventional marketing thinking was designed for situations IV and III, and even 'new marketing', with its emphasis on customer relationships, is in situation III. The reality we are experiencing in market after market is situation I – and we need new approaches, not more of the same.

Once other thing that arises out of this model is that in many markets the more sophisticated customer is also *cynical and hostile.* Consumers are increasingly sceptical about advertising and see only 'brainwashing and lies' [26] and complain loudly about advertising images that are unsubtly based on sex and violence [27]. Excuses and explanations about why products like compact music discs, cars, and clothes cost 50 per cent more in the UK compared to the USA are wearing very thin [28]. At the extreme, pressure groups abound – more than 1000, from Greenpeace to 'Surfers against Sewage' – actively campaigning to influence business policies, and Des Wilson, a former campaigner, notes, 'The militant citizen is becoming an increasing proportion of the population. The tide is still rising' [29].

'Consumers are increasingly sceptical about advertising and see only "brainwashing and lies"'

It may not be fair. It is the way things are. Traditional marketing-based strategies are increasingly questionable in these situations.

New types of competition

The paradox is that, on conventional measures of competitiveness, British firms are doing better than ever – according to an IMD survey in 1997, Britain overtook Germany in competitiveness to reach twelfth position, just one position behind Japan [30].

Yet again and again we see companies wrong-footed by innovators prepared to 're-invent' the business – like Direct Line and Virgin in financial services; like Daewoo in cars (see pp. 530); like Sears looking at the possibility of selling cut-price electricity through its Freemans mail order catalogue [31].

No market is secure from invasion and competitive turbulence, and that is the reality we have to confront. This is an issue on which we will focus later (pp. 246–51).

New types of organization

Across most of the developed world the 1980s and 1990s have been an era of *downsizing* in organizations of all kinds, to the point where many have changed radically and for ever. Depending on your viewpoint and the circumstances, you may see this as becoming lean and efficient, or simply 'dumbsizing' – reducing manpower to the detriment of business performance. Whatever else, this is the end of the road for 'company man' [32], who gave loyalty in return for a job for life. Indeed, Warren Bennis of the University of Southern California encapsulates the degree of change very nicely, when he says:

> The factory of the future will have only two employees, a man and a dog. The man will be there to feed the dog. The dog will be there to keep the man from touching the equipment.

One element of this has been the resurgence of *de-merger* and narrowing market focus in many companies. Companies like BAT Industries, ICI, Racal and Courtaulds have dramatically increased value by de-merger [33], and many others are likely to follow this trend [34]. While ICI, having de-merged Zeneca, now plans to de-merge its pigments business, at Unilever, Niall Fitzgerald is speeding up the sale of 'non-core' businesses [35].

Critical to strategic development for leaner and more narrowly-focused businesses are economies and risk sharing in the form of *collaboration* and *strategic alliances* with other organizations. This extends from the simple outsourcing of sales and marketing to specialist firms [36], to the full-blown network of collaborating partners (see pp. 254–57 below for some examples).

To the emergence of new types of organizations, where we are having to learn how to manage under new rules as we go along, we can add the new pressures for *accountability.*

In 1995 the Royal Society of Arts published its report on 'Tomorrow's Company' – a blueprint for business leadership in partnership with all the 'stakeholders' in the business: customers, suppliers, employees, shareholders and society [37]. Unipart is held up as an example of a company that has become one of the most efficient and demanding in the world by long-term partnerships with suppliers, shareholders and the community. John Neill, Unipart's chief executive, says: 'Suppliers, customers, shareholders and employees are not rivals in the battle for profits; they are partners, and will be more successful once they learn to trust each other and work together' [38].

At the same time, Anita Roddick of The Body Shop has established her New Academy of Business at Bath University to provide an 'innovative business degree addressing social, environmental and ethical issues', where Roddick tells students, 'You are the Trojan horses' – to go out and work against unethical business practices from inside big businesses [39].

In all this, one thing (and probably only one thing) is certain – the organizations from which we go to market are not the ones assumed by conventional and traditional marketing theories.

New ways of doing business

We will see throughout the book that market leaders get there by finding ways to 're-invent' the business, so they are cheaper, more differentiated in ways that matter to customers, have better products and services, or deliver the product or service in a better way. More general predictions about how the process of going to market will change in the next decade are made by Philip Kotler:

- *Target marketing* – focusing on market segments and moves to pursue 'segments of one' in 'customer-specific marketing'.
- *Electronic marketing* – transforming marketing into a genuine dialogue between customer and supplier Instead of conventional, one-way 'marketing monologue', or even a 'multilogue' between many groups of buyers and sellers.
- *Customer co-operative* – while the Internet puts power in the hands of buyers (to collect product information, to compare experiences, and so on – see pp. 336–38), correspondingly the creation of customer databases from purchase transactions compensates by giving sellers more power through enhanced customer understanding [40].

However, on top of these types of changes, there are more fundamental challenges to revise traditional ways of doing business.

We have already mentioned the spread of strategic alliances to spread risks and access new markets – and will say much more later (pp. 251–63).

But consider the advent of 'lean thinking' and 'supply chain management', and what these new management approaches may do to conventional roles about marketing – i.e. blow them out of the water.

For example, Womack and Jones [41] in an extremely influential book, tell managers how to banish waste and create wealth in their companies – a very seductive pitch to senior executives. Their approach to creating the 'lean enterprise' rests on five principles:

- Define *value* in the product or source from the end-customer's perspective – for example, they say that value for the airline passenger is convenient, hassle-free travel, yet airlines invest in large aircraft to take hundreds of passengers to 'hub' airports (i.e. places where they do not wish to be) with the result that 'passengers are miserable (this is not what they meant by value, the aircraft producers make little money because airlines can't afford new planes), and the airlines . . . have flown a decade-long holding pattern on the vicinity of 'bankruptcy' [41].
- Identify the *value streams* for each product (i.e. the activities which add to customer value) and eliminate *muda* (waste) – they use the example of the carton of cola soft drink where some three hours of actual processing of package and product requires nearly 11 months of storage in the traditional supply chain in which all companies are organized for mass production not around the value stream. A collaboration between supplier and retailers can reduce this to a few weeks.
- Organize around *flow* instead of batching and queuing everything – they illustrate this with house construction where investigations in one firm showed that five-sixths of the typical house construction schedule was occupied with *waiting* (for the next set of specialists to do their work) and *rework* (to correct work done incorrectly or out of sequence).
- Respond to the *pull* of the product through the supply chain to eliminate stocks – they give the example of Toyota's 'Daily Ordering System' for replacement car parts, where orders are placed for parts as cars come in for repair, and are met on the same day.
- The pursuit of *perfection* in all things.

This is truly impressive, and will exercise senior management's minds for some time to come. However, there are a couple of problems here – they are substituting supply chain efficiency for market strategy and not telling anyone.

For example, they see value only as measurable technical product quality and price. We know that value to customers is more complex than this, but production engineers are not interested in 'irrational' consumer requirements (until it loses us market position, and then they blame 'marketing').

They believe that supply chain efficiency will increase customer value and satisfaction. In a 'rational' world, it might. In the real world, who really believes that the fact that the can of cola has been on the shelf for three weeks instead of 11 months is of any interest to me whatsoever as a consumer, let alone increases value to me – could I care less? They believe also that branding is irrational, and in a sensible world we would all drink a generic cola – which would make the supply chain so much more efficient.

They also believe that consumer demand is inherently stable, and chaos is only created by bad marketing people advertising and promoting products to win market share, and this should stop. They say 'level scheduling needs level selling' [41]. They believe totally that the centrally planned and co-ordinated supply chain is a better way of doing business. They are persuading many senior executives and major companies that this is the way to do business in the future.

What we see is the potential re-birth of production-orientation. The last time we tried that it did not work too well, why should anyone think it will work now? And yet that is the reality in many companies right now – if you don't think so, then have a look at the Efficient Consumer Response movement (pp. 258–62).

Diversifying and challenge in how we do business is good. But it underlines the importance of hanging onto the things that matter: customers, market strategy, and effective implementation, i.e. the process of going to market, not just the supply chain.

The new challenges in managing

What this adds up to is a role for the manager which is changing and challenging. Rather than the traditional 'command and control' model of executive life, we need to think about things like the following on how to develop, train and evaluate managers.

Coping with paradox

The days of clarity and stability for managers in a largely predictable world have gone. The organizations in which we work create ambiguity and paradox:

'The days of clarity and stability for managers in a largely predictable world have gone'

- you have to focus and specialize (on key customers and market targets), but still be all things to all people (to protect company reputation);
- you have to collaborate and build relationships with suppliers and customers, but still compete 'fairly' to avoid offending the Mergers and Monopolies Commission or consumer interest groups;
- you have to deal with other companies, while a single company may be your supplier, your customer, your collaborator *and* your competitor all at the same time – I have this wonderful picture in mind of an executive from a branded goods firm sitting down with an executive from Asda because they are *collaborating* on supply chain management, but Asda is also a major *customer* for the brand and a *competitor* because they have an own-label version, and meanwhile the brand leader is *suing* Asda because the own-label infringes their brand's packaging copyright; now do they shake hands or hit each other?
- you have to control people (personal appraisal, rewards, etc.) and coach and advise at the same time (if I tell you something I got wrong, will you use it to coach me or give me a bad appraisal?);
- you have to get better at going to market – but probably without a marketing department;
- you have to manage a 'balanced scorecard' – shareholder interest, customer interests, employee interests, and so on – but find a way through conflicts of interest;
- you have to build trusting and close relationships with customers and suppliers – but you can only do that by breaking relationships (the ones your competitors have with those same customers).

This is matched by paradox in the marketplace too:

- *Situation*: A large direct mail campaign is to take place at a company. You find the direct mail pieces piled up in the mail room after they should have gone out. The reason is that the company will not send the material out until it has been blessed by a local religious leader and he cannot be found. *Question*: Where are you? *Likely answers*: the developing world, the Far East, Outer Mongolia. *True answer*: You are at the prestigious headquarters of a sophisticated health insurance company in the mid-West of the USA, where they take their religion very seriously.

● In 1996 Texaco was the fifth biggest petrol retailer in the UK. It is a major international oil company. In that year it made more money in the UK from hamburgers than from petrol (petrol prices were so low because of a competitive war that convenience foods were more profitable). This may be why Texaco is looking to open yet more McDonalds, Burger Kings, Pizza Huts and Dunkin' Donuts on its forecourts this year [42]. Also in 1996, the mighty Ford Motor Company made two-thirds of its net profit from financial services, not from selling cars [43].

● This is an era of customer service, product quality, brand equity and consumer sophistication. Yet one of the most successful business forms in the UK is the 8000 High Street curry houses. By adapting food to British tastes, by basing a menu on a single sauce and largely de-skilling the kitchen, and by getting food costs down to 5–10 per cent of the menu price (compared to 30–35 per cent in other restaurants), the Indian restaurant is a profitable business not highly dependent on volume, and has become part of the British way of life [44]. This is not featured highly in successful business stories, although many of us would aspire to equal their performance.

Coping with complexity, unpredictability and conflict within and outside the organization is one of the major challenges to managers.

Preparing for surprise

What this means is that managers have to be prepared to be surprised when the unpredictable or unlikely happens. You cannot predict when your aeroplanes are going to crash, but you know it is a risk, so you can have a response ready. You cannot predict product tampering (such as substituting cyanide pills for headache capsules in the supermarket), but if it happens you can respond, if you are prepared (Johnson and Johnson regained product leadership for the cyanide-contaminated Tylenol product by launching the first tamper-proof packs).

It may lead you into some outlandish areas of thought. Cannabis is an illegal drug in Britain – though estimated to be a £1.8 billion industry. There is a remote possibility that cannabis could be legalized. Part of strategic thinking in the UK brewing industry is to do with the substantial implications for product marketing if cannabis were legalized – and they are more than open about this [45].

On the other hand, who would have expected Gerald Ratner, chief executive of Ratner's, to repeatedly rubbish his company's jewellery products by comparing them (disadvantageously) to prawn sandwiches in front of City audiences – which led to the effective collapse of the company and the end of his career. Some things are always going to be a surprise!

Managing talent

Market strategies ultimately depend on human talent. In future they will depend on new kinds of talent – in technology, in managing ambiguous relationships inside and out-

'Market strategies ultimately depend on human talent. In future they will depend on new kinds of talent'

side the company, in 'sensing' market change and understanding new types of customer, in coping with 'empowerment' and team-based working, in building flexibility and propensity to change, in leading into new areas and working in new ways that do not depend on formal authority [46]. The challenge to managers is how to find, nurture and retain these new talents, and it is not likely to be easy to do any of these.

Managing change and innovation

We are repeatedly told that the sign of successful companies is their capacity for change – particularly radical transformational change [47] – and for innovation in products, processes and structures [48]. This is fine, but what it actually means is that we, as managers, have to find better ways of managing turbulence and sustaining change (as opposed to surviving the latest 'initiative' or 'project' and going back to the way things used to be). We will have much more to say about this challenge later (pp. 567–617).

'And if you expect more resources to do all these new things, you are probably out of luck. You are going to get fewer resources to do more'

And do it all cheaper!

And if you expect more resources to do all these new things, you are probably out of luck. You are going to get fewer resources to do more [49].

So what does all that mean?

The purpose of this chapter was scene-setting – to clarify our goals and the approach being taken. This will not be to everyone's taste.

In fact, some people will probably be deeply offended. They will probably not have lasted to this point in the chapter, so there is no point in apologizing. If you are still with me, then the introduction in this chapter has tried to do the following things:

- to turn our attention away from traditional roles of 'marketing' towards the fundamental *process of going to market* that is critical in every organization – marketing departments may disappear; the process of going to market remains critical to success;
- to put three issues centre stage for the manager's agenda: *customers*, *market strategy* and *implementation and change* – because sorting out these issues seems to be what distinguishes the winners from the losers just about everywhere you go;
- to focus on the process of going to market, and the central issues of customer, market strategy and implementation as the basis for creating and *managing market-led strategic change*;
- getting these things right is urgent, and means abandoning many of our traditional ways of doing things to cope with *new challenges* in the marketplace and how we do business and how we manage.

This book is designed to help. We will address the following critical issues to provide a framework and tools for action around customers, market strategy and the implementation of strategic change. We will do the following things:

- The remainder of Part I is concerned with *customers* – testing out whether we do take customers seriously and work for customer satisfaction or not (Chapter 2), and confronting the issue of what we have to do to create a customer-focused organization (Chapter 3).
- Building on the customer issue, Part II turns to defining a *Strategic Pathway* for a company to go to market. We will evaluate the key *market choices* that are made and how we define and segment markets around the things that matter to customers (Chapter 4); then we turn to developing a *value proposition* based on our market mission and our ability to differentiate against the competition based on our capabilities

and key marketing assets like brands (Chapter 5), next we examine the *key relationships* with customers, co-workers, collaborators and competitors, which underpin our market strategy (Chapter 6); and lastly, we provide a framework for turning our strategizing into a *plan* (Chapter 7).

- Then Part III turns to the issues we face in driving market strategy through the corporate environment – the gaps emerging between our strategic intent and reality as market strategies are turned into marketing programmes (Chapter 8); the organizational barriers surrounding the implementation of market strategy and the implications of new organizational forms (Chapter 9); the role of 'market sensing' or building shared market understanding in a company to break through cultural barriers to market-led strategic change (Chapter 10); the opportunities for managing key processes like planning and budgeting to build ownership and commitment market-led change instead of writing plans that change nothing (Chapters 11 and 12); and the critical importance of linking market strategy and marketing programmes to the sales organization (Chapter 13).
- Lastly, in Part IV we turn our attention to the need to build implementation and internal marketing strategies inside the organization to put our market strategy into effect in the customer marketplace (Chapter 14).

This agenda is contentious and controversial and it is not traditional 'marketing'. It is the agenda that matters in the process of going to market. Let's get down to it . . .

References

1. Kotler, Philip (1997), *Marketing Management: Analysis, Planning and Control*, 9th ed., London: Prentice-Hall International.
2. O'Shaughnessy, John (1989), *Competitive Marketing*, 2nd ed., London: Unwin Hyman.
3. Baker, Michael J. (1996) *Marketing – An Introductory Text*, 6th ed., London: Macmillan.
4. Cannon, Tom (1996), *Basic Marketing*, 4th ed., London: Cassell.
5. Foxall, Gordon R. (1981), *Strategic Marketing Management*, Beckenham: Croom Helm.
6. Jobber, David (1995), *Principles and Practice of Marketing*, Maidenhead: McGraw-Hill.
7. Mercer, David (1996), *Marketing*, 2nd ed., Oxford: Blackwell.
8. Doyle, Peter (1997), *Marketing Management and Strategy*, 2nd ed., Hemel Hempstead: Prentice-Hall.

9. Kotler, Philip, Gary Armstrong, John Saunders and Veronica Wong (1996), *Principles of Marketing – European Edition*, Hemel Hempstead: Prentice-Hall.
10. Brown, Antony (1995), 'The Fall and Rise of Marketing', *Marketing Business*, February, 25–28.
11. Gummesson, Evert (1990), *The Part-Time Marketer*, University of Karlstad: Research Report 90:3.
12. 'High-Tech CEOs Plugged into Marketing', *Marketing News*, 2 June 1995.
13. Freeling, Anthony (1995), 'Up the Organisation', *Marketing News*, January, 22–23.
14. Day, George (1990), *Market Driven Strategy – Processes for Creating Value*, New York: Free Press.
15. Doyle, Peter (1997), 'Go for Robust Growth', *Marketing Business*, April, 53.
16. Jaworski, Bernard J. and Ajay K. Kohli (1993), 'Market Orientation: Antecedents and Consequences', *Journal of Marketing*, Vol. 57, July, 53–70.
17. Kohli, Ajay and Bernard J. Jaworski (1990), 'Market Orientation: The Construct, Research Propositions and Managerial Implications', *Journal of Marketing*, Vol. 54, April, 1–19.
18. Narver, John C. and Stanley F. Slater (1990), 'The Effect of a Market Orientation on Business Profitability', *Journal of Marketing*, Vol. 54, October, 20–35.
19. Slater, Stanley F. and John C. Narver (1994), 'Does Competitive Environment Moderate the Market Orientation-Performance Relationship?', *Journal of Marketing*, Vol. 58, January, 46–55.
20. Brown, Stephen (1995), *Postmodern Marketing*, London: Routledge.
21. Heller, Robert (1990), *Signposts for Management*, London: Rank Xerox UK Ltd.
22. Bonoma, Thomas V. (1990), 'Employees Can Free the Hostages', *Marketing News*, 19 March, 14–15.
23. Zemke, Ron (1997), 'Quality is Not Dead; Consumers Just Expect a Lot More of It', *Marketing News*, 31 March.
24. Treacy, Michael and Fred Wiersema (1995), *The Discipline of Market Leaders*, London: Harper Collins.
25. Mitchell, Alan (1997), 'Evolution', *Marketing Business*, March, 29.
26. Johnson, Luke (1996), 'Advertising May Not Be Good For Business', *Sunday Business*, 4 August.
27. Poulter, Sean (1997), 'Bad Taste Billboards', *Daily Mail*, 15 April.
28. 'How British Consumers Pay 48 Per Cent More', *Business Age*, 1 February 1994.
29. Lynn, Matthew and Rufus Olins (1995), 'Under Pressure', *Sunday Times*, 10 September.
30. 'We've Overtaken Germany', *Daily Mail*, 28 March 1997.
31. Bernoth, Ardyn (1996), 'Sears will Sell Electricity by Mail-Order Catalogue', *Sunday Times*, 20 October.
32. Sampson, Anthony (1995), *Company Man: the Rise and Fall of Company Life*, London: Harper Collins.
33. Lynn, Matthew (1995), 'ITT Break-Up Tolls Bell for Conglomerates', *Sunday Times*, 18 June.

34. Olins, Rufus (1997), 'Revealed: Giants Ripe for Break-Up', *Sunday Times*, 9 March.
35. Wheatcroft, Patience (1997), 'Bright New Look from Persil Man', *Mail on Sunday*, 9 February.
36. Dickson, Andrew (1996), 'Passing the Field Test', *Financial Times*, 22 August.
37. *Tomorrow's Company* (1995), London: Royal Society of Arts.
38. Hotten, Russell (1996), 'The Man Who Wants To Be Everyone's Partner', *Mail on Sunday*, 13 October.
39. McKee, Victoria (1997), 'Roddick's Academy Goes Into Business Ethics', *Sunday Times*, 23 March.
40. Kotler, Philip (1997), 'Method for the Millennium', *Marketing Business*, February, 26–27.
41. Womack, James P. and Daniel T. Jones (1996), *Lean Thinking: Banish Waste and Create Wealth in Your Corporation*, New York: Simon and Schuster.
42. 'Burgers Pump Up Forecourt Profits at Texaco', *Daily Telegraph*, 15 November 1996.
43. Rubython, Tom (1997), 'Ford Faces Its Very Own 2000 Problem', *Sunday Business*, 13 April.
44. Campion, Charles (1997), 'The Great Curry House Conundrum', *Daily Mail*, 31 March.
45. Rubython, Tom (1996), 'Brewers Prepare for Legalisation of Cannabis', *Sunday Business*, 4 August.
46. Sherman, Stratford (1995), 'Leaders are Learning Their Stuff', *Fortune*, 27 November, 64–70.
47. Houlder, Vanessa (1997), 'Keep the Change', *Financial Times*, 3 April.
48. 'Innovation is the Key to Corporate Success', *Marketing Business*, January 1995, 3.
49. Harris, Lloyd C. and Nigel F. Piercy (1997), 'Market Orientation is Free', *Management Decision*, Vol. 35 No. 1, 33–39.

CHAPTER 2

Managing customer satisfaction

Do we *really* care about creating long-term customer satisfaction?

Introduction

You would think that in this day and age, because everyone tells you they take customers seriously, all we really need to do is look at the latest 'technology' – systems for measuring customer satisfaction, customer-based staff appraisal and reward systems, customer care programmes, customer loyalty schemes, and so on. (We will, indeed, look at these issues, but not until Chapter 3.) Just hold on a minute – what use are all the trappings of customer care, if they are just used in a vain attempt to cover up the fact that we do not *really* care about

'the enormous differences between lip-service to the customer and the reality in major British companies'

our customers? If you do not think that is an issue, have a look at the survey findings summarized in Table 2.1 which underline some of the enormous differences between lip-service to the customer and the reality in major British companies.

The first step in market-led strategic change is very simple – let's just see if the people in *our* company know why customer satisfaction is supposed to be the most important thing to our business, and then let's see if they really *believe* it. The evidence is that everyone *says* they believe in customers, but when you look at what they *do*, they really do not take the customer issue

Table 2.1   Paying lip-service to the customer*

The lip-service...	The reality...
100% of a sample of senior management from *Times 1000* companies say that customer satisfaction is the real measure of success	Most actually measure success by short-term financials like pre-tax profit Only 60% use any form of customer-based criteria to evaluate staff performance
70% say that customer focus is their first or second priority	Less than 24% believe that management time spent with customers is important Only 34% see it as important to train their staff in customer service skills
76% say they have a database for target marketing	At the same time they place almost no value on developing relationships with those customers

* Source: 'Marketplace', *Marketing Business*, March 1997 – describing a survey of senior management in British companies selected from the *Times 1000*, by the P Four Consultancy group

seriously. So we will start by looking at how companies treat their customers and why they need to do better. Then we can test out whether we really believe in customer satisfaction in our company.

Remember, the customer is always right-handed*

Why is it, when you look around in most markets, that companies treat their customers so badly? Is it because they don't care, or they just can't help themselves? Or don't they know what they are doing? For example:

● The new Severn Bridge between England and Wales is a £50-million-a-year sales revenue business, part-owned by the French company GTM. Adrian Evans of Cardiff is a commuter, who has paid about £7,000 in bridge tolls over ten years. One

---

* And according to Dilbert, if we could remember even that, it would be an improvement in most companies!

day he forgot to take his wallet to work, and when he got to the bridge, they refused to let him cross, causing him substantial inconvenience and aggravation. Why was this – did they think he was going to steal the bridge if they let him across without paying first? No, says the bridge company spokesman, 'It is not our policy . . .' [1].

- To check into most international flights from Heathrow, there is a mandatory two hours extra added to check-in times. This leaves most passengers hanging around the airport for about three hours. Does anyone really believe that this is for security reasons (the official excuse)? Or could it have something to do with the fact that airport profits increase by 20 per cent for every extra ten minutes that passengers are kept waiting, evidenced by the fact that sales in Heathrow's airport shops have risen five times faster than those on the high street, and contribute nearly half the British Airport Authority's profits? Who do they think they are kidding?

- Why do Blockbuster video store staff aggressively demand two 'official' addressed envelopes or utility bills (which must be less than two weeks old) and a credit card from a customer before they will rent out a video? Do they seriously believe this provides them with additional security, or do they just like annoying and humiliating their customers?

- Why do the major airlines insist on flying passengers to hubs? The definition of a 'hub' is a place you do not want to visit, but which the airline is going to make you go, because it is more convenient for them. Small airlines are leading the way – small planes flying into regional airports take passengers to the places they *do* want to go to [2].

- Why do companies like Toshiba, Canon and America On Line offer fantastic technology in their products and services and back this up with customer help lines which are useless? [3] Do they think their wonderful products are more important than their customers?

- Why is it that Land's End, the mail order clothes retailer, remembers your last order and your size, but after years of membership American Express continues to send you solicitations to join? Doesn't anyone at Amex know that you are already a customer, and that they are being very irritating and probably offensive? [4]

- Why do most retailers heat their shops to a temperature which is comfortable for someone in shirtsleeves in the middle of winter? Is it because it is more comfortable for managers and employees and no-one really cares about the customer coming in off the street wearing a winter coat and breaking into a sweat in what feels like a sauna?

In fact, more generally, if you ask around most consumers and business customers will tell you that with most of the companies that sell to them the people have bad attitudes and service stinks.

Customer service is bad all over

The critical importance to business survival and success of customer service and providing value to our customers is hardly news to anyone. With just about every sector you go to, companies tell you about their customer care policies and their focus on customer satisfaction. Who are we kidding? Just look at this random selection of examples of how organizations treat their customers:

● The National Health Service has a 'patients' charter' and boasts slogans like 'Putting Patients' Interests First' as well as a management policy of 'positive customer care'. In 1994, John Spiers, chairman of Brighton Health Care NHS Trust – an £801 million business – decided to put this to the test. He got into a wheelchair and visited the Royal Sussex County hospital in the guise of a disabled outpatient. On arrival, the hospital porter took 40 minutes to respond to his bleep, leading to the conversation:

> *Patient*: Where's your name tag?
> *Porter*: What's it to you, mate?
> *Patient*: You're supposed to wear one, it says so in the patients' charter and I'm a patient.
> *Porter*: F*** off!

Other surprises for Spiers were: getting into a hospital in a wheelchair is difficult when there are no automatic sliding doors; hospitals like this one are full of discarded litter and are very grubby, and the roof leaks when it rains; there were no pillows on the trolley; he was told to expect a five hour wait to see a doctor; there was no patient alarm to call help in an emergency; staff gave him incorrect directions, and stripped away his dignity in how they treated him – publicly humiliating him, for example, because he had failed to memorize his 'patient number'. Spiers concluded: 'If I had really been a frail and elderly patient in pain, I would have been scared and bewildered . . . whatever happened to privacy and dignity?' [5]. Two points spring to mind: how can service standards be so appalling in an expensive 'caring' business; and why is it so unusual for a chief executive to sample his or her own customer service?

- The many reports of poor service and 'nothing to do with me, guv' responses from employees to genuine customer complaints in the newly-privatized British rail industry are also illustrative. It seems that adding commercial trappings to a hostile bureaucracy simply produces a hostile bureaucracy with better excuses for the complete lack of service to its customers. What use is it changing the structure without changing the people?

  'adding commercial trappings to a hostile bureaucracy simply produces a hostile bureaucracy with better excuses'

- The retail banks in Britain spend hugely on customer service, customer care campaigns and customer satisfaction measurement, and all the other trappings of taking customers seriously. And yet customers just see the advertising slogans as the empty promises they are. Surveys show how common experiences with banks are: incorrect charges; direct debits and standing orders going wrong; and mistakes on accounts not being put right. John Beishon of the Consumers' Association concludes: 'banks are not delivering on service promises . . . Laudable exceptions apart, thousands of customers have cause to deplore the high-handed ineptitude of those they trust with their cash' [6].

- Retail business in Britain routinely promises service and value to its customers. All too often customers find a slightly different reality. A recent survey found that most retail staff will look the customer in the eye but there is a good chance they will not smile, and while shop assistants were generally perceived by customers as polite, they were less likely to be helpful or friendly [7]. Len Berry lists common customer complaints about retail staff as:

  1 *True Lies* – blatant dishonesty or unfairness, such as selling unnecessary extra services or misquoting costs.
  2 *Red Alert* – customers are treated harshly or disrespectfully because they are assumed to be stupid or dishonest.
  3 *Broken Promises* – careless, mistake-prone behaviour, or no-shows at appointments.
  4 *I Just Work Here* – powerless employees who lack the authority or desire to solve basic customer problems.
  5 *The Big Wait* – being made to wait in a queue because checkouts or service counters are closed.
  6 *Automatic Pilot* – impersonal, emotionless, no eye-contact, going-through-the-motions non-service.
  7 *Suffering in Silence* – employees who do not bother to communicate with customers who want to know what is happening.

8 *Don't Ask* – employees unwilling to make any extra effort to help customers, or seeming put-out by requests for assistance.

9 *Lights On, No-One At Home* – clueless employees who do not know, and will not take the time to learn, answers to customers' common questions.

10 *Misplaced Priorities* – employees who chat with each other or conduct personal business while the customer waits, or refuse to assist a customer because they are on a 'break' [8].

In fact, things are so bad that retailers now complain about 'store rage' – customer aggression towards shop employees, of which 350 000 incidents were reported in 1995. It is unfortunate that it is not the managers (who are responsible for making customers angry because of how they are treated) who get it in the neck – it is the shop assistants. The managerial response of issuing staff with security alarms somewhat misses the point – why not spend the money improving the horrible shopping experience so that customers are less angry? [9]

- Britain has an important tourism and leisure industry. Research by Coopers and Lybrand for the Department of National Heritage concludes that British hotels and restaurants are characterized by a 'self-perpetuating vicious circle' in which staff are poorly educated and trained, badly paid and take little pride in their work. They do not understand and cannot deliver good customer service [10]. In fact, things are so bad that in 1997 the British Hospitality Association [11] had the unmitigated gall to publish a survey accusing hotel *guests* of being ill-mannered, shouting and swearing and complaining about 'trivial things', suggesting that 80 per cent of hotel owners say that guests are making their lives a misery! I'm sorry, run that by me again, Basil Fawlty, everything is horrible, and it is the *customers'* fault?

- Why do airlines believe that treating passengers like inanimate objects to be processed in batches and held waiting in queues is good customer service? For example, Dan Jones [12] enumerates the activities involved in a family trip from England to Greece:

Total travel time: 13 hours
Time actually going somewhere: 7 hours (54 per cent of the total)
Queuing and waiting time: 6 hours
Number of queues: 10

Number of times luggage was picked up and put down: 7
Number of inspections (all asking the same questions): 8
Total processing steps: 23

Jones raises some very direct questions which would totally change the customer experience, but to which no airline seems to have a sensible answer: why can't the person at check-in do security, customs and check-in tasks, so that you pass them and walk straight onto the plane; why can't the ticket from the travel agent include baggage tags, boarding passes, taxi voucher, bus tickets and hotel registration, to be read automatically at each point; why can't the customs authorities have your passport scanned in at check-in and use the long hours while you are en route to decide whether you can enter the country (instead of making a planeload of passengers queue while the customs officials look at everyone's papers – why do they seem so surprised that you arrived; do they know something about the planes that we don't?)? The underlying answer is that no-one really cares enough to go back to basics and look at the product or service through the consumer's eyes. It is much easier to make passengers do things in the way that is convenient to airlines.

No-one has ever said that dealing with customers and creating customer satisfaction is *easy* to do. In many ways, from the internal corporate viewpoint, customers are a bit of a problem because all too often they do not think 'like we do', and they are unreasonable in a number of significant ways. So, we end up saying things like this:

'We know better than the customer'

To begin with, customers are demonstrably completely unreasonable because they persist in behaving as though *their* needs and *their* problems, and the things *they* think are important, are more central than our superb products and services, and what we think and know really matters most. In case there is any doubt that this is both true and vitally important, consider the following case.

I worked a couple of years ago with a project team, in a high-technology computer business, tasked by their company with generating a new strategy to gain market share in the UK water industry. The key target product market was that for management information systems (MIS), rather than the more traditional operating and engineering systems. I was amazed to find that a group of computer professionals (including, incidentally, sales/

marketing executives as well as technical specialists) could not cope with the simple fact shown by their market research that there was one piece of data the chief executive of a water business wants every day – the level of the water in the reservoirs. This *is* in many ways apparently quite irrational – chief executive officer or not, s/he can do nothing about rainfall. S/he would be far better off, in managing the business, with all the financial, resource and productivity data the sophisticated MIS product can provide. Unfortunately, what our sophisticated MIS product could not provide was the one thing the irrational, emotional, unreasonable customer actually wanted. In fact, in this case the customer was not being totally irrational. The truth is, of course, that to be comfortable in getting on with running a water business, what you really want to know is that you have got some water (because if you haven't, you can expect immediate pain from everyone – from the local MP whose image is at stake, to the local hospitals whose kidney dialysis machines won't work). It may or may not be irrational, but it is what matters to the customer that determines your success. In this case the computer company's whole marketing strategy began to unravel at this point: to tell the CEO what the level of water is, you have to interface with the operating systems that run the water network, and dominance of the operating systems market had been gained by another supplier, because we were so concerned with technical superiority in MIS, and so on.

'Customers are stupid'

We believe that our customers are emotional and irrational and, in some cases, just stupid in their buying behaviour. This probably merits a few more words. It has been said that nothing is ever really irrational – there are simply cases where we do not understand people's motives. Take two cases in point.

An R & D director of a high-technology manufacturing company complained bitterly to me, in a new product review meeting, that in spite of the company's massive spend on developing and launching a new electronic measurement instrument, the unreasonable, complaining customer was causing problems by turning the product down, because the on/off rocker switch on this marvel of high-technology was located at the *back* of the cabinet – not on the front where the operator could reach it without standing up from his/her seat at the workbench. He received little sympathy from me (or his customers). If the customer wants the switch on the front, there is really only one answer – move it (or better still, put it where the customer wants it in the first place)!

On the other hand, another company with whom we have been working operates a long way from the high technology end of things: it really just makes big tin boxes. Into these boxes they put bought-in electrical motors and other components, and they market ventilation and air-conditioning equipment to builders and developers. They have achieved a substantial market penetration in the highly competitive and price-oriented building site market for one reason above most others – they have always been the *only* supplier fitting an electric plug or a junction box to the wires hanging out of the back of the equipment. This does not cost the supplier much, but for the customer it reduces the use of costly labour and the incidence of wiring errors on the building site, where he has to install the product. Something this simple enables the company to achieve two things simultaneously: a substantial premium price for the product *and* a satisfied customer. In the majority of businesses, most of us would probably settle for that sort of result!

Does it have to be like this?

The answer is emphatically not. In most cases we actually have this technology and knowledge to do better, and some companies use it.

On the first point, for example, Dan Jones[12] the airline complainant in an earlier example, has a vision of perfection for a new entrant to the airline business which would overturn all the conventional barriers to customer service and value. His advice is:

- Start with small and mid-sized cities that currently only feed hubs, and think of ways for travellers to fly direct in small aircraft to other small and mid-sized cities, thus bypassing the current system.
- Re-think the terminal, so that the passenger can drive or be driven to very near the gate and walk quickly to the plane, rolling specially-designed luggage straight onto the plane.
- Make reservations by phone or computer – including the taxi, hire car and hotel reservation on the same ticket or plastic card, which gets you into the taxi, onto the plane and opens the hotel room door.
- Baggage handling would be eliminated, and there would be no need for staff at the gate.
- You save money, and the customer gets less hassle and thus better value.

This is a great recipe for powerful competitive differentiation in the airline business. It could be done, but there is little sign that it is.

The picture is not altogether bleak. Some companies have established new and better levels of customer service, and are reaping the rewards. Some of the winners in a recent UNISYS 'Customer Champions' contest were:

'Some companies have established new and better levels of customer service'

- the National Breakdown Recovery Club, which operates a guarantee that all customers will be seen within an hour of calling for help, and usually gets there in half an hour or less – if NBRC misses the deadlines, it pays compensation. The 'we try harder' mentality of NBRC staff is such that customers often refuse the compensation money. They encourage customer feedback, and 95 per cent rate them highly.
- Cellini is a jewellery business based in Cambridge that has specialized in individual service and bespoke design in a business dominated by multiple retailers selling off-the-shelf products. The company has worked hard to get right the things that actually matter to its customers.
  - opening at 8 in the morning so that customers can call in on the way to work;
  - general repairs completed within 72 hours, rings sized in one hour, and free batteries for life to everyone buying a quartz watch;
  - a free collection and delivery service;
  - no charge for site visits to do valuations after a burglary;
  - a free ten-minute polishing and cleaning service for any item, including those supplied by competitors;
  - the same care and service for a £30 pair of earrings as for a £10,000 brooch.

  The founder, John Carter, concludes: 'We have achieved a brilliant relationship with our customers virtually without any material cost, simply by being helpful, friendly, and always giving our best. It's a matter of attitude rather than resources.'
- Schein Rexodent is in the somewhat less glamorous business of supplying dental practices. This business has broken the cartel that controlled dental supplies in Britain for decades, dramatically reduced the cost of supplies to surgeries at the time of pressure on health service costs, and at the same time has used team-based management approaches backed by a large IT investment to introduce new levels of customer service in an industry accustomed to slow deliveries from sluggish suppliers. From a standing start in 1984, turnover reached £6 million in

1990 and £30 million in 1994. One of the founders, Roger Freedman, notes: 'The mistake our competitors made was thinking that all we brought to market was low prices. We didn't – it was our service that was winning us customers just as much as prices.' Dentists were used to finding that only 80 per cent of a supplier's range was in stock and available for delivery. The difference is that Rexodent has a fulfilment rate of 98 per cent across its 15 000 item product range, 99.9 per cent accuracy in order delivery and same-day despatch for orders received up to 6 p.m. Unlike its competitors, the company has no minimum order, no handling or carriage charges, guarantees prices for the 12-month life of its catalogue, gives discounts to regular buyers and takes orders direct from customers' computer systems. The company has concluded that customer care works. [13]

So, it seems not only that it *could* be done (the theory), but that it *can* be done in reality.

But what is it like dealing with our company?

The quickest way to find out is to pretend to be a customer (see pp. 30–31 above). If this does not appeal, then have a look at the Service Encounter Diary in Figure 2.1. This provides an incredibly simple (and often quite entertaining) but very effective eye-opener for executive groups and employee groups in companies. What it does is ask people to do the following things:

- to identify buying situations where they have received outstandingly good or bad service and rate them on a scale where '1' means it was appallingly bad and '10' means it was truly outstanding and excellent;
- then to summarize the things that made the experience really good or horribly bad; and
- to discuss what they have found and see what the situations they have experienced tell us about managers and employees who build service and value and those who do not – you can list the characteristics of good and bad service providers and it will nearly always come out as a list of things like reliability, employee attitude, friendliness, trustworthiness, making extra effort, exceeding expectations, providing good value and treating the customer as someone special.

The real crunch then comes – you ask people which of these characteristics sound most like *our* company and what they think

The Situations	Rating*	What Made It Good Or Bad?

Conclusions *What does this tell us about how managers and employees give good or bad service to customers?*

* 1 = Appallingly bad, 10 = Excellent

Figure 2.1   Service encounter diary

our customers would say. If you are overwhelmed by feelings of smugness and complacency (as you may well be), the answer is simple – go and ask customers to tell you their stories about what it is like to deal with your company, and bring the stories back to the company (see pp. 69–70).

The starting point for solving problems is that people accept that we have got problems. This may be the starting point for your company.

But does it really matter what customers think . . .

Customer satisfaction and customer loyalty

The conventional response is: of course it matters what customers think, because satisfied customers are loyal customers, and loyal customers bring us repeat business, a higher share of their expenditure, and referrals and word-of-mouth recommendations to other customers. That sounds pretty convincing. Unfortunately, it is wrong.

From customer satisfaction to customer loyalty

The conventional argument is that satisfied customers are loyal. This means that an important goal is customer retention, because the financial gains can be huge. The advantages of high customer retention are:

- *Profitability* – Customer loyalty reduces costs and improves profits. Frederick Reichheld of the consultancy Bain and Co writes: 'customer loyalty appears to be the only way to achieve sustainably superior profits', and using an example from the life insurance business concludes: 'a five percentage point increase in customer retention lowers costs per policy by 18 per cent'. [14]. The Bain and Co work suggests that the average company loses 10 per cent of its customers each year but a reduction in loss of customers by only 5 per cent could increase profits by 25–85 per cent [15]. This reflects increased productivity and reduced new customer acquisition costs (see below). Also, at its simplest, if we keep a customer longer, the simple arithmetic suggests we make more profit from that customer.
- *Productivity* – Gains in profitability from customer retention come because: acquiring new customers to replace those we have lost costs five times more than the cost of maintaining existing customers; the longer the 'life' of the customer the higher the sales volume over which acquisition costs can be spread; and the return in investment in marketing to existing customers can be seven times higher than with marketing to prospective customers [16].
- *Sales volume* – To hold sales volume constant, with an 80 per cent annual customer retention rate, the customer base will need renewing every five years, but if retention is increased to 90 per cent, the base needs to be renewed only every ten years. Also, the evidence is that not only do loyal customers take less

marketing effort, they buy more of the company's products [14]. Research suggests that, in retailing, loyal shoppers spend up to four times more in their first-choice store than those who are 'promiscuous' in their shopping habits [14]. Calculating 'customer lifetime value' is a powerful way of concentrating minds on the significance of customer retention.

- *Actionability* – Customer retention is one of the things you can measure and evaluate and build development programmes to improve. This is underlined by evidence that most of the customers we lose do not take their business elsewhere because of poor product performance, they switch because of our poor service and how badly we treat them.

'customer satisfaction and customer loyalty are not the same thing; and you cannot buy real loyalty that easily'

The case for focusing on customer retention is overwhelming, and has spawned huge numbers of customer loyalty programmes. This is exciting stuff, but tends to miss a couple of important truths: customer satisfaction and customer loyalty are not the same thing; and you cannot buy real loyalty that easily.

Whoever told you that customer satisfaction and customer loyalty were the same thing? – they lied to you

Put crudely: *customer loyalty or retention* is about how long we keep a customer (or what share of their business we take), while *customer satisfaction* is what people think of us – our quality, service, value, and so on. These are different things.

For example, Figure 2.2 suggests four possible links between customer satisfaction and loyalty:

- *I: Satisfied Stayers.* This is the situation that is assumed by the customer retention argument above – if you satisfy customers through your quality in product and service, then they will remain loyal, so you reap all the advantages of customer retention. But, in reality, how often do we get lulled into a false sense of security because we confuse these customers with the next type?
- *II: Happy Wanderers.* These customers show every sign of being satisfied with what you do and how you do it, but they do not (or maybe cannot) give loyalty in return. They may choose to buy elsewhere because: tempting new products and services attract them; they want things they can only get from a competitor, so they transfer their business; or a technology

innovation takes them to the competition. Alternatively, in business-to-business markets, you may lose the satisfied customer because: there is a change in key personnel; corporate purchasing policies change; the purchasing company starts a supplier base reduction strategy; or the company stops outsourcing and produces the product itself. Or maybe the customer just wants a change for the hell of it. These customers will always give you great ratings on the customer satisfaction questionnaire – they just leave you when they feel like it.

- *III: Hostages.* It is possible that some of our most loyal customers may be highly dissatisfied ones. They may be tied to us by: product compatibility (e.g. only our product works in their machines); loyalty incentives (e.g. accumulating enough frequent flyer miles with the same airline to get the free flight); the costs of switching – economic or psychological (e.g. the complications for most people in switching bank accounts are substantial, and some customers are just lazy); corporate policy (e.g. central purchasing tells you where to purchase certain products); or even a form of monopoly if your brand or product is close to being unique for the time being (in Britain, at present, households can only get gas, water and electricity from a single supplier in their area). These customers are not satisfied – but they are retained (at least for the time being).
- *IV: Dealers.* These customers are not satisfied, and move brands and suppliers frequently. Often they will be the buyers most attracted by low prices and the best 'deal' on the market.

This model is not just speculation. It comes out of a project with a well-known company which is discovering that, as its market opens up to new competitors, customer satisfaction (theirs is very high) is really not the same thing as customer loyalty or retention (theirs is falling rapidly).

Customer Loyalty

		High	Low
	High	*I* *SATISFIED* *STAYERS*	*II* *HAPPY* *WANDERERS*
Customer *Satisfaction*			
	Low	*III* *HOSTAGES*	*IV* *DEALERS*

Figure 2.2 Customer satisfaction versus customer loyalty

They are not alone in worrying about this issue. British Airways have found that the defection rate among their 'satisfied' customers was 13 per cent – *exactly* the same as with dissatisfied, complaining customers [17].

There is also an interesting question about the wastefulness in investing in loyalty programmes for customers who are Hostages, Happy Wanderers or Dealers (because those investments are unlikely to pay off), and what are the distinguishing characteristics of the Satisfied Stayers in our business. In particular, doing things to attract the Happy Wanderers and Dealers may actually undermine our position with the Satisfied Stayers – special offers and new services offered only to attract the low loyalty customer but which are not offered to the loyal customer can have this disastrous effect.

There is another problem also in confusing satisfaction and loyalty: many of the gains from customer retention reflect satisfaction, *not* loyalty, particularly in increased purchasing, word-of-mouth recommendations to others, referrals, and speaking well of the company to enhance its market reputation and standing. If customers are not satisfied, you get none of those 'soft' benefits, even if people continue to buy from you out of habit or lack of choice.

It is at this stage that executives tend to ask the really difficult question: 'Which is more important to us, then, customer satisfaction or customer loyalty?' This is a difficult call, and there may be exceptions, but the general logic seems to be that the power is in customer satisfaction, while customer retention is the result we want. The critical group is the Hostages – can we increase their satisfaction so that we retain the business when they are no longer tied to us by bribery or lack of choice (they have cashed in the vouchers, or a new competitor appears)? If we focus there, at least we may get the recommendations or referrals, even if we do not retain that particular customer.

Who said you can buy loyalty, anyway?

'The strong case for leveraging customer retention has led to what some call "a mad dash back to the dark ages of marketing"'

The strong case for leveraging customer retention has led to what some call 'a mad dash back to the dark ages of marketing' [18] in a 'lemming-like rush' [19] to customer loyalty programmes – plastic loyalty cards from financial services firms, motor manufacturers and leading retailers like Tesco and Sainsbury; customer magazines; regular customer discounts; collectable vouchers for free flights from petrol stations; the 'Air Miles' scheme where purchases in various places using various payment methods earn points towards air travel or gifts; and the 'frequent flyer' programmes operated by the major airlines (offering the business traveller who flies a lot the chance to save points so that s/he can fly some more*). In fact, the proliferation of loyalty programmes is such that Datamonitor estimates that by the year 2000 there may be 3.8 *billion* cards in circulation, and one commentator notes: 'there is only so much loyalty to go around'! [16]

As sales promotion devices some of these schemes have been highly effective – the Tesco Clubcard is seen as one of the main reasons why Tesco took market leadership from Sainsbury in the UK grocery market. They are particularly effective if they focus on the customers who are most important to us – the big spender, the potential customers for new products, or the most profitable customers.

There is, however, one problem that should be noted about customer loyalty programmes – they have very little to do with customer loyalty. As Christopher Hapton, head of the customer loyalty practice at Bain and Co, noted some time ago: 'Loyalty is not developed by simply bribing someone to come back next time.' [20]

In terms of Figure 2.2, what most companies seem to be doing is investing in developing Hostages, not building Satisfied Stayers. Is this because 'buying' a period of repeat purchases from a customer is easier than taking customer satisfaction seriously? If so, then conventional loyalty programmes are no more than short-term sales promotion, and will have little long-term effectiveness because:

- they are easy for competitors to imitate. If all the super-markets offer similar loyalty cards, and all the airlines offer frequent flyer programmes, the sophisticated customer is likely to be a member of them all, take the benefits on offer, and purchase where s/he wishes, i.e. our Hostages turn into Dealers (Figure 2.2);
- they are easy for new entrants to attack. Asda did damage to the Tesco Clubcard simply by announcing at Christmas of the first year of operation that Asda stores would honour the

---

* In fact, there is a rumour that in the USA there are some business travellers who, in theory, will never have to pay for another flight, hotel rental or hire car for the rest of their lives, because of all the Air Miles they have accumulated. The paradox is that these tend to be the last people in the world who want to travel more and stay in another hotel away from home!

Tesco discount vouchers, thus getting the sales promotion gains with none of the overhead costs of the loyalty scheme;
- smart customers can play games:
  - in the UK in 1997 a Tesco supermarket ran a bananas promotion involving extra Clubcard points. One customer worked out that if he spent hundreds of pounds buying the fruit he would get enough Clubcard points to get the bananas free. He did just this, and then gave the bananas away free outside the store, and made the national newspaper headlines;
  - in the USA one supermarket gives regular customers vouchers offering discounts off the next purchase trip. Most of the vouchers are for 5 per cent or 10 per cent off, but some are for 50 per cent off. They now get people outside the store with placards saying things like '$200 given for a 50 per cent voucher'. When asked why, one couple pointed out that most people were buying groceries, so the 50 per cent voucher would be worth $100 to them at most. They, on the other hand, wanted to buy a refrigerator costing $5000. By buying the voucher: the voucher is worth twice as much to the grocery buyer; they get $2500 off the refrigerator; and the store loses all round. The loyalty voucher has actually become a tradable commodity in its own right.

These are amusing stories – what do they have to do with customer loyalty? Not a lot.
- the big risk is that crude customer loyalty incentives will undermine the long-term value of the brand, by substituting price incentives for brand values. Retailers Sainsbury, Tesco and Safeway are heavily committed to card-based customer loyalty programmes and argue that this has become one of the costs of being a retailer, and yet other retailers like Marks and Spencer and John Lewis have achieved high customer loyalty by sticking to the basics of what their brands stand for: high quality, keeping promises and putting mistakes right quickly and unquestioningly [19].

'Customer loyalty programmes are no protection against the competitor who delights the customer'

There is undoubtedly value for us in focusing on customer loyalty and customer retention. This is not the same thing as customer satisfaction. Customer loyalty programmes are no protection against the competitor who delights the customer, offers something new that attracts customers and offers better value in the customer's terms, or simply cares enough about the customer to build trust and commitment, i.e. to work for a relationship built on something more lasting and stable than sophisticated bribery!

Once again, it seems we may be in danger of missing the point – do we really care about customers?

So, what's the problem?

Rationally speaking, one would probably believe that if a company does its best to offer high levels of service and to provide the best possible level of quality in all its dealings with customers, then it would be likely to prosper. In many cases this is true, because of the lack of competition on precisely those things in all too many markets.

To this we have to add the indisputable fact that the customers' expectations about the level of service, which is theirs by *right*, are escalating. This is most clear at the moment in the services sector, but ultimately few of us will escape this pressure upwards in minimum service and quality requirements. The reality is that many services and added-value features will not in future achieve competitive differentiation at all – they will be the customer's minimum requirements, or the cost to us of being in the business at all. In fact, some people are now saying that, far from being the route to effective competitive differentiation, customer care and service campaigns are a waste of time – forget satisfaction, unless we can positively *delight* and entrance and captivate the customer with our products, our care and our service, we have no differentiation.

In fact, the easy assumption that *maximum* service and quality pays is not necessarily true, for two reasons: we may not understand what service creates customer value and delight; and even if we do, we may not be able to deliver it. We will see in Chapter 4 that these are key issues underlying the strategic choices of markets and segments that we need to confront in building a strong market strategy (see pp. 147–54).

Do we know what service to maximize?

The first point is that customers are perverse, emotional, awkward, unreasonable people who want things done on *their* terms, not ours. Providing service and quality which is not valued by the paying customer, however well-meaning, is unlikely to gain the business that we want, and, in fact, is a good route to 'servicing' and 'total qualitying' ourselves right out of business.

Perhaps we should call this the 'RB211 syndrome'. Even if you are the greatest engineering firm (e.g. Rolls-Royce), designing in quality and technology which the customer does not want enough to pay for (e.g. the RB211 aero-engine) does not pay off (e.g. bankrupts the company).

Consider the case of an industrial equipment supplier of my acquaintance, whose engineering-led managers were committed to producing the 'best' machines on the market. They dismissed the selling problem – 'we are the best, we are out on our own, there is no problem in selling . . .'. The customer agreed that their machines were the 'best'. Unfortunately, what the customer wanted in this market was 'cheaper, and sufficient for our needs'. Even more unfortunately, the manufacturer's management would not believe or accept this, and the company started down the slippery slope of believing that they knew better than the customer, with the inevitable disastrous results.

Often the problem really does come down to simply not understanding what things really *matter most* to the customer. For instance, the management of one garage chain offered customers a free 'courtesy car' while their own cars were being serviced. They were infuriated to find that customers who only worked a few hundred yards away still took a courtesy car and left it sitting outside the office all day in sight of the garage. Management then instituted a charge for the 'courtesy car' to get rid of this 'abuse' of the service. Customers still did the same thing, but now paid for it. The motor car addict will *pay* for the personal comfort of not being cut off from transport, whether s/he actually uses it or not. Possibly irrational – but if that is what the customer wants and values, the conclusion is clear.

On the other hand, one of the cases I like to discuss with managers from sophisticated, high-technology businesses is a small businessman in Cardiff, who has nearly doubled the consumption of his 'commodity' product among his key target customers, by the addition of a service which costs him almost nothing. In doing this he has actually increased customer satisfaction *and* loyalty. Even hi-tech managers will agree that this is a result that most of us would be happy to settle for in our own businesses. He is a hairdresser, who has instituted the practice of booking your next haircut for about four weeks later, at the moment when you leave his salon. The real point is that the average period between haircuts for men in the UK is six to nine weeks – he has virtually halved this. What is more, he has done this at almost no cost to himself *and* made his most important customers feel valued! The pay-off from getting right things that the customer values is potentially enormous for us all.

The point that customer service and care create satisfied customers, from which we then get the things we want (profit, growth, value of investment, and so on), is one which the hairdresser understands perfectly. Too many of us forget it.

But this is not just about the personal service and care of the smart entrepreneur. The Training Department of J. Sainsbury Plc has a training module for supermarket staff which the company puts all its operatives through, but which is just one very tiny example of its commitment to training staff to create the standards of quality that impress its paying customers.

This training module is about what to do when the customer breaks a messy product like a bottle of orange squash or tomato ketchup, and it goes all over the floor in the store – seemingly a trivial event, but a significant problem in managing a grocery business, and a significant issue to the customer.

Now, I started my working life in discount grocery super-markets, and I *know* what the response is (or at least what it used to be): the customer is metaphorically taken by the scruff of the neck and told: 'Your kid broke it, you pay for it'! The likely result, of course, is that we certainly avoid losing a few pennies in sales, but stand a good chance of losing that customer and perhaps many others as well.

The Sainsbury training module teaches a rather different approach: first, ensure that the customer takes another product; second, make sure that the customer is not embarrassed; third, clear up the mess; and fourth, report the incident to a supervisor who will make sure that the display is secure. Result – a customer who has been treated beautifully (and has been seen by other customers to be so treated) and who will come back; we still make the sale (and because we are organized we probably get a credit from the suppliers for the broken product anyway); and the member of staff feels good about the whole thing too.

But this is not about altruism for its own sake. It is about care and attention to the small things that matter to customers, as a route to customer satisfaction and thus to high business performance.

However, in the real world we should never forget that when we are customers we are likely to be not simply harsh but also highly unfair in the judgements we make. For example, in the airline business people talk about the 'olive factor' – if you forget to put the olive in the martini, the customer thinks you will forget to put the wheels down when you land the plane, and this is not regarded as a good idea.

In a similar way, British Airways did a massive amount of expensive and sophisticated hard-nosed market research into the requirements of the short-haul air traveller, and what influenced airline choice. This led to the BA strategy of courtesy and sympathy and 'putting people first', with some considerable success. Even then they made a mistake with the critical business traveller market – they *believed* that the business traveller was mainly influenced by factors of timely arrival, availability of phones and faxes, and other 'rational' factors. The glamorous and sophisticated British Airways lost substantial market share to a small airline called British Midland because of the 'sausage factor'. The 'rational' business traveller wanted a free breakfast sausage and would change airlines to get it. British Airways had to respond with the Super Shuttle, including free breakfast.

'Customers can be very unfair in the judgements they make'

Customers can be very unfair in the judgements they make, but at the end of the day it is allowed – because it is their *money*. Maximizing the wrong service and quality (as far as the customer is concerned) is expensive and unproductive (as far as we are concerned).

Can we deliver the service we promised?

The second point is that offering the customer service and quality and responsiveness which we cannot really deliver is also potentially a route to disaster. The point is that raising unrealistic *customer expectations* (in terms of what we can really deliver) will create dissatisfied customers just as surely as poor product marketing and service delivery.

For example, one technically superb UK advertising campaign in the 1970s was the 'Wonder of Woollies' campaign, which transformed the image of Woolworths chain stores from seedy, second-choice suppliers of cheap commodities from old-fashioned, somewhat tacky outlets, to a clean, friendly, welcoming, service-oriented retailer with modernized stores. The campaign was an outstanding winner in all the usual marketing terms – consumer recall, attitude and belief change, rebuilding store image, and the like. Unfortunately, the company rebuilt store image, but did not rebuild the stores. The Woolworths of the 1970s in the UK was, in reality, much more like the seedy, second-rate position than the friendly, modernized image of the ads. The campaign was a triumph for the marketing people but a disaster for the company. To be second-rate is bad. To convince people you are first-rate, then let them find you second-rate, means they will write you off as third-rate, and you are worse off than when you started. Disappointed customers are vindictive and have long memories. Raising unrealistic expectations is a dangerous business.

Of course, managing customer expectations is a neat trick if you can do it. The car hire chain Rent-A-Wreck is a good example of managing customer expectations *down* instead of up. They advertise the offer – as the company name suggests – that they will hire you an old, beaten-up wreck of a car, for a very low rental charge. In fact, when you get to the rental office the cars are not wrecks. Certainly they are not brand-new and they may have a few scrapes, but they are fine. So you end up with a much better car than you expected *and* a low price. Most people seem quite pleased with this.

Ultimately, customer service and quality should be *consistent* with all the other aspects of the total offering that we make to the customer. A quick example. One of the most successful and dynamic businesses I have worked with in the past few years is a family-owned wholesale nursery supplier, whose core business is supplying independent gardening shops and centres with plants and seedlings. This company has a very clear product and market position with its customers: you do not get service. This company does not deliver products, once they are outside the gate they are the customer's problem. They do not wash, label, package the plants in polythene tubs and wrappers, sort, or provide information leaflets – they offer no value-added services of this type. What they do offer is a good product at a rock-bottom price. Their customers are small independent retailers, not the big chains or sheds, and their customers' major need is low-priced products to survive the competition provided by the chains and sheds. Of course, the managers of this company suffered from the major disadvantage that they had not read the books or been on the management courses that would have told them that the *only* way to compete successfully in their market is on service and quality. This is perhaps fortunate, because they have created a market position which does three significant things: it offers a particular kind of customer the one thing which is *most* important to them – low prices; it keeps customer expectations of what they will get closely in line with what they actually get; and the strategy is one that this company can deliver consistently, properly and profitably. The signs of this last point are note-worthy: if you ask the MD for his business card, he laughs and offers to write his name down for you if you cannot remember it (most people can), because the business does not pay printers for such frivolous things; very few employees have company cars and, when they do, the vehicles bought are second-hand Rovers; the people in the company are proud of each thing they do to cut costs and save money – and they brag about these things because the culture is driven by cost-efficiency. This capability and culture is supremely appropriate to delivering the company's market strategy – even though it would be a huge barrier to implementing a different strategy.

The conclusion to which I am drawing is that we should think in terms of *appropriate* service and quality strategies, which match the most important needs of our target customers but also about our ability to deliver.

For example, one way of looking round at our competitors and how well they are doing, and comparing their performance to ours, is shown in Figure 2.3. Before we jump to easy conclusions about what works and what does not, why not see what the distribution and spread of competition is – is high customer satisfaction achieved through service and quality or other issues, is low customer satisfaction associated with high or low service provision, or is there no clear relationship? Indeed, we might then look at which types of firms are doing best in market share and profitability terms, and see what conclusions that leads us to.

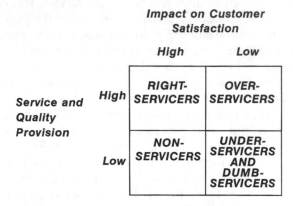

Figure 2.3 Service and quality versus customer satisfaction

Whatever else we may find, it would be good to decide whether we are currently over- or under-servicing, or if we have got it about right, and whether there are low-service opportunities in the market as well as high-service niches. There is actually some truth in the saying 'There's riches in niches'.

So, what's the real problem?

The real problem is two things: first, the very real danger that we end up becoming obsessed with the *trappings* rather than the *substance*; and, *secondly*, the issues we have raised seem symptomatic of something deeply wrong in our organizations that may be hard to get close to. Let us consider these points in turn, because they are quite important and warrant a little further thought.

Trappings or substance?

The worry is that by and large it is actually a lot easier to adopt customer care programmes, to train operatives in customer service, and so on, than to actually *care* about customers in the real sense, and to provide the services they want. Certainly I remain unrepentantly sceptical about top managements who foist such things as customer care programmes on their organizations without themselves being committed, visible participants. At worst this smacks of lip-service and lack of real commitment where it matters most in the organization, and at best of top management going for the latest 'quick-fix' (shortly to be replaced by the next fashionable panacea).

Take an extreme example of lip-service to customers rather than real commitment. In a well-known Volkswagen distributorship in the UK, the Managing Director bought the quality and service message in a big way. On the appointed day he toured all the garages in the distributorship delivering a carefully prepared and emotionally-loaded customer service message; all staff were issued with plastic cards for their wallets bearing the customer mission message, to be carried at *all* times; every single member of staff was personally briefed by the MD on that person's individual and vital role in creating quality for the customer, regardless of the effect of greasy boots and overalls on his office furnishings. No expense or inconvenience was spared to deliver the customer service message. The effect was somewhat spoiled by the fact that on the same day the MD was seen to have an abusive public row with a customer, culminating in the MD telling the customer to f*** off! The *signals* we send to our people are remembered long after our *words* are forgotten.

This may sound unfair and over-critical – and it may be just that. But it strikes me as interesting that if you talk to managers in companies pursuing quality control programmes, total quality management, and so on, they may talk a lot about the excitement and the internal changes, or even the key values of quality and the like. They rarely seem to get round to talking about what the external, end, paying customer actually *wants*, and what he/she gets that is better in his/her terms. I wonder if this is because it is a lot easier, and perhaps more fun, to introduce such programmes than to deal with the less palatable realities of customer priorities and judgements (such as those we discussed earlier and will go on discussing).

Tokens or truths?

Perhaps what is most worrying is that many tools and techniques to improve our customer service are misused on a wide scale. They are being used to treat the symptoms, not the sickness. They are token, very visible, efforts to cover up, but not solve, the underlying problem. Consider the following cases in very different companies.

Case A

A retail bank was faced with clear evidence that consumers found the attitude of its front-office staff in personal dealings off-hand, impatient and generally offensive to the paying customer. After much high-level thought and many meetings between top management and consultants, a customer care strategy was declared, and an expensive programme of training set up for front-office staff in how to deal with the customer. This itself uncovered some interesting issues – such as that it is near-impossible to train professional bank counter staff to apologize to the customer – they will *not* say 'sorry'. The best that could be devised was a conditional apology: 'I am sorry if the bank is wrong, *but* . . .'. However, this is not even the point. The point is that even bank clerks as a species are not inherently unpleasant. Their unpleasant behaviour with customers results from the way their business is run and the signals they receive from the organization that tells them the real attitudes and beliefs, and thus what is important and what matters little. Look at the example which is set by the managers of the business at all levels. For instance, one very senior executive explained to me that when he was trained in dealing with the public (a one-off event at the start of his 40-year banking career, incidentally), if a customer walked in off the street bringing his account with him, the response was clear. The appropriate response for a prudent, professional banker was to find out what was 'wrong' with the customer by writing to his existing bank manager, and probably declining the business as a result – this is how 'gentlemen' run a business. This may sound insane, but if you want to test it, go and talk to some top managers in banking. The real point of this case, however, is that you do not blame front-line operatives and supervisors for poor service in banks, you blame top, middle and junior *management*, and focus your efforts there. In fact, I have an idea about the customer service issue in banking, which I am prepared to give away for free. Instead of pressuring front-office staff and branch managers, why

'Look at the example which is set by the managers of the business at all levels'

not measure customer service perceptions (of customers) and log and investigate all customer complaints, and then let's use this information to evaluate and reward Regional Directors, Area Branch Inspectors and the General Manager (by reporting the results to shareholders)?

Case B

A prestigious multinational company in the paper goods business has been an eager adopter and a public advocate of total quality management (TQM) as the route to improving its operation. However, while on the surface this is the most valuable thing the company has ever done, scratching beneath the surface reveals that all is not quite as utopian as we have been led to believe. If we talk to managers in this company, they tell us about chasing 'brownie points' by keeping other departments happy. They tell us about massive efforts in negotiating internal 'contracts' with other departments, to avoid being put in the potentially risky position of being criticized for poor delivery of service to the other department, when they can 'sue' us in the boardroom. What they do *not* tell us about is departments jointly solving the external, paying customer's problems, which is what the TQM theory was supposed to be about in the first place. Management by slogan (however well-meaning) and by 'quick-fix' (however expensive and time-consuming in reality) is dangerous because we end up even further from delivering what the paying customer wants.

Case C

A little while ago, one of the regional companies of the UK power industry managed the interesting act of shooting itself in the foot by the very act of launching a massive customer care campaign. The top management group of this large, labour-intensive business conceived, resourced and implemented a customer care campaign, consisting mainly of a large TV and press spend, inviting the customer to voice his/her complaints, because the company now 'cared' (presumably, by implication, admitting that to date it had not given a damn about the customer). The advertising campaign was accompanied by a household ques-tionnaire and leaflet drop, reinforcing the message. Some two weeks before the campaign went live and there was no way back, management finally decided to let its staff in on the big secret. At this point, things started to go wrong. Operational staff reacted with some considerable hostility – people said unreasonable things like: 'We think it's great that you care about the customer – why don't you care about us?' Management's response was to start issuing staff with hastily-produced glossy brochures about the customer care campaign – which did not cut much ice with staff, but at least meant that management did not have to talk to them any more. The operational staff perceived that management expected them to bear the brunt of the new campaign, since quite evidently top management did not have the slightest intention of changing its behaviour or the way it runs the business. The net result is consumers who are urged to complain (who are quite reasonably not pleased when those complaints are ignored), operational staff who bear this new pressure with some lack of grace, and a well-meaning top management group who do not know what has hit them or even why. Yet again, tokenism is a dangerous game to play.

The point of these cases is two-fold. First, if we just treat the symptoms (of poor customer service and low satisfaction) without getting to grips with the real underlying problem (of management attitudes and behaviour as well as those of operatives), then we will achieve little of lasting value, and may do considerable harm to our businesses. Second, if we only adopt the trappings of these tools, then the effect may be in the wrong direction in spite of the best intentions, and any beneficial effect will be short-lived.

This brings us to the fundamental issue to be confronted and tested – our *real* attitude towards customer satisfaction as the central focus for our whole organization.

So, where are we now on the customer satisfaction issue?

Please re-read the title of this section. It reads: 'where *are* we now', not 'where would we *like* to be' or 'where *should* we be', or 'where could we *convince* ourselves we are, so we can sweep the customer satisfaction issue back under the carpet where it came from'! The real question is not just about pumping out customer satisfaction questionnaires and leaving it at that; the issue is one of *managing* the customer satisfaction issue.

Getting to grips with this issue is not easy, for all the reasons which we have gone through to get to this point. However, we have found that a good practical start is just to try asking some simple questions. The Market-Led Strategic Change Diagnostic 1 (Figure 2.4) is a set of questions which we have put together from

Company:	Market/Segment/Customer Type:
Completed by:	Date:

How good are we at each of these:	Marks out of 10*				
	1.	2.	3.	4.	5.
1. Measuring customer satisfaction					
2. Using customer satisfaction measurements to change our marketing policies					
3. Using customer satisfaction measurements to evaluate and reward staff					
4. Ensuring all staff understand our strategy on customer service and quality					
5. Setting staff measurable goals for customer service and quality, and evaluating performance					
6. Consulting staff about customers' needs, expectations, complaints — and taking notice of what they say					
7. Managers setting a good example in providing service and quality to customers					
8. Working together to remove obstacles and barriers to quality and service delivery					
9. Regularly evaluating our competitors' service and quality provision					
10. Having a clear and actionable service and quality strategy compared to our competitors					
TOTAL (OUT OF 100)					
Conclusions/Implications/Actions					

*1 = Very poor Performance   5 = Average Performance
10 = Excellent Performance/Market Leadership

Figure 2.4 Diagnostic worksheet 1 – how serious are we about customer service and satisfaction?

a variety of sources to open up this issue. (If you do not think they are exactly the right questions for your company, then change the wording as needed, but we have found the basic intentions of Diagnostic 1 to be reasonably clear in a wide variety of different organizations.) Let us consider the goals of Diagnostic 1 and how it can be used in an organization – and, perhaps most important, *who* should use it.

Goals of Diagnostic 1

The overall aim of the Diagnostic is to evaluate our performance in managing customer satisfaction as the basis for our marketing operations and strategies. More specifically, the Diagnostic tries to measure the following attributes:

- Our success in measuring customer satisfaction* – not just doing it, but being seen to do it, and being seen to do it validly, systematically and routinely (Question 1).
- Whether we use such measurements to change the way we do things for customers, and whether we are seen and are appreciated to be responsive (Question 2).
- Our effectiveness in using customer satisfaction measurements as a basis for evaluating and rewarding staff – this obviously impacts directly on front-line operational staff, but we should include management at various levels. Effective use also implies that we are positive and not negative in how we use customer satisfaction measures (Question 3).
- Our performance in successfully communicating our policies, strategies and positioning on customer service and quality to all staff. This means more than just telling them, it means getting understanding, agreement and commitment, and listening to what they say (Question 4).
- Whether we are seen to set reasonable goals for staff in delivering service and quality to the customer, and whether we are seen to evaluate and follow up performance on these goals (e.g. do we react appropriately to customer complaints, lost accounts, orders switched by customers, unfavourable informal comments about our performance, and so on?) (Question 5).
- How well do we do at finding out what our staff believe to be the customer's critical needs, expectations and why they complain – do we take notice of what they say and respond to what they say (Question 6)?
- Are managers seen to set a good example in providing service and quality to customers – or do we signal our *real* attitudes by being unavailable to meet customers face-to-face, 'in meetings' when the customer telephones, slow or recalcitrant in answering customer letters, and so on (Question 7)?

---

* We will talk in more detail about the theory and reality of customer satisfaction measurement in Chapter 3 (see pp. 84–92).

- Are we seen to be working together to remove all the obstacles and barriers to delivering good service and quality to the customer – even if it means changing company 'rules' and 'policies' and the like (Question 8)?
- Do we regularly and systematically look at our competitors' performance in delivering quality and service, and look at the effect on sales, market share, customer loyalty, profitability, and so on (Question 9)?
- Finally, do we have a strategy on our provision of customer service and quality in all that we do for the customer, which is clear, and which we are capable of consistently delivering to the customer, and which gives us a clear position compared to our competitors (Question 10)? *'do we have a strategy on our provision of customer service and quality'*

There is no difficulty in thinking up additional questions in this area, but our experience is that these are usually more than enough to get started.

Instructions for completing Diagnostic 1

As with all such instruments, the aim is to keep the exercise as simple and unambiguous as possible. The Diagnostic should be self-explanatory, but the following should make the logic clear.

- *Company* – To avoid any ambiguity about which part of our operation we are concerned with, this should be defined first.
- *Market/Segment/Customer type* – To focus attention, we should be clear whether we want to look at a whole market, just one segment, or even just one customer type. The more precise we are about what type of customer or which of our markets we are looking at, the clearer the conclusions are likely to be.
- *Completed by* – This warrants a little more consideration shortly, but for the moment we can say that it is desirable to put a name on the Diagnostic, unless this is likely to bias the results (and in some cases anonymity may be necessary to get honest answers).
- *Marks out of 10* – The form defines a simple scoring device of marks out of 10, where '1' equates to 'Very poor performance', '5' is 'Average performance', and '10' is 'Excellent performance/market leadership'. The grid or columns into which the evaluation marks are entered can be used in a number of ways, to be considered in a moment. For the present, we put our evaluations in the first column, and total to get a score out of 100.

- *Conclusions/Implications* – However we use the Diagnostic, it should not just be a list of numbers. We should carefully examine the evaluations to see what they tell us and what conclusions we can draw from the pattern we have found – and, of course, ultimately what actions are indicated.

Using Diagnostic 1

Now we get to the interesting issues – who should fill in the Diagnostic and how do we build up the grid, and how do we interpret the findings?

Who completes the Diagnostic?

There are clear options here, not all of which may be open to us, because of the way our organization works. Consider the following ways of using the Diagnostic.

- To start with, let's fill it in ourselves for each significant part of our operation – each part of the operation going in Column 1 on a separate form. Let's see what this tells us about the gaps and what actions are needed if we are going to take customer satisfaction management seriously. This is normally interesting, but we can make it a lot more interesting.
- We can ask our *staff* to complete the Diagnostic. We can ask the *Chief Executive* to complete the Diagnostic. We can ask *other departments* to complete the Diagnostic. These can then be entered in the columns of the grid, and compared item by item. The really interesting contrast is likely to be between what the operational staff tell you and what senior management tells you. This is getting closer to the real answer to the question of whether we have got our act together on the customer service and satisfaction issue.
- If we are getting somewhere on this front, we can actually do something which is so outlandish I hesitate to commit it to writing. We could actually try asking our *customers* and *distributors* to tell us whether they think we are successfully managing the customer service and satisfaction issue. Then we can put their evaluations alongside ours, our management's and our staff's, and see what the picture is then!
- The other way we should use the grid is simply *regularly.* For each of the parties involved – staff, managers, departments, distributors, customers, and so on – we should ask the same questions regularly and record the results on the Diagnostic so that we can see if we are getting better or worse over time.

One variation in using this Diagnostic, which we have tried when people find the logic a bit hard to swallow, is to fill it in for our *competitors* rather than ourselves. Even if we only use intelligence data from our sales staff and distributors, this can be fun, but it is even better if we ask the customer! It gets even more interesting if we can tie up the findings with performance in such areas as the standing of the competitor in the customer's eyes, market share, growth rates, profitability, and so on. You can also distinguish between new and established customers, for example – are the things new customers like about us the same as the things old customers like, or has the market changed?

If nothing else, this is a good way of getting some of the sceptics to take the issue more seriously.

Interpreting the findings

With all Diagnostics of this kind, the richness and usefulness of the conclusions we can reach will depend on how rigorously and seriously we use the instrument. If we pursue the possibilities outlined above, then we need to look at the completed grids, the scores on each issue and the total scores, the trend over time, and to ask questions like these:

- Where are the gaps in our approach to managing customer satisfaction, where are we seen to do badly, and what do we need to do about it?
- How does our performance differ in different markets or segments, and what are the reasons?
- How can we explain and act on the different views that we get from different sources, and what does this tell us we need to do?
- How is our performance on managing customer satisfaction issues changing over time, is this good or bad, are we making progress?
- How does our performance on customer satisfaction management relate to other critical factors: staff turnover, customer loyalty, sales and market share, other performance indicators?

'Where are the gaps in our approach to managing customer satisfaction'

No simple Diagnostic of this kind is going to tell us everything we need to know, or easily solve the problem for us. We are not in the business here of trying to provide a 'quick-fix', which produces some short-term effects and then disappears again.

However, our experiences with a variety of different organizations suggest that this type of diagnosis is a good starting point in working out where our marketing has gone wrong and identifying the things we need to do better.

The story so far

Let's consider what this chapter has tried to do by way of scene-setting for the remainder of the book and hopefully establishing a few home-truths: the evidence that, in spite of lip-service to customers, real service and real attitudes to customers are appalling and few of us can afford to be complacent on this issue – try the Service Encounter Diary (Figure 2.1) and see what it uncovers about your company's treatment of its customers when it matters; let's not confuse customer satisfaction with customer loyalty and think that customer retention statistics measure customer satisfaction – they don't; let's think in terms of customer service and customer satisfaction as part of a market strategy, not something we do for its own sake; and let's get past the trappings of customer care to how we really treat our customers (Diagnostic 1).

The next question follows directly from what we have said about taking customers seriously – if we do care and we are not doing as well as we should, how do we do better? How can we build a truly customer-focused organization?

References

1. 'Unlucky Severn for Driver With No Cash', *Daily Mail*, 28 March 1997.
2. Womack, James P. and Daniel T. Jones (1996), *Lean Thinking: Banish Waste and Create Wealth Within Your Corporation*, New York: Simon and Schuster.
3. Miles, Joshua (1996), 'Helpline Callers Left Hanging on the Phone', *Sunday Business*, 18 November.
4. Treacy, Michael and Fred Wiersema (1995), *The Discipline of Market Leaders*, London: Harper Collins.
5. Clark, Susan (1994), 'Vulnerable, Afraid and Humiliated', *Sunday Times*, 24 April.
6. 'Big Banks Slammed over Service', *Sunday Times*, 4 December 1994.
7. *The Front Line Survey*, The Grass Roots Group plc, 1994.
8. Berry, Len (1996), 'Retailers with a Future', *Marketing Management*, Spring, 43.
9. Thorpe, Vanessa (1996), 'Shop Assistants Get Anti-Violence Video as "Store Rage" Soars', *Independent on Sunday*, 22 September.
10. Marston, Paul (1996), 'Poor Staff Threatens Tour Trade', *Daily Telegraph*, 31 October.
11. 'Fawlty Manners, and That's the Guests', *Daily Mail*, 15 April 1997.
12. Womack, James P. and Daniel T. Jones (1996), *op. cit.*
13. 'Customer Champions', *Sunday Times*, 20 November 1994.

14. Summers, Diane (1993), 'Rewards for the Loyal Shopper', *Financial Times*, 2 December.
15. Reichheld, Frederick F. and W. Earl Sasser (1990), 'Zero Defections: Quality Comes to Services', *Harvard Business Review*, September/ October, 105–111.
16. Mazur, Laura (1996), 'Accountability', *Marketing Business*, July/August, 16.
17. Mitchell, Alan (1994), 'What Makes a Defector', *Financial Times*, 4 August.
18. 'Paying Lip-Service to the Loyalists', *Business Age*, 1 April 1996.
19. Mazur, Laura (1997), 'Brands', *Marketing Business*, April, 16.
20. 'The Databases of the Argument', *Marketing Week*, 18 November 1994.

CHAPTER 3

Achieving customer focus:

What do we do if we do care?

Introduction

From the somewhat acidic (though well-deserved) comments about how badly companies treat their customers, in the previous chapter, we have established that there is a major imperative for management in all types of organizations to focus better on customer needs – to be market-led, to care for customers, to create the value that matters to the customer, and so on. However, what is far less clear is how managers can evaluate and monitor, let alone change the performance of their organizations, in terms of achieving effective and productive customer focus. That is, even if we agreed on what we should be doing about this issue, there remains the problem of how we can actually do it.

'the much sought-after customer-focused organization has proved elusive'

The achievement of the much sought-after customer-focused organization has proved elusive (though not impossible).

Two things are clear, however:

- Achieving real customer focus normally needs more than management 'say so' or edict – however exalted and prestigious the managers in question may be.
- No-one ever said it would be easy (or if they did, they never tried it themselves) – there are no 'plug-in' quick-fixes for this issue.

However, what we can put on the agenda are a number of ideas, things to try and approaches to consider, in the pursuit of customer focus. None of these are total solutions, but the evidence suggests that each can achieve some good things for organizations if used thoroughly and appropriately.

The customer relationship scale

As a starting point, Figure 3.1 suggests that we can see customer focus varying on a scale, where different positions on the scale are associated with different types of customer relationships.

At one end of the scale, there is little genuine, real customer focus. In this situation, we talk of 'the market' or 'clients' or 'accounts', as some kind of anonymous entities who we hope will buy and consume our products and services. Unfortunately, anonymous entities and 'markets' are not what buy products and services – people do, and they are called customers, and that is normally how they wish to be treated.

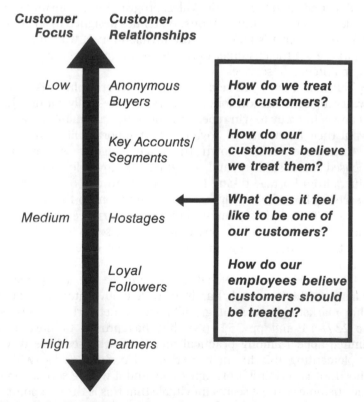

Figure 3.1 The customer relationship scale

You may get away with operating at this end of the scale – particularly if, for a time, demand outstrips supply in your industry, if you have a monopoly of some kind for a while, if you have a radical product/service innovation which only you can supply, or if you are just cheaper than anyone else can be at the time. But remember – never expect loyalty, commitment, or real satisfaction from customers you treat badly, and do not expect them to stay when a better alternative appears.

One move down the scale towards customer focus is probably where we find most marketing companies today. Some effort is made to identify and target customers as members of key market segments and/or key accounts. At least here we have some idea who customers are, and introduce some degree of customer focus into sales and market operations, though often little more than that in reality.

In the middle of the scale, we see what most modern marketing seeks to achieve – what Bonoma has called 'taking hostages'. We focus our efforts on winning 'loyalty' through customer 'satisfaction', but by doing our best to take away customer freedom. We saw in Chapter 2 that we can think of hostage-taking through: airline and credit card Air Miles programmes; consumer and trade 'collectables' and coupons; machines designed to work only with one supplier's materials; the invalidation of warranties and guarantees if the customer dares to use competitors' components or maintenance services.

This may make some sense in markets where volume is critical, switching costs are low for customers, and we really cannot think of any better way to win repeat business. But, ultimately, hostages want their freedom, and 'loyalty' is a temporary illusion.

One move further down the scale suggests we are more focused on customers and see them as 'loyal followers'. This differs from hostage-taking in that we try to win our customers' hearts and minds, rather than shackling them to the product or service. The goal is similar, but the means are more subtle. Most 'life-style' or image-based advertising seeks to achieve this effect, as do many programmes of customer care and customer calling.

The extreme on the scale is where we see customers as partners. This approach has been widely advocated in relationship marketing and strategic alliance or network theories (see pp. 237–43 and pp. 251–63), but has proved to have more limited appeal among practical managers who see little way of implementing this in their markets. (However, as we will see shortly, it is certainly not impossible, and if we are serious about the customer issue it seems inevitable that this is the real point we want to attain on the scale – see pp. 498–99).

One starting point in getting to grips with the customer focus issue is to discuss this scale with people – colleagues, employees, distributors, even customers – to figure out where our organization is and where it would like to be. The critical questions raised in Figure 3.1 suggest that we are likely to need to accommodate different viewpoints in this evaluation; our views of how our customers are treated may be very different from customers' views of how they are treated!

If the customer relationship scale is a way of putting a handle on the customer focus in a particular company, then the approaches from which we can choose the most appropriate include:

- discovering what value means to our customers;
- learning to listen to customers and to respond to what they say;
- obsessing over customers – what some call building the 'cult of the customer' in the company;
- measuring customer satisfaction and using it positively to improve how we do the things that matter to customers; and
- building and sustaining a customer-focused culture in the company.

If we were able to successfully do all those things, we would indeed have a customer-focused organization. As the cases at the end of this section show, some companies succeed in doing just this.

What is value for our customers?

To go back to basics, customers develop value expectations and make purchases based on their perceptions of a product's benefits compared to the total cost of the purchase (in price, but also time, effort, difficulty, and so on)[1]. Superior customer value is created when the buyer's experience is very favourable compared to expectations, and compared to the value provided by competitors. An overview of the sources of superior customer value is provided in Figure 3.2 and suggests them to be:

- our *capabilities, skills and resources* – what we are good at doing, that matters to the customer;
- our *customer benefit focus* – how we concentrate on doing the things that matter to customers (even if they are not the things we would most like to be doing!);

Figure 3.2 Sources of superior customer value

- our *organizational change in processes* of service delivery and value creation, to do things the way the customer wants, not the way that happens to be most convenient for us;
- the *commitment and service* for our people – what the customer finds when dealing with us;
- *innovation and change* – to get better at doing the things that matter and to find new ways of 'delighting' customers; and
- simply *listening to customers and learning* what increases value to them, and applying these terms to what we do.

There are a couple of points worth expanding here.

Customer perception is reality

The harsh truth is that value is not created in the factory or the back office; customer value exists only on the customer's terms and reflects the customer's priorities and preferences. You may say that the customer is irrational, ill-informed, misguided, short-sighted, and so on (and that is just what we do say – see Chapter 2), but value exists only when the customer decides it does.

'customer value exists only on the customer's terms and reflects the customer's priorities and preferences'

Knowing what means value to our customers is therefore rather important. We may get nice surprises: Post Office Counters is plagued by customers demanding that they cut the length of queues. They did so. Their customers believed that the (actually shorter) queues were longer than ever. Managers found the quickest way to cut customer perceptions of queuing times was to repaint Post Offices. Customers in redecorated Post Offices reported that they had queued for a shorter time, even though it was not true. The issue is not just standing in line, it is queuing in squalor. Royal Mail managers' bonuses now depend in part not just on meeting performance targets, but on whether customers believe they are meeting those targets [2].

On the other hand, if we do not know what the value drivers are for our customers, we may do the wrong things:

- One company believed that speed of service was the key to customer value, so trained telephone staff to be quicker. They lost market share because in fact customers wanted time to chat and resented being hassled [3].
- When Federal Express went for faster delivery speed to please customers, they also achieved the reverse. The extra speed caused more misdirections and errors. Customers actually value getting the parcel most!

There are a couple of complications to really knowing what value is to your customers:

- Different customers buy different kinds of value [4]. This is true both within the market (see market segmentation by customer benefits, pp. 158–88) and, more surprisingly, in different markets. For example, one of the most vilified products in Britain is the Reliant Robin – the fibre-glass-bodied three-wheeler car sold in Britain in the 1960s as the cheapest type of motoring and for those with only a motor-cycle driving licence. In 1996, Reliant almost went out of business for good. In 1997, the Robin Reliant started to sell strongly in Austria – young buyers see the three-wheeler as a 'fun vehicle' and also as environmentally-friendly because it used little petrol and does not rust. Reliant is looking to extend sales in Monaco and California [5] Or look at the portable clockwork radio, designed by a British inventor and manufactured in Africa, which is creating a sensation in the developing countries where, for large parts of the market, radio ownership is high priority, but the cost of batteries is prohibitive.
- Things change – value 'migrates' [6]. This suggests that value propositions become less effective over time, and unless you find ways to enhance or re-focus the value in your product or service, buyers will migrate to alternative value concepts.

British financial service companies have always offered trust-worthiness, prudence and financial expertise to the market, and were wrong-footed by firms like Virgin Direct offering simple products that were easier to buy.

- Even value is not enough – the best companies positively 'delight' customers. In looking at its customer satisfaction data, Xerox discovered a simple truth – satisfying customers is good, but the truly delighted customers buy six times more than the satisfied customers. Delight may be additional product features or absolute guarantees of quality and price, but the winners seem to be the companies that dramatically exceed customer expectations on critical dimensions of value.

One-to-one marketing

Don Peppers uses the term 'one-to-one marketing' to focus on the value issues at the individual customer level, and to customize products and services accordingly. This sounds outrageous, but it can be done:

- Value to young buyers of jeans is that they fit tightly round the butt. The giant Levi Strauss and Co has developed a 'Personal Pair' customized tailoring service for its famous blue jeans. Customized software is used to design tapered-leg jeans to the individual customer's body measurements, input by a trained sales assistant. The program identifies a 'prototype' which is closest to the customer's size, final adjustments are made to perfect the fit, and these measurements go by modem to the factory, from where the perfect fit, individually-tailored Levis go to the customer. The product is coded to allow easy re-ordering of an identical fit.
- Value to sophisticated home computer buyers is to choose their own specifications for the machine. This is essentially what Dell Computers offers in its direct-selling channel. From a standing start Dell has got to a position in the top ten computer manufacturers in a decade. Virtually every computer with a Dell badge is built to individual order [7].

It may mean massive change in the process of how you go to market, but focusing on what creates value for customers is incredibly powerful.

But how do we find out what our customers value? We could try listening better and learning.

Listening to customers and learning

Perhaps one of the hardest things we have to do in building customer focus is simply to learn to listen better to customers. This is not about sophisticated surveys and tests or huge computer databases, just about listening and being prepared to learn. Besides, we saw in Chapter 2 that we get customer satisfaction scores at satisfied/very satisfied when we do the surveys – but the same customers still defect to the competition. Indeed, we will see in Chapter 10 that the issue is really market 'sensing' or understanding.

If you can find better ways of listening to customers, the pay-off may be enormous. The surprise again and again is that customers will actually talk to you and help you learn how to be better if you are just prepared to listen.

Storytelling

Some major organizations have adopted storytelling as a way of listening and learning – not as silly as it sounds because it comes out of the insights of Gerald Zaltman at Harvard Business School. The goal is to find out the things that are missed by the conventional surveys and focus groups, and the method is to get real-life stories for customers about how they behave and what they really feel [8]. Some of the results are impressive:

- Kimberley-Clark has reinvented the baby's disposable nappy business. The paradox in this market is that every time a baby graduates to underpants from nappies you lose the customer for ever. The issue was, would people buy 'training pants' a transition product that looks like underpants but works like a nappy. K-C sent a small team of individuals (many themselves in the midst of the trauma of toilet-training their own children) into consumers' homes to hear real-life stories. What they discovered was that the real stress in toilet-training came from parents' feelings of failure, and dread of someone looking at their child in horror and asking, 'Oh, is your child *still* in nappies?' Nappies are an indicator of child development, not just a waste-disposal product. This is what really matters to young parents, but it is *not* what they say in conventional surveys and focus groups. K-C launched Huggies Pull-Ups training pants in 1991, and by the time the competition caught up they had a $400 million business [8].

- Intuit is a computer software company, whose world-wide success with Quicken personal finance software grew out of listening to customers' problems in balancing their cheque book, let alone getting a computer to do it for them. Chairman, Scott Cook, says: 'People don't buy technology. They buy products that improve their lives.' He concluded that personal finance software that could only be operated by the computer-literate 12-year-old in the family would just get turned off. They have gone to a lot of trouble to listen to customers. They have 'usability labs' where non-users come in and try to make the product work. They have a programme called 'Follow Me Home' – a kind of formalized stalking where employees go home with customers, have a 'tour' of their cheques and bills boxes, and look over their shoulders while they use the Intuit software. They also leave a cassette recorder so that when it all goes wrong the customer can hit the Record button and say what happened. Customer stories are the basis for product improvement and the creation of highly user-friendly software and also new products – they found that small business owners were using Quicken home finance software to keep their business accounts. The product was not designed for this purpose, but people preferred it to conventional business accounting software that forces you to learn double-entry bookkeeping when you don't need to. Today, Intuit's 'QuickBooks' is used in thousands of small businesses around the world.
- Even the mighty IBM is prepared to listen and learn – customer feedback showed one business unit that less than 1 per cent of customers preferred to make contact with the company by sales calls, but 82 per cent wanted more regular telephone contact. What customers said they wanted (and now get) actually saves IBM money.

This is not high-technology stuff. But when was the last time anyone in your company came back with some 'war stories' from customers and got taken seriously?

Watching customers

'The fancy name is generating "holistic customer insights", but it's really just about watching and learning'

Other companies have discovered that you can learn just by watching the people who set the standards. The fancy name is generating 'holistic customer insights', but it's really just about watching and learning:

- The power tools company Black and Decker achieves its innovative product designs and features by watching people using the tools and asking them about the experience and what would make it better (in the context, of course, of the well-known male bonding ritual with power tools).

- At Wiremold, a 'low-tech' producer of wire management systems (to route wiring through buildings), they have coined a wonderful phrase to describe how the voice of the customer drove their highly successful new product development and launch: they say, 'We designed it with our ears' – their product design comes from listening and watching and learning.
- At Sony, marketing innovative consumer electronic products, they have an even simpler logic: they say: 'Our employees are our customers, so let's give them the product to take home and test, and then they can tell us about it.'
- At Nike, the business is not really sports clothing, it is fashion – so they employ 'trend observers' to follow and observe the setters of trends in fashion (urban youth, sports stars, pop stars and so on).

This is simple stuff, but the evidence is that few of us do it, or do it well . . .

Meeting customers

There is actually a big learning experience for most of us, not just in meeting customers, but meeting them in the real world, where the product or service is consumed. This is likely to tell you things you will not otherwise learn:

- Talking to passengers actually on the long-haul flight or waiting in the airport will tell you how angry and frustrated they are at their loss of control over the process and what really irritates them more than nice controlled interviews later when the flight is a (bad) memory.
- Just talking to people walking round the supermarket will tell you more about what they like or don't like than questionnaire surveys will.
- One bank went for a glass-wall design for its offices for customer contact staff. The design won prizes, and was received favourably in market tests. The bank thought it made staff more approachable. In the actual event, customers felt robbed of their privacy and were very uncomfortable, and were prepared to say so when asked [9].
- Computers for word processing are not used in quiet controlled laboratories, they are used in noisy, busy offices where

interruptions are constant and people want things done fast – that is the environment where you can find out what value means to the customer!

More generally, many salespeople will tell you that if you are going to do a deal with someone, then it is important to meet them socially, and to eat and drink with them. Many of us may be tempted to write this off as an excuse for sales to build a big entertainment budget! But if the people who earn their living by doing deals and building relationships tell us that socializing with customers matters, perhaps we should listen.

This may be most obvious in the business-to-business setting. For example, a key aspect of implementing a vertical marketing strategy with one manufacturer was that the company was not organized around markets, it was structured around products, and that was the way managers liked things. There was much resistance to an industry sector-based strategy which cut across different product departments, to put together the product range customers wanted. One of the most influential ways in which this resistance was reduced was simply by organizing events and social functions around the target industrial sectors (actually in the form of training seminars and charity events). The effect of having senior managers meet customers informally and talk to them was fundamentally to shake the corporate belief that strategies were about products, not markets.

The same thing can be done in consumer markets. In the USA, the car manufacturer Saturn (a small GM subsidiary) is achieving quite amazing things in customer loyalty and retention simply by meeting its customers. The company says, 'Saturn cars are bought not sold', so the distributors run parties for customers, called 'familiarization' days, when new car buyers are taught the basic features and maintenance requirements of their cars, fed from a pit barbecue, treated as important, and sent on their way to spread the Saturn message. The factory in Georgia also holds events where large numbers of buyers visit and are fed and entertained, and made to feel like valued members of the 'Saturn family'. This may sound trite and trivial, but the effects are remarkable (particularly since publicizing the events is also the main platform of the company's advertising). If this sounds exaggerated, in 1993 this small producer was the leading US brand in the J.D. Power Customer Satisfaction Index.

Before we dismiss this as unworkable, maybe we should ask when we last talked to a customer in a social setting (and when did our chief executive do so) – and if the answer reveals that we never do, then perhaps we should, even if it is difficult to arrange.

However, do not expect 100 per cent success from the word go. Life is rarely this simple. In a medium-sized manufacturer of fire alarms, there was a major source of friction between the accounts office and customers – customers were being chased very aggressively for payment in the minimum time period (in at least one case before the product was delivered!). So the company was advised to take the head of accounts out to meet some customers and listen to what they had to say. This they did, over an excellent lunch at the customer's expense. On return to the office, the head of accounts said, 'Well, if they can afford lunches like that, they can afford to pay our invoices quicker', and returned to harassing customers with renewed vigour!

Indeed, I made this point about managers visiting customers in an after-dinner speech to one prestigious company's senior management. These managers spent some four hours until 3 in the morning rehearsing all the reasons why it was not appropriate for managers from production and logistics and service to 'waste' time on visiting customers. They still do not visit customers.

Customer days

Following the same logic, one very powerful way of getting customers taken seriously in the company is if we can get them to come to us – to enter the corporate lair and tell us what they think of us and our products.

The conclusions may be remarkable. For instance, in one high-technology company (which must remain nameless), customers visited to view a new machine which dispensed a pharmaceutical product for injection into humans. The company was very proud of this machine, which was a new design and very sophisticated. Customers showed that, by ignoring the instructions for use, it was possible to use the machine to squirt a fine spray of the injectable material over a wide area. Since the material in question was radioactive, this was not unparalleled good news. It would have been far worse if the product had gone into the market and patients had been sprayed with the material. The company redesigned the product.

Although this is most obviously applicable to business-to-business markets, it can be done anywhere. For instance, CIGNA, a major health insurance organization in the USA, has faced a process of strategic change from marketing to employers, to marketing to employees. One problem the company faced was that managers believed that what they knew about their old markets would apply to their new markets. It did not. The marketing vice-president confronted this problem in stages. First, he asked teams of managers to specify the key customer needs and preferences for the new market. Secondly, he organized Customer Days, when groups of customers visited the company to tell managers what *they* believed were their needs and preferences. Stage three was to wait for a short period while managers licked their wounds. Stage four was to ask managers to compare the two lists and their recommendations of how the company needed to change its approaches to attack the new market. He says this was a brutal process, but changed managers' minds about a few important issues.

Similarly, at Xerox's famous Palo Alto Research Center, R & D executives are required to spend a full 20 per cent of their time interacting and participating with customers. This is a very expensive investment – the measure of success is simple: 'what have we learned?'

Surveys and research reports may be excellent things – but generally they do not seem as powerful a form of communication as real customers who come to spit in your eye and tell you face-to-face what they really think of you.

Put it this way, if Lou Gerstner can run IBM and still spend 40 per cent of his time talking to customers – what are the rest of us doing?

Listening, not evaluating

If we are privileged enough that our customers will tell us things, our role is not to evaluate and disagree because we know better. Our role is to keep quiet, listen and learn.

In fact, perhaps the single most difficult thing to
'Our role is to keep   confront in this whole area is that customers may see
quiet, listen and   things differently to us. They may have very different
learn'   ideas about what matters about our products and
services. This is very unfair – we are the experts, after all. If we say the computer switch belongs on the back of the box, or you cannot have a TV rental delivered on a Sunday or in the evening, or the office has to shut at lunchtime so that people can eat, or guests should not walk on the grass in front of the hotel, then surely people should bow to our superior wisdom and professional expertise? I think not.

One stunning piece of corporate arrogance was displayed in a recent edition of the *Wall Street Journal* by a leading computer manufacturer. The article in question reported the war stories collected in the 'Customer Service' department (the reason for the quotation marks will become apparent shortly). These stories concerned the pathetic inadequacies of customers, who surely do not deserve to own the manufacturer's fantastic products:

- the lady who could not get the computer 'foot-pedal' to work, and had to be told that the computer was not a sewing machine, and to take the 'mouse' off the floor. . .
- people who feed computer disks through a manual typewriter to type nice neat labels on them, thus corrupting the disks and rendering them useless . . .
- people who phone up to complain that their software says 'Press any key', but the keyboard has no key marked 'any', so there must be something wrong with the keyboard.

Such instances lead to customer service reports of RTFM (the clean translation being: 'read the 'flaming' manual').

This is terrifically amusing, and we may permit ourselves the self-satisfied smirks of those who know better. But how profoundly depressing that a major company like this can display such overwhelming arrogance and offensiveness to its paying customers, and, what is more, sees nothing wrong with doing this in the pages of the *Wall Street Journal*. What does this say about the attitude of these 'service' employees towards the people who pay their wages? What does it say about this company's inability to grasp the basic needs of customers for clear and unambiguous guidance in using the products? What does it say about the underlying beliefs of the managers of this company as far as customers are concerned?

Taking the trouble to find out what matters to paying customers, respecting, not rubbishing those priorities, and doing something about them is likely to be a painful process for many of us. It may be one of the most powerful sources of competitive advantage and real customer focus, and it may be staring us in the face.

But what about the complainers?

In an ideal world where we got everything right, there would be no customer complaints. However, we do not live in an ideal world. If we do not receive any customer complaints, it does not mean all is well – do not confuse silent customers with satisfied customers. It probably means our customers think so poorly of us that they cannot even be bothered to tell us how bad they think we are.

The figures about dissatisfied customers and complaining behaviour are well-known [10]:

- *Most dissatisfied customers do not complain to us – probably only 4–5 per cent bother.* One estimate is that for every single customer who brings us a complaint, another 26 probably also have problems, six of which are likely to be serious, and do not complain to us. The silent majority defect to a competitor, or put up with us being bad and then defect.
- *Dissatisfied customers tell everyone except us.* In consumer markets the estimate is that the disgruntled customer tells around 14 others.
- *Dissatisfied customers buy less* – and seem to do their best to get others to buy less as well.
- Typically the *cost* of complaint resolution is 10–25 per cent of the cost of finding a new customer [11].
- When complaints are *resolved satisfactorily* these customers tend to be more loyal than those who never experienced a problem in the first place.

But why do so many customers not complain and give us the chance to do better? Conventional answers might be:

- They did not think it would make any difference.
- They did not think it was worth their time and effort.
- They did not know what they had to do to get help.
- They never got round to it [12].

Or maybe they thought we were so crass that we would make complaining a horrible and demeaning experience? Consider the following situation. A young lady buys an expensive, branded face cream in a well-known department store, having ascertained from the salesperson that it did not contain skin-tightening agents to which she is allergic. Nonetheless, she was allergic to the cream and took it back for a refund. She explained this to the salesperson at the counter, whose attitude immediately became hostile, and who accused the customer of ignoring the instructions and buying the wrong product – all this takes place at the counter in a busy shop. A refund is not forthcoming. The customer asks to see a supervisor. The supervisor arrives, apologizes, provides a chair in a private area, and basically provides an instant refund but asks for the chance to work with the customer to find an alternative product that would be suitable. Now, that is the difference between someone who has been trained to handle customer complaints positively and someone who has not*. Which sounds more like your company?

In fact, the real question is, how would you like to be treated the way your company treats customers who complain? *Find out.* Act like a customer and *see* what it is like and what it *feels* like.

What you will probably find is that much of what loses us business is things which are trivial for us, but that turn customers off – how long it takes to get a reply to a letter, the time it takes for the phone to be answered, whether the salesperson knows anything about the product (or the company), whether the sales literature tells you anything, 'company policies' that make sense to the company but not to the customer. That last one is a joy. When *you* are the customer, see how *you* feel about being passed from salesperson to salesperson because you contacted the 'wrong' one, the corporate 'policeman' who does credit checking and billing, the queuing procedures, the routine attempts to disprove warranty claims, and all the other 'rules' that seemed to make sense inside the organization, but which are irritating obstacles and insults for the customer. The reality is that when *you* are the customer you want things done *your* way. Something as simple as this is a good start to getting to grips with the real customer satisfaction issue, and the joy is that in practice so many of the problems and idiocies that you find can be solved instantly, and at little cost – it just takes the effort of taking them seriously.

In fact, if you look at things from the customer's perspective, you may find yourself amazed at how your company seems to have set out to positively irritate and annoy the paying customer when it costs so little not to, and how astounding it is that so few customers do actually complain.

Perhaps the best example of the pay-off from something as simple as this is Marks and Spencer. In this company's phenomenally successful retail operation, the Board members regularly visit stores as customers, and use new products in their own homes to evaluate them. It is good that they do this, it is even better that they are seen by staff to do this, and still better that they are known by customers to do so.

Apart from anything else, disgruntled, complaining customers offer us a marvellous opportunity. The research evidence is that it makes a big difference to the chances of doing repeat business with a complaining customer if we just *listen* to the complaint, although this pales into insignificance compared to the effects

---

* This is a true story. The customer was my wife, Nikala – as formidable a consumer as any shop assistant is ever likely to meet!

'If we can find the unhappy customer we have the opportunity to convert him or her into our most loyal customer'

achieved if we listen to the complaint *and* do something about it. If we can find the unhappy customer we have the opportunity to convert him or her into our *most* loyal customer of all time, by virtue of the way we treat him or her as an individual.

Take a case in point. A little while ago, I stayed for a few days of a business trip in the Chicago Downtown Marriott hotel. The room was expensive, but very good. On my last day I had to catch an afternoon flight, and I wanted to take late breakfast at about 11.30 in the morning. Unfortunately, this was the precise moment that the hotel chose to close the breakfast area for an hour to clean it. As a typically emotional and unreasonable customer I complained on my Customer Satisfaction Questionnaire. This made me feel better. However, on my return to the UK I received an airmail letter of apology and thanks from Bill Marriott's office, a personal letter from the hotel manager apologizing further, and offering me a free night's accommodation on my next visit to Chicago, and a personal airmail letter from the departmental manager apologizing and offering to upgrade my accommodation on my next visit. I have got to the stage where I am frightened to open the front door in case there are personal representatives of the catering staff from the Chicago Marriott offering yet further apologies and compensation, and trying to force-feed me blueberry muffins. The result is that I would not dream of taking the free offers, but I am a far more loyal Marriott customer than ever before.

In fact, the results of pursuing these types of questions with customers who complain can be surprising as well as productive. In one Volkswagen dealership in the UK, management had made determined, systematic efforts to regularly *listen* to what their customers thought about the level of service provided by the garage. Top management's message to staff in dealing with customers was, 'you have two ears and one mouth, so use them in proportion'. All was going well except for one particular customer, who *every* quarter complained lengthily, bitterly, and in detail about the poor quality of the servicing of his car and the intractability of the service people in acting on his complaints. The General Manager finally phoned him and said that clearly the company did not deserve to keep his business, but would he help them avoid the problem happening again. He was persuaded to visit the General Manager to tell the company how it could do better. He provided a list of service tasks which were *never* done on his car and which service staff refused to put right – greasing ball-joints, and the like. Further questioning showed that *all* his expectations were wholly based on the old 1968 owner's workshop manual. It was 1988 – ball-joints no longer *have* to be greased, and so it went on through his entire list of 'complaints'! The problem was solved by the free gift of the 1988 owner's workshop manual, and the customer was converted. Understanding expectations is as important as seeing how delivery of the service goes wrong.

In summary then, what is so special about complaining customers? Well, they are the ones who actually want to talk to us, which makes listening easier. The opportunities we face with complaining customers are:

- to *learn* about the areas where we need to improve the way we do business;
- to satisfy these customers by replacing the service or replacing the product and get the repeat business and refusals;
- to potentially build real customer loyalty.

There may be problems – if we see the customer as the enemy, then we probably do not like complaints or the people who make them. Indeed, dealing with angry customers or ex-customers can be tough. The example set by managers is critical.

Most organizations do have formalized procedures for reacting to complaints – but too often this is too low in the organization, and is no more than a tactical coping mechanism, which has little impact on the rest of the company.

One chief executive of a highly successful European company takes a different view of the complaints issue. He insists that all senior managers in the company take responsibility for investigating three customer complaints each month, and for one of these it is expected that a customer visit will be made. Incidentally, he includes himself in this rota. He says it is easy to do this, because when you go and ask Customer Service to give you three really bad complaints to deal with, they are delighted and give you really difficult ones! This is expensive, but a superb way to get customer complaints taken very seriously by everyone in the company. Besides, he says the things they have learned about how their products work in the real marketplace and what annoys customers is far more effective than all the market research surveys in the world, and this alone makes the policy worthwhile.

Be sure, though, that this is about developing ways for effectively listening to customers, responding positively and building customer loyalty through this care and attention. It should not be a police action, over-reacting to isolated complaints, or a negative control mechanism to punish people in the organization.

In fact, you have to learn to *trust* the people in the company and give them the power to solve customer problems. Easy to say, but often not so easy to do. For example, in one company managers said to this that you cannot trust front-line operatives to give refunds or replace products because 'the kids would give the store away!' A test was set up: groups of managers and groups of front-line employees were given simulation exercises in handling customer complaints. At the end we compared who gave away most in solving customer problems – guess what, it was the managers. At that company front-line employees are now trusted with handling customer complaints.

A learning organization?

Many leaders in management thinking advocate the 'learning organization' [13]. This is ambitious. A start for most of us is to learn, to listen, to share the lessons throughout the company, and to retain the knowledge we are building for future use [14].

However, be aware of the other trap – learning is not the same as policing. Listening to customers, and particularly analysing customer complaints, can be turned into a disaster. We can make the whole thing negative by:

- *Over-reacting to isolated, ad hoc criticisms* – a single isolated complaint may really not be enough evidence sensibly to take action on how we do things in the future (although this does not mean we should not do what we can do to make the unhappy, complaining customer happy).
- *Over-reacting to complaints about sensitive issues* – there is a risk that we only respond to complaints about the things *we* think are most important, not what the *customer* thinks are most important. This misses the whole point.
- *Under-reacting to major criticisms* – when we start, we may well be shocked by the extent and spread of criticisms. This should provide an agenda for action, not a rejection of the results because 'we can't be that bad'. (See the question of the elephant, p. 393.)
- *Poor quality reaction because of defensiveness* – we may easily achieve disastrously negative effects if we simply use customer feedback as a big stick with which to beat up people in the organization. The idea is to help us all improve the way we do our jobs, not a ritualistic blood-letting.
- *Politicking* – finally, there is a substantial danger with some organizations that customer feedback becomes a political weapon in the inter-departmental vendettas and struggle for power. Management uses the results to criticize Marketing, Marketing uses them to attack Production, the Accountants

use them to fight back budget requests, and so on. Certainly, some marketing executives have said to me that to publish customer views would simply be to create a 'hostage to fortune' – a basis for them to be attacked and sniped at by others in the company.

If we do it badly, then there is no doubt that customer feedback and complaints handling can be a disaster. However, note that most of the ways it can go wrong reflect how the results are *used* and *abused* – not something fundamentally wrong with doing it in the first place. The goal is to learn and improve, not to 'police' the company.

Obsessing over customers

In fact, if you look at companies that do focus on what is value to their customers, and who do listen and learn, it goes much further – they are obsessional and almost overpowering.

International examples are well-known, and centre on companies like Marriott, Disney, Delta Airlines and McDonalds – Ray Kroc was renowned for his stubborn insistence on QSCV (Quality, Service, Cleanliness and Value), and McDonalds outlets not conforming to his standards were in big trouble.

There are examples in successful companies closer to home. Tesco has recently won market leadership in the UK grocery sector. The man who has driven the transformation of Tesco from 'pile it high, sell it cheap' discount retailing is Terry Leahy, Marketing Director under Ian MacLaurin, and in 1997 made Chief Executive. Behind the scenes, Leahy has driven major customer-focused changes by listening to customers, learning and doing:

- he drove a programme to make the stores nicer places to shop because customers wanted it – shorter queues, better decor, higher quality products and new ways of shopping, such as the Tesco Metro providing a food store near the office that opens early and shuts late;
- he championed the Tesco Clubcard loyalty scheme, and is using it to target individual customers with special offers, such as the 'Babyclub';
- he is increasing investment in customer service – hiring 5000 new customer assistants, reducing the time employees spend on administrative work and encouraging them to spend more time with customers.

What they say about Leahy is things like this:

> Leahy's obsession is not the graphs that show good performance, but rather the customers who shop in the stores. Leahy's mantra is 'customer'. The word creeps into every sentence to the point of irritation. But to Leahy . . . it is the crux of the business and the focus [15].

Maybe this is how you go from being a shelf stacker to the chief executive's job (which Leahy has)?

There is nothing like a true obsessive, is there? You may prefer to call it leadership (but 'obsession' works for me).

Another view is that it is about 'creating the cult of the customer' [16], where everything everyone does is judged by what it means to the customer.

'creating the cult of the customer'

Some of the obsession is about managing the symbols – managing rewards to give incentives, giving employees the power to do the things that matter, and to behave as though customers matter.

One way of approaching this is to ask what we do to reward those who foster and develop productive customer relationships or, even more apposite, what we do to avoid the organization punishing those who do their best for the customer.

The best companies reward and value those who break the rules to do a better job for the customer. For example, in the Marriott hotel business, one valued manager diverted the budget for putting televisions in the bathrooms to providing ironing boards in all bedrooms. His thinking was very clear – customers repeatedly ask for ironing boards, and there is a lot of time spent on taking them around and collecting them and there are not enough to go around. No-one has ever complained of the lack of a TV in the bathroom. The solution was obvious, and the company applauded his decision.

Another well-known example is from a courier delivery business. This company promises its customers overnight delivery. A depot manager was faced with the problem that this promise apparently could not be kept for one customer's package, because of public holidays and uncompromising haulage schedules. The answer was obvious – he chartered a plane to take the parcel to its destination. Far from being punished, the manager has been rewarded and turned into a hero in the company (although it is rumoured that at his presentation the CEO did take him on one side and suggested that if the same thing happened again, could he possibly find a *small* plane . . .).

In case we think this is the province only of the large organization, Tom Bonoma tells the story of the proprietor of a garage who solves the problem of how to get his staff to clean the customer toilets regularly – a job which no-one wants to do. A couple of times a year the garage owner hid a $100 bill taped to the porcelain in the toilets, to be kept by the lucky individual cleaning them! Or, in fact, if found by Tom Bonoma to be handed back, because the proprietor was his father.

Conversely, how many times, when we find customers being treated badly, do we find the reason being that the organization rewards precisely this type of behaviour towards customers? Tom Peters tells the story of the R & D manager of a major US firm, who still recalls, when he was a line manager, buying equipment from a reputable supplier who treated him badly when the equipment malfunctioned – they claimed it was the customer's fault, were rude in correspondence, did not return telephone calls and refused to allow anyone in his company to buy from that supplier (and this is some 20 years later). However, that is not the point of the story. The real point is that you can guarantee beyond a shadow of a doubt that someone in the supplying company was applauded and rewarded for his/her efforts to cut down on the costs of warranty replacements.

One Japanese photocopier supplier understands this and has changed the way maintenance engineers are rewarded. Maintenance engineers get a bonus which reduces as the number of customer callouts increases. The logic is clear. If maintenance is done thoroughly and effectively, there should be fewer callouts for breakdowns. This is what is rewarded, not the number of calls made.

The question which arises is simple – if we know what matters to our customers, what are we doing to honour and reward those who do the things that win customers' hearts and minds, and to protect them from company systems set up to punish and sanction such actions? If the answer is nothing, then that is probably where we need to start in taking customers seriously.

This includes managing less tangible things as well. Radio Cornwall, a BBC local radio station, was widely criticized for one of its policies in 1996. That was very unfair because their policy was exactly right. The company's internal memo to staff using company cars read as follows:

> If you listen to anything other than Radio Cornwall in our cars you will be banned from using them. This is no longer a warning, it is a statement of policy. And if the station which is paying your money isn't good enough for your listening needs, go and work for another station. If you get in a car that isn't tuned to Radio Cornwall, then retune it pronto. Otherwise, you will be spending a lot of money on petrol. From today there will be spot checks on the cars – if they aren't tuned to Radio Cornwall, you are banned. [17]

OK, marks out of ten: tact, diplomacy and internal communications skills, zero; obsessing with the customer, ten. The moral? Obsessing with customers may not always make you popular with your colleagues.

Don't forget that you attract new customers by honouring employees who go the extra mile to deliver excellent service to existing customers. For example, Marriott has run entire international advertising campaigns based on what customers say about how Marriott employees treat them when the chips are down. The wording of one such ad reads as follows:

> There were no taxis and no chance of catching my plane until the Marriott receptionist took a *personal* interest in the matter. Without hesitation she made an executive decision. If she couldn't order a car in time to get me to the airport, she'd take me in her own. It was no stretch limo but thanks to her I made the flight. I believe at Marriott they call it Empowerment. It means that the staff see their roles as being more than just a duty. They're really sensitive to guests' needs and assume responsibility for attending to them. I needed to catch that plane and they ensured I did. It's been the same wherever I've stayed at a Marriott...'

Call me sentimental if you wish, but if your customers write your advertisements for you, you have to be getting something right.

If you believe in customers and want to do something about customer focus, it may take just such obsessive management behaviour. If our goal is to 'reach an interaction with customers that so utterly distinguishes you from others that it is a brand in itself – a unique impression that sets your company apart from others', then every contact between the customers and the company must prove how much the company values them [18].

Measuring customer satisfaction*

About the most popular way of listening to customers has become the boom in customer satisfaction measurement. So,

---

* This section is based on: Nigel F. Piercy (1996), 'The Effects of Customer Satisfaction Measurement', *Marketing Intelligence and Planning*, Vol. 14, No. 4, 9–15, and Nigel F. Piercy and Neil A. Morgan (1995), 'Customer Satisfaction Measurement and Management: A Processual Analysis', *Journal of Marketing Management*, Vol. 11, 817–34.

do you want the good news or the bad news? Try separating out two issues here:

- how we measure customer satisfaction; and
- how we use it once we have measured it.

How do you measure customer satisfaction?

The world and his uncle want to sell you systems and methods for customer satisfaction measurement (CSM). There is a massive technical literature available to support moves towards formalizing the measurement of customer satisfaction. This supporting base is concerned with such issues as:

- developing different concepts of customer satisfaction which can be evaluated [19];
- designing effective customer satisfaction data collection and reporting systems, varying in sophistication [20];
- adopting methods for institutionalizing customer satisfaction measurement into organizational control systems [21];
- developing systems for responding effectively to customer dissatisfaction and customer complaints [22].

In fact, customer satisfaction measurement has proved to be one of the most successful products for market research agencies through the recent recession [23]. Certainly, the market research industry offers a full range of products in this area: customer satisfaction survey methodologies; focus groups to study customer satisfaction issues; standardized packages for monitoring customer satisfaction; and the computer software needed to analyse and report customer satisfaction data to management.

'the real issues for managers are not so much about the data collection, but what happens to the information after it is collected'

However, the real issues for managers are not so much about the data collection, but what happens to the information after it is collected.

But what do we do with it?

A good question – but do we know the answer? Well, one source of insight into what happens in companies that measure customer satisfaction comes from exploratory workshop discussions held with managers. Simply looking at the themes emerging from what managers say about customer satisfaction measurement raises some very serious concerns about what effects are achieved. The themes emerging from those discussions are as follows:

- *Companies which trivialize CSM.* Many say that in practice CSM becomes a superficial and trivial activity, which is significant only at the customer service level. They suggest that CSM is not related to market strategies and strategic change in their companies, but rather is about monitoring customer service operations, and responding to customer complaints (sometimes quite disproportionately and inappropriately to boot).
- *CSM and interdepartmental power struggles.* Some executives describe CSM as little more than a weapon used in the power struggles between functional areas, in attempts to 'prove' to management that other departments are responsible for losing market share and declining customer satisfaction.
- *The politics of CSM.* Others describe CSM as characterized by gaming behaviour by company personnel to 'beat' the system, and to avoid being 'blamed' for customer complaints – often resulting in behaviour not anticipated by management and not supportive to customer satisfaction policies and market strategies; for example, sales and distribution personnel giving price and service concessions to customers simply to win 'brownie' points in the CSM system. Others describe CSM as a 'popularity poll' for the salesforce, where 'popularity' is rewarded and 'unpopularity' is penalized.
- *CSM as management control.* Some see the implementation of CSM in a negative way, as a crude control device used by management, to police the lower levels of the organization and allocate 'blame' for customer complaints. Others describe CSM systems as wholly negative and focused on criticism, with no balance of positive feedback or praise for what is good. In some cases the data are seen only by management and only 'conclusions' communicated to employees – often in a negative and critical way. Others see CSM as a crude attempt by management to coerce employees to change their behaviour in the ways desired by customers (or at least the desire of those customers who have complained most recently and most vociferously).
- *The isolation of CSM.* Many executives talk about situations where CSM data are collected and stored but not disseminated in the organization. For example, in some cases CSM information is collected by the marketing department but not shared with the production or even the quality departments.
- *Poorly diffused CSM.* In some cases people describe a general lack of acceptance of CSM. For example, in one high-tech

company a monthly management information report is circulated with sales, profit and CS results summarized, for the use of all senior managers. The executive responsible described how every month there were queries and arguments and protests about the accuracy and validity of the sales and profit figures, but no-one had ever questioned the CS data – they simply did not matter to managers. Another company described how they knew that distributors completed CS questionnaires themselves, because they did not see the point of the exercise and did not want to 'bother' their customers.

It would be unwise to claim that these findings have any general representativeness, since they reflect only exploratory discussions with executives. However, they do appear to offer some novel insights into the reality of the operation of CSM systems in organizations, which are largely ignored by conventional approaches.

In fact, we went deeper into this issue, and did a survey of several hundred British companies using CSM. The results of the survey are summarized in Figure 3.3, which shows the managerial uses of customer satisfaction measurements, the internal processual barriers found, and the market strategies managers identified:

- *Managerial uses of customer satisfaction measurement.* Managers were asked to evaluate the degree of use of CS measurements in a number of decision-making areas, which were reduced by factor analysis to the use of CS measurements in:
  - *quality/operations management*, which linked the use of CS data to monitor and manage quality, to guide R & D, and to manage production;
  - *staff pay and promotions*, linking pay and promotion decisions for operational and management staff;
  - *staff training and evaluation*, linking the training and evaluation of both operational and managerial staff; and
  - *strategic management control*, linking the development of company-wide strategy, control of the business and the management of customer service and marketing programmes.
- *Internal processual barriers.* The central issue in the study related to the characteristics of the CS measurement process in terms of the perceived beliefs and attitudes of the people involved and the organizational context provided by the company in question and its management. A list of statements

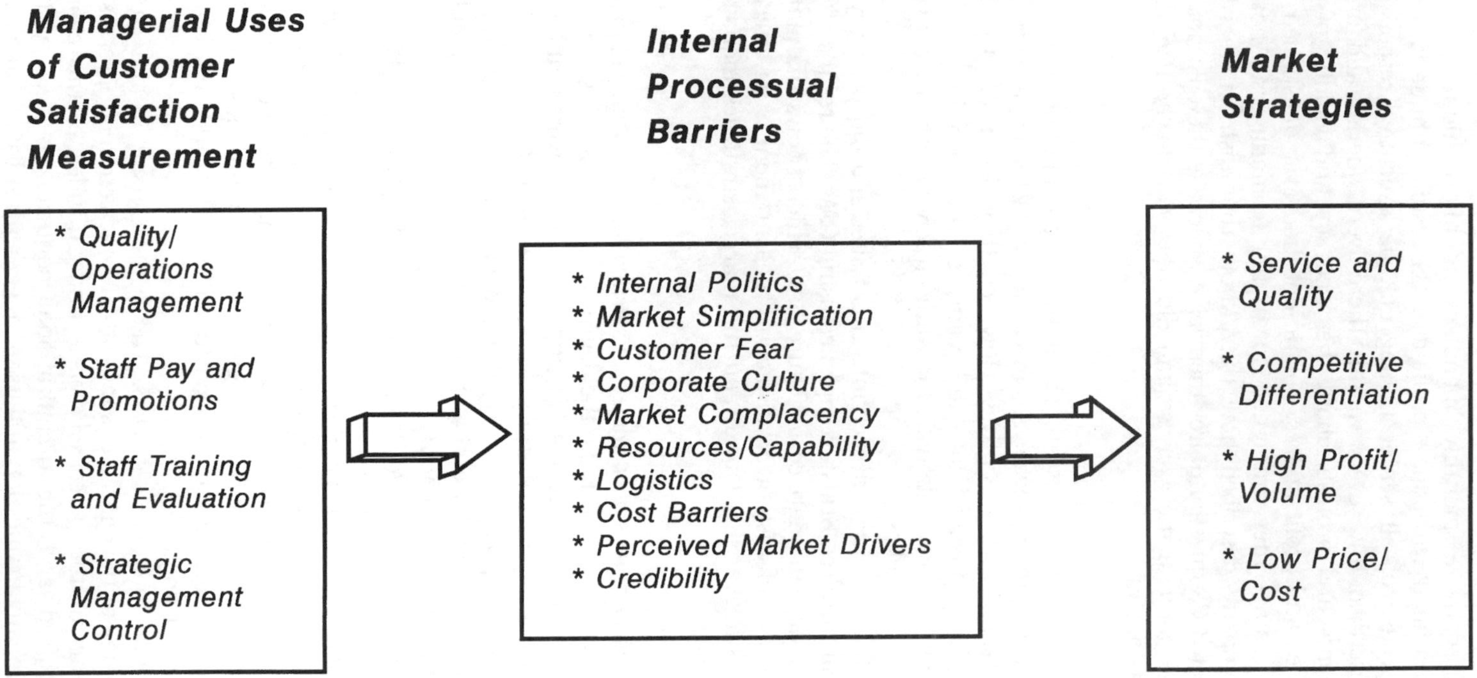

Managerial Uses of Customer Satisfaction Measurement

* Quality/ Operations Management

* Staff Pay and Promotions

* Staff Training and Evaluation

* Strategic Management Control

Internal Processual Barriers

* Internal Politics
* Market Simplification
* Customer Fear
* Corporate Culture
* Market Complacency
* Resources/Capability
* Logistics
* Cost Barriers
* Perceived Market Drivers
* Credibility

Market Strategies

* Service and Quality

* Competitive Differentiation

* High Profit/ Volume

* Low Price/ Cost

Figure 3.3 The customer satisfaction measurement process

was evaluated by respondents and their responses factor analysed to produce the following structure:

- *internal politics*: CS measurement is believed to generate internal conflict and political squabbles, to produce a 'hostage to fortune' and bring increased management control, areas of customer complaint are politically sensitive in the company, CSM undermines management, and people cheat in the CS system;
- *market simplification*: word-of-mouth recommendation by customers is believed to be unimportant, customer loyalty is thought to be non-existent, repeat sales do not matter, the company is not believed to be a service and quality provider, the company cannot change to respond to complaints, people do not believe that CS matters;
- *customer fear*: if asked about satisfaction, customers think something is wrong, asking about CS reduces satisfaction, it raises unrealistic customer expectations, it invites unwelcome complaints, it is badly received by people in the company;
- *corporate culture*: a lack of management support for CSM, a perception that CSM is not appropriate to the company or the market, a lack of attention to the results, a lack of a customer service policy, a low priority for CSM;
- *market complacency*: beliefs that the company already knows what matters in the market and what customers think, the belief that what matters is having the best product, CSM is believed to be difficult and to invite unwarranted criticisms from customers;
- *resources/capability*: CSM makes excessive demands for technical expertise, systems, people and time;
- *logistics*: beliefs that identifying the real customer is problematic, and that it is a role for the distributor, not the manufacturer;
- *cost barriers*: links the finance and expense implications of CSM;
- *perceived market drivers*: links beliefs that the market is driven only by technical specifications and price;
- *credibility*: people do not believe the results of CSM.

- *Market strategies*. Respondents were asked to prioritize their market strategies, and factor analysis revealed the following imperatives:
  - *service and quality* – links goals of achieving the highest perceived quality in the market, providing excellent customer service and achieving high buyer loyalty;

- *competitive differentiation* – links issues of managing distribution networks, building brand image, and differentiation by design and technical specifications;
- *high profit/volume* – links goals of sales growth, higher market share and improved profitability;
- *low price/cost* – links strategies of being price-competitive and minimizing market costs.

This model, based on what we found in companies, suggests that we need to think about a hidden management agenda, to be addressed by executives in organizations adopting and using customer satisfaction measurement approaches. Conventionally, the agenda is concerned primarily with data collection, measurement techniques and reporting formats. Our findings suggest that, to realize the promises for CSM, this approach is inadequate.

First, the findings from the workshops and the survey underline the need for clarity regarding customer service policies and customer satisfaction targets. It is not enough to pay the usual lip-service to these ideals and to expect success in attaining them. The starting point must be to identify what has to be achieved in customer satisfaction to implement specific market strategies, and to position the company against the competition in a specific market. It is unlikely that achieving what we want will be free. We need to take a realistic view of the time needed and the real costs of implementation.

'The starting point must be to identify what has to be achieved in customer satisfaction to implement specific market strategies'

Secondly, the internal processual barriers uncovered here suggest the need to consider what both the internal and external markets face in implementing customer satisfaction measurement and management systems (see Chapter 14, pp. 593–600 regarding internal markets). To ignore the internal market is to risk actually damaging the company's capacity to achieve and improve customer satisfaction in the external market. If, for example, management uses CS data in a negative and coercive way, then it may reduce employee enthusiasm for customer service, or create 'game-playing' behaviour where people compete for 'Brownie points' in the systems, at the expense both of the company and the customer. This said, we have also to recognize not just the complementarity between internal and external markets, but the potential for conflict of interest. Achieving target levels of customer service and satisfaction may require managers and employees to change the way they do things and to make sacrifices they do not want to make. This may take more than simple advocacy or management threat.

Thirdly, and related to the above argument, recognizing the internal market suggests that there may be a need for a structured and planned internal marketing programme to achieve the effective implementation of customer satisfaction measurement and management. This has been described elsewhere as 'marketing our customers to our employees' [24], and can be built into the implementation process to address the needs of the internal customer and to confront the types of internal processual barrier we have encountered.

Fourthly, also related to the recognition of the internal market, is the need to question the relationship between internal and external customer satisfaction. This was discussed with one company using the structure shown in Figure 3.4. This suggests four possible scenarios that result when internal and external customer satisfaction are compared:

- *Synergy*, which is what we hope for, when internal and external customer satisfaction are high, and we see them as sustainable and self-regenerating. As one hotel manager explained it: 'I know that we are winning on customer service when my operational staff come to me and complain about how I am getting in their way in providing customer service, and tell me to get my act together!' This is the 'happy customers and happy employees' situation, assumed by many to be obvious and easily achieved.
- *Coercion* is where we achieve high levels of external customer satisfaction by changing the behaviour of employees through

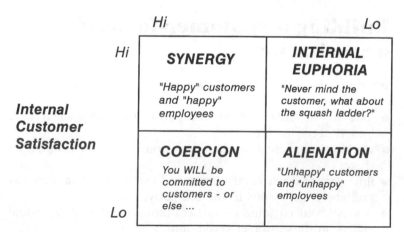

External Customer Satisfaction

	Hi	Lo
Hi	**SYNERGY** *"Happy" customers and "happy" employees*	**INTERNAL EUPHORIA** *"Never mind the customer, what about the squash ladder?"*
Lo	**COERCION** *You WILL be committed to customers - or else ...*	**ALIENATION** *"Unhappy" customers and "unhappy" employees*

Internal Customer Satisfaction

Figure 3.4 Customer satisfaction and the internal market

management direction and control systems. In the short term this may be the only option, but it may be very difficult and expensive to sustain this position in the longer term, and we give up flexibility for control.

- *Alienation* is where we have low levels of satisfaction internally and externally, and we are likely to be highly vulnerable to competitive attack in the external market and low morale and high staff turnover in the internal market.
- *Internal euphoria* is where we have high levels of satisfaction in the internal market, but this does not translate into external customer satisfaction – for example, if internal socialization and group cohesiveness actually shut out the paying customer in the external market. These scenarios are exaggerated, but have provided a useful way of confronting these issues with executives.

Lastly, and simplest, we suggest that a critical mistake is to ignore the real costs and challenges in adopting customer satisfaction measurement as a management approach, and the limitation which may exist in a company's capabilities for improving customer satisfaction levels. While advocacy is widespread and the appeal is obvious, achieving the potential benefits requires more planning and attention to implementation realities than is suggested by the existing conventional methodological literature.

So customer satisfaction measurement may not be the answer to all your customer-focus problems. It has great potential value, but used badly it can do more harm than good. If you do it, do it for the right reasons, and do it carefully.

Building a customer-focused organization

What we have said so far is to achieve customer focus:

- look at your current relationship with the customer and see how it needs to change;
- work out what creates value for customers and focus attention there;
- find ways to listen to customers and learn from what they say and apply the lessons in the company;
- obsess about customers – focus management leadership and efforts on the customer credo; and
- measure customer satisfaction and use the results positively.

But this leaves the question of packaging these things together and finding the key drivers to make it real – i.e. building a customer-focused organization. A number of things are worth considering.

Customer care programmes

This is the first thing people try. After all, it is a great way for managers to convince themselves they are taking customers seriously, while dumping the issue on their people instead.

There is a lot more involved in genuine customer care and service than 'slapping in some training and accompanying it with hype' or sending employees to 'smile schools' [25]. The results of trying to 'enforce' smiling and customer care are shown in the retail business: store operatives accepting their compulsory name-badges, but deliberately wearing them upside down; smiles which last as long as the video surveillance of the checkout; management policing of 'false smiles', and the use of *agents provocateurs* to test staff without warning, leading to a predictably resentful staff[26]. These people are trying to tell us something!

On the face of things, customer care and customer service training programmes are a way to improve our performance where it counts most – at the place where the customer experiences what we do. Great things can be achieved by such efforts and they should not be ignored or denigrated. We may actually improve on the 'service with a snarl' that all too many customers get when they pay their money. However, there is a worry that how we actually use these things is as something we 'bolt-on' as an afterthought to cover up our real inadequacies and our real disregard for what matters to customers.

David Clutterbuck [27] has estimated that up to 90 per cent of customer care programmes have failed or are likely to. He points to the absence of objectives and evaluation, with companies viewing customer care as the latest, plug-in 'quick-fix', and (the real point of significance) no real change in *management* behaviour.

The reality of customer care is about how we run the whole operation from top to bottom, not manipulating front-line employees, and what I have come to call the 'have a nice day syndrome'. Real customer care is not about building new bureaucracies and lip-service, it is about anarchic commitment to the customer. It is not about adding a bit of customer service training at the end of the process of going to market – it is about how we manage the whole process. It is about commitment at the top and customer care as an integral part of market strategy. The best customer care programmes recognize precisely this, but I am somewhat less convinced about others.

'Customer care
programmes **can**
be used to manage
change'

Customer care programmes *can* be used to manage change*. But then they are likely to be 'root and branch' programmes of change, not afterthoughts.

For example, UNISYS has used the word 'customerize' to describe this type of approach to customer care. Customerize is defined as '1: to make a company more responsive to its customers and better able to attract new ones, 2: to customerize an organization's information strategy, e.g. to extend systems capabilities to field locations and other points of customer contact and support.' The UNISYS customerizing process is linked to:

- Top management commitment – providing leadership and role models;
- Understanding customers;
- Setting customer-centred strategies;
- Cultivating pro-customer employees and service programmes;
- Focusing on customer retention;
- Gaining new customers;
- Using technology-enablers and measurement systems to achieve this.

Then, add to that something like Customer Management Teams [28], and we see something powerful coming together.

Now that adds up to a bit more than management lip-service and 'smile schools' for the employees.

Look, for example, at the volunteer 'ambassador' programme launched at Southwestern Bell, the US telephone company, in 1995. Non-sales employees volunteer as ambassadors to establish relationships with their designated customers – a very powerful way of putting a face to the company and letting the customer know that the company really does care about them. The ambassador visits the customer quarterly, and gives out his/her office phone number for the customer to call with any query or problem. The company says it has stronger, smarter, problem-solving employees as a result of the ambassador programme, and

---

* If you want a source of ideas of the sorts of training and development that can be done in customer service, have a look at: Kristen Anderson and Ron Zemke (1991), *Delivering Knock Your Socks Off Service*, New York: AMACOM; Chip R. Bell and Ron Zemke (1992), *Managing Knock Your Socks off Customer Service*, New York: AMACOM.

gives better service to more loyal customers. Indeed, some of the customers are paying the ultimate compliment – they are copying the ambassador programme for their own companies.

People buy from people

. . . or more probably they only buy from people they like (who are not rude, arrogant, off-hand or unhelpful). It is the people in the company who are the 'value creators' [29], and it is the people in the company who can undermine any customer-focused market strategy you care to name.

One commentator all too rightly notes that 'too many employees who deal directly with customers are damaging the product, service or corporate brand every time they open their mouths' [30]. Karl Albrecht [31] goes as far as to say that unhappy employees can work as 'terrorists' in the company. Others go even further and say that it is company employees, not customers, who have to be 'number one' if the company hopes to truly satisfy its customers [32].

But why don't our people do what we tell them, and be nice to customers? John Crump, of Kaisen Consultancy, works on these issues and his views can be summarized along the following lines. He says people do not always deliver the best possible service because of:

- The human factor – in the real world people make mistakes and become demotivated or have an 'off-day', and we often assume that they have knowledge and capabilities which they do not have.
- They do not always know what 'right' looks like – and why should they, unless we provide a model of what is good and bad in customer service.
- They do not always know if they are being effective – because we fail to give them regular feedback as customer satisfaction (and customer complaints!).
- They are not always rewarded for doing the right thing.
- Sometimes jobs have conflicting demands that cannot be met – time with the customer versus time doing administration, for example, because managers pass on paradox (see pp. 20–21) instead of simplifying, so people do the minimum they have to do to stay out of trouble.
- Sometimes they get stuck in the 'old way' of seeing things and we do not help them to change.
- They simply may not understand what we want from them, because we have failed to communicate properly [33].

For example, thinking about that last point, psychologists have been employed to try to teach Berlin's notoriously rude transport workers to be nice to passengers, with the following results:

We say . . .	*They say . . .*
Say 'please' when you ask passengers to stand back from the doors when they close	Why should we say 'please', it is an order!
Help passengers with their luggage	Why – if they can't carry it, they shouldn't expect others to do it for them
Look customers in the eye and speak slowly	Why – if they ask us questions, they should listen to the answer carefully
Wish people a nice day	We only say what we mean, and we do not care if they have a nice day or not
What matters is customer service	No, what matters is speed and efficiency [34]

And you thought you had problems?

So, if the real problem in building a customer-focused organization is the people – who can help us? Maybe the Human Resource Management* people can?

Collaboration with human resource management

The fundamental case we are making is:

- The single most important factor for most companies in maintaining competitive strength is employees.
- A major source of competitive differentiation is achieved by managing our people more effectively than the companies do.
- Distinctive human resources provide the real core competencies of the business as the real source of competitive advantage.

---

* And does anyone know when we allowed Personnel Departments to put on airs and graces and call themselves Human Resource Management, let alone why?

So, the question is, how can it make sense to have one group of people doing HR types of things (recruitment, selection, training, appraisal) and another bunch of people somewhere else doing customer sorts of things (managing customer service, measuring customer satisfaction, collecting customer feedback)? (Which is close to the situation you find in most companies.) Is there likely to be an explosion of synergy if we put these two sets of people together and line up workforce capabilities with customer-focused market strategies? The answer is yes, and if you do not believe me, try reading the Avis case (p. 100).

In fact, some argue that the major issue facing modern business is how to integrate 'marketing' with human resource management, because neither can be effective as a separate function – this may be the most critical strategic partnership we need to manage in creating market-led strategic change and building a genuinely customer-focused organization [35, 36].

This is a central theme in market-led strategic change – it is reflected in several of the case studies that follow, and we pick it up again in Chapter 14, where we look at internal marketing.

So, where have we got to?

So far, I have tried to do three things:

- to set the scene as *the process of going to market*, instead of conventional 'marketing', where managers need to know about customers, market strategy and implementation more than anything else;
- to test out just *how serious we are about customer satisfaction*, given how poor customer service tends to be in so many companies; and
- to look at what we know about *building a customer-focused organization*.

This is the foundation. Now we can talk about building a market strategy.

References

1. Cravens, David W., Gordon Greenley, Nigel F. Piercy and Stanley F. Slater (1997), 'Market-Driven Strategic Management', *Long Range Planning*, Vol. 30 No. 4. 493–506.
2. Summers, Diane (1995), 'Letters Chiefs Aim to Deliver Quality', *Financial Times*, 6 March.

3. Heller, Robert (1995), 'The Art of Delighting Customers', *Mail on Sunday*, 6 August.
4. Treacy, Michael and Fred Wiersema (1995), *The Discipline of Market Leaders*, London: Harper Collins.
5. Self, Alastair (1997), 'Hello Johann, Got a New Motor', *Mail on Sunday*, 13 April.
6. Slywotsky, Adreian (1996), *Value Migration*, Boston, Mass.: Harvard Business School Press.
7. Hewson, David (1995), 'Jean Genius: One to One Marketing', *Sunday Times*, 11 June.
8. Leiber, Ronald B. (1997), 'Storytelling: A New Way to Get Close to Your Customer', *Fortune*, 3 February.
9. Kay, David (1997), 'Go Where the Consumers are and Talk to Them', *Marketing News*, 6 January.
10. Doyle, Peter (1997), *Marketing Management and Strategy*, 2nd ed., Hemel Hempstead: Prentice-Hall.
11. Walther, George R. (1994), *Upside-Down Marketing*, New York: McGraw-Hill.
12. Barley, Peter (1994), 'Looking for Trouble', *Marketing Business*, September, 21–24.
13. Slater, Stanley F. and John C. Narver (1995), 'Market Orientation and the Learning Organization', *Journal of Marketing*, October, 63–74.
14. Cravens, David W. *et al* (1997), *op. cit.*
15. Oldroyd, Rachel (1997), 'Man With Plenty In Store', *Sunday Business*, 13 April.
16. Treacy, Michael and Fred Wiersema (1995), *op. cit.*
17. Muir, Hugh (1996), 'Stay Tuned or Start Walking', *Daily Telegraph*, 30 September.
18. Long, Pat (1997), 'Customer-Loyalty, One Customer at a Time', *Marketing News*, 3 February.
19. Griffin, A. and J. R. Hauser (1992), *The Voice of the Customer*, Cambridge, Mass.: Marketing Science Institute.
20. McQuance, E. and S. McIntyre (1992), *The Customer Visit*, Cambridge, Mass.: Marketing Science Institute.
21. Lele, M. M. and J. Sheth (1988), 'The Four Fundamentals of Customer Satisfaction', *Business Marketing*, June, 80–84.
22. Richins, M. L. (1987), 'Negative Word-of-Mouth by Dissatisfied Customers', *Journal of Marketing*, January, 68–78.
23. Coleman, L. G. (1992), 'Learning What Customers Like', *Marketing News*, 2 March.
24. Piercy, Nigel F. (1995), 'Customer Satisfaction and the Internal Market: Marketing Our Customers to Our Employees', *Journal of Marketing Practice: Applied Marketing Science*, Vol. 1, No. 1, 22–44.
25. Thomas, Michael (1987), 'Coming to Terms with the Customer', *Personnel Management*, February, 24–28.
26. Jenkins, Jolyon (1990), 'Say Cheese', *New Statesman and Society*, 20 April, 24–25.
27. Clutterbuck, David (1989), 'Developing Customer Care Training Programmes', *Marketing Intelligence and Planning*, Vol. 7, No. 112, 34–37.

28. Monaghan, Robert (1995), 'Customer Management Teams are Here to Stay', *Marketing News*, 6 November.
29. Band, William A. (1991), *Creating Value for Customers*, Toronto: Wiley.
30. Mazur, Laura (1996), 'Accountability', *Marketing Business*, September.
31. Albrecht, Karl (1988), *At America's Service*, New Jersey: Irwin.
32. Rosenbluth, Hal F. and Dianne McFerrin Peters (1992), *The Customer Comes Second*, New York: William Morrow.
33. Crump, John (1996), 'Changing the Culture', The 8th UNISYS Life and Pensions Seminar, Nice.
34. Fronchetti, Mark (1996), 'Germans Learn to Grin and Bear it', *Sunday Times*, 7 April.
35. Glassman, M. and B. McAffee (1992), 'Integrating the Personnel and Marketing Functions: The Challenge of the 1990s', *Business Horizons*, Vol. 35, No. 3, 52–59.
36. Hulbert, J. M. and L. Pitt (1996), 'Exit Left Centre Stage', *European Management Journal*, Vol. 14, No. 1, 47–60.

Case I   Avis Europe Ltd:
Synergizing customers and employees to create competitive advantage*

'We try harder' is the slogan that captivated the American public in the early 1960s. It created one of the ten most famous advertising campaigns of all time, and encapsulated the competitive edge that was to turn Avis from a tiny American company with an unbroken record of financial losses to a global service leader with over 333 000 vehicles, operating through 5000 locations in 163 countries, and characterized by one of the most powerful corporate cultures in the world.

Avis Europe was created in 1965 as a separate operating division to spearhead international expansion into Europe, Africa and the Middle East.

'building the best and fastest growing company with the highest profit margins in the business of car rental'
With the singular vision of building the best and fastest growing company with the highest profit margins in the business of car rental, and boosted by the impetus of 'We try harder', the company climbed from 'greenfield' start to market leader in just eight years, and has remained there ever since. The company has gone through a number of changes in ownership structure, including three years as a highly successful plc in the late 1980s. Since 1989, Avis Europe has been privately owned, and while legally separated from its former parent, Avis Inc in the USA, it retains strong and cohesive operational links with the rest of the Avis system, presenting a global brand and customer service image to the world's travelling public. Its operating revenues this year will be in excess of £500 million, representing a growth of over 40 per cent since 1994.

This case describes how Avis Europe has built its organization and management processes around those early principles of 'We try harder', and taken its famous slogan from an 'underdog' strap line in an advertising campaign to a market leadership strategy in a highly competitive industry.

The 'We try harder' story

In 1962 Avis was a small American company, with an unbroken record not of service excellence but of financial losses in the previous six years. The newly appointed president of that time, Robert Townsend, took a number of actions to turn the company around, including hiring a new advertising

---

* This case study was prepared by Lesley Colyer, Vice President – Personnel, Avis Europe Ltd.

agency. He went to Doyle Dane and Bernbach, a prestigious Maddison Avenue house. Townsend didn't have much money to spend on advertising – in fact, he had only one fifth of the funds spent by Avis's major competitor, Hertz. He struck an unusual deal with the owner of the agency, Bill Bernbach. Bernbach's deal was: 'If you want five times the impact, give us 90 days to learn enough about your business to apply our skills ... then run every ad we write, as we write them and where we tell you. Agree to this and we have a deal.' Townsend did.

The agency began their research to find a positive differentiating factor between Avis and its competitor. They concluded that there wasn't one! Ninety days of research revealed that Avis did not do anything better than its competitor; the only difference was the Avis employees – they seemed to try harder than the rest, but probably because they had to!

From this remark, a revolutionary campaign was born – revolutionary because it was the first time in history that *any* company publicly admitted that it wasn't the best ... but it was trying to be. None of the Avis executives liked the campaign, but Townsend honoured the deal and ran it anyway. The rest is history.

'We try harder' now holds the distinction of being one of the ten most famous advertising campaigns of all time. The slogan appealed to people's natural inclination to support the underdog – they tried Avis once to see if the ads were true. Having tried Avis once they came back again and again – not because of the ad campaign, but because of its most remarkable impact on the employees. 'We try harder' literally inspired the Avis people to deliver new heights of service. It turned good people into star performers because of the onus placed on the individual to excel.

Each ad was distributed in every employee's pay packet before being launched externally – and we mean every employee – from managers to front-line staff and those who washed and delivered the cars. Each ad told customers and employees what the car was to be like, what the service was to be like, and how the company was to perform. 'We try harder' created a charter of standards and expectations that became the company's new birthright. And most important ... within three years the company was solidly in the black and sales had tripled.

'We try harder' recognized that we could not take customers for granted and that each employee, no matter what their role in the company, would try harder to make sure that customers would come back again ... and all this in an era before the concept of customer service and satisfaction was embedded in the USA or, indeed, anywhere else in the world.

From these early years Avis Europe developed a set of beliefs and values that remains at the heart of our organization and management processes. At the core of these is the 'We try harder' ethos:

We believe that sustainable competitive advantage comes from our ability to continuously innovate ahead of the competition. In achieving this we look for continuous improvement, no matter how

Avis needs you.
You don't need Avis.
Avis never forgets this.

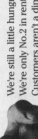

We're still a little hungry.

We're only No.2 in rent a cars.

Customers aren't a dime a dozen to us.

Sometimes, when business is too good, they get the short end and aren't treated like customers anymore.

Wouldn't you like the novel experience of walking up to a counter and not feel you're bothering somebody? Try it.

Come to the Avis counter and rent a new, lively super-torque Ford. Avis is only No.2 in rent a cars. So we have to try harder to make our customers feel like customers. Our counters all have two sides.

And we know which side our bread is buttered on.

A copy of this ad
is going into
every Avis pay envelope

People in this country don't believe everything they read in ads any more.

And with good reason.

Most advertising these days is long on the big promise–a promise that the product doesn't always deliver.

And at times Avis is no exception. A shiny new Plymouth with mud in the trunk or a spare tire with no air in it makes a liar out of Avis ads.

So they can't miss it. We can't police all the other advertising in this country. But we can live up to our own.

In our next ad we're going to promise customers that we'll get the rental form filled out within 2 minutes.

You can do it, girls. You've been trained to.

Let's see if we can keep Avis ads honest.

small, in everything we do and at the same time quantum improvement in the way we do business. We will never hesitate to adapt to new and more profitable ways of working provided that the honesty and integrity we apply to our business is not compromised. We actively encourage a 'try harder' and 'can do' mentality and operate a climate of trust at all levels. The only mistake is not to try something.

One of the key lessons we learned all those years ago is that no matter how successful an organization becomes, it must seek to continuously improve, if it is to compete in tomorrow's marketplace. However, continuous improvement will not increase shareholder value or long-term profitability unless it focuses on what matters to the customer. It is all too easy to lose track of this in times of business success. We have tried very hard to avoid this trap and to translate those same customer philosophies and principles we employed as a small loss-making company, with a handful of employees in one country, to a global enterprise at the leading edge of service delivery, with 21 000 employees in 163 countries.

Continuous Improvement Cycle

Listening to customers

A company cannot know what matters most to customers unless it asks them. In 1989, we took a quantum leap forward in the way we 'listened' to customers, by leveraging our technological advantage. Since the 1960s, Avis has invested over \$1 billion in developing the most advanced global computer network and information processing systems in our industry, which today links more than 350 000 terminals around the globe. This has given us a major competitive edge in many areas, and not least in the area of customer satisfaction. Through our technology we capture virtually every single customer transaction and obtain a wealth of data that can be linked to customer and employee opinion and used to drive improvements in areas that most affect customer satisfaction and loyalty.

We began this process by launching a significant piece of pan-European research. We talked to thousands of our customers in eleven countries, asking them what they thought of their experiences with Avis, and what they wanted from car rental. At the same time, we surveyed every one of our employees, asking them the same questions as the customers in addition to specifics about working practices and company processes.

The results of this baseline research formed the basis of a number of initiatives that we have implemented in the last five years – many of which have already reaped additional customer loyalty, additional profits and more awards for service excellence than anyone else in the industry.

The Avis baseline research

The key findings of the baseline research were:

- The research showed that only a very small percentage of our customers ever communicated about service issues – good or bad. Of those who had an enquiry or service issue, only 6 per cent actually contacted the customer service department. Each one of these contacts, handled to the satisfaction of the customer, resulted in a retention factor of over 90 per cent – almost as high as customers who were happy with the service they received in the first place!

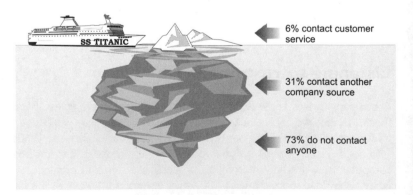

Customer Contact Iceberg

6% contact customer service

31% contact another company source

73% do not contact anyone

- Of the remaining customers who had an enquiry or service issue, 31 per cent contacted someone else in the organization – usually front-line staff. This was valuable customer data, not captured or fed into the company's continuous improvement and root cause improvement processes. Moreover, service issues dealt with at the front line generated a lower level of satisfaction, some of which resulted in a second contact being made by the customer, usually to the customer service department. This 'escalation' phenomenon is costly in terms of customer retention and profit for a number of reasons:

  'This "escalation" phenomenon is costly in terms of customer retention and profit'

  - negative word of advertising occurs between the first and second contact;
  - the second contact may not happen at all ... leaving a dissatisfied customer, unlikely to come back;
  - between the first and second contacts, the problem is likely to escalate in the customer's mind and become more costly for the company to resolve.

Service Issue Escalation and Impact on Customer Loyalty
(% loyalty)

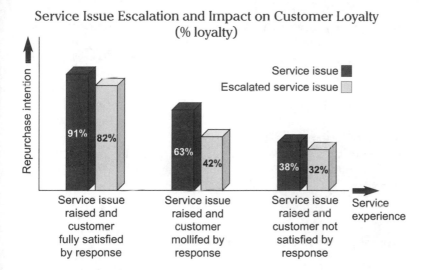

- The vast majority of customers with enquiries or service issues did not contact anyone at Avis, but they did, however, tell other people! We call this 'negative word of mouth advertising', and we know from research across many industries that unhappy customers tell three to four times as many people about their experiences as happy customers do. Even worse is that these customers take their business elsewhere the next time. Research showed that only 78 per cent of these customers would use Avis again, compared with 92 per cent of customers who were satisfied with their service encounter. This difference of 14 per cent represents lost customers, lost revenues, lost profits and lost reputation.

Customer Loyalty vs. Service Experience

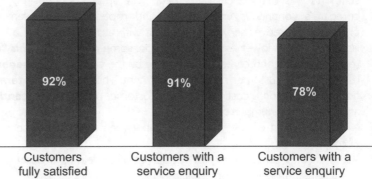

92%	91%	78%
Customers fully satisfied with service experience	Customers with a service enquiry who are fully satisfied with the response	Customers with a service enquiry who do not contact anyone

- The employee research indicated a 'positive morale' problem! Employees were committed to delivering excellent customer service, and wanted to resolve customer queries, but found insufficient flexibility to do so in some company processes.

The key actions that resulted from this research involved:

- making customer service a profit centre;
- transferring ownership of the service encounter to employees;
- aligning training processes with this strategy; and
- continuously tracking both customer and employee satisfaction with Avis.

Customer service as a profit centre

The research clearly showed that customer service departments were key to customer retention and should be profit centres in their own right. Customers with service issues, who are satisfied with the way their query is handled, are the most loyal, give repeat business and champion the company with positive word of mouth advertising to others. Since it costs a company at least ten times as much to solicit a new customer as it does to retain an existing one, investment in our customer service units became a priority. Our approach involved the following:

- We invested substantially in state-of-the-art call management systems, linked directly to customer transaction data and receivable and billing systems.

- We fully empowered and trained our customer service employees to do whatever it took to resolve a customer issue there and then on the telephone, and to action the resolution of the problem directly into the billing systems.
- We implemented a complainant satisfaction tracking system to assess effectiveness at retaining customers.
- We made it easier for customers to contact our customer service centres, publishing the telephone number on all rental material, and providing dedicated and unique numbers for major customers.
- We implemented a process of root cause analysis, to identify and resolve service issues at source, and a monthly feedback system to rental locations, giving them customer feedback – good and bad – about their specific location, thus providing a mechanism for root cause resolution at all levels in the company.
- Customer service representatives began to regularly attend meetings with major customers, along with operational employees, to ensure that service requirements are understood and any issues quickly resolved.

These actions have had a significant impact on customer retention. Some of the key achievements of the UK customer service centre are: (1) today, over 90 per cent of customer service calls are resolved live, while the customer is on the phone and on the first call; (2) overall complainant satisfaction levels this year are running on average 10 percentage points above last year; (3) a multi-functional task team developed substantial process improvement programmes to address the top three service issues in 1995 – all of these are now in the process of implementation; (4) a new complainant satisfaction tracking system fully integrated with Avis technology and enhanced to reflect state-of-the-art contact measurement is under development.

Employee ownership of the service encounter

Responsiveness to customer needs is key to the longevity of any business. Our research re-emphasized the critical role front-line employees play in customer retention, and the need for us to remove any organizational obstacles to delivering good service. Today, this is fashionably called *empowerment*, and to many it is simply devolving responsibility to the lowest possible level in the organization, to prevent escalation of customer problems – something that can be instilled in a two-day training course. To us, it means much more than this. It means creating an organizational and management climate that encourages responsiveness to customer needs. It means employees who are both willing and able to make exceptional service the norm, rather than the exception. It means employees who are willing to give a little extra: to create customer value every time – not just when there are problems; and everywhere – not just at the front line and the interface with the customer.

This is an extract from a customer letter about Dawn Swadling, a front-line employee at Heathrow:

> 'I had to travel to the UK to attend my father's funeral. I required a small auto ... had to wait ... she tried her utmost to solve my dilemma. I marvelled at her professionalism, courtesy and kindness ... carried my suitcase to the car and put her arm around me in a very tender and consoling manner as she wished me well. My company requires all its 30,000 employees to attend 'Customer First' training. Whenever examples of the ultimate in customer care were given, Dawn always came to mind. She could have written the book!'

Dawn is what we mean by empowered – customer retention through total responsiveness to customer needs. You cannot buy Dawns ready-made or from an advertising agency (any more!).

At Avis we had most of the necessary organizational characteristics and management processes in place, including most importantly, as the research told us, a workforce that actually wanted to do it! The challenge was to adjust and implement the necessary mechanisms to develop total employee ownership of the service encounter.

Alignment of training processes

The first thing we did was to critically re-appraise our training processes, to ensure that we were delivering high levels of competence and clarity. As a result, we set up a project to develop a completely new and innovative training process for front-line staff which would lead to customers experiencing a unique level of value and service that would not be experienced with any other service provider. The project team comprised operational management, the training manager and rental sales agents – those who actually do the job! We believed that a programme conceived, designed and written by actual end users would be far more effective than one solely devised by 'training professionals'.

It took the team three years to produce a competence-based distance learning programme. In excess of 140 competence statements were produced to cover all the key elements of service excellence in our environment, and grouped into five stages. The programme was designed to be completed in the workplace, and it takes a new recruit between 18 months and two years to successfully complete it. The programme has BTEC accreditation, and the successful completion of the final stage requires completion of a business improvement project. The programme was officially launched in the UK in 1993 by Alun Cathcart, Chairman and CEO, Keith Dyer, UK Managing Director, and Sir Geoffrey Holland.

Since its inception, more than 500 employees have been enrolled on the programme, 30 per cent of whom have successfully passed stage 3, which makes them fully competent as professional rental sales agents. The majority are now taking the optional stage 4 and 5 levels, designed to promote a greater understanding of the business and prepare individuals for supervisory and management positions. Forty per cent of those who have finished stage 5, have already been promoted, and some substantial business improvement projects have been presented. This is the world's first formal standards-based front-line employee training programme in the car rental industry and, whilst it is too early to offer proof of impact on employee turnover and customer satisfaction, it is clear that this programme is having a positive influence in both of these respects.

Continuously tracking customer and employee satisfaction

From what our customers and employees told us in the research we conducted, we developed comprehensive and *meaningful* customer and employee satisfaction tracking systems. Customer expectations are constantly changing and increasing. What the customer perceived as excellent yesterday is mediocre today, and will be unsatisfactory tomorrow. It is therefore critical to continuously listen to customers and to have on-going customer and employee satisfaction and retention measurements integrated with the key business monitors of the organization. This ensures that improvements are focused on what matters to the customer and avoids the trap of 'customer arrogance' into which otherwise successful companies can fall.

Customer satisfaction tracking system

We have developed one of Europe's most extensive independent measurement systems for tracking customer reaction to the service they have just received from Avis. Each month, over 13 500 customers are randomly selected from the total number of customers who rented in the previous month. These customers are contacted and asked to record the level of satisfaction they have experienced with our service, our product and our people for a particular rental. There are two important points here.

First, the service attributes measured are those that have the greatest impact on satisfaction and retention in our particular operating environment, as identified in our baseline research. Secondly, *all* of the attributes measured can be directly influenced and affected by our employees.

'the service attributes measured are those that have the greatest impact on satisfaction and retention'

Customers are also asked to express their overall satisfaction, and how likely they are to use our service again. Therefore, we are not asking a generic set of questions, but what they thought about our service on a particular occasion. Our technology links each response to a specific rental contract, containing substantial data that we do not need to ask the customer for.

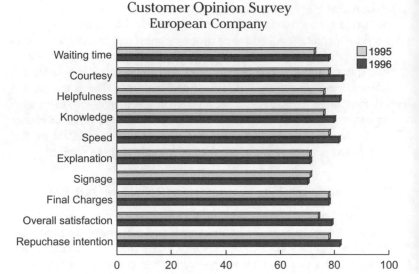

From the responses we receive from customers, comprehensive information is produced which is filtered from Board level to every single rental location in our network. Each location receives regular and recent feedback from its customers – not just a set of average numbers, but individual customer scores, together with the contract number. Local teams are, therefore, not only able to look at the survey results, but to view the full details of the transaction on their computer screens. This is very powerful because it helps each team to identify what likely actions, circumstances or behaviours were responsible for the specific customer feedback. Continuous improvement is thus driven at local level by those who deliver the service, and is in absolute response to *their* customers' feedback.

An example of local initiatives is the launch of 'full-service return' in the Scottish district, to improve performance on 'accuracy of billing'. This meant using the Wizard system real-time with the customers to calculate the rental charges and explain and agree them with customers. The district improved its accuracy of billing scores from customer opinion by 5 points in a six-month period. The District Manager responsible for this initiative is, today, the Director of Training for the Avis Group.

But customer feedback is not just used in our operations. It is used by every function, to continuously improve what matters most to the customer. Our marketing functions are able to track satisfaction by product, by day of the week, by location and by nationality, enabling improvements in product development. Our fleet functions are able to track satisfaction by make and model. As we are the largest purchaser of fleet cars in Western Europe this is of significant importance, not only to us as a factor in fleet purchase decisions, but also to the vehicle manufacturers in terms of their fleet design and model acceptability. Our training and customer service functions are able to identify where changes are needed to processes and procedures; what are the root causes of customer dissatisfaction; what new knowledge and skills need to be emphasized.

In addition, we use the data externally in a number of ways. We are able to assess and improve partnership products such as frequent flyer programmes. We also produce customer satisfaction reports for our major customers regarding the satisfaction of their travelling employees. This process forms a key part of contract negotiation and acts as a powerful tool to demonstrate that service standards are being achieved and to agree service guarantees. This has undoubtedly created a competitive advantage for Avis.

A truly effective customer quality process is not just an internal and insular activity. Its ultimate success depends very much on the extent to which it also recognizes and integrates the interests and needs of customers, suppliers and partners alike.

In the spirit of continuous improvement, the customer satisfaction tracking system itself underwent significant enhancements last year to ensure that it continued to reflect what matters most to our customers and that it remained at the leading edge of customer opinion measurement systems. The key changes were:

- An updated customer communication vehicle, creating a more customer-friendly image and encouraging greater response levels;
- A substantial reduction in the process cycle from mailing to customers, to results being received by rental locations, together with increased frequency of rental location reporting (the latter being an enhancement requested by operations themselves!). Cycle times have been reduced by over 71 per cent, providing more meaningful and timely data for operational action;
- A broader base of questions on service and rental processes, together with customer buying patterns and perceptions on competitor performance;
- The development of an exception reporting process on a routine basis to continuously focus attention on key areas.

Whilst only operational for a few months, we are already reaping substantial benefits from the new survey: response rates have increased by 15 per cent with an average pan-European response rate of 30 per cent; significant volumes of 'white mail' have been received, providing a valuable source of customer feedback; and there has been a substantial improvement in quality of name and address capture at the time of rental.

Employee satisfaction tracking system

The linkage between customer satisfaction and employee satisfaction is very strong. This was bought home to us back in the 1960s. It is a lesson we have never forgotten.

We used our baseline research to develop an employee satisfaction tracking system to provide linkage with our customer satisfaction data. This survey embraces all employees in all parts of the organization, and measures the 28 attributes that customers and employees told us were essential to delivering excellent service. The data is fed to countries, to functional teams and directly to employees and, when linked to customer satisfaction data, it provides a powerful information base for local action and continuous improvement initiatives.

The chart below shows the cumulative increases in employee satisfaction in one of our countries, Spain, over the last two years. It is no coincidence that over the same time-frame overall customer satisfaction in Spain increased, with satisfaction increasing on five service attributes and exceeding 90 per cent in two key areas. During this same period, the Spanish company grew its customer base by 45 per cent.

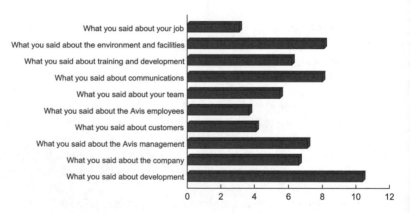

Employee Satisfaction Survey, Spain
(% Change FY96 vs. FY94)

Employee satisfaction results at the headquarters of the Avis Europe Group in the UK have led to the development of a number of corporate initiatives over the last two years, which we are in the process of rolling out and integrating into our operating units:

- A new performance and development review process, linked to an employee development programme, providing both Avis-specific and professional training opportunities and qualifications;

- Bi-annual business awareness initiatives, featuring 'hands on' experience of the latest developments in the business for all employees – examples are:
  - *Global branding*: Prior to externally re-launching our global branding this year, we invited employees to attend workshops to understand the external positioning and enter a team competition by creating, designing and making brochures themselves using the new Avis guidelines;
  - *Internet*: Avis established the industry's first World-Wide Web site on 12 April this year. All employees had the opportunity to 'surf the Avis site' and view the Avis features offered to millions of customers worldwide;
- Opportunities for all newly-recruited HQ clerical staff to 'hear the tills ringing' with some time spent at a rental location;

  'Opportunities for all newly-recruited HQ clerical staff to "hear the tills ringing"'
- Bi-annual business performance briefings by the Chairman and Chief Executive;
- Social events, giving all employees regular opportunities to meet the directors and discuss anything they wish to raise.

Maintaining the momentum through people

Today, the satisfaction tracking systems are closely integrated with our key organization and management processes and fully aligned to a strategy of customer retention.

All of these issues are important, but we firmly believe that the single most important factor in sustaining our momentum, and the competitive advantage of 'We try harder', lies with our people: the way we recruit, train, develop and manage them. We look for people who have a strong orientation to working with other people, who like a 'hands on' approach, and also know how to enjoy themselves and have fun in their jobs.

We have evolved an operating structure that minimizes bureaucracy and encourages initiative. Our vertical lines are short, with a maximum of

Avis Europe corporate beliefs and values

The following statements encapsulate our beliefs and values and our approach to doing business throughout our operating territories

Business ethics

We believe it is in the interest of our shareholders, our customers and our employees that we maintain a highly acceptable public image supporting a progressively profitable company. Honesty, integrity and fairness in dealings must and will be absolute and an integral basis of our total philosophy.

Customers

We believe in providing consistently high standards of integrity, service, quality and value in satisfying customer needs. This operating ethos maintains our industry leadership and retains the loyalty and respect of our customers.

Employees

We aim to stimulate duty, mutual loyalty and a sense of pride in working for Avis through employee involvement at all levels, continuous updating of knowledge and skills and attractive and competitive recognition and reward systems. We believe that employees should be actively encouraged to grow and develop their careers with Avis and we always seek first to appoint candidates from within the Company to fill positions at every level - both nationally and internationally. To this end, we will provide the environment to help employees improve and develop themselves.

Management and leadership

We believe in local autonomy, working within broad guidelines and underpinned by strong support services at the centre. We are committed to professionalism in leadership; clear direction, clear team work development, clear communication, clear and sensibly quick and consistent decisions based on 'what' is right rather than 'who' is right. We recognise that excellence and professionalism amongst Avis management and employees is a key marketing tool. It gives customers confidence and competitors an inferiority complex.

'We try harder.'ethos

We believe that sustainable competitive advantage comes from our ability to continuously innovate ahead of the competition. In achieving this we look for continuous improvement, no matter how small, in every thing we do and at the same time quantum improvement in the way we do business. We will never hesitate to adapt to new and more profitable ways of working provided that the integrity and honesty we apply to our business is not compromised. We actively encourage a 'try harder' and 'can do' mentality and operate a climate of TRUST at all levels. The only mistake is not to try something.

Community

We operate as responsible members of the community and within the laws of the countries within which we do business. We recognise and respect the attitudes, characteristics and customs of local populations.

Environment

We recognise our corporate responsibility to the community at large for public health and safety and environmental protection. We fully comply with all legislation in this respect and actively pursue environmental and safety initiatives on a local, industry wide and global basis.

Suppliers

We ensure integrity and professionalism in all dealings with suppliers and expect the same in return. We seek economic quality and efficiency of service in all supplier relationships and, where possible, 'added value' to the mutual benefit of both. We continuously foster strategic alliances and partnerships with major travel industry organisations who share a mutual respect of the customer, a commitment to quality and a desire to maximise and enhance the reputation and value of the brand.

Costs

We regard efficiency as central to our whole business philosophy and we continuously search for means to reduce the cost of delivering a better product for the customer.

six levels between the Chairman of the company and a car washer in downtown Rome. We operate a philosophy of decentralized management and a high degree of local autonomy, underpinned by strong support services at the centre and a shared vision of beliefs and values. We have achieved significant continuity and longevity in our workforce:

- We are only 30 years old as a company, but over 50 per cent of our employees today have more than five years' service with us – next year almost 15 per cent will achieve a long service award.

- Over 90 per cent of the 200 most senior managers in Avis today came up through the ranks – many began their careers serving Avis customers and they continue to do so today. Visible management is the oldest corporate management process in Avis. For 25 years, and long before Tom Peters popularized 'walk the talk', the Chairman and managers across the network regularly set aside days to work at the rental counter, wash cars, take reservations and handle complaints. This is not stunt management, it is a key process for listening and staying close to customer and employee opinion – continuously.
- Cross-functional and cross-border appointments are a regular feature of Avis Europe's management development programme, minimizing the trap of 'functional' mind set and inter-departmental politics.

The future

We believe that 'We try harder' is a unique organizational capability and a primary source of competitive advantage for us. Looking to the future, we have undertaken a comprehensive review of our reward and recognition processes and developed a holistic programme for all employees in each of our operating territories to encourage and recognize the 'We try harder' service values and to tap the creativity of our workforce in a way that, we believe, will see Avis continue to thrive and be successful well into the next century.

Known as 'The Spirit of Avis', the first element of the programme is a recognition process for delivering the promise of 'We try harder'. A customer, supplier, partner or fellow employee can nominate anyone in the company for recognition for giving a little extra. There are various levels of recognition within the programme – for teams as well as individuals – culminating in a gold award from the Chairman and CEO. The programme is explained to all new employees at the time of their induction into the company, and includes a 15-minute silent movie, made in the early 1970s, which demonstrates what the 'We try harder' promise means on a day-to-day basis. This recognition process is very powerful in perpetuating the cultural behaviours that drive responsiveness to customer needs – internal and external.

The second element of the programme is about putting 'We try harder' into action and bringing the 'We try harder' operating ethos of innovation and continuous improvement to life – permanently. Essentially, it actively encourages idea generation and provides reward for it. Each Avis territory has a multi-functional team, led by a member of the senior management team which receives and rewards ideas generated in their country. A unique automated process is designed to capture the input from more than 90 countries to a multi-functional team at Group headquarters who, in addition to capturing ideas from Group headquarters' employees, are responsible for disseminating and progressing ideas from different territories across the Group. This new process will be fully implemented in all our countries by the end of 1996, when it will become the system that captures improvement ideas from many other company measurement systems and, critically, those described in this case study: customer satisfaction tracking, employee satisfaction tracking and complainant satisfaction tracking.

Evidence of success

How successful have we been with our approach, our management practices and measurement systems, and how valid are our presumptions that service values will continue to provide a competitive advantage in the years ahead? We have given specific locations and country results as illustrations throughout this case. For the total company, there is substantial external recognition of our approach: more innovation in product development than our competitors; more service awards than any other car rental company; and the only car rental company to receive site visits for major quality awards, spanning three continents. We could point to sustained market leadership, a profit record that consistently outstrips our competitors, growth in shareholder value and many other indicators of success.

In 1997 Avis Europe announced its intention to refloat on the stock market with an expected value of £700 million, leading to the buying-out of minority shareholders and gaining access for Avis Europe to the whole of Asia, as well as funding expansion into Central and Eastern Europe. In March 1997, market enthusiasm for the Avis share offer was shown by the fact that it was oversubscribed fivefold.

For us, the most important indicator is what our customers think, and we would like to leave the final word on 'service' to a customer – the Chairman of a major plc who sent us this letter just a few weeks ago. It demonstrates that the service values inherent in the 'We try harder' promise are as fresh as ever and as relevant today as they were in the 1960s.

> *'I can't tell you how enormously impressed I have been with the efforts of your operation at Derry airport. It is the epitome of 'We Try Harder' in action. A recent example is that I arrived in Derry at 5.30 pm on Friday 3 May, without having booked a car (by mistake). Martin Hankin not only came up trumps immediately with a car, but was then kind enough to deliver to my address in Ireland a more suitable car much later that evening. I can tell you that it is rare to receive that kind of help from an organization and I am deeply impressed and thankful for it. If it represents your quality of service around the world then your competitors have a lot to be frightened of.'*

Questions to consider

1 What does the Avis experience tell us about the power of customer focus and the cost of customer focus?

2 Does advertising always say the right things to employees as well as customers – or is this actually the result of careful strategy? Are there examples where advertising by companies can have a negative effect rather than the synergy achieved by Avis?

3 What are the most important internal organizational practices at Avis that drive 'We Try Harder', and how could they be applied in other companies?

4 If Avis can manage customer and employee satisfaction in parallel, why do other companies have problems putting these two things together?

5 How much will Avis have to change its strategy for Asia and Eastern Europe?

6 What are the most important lessons we can learn from the Avis story about building and sustaining customer focus in an organization?

The CIGNA Corporation is one of the largest health insurance providers in the USA, based in Philadelphia, and with revenues in excess of $35 billion. In the USA, CIGNA is the largest investor-owned provider of health benefit programmes, and provides cover for more than seven million people. Around 17 per cent of CIGNA revenues come from outside the USA, where the company operates in 120 different countries, and CIGNA Employee Benefits is in the international division of the corporation, based in Greenock, Scotland. The Greenock headquarters employs around 150 people, and provides private medical insurance cover for some 200 000 people across the UK and earned annual revenues in excess of £90 million in 1994.

CIGNA's UK product range has included life, medical, sickness and permanent health insurance, but the primary focus is on providing high quality healthcare benefits to individuals, through the benefits provided by their employers. Most of the client base comprises large corporate bodies attracted by the idea of including private medical insurance as part of their staff benefits package. A recent advertising slogan was 'CIGNA – The Way You Want To Be Treated', and the company's strategy rests on achieving a high level of service quality in the areas most important to its customers. The company has won major awards for its customer service excellence, while at the same time dramatically increasing productivity and profitability.

When he was manager of the Customer Service Centre at Greenock, Douglas Cowieson wrote: 'within the CIGNA organisation we are seen not as *a* centre of excellence, but *the* centre of excellence for **'we are seen not as a centre of excellence, but the centre of excellence for reengineering and customer service'** reengineering and customer service.' While many client organizations visit Greenock to see how excellent service is provided for them as CIGNA customers, they are out-numbered three to one by other visitors going to find out how CIGNA changed its strategy and developed a new culture of customer focus.

---

* This case study has been prepared by Nigel Piercy, Cardiff Business School, from company documents and discussions, and secondary sources. Grateful acknowledgement is made to the input of Douglas Cowieson and Ian Ferguson of CIGNA.

CIGNA in the UK was not always the success story it now is. The business has been through a major strategic change and turnaround during the 1990s.

The starting point for a new customer-focused strategy

The US CIGNA Corporation purchased the Surrey-based insurance company Crusader Insurance in the mid-1980s, expecting to use CIGNA expertise to turn the business around financially. It failed. By 1990, the business was running at a £9 million annual loss, and was very clearly stagnating. Crusader was a conventional insurance business with a hierarchical organizational structure. Customer and staff retention rates were dangerously low. Customer perceptions of CIGNA were unfavourable. The business showed little ability to grow profitably, and was under pressure to perform better by the US owners.

Critical problems facing the business at this time were: the high operating costs in the South-East of England; an organization structure not designed to manage change; a lack of market focus; and a traditional insurance industry culture.

A new start

The turning point in the CIGNA story in the UK came with the move from Surrey to Greenock, on the outskirts of Glasgow, in response to pressure to reduce operating costs. This move, however, was associated not just with reducing costs, but also with shedding the majority of the existing staff, who did not move to Scotland. The move led to a radical change in the way the company operated both internally and particularly in how it dealt with its customers. The result was that by 1994 the £9 million loss had been turned into a £1 million profit, productivity measured by things such as claims processed had increased by 30 per cent, staff retention was up to 95 per cent, and the company was the overall winner of the UK Best Practice Awards for Service Excellence. The key issues underpinning this turnaround were: changed market focus; developments in the product line; refocusing on customer needs; identifying the barriers to change; and undertaking a programme of radical change in the way the business operates and the culture that drives it.

Market focus

The Greenock operation started out as the European Service Centre – following the logic common in many US-based multinationals that Europe is a market that can be managed as one. This strategy was dropped, and the focus described below is on the UK. The major customer focus is on corporate customers, not individual consumers. The positioning is on the high-value end of the UK corporate health insurance market, based on customer service and value rather than price.

Product-line changes

The CIGNA business in the UK is primarily involved with providing group life, group medical, group dental and group private health insurance to employers providing these services to their employees. However, the original product line was made up of insurance policies that the company systems and processes could handle, rather than those the customers wanted. The new product line is built around customer needs, in terms of the policies on offer and the way they are handled.

For example, one response to an identified customer need in the corporate market was the 'managed care' policy, in which trained CIGNA nurses map out treatment plans with individual patients. Since moving to Scotland, in excess of 40 per cent of the business has been converted to managed care. The underlying process has been one of developing products closely tailored to customer needs. By 1995, in four years the company had built managed care into a £16 million business, covering 90 000 lives, with a customer retention rate of 95 per cent, and no customer losses because of service issues.

Patrick Brennan, Managing Director, says that marketing an employee benefit to corporate customers involves paying attention to the politics and culture within individual companies to find out exactly what *'marketing an employee benefit to corporate customers involves paying attention to the politics and culture within individual companies'* they want to accomplish by offering private medical insurance, and concludes: 'That kind of customer is interested in our approach because we ask them what is important to them about PMI (personal medical insurance), we go back and design a product to meet their objectives and then the company can tell us how much extra service they want to add on to that design'. It is this market-led approach that produced the highly successful managed care products, and it is also part of the reason why CIGNA is rarely the cheapest supplier.

The company also refocused by selling off its main business lines of pensions and individual life products, because the company was too small to be a major player in a commodity market, where market share drives profitability. The understanding of the customer which the company has built has been a driving force in making CIGNA a specialist in healthcare.

Customer understanding

Ailie Ferrari, Marketing Intelligence Manager, describes the intense programme of research that CIGNA used to gain an understanding of who their customers were, and what those customers wanted, as the basis for building competitive advantage. The investigations encompassed existing corporate medical clients, intermediaries who advise such clients, and companies choosing not to buy corporate medical insurance from CIGNA. They used face-to-face interviews and a questionnaire-based approach to identifying the service areas with the maximum potential for improvement.

With existing corporate clients, satisfaction with CIGNA service was high, as would be expected, but six key areas for service improvement were identified: (1) clients had to talk to too many people before finding someone who could help them; (2) clients found it easier to have one point of contact at CIGNA; (3) there was dissatisfaction with the availability of claims personnel; (4) there was dissatisfaction with the accuracy of claims payments; (5) CIGNA literature was not of a high standard; (6) the CIGNA representative did not clearly explain changes being made in client company plans. These findings were fed directly into the company's programme of change.

Investigations with intermediaries advising corporate clients found a lower level of satisfaction (probably reflecting CIGNA's direct selling to clients in parallel to sales effort by the intermediaries). However, again the studies identified specific service elements that would lead to a significant improvement in overall satisfaction, which involved improving communications with intermediaries, particularly regarding claims, quotes and renewals. This too was fed into the re-engineering of customer service.

Market studies of companies not buying from CIGNA involved using a research agency to evaluate purchasing criteria and competitive rankings. The findings suggested that these companies generally saw all private medical insurers as offering much the same product, and that the key issues affecting the ability of CIGNA to gain new business were: *inertia* – the difficulty of dislodging the established insurer; *low name awareness* – making companies reluctant to offer CIGNA cover to their employees, rather than that of a better known supplier; and *lack of price competitiveness* – CIGNA was seen as expensive.

The overwhelming need identified by the market research was for greater customer responsiveness and higher service standards, but the problem remained of creating the change in the company necessary to deliver this.

Barriers to change

Douglas Cowieson suggests that the greatest challenge faced was the need to change the *culture* of the company. He has described the problems he faced in driving a programme of service excellence through a culture wedded to traditional insurance company values. A traditional industry measure is 'denial rate', i.e. the proportion of claims turned down. To the traditional culture this is money saved; in a customer-led culture it is dissatisfied customers. Cowieson took his 'denial rate' to incredibly low levels by avoiding dubious claims coming through the door. In the traditional culture, delaying payments is good – because interest is earned on the balances waiting to be paid out. In a customer-led culture, slow payments create unhappy customers who complain – to CIGNA and to their employers. Cowieson took the industry average payment time of 14 days down to a norm of three days (and five days for difficult claims) on the grounds that it pleases his customers, and besides, it means he employs fewer staff to deal with phone calls from people saying: 'Why haven't you paid my money?', because he knows that after seven days the number of phone calls about a claim goes up 75 per cent. The change in culture was facilitated by the change in workforce in CIGNA's relocation and replacement by people from outside the industry, but this is far from being the whole story.

Another barrier to achieving the turnaround of the business was provided by the inherited hierarchical *organizational structure* and the *functional specializations* within it. Hierarchies are efficient, but not well-suited to managing fast change and being flexible and responsive to the outside world. The functional specialisms are efficient, but explain why customers are passed from department to department to deal with simple queries and problems. Executives observed that the scope for individual initiative and job satisfaction was minimal, and the management challenge had become confined to maintaining a command and control structure that placed little trust in the front line.

The programme of change

In 1994, Douglas Cowieson was quoted as saying: 'By the end we had reengineered the whole company, but people did not necessarily set out on a march like that. If we are completely honest, we decided to survive – which meant moving to a low-cost area, sorting out our business priorities, dropping certain lines of business and picking up new ones, and changing the way we worked so that we reduced the overhead.' CIGNA managers emphasize that change on the scale they have experienced is costly, and sometimes traumatic. Cowieson makes it clear that the driving force was company survival, not some ideal of perfection.

The company used the springboard provided by the market research studies and the new understanding of the customer as the basis for a business process re-engineering programme across the company. The results of that programme are dramatic, and underpin the turnaround of the business and the successful implementation of its market strategy. The underlying theme of change is summarized by Cowieson in the following terms: 'The organisation was to a certain extent designed by the customer. We said to them: 'How do you want it to look ... they don't actually tell you how it is going to look, they just tell

'The company used the springboard provided by the market research studies and the new understanding of the customer'

you the attributes they want within it. They wanted it to be flexible, understanding, and caring. ... You have to figure out what you are going to have to do to actually meet those needs.'

A flatter organization

From a traditional hierarchy, CIGNA has developed into a much 'flatter' organization. Four layers of middle management have been removed, and there are now only four organizational levels between the Managing Director and the most junior member of staff.

Multi-functional teams

CIGNA's operation is based on team-based working across all sections, including senior management, and including 'virtual teams' formed for a specific task and then disbanded. The team structure replaces the traditional functional specialization in the company. To provide the one point of contact with the company that customers want, CIGNA now assigns each corporate customer (and the employees covered by its health scheme) to a named individual with a direct phone line, who works in a customer service team of six or seven people. Members of that team have the information and authority to resolve most customer service issues. These members of staff now have responsibility for the client relationship, not just for processing pieces of paper. The teams set their own work targets and measure their performance against those targets. Executives have been amazed at the release of energy and empowerment in team-based working. Doug Jamieson says: 'The devolution of power and responsibility has now gone so far that the team members can, in effect, hire and fire. In extremis, they can get rid of their own team leader if he or she isn't making the grade.' The power of the teams also stretches to decisions on the division between team members of performance bonuses.

Communications with employees

Re-building the company around the concept of customer satisfaction has also involved recognizing employees as internal customers, whose satisfaction also matters to performance. Executives stress the importance of constant, consistent and honest communications with staff. One sign of listening to customers inside the company as well as outside, is an annual 'climate survey', in which an external agency surveys employees' opinions and publishes the results in the company. The company's executives respond carefully and systematically to employee views.

Customer focus

The CIGNA strategy has been of a move from a traditional insurance industry culture to one dominated by achieving customer service excellence. Intangible signs are many. More tangible confirmation symbolizing the change also exists. The company has established a Customer Advisory Board, to communicate directly to management and employees. Confidence in the strength and competence of the teams to deliver superior customer service is such that CIGNA offers a compensation scheme making cash payments to customers who receive service which falls short of the published standards – those standards cover such things as strict time limits for responding to enquiries and settling claims, and guaranteed regular customer contact and reporting.

New metrics
New metrics have been established for virtually all areas of the business, for example in quality, productivity, timeliness and credit control, which have meant abandoning many of the old ways of assessing performance. The emphasis has been intentionally changed from efficiency to effectiveness. This too has meant overturning some of the old culture.

Information technology
Underpinning the move towards improved service has been IT development. For example, a customer information system has been developed to automatically track all quotation and group profile data for any company with which CIGNA deals. The time taken to underwrite and produce a quotation has been cut from 15 days to two, and staff who used to process between 35 and 40 claims a day now get through 75 to 90 per day.

Business process re-engineering
The driving force for the change in the company has been the use of a highly participative and transparent BPR methodology.

The result of the programme of change is summarized by one company manager in the following terms:

> CIGNA UK is now a consistently profitable manager of employee benefits providing excellent service to select market segments through successful people.

Sources: 'Championing a Healthy Dose of Private Care', *The Scotsman*, 10 November 1994. 'CIGNA Services UK', *Management Today*, June 1994, pp. 94–5. 'CIGNA: Setting New Standards in Corporate Customer Service', Ailie Ferrari, *Managing Service Quality*, Vol. 5, No. 1, 1995, pp. 30–4. 'Culture Change: Making it Happen', Douglas Cowieson, Presentation at Unisys Seminar, Nice, February 1995. 'Reengineering from Top to Bottom', Ian Ferguson, *Banking and Financial Training*, March 1994, pp. 7–12. 'The Hard Road Back to Health', *European Quality*, Vol. 1, No. 5, pp.40–3.

Questions to consider

1 What does this case suggest are the key elements of changing a company's focus from products to customers?

2 What mechanisms did CIGNA exploit to understand the customer and to incorporate those lessons in how the business is run? Could those mechanisms be applied in other companies?

3 What were the prerequisites for successfully handing power to the multi-functional teams – and how common are these in other companies?

4 Is employing people who are not 'experts' (few CIGNA customer services staff have experience or qualifications in financial services) a strength or a weakness?

5 How can a company that has achieved customer focus sustain that focus in the longer term?

Case 3   Ford Cellular Systems*

Ford Cellular Systems (FCS) is an operation within Ford Motor Company's European Division, based in Swindon, Wiltshire, and employing around 130 people. The Chief Executive is Nigel Bunter, who returned to the UK from a job as a Business Planning Manager with Ford in the USA, with a track record of success in projects which were unconventional in Ford, a brief to start up the new mobile communications venture in the UK, and a supervisor located 5000 miles away in the USA.

From the start-up with five staff, it was clear that there was no Ford 'blueprint' for running this type of business and every process had to be designed from new. Also, Bunter was aware that as a global company Ford had a very limited appetite for high-risk ventures outside the conventional realm of automotive manufacture, and that the structure of the UK mobile communications market was unattractive to a conventional manufacturing company.

That structure had two cellular communications networks (Cellnet and Vodafone), which were allowed by the UK government to operate only through service providers, who sell airtime direct to customers or via dealers to customers. Within this structure, service providers earn commission on the airtime consumed by their customers, but customers are gained only by the offer of heavily-subsidized mobile phone equipment, the cost of which has to be absorbed by the service provider and recouped from the commissions paid by the network. This places the service provider at a high risk of loss if customers are not retained long enough to recoup the subsidy on the phones.

Four years into the new operation FCS had achieved a customer base of around 20 000, in an industry which recognizes a base of around 50 000 to be the minimum critical mass. Bunter's problem was to design a market strategy to grow his business to this critical mass, but to do this in a way which was attractive to Ford in avoiding the uncertainties and loss exposure inherent in the existing industry structure.

The 'Ford Call' strategy

The core of Bunter's strategy was to exploit the synergy with Ford Motor Company by offering the mobile communication networks access to the

---

* This case study has been prepared by Ian Irving, Ian Irving Ltd, Lynda Irvine, Price Waterhouse, and Nigel Piercy, Cardiff Business School, from in-company research. At the time of the events described in the case study, Ian Irving and Lynda Irvine were employed by Robson Rhodes Consulting to work with Ford Cellular Systems. The case study also benefited from the comments of Nigel Bunter, Managing Director, Cellular Operations Ltd.

large customer base represented by Ford's UK car sales, with FCS acting as the service provider between the network and the customer. This base is highly attractive, because it consists of around 500 000 people a year who have just acquired a Ford vehicle and shown themselves to be attractive targets for mobile communications providers.

The customer offering developed for Ford car buyers is extremely attractive:

- free mobile phone equipment;
- free connection to the network;
- one-month contracts (instead of the 12- or 18-month contract required by other service providers);
- a pre-programmed link to the RAC;
- a pre-programmed link to the 'Ford Call Connection' to access fax service and other information services.

The upgrading of the product offer is developing, for example in offering security, navigation and other services linked to the cellular phone. The implementation of this strategy quickly developed FCS's customer base from some 20 000 to around 75 000 customers.

The market conditions were not easy. It is important to recognize the volatility of the mobile phone market, which has grown at phenomenal rates during the 1990s. Ford began operation late in 1993, and the subscriber base grew from 0 to over 50 000 in 18 months, with around 40 per cent of connections in the months of August and September, coinciding with new car registrations. Over 95 per cent of this base were connected to a low user tariff and were seen as consumer rather than business users. The consumer users in this market are characterized as promiscuous, treating mobile phones like a 'Christmas puppy' – getting rid of the handset when they realized the true cost of ownership, or switching service providers to get a better deal.

'The consumer users in this market are characterized as promiscuous, treating mobile phones like a "Christmas puppy"'

The implementation problem

Bunter's problems in driving this strategy in a difficult market fell into two main areas. The first was the cost of operations in his new organization and the need to redesign the business to cope with a totally new scale of operations. His staffing had grown to 130 from 40, and he knew this escalation could not continue. He had to find ways of servicing the new customer base to a high quality level by improved efficiency, not by acquiring yet more human and physical resources.

The second problem was that his market strategy depended critically on delivering high customer service quality which had to be demonstrably superior to the competition, and differentiating his market offering by the type and level of service provided. The harsh reality of the market is that any Ford car buyer can deal with another service provider if s/he wishes at the time of car purchase or later. Indeed, there was no room for failure here, as Bunter points out, when Ford Motor Company spends £6 million on TV advertising for a new service, the company does not expect or accept anything less than the best, and failure is not an option!

The difficulty he faced was that, using the metrics in place at the time, the company's service levels to customers had, in fact, dropped to unacceptable levels, and the success of his market strategy was at risk.

The company also faced the problem of gaining high service levels and a strong market position quickly. The basic strategy is easily imitated – British Airways and American Express have both entered the cellular market with special offers for their existing customer bases.

It was at this time, with the support of his management team, that Bunter looked to business process re-engineering as a way forward, in achieving both the efficiency levels he needed and the customer service excellence on which his strategy relied. Nine months into the Ford Call strategy, Bunter's reasoning was straightforward: performance improvement was urgent; the management team in the company was fully committed to running the day-to-day operation; and he needed outside involvement to benchmark his standards, not just against mobile communications but against the best service providers in any industry.

The Business Process Re-engineering experience

The market has an ever increasing number of low-revenue/low-margin customers, notorious for their propensity to switch service providers, so core requirements are low subscriber maintenance cost and excellent customer service (to retain customers). This pressure on profit margins, and the need to recoup the subsidies offered in supplying equipment to customers, made a lean and highly efficient customer services operation essential – while maintaining and improving service standards.

Benchmarking carried out for FCS established that the company simply was not cost- or service-competitive in the key business processes:

- the connection process;
- the billing process;
- the collection process; and
- the customer service process.

The first three of these processes are required for every single subscriber, while the fourth is largely dependent on the successful completion of the first three. These processes describe the fundamental activities in the business – their efficiency and effectiveness directly determines the cost of customer maintenance, profitability and customer service standards.

What the consultants found was that FCS was organized on a traditional functional basis. These functions were: order entry; billing and receivables; customer services; warehousing and distribution; and finance. Responsibility for the core processes of the business were divided among these functions and outside collaborators: the *connection* process – divided between Ford Motor Car distributors, an external marketing company, and the order entry, finance and warehousing functions; the *billing* process – relied on the order entry, finance, billing and receivables, and customer services functions; the *collection* process – the shared responsibility of the billing and receivables, finance, and customer services functions; the *customer service* process – the sole responsibility of the customer services department.

The team also found that the different functions in the business experienced their peak activities at very different times. For example, the order entry department had to input all orders by 2.00 pm each day, so that warehousing and distribution could pick and despatch all orders by around 6.00 pm. On the other hand, the customer services department had its peak level of activity between two and four days after the despatch of customer bills (which generated a huge surge of account queries) – driven by billing and receivables sending all bills out on the same day each month (because of IT problems).

The BPR team formed two broad objectives in collaboration with Nigel Bunter:

- to design, develop and implement more robust and flexible core processes at the lowest possible cost; and
- to achieve a 'best in class' customer service organization which could offer value-added services to the consumer market at the lowest cost.

Their reasoning was that the FCS market strategy was to retain and acquire customers by offering an increasing range of value-adding features – fax facility, hotel advice, travel advice, emergency breakdown service, etc. None of these could be launched to generate revenue until the core processes were effective.

The BPR project concentrated on removing the imbalances, and unnecessary control and checks, which drove staffing costs up and the quality and speed of the core processes down. Central to the changes was the billing system – which drove the customer service process and created the unmanageable peaks of customer queries each month. In fact, this required work with an external software developer to solve the billing system limitations and spread billing across the month.

However, even more central was the change in attitudes and behaviour needed to move from traditional functional responsibilities and jurisdictions to a customer-focused culture.

'the change in attitudes and behaviour needed to move from traditional functional responsibilities and jurisdictions to a customer-focused culture'

The human side of Business Process Re-engineering

BPR is about developing high quality processes to run the business more effectively, but this is only one element in the type of organization change needed at FCS. What was also required was a radical overhaul of the management and development of people in the new organizational framework. Real leverage on competitive advantage depended on achieving that shift.

The traditional functional orientation of FCS was mirrored in its approach to serving customers – customers had to fit in with internal departmental ways of doing things. The BPR team focused on building a 'Customer In' philosophy based on satisfying customer needs, rather than serving the organization's internal processes and structures. This philosophy relied on moving towards working with multi-disciplinary teams, built from staff who were fully conversant with the total 'customer handling process', not just one functional 'job' within that process.

The initial findings of the BPR team on entering the FCS organization were as follows:

- FCS was run with traditional functional processes, with little cross-functional communication;
- There was no truly integrated business strategy to guide internal decision making and resource allocation;
- There was considerable management 'in-fighting', and only 'lip-service' to group decisions;
- Managers had little understanding of the total business;
- There was little staff training, and recruitment processes lacked metrics;
- There was an 'anti-structure' culture, with isolated management decision making in the functional departments causing major problems downstream in the customer handling process;
- However, FCS had many positive and committed employees with room to grow.

Critical to the success of the project was that Nigel Bunter, the Managing Director, was willing to accept the existence of these problems in his organization, and his positive attitude towards the change project. Together with an organization development specialist, Bunter created a series of management principles to guide the future:

- A statement of vision and values would underpin the transition process.
- Once fully trained and competent in their roles resulting from a massive investment in training and staff development, staff would be 'freed' to make decisions within agreed boundaries.
- A business plan would be developed with key managerial performance metrics, to allow objective team decision making.

- There would be investment in developing a series of 'universal skills', to enable the creation of a sales and marketing-led culture focused on satisfying the customer. These skills were defined by employee focus groups, to gain their 'buy-in' and to overcome scepticism early in the project. These skills included task orientation (customer handling, telephone technique, computer literacy, selling skills and financial awareness), but also maintaining a problem-solving team-based process.

The transformation programme began by informing all staff of the new goals and strategy and encouraging direct questioning of Bunter and the management team, and included the involvement of staff in all aspects of the change – including design of training events and participation in team-building events to build the change to 'customer-facing' processes driven by multi-functional teams.

The results?

The bottom-line result is that FCS has gone from supporting 56 000 subscribers with 121 staff to serving 72 000 subscribers with 99 staff – while at the same time increasing measurable service standards and losing staff only through attrition, not redundancy. The fact that the organization has become more able to meet the needs of both customers and employees is underlined by the winning of the 1996 Cellnet award for customer service excellence.

At another level, the results of the programme of change are clearly visible. On the stairway behind the company's reception area is a hand-written sign with up-to-date sales information seen by all employees – previously no-one had ever known how sales were going. The Customer Service Office hums with concentrated effort – concentration assisted by electronic signs visible throughout the office, up-dated every 30 seconds and detailing the following information:

WAI = the number of customer calls waiting

ACD = the number of customer calls in progress

NRD = the number of operatives between calls or doing other work

NOW = the number of operatives waiting for a call

AVE = the average time to answer calls in the last 10 minutes

SVL = the service level – in the last 10 minutes, the per cent of calls answered within 10 seconds

On the wall of the Customer Service Department are the written objectives to achieve the goal of 'Best in Class Customer Service Operation':

Key objective	Measurables
1. Continuous improvement in customer service level	Quarterly customer satisfaction survey
2. Provide best in class response time	Answer incoming calls within 10 seconds Process all orders within 24 hours All account maintenance completed by cut-off Benchmark to continuously review targets
3. Best in class resolution at first contact	Incoming calls Incoming correspondence Benchmark to continuously review targets
4. Achieve 100 per cent core competence in base skills of multi-skilled teams. Broaden skills to include sales, churn busting, credit collection	Develop varied core competence tests Quarterly appraisals Continuous training and development Call grading (by supervisor monitoring)
5. Reduce churn	Complete checklist for every cancellation request

This is taken very seriously, not least because all the employees of the company (not just those in Customer Service) are paid a bonus depending on continuous customer satisfaction and service improvement.

More generally, it is recognized that managers have become more able to make business-aware decisions about resource use, while employees are better trained and understand the process of change for continuous improvement.

What did it take to get these results?

Bunter's view is that the BPR approach was the *only* way forward to drive his market strategy effectively, and the results justify an investment he estimates as £¼ million. However, he does believe that the changes worked better in some areas than others, and that adaptations had to be made to make the new process-driven organization effective.

Along with Marc Tielemans, the Project Manager for the BPR programme, Bunter enumerates the lessons that were learned in the following terms.

The change programme was initiated with the support of the company's management group, and Bunter made an explicit statement that there would be no redundancies as a result of the BPR programme. Nonetheless, the programme was characterized throughout by management resistance, in-fighting and conflict. Tielemans describes how operatives saw new ways of working as interesting and challenging, and were willing to give the new methods a try, but were often undermined by negative and hostile management attitudes and behaviour.

BPR rests in large part on multi-skilling and the use of process-based teams. For example, one innovation in customer handling was the 'one-stop shop' for the customer, i.e. a single point of contact for each of the 1000 customer calls a day, instead of separate contacts with the front desk, order processing, customer accounts, and so on. The strength of resistance from the traditional functions and managers is causing the company to pull back from this ideal, to settle for something less radical and more workable.

While BPR suggests the empowerment of teams so that they are self-directed and self-managed, FCS's experience was that many of its operatives were uncomfortable and unsure in this type of team and found it difficult to cope with self-discipline and rotational leadership, and personality clashes were common. The company has reverted to the role of a supervisor as permanent team leader, on the grounds of effectiveness and clarity. Indeed, the weaker multi-skills teams have reverted by consent to a functional division of tasks, in spite of the obvious disadvantages.

Managers chose the pilot teams without using psychometric diagnostic tools, which produced a highly volatile, enthusiastic and headstrong group. The company has also learned that recruitment to teams is critical, and has adopted psychometric testing for this key selection process. This has had the effect of greatly increasing the 'quality and fit' of new employees to the teams.

Bunter also notes the problem of ownership. With a group working on initial strategic changes across the whole company, he says he reached a point where it felt as though the change agents were managing the whole business. He suggests that a substantial problem in such radical change is getting the managers and employees to regain ownership of their business, and he worries that this has not yet been fully achieved.

> *'it felt as though the change agents were managing the whole business'*

Although the consultants have departed, the change process continues, based on a new 'can do' attitude and an enhanced company-wide understanding of the core processes that matter in going to market.

A footnote

1997 marked major changes for FCS. On 27 March 1997, a new company, Cellular Operations Ltd, acquired Ford's European cellular business. The new company is a management buy-out by Nigel Bunter, with a partner and with an outside investment by a single investor. The company retains its links with Ford and Jaguar in the form of a long-term contract to supply cellular services to Ford and Jaguar cars. A Ford Motor Company strategy of divesting non-core business has given Bunter the chance to go further down the entrepreneurial path, and the opportunity to use his company's expertise in the automotive area with new clients.

Questions to consider

1 What does the FCS experience tell us about the real sources of competitive advantage in the process of going to market?

2 FCS is facing a volatile, fast-moving, low margin, low customer loyalty market. What are the demands that this places on a company?

3 What are the most important barriers to moving from a functional department to a customer-facing culture in a company? What lessons from the FCS experience can be applied to other companies?

4 What are the most critical aspects of the implementation strategy that led to greater efficiency, and what led to enhanced customer service standards?

5 What agenda should the Managing Director be addressing now to sustain the high customer service standards and continue to improve performance?

6 Now that the company is separate from Ford Motor Company and is privately owned, how should its market strategy develop?

PART II

What Going to Market is About: Defining the Strategic Pathway

CHAPTER 4

Market strategy:

The market – Definition, segmentation and choices

Introduction

The goal in Part II is to sort out the 'what' of the process of going to market, by trying to simplify the somewhat rambling, disjointed and extensive literature of marketing and strategy to a few basic issues, so that at least we are all talking about the same thing, before we talk about how to do it.

The way we plan to achieve this goal is as follows. In this chapter we will distinguish market strategy from marketing programmes. Our simplification mechanism for market strategy, to move from the theory to the reality, is the *Strategic Pathway* that reduces the strategy issue to key questions about *market choices*, the *value proposition* that we make to customers, and the *key relationships* that drive the strategy. This chapter will focus on market issues, and the next two chapters on the value proposition and key relationships in turn. Chapter 7 then provides us with a framework to turn from strategies to plans – to structure, test and communicate our market strategy in the company.

'the **Strategic Pathway** *that* ***reduces the strategy issue to key questions about*** **market choices,** *the* **value proposition** *that we make to* **customers,** *and the* **key relationships** *that drive the* **strategy'**

Making sense of market strategy and marketing programmes

The focus we are taking here is in the process of going to market for the reasons given in Chapter 1. However, in the real world companies do not just go to market, they 'do marketing' as well. If we are going to talk about a process of going to market which contains market strategies and marketing programmes, then we need to sort out what these things mean. This is easier said than done. As we saw in Chapter 1, one of the problems arising from the growing sophistication and diversity of marketing methods and technologies, is that it is actually quite difficult to pin down exactly what marketing involves, and what it means to different people. This confusion is assisted by the conflicting views presented by the textbooks, articles in management magazines, the technical literature, the marketing 'gurus' of the moment, trainers, consultants, business advisers, and so on. This is a bit of a problem – if we cannot pin down exactly what we are supposed to be managing, how can we manage it?

The bottom line in all this is that we are being told on every side that: marketing is the greatest thing since sliced bread (indeed was almost entirely responsible *for* sliced bread); is something of which we should all have a lot more; is what our international competitors beat us on; is an area where we have to train and become more effective; and so it goes on. Unfortunately no-one seems to be able to tell us exactly what it *is*. Well, we may not be able to say exactly what it is, but at least we can organize better our ideas about what it can be!

Sorting out the theories

A simple structure to achieve this 'sorting out' with executives is shown in Figure 4.1, and can be explained as follows.

Much writing and consultancy is mainly concerned with issues of *Market Strategy*, where the theme addressed is the positioning and overall direction of a business in each of its various marketplaces. This is a broad area and it is probably the most difficult, but the most important, for executives to get to grips with. For practical purposes, our view of market strategy is structured around: *market choices* (market definition, segmentation and setting priorities on the basis of market attractiveness and position), the *value proposition* (our positioning in the market drawing on our market mission, competitive differentiation and use of key marketing assets like brands); and the *key relationships*

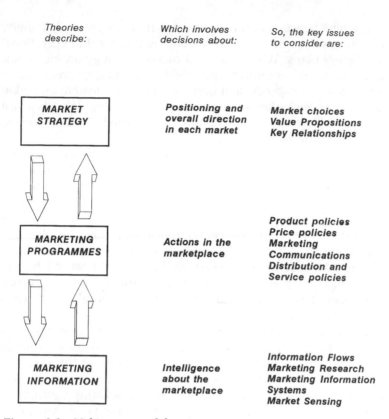

Theories describe:	Which involves decisions about:	So, the key issues to consider are:
MARKET STRATEGY	Positioning and overall direction in each market	Market choices Value Propositions Key Relationships
MARKETING PROGRAMMES	Actions in the marketplace	Product policies Price policies Marketing Communications Distribution and Service policies
MARKETING INFORMATION	Intelligence about the marketplace	Information Flows Marketing Research Marketing Information Systems Market Sensing

Figure 4.1 Making sense of theories

that drive the strategy (with our customers, our employees, our partners or collaborators and our competitors). It is these issues which define a company's Strategic Pathway. These are the most fundamental questions, and the ones where typically concrete structures for planning and decision are least apparent. This is not about producing a plan. The goal is to produce a strategy. Then we can plan. Bear in mind, that the fact that these issues are difficult to work with in practice does not mean that they do not matter – quite the reverse is the case, and this is almost inevitably where we have to start to develop any real movement towards market-led strategic change.

Figure 4.1 suggests that our market strategies are directly connected to *Marketing Programmes*, concerned with planning and implementing specific actions in the marketplace. Although it has some limitations, and trendy marketing academics will hate me for this, we can open up the issues here by using the traditional model of the marketing mix or programme, consisting of the following elements: product policies; pricing policies; marketing communications; and distribution and service policies.

The main attraction of this structure is that it is generally familiar to executives as the basis for developing and writing operational marketing plans. Where issues of market strategy are nebulous, qualitative and emphasize intangibles, marketing programmes are much more specific and down-to-earth and lead to an action plan – or at least, they should. It is in this area that there is a vast technical literature of techniques and methods to handle each element of the marketing mix.

Finally, *Marketing Information* is concerned with gaining intelligence about the marketplace and impacting both on the market strategies we choose and the marketing programmes we implement. The role of marketing information is in both analysis and planning, but also in evaluation and control. The principal issues to consider are: marketing information flows for planning and control; marketing research; and marketing information systems. Most of what we know, and certainly most of what we train into our marketing executives, in this area is concerned with techniques – of data collection, data analysis, systems design, and so on.

However, the interesting point about marketing information is that most of this totally ignores the *real* function of information in organizations – which is to construct the model of the world we all have to assume to be true (in order to do our jobs), even though we know it is *not* true. This view of marketing information – 'market sensing', or how executives understand and react to the marketplace – is important enough to gaining the leverage we need to change the way things are done that it provides the content of a separate chapter (Chapter 9) with its own worksheets.

That is the broad scope of what we have to manage in the process of going to market. Now we can go into more detail. This chapter focuses on market strategy and particularly market issues, and then Chapters 5 and 6 examine value propositions and key relationships in building strategy, and Chapter 7 highlights the problem of trying to put it all together in a plan.

Market strategy

Market strategy may sound esoteric and academic and daunting. Let us remember what we established earlier:

- it is all about doing best what *matters most* to the customer;
- it is all about getting what *we* want through long-term *customer* satisfaction; and

- it is about finding new and better ways of looking at important things (the customers) to get some leverage for changing the way things are done (in the company).

All the complex strategic issues are really just ways to help in doing exactly this (and if they are not, then maybe we should not bother with them). It is as simple as that. This may be worth remembering.

But, what is strategy?

To paraphrase two major milestone publications about strategy in the 1990s by Michael Porter[1] and Gary Hamel and C. K. Prahalad[2], strategy is about *breaking free*. It is about breaking free in the following senses:

- Breaking free from an obsession with *management tools* that are spectacular and seductive in improving operational efficiency but are not strategy – such as total quality management, benchmarking, time-based competition, outsourcing, re-engineering, lean supply chain management, efficient consumer response, and so on – on the grounds that while operational effectiveness and strategy are both essential to superior performance, operational effectiveness does not substitute for strategic direction.
- Breaking free of *industry dogma* – John Kay has pointed out that an *industry* is a group of organizations with similar capabilities and supply technologies, while a *market* is defined by customer needs and demands[3]. Customers do not care about industries, just about meeting their needs, as shown by the entry of supermarkets into banking and financial services (not their industry, but definitely their market).
- Breaking free from the *industry 'rules'* – Gary Hamel says there are three kinds of companies in all industries: *rule makers*, who built the industry; *rule takers*, who follow and imitate; and *rule breakers*, like IKEA, the Body Shop and Virgin, who implement revolution in the industry and re-invent the business[4], and he challenges us to recognize the 'nine routes to industry revolution', summarized in Table 4.1. This list is a good way to figure out if we ever even take market strategy seriously in our company.
- Breaking free of *the present* to create the future, and particularly from trying to preserve the past – Hamel and Prahalad estimate that senior managers spend only 1–3 per cent of their time looking at the future (see Table 4.2 to test that out – and

be prepared for a shock, because few companies stand up well against these criteria).

● Breaking free from *tactics* – 'Strategy is revolution; everything else is tactics' [4] – Gary Hamel also challenges us to consider ten key principles in becoming an industry revolutionary, which are summarized in Table 4.3 – again, these points are an excellent way to get started on a fundamental strategy debate in your company instead of just planning and budgeting for the same things every year.

' "Strategy is revolution; everything else is tactics" '

● Breaking free from '*sameness*' – Michael Porter argues that a company can only outperform its competitors if it establishes a difference that it can preserve, that delivers greater value to customers or creates comparable value or a lower cost (or both). Consider the impact of Virgin Direct on the financial services industry, attacking with a better value product sold direct. Or look at the impact of Daewoo Cars on the UK car market by a strategy of value and a differentiated channel of distribution – and in both cases, remember to ask what differentiated conventional insurance companies and car companies from each other (and the answer will be 'not a lot').

Table 4.1 Ten Principles for Building Revolutionary Strategy*

● *Principle 1: Strategic planning is not strategic* – distinguish planning from strategizing, the first produces ritualistic plans, the second produces strategy.
● *Principle 2: Strategy making must be subversive* – relax the fundamental beliefs shared by people in your industry, and see what new business opportunities appear.
● *Principle 3: The bottleneck is at the top of the bottle* – senior management is often the repository of orthodoxy, not the source of radical innovation.
● *Principle 4: Revolutionaries exist in every company* – in middle management, at the operating level, muffled by the bureaucracy, but liable to leave and become competitors if they are denied a voice.
● *Principle 5: Change is not the problem, commitment is* – strategy-making process should give people the responsibility for creating change, not impose it on them.
● *Principle 6: Strategy making must be democratic* – supplementing the hierarchy of experience with imagination and innovation.
● *Principle 7: Anyone can be a strategy activist* – front-line managers and employees should be activists, not victims in the strategy process.
● *Principle 8: Perspective is worth 50 IQ points* – innovation in strategy requires a change in perspective.
● *Principle 9: Top-down and bottom-up are not the alternatives* – the strategy process should be deep and wide in the organization.
● *Principle 10: You can't see the end from the beginning* – the strategy cannot be set at the outset, or why would we go on a quest for it?

---

*Source: Adapted from Hamel, Gary (1996), 'Strategy as Revolution', *Harvard Business Review*, July/August, 69–82

Table 4.2 Strategies for the future*

How well does management in this company perform in the following areas:

	Conventional and reactive				Distinctive and far-sighted
Senior management's view of the future compared to that of our competitors?	1	2	3	4	5
	Re-engineering core processes				Regenerating core strategies
What absorbs more senior management time?	1	2	3	4	5
	Mostly as a rule follower				Mostly as a rule maker
How do competitors view our company?	1	2	3	4	5
	Operational efficiency				Innovation and growth
What is our greatest strength?	1	2	3	4	5
	Mostly catching up				Mostly getting out in front
What is the focus of our company's attempts to build competitive advantage?	1	2	3	4	5
	Our competitors				Our foresight
What has mainly set our company's agenda for change?	1	2	3	4	5
	Mostly as an engineer				Mostly as an architect
Do we spend most of our time monitoring the status quo (the maintenance engineer) or designing the future (the strategic architect)?	1	2	3	4	5

*Source: Adapted from Hamel, Gary and C.K. Praharad (1994), 'Competing for the Future', *Harvard Business Review,* July/August, 122–8

Table 4.3 Nine routes to reinventing an industry*

Route	Methods	Examples
Reconceiving the product or service	1. Radically improve the value equation	Hewlett-Packard and Canon in computer printers
	2. Separate function and form	The credit card that opens the hotel door and acts as an international passport
	3. Achieving joy in use	Making shopping fun
Redefining market space	4. Pushing the bounds of universality	Transforming the expensive camera into a cheap disposable product for any consumer (even children)
	5. Striving for individuality	Levi's 'Personal Pair' system to make jeans to the individual consumer's measurements
	6. Increasing accessibility	Twenty-four-hour banking with First Direct
Redrawing industry boundaries	7. Rescaling industries	Increasing scales in a fragmented industry, e.g. funerals. Decreasing scales for specialized advantage, i.e. local microbreweries or bakeries
	8. Compressing the supply chain	Xerox plans to transmit information electronically to cut out freighters and suppliers of documents
	9. Driving convergence	A credit card for a car supplier. A bank account at the supermarket

*Source: Adapted from Hamel, Gary (1996), 'Strategy as Revolution', *Harvard Business Review*, July/August, 69–82

● Breaking free from hostility to *change* – change is seen as unpleasant and is resisted mainly when it is something nasty imposed on us from above (and when it is a synonym for cost-cutting and downsizing), not when it is about growth, new ways of doing things and new activities that we choose for ourselves.

But these examples show that strategy is about more than breaking free of these constraints and burdens – it is about defining what we are going to be in the marketplace, or what Hamel and Prahalad [5] have called building a 'strategic intent': a stable but stretching perspective of how to win based on our core competences as an organization [6].

These ideas about core competences and re-inventing the business, differentiation against the competition and the routes to market leadership will come into play in the next chapter, when we look at developing a value proposition.

But does strategy make any difference?

Some corporate leaders will tell you they do not do things with a strategy in mind. Richard Branson of Virgin says they usually make up the strategy after they have decided what to do. (This somewhat neglects the careful development of a classic brand extension strategy and detailed market evaluation by teams of analysts at Virgin headquarters, but who are we to disagree with Richard Branson?)

The simple fact is that you can *tell* if a company has a strategy – it knows where it is going and develops the capabilities needed to get there. This is something that stands behind planning and systems and structure – it is more fundamental.

This is why some companies prosper in hostile environments. In the USA, Southwest Airlines made profits throughout the period when American Airlines, Delta and United Airlines all recorded huge losses – because Southwest had a low-cost, city pair strategy and a loyal customer base; Singapore Airlines has shown impressive performance among global airlines, while many international carriers have made losses. Innovative strategies can produce successful performance in unattractive markets [7].

The link is that these companies have each mapped a pathway to organizational competitive strength.

But why change?

Change comes from strategy because only an unassailable market leader has an interest in maintaining the status quo, and there are no unassailable market leaders. Microsoft is probably in one of the strongest market leadership positions in any industry, and that company is far too smart to see itself as unassailable. They used to say IBM was unbeatable. . . .

Pause for thought

Stop here for a moment. Read through the previous section about strategy. If these are not the most exciting and challenging issues for you – then this part of the book is not for you. If there are no new ideas here that can do incredibly valuable things in your company, then either (a) your name is Bill Gates, Richard Branson, or Anita Roddick, and you should not be reading this book, or (b) you are wrong – so have another look.

But the question now is – how do we start using these ideas, and this is the role of the *Strategic Pathway*.

Finding the Strategic Pathway

The Strategic Pathway is about getting from the challenges and open-endedness of the strategy issues mentioned above to something more specific. It provides us with structure and tools to address in a practical way the issues that matter. The Strategic Pathway is a simple model of the market strategy process as shown in Figure 4.2.

The logic is that market strategy issues can be grouped into three highly interrelated categories: market choices, our value proposition, and the key relationships underpinning the strategy.

Market choices are about how we define our markets in terms of customer groups and products and services, and how we develop market segments to target that are compatible with our capabilities. This is about making choices based on how attractive different markets or segments are, but also how well we can perform in those markets.

Linked to this, how well we perform and our choice of market targets should be informed by how we build a *value proposition*: what role do we want to play in the market (our market mission); how will we establish competitive advantage in the customer's eyes through differentiation and positioning; what intangible market-

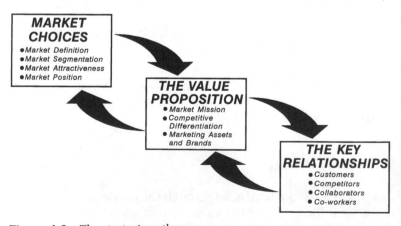

Figure 4.2   The strategic pathway

ing assets and brands can we use to achieve this; what is our promise to the customer that represents value to the customer?

This links in turn to the *key relationships* in the strategy: with the customer, with collaborators and distributors, with existing and new competitors, and with our own employees and co-workers who have to deliver the real quality and service to our customers. In turn again, this leads back to the issue of which market targets we should choose.

This model is far from perfect. It does, however, provide a practical tool for defining strategic direction and positioning and acts as a framework within which we can plan market strategy.

We will open up each part of this model in turn.

Market choices

Figure 4.3 suggests that a way of starting the quest for an effective market strategy is with the key choices we make about markets:

- *Market definition* – how we select a piece of the marketplace and identify it as our market;
- *Market segmentation* – how we identify groups within the market as targets for our products and services;

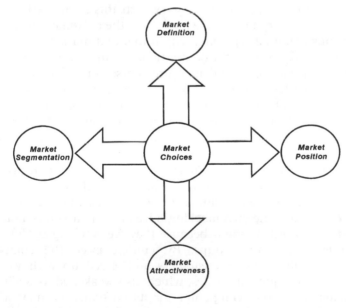

Figure 4.3   The key market choices in market strategy

- *Market attractiveness and market position* – what we decide makes a market or segment attractive to us and a position we take good or bad, and the choices we make about where to concentrate and establish our marketing priorities.

Each of these areas moves from generalization to a specific analysis.

Market definition

Incredible though it may seem, there are valuable insights to be gained in most organizations by looking at, and frequently reviewing, the practical *definition* of our markets, in terms of specific products and services and specific customer types. And yet very few people do this on a regular basis. This is silly. We know that markets change – so surely how we define the markets that matter to us should be constantly under review and revision?

To start with, there are obviously some basic parameters which should be defined so that we know where we are competing and planning, and so on: the geography of the market; the industrial sectors included; the type of consumer in demographic terms; the product/service applications or customer needs; the range of products/services which go into the market to meet these needs; and the broad types of customer within this need market. This can lead to a very productive analysis of the customer differences and thus potential segments within the total market.

But this is not about a conventional statistical analysis using traditional categories and measurements. Conventional market definitions reflect *industries*. We have already seen that industries are groups of companies linked by technology or product similarities. What we are interested in is *markets*. Markets are based on customer needs and demands. This is where market strategy must focus.

The results of re-thinking market definitions may be surprising. For example, one well-known whiskey brand cut its price in response to a similar move by an own-label version. In

'The results of re-thinking market definitions may be surprising.'

fact, the own-label initiative had had no impact on the whiskey brand because they were selling to different customer groups. By cutting price the company alienated its customers and ended up with weaker margins and sales, which also weakened its ability to respond to its real competitor for its customers – new white spirits. The truth is, customers just do not fit traditional industry definitions of markets – you think you make crisps, the retailer thinks that the category is salty snacks, but the customer-defined market is lunch [8].

To open up this issue for a company, one practical approach, which is deceptively simple, but which has proved to have great leverage in helping to get executives to look at the market in a new way, is described below – the Product–Customer Matrix (Figure 4.4). This matrix is simple – all it asks us to do is to identify the five or six different types of product or service going into the market we have chosen, and the four or five different types of customer, which defines the total market. But there are some important angles here.

Let us consider *products* first. The initial reaction of most companies is that this task is *completely* impossible, unless we are prepared to give them a 20-foot wall for the matrix, because they have 500 products, or 5000, not 5 or 6. This is the first catch – we are only interested in products as they are seen to be different by the *customer*, i.e. they meet different *needs* as they are felt by the customer.

For instance, in attempting this exercise with managers from one of the retail banks, when the executives had finally finished falling off their seats laughing at the impossibility of the task, and the naivety of consultants, they produced a computer printout listing their retail bank products which was fully five inches thick, because they had some 600 or more different products. The task was self-evidently impossible.

In fact, if you think not about production or technology or our bank's back office operations, but what matters in the *front* office to the customer, there are only *six* customer benefits in the retail bank market and thus only six types of product. Quite simply, as a retail bank customer I want:

- to lay my hands on ready money when I need it;
- to have my savings held safely;
- to buy things before I have the money to pay for them;
- to pay bills via cheques and debits;
- to get income from my savings; and
- to acquire some services such as insurance, investment advice, and so on.

I do not really care how many different ways the bank has of giving me an overdraft, I just want to buy a car before I can really afford it! There are only *six* retail bank products, so that side of the matrix is done – impossible it is not!

Now we can talk about *customers*. This too is normally seen as impossible (we either have too many customers or not enough to

Market:						
Products Customers	1	2	3	4	5	Total
1						
2						
3						
4						
5						
6						
Total						

Figure 4.4 Poduct–Customer matrix

Instructions for Completing the Product–Customer Matrix

1. Enter the name of the market to be analysed — indicating what the customer base is, the geography of the market, and the basic customer need to be met

    e.g. The UK Market for Financial Services in Medium and Large Corporate Customers

    The European Market for Personal Computers.

2. List separately all the products going into this marketplace. Group these into five or six categories, and list these across the top of the matrix. We are only interested in what products do for the customer — not how they are produced or by who.

3. List separately all the types of customer in this marketplace. Group these into five or six categories and list these down the side of the matrix. We want to group customers by the most significant differences between them (e.g. the primary benefits they seek, their most important product needs and priorities, how they buy products, etc.).

4. We have now defined the product-customer cells which make up the total marketplace. This can be used for building up a picture of market size and growth, our areas of current strength versus the competition and vice versa, the growing and declining areas within this total market, our 'competed market' within the total market, and taking a new view on the underlying segments in the market (i.e. the single product-customer cells or the groups of cells which make up potential niches or segments as our targets).

5. It is unlikely we will get this right first time. It is worth taking a first-cut, and then revising the product and customer definitions to see what effect such changes make on the picture we can build.

---

make up five or six groups or types), or this is something which is so obvious we already know about it.

For example, in another case, working this time with a corporate bank (i.e. one dealing only with companies, not retail customers), on being asked to do this the bank executives were exultant; they said they had done this *before*. We pointed out that the object of this analysis is to group customers together according to their most important needs, their priorities, significant differences in their behaviour, and so on, so that we can use them as distinct market targets. They said, 'yes, yes, we've done it before'. We were astounded but pleased. We asked them to complete the matrix. The sum result of hundreds of years of combined banking experience, university-level education and professional qualifications was the following definitive list of customer types in the corporate banking market: *small* companies; *medium-sized* companies; and *large* companies. (This incisive and deeply analytical model, incidentally, represents how most bankers traditionally view this market.)

This was not very helpful. But we persevered – or tried to. If you then use the matrix to ask a couple of basic questions, the insight into customer needs, generated by the customer base divided in the conventional way by company size, is almost zero:

We asked . . .	*They said . . .*
Which customers take which products?	They all take everything (or at least some in each category do).
Which are the most important products for each type of customer (i.e. the ones you have to get right to be a player in this market)?	Impossible to say – different products are the most important to some companies in each size category
What are the critical success factors for each type of customer?	Impossible to say – it depends which customers you mean in each category.

In fact, this group of executives persevered manfully with the matrix and, after much hard work, heart-searching and substantial cost in human suffering (theirs and ours), classified corporate customers according to the *strategy* the customer is pursuing – because that predicts the customer's need for financial services, and the critical products and success factors. For example, 'market share strategy' companies need good liquidity products, but companies pursuing a 'profit-reconstruction strategy' are likely to value most highly financial efficiency products, and so on. This provided them with a novel and creative way of choosing customer targets and specializing the total 'offering' around the customer's needs.

Incidentally, if you try to use the Product–Customer Matrix and it really *is* impossible to group products and customers in the way described above, then you have probably not defined a market at all – i.e. a group of customers sharing a set of common problems buying products to solve those problems. The way round this is to split the 'market' up and then try the matrix for each part. You are likely to find that you are really talking about a number of markets, not just one. Perhaps the greatest value of this approach is that it is capable of generating new ways of segmenting the market, which we will consider in more detail in the next section.

Once the matrix is constructed, however, it can be used for a number of significant purposes:

- to look at market size and trend, product by product and customer by customer;
- to look at the market and product life cycle stage, product by product and customer by customer;
- to look at our present strategic position, product by product and customer by customer (see pp. 194–98 below), to evaluate whether our real strength is in products or relationships with particular customers, and thus the best way to grow the business;
- to find out where we make most of our profit in the market, i.e. from different products and services going to different customers;
- to identify where we are achieving the highest levels of customer satisfaction and loyalty;
- to isolate those parts of the market where we have the greatest competitive advantage over our competitors;
- to identify the parts of the market in which we are actually doing business (the 'competed market');
- to look at our real market share in the competed market.

On the last two points, for example, we were told by one medium-sized manufacturer of varnish products that they were part of a market worth about £1000 million a year, and since they only had 0.05 per cent of the market they saw no need to worry about market strategy. Actually they had the figures wrong anyway, but this is not the point of the story. Completing the product–market matrix showed that the supposed £1000 million was *all* paints and surface coverings for industrial and consumer uses, not the market for small tins of varnish sold to the retail customer for use in the home. In addition, this firm was effectively in business only in the South of England and through only one type of retailer. In the *competed market* they had 10–15 per cent of a declining business sector. They had market strategy problems after all.

The point of putting this analysis of market definition at the start is that it is a practical vehicle for re-thinking segmentation as well, i.e. moving from the basic customer needs in our market to ways of setting specific strategic targets for our marketing programmes. Let us move on to the question of *market segmentation*.

The value of this type of analysis is demonstrated by the performance of Federal Express – one of the most successful companies in the world – in a strategy of improving customer satisfaction and profitability by defining the needs of different customer segments in a better way to offer customers in each target segment expertise and service tailored to their specific needs – the value proposition is different for each customer segment. For example, companies like Intel are offered a specialized international logistics support system because this is a critical customer need – the effect, for example, is that Intel does not have warehouses in China, the FedEx planes are the warehouses.

Incidentally, experience suggests that one of the main sources of company short-sightedness and inflexibility in how markets are defined is not lack of executive vision or understanding of customer differences – it is company information systems, which contain fixed and historical assumptions about what the market is.

Market segmentation*

'The biggest difficulty we face in working on market segmentation is that everyone thinks they know what it is, and no-one thinks it is strategic. They don't. It is.'

The biggest difficulty we face in working on market segmentation is that everyone thinks they know what it is, and no-one thinks it is strategic. They don't. It is.

The theory is simple. We divide a market into groups of buyers who make coherent targets – for example, by age, gender, geographic location, socio-economic group or lifestyle for consumers; or company size, industrial sector and the like for industrial buyers. Conventional thinking is that we can then develop consistent marketing programmes based on the important characteristics of the customers in a segment, with potentially different marketing approaches for each segment – see Figure 4.5.

To many operational marketing and advertising executives, market segmentation is quite simply about tactical issues like where to advertise to get the best audience 'reach' for our promotional messages; which types of distributive outlet have the optimum customer profile; and where the salesforce can locate potential customers. This is one of the many reasons why markets are too important to be left in the hands of marketing executives.

---

* This section of the chapter leans heavily on Nigel F. Piercy and Neil A. Morgan (1993), 'Strategic and Operational Market Segmentation: A Management Analysis', *Journal of Strategic Marketing*, Vol. 1, 123–40.

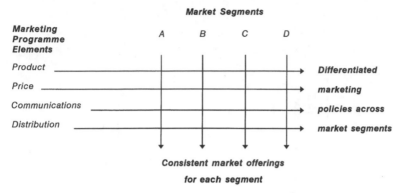

Figure 4.5   Consistency versus differentiation in market segmentation

In fact, segmentation is a fundamental issue of market strategy with far-reaching effects – indeed, ultimately the only real logic for how we organize the whole company is our understanding of the structure of the market (i.e. market segmentation).

The other misconception about segmentation is that if you could simply collect enough statistical information about the market, then the 'right' segments could be automatically identified by the computer. In the real world, notwithstanding the wonder of database marketing (see pp. 239–41), in most cases you cannot get 'enough' information anyway, but even if you could, approaching segmentation like this would miss the whole point about the power of creativity in segmenting markets to create competitive differentiation.

At the strategic level, segmentation is really about one thing and one thing only – the *customer benefit* from the product or service. This brings us right back to our central theme – what matters most to the customer.

Take the classic example of segmentation in the toothpaste market. A major piece of market research conducted by Haley [9] in the USA in the late 1960s remains the model for this marketplace, more than a quarter of a century later. Surely, if ever a product should rationally be an undifferentiated commodity product, it is toothpaste. Functionally the product is a grinding compound, chemically very similar to the compound used to remove surface blemishes on the paintwork of a car (although there may be differences in flavour).

However, the customer benefit segmentation of this market shows that it is far from being a price-led commodity market, as summarized in Figure 4.6. In customer benefit terms, there are

	The Sensory Segment	The Sociable Segment	Segments The Anxious Segment	The Independent Segment
Demographic Characteristics	Children	Young Adults	Families	Men with a higher level of education
Personality Characteristics	Self-involvement, little interest in others	Sociable, looking for sexual partners	Hypochondria, because of the disruption of family illness	Autonomous
Lifestyle Characteristics	Hedonistic, i.e. pleasure and sensation seeking	Active, gregarious, outward looking	Conservative and security conscious	Value-oriented
Most Important Product Benefits	Flavour Appearance	Cosmetic	Decay prevention promises	Price
Product Features Required	Specialist flavours Stripes Shaped extrusions	Promise of sexual attractiveness	Promise of health care, reassurance of fulfilling duty to the family	Low price/no branding e.g. retailer own-labels and/or special offers

(Adapted from Haley (4))

Figure 4.6 Customer benefit segmentation of the toothpaste market

quite different types of customer in this market – i.e. groups of customers to whom quite different things are the most important thing about the product. Maybe the strategy that drops out is one of developing separate brands for each customer, or maybe we attempt the trick of developing a multiple-benefit brand that has appeals matching the critical requirements of each customer, or maybe we do both. The real point is that if we focus on the *customer benefits* in the market, we are going to create a different model of the world and how it works than if we simply think about prices and products.

Lest it be suspected that this is all a bit theoretical and you can only get into customer-benefit segmentation if you have a king's ransom to spend on clever market research, consider the following case.

We were approached a little while ago by the General Manager of the Spares Division of one of the import car firms in the UK. His beef was about replacement exhausts. He could not understand why his potential customers for replacement exhausts were so 'irrational' – or, as he actually put it, 'stupid'. His case was that with the first exhaust replacement, in the majority of cases, only the back pipe needed replacing, costing on average £40 if purchased from the manufacturer's distributor. If the customer went to a high-street exhaust and battery outlet, he would probably be sold a complete new exhaust system for about £100. This appears to be economic madness to an engineer with expert knowledge of the motor business.

We worked out a benefit-segmentation model in a couple of hours over discussions with him. The sort of segments that appeared were:

- the *Wealthy High-Dependence Driver* – people like the self-employed, who rely on the car for income, whose primary product benefit is dependability;
- the *Impoverished High-Dependence Driver* – people like single-parent families, or the elderly, whose lifestyle crashes if the car breaks down, and who also seek dependability above all else;
- the *Scared Driver* – who just wants the fear of mechanical breakdown taken away;
- the *Ignorant Driver* – who wants expertise to solve the problem; and
- the *Value-Seeking Driver* – whose main goal is value.

The model is probably not exactly right. What it does do is suggest why the majority of the car exhaust market is not driven by price (or even in most cases value). In fact, the conclusion reached was that whatever customer-benefit you identify, Kwik

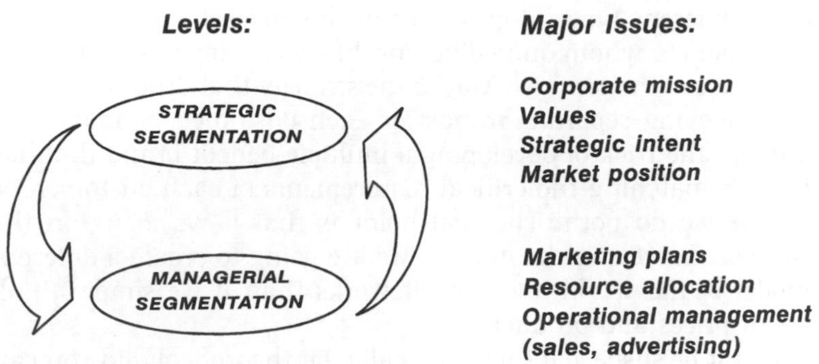

Levels:

Major Issues:

Corporate mission
Values
Strategic intent
Market position

Marketing plans
Resource allocation
Operational management
(sales, advertising)

Figure 4.7   Strategic and managerial levels of market segmentation

Fit has beaten you to it! The General Manager concluded that this was not a market worth the cost of fighting.

One way of opening up the market segmentation issue is to distinguish between strategic and managerial segmentation issues – as suggested in Figure 4.7. *Strategic* segmentation is led by customer benefits and relates to issues like corporate mission and value and strategic intent and market position. *Managerial* segmentation is the more familiar level of managerial planning and resource allocation and operational issues of sales and advertising allocation. Most people only see the managerial aspects of segmentation and ignore its strategic significance. Let us consider the conventional view of segmentation and then get a bit more real about segmentation strategy.

Conventional views of market segmentation

The traditional view of segmentation is concerned with:

- the *methodology* of identifying segment targets – for example, dividing markets by geographic or demographic characteristics, or more sophisticated statistical clustering techniques;
- *criteria* for testing the robustness of the segments identified as marketing targets – are segments measurable, accessible, sustainable, actionable and stable enough to make good targets; and
- the *segmentation strategy* decision – do we develop separate products and/or marketing programmes for different segments (*differentiated* marketing), focus efforts on certain segments (*concentrated* marketing), or ignore segment differences and treat all customer groups the same (*undifferentiated* marketing)?

Chapter and verse on the statistical techniques and complex methodology of market segmentation can be found in any conventional textbook on market strategy or marketing research (see p. 4).

The only problem with this conventional approach is that it largely misses the point. It is concerned only with the operational aspects of marketing. It ignores the strategic issues almost entirely. This may explain why there is growing evidence that companies do not use segmentation theory to a great extent, beyond targeting advertisements into media based on demographics.

Indeed, the typical (but recurring) responses of managers in workshops to conventional segmentation are revealing. They say things like:

- 'Is the fact that we *can* segment markets any reason why we *should* segment markets?'
- 'Should we allow our marketing strategies to be driven primarily by the availability of the information technology that facilitates sophisticated market segmentation?'
- 'If, as competitors, we all pursue the conventional, mechanical approaches, using the same techniques and often the same databases – surely we all end up with the same segments and no competitive advantage (indeed, maybe more competition in the critical segments because everyone goes after them)?'
- 'What's the use to anybody of identifying and choosing market segments that nobody in the organization owns?'
- 'Fancy segment labels are all well and good, but they do not fit the marketing plan and they don't get budgeted for.'
- 'It is fine being imaginative about basing segments on customer needs and benefits sought, but how do you turn that into quantifiable targets with specific customers for the salesforce?'
- 'Don't we have to revert to demographic and geographic segmentation anyway, because those are the only things we can easily measure, and see what we've got and where we're going?'

Such responses have led us to build an extended model of segmentation to use with executives to work on market segmentation questions.

An extended model of market segmentation

Our extended model – which can be used as a diagnostic framework to sort out segmentation issues for a company – is *'there is a need to distinguish between strategic and operational organizational levels in dealing with the segmentation issue'*

shown in Figure 4.8. This model is based upon two important propositions: *first*, that there is a need to distinguish between strategic and operational organizational levels in dealing with the segmentation issue; and *secondly*, that in order to address the issue of implementation it is necessary to examine the internal organizational context, as well as the external marketplace, in considering segmentation. The suggestion is that in each of these areas the managerial agenda to be addressed is different, as suggested in Figure 4.8 and outlined below.

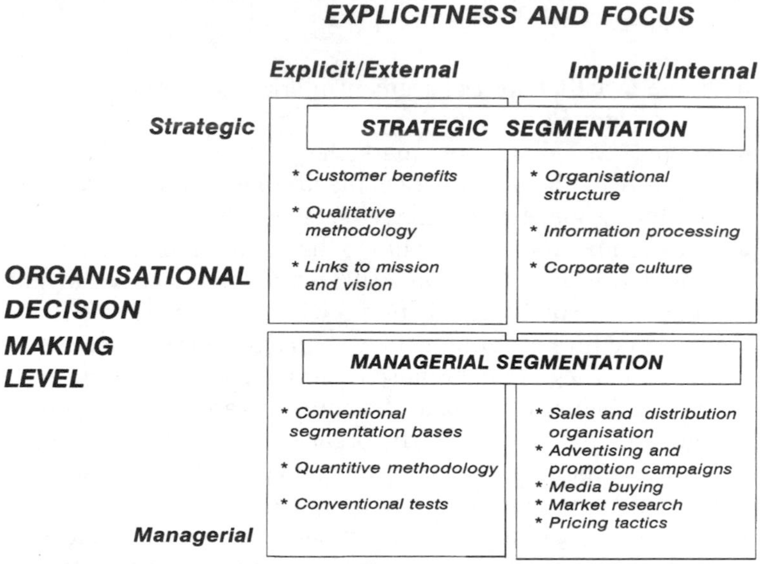

EXPLICITNESS AND FOCUS

	Explicit/External	Implicit/Internal
Strategic	**STRATEGIC SEGMENTATION**	
ORGANISATIONAL DECISION MAKING LEVEL	* Customer benefits * Qualitative methodology * Links to mission and vision	* Organisational structure * Information processing * Corporate culture
	MANAGERIAL SEGMENTATION	
Managerial	* Conventional segmentation bases * Quantitive methodology * Conventional tests	* Sales and distribution organisation * Advertising and promotion campaigns * Media buying * Market research * Pricing tactics

Figure 4.8 An extended model of market segmentation

Strategic-Explicit issues

These issues relate to *strategic segmentation*, and the goal is to focus on the fundamental customer benefits sought in different parts of the market, whether from physical product differences or from non-product attributes. It is quite possible that the conventional criteria of segment evaluation do not validly or usefully apply to what is built here. The pursuit of a strategic market vision may quite reasonably be judged by criteria other than measurability and the like.

At this level, segmentation models might be better judged by such criteria as: the ability to create and sustain competitive differentiation and advantage; innovativeness in how the market is attacked; the compatibility with mission; providing a coherent focus for thinking in the organization; and consistency with corporate value and cultures.

Indeed, the relevant techniques for generating 'strategic segmentation' in the first place are more likely to be qualitative and creative than quantitative and 'scientific'. This is arguably the practical link between corporate mission and the marketplace – it is where the broad concepts and ideas in the mission statement can be related to customer needs and benefits in a specific marketplace, or conversely where market insights provide feedback to those building mission statements. However, it is at this decision-making level that we must also recognize the other characteristics of strategic decision making: levels of uncertainty and ambiguity are high; information is scarce; and the market environment is enacted or constructed rather than objectively known (see pp. 388–96).

Managerial-Explicit issues

Here the critical issues are the most familiar ones: the choice of conventional segmentation bases and the application of quantitative methodology to identify segment characteristics. Here the conventional tests probably do apply, and the goals are primarily managerial in allocating resources and operational in the tactical management of marketing programmes.

Strategic-Implicit issues

This is where it gets more interesting. We refer here to a set of issues that have been largely neglected by conventional segmentation, although they are likely to be critical to successful implementation of segmentation strategies. These issues are concerned with the fundamental implications of market segmentation for the 'inner workings' of the organization. These issues are likely to include the following areas:

● *Organizational structure.* Strategic market vision may be incompatible with marketing organization structures (and the related organizational decision-making processes and information flows), raising a variety of practical questions which are central to the ability of an organization to implement a segmentation strategy: how well can existing organizational structures of departments, functions and divisions service the segments targeted; does mismatch between a segmentation model and the reality of the organization mean that segments are never 'owned' or taken seriously, because they fall between the jurisdictions of existing departments or SBUs?

- *Information and reporting.* Fundamental problems may be that: new segment targets may be incompatible with existing information processing systems (i.e. data collection and dissemination), and unfamiliar to managers and difficult to identify and evaluate in conventional terms; if existing reporting lines do not put sales and market achievements in terms compatible with the segmentation model, it may be very difficult to set targets, allocate responsibilities, monitor progress, or even have target segments taken seriously within the organization.
- *Internal decision-making process.* If segments are conceived and defined in a radically different way to the conventional market targets, a major implementation barrier may arise concerned with whether the new segments will become a genuine focus in marketing plans and whether they will be recognized and gain resources in the budgeting process.
- *Corporate culture.* Here the issue is the acceptability of new segments to the people in the organization in terms of values, ethos, internal rules, evaluation systems and the like. If new segments represent radical change and are potentially threatening to the status quo and the current distribution of influence and control, there may well be hidden barriers to implementation which are powerful. It is the neglect of issues such as these that really lies behind the observed failure of many innovative customer-benefit-based segmentation models, when this construction of the market produces segment targets that: fall between the responsibilities of different organizational units, so are not 'owned' by anyone; are not easily measurable or monitored in the existing information system, and are not the focus of conventional reporting; are not part of existing planning and budgeting processes; and in which the people in the organization have little belief or confidence.

Managerial-Implicit issues

Here the concern is also with internal organizational issues, but now at an operational level:

- *Sales and distribution organization* – are the segment targets easily identifiable by salespeople and accessible through existing distribution channels, and are they compatible with the way these processes are currently structured?
- *Advertising and promotion campaigns* – are the segment targets reachable as separate targets through our existing procedures and capabilities for marketing communications?

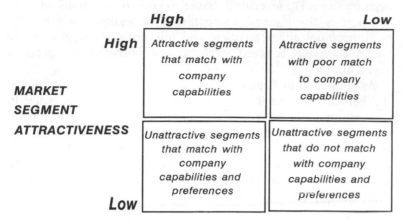

Figure 4.9 Conventional segment attractiveness versus internal compatibility

- *Market research* – do we have information organized around these segment targets to identify them, to size and measure opportunities, and to evaluate our performance?
- *Pricing tactics* – do we currently have the facilities to price differently to segment targets?

These issues, though frequently hidden and ignored, are with tactical problems in implementing segmentation: where segments cut across sales and distribution systems and cannot be adequately serviced by either; where marketing communications, pricing and market research systems are not set up to deal with, or differentiate between, segments of the type proposed.

The practical conclusion is that we should screen segments not just in terms of 'market attractiveness' (the conventional criterion), but also in terms of 'internal compatibility', in the way suggested in Figure 4.9. The critical implementation issue is compatibility and consistency between segment targets and organizational attributes, both overt and covert.

However, to identify such issues of internal compatibility may require more detailed analysis of the kind discussed below.

Consistency and integration

The argument above suggests that overall we can reduce the market segmentation issue to two critical questions to evaluate relevance and the practical usefulness of a given segmentation model, in terms of whether it can be implemented at all by a given organization. These critical issues relate to questions of consistency, or the internal compatibility of segment targets with organizational characteristics; and questions of integration, or the relationship between strategic and operational aspects of segmentation.

As suggested in Figure 4.9, *consistency* is concerned with the 'fit' between the explicit/external and implicit/internal issues in segmentation, at both the strategic and the managerial/operational levels. On the other hand, *integration* refers to the 'fit' between the strategic segmentation model and the managerial/ operational level; and between internal issues at both these levels. Figure 4.10 provides a framework for addressing these issues. Stimulus questions for executives are:

- What is the existing or achievable 'fit' or internal compatibility between the 'strategic segmentation' model of the external customer marketplace and the internal organization structure, information systems, processes like planning and budgeting, and corporate culture?
- What is the existing or achievable 'fit' or internal compatibility between the 'managerial/operational segmentation' model of the external customer marketplace and the sales and distribution organization, advertising and promotion management, media buying, market research systems and pricing administration?

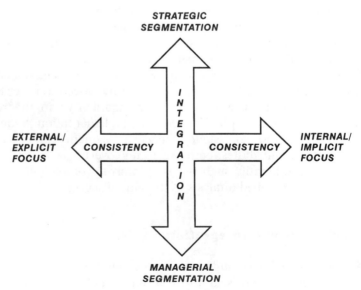

Figure 4.10 Segmentation consistency and integration

- How compatible is the 'strategic' segmentation at the managerial/operational level? Can customer benefit groups be translated into accessible target segments?
- How compatible are the internal issues at the 'strategic' level with their counterparts at the 'managerial/operational' level – in terms of organization, information, planning, budgeting, people and so on?

Although it cannot provide easy answers, the framework provided by Figures 4.7 to 4.10 provides a structure by which managers may evaluate the real nature of market segmentation for their companies and for identifying implementation barriers to segment-based strategies. In practical terms, this is a useful device for bridging the gap between the conventional theory of market segmentation and the implementation of segmentation strategies.

'provides a structure by which managers may evaluate the real nature of market segmentation for their companies and for identifying implementation barriers'

What happens if you stick to a narrow view of segmentation?

A no-brainer – it does not work. Also the consequences may be painful.

For example, pursuing the corporate banking example cited earlier – the strategic vision of top management was to target corporate customers for financial services according to the customer's own corporate strategy (which would predict customer needs and priorities for financial services), with product offering and marketing programmes built around, for instance, 'market-share driven' companies as compared to 'profit-reconstruction strategy' companies. As we saw, this defined an unusual and novel strategic segmentation model which offered considerable potential competitive advantage. However, many problems emerged in attempting to implement this segmentation model in the bank:

- the powerful branch network in the bank saw the new corporate market segmentation as a threat to their own business – they called it 'cherry-picking' – and lobbied against it, as well as effectively withholding co-operation;
- it was impossible to value or target the new segments because the bank's information system coded only customer size and industry type;
- the new segments did not 'fit' with the established planning system and were largely ignored when targets were set and when promotional resources were allocated;

- lack of information meant that salespeople were given little support in how to identify corporate customers in terms of the new segments, and so largely ignored them;
- the new 'marketing' idea of segmenting the bank's customers by need and benefit found little support among management, who defended the *status quo* as 'prudent banking practice';
- the strategy was a complete failure.

This may be an extreme case, but it illustrates the pointlessness of market segmentation – however innovative – that ignores issues of integration and consistency inside the organization.

More publicly, John Coleman at House of Fraser has been struggling with the implications of segmentation in the women's fashion clothing market, in a traditional department store chain of 50 stores with declining performance [9]. His plan is based on attracting women clothes shoppers in three highly attractive, high-spending segments:

- the '*Quality Classic*' buyer;
- the '*Smart Career Mover*'; and
- the '*Fashion Lover*'

and he has controversially rejected the 'Young Mother' clothes buyer as a target. However, his problem is that House of Fraser brands are not particularly appealing to these target segments – these consumers visit House of Fraser stores, but to shop at concessions like Oasis, Mondi, Liz Claiborne and Windsmoor. His target is 'the affluent woman with aspirations' and his products are positioned against Marks and Spencer (where they fail), and his buying operation has struggled to achieve any re-positioning. The strategy involves a new own-label range for the segment targets, which has so far failed to appeal, and in 1997 prices are being discounted before the products even get to the stores.

There is a simple and obvious fact to bear in mind: if you do not have a competitive advantage in a segment, then it is not attractive – however big, free-spending and dynamic it may be. Segmentation strategies that cannot be implemented are dreams, not strategies.

Segmentation is a powerful strategic tool for focusing on customer needs and building competitive advantage from that focus. The Product–Customer Matrix analysis (Figure 4.4) provides a mechanism for identifying and evaluating market segments. But we have to be realistic and think segmentation through to the capabilities and characteristics of the organization as well, or we end up with a brilliant market strategy that does not work.

However, markets are dynamic . . .

Market segments that stand up and bite

It is worth noting that ignoring the existence of distinctive segments in our markets may involve more risk than simply missing opportunities to build competitive strength. In sophisticated modern markets some segments are proactive – they judge us and attack us for not adapting our products and services to their needs!

There is a compelling argument, for example, that in Britain in the 1990s ethnic or cultural identity is a powerful lever for analysing markets:

- Ethnic minorities comprise 5.5 per cent of the UK population and the number will double in the next 50 years.
- Ethnic minorities spend £10 billion annually.
- Ethnic minorities include many socially mobile and increasingly affluent groups [10].

These groups are rarely targeted by companies, which is a missed opportunity. However, while they may be ignored, ethnic groups do not ignore companies, and their perceptions impact on brand equity:

- Brands perceived as *ethnically insensitive*:
  - Persil (TV ad showing Dalmatian shaking off black spots)
  - McDonalds (TV ad showing stereotype of young black man listening to very loud music while driving)
  - TSB (ad showing two short planks with Irish accents)
- Brands perceived as *ethnically sensitive*:
  - BT (radio ads in Hindi promoting long-distance calls)
  - Persil (TV ad with black family)
  - Sainsbury (catering for local ethnic minorities)
  - WH Smith (stocking ethnic greeting cards) [10].

Similarly, consumer attitudes towards 'green' issues remain on the agenda, even if we prefer to ignore them. The National Consumer Council identifies:

- *Affluent Greens and Young Greens* (36 per cent of the population) – committed to green consumerism;
- *Recyclers and Careful Spenders* (38 per cent of the population) – act in an environmentally friendly way, but do not usually 'buy green';
- *Sceptics* (26 per cent of the population) – determined not to buy 'green' under any circumstances [11].

As markets change, market strategies like segmentation have to evolve as well. Companies do not miss just market opportunities, they risk being judged and written off by significant parts of the market if they do not stay in touch.

Indeed, some new segments may be both judgemental and hostile. 'Generation X' (the youth of the 1990s) consumers are not differentiated by age and gender but by attitude – disillusionment, knowingness and cynicism. Nike understands this market. A Nike sports shoe advertising insert in *Loaded* (a magazine for 'new lads') reads:

> 'We don't sell dreams. We sell shoes. . . . Don't insult our intelligence. Tell us what it is. Tell us what it does. And don't play the national anthem while you do it'. [12]

In similar media, Hugo Boss's advertising for its male fragrance, Boss, reads:

> 'No fancy women, no passionate embraces. No silly sunsets. Just a great fragrance.'

This is a market where 'maverick' brands like Virgin, Body Shop and Benetton have enormous competitive advantage. How many other companies have taken seriously an anti-marketing, anti-advertising 'Generation X' market segment?

And thinking forward

It should be remembered that we also have to think about our value proposition and the key relationships before we finalize our thinking about market segments – who said it was going to be easy?

Market attractiveness and position

Re-thinking market definitions and market segments and targets is likely very quickly to confront us with choices. If we cannot pursue all the markets we have identified, if we cannot attack all the segments we can see – then how do we see priorities and decide where to focus? We have been warned of the strategic weakness in trying to be all things to all people – but how do we set our priorities?

'how do we see priorities and decide where to focus?'

The results of this type of focus can be surprising. ANI Bradken is a Scottish foundry which continues to improve profitability in a declining and highly price-competitive market. The firm has been 'sacking' unrewarding customers. The role of the business development director is to sift through potential clients to choose which ones to do business with, and the salesforce interviews prospective customers as though they were applying for a job. Bradken has taken its customer base in this unusual way down from 212 to 25, and focuses all its efforts on these customers [13].

At the larger corporate level, more and more strategy is driven by market focus in the fight for market leadership. The thinking is that focus creates a strong position in the minds of customers: Volvo owns safety, Xerox owns copiers, Coke owns cola, Kleenex owns tissues. One analyst suggests that the reason that Pepsi has failed to win market leadership over Coke, in spite of the fact that consumers prefer it, is that Pepsico lacked market focus, and has only now started to divest businesses such as its restaurant chains [14].

But how do we confront the market choices important to our business? The world is full of portfolio models and decision aids. Perhaps the most straightforward is one that prioritizes by looking at:

- *Market (or segment) attractiveness* – the degree to which an opportunity fits with our goals and capabilities;
- *Market position* – how well we believe we can do in this market or segment.

Obviously, neither of these things is static. Market attractiveness can change. In 1997 Texas Instruments sold off its notebook computer business. The notebook computer market is large, growing and, on the face of things, an attractive market. In fact, margins are pressured by price-cutting, and only Intel (supplying the computer chips) and Microsoft (supplying the software) make money – the suppliers of the boxes do not.

In the US telecoms business, costs of long-distance phone calls have declined dramatically. Five years ago they averaged 37 cents/minute, now they are 10–15 cents/minute unless you are a large corporate, when it may be as low as $1\frac{1}{2}$ cents/minute. The cost may soon be zero – a new service provider offers free long-distance calls, with revenue generated by 10–15-second advertisements during the phone call. As a profit centre this market is not attractive (though for telecom companies it is a strategic platform on which to build other things).

The market position you can take will depend on what you do – the strategy, the value proposition, and so on. For example, the Body Shop International is expanding its branch and distribution network to channel its cosmetic products to new international markets – but in different retail formats depending on customer needs and behaviour in each market. While direct marketing operations are planned for Switzerland and Canada, the 'micro-store' outlet is more suitable for expensive large city sites and markets like Japan.

Market position can change dramatically, and quietly too. Mathew Clark, the UK drinks group, reported at the end of 1996 that sales of Diamond White and K Ciders had dropped 40 per cent and profits had fallen dramatically – share price instantly fell by 45 per cent. The reason – the switch by young drinkers to 'alcopops' like Bass' Hooch brand of alcoholic lemonade. Professional analysts regarded brands like Hooch as a joke – a temporary fad at most. A year in, from a standing start, alcopops were selling 100 million litres a year. Market position depends on customers, and they have a nasty habit of changing their minds when something new comes along.

Indeed, one of the most spectacular success stories in British business in the 1990s demonstrates just how vulnerable your market position can be. James Dyson was the man who transformed the wheelbarrow by replacing the wheel with a plastic ball, but he also designed and developed with his own hands the first vacuum cleaner that uses a vortex of air to suck in dirt and cleans better and does not need a bag – the Dyson Cyclone vacuum cleaner. The vacuum cleaner market had been dominated by companies like Hoover and Electrolux since the 1950s with conventional designs of cleaner. Dyson offered his design to Hoover and they laughed at him. After many problems, Dyson launched the product himself with the slogan 'The world's first bagless vacuum cleaner – 100 per cent suction, 100 per cent of the time'. His machine is priced fairly high at £199 and was launched in 1993. He had a lot of difficulty getting into conventional retail outlets, and initially relied on mail order. He sold £3 million in the first year, tripled his business every 12 months, and now has £200 million annual worldwide revenue. Dyson is now actually doing the amazing thing of selling his electrical appliances *to* Japan. His is the fastest growing brand in the market, outselling Hoover and Electrolux. Hoover had for years held 50 per cent of the upright vacuum cleaner market – this has halved. By 1995 Dyson had 58 per cent of the market for cleaners priced over £180, compared to Hoover's 14 per cent. The traditional firms are tied to a product technology that now looks obsolete, and the only response has been a rearguard action to try to persuade Comet and other major electrical goods retailers not to stock the product. No market position can be assumed to be safe indefinitely, as Hoover and Electrolux have discovered the hard way.

Accepting that things change, our logic is shown in Figure 4.11 – assuming we grade a market or segment as high or low in attractiveness, and the position we take as strong or weak, then the options and priorities are:

- *Core business* – areas where the market offers the potential for us to achieve our goals and which fits our capabilities and competence, *and* where we believe we can take a strong market position. Such areas are a high priority for investment.
- *Peripheral business* - where the market is less attractive to us (there is no growth, competition is tough, margins are low, and so on), but we can take a strong position. These may be areas where we continue to do business, but unless they bring us other benefits they are not a high priority for investment.
- *Illusion business* – these are highly attractive markets which offer everything we want, but where we can or do take a weak position. These markets and segments are an illusion because the market looks great – but we can never get a pay-off.
- *Dead-end business* – These are the lowest priority because the market is not attractive to us, and we can only take a weak position.

Clearly, this is a crude and often uncomfortable view of the markets and segments we have identified. It can be a very useful tool, because it forces us to face up to realities.

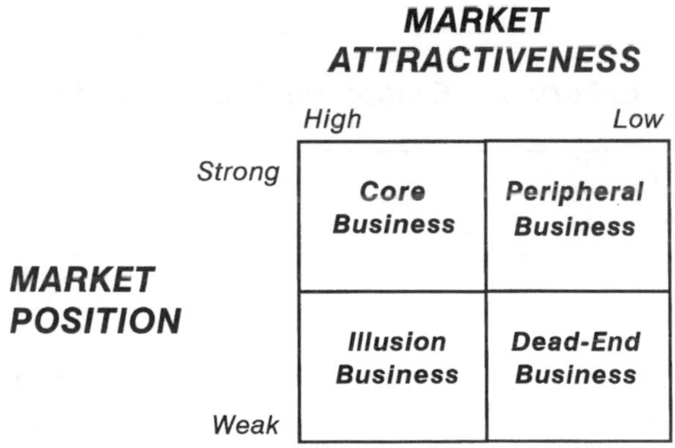

**MARKET
ATTRACTIVENESS**

	High	Low
Strong	**Core Business**	**Peripheral Business**
Weak	**Illusion Business**	**Dead-End Business**

MARKET POSITION

Figure 4.11 Market attractiveness and position

When we add to this our thoughts about our strategy – our competitive advantage with different customer groups, the sustainability of our market position, the robustness of our brand or value proposition, i.e. movement from one issue to another within the market strategy – then the picture may be even more valuable.

Our way of using this sifting mechanism operationally is shown in the worksheet in Figure 4.12. This provides a structure to do the following important pieces of analysis:

● put down what are the criteria that make a market or segment attractive to our company – these are not the same for all companies – and what makes a market or position strong or weak as far as we are concerned;

Criteria for Evaluating Market Attractiveness

Rank	Criteria	Weight
1		
2		
3		
4		
5		
6		
7		
		1.00

Criteria for Evaluating Market Position

Rank	Criteria	Weight
1		
2		
3		
4		
5		
6		
7		
		1.00

Figure 4.12   Market attractiveness and position worksheets

Market Attractiveness

Criteria	Weight	Market 1		Market 2		Market 3		Market 4		Market 5		Market 6	
		Score	Wtd Score	Score	Wtd Score	Score	Wtd Score	Score	Wtd Score	Score	Wtd Score	Score	Wtd Score
1													
2													
3													
4													
5													
6													
7													

Market Position

Criteria	Weight	Market 1		Market 2		Market 3		Market 4		Market 5		Market 6	
		Score	Wtd Score	Score	Wtd Score	Score	Wtd Score	Score	Wtd Score	Score	Wtd Score	Score	Wtd Score
1													
2													
3													
4													
5													
6													
7													

Market Attractiveness

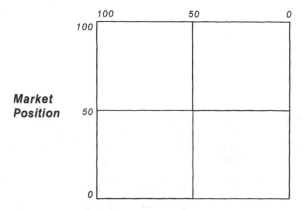

Figure 4.12   continued

Instructions for Completing the Market Attractiveness and Market Position Worksheets

1. The first part of this worksheet asks us to define the criteria which we wish to apply to two aspects of each market or segment:

   - the *Market Attractiveness* to our company, and
   - the *Market Position* we could take, with a given value proposition and collaboration strategy.

2. Evaluating the *Market Attractiveness* of a possible area for investment and exploitation will involve considering a variety of issues. Suggested issues to be considered are:

   - the size of the market opportunity,
   - the prospects for market growth,
   - the absence of entrenched competition,
   - the existence of barriers preventing competitive entry,
   - the ease of servicing the market,
   - the 'fit' with internal company needs – corporate strategies, size and profitability thresholds, exploitation of existing technology investments,
   - the availability of promising collaborative relationships.

   These are only suggestions about what may be important – you should brainstorm a list of all the things that the company requires and that you believe should be evaluated in deciding how attractive a market is to your company. Bear in mind that at this stage we are only specifying the criteria, not making judgements about a particular strategy.

   A weight should be included, showing our judgement of the relative importance of the different criteria identified and entered in the Worksheet (these should total to 1.00).

3. This part of the worksheet follows a similar procedure, but asks us now to specify what are the important things in judging the position that we could take in this market, i.e. how competitive could we be and what results could we offer the company? The issues that we may wish to consider including are:

   - the sales and market share that we could achieve versus the known competition.
   - the competitive position we could achieve,
   - the lack of vulnerability to competitive attack,
   - the strategic platform for developing other business.

   In this case we are concerned with how competitive a given strategy could make us in this marketplace and the strength of the position we would hope to build. Again at this point we are doing no more than building the most relevant list of criteria to be used in evaluation, we are not evaluating any particular strategies.

4. In both cases we should list the most important 6 or 7 rating criteria in the boxes in the worksheet, together with the weights, after we have agreed these. We then have a basis for a careful evaluation of the market attractiveness and the potential market position we could build.

5. The worksheet asks us to list up to five potential markets or segments to be considered, and then to use the criteria specified to evaluate each in terms firstly of the market attractiveness, and secondly the market position that we could take using this strategy in this market. The procedure is:

- List the market or segments across the top of the two grids.
- Using the criteria specified, evaluate each potential market on its market attractiveness and market position characteristics. In each case enter a raw score (out of 100) on each criterion.
- When each potential market has been scored on each criterion of Market Attractiveness and Market Position, the weights can be used to calculate a Weighted Score on each criterion.
- The Weighted Scores are totalled for each market, to give each a Weighted Score for Market Attractiveness and for Market Position.
- The scores can then be used to position each potential strategy in the matrix.

6. The picture we have built up is based on two dimensions: the attractiveness of a market to us (based on the criteria we have said are the most important), and the market position we might take (again based on our own criteria of importance and priorities). It is worth considering this picture in various ways.

We should also consider what would need to be done to change the positioning of a market option in the matrix. The sort of question that we might raise is what would have to change about how we have modelled the market to make it attractive; and what would have to change to make our Market Position stronger (perhaps a different form of collaboration, or a different value strategy).

We should not draw conclusions from the model until we have exhausted these possibilities.

When this is complete, we should be able to make a judgement as to the most appropriate and potentially productive market choices and priorities.

- rate or score the markets or segments against the specific criteria we have identified – subjectively or through more detailed market analysis;
- use these ratings against the things that matter to our company to prioritize the opportunities we have identified.

This may look bureaucratic, but it is actually very easy to do, and experience suggests can flush out some interesting things:

- cases where all our thinking is about defending our market position in Peripheral business – because it is where we have always been;
- executives who champion new markets and segments but can see no way of taking a strong position – they drive us into the Illusion business;

'all our thinking is about defending our market position in Peripheral business – because it is where we have always been'

- the deep-seated and vigorous defence of markets which are Dead-end business, because we just refuse to accept that one of our traditional markets has become less attractive or that we have been overtaken by new competitors.

These are vitally important questions to confront before we commit to a market strategy. Do not forget, however, that we need to think also about the value proposition and key relationship components of market strategy in making these judgements – how else can we be sure about the strength of our market position, unless we know what it is based on and whether we can sustain it through collaborations and employees and defend it against competitors?

Where are we now?

What we tried to do in this chapter was to break down the important issues into strategy, programmes and information and then to focus on market strategy. We saw that thinking about strategy hurts – it is open-ended, disruptive, uncomfortable, long-term, subversive and revolutionary. But strategizing matters.

To turn the brave ideas about new market strategy into reality, we look to the Strategic Pathway approach. This separated our market choices, the value proposition and the key relationships as the critical elements of market strategy.

The remainder of the chapter looked at market choices: market definition, market segmentation, and making market choices based on market attractiveness and market position. These are incredibly important questions which underpin most of what follows. They are also difficult to sort out – which is why we often neglect them.

However, it is clear that market choices are also informed by how we can compete – the value proposition and the key relationships to which we turn our attention next.

References

1. Porter, Michael E. (1996), 'What is Strategy', *Harvard Business Review*, November/December, 61–78.
2. Hamel, Gary and C.K. Prahalad (1994), 'Competing for the Future', *Harvard Business Review*, July/August, 122–128.
3. Kay, John (1995), 'Learning to Define the Core Business', *Financial Times*, 1 December.

4. Hamel, Gary (1996), 'Strategy as Revolution', *Harvard Business Review*, July/August, 69–82.
5. Hamel, Gary and C.K. Prahalad (1989), 'Strategic Intent', *Harvard Business Review*, May/June, 63–76.
6. Prahalad, C.K. and Gary Hamel (1990), 'The Core Competence of the Corporation', *Harvard Business Review*, May/June, 79–91.
7. Cravens, David W, Gordon Greenley, Nigel F. Piercy and Stanley F. Slater (1997), 'Market-Driven Strategic Management', *Long Range Planning*, Vol. 30, No. 4, 493–506.
8. Mitchell, Alan (1996), 'Marketers Seek Oasis From Blur', *Marketing Business*, 27 September.
9. Rankine, Kate (1996), 'Not a Happy House', *Daily Telegraph*, 5 October.
10. Dwek, Robert (1997), 'Losing the Race', *Marketing Business*, March.
11. Clover, Charles (1996), 'The Green Shopper Is Alive and Well', *Daily Telegraph*, 11 December.
12. Dwek, Robert (1997), 'Cool Customers', *Marketing Business*, February.
13. Mitchell, Alan (1997), 'Putting Customers First', *Marketing Business*, April.
14. Ries, Laura (1997), 'Welcome to the Focus Generation', *Marketing News*, 14 April.

CHAPTER 5

Market strategy:

The value proposition – Market
mission, competitive differentiation
and marketing assets and brands

Introduction

In the previous chapter we developed the Strategic Pathway as an
approach to systematically building market strategy, and we
considered the critical market choices that start the Strategic
Pathway. We now turn to the question of our value proposition –
what do we have that will enable us to build and sustain a strong
competitive position in a market or a market segment? As shown
in Figure 5.1, the issues for us to confront here are:

- *Market mission* – what do we want to *be* and to *stand for* in this
  market, and how does this relate to corporate goals and
  mission (if it does)?
- *Competitive differentiation and positioning* – what do we have to
  build a difference between what we offer and what our
  competitors offer in the customer's eyes, and how do we use
  this to build a sustainable and profitable competitive position in
  the market?
- *Marketing assets and brands* – what competitive advantages do
  we have in intangible assets like company reputation, unique
  capabilities and brand identity, that can be used to build our
  market strategy?

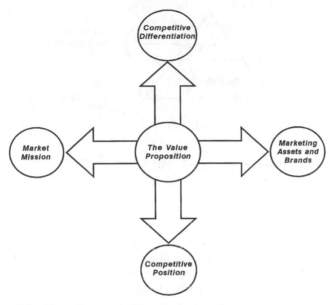

Figure 5.1 The value proposition in market strategy

Just a reminder – these questions are highly interrelated and also inseparable from the market choices (previous chapter) and key relationships (next chapter) components of market strategy. To build the strategy step-by-step, we take the components individually – but it is the total market strategy that matters.

Mission analysis*

Perhaps the strategic analysis most demanded by companies and executives at the moment, but all too often the least rewarding aspect of working with companies on market strategy, is *mission analysis*. In theory, mission is where we start, because it tells us the broad purpose of the operation and gives us the framework within which to develop sets of specific objectives and programmes – as suggested by Figure 5.2. The logical sequence is that we start with basic purposes (mission), determine

'all too often the least rewarding aspect of working with companies on market strategy, is mission analysis'

---

*This section draws heavily on Nigel F. Piercy and Neil A. Morgan (1994), 'Mission Analysis: An Operational Approach', *Journal of General Management*, Vol. 19, No. 3.

Figure 5.2 Mission and market strategy

specific goals (objectives), figure out what we need to do to achieve these things (market strategies) and how we are going to do it in the marketplace (marketing programmes).

The results of mission analysis tend to be statements of varying length that state what we want our business to be. Examples include:

- *Pepsi* – 'We will be an outstanding company by exceeding customer expectations through empowering people guided by shared value';
- *Kentucky Fried Chicken* – 'To provide families with affordable, delicious, chicken-dominant meals';
- *Lada* – 'To provide the lowest price and best value for money in Britain';
- *Sony* – The 'BMW' slogan: 'Beat Matsushita Whatever'.

Other mission and vision statements run to many pages and hundreds of words, and consume many hours of management time in their construction.

Results seem mixed. McDonalds has the mission of existing to 'provide great-tasting food backed up by excellent operations and friendly service in a relaxed, safe, and consistent restaurant environment'. The effectiveness in creating service quality should be considered in the light of the (hopefully untypical) customer experience in Chester in 1994 of receiving a printed receipt reading 'One regular Coke – no f***ing ice' [1]!

If mission statements are to contribute anything, then they must:

- reflect our core competences and how we intend to apply them and sustain them;
- be closely tied to the critical success factors in the marketplace – the things we have to be good at to survive; and

● tell our employees, managers, suppliers and partners what contribution is required from them to deliver our promise of value to the customer.

If they do not do this, they are of no use in building market strategy. But, in reality, how often do they do these things? Often they do not. Frankly, most of the time they do not.

The trouble with talking about mission is that at the extreme it becomes top management ego-massaging and 'holier than thou' posturing, and has little to do with running the business and satisfying the customer.

For instance, to give you an idea of what I mean, I used to run an ice-breaker game with top manager groups on executive development programmes, where I asked them to play the 'car game'. This is where you have to imagine your business is a car, and then tell everyone what car it would be now, and then what car you would like it to be. This is great fun, until you suddenly realize that about 90 per cent of top management want their businesses to be Ferraris, Lamborghinis and small-badge sports cars with exotic names that I have never heard of before. No-one seems to want to be a Ford Escort. The point is that there is actually room in the world for a lot more Ford Escorts than Lamborghinis.

Indeed, I have been driven to suggest to some companies, whose version of mission analysis is pure, non-operational motherhood, that we are prepared to provide them with the 'Instant Mission Kit', shown in Figure 5.3.

This kit is guaranteed to produce a mission statement of bland, non-operational motherhood, with which no-one will disagree, but which will not change a single thing in the business and its service to the customer – but at least it is quicker than the usual weeks of heart-searching, so you will not waste as much time!

Mission Statement Components	*Tick as required*
. . . a market leader . . . a total quality supplier . . . a socially responsible producer . . . a green/environmentally friendly firm . . . a caring employer . . . a safeguarder of shareholder interests . . . a global player . . . a provider of service . . . a good corporate citizen . . . a customer-oriented organization . . . a responsible partner with distributors . . . a builder of human dignity	

Figure 5.3 Piercy's instant corporate 'mission kit'

This is perhaps a little too cynical, and probably reflects battle fatigue from too many fatuous mission analysis sessions with company top managements. Please note, however, that I am not alone in such cynicism. Dilbert, the world's greatest business cartoon character, informs us that:

> If your employees are producing low-quality products that no sane person would buy, you can afford to fix that problem by holding meetings to discuss your Mission Statement. A Mission Statement is defined as 'a long awkward sentence that demonstrates management's inability to think clearly'. All good companies have one. [2]

Does it ever work?

Perhaps surprisingly, yes – it does seem to work for some companies.

'customer needs are fundamental, and, by contrast, our specific products and technologies are no more than one way of satisfying that fundamental customer need'

In fact, the whole customer mission thing was started off by Theodore Levitt's classic paper 'Marketing Myopia' in 1960 [3]. This paper laid down the argument that has become an article of faith for generations of marketing executives. Levitt tells us that customer needs are fundamental, and, by contrast, our specific products and technologies are no more than one way of satisfying that fundamental customer need (so far, so good). The examples given of companies incorrectly defining their businesses have also become classics.

The basic questions we are urged to ask are:

- What business *are* we in?
- What business *should* we be in?
- What business *can* we be in?

Our answers are required to be given in terms of customer needs, not products. Levitt's examples included:

Traditional, but inappropriate product or technology-based definitions of the business:	Appropriate customer need-based definitions of the business:
Railways	Transportation
Oil	Energy
Computers	Information processing
Photocopiers	Office productivity

Things that give us greater insight into the real sources of competition and what really matters to the customer – i.e. meeting the need or solving the problem, not buying our product – cannot be all bad.

For example, Levitt's view of railways as being in the transportation business in the 1960s could be up-dated for the 1990s to say that the railway company is actually in the 'communications' business. If this seems far-fetched, consider the following advertising message at the centre of a major advertising campaign run in the UK:

Picture the scene: a tired, scruffy, dishevelled executive arrives home from yet another trip away on business. He finds his wife in the arms of a Spanish dancing instructor, and less than enthusiastic at his arrival. His small child appears and screams at the stranger before him. His dog arrives and bites the ankle of this forgotten intruder. *The message*: do not *travel* on business, use the phone, the fax, the telex, the confraphone, the electronic mail system, and regain your quality of life. *The significance*: all of a sudden, British Telecom and British Rail are direct competitors in the business communications market. And before we discuss that preposterous thought, let us not forget that the much-maligned British Rail has a major expertise in electronic communications and substantial potential synergies with the computing and telecoms industry.

This style of analysis is often difficult, but it can produce some very real insights into ways to grow a business, to reposition it, to understand its core strengths and to fend off emerging competition.

For instance, mission analysis was useful in identifying different ways to define the business of a British garden centre firm, at different levels of abstraction from its core business of simply growing plants and selling them. The levels that mission analysis identified were:

- *horticulture* – we grow plants and sell them, and can develop the business by doing more of the same;
- *gardening services* – we add value by providing advisory and information services to support the sale of plants and equipment. We may grow into new markets like garden design services, landscaping, estate maintenance;
- *leisure/entertainment* – we see our role as filling people's leisure time. We add leisure facilities – catering, children's entertainments, to create a 'day out'. We develop (probably by leased areas) into new outdoor leisure product areas – camping, caravanning, do-it-yourself;

- *dream fulfilment* – we specialize in meeting the needs of the person to whom the perfect home and garden is the ideal and central to their lifestyle*.

In fact, this company chose to pursue the leisure/entertainment mission, and rationalized their operation around this. For these managers, mission analysis was central to the practical issue of sorting out how they identified the market, the target customer and the appropriate direction in which to take the business.

The danger is that we get carried away with the excitement and creativity in mission analysis and with the insights it can provide. Mission analysis which forgets the realities of our core business is dangerous, and unhelpful to the people who actually have to run the business.

For example, John Kay[4] links Levitt's analysis of the petroleum industry (meeting energy needs, not supplying petrol) to the diversification of oil companies into other energy markets after the 1974 oil strike. The results of this diversification ranged from the disappointing to the disastrous. Few of these activities survive. Oil companies showed little capability for these new areas – they make money by selling oil products, which is what they are good at. Kay argues that Levitt confused industries and markets – washing machines and laundries are in the same market, defined by customer needs to clean clothes, but washing machines and refrigerators are in the same industry, defined as producers of white boxes with motors. Confusing industries and markets is dangerous.

'Confusing industries and markets is dangerous'

Defining core business is about identifying our distinctive skills, resources and capabilities and using these in markets where they give a competitive advantage. This is why Marks and Spencer has done well in financial services (capitalizing on its reputation with customers) while BT has done badly in buying equipment manufacturers (BT is a phone company). The critical issue is whether an activity matches our core capabilities.

---

*I have referred to this case in a lot of speeches and talks over the last couple of years. I used to scoff at the 'dream fulfilment' mission. I stopped after being attacked by a group of very affluent senior managers, who came up to me after my speech and pointed out that the one thing they loved in life was their house and garden – and they would willingly drive hundreds of miles to get to a garden centre which understood their dreams, if only I could tell them where it was! This just goes to show that none of us should forget about finding out what really matters to the customer, before jumping to 'obvious' conclusions!

This said, certainly many companies will tell you that mission analysis was the single most valuable thing they have *ever* done. Indeed, in some organizations, mission analysis has provided the broad logic for divisionalizing and developing strategies for complex businesses in very simple terms.

One well-known example was a UK brewery which undertook mission analysis at the corporate level with the results described below:

The brewery's missions	Organizational and market characteristics	Strategies developed
Drink	A static market leading to a traditional bureaucratic organization driven by the pressure of production efficiency and economies of scale	Compete for market share against competitors by large advertising spends and new brands. Acquire new outlets where possible
Catering	At the time a by-product of being in the business of running public houses	Compete for customer spend by greater variety of food in pubs. Acquire restaurant groups. Acquire hotel groups
Entertainment	Pubs are leisure centres. We have expertise in filling people's social needs	Acquisitions: gaming clubs, gambling machine manufacturers, holiday camps, holiday tour operators, private sports clubs.
Chemicals	The unavoidable by-product of brewing	Strategy of R & D-based collaborations with third parties to exploit the biochemical material for new markets as diverse as blood replacement, fish food and genetic engineering.

In this instance, mission analysis provided an enduring structure (now 20 years old) for developing organizational planning and identifying strategies, on the basis of capabilities in the different customer or user markets to be competed.

At a much more detailed level, mission analysis can certainly provide us with insight into why things have gone wrong. Assessing the failure of a medical clinical diagnostic product (the XYZ test) in the pregnancy healthcare market, which used radioactive-labelled compounds for precise measurement of hormones, and which had been produced by a science-led company in the UK, the following picture emerged:

The *company* saw the market as . . .	the 'XYZ' test market
The *competition* saw the market as . . .	all radioimmunoassay tests (regardless of which substance they measured, because generally in the NHS the patient only gets one test per pregnancy)
The *laboratory* saw the market as . . .	all clinical diagnostic testing, dominated by chromatography (i.e. essentially the sophisticated technology of dipping pieces of chemically-treated paper in urine samples and looking at the degree of colour change)
The *doctor* saw the market as . . .	pregnancy monitoring (the real competition is the traditional 'laying on of hands' by the God-like clinician, and then later high-technology scanning devices that give the doctor, the pregnant patient and proud father-to-be pretty pictures, not graphs and technical measurement data)

The sorts of benefits that this kind of market-based mission analysis can give us are:

● defining the market from the customer's perspective, i.e. the need or problem to be solved, so we get better insight into what matters to the customer;
● mapping out the different types of customer market in which we need to develop different types of market strategies and programmes if we are to be a serious player;
● helping us to see where the real competition is coming from, and where it is going to emerge;
● finding us new areas into which we can develop, where the link to our current business is our customer base and our capabilities.

On this basis, mission analysis can be used productively, but needs to be used with care to avoid some of the stranger conclusions to which I have alluded.

There is another type of mission analysis of which we should be aware – the *key value mission*. This is mission analysis which identifies the key values, goals and constraints that we want people to share in running the business.

This is more about motivation and team-building than defining markets, but it too may have something to offer us. One example of this type of mission analysis was the one-time mission statement for Coca-Cola in the UK, which is '3As':

- Acceptability
- Availability
- Affordability.

The attraction of this is that it tells us snappily and succinctly the things that are most important to the company, which are actually all about protecting the integrity of the Coke brand at all costs (because that is the single resource on which the business relies for survival and success).

A less snappy statement, but fundamental to Lou Gerstner's programme of cultural change at IBM, is the written statement of 'IBM's New Principles' shown in Table 5.1. The goal is to provide a benchmark in the company's attempt to break free from the past and IBM bureaucracy and build customer focus driven by empowered managers.

Table 5.1   IBM's new principles in 1994*

---

1. The marketplace is the driving force behind everything we do.

2. At our core, we are a technology company with an overriding commitment to quality.

3. Our primary measures of success are customer satisfaction and shareholder value.

4. We operate as an entrepreneurial organization with a minimum of bureaucracy and a never-ending focus on productivity.

5. We never lose sight of our strategic vision.

6. We think and act with a sense of urgency.

7. Outstanding, dedicated people make it all happen, particularly when they work together as a team.

8. We are sensitive to the needs of all employees and to the communities in which we operate.

---

*Source: *Wall Street Journal*, 13 May 1994

So, how do we sort out our market mission?

It is clear from the above that mission analysis is potentially confusing and open to abuse – personally I *hate* being asked about mission. Nonetheless, executives show great enthusiasm for building statements of their vision and mission. If we are going to get involved in this analysis as part of building market strategy, then at least let's do it systematically.

The problems seem to be lack of clarity, lack of focus on markets (which is certainly not what Ted Levitt intended) and ambiguity. In fact, what managers say about mission analysis in workshops is things like this:

- the Mission Statements that are produced are qualitative, non-specific, unclear and ambiguous, and so serve little useful purpose in the organization;
- the Mission Statements constructed inevitably seem to represent a trade-off or compromise between the interests of different groups inside and outside the organization – in trying to be 'all things to all people' they end up as largely valueless to anybody;
- to avoid conflict, Mission Statements contain nothing but 'motherhood' – no-one can disagree with what they say, but they have no influence on what people in the organization *do* or *how* they do it;
- Mission Statements are inconsistent – they are self-contradictory in the demands they place upon managers; for example, often in social responsibility imperatives compared to required market position and financial performance;
- Mission Statements are poorly integrated – the different components all make sense on their own, but they look as though they have been produced in isolation, and they are not compatible and lack realism; for example, injunctions from corporate levels to behave in ways that ignore market and competitive realities;
- Mission Statements try unsuccessfully to encompass everything, rather than recognizing market and SBU differences;
- Mission Statements are so 'visionary' that they lose touch with reality in the organization and the marketplace, and have no credibility with line managers – the 'Field of Dreams' approach to mission; and
- Mission Statements are produced that are inward-looking and historically-based, when we desperately need to be market-focused and future-oriented.

These statements are simply compiled from managers' reactions to the mission issue in planning workshops and similar venues. Such comments suggest a pathology of mission in practice, or simply that the reality of the implementation of mission analysis may not be all that is promised by the conventional literature. We should be able to do better than this.

Structuring mission content

Views about the desirable content of Mission Statements are many and varied. However, we can distinguish four major areas of development:

'Views about the desirable content of Mission Statements are many and varied'

- statements relating to *organizational philosophy*;
- the specification of the *product-market domain* or scope for the organization;
- definition of *organizational key values* for participants; and
- the identification of *critical success factors* in the marketplace or industry faced.

These issues vary in *focus* – internal or external – and *scope* – broad and narrow, as shown in Figure 5.4.

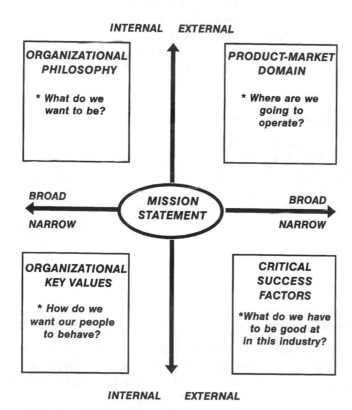

Figure 5.4   A model of mission

Organizational philosophy

Many views suggest that at the centre of mission lies the definition of the central purpose, or philosophy of the organization, or even creating a form of 'corporate constitution'. Some see this area as encompassing the broad issues: the grand design, quality orientation and atmosphere of the enterprise, and the firm's role in society, or the combination of managerial culture and ethos with social responsibility and public image. More focused perspectives emphasize specific service to internal and external stakeholders, and the identification of values, beliefs, guidelines, aspirations, and thus the creation of a unifying force in the organization. In the simplest terms, the underlying question here is: 'What do we want this organization to *be* and to *stand for?*'

Product-market domain

Others look to mission to define where the organization is to operate, which is shifting from a focus on internal to external issues: the definition of the customer base, the product/service offering, location or geographic coverage, and the core technologies or capability to be exploited. In the simplest terms, the central question to be addressed here is: '*Where* are we going to compete', or 'What is our *field of operation* and what are our *core capabilities?*'

Organizational key values

This relates to ideas about defining the core values or principles which provide guides to action for members of the organization, or the 'policies and behaviour that underpin the distinctive competence and value system'. Some see this area as building corporate culture and 'selling' corporate beliefs to employees, or motivating employees to achieve the organization's objectives, and even providing the basis for appraisal and reward. In the simplest terms, the central question here is: 'What do we want people in this organization to be *good at*, and how do we want them to *behave?*'

Critical success factors

Less easily identified in the traditional approach are suggestions about the external impact of mission. These are taken here as the identification of critical success factors in the market or industry faced. In the simplest terms, the central issue here is: 'What do we have to be *good at* to *succeed* in this market or industry?'

**Are the External
Dimensions Covered?**

Yes   No

		Yes	Global Mission	Organizational Mission

**Are the
Internal
Dimensions
Covered?**

	No	Market Mission	No Mission

Figure 5.5   Types of mission statement

This structuring of issues suggests that there are several possible types of Mission Statement, reflecting the internal/external and broad/narrow dimensions of mission, as suggested in Figure 5.5. The suggestion is that if all the dimensions are covered by our mission analysis, then we may consider that we have a *Global Mission Statement*. On the other hand, a view of mission that is concerned only with beliefs, philosophy and internal values can be labelled an *Organizational Mission Statement*. However, where analysis leads to a view of mission that is dominated by defining the market base and critical success factors in the marketplace, this may be seen as a *Market Mission Statement*. Of course, a Mission Statement in which we can find no sign of internal value or external domain is really *No Mission*. Our interest here is in market mission – though extending to the consistency of market mission with internal organizational issues.

Analysing Mission Statements

We can use the structures in Figures 5.4 and 5.5 as a diagnostic tool to confront the mission issue in organizations, either in building a Mission Statement for the first time, or in evaluating an existing statement. The procedure is:

- Summarize the key points of our existing or proposed new Mission Statement. For a new Mission Statement this may mean brainstorming and information gathering, while for the testing of an existing Mission Statement it may be more a process of extracting the key points from the available documentation.

- From those key points, identify the following dimensions of mission: *Organizational philosophy* – what do we see as the enduring purpose of our organization, its unique characteristics, and what it wants to achieve?; *Product-market domain* – where do we intend to operate and compete, what are our products, what needs do they meet, who are our customers, what technologies will we apply, what are the boundaries of our markets, what are our core capabilities?; *Organizational key values* – what values, norms, guidelines, do we think are important in our organization, what things do we want people to have in their minds when they make decisions and carry things out for us?; *Critical success factors* – what things do we have to be good at to survive and prosper in our marketplace?

- Using the structure in Figure 5.4, look at the consistency between the different parts of our mission: do the critical success factors derived from the mission actually make any sense in terms of the product markets the organization has chosen – or are we trying to be good at things that don't matter? Does the organization's 'philosophy' relate to the key values we try to transmit to people who make decisions in the organization, or are there inherent conflicts because we have not thought things through enough? Do these key values (services, quality, social responsibilities, or whatever) relate directly to the critical success factors in these product markets – or do our internal values have nothing to do with what matters in the marketplace? Has the organization chosen sensible product markets where its philosophy or sense of purpose makes sense? If we work through this process, what conclusions can we reach about: the adequacy of our mission statement; the consistency between internal issues of philosophy and key values and external issues of product-market domain and critical success factors?

- Our conclusions may lead us to revise what we want to reflect in our Mission Statement, or to revise the draft Mission Statement. The critical requirement is to move backwards and forwards between these stages – discussing, revising, testing, re-thinking – until we can move from the draft Mission Statement to the final version.

- Finally, we can test our Mission Statement in the way suggested in Figure 5.6, with our managers, our employees, our shareholders, our customers and our suppliers.

Give a score to the Mission Statement for each of the following questions

Score
0 = very poor
5 = medium
10 = excellent

1.	Does the mission statement make it clear what the organization stands for and why it exists?	
2.	Does the mission statement make it clear where we have to compete and who are our customers?	
3.	Does the mission statement tell us the values we should adhere to in working for this organization?	
4.	Does the mission statement make it clear what we have to be good at to survive and prosper?	
5.	Do the different parts of the mission statement hang together - does it make sense?	
6.	Is the mission statement short enough so that people can understand it?	
7.	Is the mission statement well-written enough so that people will remember it?	
8.	Is the mission statement believable as a view of what this organization is all about?	
9.	Is the mission statement challenging and exciting - will it motivate us?	
10.	Does the mission statement tell us what we should be doing and what we should not be doing?	
	TOTAL	
	Conclusions/Implications	

Figure 5.6   Testing mission statements

If nothing else, a systematic structural analysis of the mission issue takes us forward from the vague, open-ended waffle that some executives produce. Experience in testing this approach in-company suggests it can be a good way to find out if there is anything useful here to build market strategy, and to highlight the process of matching our core capabilities with our internal values and with the critical success factors we need outside. In fact, if we regard our company's reputation as an important marketing asset – customer judgements about our philosophy and values may be important in the marketplace as well (see pp. 214–15 below) – crudely being seen as ethical and socially responsible may have a marketplace value.

However, we keep using the words 'core capabilities' and 'competitive advantage' and 'competitive differentiation'. These need much more clarification in progressing the development of market strategy.

Competitive differentiation and positioning

One of the more difficult issues on which to work with companies is that of *competitive differentiation*, and the result that it achieves in positioning one company's offering as distinctive in the customer's judgement – and hopefully, in the target customer's eyes, better and preferable to the alternatives. These words seem to be ones which create problems for executives, perhaps because they sound like vague theoretical notions. Competitive differentiation and positioning are neither vague nor academic; they are about delivering what the customer values, to get the results we want, and to do this we have to find and exploit our core capabilities.

Competitive differentiation

The best-known approach to simplifying this issue is that provided by Michael Porter of Harvard Business School [5]. Porter tells us that in spite of the apparent complexity of competitive strategy there are two, and only two, sources of competitive advantage: low cost and differentiation. This leads to the identification of three generic strategies, as in Figure 5.7. Porter's view of our competitive choice is that we can compete on a broad or narrow scope (in the same way as we have already discussed segmentation), but that we are then either a *price leader* or a *differentiator*.

The two most relevant points from Porter's work for our present purposes are: first, we should think in terms of our *own* competitive strategy type (to avoid the danger of becoming a 'stuck in the middle' firm which is weak and vulnerable because it is neither one thing nor the other – neither a differentiator nor a price leader); and second, we can use the structure to see how groups of our competitors are positioned in terms of their strategies – i.e. what are the 'strategic groups' and how well these groups perform.

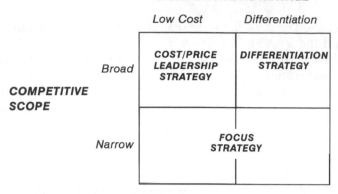

Figure 5.7   Porter's generic strategies

For instance, we might be able to break the complex market for personal writing instruments into:

- *Broad scope/Price leadership* – throw-away ball-point pens, generics;
- *Broad scope/Differentiators* – mass-market brands, Parker, Schaeffer, etc., differentiated by branding, design, packaging, and so on;
- *Narrow scope/Price leadership* – own-label pens, badged hotel pens, etc.;
- *Narrow scope/Differentiators* – exclusive brands like Cross, Mont Blanc, etc.

It is often very revealing of the reality of what works competitively and what doesn't (i.e. what value means to different customers) to try this simple way of reducing a complex competitive market to a few basic groups. However, this leaves untouched the question of *how* differentiation can be achieved.

Porter is adamant that differentiation must be added to operational efficiency if we are to perform well:

'differentiation must be added to operational efficiency if we are to perform well'

A company can outperform rivals only if it can establish a difference that it can preserve. It must deliver greater value to customers or create comparable value at a lower cost, or do both. The arithmetic of superior profitability then follows: delivering greater value allows a company to charge higher unit prices; greater efficiency results in lower average unit costs. [6]

This comment is important, and raises three significant questions for us in building a market strategy:

- What differences can we establish or exploit between ourselves and the others in this market?
- In what ways do these represent superior value to all or some of our customers in this market?
- Can we sustain this form of differentiation and defend it against 'me-too' imitation by existing or new competitors?

One of the problems we face is that in many markets the spread of approaches like benchmarking, 'best practice', shared technology and distribution drives out real differentiation between competing firms and products. Superficial differentiation of products and services that are essentially identical does not fool customers indefinitely (if at all):

- as the manufacturers of vacuum cleaners found when confronted by Dyson (see pp. 170–71 for the story);
- as the UK car manufacturers discovered when outflanked by Daewoo (see pp. 530–40); and
- as the Andrex brand of toilet paper discovered in the UK – the emotion-tugging Labrador puppy in the TV advertising could only hold prices high for so long, he had a cuddly and soft underbelly wide open to attack from rivals offering better value. In 1996 alone the brand lost a third of its market share;
- indeed, consider the spectacular market success achieved by Direct Line. This operation pioneered telephone-based selling of insurance products with the effect of transforming standards as to how insurance is sold in Britain, drastically reducing the prices of policies and stunning the traditional competitors, and yet by mid-1997 this operation had dropped into a loss-making position. Virtually every competitor can imitate telephone selling, and after recovering from the initial shell-shock, this is exactly what they have done.

The issue is real differences that matter to customers – which we can sustain.

Porter's argument is that if competitive strategy is about being different, then the essence is positioning ourselves by choosing to perform activities differently, or choosing to perform different activities than our rivals. For example, all banks and insurance companies offer the same products (as far as customers are concerned), but First Direct and Direct Line introduced direct marketing, compared to conventional branch networks and face-to-face selling. On the other hand, IKEA is differentiated from conventional furniture stores by substituting self-service for personal selling and having customers do their own pick-up and delivery.

The logic is that competition can be seen as 'the process of perceiving new positions that woo customers from established positions or draw new customers into the market' [6], and in this sense it is highly entrepreneurial. Strategic positions are suggested to come from three distinct sources:

- *Variety-based positioning* – producing a specialized sub-set of an industry's products or services. For example, Kwik Fit replaces car exhausts, batteries and tyres, but does not offer general repairs and servicing. Conversely, HFS Inc in the USA has achieved market success by offering the home-buyer and business traveller 'one-stop shopping' – it links car hire, hotels, estate agencies and residential renting into one product.
- *Need-based positioning* – targeting a particular group of customers, for example in exclusive private banking, or in home furnishings by specialized firms like IKEA and Habitat.
- *Access-based positioning* – where customers differ on the best way of reaching them. For example, the rural cinema company Carmike provides small cinema services tailored to the needs of rural communities, or First Direct's 24–hour telephone banking service in the UK reaches those who work through conventional banking hours.

In broad terms, this asks us to choose: are we a product specialist or a customer specialist? To test that out in real terms for your own business, go back to the Product–Customer Matrix (Figure 4.4), look at each cell in the matrix and ask: Will we achieve better results by taking our existing product/service to new customer types, or by adding new products/services to what we sell to existing customers? Or, do we aim to sell more existing products to existing customers (grow within the cell)? This quickly highlights what we believe to be our greatest competitive strength.

Porter also points out that approaching competitive differentiation and positioning in this way only produces a sustainable competitive advantage if two further conditions exist:

- competitors cannot imitate or equal our position with their current operations; and
- the activities needed to support the position we want to take in the market fit to each other and to our capabilities.

In short, this says that for our strategy to be effective, it needs to reflect what we are best at doing – our core capabilities – not what our competitors can do just as well.

Core capabilities

At the broadest level, Prahalad and Hamel[7] give us an interesting view of the 'core competence of the corporation', which we can combine with the model of competitive differentiation and positioning – how can we differentiate effectively if we do not understand our capabilities? But we can then focus on the issue of value to the customer, and the marketing assets we have at our disposal to create the value which underpins competitive positioning.

In a widely-admired *Harvard Business Review* article in 1990, C.K. Prahalad and Gary Hamel examined the characteristics of companies that have succeeded in inventing new markets, quickly entering new markets and dramatically shifting patterns of customer choices in established markets. They concluded that the common characteristic is that these companies understand, exploit, invest to create, and sustain core competences. Examples include:

- *Sony* – the capacity to miniaturize;
- *Philips* – optical-media expertise;
- *Citicorp* – competence in systems;
- *3M* – competence with sticky tape;
- *Black and Decker* – expertise with small electrical motors;
- *Canon* – skills in optics, imaging and microprocessors;
- *Casio* – competence in display systems.

They see these as the most basic corporate resources, which lead to success in apparently diverse markets and products, and suggest that even the largest company is unlikely to have more than five or six core competences.

For example, the transformation of Rentokil in the UK from a pest control business into a diversified services company has been achieved through a radical focus on the company's core competence: 'the ability to carry out high-quality services (from pest control through healthcare to manned guarding) on other people's premises through well-recruited, well-trained and well-motivated people' [8].

This view of core capabilities can be combined with our earlier view of competitive differentiation and positioning in the way suggested in Figure 5.8. This suggests that the underlying

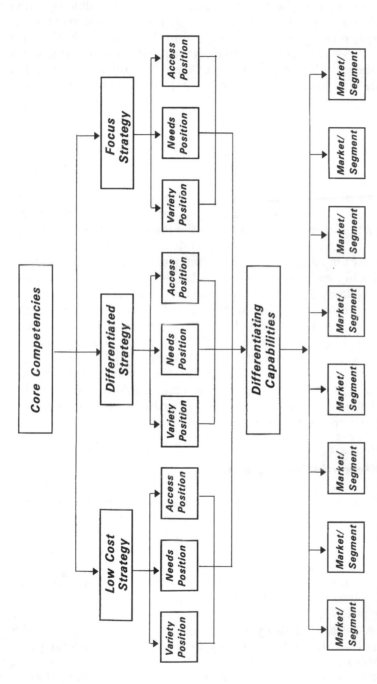

Figure 5.8 Corporate differentiation and core competences

corporate issue is 'core competencies' – what this company is best at. This leads to the generic strategies of low cost, differentiation and focus, and the potential for positioning within each of these is based on variety, needs and access. But this leads to a further idea which takes us from corporate issues to market strategy – *Differentiating capabilities*. This turns our attention from broad corporate competencies and strategies to a more specific issue – at the level of the market, segment and customer, which of our capabilities or competencies create value for a customer, around which we can build a sustainable market strategy?

'at the level of the market, segment and customer, which of our capabilities or competences create value for a customer, around which we can build a sustainable market strategy?'

It is worth bearing in mind that a company's core competences may *not* produce differentiating capabilities at the market or customer level. For instance, IBM built an amazingly strong position in the world computer market – in the mid-1980s IBM had 40 per cent of the industry's entire worldwide sales and 70 per cent of all profits. The core competence at IBM was 'big iron' – dealing with big customers and big computers. As the market moved towards the personal computer, IBM was poorly positioned to compete – basically smaller suppliers dealing with smaller customers ran rings around IBM. The strategy under John Akers of attacking Microsoft and Intel was a failure. The most critical IBM core competence gave little differentiating capability in the PC market. In fact, the company has been turned around by Lou Gerstner in the 1990s by his vision for an IBM Global Network – global networking requires IBM's expertise in 'big iron'. This area exploits IBM's most basic core competence [9].

Differentiating capabilities

Differentiating capabilities put together the theories of differentiation and core competences in a specific market. At this level, our concern is when we have to build a market position – what competitive differentiation can we use to create value for a customer in this market or segment?

We need to think very hard about which of our company's core capabilities are valuable to us in a particular market:

- Does this capability create value for the customer in this market? If not, it is of no use to us in developing a strategy for this market.
- Will competitors find it hard to copy this capability? If every company can do this as well as we can, there is no competitive advantage.

- What is the probable duration of the uniqueness? How long have we got before the competition can catch us up?
- Who is the primary beneficiary of the capability? Does it relate to particular segments of the market on which we should focus?
- Does another capability satisfy the same market need? Do we face competition from substitution?
- Is the capability we believe we have really superior to the competition, or are we kidding ourselves? [10]

In the real world, competing on capabilities is a moving target.

However, perhaps the greatest single barrier to getting market strategy to work effectively is the fact that many executives will tell you that in their business the market is a *commodity* market, and consequently the only thing that matters is price and product specification. The reality is, of course, that price and product specifications *do* matter in most markets, but anything and everything can be differentiated. This may sound preposterous, but let us consider it for a moment.

Tom Peters [11] uses the example of the launderette, turned by one company into a fast-growing success story by twinning it with the wine-bar under the slogan: 'Enjoy Our Suds While You Wash Your Duds'. Theodore Levitt [12] has taken examples of basic chemicals like isopropanol, an undifferentiated chemical, and shown large variations in the prices paid by customers in the same market at the same time.

On the other hand, the retail bookselling business in Britain has been traumatized by the abandonment of price protection (the end of the Net Books Agreement) and the entry of multiple supermarkets as discount book retailers. Much of the traditional industry was prepared to simply curl up and die. Waterstones has in 1997 opened a massive new flagship store in Glasgow which fights off price competition with a highly differentiated offering to customers that exploits the company's strength and delights its customers. The differentiation is not based on outside research but the 'market sensing' of a team of six 'advocates' – senior managers who brainstormed ideas about what sells books and toured the world for new ideas. They defined six key qualities that a bookshop needs to offer its customers: friendliness, service, excitement, generosity, community commitment, and an appealing combination of space, comfort and atmosphere, termed 'browsability' – they say: 'Everybody wants to sit down and read the book they have purchased right away', so this is the kind of bookstore they provide. This provides a highly differentiated market position which discount retailers cannot emulate. [13]

People in the oil business believe they are in a commodity market. An interesting game to play with oil company executives is to challenge them to conceive of a situation where it would be possible to get a 50p a gallon price premium for petrol from the buyer. (I admit to being motivated by the desire to irritate certain such executives, who appear to have been cloned by the 'Smug Corporation'.) This game normally fails because the oil industry's deeply-ingrained belief is that only price and outlet location matter in selling petrol. Interestingly, it is executives from other industries who observe this dialogue and often admit they actually do not *know* the price of a gallon of petrol, and, since they do not pay for their own petrol on business trips, probably *would* pay a premium price for such things as: preference in queues, delivery of petrol by an attendant, a quick car wash, a 'free' cup of coffee, clean toilets and bathrooms for 'club members' with keys, preferential access to a phone and fax machine, and a few other services that matter to people travelling on business. This may sound outlandish, but consider the proven efficiency of offering truck drivers in the USA a 'free' breakfast in return for their diesel fuel business (which admittedly may amount to several hundred pounds worth of fuel each time, given the size of the trucks), as opposed to conventional price competition. (It is also highly predictable that if anyone does something like this in the UK, it will be a company like Virgin, not the established oil companies!)

Then consider what Tom Farmer has done to the car exhaust and tyre business in the UK. Replacement exhausts and tyres are a 'distress' purchase, which none of us want to make, but we *have* to. Farmer's Kwik Fit operation dominates the UK market and has turned a commodity market into a brand-loyal one – where the loyalty is to Kwik Fit, achieved through a variety of means: an obsession with customer satisfaction; a highly idiosyncratic management structure and approach; a large advertising spend; *and* good price deals.

No-one is saying it is *easy,* or necessarily *cheap,* but with creativity and a simple focus on innovation and novelty in what matters to the customer, there are differentiation opportunities *everywhere.*

At the simplest level, competitive differentiation comes from the three sources identified in Figure 5.9 – the product itself (even if it is a service product); the surround of added-value services which are available (or can be); and a whole set of marketing intangibles (or assets, to which we turn our attention in the next section).

But this leaves open the question: But what sources of competitive differentiation open to us will create *value* for the

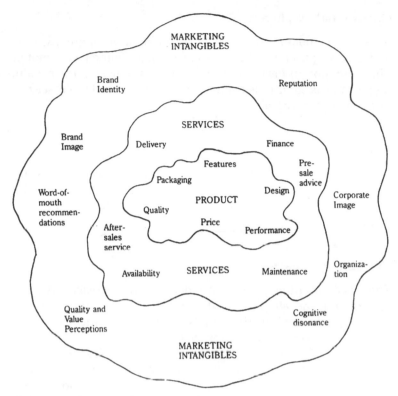

Figure 5.9 Sources of competitive differentiation

customer, and build competitive advantage for us in this market – i.e. what are our differentiating capabilities?

Useful insights into this question came from Treacy and Wiersema's study *The Discipline of Market Leaders* [14]. Their view is that market leaders dominate their chosen areas by achieving the highest value in the customer's eyes in a new world of competition, where:

- different customers buy different types of value – few companies excel at everything, so the issue is one of choosing customers and narrowing the value focus, because market leaders excel in offering a specific dimension of value;
- as value standards rise, so do customer expectations, so you have to improve every year or be outpaced by competitors;
- producing an unmatched level of a particular value requires a superior operating model dedicated to that kind of value.

This leads Treacy and Wiersema to identify the 'value disciplines' followed by market leaders as operational excellence, product leadership, and customer intimacy.

Operational excellence

These are companies that deliver a combination of quality, price and ease of purchase that no-one in their market can match. They are not innovators or relationship-builders; their value proposition is guaranteed low price and/or hassle-free service. Prime examples are discount retailers.

Product leadership

These are the competitors who continually push products and services into the realm of the unknown, the untried, or the highly desirable. Examples of such firms include Intel, Canon and Nike.

Customer intimacy

'at the market level, the leaders choose a value discipline and ruthlessly specialize in it'

The customer-intimate company delivers the message: 'We take care of you and all your needs' or 'We give you the best total solution', in the way that IBM did in the 1960s and 1970s in the computer market.

In the same way that Porter tells us not to be a 'stuck in the middle' company, which is neither low-cost nor differentiated, neither fully broad nor focused in scope, Treacy and Wiersema argue that, at the market level, the leaders choose a value discipline and ruthlessly specialize in it.

Developing a specific value proposition and establishing a value discipline is described by Treacy and Wiersema as three phases.

Phase One: Understanding the status quo

Developing a common understanding of the market based on five fundamental questions:

- What are the dimensions of value that customers care about?
- For each dimension of value, what proportion of customers focus on it as their primary or dominant decision criterion?
- Which competitors provide the best value in each of these value dimensions?
- How do we perform compared to our competitors on each value dimension?
- Why do we fall short of the value leaders on each dimension of value where we perform less well than they do? (We will provide a framework for tackling this in the next section.)

Phase Two: Identifying realistic options

For each dimension of value, we should ask:

- Regardless of industry, what are the benchmark standards of value performance that will affect customer expectations, and how do firms achieve these?
- For the value leaders in this market, what will the standards of performance be in three years' time?
- How are the operations of the value leaders designed to attain these levels of performance?

Phase Three: Design and choices

If we have options for how we would close the gap, then we must ask:

- How will this operating model produce superior value?
- What threshold levels of value will the market require in the other value dimensions, and how will these be attained?
- How large will the market be for this value proposition?
- What is the business case – costs, benefits, risks – for pursuing this option?
- What are the critical success factors that can make or break this value proposition?
- How will the company make the transition?

This choice of value discipline commits the company to a particular Strategic Pathway. Dealing with these questions may force us back to reconsidering how we define and segment the market, and we may not be able to make decisions here until we have worked through issues of marketing assets and the key relationships involved in the strategy.

Nonetheless, the important point at this stage is to force us to confront issues of competencies and capabilities, the scope and form of differential advantage and whether any of this creates value for the customer – because no advantage in customer value equals no strategy.

Competitive mapping

If this all starts getting confusing (and it usually does), then looking systematically at what the various suppliers to a customer market offer and how well they are performing helps. Figures 5.10, 5.11 and 5.12 provide a structure for these comparisons:

- to find out if we can identify important differences between customer groups in their value priorities (Figure 5.10);

- for each important customer group to see how well each competitor performs on each dimension of value (Figure 5.11);
- to see what this produces as a competitive map for this market (Figure 5.12).

Value Dimensions	Customer Groups/Segments*									
	1.	2.	3.	4.	5.	6.	7.	8.	9.	10.
1.										
2.										
3.										
4.										
5.										
6.										
7.										
8.										
9.										
10.										

*** Enter rank of each Value Dimension for each customer group/segment**

Implications

Instructions for Completing Customer Value Matrix

1. Produce a list of the items that produce value for customers in this market – try brainstorming at first but you may need market research inputs. List these on the left of the matrix.

2. List up to 10 customer groups or segments across the top of the matrix – you can take these from the Product-Customer Matrix completed earlier.

3. For each customer group or segment, rank the value dimensions in order of their importance to that type of customer.

4. Compare the customer groups and note the differences in their value priorities. What does this tell us - how different are customers in the value they want to buy, what opportunities does this offer for developing a value proposition for each major customer type?

Figure 5.10 Value priorities for different customer groups

Value Dimensions	Competitors in this Segment*									
	1.	2.	3.	4.	5.	6.	7.	8.	9.	10.
1.										
2.										
3.										
4.										
5.										
6.										
7.										
8.										
9.										
10.										

* Enter performance score out of 10 for each major competitor for each value dimension with this type of customer

Implications

Instructions for Completing Competitor Value Matrix

1. For each important customer group, list the major competitors across the top of the matrix.

2. Enter the value dimensions on the left of the matrix, in order of priority for this type of customer.

3. Rate the performance against each value dimension in turn of each competitor.

4. What does the resulting picture tell us about competitors' strengths and weaknesses, and value dimension where higher performance will create a competitive advantage with this type of customer?

Figure 5.11 Value performances by competitors

Market/Segment/Product/Customer Type:							

		Competitors					
Price Positioning		Us	1	2	3	4	5
Sales £K							
Market Share %							
Prices £							
Prices Index (market average = 100)							
Non-Price Factors	Weight	Scores on Non-Price Factors*					
1							
2							
3							
4							
5							
6							
7							
8							
9							
10							
Total	1.00						
	Averages						

*1 = Very poor on this factor   5 = Average on this factor
10 = Market leader on this factor

Figure 5.12 Mapping the competition

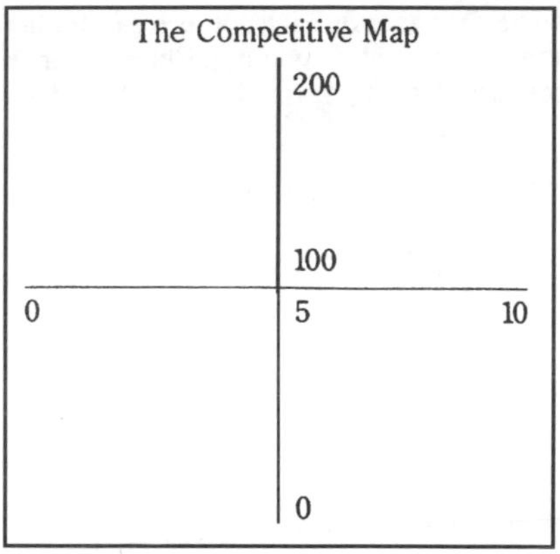

The Competitive Map

200

100

0   5   10

0

Instructions for Completing The Competitive Map

1. Identify which market or segment, which product or customer type, and enter this at the top. All that follows is limited by and to this definition.

2. List the most significant competitors across the top of the form.

3. Estimate the sales to this market by each competitor we have identified, and enter this. Use these figures to calculate the rough market shares (the last category may have to be 'Others' to get to 100% of the market).

4. Enter an indication of prices paid by customers for each competitors' products in the next line. Use these figures and the market share figures to calculate the average market price level, e.g.

	Competitors		
	A	B	C
Sales £K	120	50	30
Market Share %	60	25	15
Prices (£ per unit)	10	15	5
Prices Index (Weighted Market Average = £10.50 = 100)	95	143	48

5. Identify the most significant non-price factor important to customers in the market, list them in order of priority, on the form. You can add weights if you think that some of the factors are much more important than others (but the weights must total to 1).

Figure 5.12 Continued

6. Rate our own performance on each non-price factor in turn, and score out of 10 ourselves and each competitor. Enter either this score, or the weighted score if preferred (the raw score multiplied by the weighting), e.g.

		Competitors					
		A	B	C	A	B	C
Non-Price Factors	*Weight*	*Raw Scores*			*Weighted Scores*		
1. After-sales service	.60	6	9	2	3.6	5.4	1.2
2. Design aesthetics	.20	7	10	3	1.4	2.0	0.6
3. Availability from stock	.10	5	6	8	0.5	0.6	0.8
4. Packaging design	.05	6	5	7	0.3	0.25	0.35
5. Brand image	.05	8	7	2	0.4	0.35	0.10
TOTAL	1.00	32	37	22	6.2	8.6	3.1
AVERAGE		6.4	7.4	4.4			

7. For each competitor we now have a price index (computing the price each charges to the market average) from 4 above; and a score out of 10 on non-price competitive strength from 6 above.

8. Use these scores to locate each competitor on the map, and then draw a circle around each of those points representing the size of each competitor's sales, e.g.

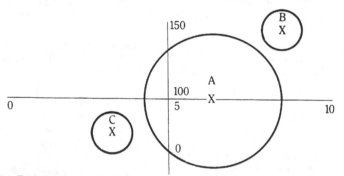

9. Evaluate the resulting map to compare the relative success of price and non-price factors and the impact of non-price factors on prices that can be charged, to see what can be concluded about the sources of competition in this market.

Figure 5.12   Continued

Looking at competitive differentiation and positioning should have involved us in some painful soul-searching about our core competences and capabilities, our strategic positioning options and the route to achieving higher value for a target customer through our differentiating capabilities.

However, we cannot finalize our views on competitive differentiation and positioning without examining also our available marketing assets, and brands in particular.

Marketing assets and brands

As we move from corporate issues like core competences and strategic position to asking what we have got that can create value for a customer in our market, it is often useful to ask what *marketing assets* we have (and in some cases, as we will see, *marketing liabilities*). Marketing assets refers to all those intangibles which may impact on the customer's perception of us and our products and services. This includes our history, our reputation, our expertise and, perhaps most importantly, our brands. We will review marketing assets generally, but then focus on branding.

One way of underlining the importance of recognizing marketing assets is in Hugh Davidson's view of *asset-based marketing* shown in Figure 5.13, and contrasted with the more traditional concept of marketing [15]. The point of this is that it emphasizes the need to look for how we exploit more effectively what we've got (our assets), but to constantly balance this with customer

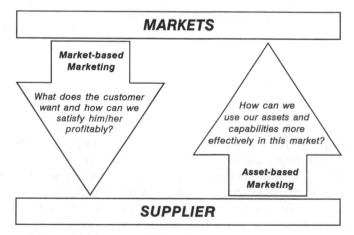

Figure 5.13 Asset-based marketing

satisfaction demands. Life is a constant balancing act – we iterate around these issues until we find a balance or match that achieves what we want (or as much as we can get) by giving target customers what they want (or as much as we can give them).

This is a nice way of summarizing the matching problem, but brings us inevitably to the difficult issue of marketing assets. What do we mean by marketing assets? In fact, these are revenue, and income generating resources of the business, which normally cost us a small fortune to create and maintain, and which probably distinguish between the winners and the losers in most markets. However, marketing assets are a bit of a problem for three reasons: they are *intangible*; most businesses do not place any *accounting value* on them (or if they do, it is written off as quickly as possible as 'goodwill'); accordingly, they are almost impossible to *monitor* or even to measure in most conventional management accounting systems.

What are marketing assets?

There is no accepted framework for listing marketing assets, but we can make a start by thinking about:

- our differentiating capabilities;
- our customer relationships;
- our channel power;
- our company reputation; and
- our brands.

Differentiating capabilities were discussed earlier (see pp. 200–11) as our cutting edge in the marketplace that grows out of our core corporate competences and our strategic positioning choices. The test for whether something is a differentiating capability is simple – does it use our resources to give us an advantage over the competitor in the customer's eyes? Examples of what this can mean in practice include:

- Singapore Airlines – while performing a great many commercial air transportation functions well, is widely acknowledged as the industry leader in *customer service delivery.*
- Amersham International – a specialized producer of radioactive and related products for medical diagnosis and treatment, is renowned for its R&D and new product development, but has a *logistics system* that can process orders for radioactive products instantly and deliver them safely and quickly to

locations anywhere in the world. With products that are decaying from the moment of production, where the documentation needed to take such materials across national boundaries is fiendish, and where the doctor needs the product tomorrow at the latest, Amersham's expensive expertise in logistics gives a unique competitive advantage from the customer's point of view.

- Intuit's 'Quicken' personal finance software dominates the market because this company's culture and organizational processes are totally connected to making the product so *customer-friendly* that anyone can use it (see below for more information about how they do it, and put to shame so many other software producers).

Customer relationships provide a marketing asset, in the sense that loyalty and trust give us the ability to defend market share and open up new markets. Perhaps the prime example is Marks and Spencer – dominating the High Street merchandising of middle-of-the-market clothes, but exploiting its unique position in the customer's mind to move into food, wines, furniture and financial services.

Channel power concerns our dominance or weakness in the distribution channel – our market share in key outlets and share of shelf space in supermarkets for consumer-packaged products. If this does not sound important, consider the following case.

Mars launched the Mars Ice-Cream bar (in fact, an obscenely wonderful product) as a major new market entry. The product created a new quality threshold – it turned a child's treat into an adult indulgence. The strategy of turning chocolate bars into ice creams has been imitated by countless competitors. However, Mars lost money on this product. The reason – Unilever-owned Walls, the market leader, *owns* the distribution channel that matters: it has a stranglehold on impulse buying outlets like local newsagents. Walls literally owns the freezers in these outlets and does not allow other manufacturers shelf space. With the best branding and marketing communications in the world, Mars cannot compete effectively in this market because it does not have the critical marketing asset in distribution needed to succeed [16].

Market information can be a critical marketing asset, in the sense that being able to understand the market or customer better and to respond faster and more effectively to customer demands creates competitive advantage. We discuss organizational learning and the importance of superior 'market sensing' in Chapter 9, but to underline the point about information as a

'being able to understand the market or customer better and to respond faster and more effectively'

marketing asset, consider the customer databases now being built by companies like Tesco and Sainsbury through their loyalty card schemes or through the direct marketing by Virgin Direct in financial services (and it is better quality information too – you may describe yourself as named Santa Claus, aged 102 and of a hermaphrodite inclination in yet another nosy and intrusive questionnaire, but not to people you buy your pension from!). Or consider the scenario below and ask where the competitive advantage comes from:

> Check into any Ritz-Carlton hotel anywhere in the world and you will be greeted not only by the doorman, but also by a number of small, pleasant surprises. The hotel does not need to ask the name of your employer, your home address, whether you want a non-smoking room, or if your preference is for a non-allergenic pillow. All this information was obtained during your previous visit to the Ritz-Carlton ... you sense that the hotel staff is somehow able to anticipate and respond to your every need, providing you with a feeling of satisfaction that comes from being among people who care about you as an individual. 'Why would I ever stay anywhere else?' you wonder. [17]

Company reputation has always been recognized as a marketing asset (or liability). As buyers become more sophisticated and judgemental this is becoming an even more significant factor – the company's reputation may impact very directly on brand value for customers. For example, British Gas's entry into the financial services market with its Goldfish card represents the use of corporate reputation and identity to open up a new market opportunity.

The impact of company reputation on brand value is far more important than the endless (and boring) debate about corporate logos and headed notepaper. (This said, it is true that companies like BP, Shell, Coca-Cola, Apple, Orange and Nike *do* have clear, concise, constantly recognizable identities that reflect core brand values, while the same cannot be said for companies like British Aerospace, Grand Metropolitan, the City institutions and most pharmaceutical companies [18].)

However, what started off with concern about a company's reputation for service, value and quality has now become involved with what customers think about our ethics and environmental responsibility.

An Ogilvy & Mather survey in 1996 contrasts the views of consumers of some companies as 'efficient bastards' compared to the 'Mr Cleans' at the other end of the scale. The top end of the ethical chain in consumers' eyes was represented by companies like Marks and Spencer, Boots, Virgin Atlantic, Cadbury and Body Shop. At the other end were Camelot (the National Lottery company), *The Sun*, Yorkshire Water, William Hill, Ladbrokes and Sky TV [19].

Add to this suggestions that customers may be reluctant to deal with companies they perceive as unethical and we may have a problem – one recent survey suggested that 55 per cent of consumers would not deal with a company if they disliked its ethics. Being seen as a 'good corporate citizen' may be a substantial asset that impacts on competitiveness and opens up new opportunities [20].

For example, the Co-Op Bank has a reputation described variously as 'cuddly' or 'woolly'. However, the bank has grown significantly with its 'ethical banking policy' – no investments or loans to companies that transgress its standards of ethical business practice, and a £10 payment to customers to say 'sorry' for mistakes in accounts. This is a source of competitive differentiation against other banks, which matters to their customers.

The Centre for Tomorrow's Company has pioneered a 'stakeholder approach' to make social and ethical responsibilities even more explicit (see pp. 16–17). A final word – the evidence is that these issues matter far more to customers than executives think. There is the prospect of nasty surprises here for the unwary [21].

Perhaps the most widely-recognized marketing asset is the *brand*. Let's open this up as a separate issue, for two reasons: branding is critically important in its own right in many markets, but also it provides a model for the other intangible marketing assets in our portfolio.

Brands and branding

Everyone talks brands these days – the company as the brand (e.g. Tesco), the product as the brand (e.g. the Mars bar), the person as the brand (e.g. Richard Branson), the customer as the brand (yes, we'll come back to that one). This is an important issue to sort out in building our market strategy. Let us look at the following questions:

- different types of branding that occur, and what the 'top brands' are;
- why branding remains important to market strategy;
- the issue of brand extension strategies, and whether they work; and
- the future of the brand as a central part of market strategy.

Types of branding and the big brands

Perhaps the first point is, if you want to know what branding is, *never* ask someone from an advertising agency, unless you like lectures on the philosophy of meaning and have plenty of time. The simplest explanation of a brand was Stephen King's view that: 'A product is something that is made in a factory. A brand is something that is bought by a customer.' In other words, the brand is the 'core identity' we are selling. Advertising people like to talk about the 'brand personality' and to give brands human identities – Martini and Coke as 'extrovert' brands that want you to join in, but Timotei shampoo as an 'introvert' brand saying shyly 'You can come to me if you want' [22]. There is much talk of the 'soul' of the brand. (Or, as Dilbert would say: 'Isn't it amazing we actually get paid for doing this'! – Now look, I have been very serious and well-behaved so far this chapter, but there are limits!)

Brand strategy is frequently associated with 'creativity' and advertising-based positioning, and, not surprisingly, comes largely out of consultancies and advertising agencies. For example, Anthony Freeling of McKinseys identifies seven models for creative brand strategy:

- *Classic FMCG* – the fast-moving consumer good route based on large advertising spend, and practised by companies like Procter and Gamble, Mars, Kraft and Unilever;
- *The Enticer* – frequent changes to product, price and promotion are made to generate constant excitement for the consumer, as used by major retailers and consumer electronics companies;
- *The Individualist* – building sales one at a time, through close personal dialogue with individual consumers, as attempted widely in the financial services market;
- *Transparent Marketers* – whose unique selling point is their honesty about how the market works, for example, Daewoo in the car market;
- *Monogamists* – who try to build lifetime relationships with special customers, such as the British Airways customer loyalty approach;
- *Benefit Unbundlers* – who over-deliver on what matters most to their customers, but strip out the rest, making consumers a 'partner in value delivery', as with IKEA in furniture where the customer has to pack, transport and assemble the furniture; and
- *The Helpful Brand* – which endears itself to customers by delivering quality and minimizing the time and hassle of shopping. For example, Lexus has bundled up manufacturing with service and repair, and claims to be 'an integrated personal transport package', not just a car brand [23].

Yes, well . . . if nothing else, this does firmly underline the link between brand and value proposition (and let's be charitable, even McKinsey consultants have to make a living).

A more basic view of different types of branding is illustrated in Table 5.2, reflecting differences in company and product brand identities for products. Much debate occurs on the relative merits of individual brands versus company brands and the implications for risk and brand extension. This is very boring.

Table 5.2 Types of branding*

Type of branding strategy	Examples
1. *Company brand* – the company is the brand name	Heinz Baked Beans ICI Polyurethane
2. *Umbrella branding* – the company name and product name identify the product	Ford Escort – company name plus sub-brand name Sainsbury's Novon and Gio products Kellogg's Cornflakes
3. *Linked branding* – the brand name leads, but is linked to the company	Kit Kat – chocolate bars, endorsed by Nestlé
4. *Range branding* – Product 'families' with different branding	Matsushita electronics products – National, Panasonic, Technics and Quasar brands
5. *Product brand*	Silk Cut cigarettes Persil detergent

* Source: Adapted from Mihailovic, P. and de Chernatony, L. (1994), 'Brand Bonding', *Marketing Business*, October, 31–4

More interesting is the concept that the customer *becomes* the brand. If I sit here typing onto a Virgin computer disk, while the computer's CD-ROM plays the Spice Girls on the Virgin CD purchased from a Virgin Megastore, wearing my Virgin jeans, smelling of my Virgin deodorant, occasionally sipping my Virgin vodka mixed with Virgin cola, while fantasizing about my forthcoming Virgin flight to the USA, secure in the knowledge that Virgin Direct is safeguarding my insurance needs and pension requirements, then who or what is the brand? Virgin or Richard Branson? Or me? Certainly more of our thinking should be directed to share of *customer* rather than share of market achieved by a brand.

> *'More interesting is the concept that the customer becomes the brand'*

However, the reality is that currently most of our thinking about brands is dominated by the big brands. Table 5.3 lists the Top Ten Brands identified by Interbrand in 1996 [24]. This list significantly represented the overtaking of Coke by McDonalds for the first time, which has attracted much comment about the growing importance of corporate brands compared to product brands. The highest-placed British brand on the Interbrand list was The Body Shop, placed 36th. Other notable placings were: Heinz (30th), Harrods (41st), *Time Magazine* (46th), the BBC (50th) and Virgin (91st).

I am all in favour of a law which says that all advertising agency personnel must learn this list off by heart, and their salaries will be based wholly on the accuracy of their recall (mainly because it would keep them out of our way for a substantial period of time). Other than this very useful contribution, such lists are no more than a hopeless conceit. They tell us nothing about the real power of a brand, its 'stretchability' into new products, the significance of 'widget' brands like Dolby sound or Nicam stereo components of music and video systems, they ignore the niche characteristics of brands like Virgin, they tell us nothing about branding as a barrier to market entry, and they exclude the importance of brands or products bought mainly by industry or business – photocopiers, industrial machines, and so on.

Top brand lists have amusement value only – they are self-selecting by virtue of the ranking criteria anyway (see Table 5.3).

Table 5.3   The top ten brands in 1990 and 1996*

Rank**	1996	1990
1.	McDonalds	Coca-Cola
2.	Coca-Cola	Kellogg
3.	Disney	McDonalds
4.	Kodak	Kodak
5.	Sony	Marlboro
6.	Gillette	IBM
7.	Mercedes Benz	American Express
8.	Levi's	Sony
9.	Microsoft	Mercedes Benz
10.	Marlboro	Nescafé

* Source: Interbrand [21]
** Ranking based on: (1) Weight – dominance of the market;
(2) Length – extension into other markets; (3) Breadth –
approval across age, religion, or other divides; and (4) Depth –
customer commitment

Besides which, there are major difficulties in establishing new brands in existing markets. If you look at the top 50 grocery brands in the UK, very few are new:

4 – launched when Queen Victoria was on the throne
16 – launched between 1900 and 1950
21 – launched between 1950 and 1975 (including the impact of the launch of commercial television in the UK)
9 – launched since 1975

This means that more than 80 per cent of Britain's top grocery brands are more than 20 years old. A somewhat less than dynamic rate of change and innovation.

Why branding is strategy

So why do we need to think about branding in developing a market strategy? Because *brands add value* in the consumer's eyes. Consider how else we could explain the following cases:

- *Coke versus Pepsi* – A panel of consumers was asked to taste samples of Coke and Pepsi – half in *blind tests* (they did not know the brand identities) and half in *open tests* (they could see the containers, the packaging, the logos, so knew which brand was which). In the blind test, 51 per cent preferred Pepsi and 44 per cent preferred Coke. In the open test, 65 per cent preferred Coke and only 23 per cent preferred Pepsi. There are few more literal illustrations of the power of the brand in adding to value in the customer's eyes [25].
- *Toyota versus General Motors* – In Fremont, California, a joint venture factory produces two virtually identical cars, but one is branded as the Toyota Corolla and the other as the GM Geo Prism. Both cars cost $10,300 to manufacture. In the US car marketplace, the Toyota Corolla sells at a 10 per cent higher price than the GM Geo Prism, holds its value better (so after five years the Toyota trades in for 18 per cent more than the GM), and its market share is twice that of the Geo Prism. It is estimated that Toyota made $128 million more profit than GM from the joint venture. The Toyota brand simply adds more customer value to the product [26].
- *The Savoy Hotel* – In 1997 a letter arrived in the UK from the Czech Republic addressed simply: 'The Manager, the Greatest Hotel in London'. The Royal Mail wrote on the front: 'Try

Savoy Hotel, WC2'. That envelope is now the basis for Savoy Group advertising in the USA!

● *Heinz Baked Beans* – An old brand, something of a cliché, Heinz Baked Beans survived a grocery price war in 1996, when some of the supermarkets own-label beans were priced as low as 3p a can. The power of this brand is such that not only did Heinz customers stay loyal while paying prices nine times higher than the own-labels, the company was actually able to *increase* its price in the same period. In this whole price war, Heinz saw sales revenue dip only by 4 per cent.

Quite simply, brands can *transform markets*, and change competitive structures, because they change how customers look at products, services and suppliers. Consider the following illustrations:

● *Financial services* – The financial services sector in Britain – banks, insurance companies, etc. – has been characterized for years by very weak branding. The words Provident, Perpetual or Scottish may imply thriftiness, but no distinct brand personality or positioning. Virgin Direct, The Sainsbury Bank (and some others) have been able to take market share in this sector quickly and cheaply by exploiting their brand strength, and the existing players are largely powerless to prevent this. Branding can be a major barrier to entry by new competitors – or not, as the case may be.

● *Cola wars* – In 1996 Pepsi changed its package colour and design from red to blue at the cost of some $500 million, to deliver more impact for the brand and to differentiate more effectively from its stronger rival, Coke. Coke fought back with a $500 million advertising spend. The products are heavily reliant on image-based advertising – Coke standing for 'America and friendship' and Pepsi as 'California and youth'. Competition between the two companies is fierce and unrelenting. They will do anything to gain or defend market share. Anything, that is, except one thing – they will *never* get into a price-cutting war with each other. They tried this in the 1930s and the early 1990s and did not like it. This makes both players vulnerable to new entrants who *will* compete on price. In the UK this attack has been by Virgin Cola and Sainsbury Cola, both supplied by the Cott company in Canada. Taylor Nelson AGB figures show that in 1993 Coke held 55.2 per cent of the British market and Pepsi 19.8 per cent. By 1995 Coke was down to 42.9 per cent and Pepsi to 16 per cent. In 1996 the combined Coke and Pepsi consumer share was down to 65 per cent, with Virgin taking

7 per cent* and own-labels 24 per cent [27]. Commitment to branding may actually restrict the freedom of brand leaders to respond to new competitors.

- *Tango* – Tango is a Britvic Soft Drinks brand which has been transformed during the 1990s. In 1990 Tango was an 'also-ran' – a boring minor brand of orange fizzy drink in a can with pictures of sliced oranges on the can. The re-launch in 1991 was characterized by anarchic advertising and promotion – a fat, bald, orange man who slapped the faces of the unsuspecting to 'Tango' people (a practice widely imitated for a time in play-grounds around the country), exploding grannies (less widely imitated), holiday postcards from fictitious characters sent to consumers' homes, and a mock TV 'appeal' not to buy the new drink because it had nothing to do with Britvic. The brand personality is based on a continuing joke, appealing to the key 16–24-year-old consumer who reacts badly to being patronized – the joke has frequently led to the company being criticized for being irresponsible, but they do not seem to mind. From almost a standing start, by 1996 the brand was growing at 30 per cent a year and was valued at around £50 million [28].

However, it is also true that in building a market strategy brand identity may also be the biggest *liability* you have to overcome in a market:

- *Skoda Cars* – The Czech Republic's main contribution to the motor industry is Skoda Cars. For several years, Skodas have been the butt of many jokes:

  Q: Why do Skoda have heated rear windows?
  A: To keep your hands warm when you are pushing them.

  Q: How do you double the value of a Skoda?
  A: Fill the tank with petrol.

  Q: What do you call a Skoda with a sun roof?
  A: A skip.

  Q: What do you call a Skoda with twin exhausts?
  A: A wheelbarrow.

  Q: What do you call a Skoda driver with more than one brain cell?
  A: Pregnant.

---

*Some analysts say this is a very small market share – hardly market dominance. But as Anita Roddick of The Body Shop has said: 'If you think being small means you cannot make any difference - try sleeping in a tent with a mosquito'.

These jokes are based on a widespread belief that Skoda cars are low-quality. The cars are *not* low-quality – they are fine cars which are extremely cheap but robust basic vehicles. In fact, Skoda buyers are extremely loyal to the brand – it is estimated that 72 per cent of first-time Skoda buyers return for a second Skoda purchase. In 1996 Skoda was the highest-ranking European car in the J.D. Powers British customer satisfaction survey, and the company is actually now part of the Volkswagen group. Nonetheless, in 1995 Skoda was preparing to launch a new model in the UK. They did a 'blind and seen' test – with the badges removed, and with no way of identifying the car as a Skoda, consumers were impressed with the design of the new vehicle, but with the badge and identity revealed, perceptions of the design were markedly less favourable, and the estimated value by potential customers (i.e. the price they would be willing to pay) was several hundred pounds lower. To break out of its current niche, Skoda has to overcome *negative* brand equity – where the branding reduces the market value of the product. It looks as though they are doing this, incidentally – in 1996 there was a six-week waiting list for new Skodas across most of Europe.

'brands have become a major point of strategic focus'

Even so, in recent years, brands have become a major point of *strategic focus* in companies, and the concept of the brand has been widely applied:

- BMW, the German car company, bought the troubled British car manufacturer Rover in 1994. Part of the BMW approach to strategic change at Rover is to embed the vision of the brand as the unifying focus. While Rover's traditional multi-brand approach around brands like Land Rover and Mini was clear in the market, the strategy was less clear to employees and suppliers. The focus throughout the supply chain is now the Rover brand.
- In many traditional sectors, like financial services, growing emphasis is on the brand concept instead of individual products and companies, as a way of building greater customer focus.
- The 1996 purchase of the remaining shares in 'The Hard Rock Café' was to unify the Hard Rock brand under Rank ownership, as part of corporate development by Rank as a themed catering and leisure company.
- One of the most dynamic businesses in the UK in 1996 was the 'Toni and Guy' franchised hairdressing salons. Owned by the Mascalo brothers, the Toni and Guy brand stands for trendy, youthful hairstyles. The brand range is highly fashionable – the image in the Toni and Guy advertising begs the trendy young person to ask the stylist: 'Make me look like that'. From

franchising the brand name Toni and Guy, the Mascalo brothers turn over around £12 million a year, with another £8 million from Toni haircare products, and they are taking the brand international.

- 'Brand culling' – brands have become recognized as tradeable assets with a market value, and removing brands from the portfolio is now a major strategic issue in companies watched closely by the City:
  - in 1996 the Swiss drugs giant Novartis started a sale of brands like Ovaltine and Isostar, as non-core activities, to City approval that sidelining the consumer brands would allow greater focus on the core drugs and pharmaceutical business;
  - in mid-1996 Interbrew, the world's fourth largest brewer, announced the sale of beer brands like Labatt Ice and Rolling Rock to solve debt problems;
  - corporate strategy at Grand Metropolitan has involved the sale of brands worth £300 million (like the 205-year-old Shippams Paste brand, Memory Lane Cakes and Peter's Savoury Products) to concentrate resources on four key global brands: Pillsbury, the chilled dough ranges; Green Giant, in canned sweetcorn; Haagen-Dazs ice-cream; and Old El Paso Mexican foods;
  - at Unilever in 1996, Bird's Eye decided to drop all sub-brands (e.g. MenuMaster, Healthy Options and Country Club) to improve margins through focus on the Bird's Eye identity;
- Brands have a balance sheet and income value (as shown above) – in 1997 Highland Distilleries has valued the Macallan brand of whisky in its accounts at £60 million, and Manchester United Football Club showed a £2.2 million exceptional profit from selling 'goodwill' (in fact, a trademark licensing agreement for the Man U brand).
- 'Brand extension' – using brand names to enter new product markets and new geographical markets had become a critical issue in many companies. This deserves more detailed consideration below.

It does seem, however, that we can make a powerful case for not neglecting the importance of brands (and other intangible marketing assets) in building market strategy, and the value proposition in particular.

Brand extension strategies

The value of brands, the difficulty and cost of establishing new brands, and the large on-going investment in maintaining a brand all push in the direction of extending or 'stretching' brands into new markets. As executives increasingly talk about 'leveraging brand equity', we need to talk more about being realistic about brand extension possibilities.

Brand extension can be effective, but it carries *risks*.

Global brands like Coke, Toyota, Microsoft and the like have little trouble crossing national and cultural barriers. However, the Interbrand agency's 'black museum' of failed brand moves includes:

- products that have failed to transfer to the UK – a Swiss perfume called 'Kevin', 'Cunto' coffee from Spain, 'Craps' chocolate from France, 'Skum' marshmallows and 'Bums' biscuits from Scandinavia, and the 'Homo Sausage' salami stick from Japan;
- a large Japanese travel firm was surprised at the enquiries it got when it started operating in English-speaking markets, and eventually decided to change the name from the Kinki Nippon Tourist Company;
- the launch of the Ford Pinto in Brazil was not helped by the car's name translating into Portuguese as 'tiny male genitals';
- Rolls Royce's 'Silver Mist' had to be re-named for Germany, where the original branding means horse manure; and
- major question marks surround the use of the Orange brand in Northern Ireland [22].

However, moving a brand identity can be highly effective – Cadbury brands a cream liqueur, Del Monte brands cook-in sauces, and Sainsbury runs a bank. On the other hand, Kellogg, the 'king of cereals', tried to become the 'king of breakfast' with orange juice, and failed. Cadbury's brand was extended onto salted snacks, teabags and instant mashed potato with poor results – the Cadbury name now only appears on chocolate-related products [29].

Currently, in the fashion world, the exclusive haute couture designer brands are being extended into the middle of the market. Exclusive houses like Ralph Lauren, Calvin Klein and even Tommy Hilfiger are taking 'diffusion ranges' into the middle of the fashion market with great international success – Ralph Lauren sold £3 billion worth in 1995 and Calvin Klein £2 billion [30].

However, the key issue facing companies is 'brand stretchability' – can you extend the brand and where can you extend it?

Jeremy Bullmore, a director of WPP, has developed a game for advertising and marketing executives that he calls 'Brandicide'. The challenge to players is simply to choose a well-known brand and think of extending its name into a new area that would kill

the brand stone dead. Bullmore's best effort is: After Eight
Bubblegum. Cruder and less subtle opponents might suggest:
Persil chocolate, Cadbury washing-up liquid, a Listerine whisky,
Harpic baby food, and so on [29].

Peter Wallis, founder of the consultancy SRU, suggests we need
to consider both the degree of stretch we are proposing for a
brand and whether the brand personality is suited to that
stretch [29]. Wallis distinguishes *degree of brand stretch* as:

- *Licensing* – a strong brand like Harley-Davidson allows the
  name to be used on cosmetics, and Manchester United's
  branding goes on clothes and publications.
- *Gentle stretch* – the new branding is in the same sector; for
  example, confectionery brands like Mars badging ice-creams,
  the Persil brand extending to washing-up liquid from the
  detergent brand.
- *Unknown territory* – we rely on the relationship with the customer to transfer into a radically new product market – Virgin
  from music to airlines, Sainsbury's from groceries to financial
  services, retail banks into stationery and office supplies.

Wallis's test for stretchability is the trust and credibility in the
brand – the *brand personality*, which we fail to understand at our
peril. Table 5.4 lists some of his views about the stretchability of
major brands.

Table 5.4 Brand stretchability for brand extension strategies

Brand name	Brand personality	Brand stretchability*
Marks and Spencer	Editorial ability, innovative luxury	3
Virgin	David vs Goliath	3
Levi's	Classic style, authenticity	2½
Nike	Just do it (youth and attitude)	2½
Sony	Innovative design in 'gizmos'	2½
Cadbury	Small purple pleasures World of chocolate	2
Coca-Cola	America for everyone	2
Sainsbury's	Middle-class quartermaster	2
Barclays Bank	70s-style high-street banking	1
Mars	Countlines	1
Nescafé	Suburban niceness, familiar product brand	1
Persil	Caring household cleaning	1

*3 = Outstanding – superstretchy; 2 = Good – very stretchy; 3 = Average – only
slightly stretchy
Source: Adapted from Olins [26]

This is an important perspective, and it should be remembered before we make big assumptions that our brand's value proposition will transfer and extend to a new product or a new market. The big risk is that a failed brand extension will undermine the customer's relationship with the whole brand, not just the extension.

The dilemma remains. Take the case of Xerox. Xerox invented the photocopier and built a $16 billion business out of office products. The company's copier patents expired in the 1970s, and a move into personal computers failed. Xerox's newest incarnation is as 'the document company'. The extension strategy is to combine print technology with the software that manages the electric media on which documents are created and stored. The question exercising executive minds of Xerox is, will the Xerox brand transfer from office machinery to software? [31] There is no easy answer.

The future of the brand?

'the traditional brand, and traditional brand management, is under attack'

Notwithstanding all this, the traditional brand, and traditional brand management, is under attack from several quarters:

- 'Marlboro Friday' and 'Sainsbury Wednesday', which shook the faith of many in the sustainability of brand-based competition;
- own-labels – the undermining of manufacturer brands by retailer brands;
- the vulnerability of brands to copying and counterfeiting; and
- the impact of category management in retailing.

'Marlboro Friday' was 2 April 1993, when Philip Morris took the huge gamble of cutting the price in the USA of its top-selling cigarette, Marlboro, by 20 per cent – 40 cents a pack. This was a desperate attempt to protect eroding market share being taken by low-price, unbranded, generic cigarettes. The immediate result was that Philip Morris stocks plummeted on the market. As Philip Morris extended deep price-cutting to other premium brands – Benson and Hedges, Virginia Slims, Merit and Parliament – branded competitors across the industry were forced to follow the prices down on their brands as well (two companies were driven quickly into loss-making positions). The result was a worldwide loss of confidence and share value in branded goods companies. Much of the market situation was recovered, but the question mark over the real robustness of branding as a sustainable strategy remains in many minds. The fear is that even after huge investments in building brands, when times are hard brands cannot survive against low price competition. Some analysts saw the British version of 'Marlboro Friday', as 3 November 1994, when on 'Sainsbury Wednesday' the supermarket group cut prices on 300 own-label lines to attack the manufacturer brands [32]. This has fuelled beliefs that however strong brands are, when the chips are down they lose to price cutters.

More generally, the impact of *retailer own-labels* is enormous in many consumer markets. In the UK around 30 per cent of all grocery sales are own-label – own-labels account for around 80 per cent of milk and wrapped bread, 60 per cent of frozen peas and fruit juices, more than 50 per cent of yoghurts and fizzy drinks. As we see below, own-labels have even impacted on goods as heavily branded as colas. The dilemma facing brand leaders is to decide whether or not to produce the own-label products which will ultimately undermine their main brands. This is complicated by the continuing belief among many customers that retailer own-labels are actually produced by the brand leaders anyway – this consumer perception has plagued Kellogg over the years in the highly competitive breakfast cereals market (Kellogg does *not* produce own-label breakfast cereals and even says so in its advertising, but consumers still believe that it docs).

Even heavily branded markets are vulnerable to own-label competition. The cola market, dominated by Coke and Pepsi, is probably the most heavily branded market in the world. When Sainsbury's supermarkets in the UK launched 'Classic Cola' (supplied by the own-label soft drinks specialist, the Cott Corporation) in 1994, within two months the own-label brand had taken 60 per cent of Sainsbury cola sales, which gave it 15 per cent of the entire UK market. By 1995, Coke's share of the UK market had fallen to less than 50 per cent for the first time. In the USA, the Cott Corporation supplies 'Sam's American Choice' cola to Wal-Mart (named after Wal-Mart founder Sam Walton), which now outsells Coke and Pepsi combined in the vast Wal-Mart chain. If Coke and Pepsi are not safe from low-price own-labels, then no-one is.

Yet more aggressive competition which has emerged in UK branded goods markets has been *brand copying* – again primarily by retailer own-labels. In polite circles this is discussed as 'parody as marketing strategy'. While Asda vehemently denies the accusation, interesting parallels exist between a number of its own-label launches and manufacturers' brand leaders:

Manufacturer brand	*Asda brand*
'I Can't Believe It's Not Butter' from Van Den Bergh Foods – a spread in a flat yellow tub with blue print	'You'd Better Believe It' from Asda – a spread in a flat yellow tub with blue print
'Rice Krispies' from Kellogg – a breakfast cereal in a blue box and with a picture of milk being poured on cereal	'Rice Snaps' from Asda – a breakfast cereal in a blue box and with a picture of milk being poured on cereal
'Penguin' – chocolate biscuits from United Biscuits in a flat orange and blue pack	'Puffin' – chocolate biscuits from Asda in a flat orange pack with blue print
'Jack Daniels' – bourbon whiskey distributed in the UK by IDV, in a brown bottle with coloured cap and 'Old South' label design	'Daniel Boones' – bourbon whiskey from Asda, in a (shorter, flatter) brown bottle with coloured cap and 'Old South' label design
'CK One' – the world's top-selling prestige perfume from Calvin Klein in a flat, translucent bottle	'George I' – unisex fragrance from Asda in a round, translucent bottle

Various brand owners are suing Asda (in some cases very reluctantly because Asda is a major customer for them as well as a competitor) – Asda says it has *not* copied anyone's brand and will fight. The lawyers will probably find for the brand owners, at least in part, but in the meantime own-labels continue to eat into the sales of brand leaders because they are substantially cheaper.

In a total different category is straightforward, criminal *brand counterfeiting* – i.e. the illegal branding of foods as brands which they are not. Counterfeiting has become a substantial problem for brand leaders like Adidas sportswear, Nike and Reebok sports shoes and fashion clothes labels as diverse as Levi-Strauss, Polo from Ralph Lauren, Armani and Paul Smith. However, the same issue exists for BP with motor oils and for computer software producers[30]. It is illegal, but it is difficult to trace, and it undermines the brand – the brand leader gets the blame for the low quality product, not the counterfeiter. It is a further serious indication of the vulnerability of a market position that relies on branding.

A major change overtaking retailing is *category management*. The retailer increasingly defines a category of goods as the focus for merchandising, instead of manufacturers' brands – lunchtime snacks, Friday evening take-homes* , and so on. The retailer's interest is then on what each manufacturer can offer to improve the performance of the category in the store. This question replaces the issue of brand leadership – the issue is position in the category. The implications are enormous – at Elida Gibbs, for example, brand management has disappeared as new category managers work with the salesforce and each retail customer.

Related to this retail focus are the *category killers* – emerging large-scale discount retailers in specialized product areas. They are characterized by limited product ranges but very low prices – examples include IKEA in furniture, Toys'R'Us and Costco in grocery. The transfer of customer priorities to low price further undermines the traditional brand-based strategies of companies in these markets [34].

A variation on category killing with similar results is where a retailer chooses to sell a branded product in circumstances that the brand manufacturer does not want. For example, in 1997 the supermarket firm Tesco began to sell Levi 501 blue jeans – a heavily branded product supported by its famous image-building advertising – at a price discounted by nearly 50 per cent. Tesco went into the national press with full-page advertisements and the copy line:

'SAFE SEATS.

£30.

(LEVI 501s AT ROCK BOTTOM PRICES)'

Levi are not terribly amused – their view is that the integrity of their brand is compromised if your mum can buy Levi's for £30 with the groceries. They tried to prevent Tesco from obtaining supplies. Tesco has played this game before – they sourced the product from Mexico to avoid the Levi embargo. As we saw earlier, Tesco has adopted a similarly robust approach to stocking

---

*Wal-Mart, the huge US discount retailer, found a strong link between the purchase of nappies and multi-packs of beer on Friday evenings. This reflected young men being told by their partners to pick up some nappies on the way home from work, who then figured that this was a good chance (and maybe a good reason) to stock up on beer as well. It makes sense for the retailer to build displays on Friday afternoon of beer and nappies side by side.'

other brands, like Chanel and Clarins, without the approval of the manufacturers concerned. The manufacturer's risk is clear – you spend a fortune creating and maintaining a brand image, which is then undermined by a retailer, and there is little you can do to prevent it happening.

Branding, value proposition and market strategy

Along with other intangible marketing assets, brands remain a central issue in developing what we will offer the customer as our value proposition. Branding issues are also a main input to our evaluation of market attractiveness and market position (see pp. 168–76 above). However, there are some major questions to be raised about the implications of relying on brands for sustainable competitive advantage, and the vulnerability of a market position based on branding to competitive attack.

'the vulnerability of a market position based on branding to competitive attack'

Do we have a value proposition?

If we have got a good idea about our target markets and segments, and have linked our vision and mission to our strategic positioning and thought through our differentiating capabilities, particularly in terms of our marketing assets and brands – the question is: do we have a value proposition for our customer?

Do not just say 'yes' and move on! Try writing it down. If we do not know what we have to offer each of our customers that makes us more attractive than the next to that customer, that we know we can deliver to that customer, then we do not have a market strategy. If that sounds vague, look at the Daewoo case study (pp. 530–40) and see how they got to a market-beating value proposition.

For example, the written value proposition for a leading financial services company called their Customer Proposition reads as follows, and describes the position they aim to take in the customer's mind:

● I am more than just a customer with . . .
● All my personal financial needs are met by . . .
● I get top value prices from . . .
● My money is safe with . . .
● I can understand . . .
● I would always recommend . . .

- I find it easy to deal with . . .
- I get the best possible service from . . .
- I can trust . . . to look after my interests
- . . . is where I want to work
- I know that . . . supports people with more than money.

There is no fixed format for what a value proposition should look like – but a summary of the factors that should be taken into account is given in Figure 5.14.

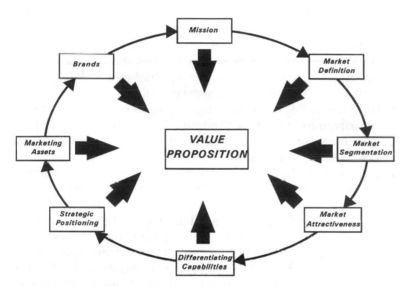

Figure 5.14 Building the value proposition

You can use the framework in Figure 5.14 to check that you have considered all the issues we have raised and how they are linked, and see how each contributes to building a statement of the value for our customers that will establish a strong position for us in this market:

- Have we got all we can from evaluating the issue of mission – company philosophy and key values, product-market domain and critical success factors – if this defines what the company is all about, what does this contribute to our value proposition?
- Have we systematically re-evaluated the definition of our markets and the segments within them, to focus on customer needs instead of our products, leading to the role of different products and services (maybe from outside our industry) in meeting those underlying customer needs?

- Have we got a model of market segmentation that reflects customer needs and customer benefits, not just the easily measured factors like demographics, and which we can link effectively to our planning, budgeting and internal systems and structures?
- Have we systematically evaluated our priorities in terms of markets and segments, on the basis of analysing what makes markets attractive to us, and the strength of position we can take in each market?
- Have we looked at the possibilities for a strategic position built on variety, needs or access specialization, as well as the value disciplines of operational excellence or product leadership?
- Do we have a clear view of our differentiating capabilities – drawing on corporate competencies to establish what will give us sustainable competitive advantage that clearly differentiates us from the rest as offering superior value?
- Have we studied our base of marketing assets to see what they contribute to building a strong market position – do we have advantages in company reputation, channel control, market information, and so on?
- Have we looked at our branding to see if it provides a sustainable platform for the value proposition that is developing?

These are rich and complex issues, but they are the ones which are essential to building an effective and strong market strategy.

However, we have not finished yet. The last strand that links to our market choices and our value proposition is the key relationships that will drive the strategy. We turn our attention to this in the next chapter.

References

1. Thomas, Lesley (1995), 'Millions Spent on Firing Firms with Missionary Zeal', *Sunday Times*, 25 March.
2. Adams, Scott (1996), *The Dilbert Principle*, London: Boxtree Press.
3. Levitt, Theodore (1960), 'Marketing Myopia', *Harvard Business Review*, July/August, 45–56.
4. Kay, John (1995), 'Learning to Define the Core Business', *Financial Times*, 1 December.
5. Porter, Michael E. (1985), *Competitive Advantage: Creating and Sustaining Superior Performance*, New York: Free Press.
6. Porter, Michael E. (1996), 'What is Strategy?', *Harvard Business Review*, November/December, 61–78.
7. Prahalad, C.K. and Gary Hamel (1990), 'The Core Competence of the Corporation', *Harvard Business Review*, May/June, 79–91.

8. Simms, Jane (1996), 'Mission Control', *Marketing Business*, July, 18–21.
9. Lattice, John (1996), 'Blue's Legend', *Sunday Business*, 21 April.
10. Cravens, David W, Gordon Greenley, Nigel F Piercy and Stanley Slater (1997), 'Market-Driven Strategic Management', *Long Range Planning*, Vol. 30, No. 4, 493–506..
11. Peters, Tom (1986), *Passion for Excellence*, New York: Harper and Row.
12. Levitt, Theodore (1980), 'Marketing Success Through Differentiation – of Anything', *Harvard Business Review*, January/February, 83–91.
13. Brayfield, Celia (1997), 'Bookshops will Never be the Same Again', *Daily Telegraph*, 28 March.
14. Treacy, Michael and Fred Wiersema (1995), *The Discipline of Market Leaders*, London: Harper Collins.
15. Davidson, Hugh (1983), 'Putting Assets First', *Marketing*, 17 November, 35–40.
16. Mitchell, Alan (1995), 'Changing Channels', *Marketing Business*, February, 10–13.
17. Hart, Christopher W. (1996), 'Made to Order', *Marketing Management*, Summer, 11–23.
18. Jones, Helen (1997), 'Identity Crisis', *Marketing Business*, January, 38–41.
19. Bell, Emily (1996), 'Bastards are Losing Out to Mr. Clean', *Observer*, 30 June.
20. Bernoth, Ardyn (1996), 'Companies Show They Care', *Sunday Times*, 8 December.
21. Carter, Meg (1996), 'Consumers Rally to Good Causes', *Independent on Sunday*, 17 November.
22. Bennett, Oliver (1996), 'I'm a Tall Blonde Burger', *Independent on Sunday*, 17 November.
23. 'Get Ready for a Brand New Battle', *Marketing Week*, 23 September 1994.
24. Trapp, Roger (1996), 'Brands With No Barriers', *Independent on Sunday*, 17 November.
25. de Chernatony, Leslie and Malcolm H.B. McDonald (1992), *Creating Brands*, Oxford: Butterworth-Heinemann.
26. *The Economist* (1996), 6 January.
27. Bell, Emily (1996), 'Any Colour as Long as it's Blue', *Observer*, 31 March.
28. Teacher, David (1996), 'Tango and Cash', *Independent on Sunday*, 5 May.
29. Olins, Rufus (1996), 'Elastic Brands', *Sunday Times*, 3 November.
30. Bernoth, Ardyn (1996), 'Designers put London in Fashion', *Sunday Times*, 3 November.
31. Lamb John, (1996), 'Can Xerox Take it in the Software Business?', Sunday Business, 12 May.
32. Lorenz, Andrew and Garth Alexander (1994), 'Brands Fight Back', *Sunday Times*, 3 April.
33. Brown, Malcolm (1995), 'Faker Breakers', *Marketing Business*, June, 30–33.
34. 'Killing off the Competition', *Marketing Business*, April, 11–14.

CHAPTER 6

Market strategy:

The key relationships: Customers, competitors, collaborators and co-workers

'what are the key relationships that will drive this through, and can we rely on and successfully manage those relationships?'

The issue considered here is: if we are going to deliver our value proposition to our target markets and segments, what are the key relationships that will drive this through, and can we rely on and successfully manage those relationships? Critical issues include the following types of relationships:

- with the *customer* – can we keep the promises we have made in the value proposition?
- with *competitors* – how vulnerable is our market strategy to competitive attack, how well do we understand our competitors' capabilities, and will the strategy survive?
- with *collaborators* – does our strategy rely on partnerships with other organizations such as suppliers, distributors and so on, and can we manage these relationships effectively?
- with *co-workers** – can and will the employees and managers in this company deliver the quality, the service and the brand values on which the market strategy relies?

These are the areas identified for attention in Figure 6.1.

---

*Apologies to the reader for using the word 'co-workers' to refer to the employees and managers in our company, but it all alliterates too well with the other relationships and I could not resist!

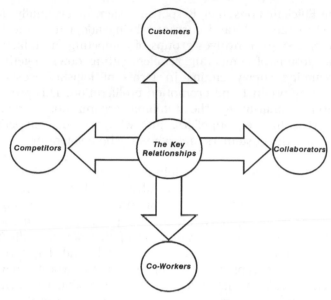

Figure 6.1   The key relationships in market strategy

This is a very neat and tidy model. Do not be surprised if things are somewhat less clear-cut in the real world. It is often difficult to sort out the type of relationships we have with different parties. Ask who is the customer, competitor, collaborator and co-worker in the following cases:

● Company X produces speciality pharmaceutical chemicals for the healthcare industry. They were approached by a customer for a new material to be supplied for clinical diagnostic purposes, which had been designed by the customer's R&D department. Company X had the production facilities for the new compound, but did not have access to the raw materials needed or the packaging plant required. The customer agreed to supply the raw materials from another source, and arranged for Company X to lease packaging line time at Company Y (Company Y also supplies the customer, but is the major competitor of Company X). Company X supplies the new material to the customer in bulk for re-packaging and in specialized packaging for laboratory use. The customer packages the bulk material itself. Company X and the customer both sell the bulk material and the packaged material to other healthcare companies, including Company Y. (This is a real situation, but the companies concerned would just as soon not have their names published.) This arrangement has proved profitable for all concerned, it just isn't neat and tidy.

- The Efficient Consumer Response system as originally developed in the USA (and currently being adopted in the UK – see pp 258–62) involves groups of competing manufacturers and groups of competing retailers sitting down together to streamline supply chains in terms of logistics, costs and reducing product and promotion proliferation. This process is driven primarily by the retailing organizations providing expertise to their suppliers. Just who are the competitors, who are the customers and who are the collaborators in this scenario?

- In 1996, Kodak and Fuji jointly brought to market a new film and camera system – the Advanced Photo System under the Adnatix brand name – that uses digital technology to improve picture quality (magnetic signals in the film coating tells the processing laboratory computer how to adjust for colour and lighting conditions). Kodak and Fuji are the largest photographic film companies in the world. They are intense rivals in that industry. In 1996 Kodak was involved in fighting Fuji over what Kodak claims is the protection of the Japanese market from outsiders. Yet both companies see their collaboration as a route to superior international performance.

- There are many cases where companies end up competing with their own distributors. For example, insurance companies sell through Independent Financial Advisers (independent firms and individuals who have direct salesforce operations) and increasingly direct marketing operations. They compete directly (though frequently covertly) with their own distributors.

This does not get us off the hook of evaluating the key relationships that underpin our market strategy. It just means that in reality it gets messy. We may have to look at customer, competitor and collaborator relationships when it is the same company we are talking about in each relationship, and this may pose particular problems – if we attack a competitor with a new product which is also a customer for existing products, do we undermine the original business, for example?

The important point is that if our evaluation here is unfavourable – our people cannot deliver the values promised to the customer, our partners will not support our brands, and our strategy can be wiped out by the competitors – then we have to think again about our market choices and value proposition, because we have not yet developed a robust market strategy.

We will consider each of these areas in turn. However, first, let's talk about *relationship marketing*.

So, what is the deal with relationship marketing?

The 1990s has seen just about everyone telling businesses that they have to get with relationship marketing as the only way to do 'new marketing' in modern markets – a major 'paradigm shift' for marketing theory and practice [1]. The difference between conventional marketing and relationship marketing is the move from emphasis on the transaction (the single sale of a product or service) to a focus on the continuing relationship with the customer. Critical differences between the two approaches are summarized in Table 6.1.

Table 6.1   The differences between transaction marketing and relationship marketing*

	Traditional transaction-based marketing	**New relationship-based marketing**
Focus	Individual sale to a customer	Total sales to a customer in the long term
Evaluation	Sales volume Market share Overall customer satisfaction	Customer retention Share of customer Individual customer satisfaction
Time perspective	Short-term	Long-term
Marketing dominated by	Marketing mix	Interactive marketing (supported by marketing mix)
Price sensitivity	Customers tend to be more sensitive to price	Customers tend to be less sensitive to price
Quality issues	Technical quality of product/service dominates	Quality of interaction with customer becomes more important
Customer information	Surveys of customer satisfaction	Continuous customer feedback system
Integration of marketing, operations and personnel	Limited importance	Strategic importance
Internal marketing	Limited importance	Strategic importance

*Source: Adapted from Gronroos [1]

But what does relationship marketing do for us?

'relationship marketing is an exciting and major force for revitalizing marketing'

In fact, relationship marketing is an exciting and major force for revitalizing marketing. It can do the following types of thing for us:

- It tells us that what matters most is the *relationship* we build with the customer, because this is the real source of enduring competitive strength.
- It tells us that we have to have a broader perspective which recognizes that we have more than one type of customer and market. Martin Christopher and colleagues[2] point to the importance of five markets: *supplier, employee, referral, influence* and *internal* markets, and this means that relationship marketing involves all employees across traditional boundaries in building and sustaining customer relationships – the role of the 'part-time marketers'[6].
- Because we focus on relationships in all these areas – customers and partners – instead of just transactions, then we turn from competition and conflict to *mutual co-operation and mutual interdependence*[3].
- Our market strategy has also to be into the broader setting of *networks* of interdependent firms linked by strategic alliances, joint ventures and new types of joint trading agreements[4,5].
- It focuses our attention on *customer retention* – the efforts we make to build a lasting relationship with the customer, not just selling a product or service in a one-off transaction.
- It offers competitive strength from *micro-segmentation and customizing* – using our enhanced knowledge of the customer to take our value proposition down to the segment of one customer with customized or adapted offers and products.

Academics and consultants wax lyrical about the emergence of relationship marketing as a new approach. It is actually incredibly valuable in practical terms as well. What relationship marketing gives us is a framework and a rationale for doing the following things:

- Focusing everyone's attention on our total offering to the customer and the value it creates for that customer – this is a greatly superior basis for building strategy than wonderful products (we think) *or* clever advertising programmes (the advertising agency thinks).
- It is the closest we have got so far in most companies to recognizing the need to manage the whole of the process of going to market, instead of just 'marketing' in the conventional sense – see Chapter 1, pp. 6–8.

- It gives us leverage against accountants who want to see a margin on every transaction. Everyone does some deals where they lose money – the point is whether we make money from the customer relationship through its life cycle.
- It gives us a logic for breaking free of traditional functional departmental boundaries, to build focus on value for the customer all the way from production to sales.
- It is exciting and innovative and offers us the chance to revitalize marketing in companies – because, let's be honest, in some firms marketing departments are looking a bit tired and bureaucratic.

However, there is one thing that relationship marketing is *not*. It is not *new*.

'However, there is one thing that relationship marketing is not. It is not new'

What do you mean – of course it is new!

If you want to be precious, you can probably trace the relational exchange approaches to doing business back several thousand years in the eastern cultures[7] and certainly to the industrial revolution in Britain[8].

Certainly, the label 'relationship marketing' has emerged as common terminology in the 1990s, and, depending on your perspective, has either been pioneered by the Swedish and European academics led by Christian Gronroos and Evert Gummesson, or by a group of US academics led by Jagdish Sheth at Emory University (this conflict has no practical significance whatsoever, but it is always fun to see distinguished academicians squabbling in public).

However, if you look at the content of relationship marketing, there is little here which has not been known about for a long time:

- We have actually known about the importance of customer focus and retention for quite a while – this is not news, and even now most forms of customer retention and loyalty programmes are little more than sophisticated attempts to take customers hostage, not build relationships or partnerships (see pp. 39–45).
- The importance of building a total market offer to the customer that involves service employees, technical specialists, purchasing experts, and so on, to sell to the customer may be a new idea to some marketing executives, but salespeople could have told you about it a long time ago, and it is what firms like Marks and Spencer have always done.

- Another name for 'mutual co-operation and mutual interdependence' with customers and collaborators is *key account selling*, and it is not a new idea for anyone dealing with multiple retailers, for example.
- Much of what passes for 'micro-segmentation and customizing' is simply exploiting new computer stores of customer data to make direct contact. Linking customer information to sales promotion is also not new, it used to be called (and still is) direct marketing, or database marketing, or even mail order marketing – it is simply using technology to do better what we have always done. This is about an IT revolution, not a marketing revolution. It is an incredibly important development in marketing practice – but a new paradigm or theory of marketing? I think not.

We also need to be very cautious about making promises we cannot keep in the guise of relationship marketing. Speaking as a 'segment of one' – is British Airways really going to give me more leg-room in an economy seat and let me smoke on the flight because I tell them this is what I want; is the Sainsbury Bank actually going to give me a different account to anyone else's; is Marks and Spencer going to use its database to stock trousers that are long enough for me; is BMW going to change more than the marginal extras on the vehicle to retain me as a customer? I really do not think so. This may sound unduly cynical. It may even be untrue. But I really do not think they will. All the evidence is that what they actually want to do is to sell me financial services.

In fact, a 1997 survey by Harris International Marketing[9] found that notwithstanding loyalty cards, relationship managers, customer service strategies, and so on, shoppers continue to report that: retailers' customer service is poor; shopping is boring; all the supermarkets are very similar to each other; and overwhelmingly they buy groceries at the closest supermarket (i.e. the most convenient measured in distance and time). Perhaps consumers are trying to tell us something about relationship marketing?

Part of what they are saying may be that some customers simply do not *want* to have a relationship with you. A conundrum for the financial service sector – where many of the firms see relationship management as their salvation – is that many of their most attractive, affluent customers are saying things like: 'Do not telephone me to tell me that you are my personal banker and that you have some wonderful new products. Stop sending me letters and leaflets about your products. I do not want to have lunch with you, play golf with you or go to the races with you. I just want you to leave me alone!' Now that puts a different perspective on relationship marketing!

There does seem to be a danger that because marketing people have just discovered relationship marketing, they assume that relationship strategies will be greeted with open arms by their customers. The evidence suggests that this is not the case. Before getting carried away, ask the question: are we embracing relationship marketing because it is a better way to meet our customers' needs, or because it meets our needs inside the company? If the answer is the latter, there is nothing necessarily wrong with this – just don't expect your customers to get excited about it.

It is also strange that enthusiasts for relationship marketing make so little of the negative side of relationship marketing – our goal with our database analysis, customized product, direct marketing communications and retention and reward systems is to *break up* relationships, i.e. the existing relationships that customers have with their present suppliers. The reality is not quite as cuddly as the theory in this respect, so let's drop the 'holier than thou' stuff.

On the other hand, when we find it is our customers who *demand* a relationship focus, then we really are talking about incredibly powerful leverage for competitive advantage. This pressure comes mainly in business-to-business marketing – either to distributors or industrial end-user customers. Here there is a major change in customer priorities that puts relationship management high on the agenda. We consider this as a sales management issue in Chapter 13.

One neglected idea that arises from the above is that relationship requirement is potentially a very revealing way of *segmenting* markets (see pp 154–58 above). If we genuinely seek to distinguish important differences between customers, then maybe one way is to look at what they want from us in terms of a relationship (both type and degree of involvement). At least then we could focus on the customer groups where we are best able to deliver the relationship that they want. Try that one in the Product-Market Matrix (see pp. 150–51). For example, Figure 6.2 suggests that if we look at the customers in our market in terms of whether they want a long-term relationship with their suppliers, and the closeness of the relationship they want, we may find very different types of buyer:

- *Type I: Relationship Seekers* – the type of customer becoming a major force in industrial marketing, who wants a long-term relationship with the supplier and a high degree of closeness or partnership in things like developing new products (see pp. 496–99);

- *Type II: Relationship Exploiters* – customers who will take every advantage they can get from relationship offers for whatever they can get, but at the end of the day shop around, and your investment in the relationship does not buy you customer loyalty or retention;
- *Type III: Loyal Buyers* – customers who want a long-term relationship, but not a close one – think of the financial services example above (p. 240);
- *Type IV: Arm's Length Transaction Customers* – will shop around for the best deal, will probably buy on price, and do not want a close relationship with the supplier. An example might be buyers of staple chemicals for industrial applications.

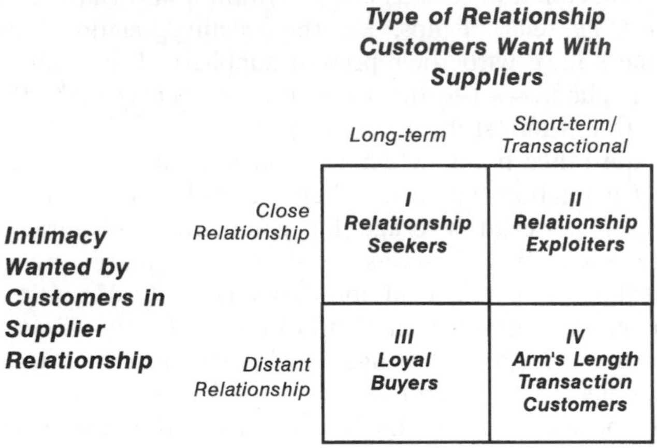

Type of Relationship Customers Want With Suppliers

		Long-term	Short-term/ Transactional
Intimacy Wanted by Customers in Supplier Relationship	Close Relationship	I **Relationship Seekers**	II **Relationship Exploiters**
	Distant Relationship	III **Loyal Buyers**	IV **Arm's Length Transaction Customers**

Figure 6.2   Segmenting markets by relationship requirements

This is not particularly profound. It is just something worked out on a flip-chart in a company strategy workshop. However, executives have suggested it is a good way of re-thinking our priorities in investing time and effort in building customer relationships, and it may be a useful balance to the current consultants' euphoria over relationship marketing as the solution to any problem you care to name.

So, where does that leave us with relationship marketing?

Actually, what all this means is that relationship marketing is the most fantastically useful thing for executives – it gives a new life to marketing and market strategy in particular, but you don't have to learn anything new! Don't dismiss relationship marketing as a fad (which it may turn out to be) or 'putting old wine in new bottles' (which it probably is) or 'academic theory' (which it certainly is) – take the opportunity to *use* relationship marketing to build customer focus in the company, to involve the people you need, and to drive market-led strategic change. You get this for free – it would be churlish not to take advantage!

The opportunity is to use relationship marketing to help in:

- putting the marketing process (not the marketing department) back on centre-stage in companies which have been looking elsewhere for leadership;
- getting the management focus back to the customer;
- involving every part of the company in concentrating on value for the customer; *and*
- putting the customer higher on the agenda than advertising and marketing programmes.

'focus on the key relationships on which our market strategy relies for success'

For most of us, this is just too good to miss out on!

The remainder of this chapter is not selling you relationship marketing, which it is up to the reader to take or leave. What it does is to focus on the key relationships on which our market strategy relies for success, and to test whether they are compatible with our value proposition in our chosen markets and segments.

'test whether they are compatible with our value proposition in our chosen markets and segments'

Customer relationships

A huge amount of what has led up to this point is based on the customer. Our starting point was with customer satisfaction and building customer-focused organizations (Chapters 2 and 3). In building a market strategy, the customer has been our point of focus throughout:

- in defining and segmenting markets around customer needs to establish a competitive position;
- in building a value proposition that is based on our market mission, our differentiating capabilities and our marketing assets.

However, before we go further, it is time to ask some tough questions.

- Do we know what the relationship with the customer has to be for our market strategy to work?
- Does the customer know and accept this?
- Can we actually deliver that relationship in the customer's terms?

Do not forget that what customers actually see of your 'relationship strategy' is sales promotions and direct communications based on database information – and I personally am delighted to get a personalized letter from Tony O'Reilly about Heinz Baked Beans, it certainly made my day (not) – and loyalty programmes, or, as they have been called, 'customer detention' programmes, that are intended to tie in business (or restrict the customer's freedom and choice, as some would say). None of this seems particularly related to the philosophy of mutual interdependence that *we* know is what relationship marketing is really about.

Do we know what we want the relationship to be?

If we have got this far and the answer to the question is 'no', then we need to think again! We should be able to write down the relationship with the customer that grows out of our market focus, and our value proposition. Try it.

That statement should tell us, if our strategic position and value proposition are going to stand up:

- how *close* does the relationship have to be – the choices range from essentially a transactional relationship (we are only interested in the one-off sale) through to almost a partnership with the customer (see Chapter 13 for examples of the demands of business-to-business customers for partnership with suppliers);
- the *qualities* needed in the relationship – what do we need to have customers believe about us, e.g. our integrity, our service level, our quality, our technology compared to the competition?
- the *life cycle* of the relationship – how long has it got to last for the market strategy to be viable?

Do we have that relationship or can we get it?

This is about getting realistic and challenging any belief that we can take a strong competitive position just by telling customers that we are going to be nice to them (countless millions have been spent over the years on advertising to do just that, and it has not proved very effective).

If the relationship positioning we want depends on customer *beliefs* about us, let us find out what they do believe about us by asking them. A lot of companies are shocked to find that customer have long memories – they remember you and what you did before you got the relationship marketing religion. One of the things happening in markets across the world is that customers are getting far more marketing-literate – they *know* what you are doing and why.

Years ago, somewhat arrogant marketing and advertising executives used to say things like: 'You never lost money by underestimating the intelligence of the housewife'. To paraphrase David Ogilvy's comment: 'Excuse me, that's my wife you are talking about!' More apt today would be: 'You never lose money by underestimating the intelligence of people who underestimate the intelligence of the housewife'.

The critical issue is, are customer beliefs about us supportive to our market strategy or a barrier to it?

The same applies to *trust*. If our market strategy rests on the assumption that customers trust us, then maybe we should find out if they do. Does our company reputation support our market strategy or create a barrier to it?

Customers do not have to believe that you are a wonderful company or trust you with their lives in order for you to do business. People do business with companies they do not trust (see pp 214–15). What we have to avoid is building a market strategy that relies on beliefs and trusts which do not exist.

Can we deliver that relationship?

Getting customers is not the same thing as retaining them, as we saw in Chapter 3. Attracting customers is largely about *making* promises. Retaining customers is much more about *keeping* those promises.

The question at this stage is: when we look at the customer relationship defined by our market strategy, do we have the capabilities to maintain and enhance that relationship?

This forces us to look at our internal resources (our people, systems, procedures and structures), but also at the other key relationships we have to manage to maintain the customer relationship.

How seriously major firms are taking the management of customer relationships is well illustrated by the Customer Relationship Management initiative at IBM. The main characteristics of this programme are summarized in Table 6.2.

Table 6.2 Customer relationship management at IBM*

- Most of IBM's marketing activities are now embedded in a global initiative called Customer Relationship Management (CRM).
- CRM works through core processes:
  - Market management – to identify and select key market segments
  - Relationship management – handles interactions between IBM and the customer with established customers
  - Opportunity management – as soon as a sales opportunity is identified, the opportunity manager has the role of finding the right 'opportunity owner' who can offer the right type of expertise and the right level of interaction (e.g. mass customization versus one-of-a-kind), drawing on the next processes
  - Offering information – keeping track of every product or solution developed by the company or its business partners, so no-one in IBM has to waste time re-inventing the wheel
  - Skills management – a worldwide database of IBM personnel's skills, graded on scales from levels 1 to 5
  - Solution, design and delivery – each offer and bid is tracked to check the result
  - Customer satisfaction management – handling customer feedback and complaints
  - Message management – handling communications.
- The goal is co-ordination of customer relationships through managing business processes that cut across boundaries to achieve maximum effectiveness.

---

*Source: Adapted from Mitchell, Alan (1997), 'Speeding up the Process', *Marketing Business*, March

If we cannot resolve this issue, we need to go back to the value proposition and think again. Making promises to customers that you cannot keep is dangerous.

Competitor relationships

We also need to be pretty realistic about the type and level of competition in our target markets. This sounds so obvious, but many companies are very poor at putting strategy development into the real competitive environment. This is a route to nasty surprises. We need to give some serious attention to issues like:

- really understanding the competition, particularly in terms of their ability to respond or retaliate to our market strategy;
- continually up-dating our view of the sources of competition in our market – not just the existing 'me-too' competitors but new entrants, because then we can focus on the level and type of competitiveness in this market.

However, let us get some fundamental issues out in the open before continuing:

- *Every organization has competitors* – whether you accept it or not. Talk to senior people from the police service. These managers say they had no competitors – there is only one police service. What else do you call the amazing growth in private security firms for the home and the business? We look later at a clothing firm who believed that their brand strength meant that they had no 'competitors', only 'imitators' (see pp. 418–22) – those non-competitive imitators are now the market leaders in that clothing market.
- *We know who our competitors are* – just about every organization says this. An awful lot of them are wrong. Take the examples we looked at earlier: the high-tech medical company that looked only at diagnostic test kits, not electronic scanning, and ended up with no market (see pp. 186–87); the retail banks who persistently claimed that building societies and insurance companies could not compete in the retail banking market (see pp. 284). Competitive myopia is a common condition and can prove fatal.
- *Competitors are in our industry* – many of us tend to identify competitors as firms with the same technology, the same type of products and services, as us: this is the *industry.* Customers are not interested in the 'industry', only in meeting their own needs. The real competition may come from outside our industry: electronic communications reduce the need to travel or freight paper around the world; music competes with clothing for the young consumer's leisure spend; management consultants compete with corporate banks by reducing the need for companies to borrow (e.g. to fund stockholding); industrial companies produce their own raw materials instead of outsourcing and turn from customers to competitors.

Sorting out these basics goes before evaluating our relationships with competitors.

Really understanding the competition

Getting to grips with competition is about far more than just listing the companies that sell similar products and services to us. It is far more about challenging conventional assumptions about what drives our key competitors, understanding their strengths and weaknesses, their limitations and

'challenging conventional assumptions about what drives our key competitors, understanding their strengths and weaknesses, their limitations and problems and their likely strategies'

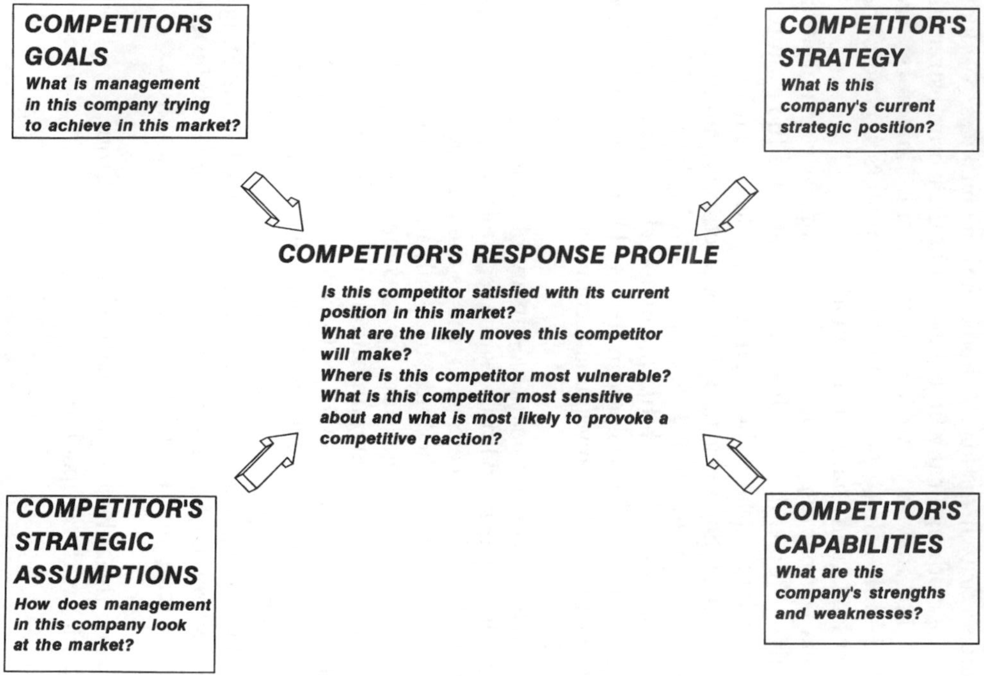

COMPETITOR'S STRATEGY

What is this company's current strategic position?

COMPETITOR'S CAPABILITIES

What are this company's strengths and weaknesses?

COMPETITOR'S RESPONSE PROFILE

Is this competitor satisfied with its current position in this market?
What are the likely moves this competitor will make?
Where is this competitor most vulnerable?
What is this competitor most sensitive about and what is most likely to provoke a competitive reaction?

COMPETITOR'S GOALS

What is management in this company trying to achieve in this market?

COMPETITOR'S STRATEGIC ASSUMPTIONS

How does management in this company look at the market?

Source: Adapted from Porter, Michael E. (1980), Competitive Strategy, New York: Free Press.

Figure 6.3   A framework for competitor analysis

problems and their likely strategies. A conventional framework for structuring this is shown in Figure 6.3.

This framework suggests that we should build a competitor response profile for each key player in the market and constantly revise it. This should help in confronting the likely reactions to our market strategy from each competitor.

The profile should also take into account the psychology of the competition in this market – basically how mean and aggressive are the competitors. For example, try categorizing your competitors in the way shown in Figure 6.4. This involves identifying competitors who will:

- fight to the death in this market, possibly regardless of the short-term commercial consequences;
- show disdain by not reacting to our strategy, because they do not see us as a threat or because they do not have the capability to respond;
- counter-attack to protect their own position, but not very aggressively; and
- simply leave us alone, for one reason or another.

Analysing like this can be surprisingly revealing. It is not a wasted effort if you identify the real threats of aggression in the market.

In case this sounds dubious, consider the continuing competitive war between Tesco and Sainsbury. The nature of Tesco's competitive stance can be judged from an often-repeated anecdote from the days of restricted Sunday trading. A Tesco store was reported on Sunday for illegal trading and was fined and ordered to close. The following Sunday, every Sainsbury within a 50-mile

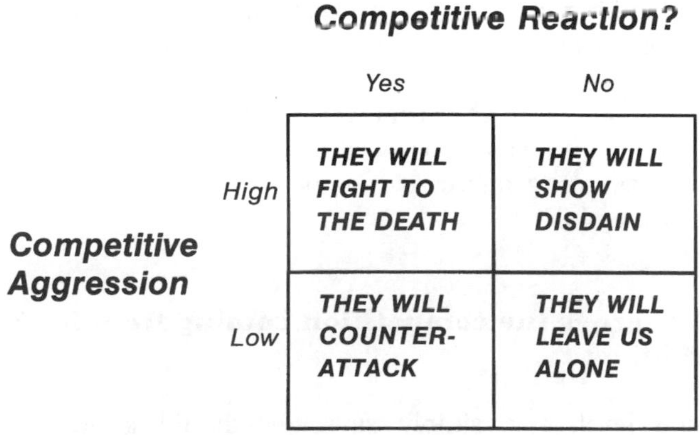

Competitive Reaction?

		Yes	No
Competitive Aggression	High	**THEY WILL FIGHT TO THE DEATH**	**THEY WILL SHOW DISDAIN**
	Low	**THEY WILL COUNTER-ATTACK**	**THEY WILL LEAVE US ALONE**

Figure 6.4 How mean are the competitors around here?

radius of that Tesco store was systematically reported for illegal trading and consequently ordered to close. This may have been an unhappy coincidence, but most people suspect not. It does not matter whether this story is true – it is probably not (it was more likely a 100-mile radius), and we should never let the facts get in the way of a good story. The point is that when Sainsbury talked about the possibility of a price-cutting campaign in January 1997, and Tesco immediately said it would match every price cut made every inch of the way – everybody believed that Tesco would do exactly that. The market knows that if the major competitor attacks Tesco on price, they will hit back immediately and fully.

On the other hand, look at the behaviour of the big manufacturers of electrical household goods – washing machines, fridges, and so on. Far from competing on price, these firms stand accused of deliberately restricting supplies of product to discount outlets. They simply do not want to get into that sort of competition [10]. This is not suggestive of cut-throat, fight-to-the-death relationships between these suppliers, but something rather cosier.

Contrast that with the relationship between Ted Turner, vice chairman of Time Warner Inc, and Rupert Murdoch. Murdoch's new American Sky Broadcasting satellite broadcasting company has led Turner to declare war in highly vitriolic terms, even though the war may damage his own company. The reason seems to lie in pure, mean hatred between the two men. There will be no cosy deals between these companies [11].

Part of the objective in putting strategy into a competitive context is to avoid being trapped in vulnerable positions. If you get into head-on competition with an aggressive market leader they will fight back, and if they are strong enough they will win. Success comes by avoiding head-on conflict and outmanoeuvring the competition – as Daewoo did in the car market, as First Direct did in banking, as Avis did in overtaking Hertz. That success is also about playing to your own strengths and your competitors' weaknesses.

If our analysis suggests that we are targeting the same markets with the same value proposition and the same marketing methods as strong, aggressive competitors – why would we expect to be successful?

But where is the competition coming from in this market?

At one level, this simply says we should know who the competitors are in this market. Undoubtedly true – but not the full story. We also want to know where the *new competitors* will come from:

- potential new entrants to the market – such as retail firms entering the financial services industry; and
- the threat of substitute products and services that meet the customer's needs but may come from a different industry or technology, for example, Dyson's entry to the vacuum cleaner market (see p. 170).

Both are vital to know, both are difficult to track. At least, so it seems. In fact, if you look at the examples given above, the financial services sector had been told for the best part of two decades that multiple retailers could easily and forcefully attack the sector; and the Dyson product innovation was actually offered to the main competitors (Hoover and Electrolux) before Dyson launched it himself (see pp. 170–71 for the full story). Maybe some nasty surprises shouldn't be?

Nonetheless, the point to be made is that we need to continually monitor for new competitive threats which may radically change the attractiveness of the chosen market and undermine our value proposition. The test of whether we are getting there is:

- Do we understand the competition well enough to predict their strategic moves and to maintain our competitive advantage?
- Does this include existing and potential competitors and potential new technologies coming into the market?
- Does our value proposition give us a specific positioning that plays to our strengths and avoids head-on competition, so that we can build a strong position and defend our foothold in the market? If we do not have a competitive differentiation that separates us from the competition in the customer's eyes, then we have no competitive advantage and this market strategy will fail. In this case we need to think again.

This issue has proved so problematic in working with executives that we have developed a specific 'market sensing' technique which focuses on competition (see pp. 415–18).

Collaborator relationships

For most firms, going to market has always involved dependence on other firms – suppliers of raw materials and components, advertising agencies, distributors, and so on. The idea that our market strategy relies for success on collaborating effectively with others to get the product or service to the customer is hardly new. We have always been vulnerable to failure in supply or blockages in the distribution channel. However, the issue of collaboration goes a lot further – it includes various forms of *partnership* with other organizations. This increases our dependence on others to drive our market strategy and suggests areas of risk to consider in putting the strategy in place.

Let us consider the following issues:

● the move from outsourcing (buying-in products and services) to strategic alliances and networks (partnerships of various kinds);
● the emerging pressure to focus on supply chain management and the Efficient Consumer Response programmes; and
● the problems of managing partnerships in implementing market strategy.

The goal is to identify the critical collaboration links that lie under our market strategy, and to see how vulnerable this makes us.

From outsourcing to alliances and networks

One way of categorizing collaborative relationships is shown in Figure 6.5. This suggests that, getting progressively closer to collaboration with others, we can distinguish between:

● *Outsourcing* – an 'arm's length' relationship where we simply contract to buy goods and services on a normal basis, e.g. advertising, market research and direct marketing expertise are typically bought-in expertise. However, we need to consider also the trend towards outsourcing critical activities like personal selling, and for most firms, the unavoidable reality that they will rely on distributors to get their products and services to customers. Some outsourcing may involve enduring relationships and close co-operation.
● *Partnership* – a closer type of relationship where companies recognize each other as partners, and there are varying degrees of inter-company co-ordination and integration.
● *Alliance* – a joint venture where ownership of an activity or operation is shared with a collaborator.
● *Vertical integration* – we fully own the activity or operation [12].

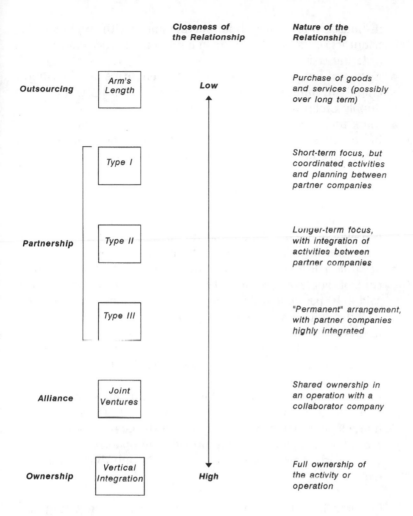

Source: adapted from Lambert et al (12)

Figure 6.5 Types of collaborative relationship

There are many factors driving companies to explore partnerships and strategic alliances as critical components of their market strategies. Quite simply, the use of collaborative arrangements has escalated because of conditions of rapid change and high risk in the marketplace, together with demands for skills and resources that exceed a single firm's capabilities. The goals we seek in partnering and alliance include:

'There are many factors driving companies to explore partnerships and strategic alliances as critical components of their market strategies'

- *Cost efficiency* – it may be cheaper to use the expertise of a specialist than to do something

in-house: McDonalds has partnerships with regional distributors servicing all outlets in a region to reduce delivery and
ordering costs.

● *Customer service* – integration between firms in the supply
chain can improve service (and prices) for customers (see the
Supply Chain commentary below).

● *Marketing advantage* – integration can acquire greater marketing expertise, gain entry to new markets, and provide better
access to technology and innovation. For example, in marketing office equipment in the USA, Xerox partners with Ryder,
the transportation firm, to deliver and install equipment,
reducing costs and retaining price competitiveness. In 1997
British Aerospace announced a deal with Vickers, under which
BAe will market Vickers tanks and armoured vehicles in areas
like Qatar and Saudi Arabia, where Vickers is weak.

● *Strategic advantage* – an alliance may offer greater market
control. For example, in 1997 Dixons, the electrical retailer,
sold a 40 per cent stake in its communications offshoot, Link,
which retails mobile phones, pagers and faxes. This has two
main effects. First, joint ownership commits both Dixons and
Cellnet to the Link venture. Secondly, it is likely that Vodafone,
Cellnet's competitor, will have some trouble finding space for
its products in the Link shops.

● *Profit stability and growth* – for many companies, prospects of
reduced costs and enhanced profits, and access to more
markets and higher market share are the goals of partnership.
More broadly, alliances may provide the opportunity to learn
and absorb other companies' skills (although that works both
ways).

In some industries now, commentators are suggesting that
competition in the future will no longer be between individual
firms, but between *alliances* of firms. This is already becoming a
significant issue in the airline and computer businesses, and
areas like utilities.

For example, early in 1997 Microsoft announced a corporate
computing alliance with Hewlett-Packard, to counter the anti-
Microsoft alliance created the previous week between IBM,
Netscape Communications, Sun Microsystems and Oracle. The
Microsoft alliance will further the spread of the Windows NT
operating system, while the IBM alliance aims to weaken
Microsoft's control over technology standards. In the British
market for electricity and gas supply, rumours in late 1996 were
of a prospective alliance between British Telecom and certain of
the power companies, for BT to market energy and telecom
services together.

Indeed, in the international telecoms market, British Telecom is partnering with MCI, the second largest US long-distance carrier, to create Concert, a holding company for the two groups, which will compete against AT&T's Unisource consortium and the Franco-German alliance of Deutsche Telekom and France Telecom.

These examples are all illustrative of a new type of competition – between alliances and consortia, not individual organizations – which may cause us to re-think some of our assumptions about who can do what.

In fact, there is more – the spread of collaboration, partnership and alliance strategies has led in many industries to the emergence of a wholly new organizational form: *the hollow* or *network organization.*

For example, in the USA, Calyx and Corolla (C&C) is a good example of a prototype for the network organization. C&C have in effect re-invented the way Americans buy flowers, by selling perishable cut flowers from catalogues (and an Internet site). The C&C network is shown in Figure 6.6 – customers order flowers from C&C's catalogue pictures, C&C passes the order electronically to the selected grower (based on stock availability), and Federal Express collects the flowers from the grower (branded with the C&C logo and packaging) and delivers them to the customer. This case is remarkable in two respects. First, it cuts out

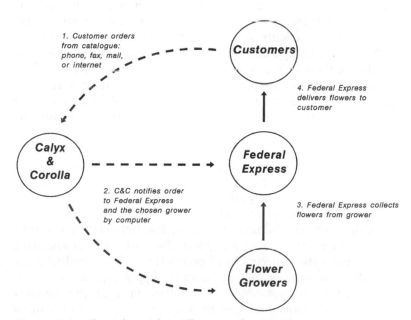

Figure 6.6 The Calyx and Corolla network organization

three middlemen from the traditional channel for cut flowers (wholesalers, distributors and retailers) and gets flowers to the customer that are up to nine days fresher than flowers bought from a conventional retailer. Secondly, this is a 'virtual' or 'hollow' organization – C&C adds value through a catalogue and computer links, it does not grow flowers, own warehouses, operate retail outlets, or run a distribution or delivery fleet, and it operates with only a small core staff, so can quickly re-position to follow changing customer requirements [13].

A similar re-thinking of a business based on a network of collaborators is shown by the Smart Card announced by Shell, the oil company, in 1997 [14]. Shell is at the centre of a consortium of retailers and other companies (Dixons, Currys, Victoria Wine, Vision Express, John Menzies, The Link, Commercial Union, the RAC, Hilton Hotels – with Sainsbury, Next, Allied Domecq and Cellnet potentially joining). The Shell strategy is to take its Smart loyalty card into general shopping, allowing card users to shop, bank, make phone calls, while collecting discount points and Air Miles in the process. The discount points earned are cashable in any of the consortium members' operations – money spent on Shell petrol could give money off a product in Victoria Wine, and so on. The goal is for the one card to service 70 per cent of the average consumer's expenditure. This strategy too is based on a 'virtual' organization.

Another 'hollow' or 'virtual' organization is The Registry Inc. in the USA. The Registry's core competence is its skill in recruiting software engineers, programmers and technical writers to work on clients' computing and IT projects. Founded in 1987, The Registry's customer account managers identify client needs and then form customized technical teams to service client projects, such as computer system conversions and software development. The Registry has a database of 55 000 technical specialists, with 30 recruiters to locate technical talent and 55 salespeople to put together teams around customer needs. Sales in 1995 were around $100 million [15].

However, network organizations do not always involve such a high degree of collaborative relationship to succeed. The Bombay Company is an extremely successful speciality furniture company in the USA – its stores are full of ornaments and household items from the East. The Bombay Company has links with more than 150 speciality producers throughout the world, and this network co-ordinates the sourcing and production of the products. For example, one supplier may contract to supply a quantity of table tops, which are assembled by another firm in the network together with items produced by other suppliers for the Bombay core organizations, to produce tables. Members of the network are specialists in performing certain value-adding functions at low cost. The Bombay Company's very successful market performance is based on a unique product assortment, and the flexibility to quickly change the assortment in the light of consumer preferences [13].

In some cases collaboration is simply a fast way to get access to a market by using the existing resources of other companies. For example, a niche of the highly competitive UK grocery market is the time-pressed mobile customer who wants easy one-stop shopping – someone on the way home from work who has no dinner in the house and no catfood. The Budgens supermarket group has outmanoeuvred its larger competitors by a collaboration with Kuwait Petroleum and BP, to open co-branded petrol station forecourt grocery stores, selling ready-meals and fresh and chilled food (and catfood).

One remarkable example of the degree of transformation that may be involved in these new types of organization is shown by ICL, the troubled 'British' computer company, now owned by Fujitsu. The transformation of this company during the 1990s is so radical that by 1997 ICL no longer had any factories. The company has gone from a traditional manufacturing organization to a computer services company focused on consultancy, outsourcing, electronic commerce, computer training and the delivery of systems to the retail and finance sectors. ICL's move into new areas, after a period of restructuring and divestment, means that it no longer needs to own production facilities – ICL is a hollow corporation.

However, the search for competitive advantage by developing networks based on strategic alliances and partnerships has also seen some major failures:

'the search for competitive advantage by developing networks based on strategic alliances and partnerships has also seen some major failures'

- When Rover was purchased by BMW, the Rover chief executive actually seemed to believe that the 15-year-old R&D and marketing partnership with Honda would continue. Honda's view about Rover attempting to sell Honda's expertise to BMW was somewhat different, and Honda has effectively ended the collaboration.
- IBM and Microsoft were at one stage partners in a strategic alliance, which collapsed because of conflict of interest between the partners.
- British Airways and USAir ended up in court, because BA decided it was better served by an alliance with American Air, and that partnership is dead.
- The alliance between KLM, Royal Dutch Airline and Northwest Airlines was formed in 1990 and took Northwest back into

profitability by generating $100 million in new revenue for the partners, but has involved clashes between the partners, such as KLM's threat to sue if Northwest carried out a threat to change shareholder rights, and the battle for power continues[16].

- In 1994 the strategic alliance between Intel, the microprocessor manufacturer, and its biggest customer, Compaq, crumbled as a result of the 'Intel Inside' advertising campaign, which undermined Compaq by promoting its competitors' computers (which also have Intel chips) [17].
- One recent study of 82 large multinational companies found that less than half the companies operating strategic alliances were satisfied with the effectiveness of those alliances[18].

Developing networks of collaborating and allied organizations can provide powerful competitive leverage. However, collaboration creates dependence, and we need to think very hard about that vulnerability – how good are we at managing in partnerships, and where will we be left if the partnership fails?

A particular area of collaboration and partnering that should be noted is in *supply chain relationships*. For consumer goods manufacturers these are of particular note because, as with so many deals with powerful retailers, collaboration largely means doing what you are told. At the extreme, control of supply chains may even take away the manufacturer's right to brand, in favour of the retailer's. Consider the following example.

The focus on the supply chain is seen in the Efficient Consumer Response (ECR) programme in the USA, started in the early 1990s and launched in the UK in 1996. ECR has been pioneered in the grocery business, but is being extended into the healthcare, airlines and food processing sectors in the USA.

The ECR movement is based on 'co-operative partnerships' between retailers and manufacturers, who commit to collaborate in reducing costs in the supply chain. Leading players in the USA were Krogers, the leading national supermarket chain, and Procter and Gamble – but by 1995 nearly 90 per cent of firms in the grocery business were applying ECR. In the UK, the participants at the 1996 launch were Tesco, Sainsbury, Waitrose, Safeway, Asda and Marks and Spencer from retailing and Procter and Gamble, Unilever, Mars, Nestlé and Kraft on the supplier side. ECR represents the application of 'lean supply chain' principles to the branded goods business (see pp. 18–19).

The US pioneers of ECR in the grocery business point to the key drivers of what they believe was a survival strategy, as factors in traditional channels like:

- *forward buying and diverting* – where retailers do not pass on manufacturer price cuts, but buy-in at low prices and take on 'internal' profit, or buy locally where manufacturers have discounted prices and ship the goods elsewhere again to show an internal profit;
- *excessive inventories* – retailers were holding an average of more than three months' supplies;
- *damaged and unsaleable goods* – were at unacceptably high levels;
- *complex deals and deductions* – negotiated deals were so complicated that as much as 80 per cent of invoices had to be processed manually;
- *promotion and coupons* – it is estimated that in the USA, in 1996 261 billion promotional coupons were issued, with less than 2 per cent redeemed;
- *new products* – in 1996, 22 400 new products were launched in the US grocery business, dominated by imitative 'me-too' brands, with the expectation that 90 per cent would last less than two years, while the bottom 25 per cent of brands stocked in the supermarket gave retailers less than 1 per cent of their sales.

The ECR programme was a response to this situation, and the goal was to take some $30 billion a year of cost out of the grocery supply chain in the USA, by making retail assortments more efficient, by making sales promotion more efficient, by making product replenishment systems more efficient and by handling product introductions better. The central issue is one of managing flows in the supply chain – flows of product, information and cash. The key elements of ECR are:

- *Category management* – collaborative planning by retailers and manufacturers around groups of products in the store as they are perceived by customers, not brands as produced by manufacturers, e.g. 'ready-meal solutions' grouping together products that replace the home-cooked meal, 'laundry' or 'photoprocessing'. Typically this has taken 20 per cent of product items off the shelf for good;
- *More efficient promotions* – drastic reductions in the number of coupons and special offers and the substitution of 'value pricing';
- *Continuous replenishment* – the continual flow of product from manufacturers, with no stock-keeping at retail or wholesale levels, with direct store delivery, with the result that by the end of the first three years of ECR around 20 per cent less stock was held. For example, a package of Procter and Gamble soap

powder typically gets to the customer seven days after manufacture instead of four to six weeks (and, incidentally, contains less preservatives as a result);

- *Electronic Data Interchange* – the computerization of ordering and payment systems, in a paperless information flow through the supply chain;
- *Performance measures* – new ways of evaluating performance;
- *Organizational change* – for example, Procter and Gamble has replaced its sales organization with its Customer Business Development organization, as part of its commitment to ECR.

Enthusiasm for the power of the ECR strategy in reducing supply chain costs has crossed the Atlantic to Europe. Claims are widespread that across Europe it should be possible to take out £21 billion a year from grocery supply chain costs, or between 5 and 6 per cent of cost. The principles are the same: automated store ordering (point-of-sale scanning data triggers new orders automatically); cross-docking (goods go from suppliers' trucks to retailers' trucks with no time spent in a warehouse); continual replenishment (to avoid stockholding); and more reliable ordering and payment systems.

This pursuit of operational efficiency in distribution is in many ways superb. However, at the risk of appearing a little cynical it is worth raising a couple of questions about the impact of ECR on market strategy and customer value, rather than just operational efficiency:

- When Don Dufek, ECR Operating Committee Chairman in the USA, a champion of ECR and former Senior Vice-President of Krogers, says that ECR is about increasing customer satisfaction and that 'the real power is with the consumer', we all get excited and think ECR is wonderful [19]. But then he tells us how at Krogers they have used ECR to drastically reduce the number of brands on the shelf in collaboration with major suppliers, and how they found that with ECR they could increase some product prices to improve profitability. Am I the only one who cannot see how less choice and higher prices will increase my satisfaction as a Krogers' customer? Am I the only one who wonders how small brands from smaller suppliers are ever going to get onto Krogers' shelves, now that they are neatly shared out between the big suppliers?
- ECR is an excellent vehicle for reducing operating costs in mature channels of distribution, but its importance is to cost saving (particularly for retailers), not customer satisfaction. I am very pleased for companies that save money, but where is the benefit to me as the customer? The most they could

possibly offer is a 5 per cent price cut (and it will probably be much less), and that is not very impressive to me as a customer.

- Why does anyone think that as a customer I care how long the product has been on the shelf? It really makes no difference to me whether the can of Coke is three months old or one week old, because it still *tastes* the same; I am not really interested if the pack of soap powder left the factory eight weeks or eight days ago, it does nothing to increase the value of the product to the customer. Great increases in operational efficiency – yes. Increase in customer value – no.
- It is also perhaps too cynical to note that Procter and Gamble's disappointing 1996 results brought a large share price fall, and this was attributed mainly to its Efficient Consumer Response programme and particularly its 'value pricing' component [20].
- Why does it seem strange that after years of confrontational and adversarial conflict between retailers and manufacturers we can accept the 'cease-fire' because of ECR – it looks very fragile in the longer term? Why does it look more like retailers using their market power to demand more cost savings from manufacturers?
- Why do I feel uncomfortable when I hear Paul Polman of Procter and Gamble (UK) talking about 'confusing consumers with meaningless choice', and telling us that even if 40 per cent of existing laundry stock-keeping units (product items) are cut, the category would still meet 95 per cent of consumer needs; and why do I start speculating about the consumers who like choice and the niche market opportunities in the 5 per cent of the market that P&G does not seem to want [21]?
- Why, when a branded goods marketing manager says: 'If your top five retail outlets say you are joining this club, or face the consequences . . . you join the club and pay your dues', does this sound a bit more like the real world?

Whatever view we take, ECR is a reality for those in the grocery business, and it may well spread to other sectors in time. In this situation, the real issue is how the total surplus in the supply chain is divided between manufacturer, supplier and distributor. The question for us then is how it impacts on our value proposition and our process of getting to the market.

More generally, the potential attraction of collaboration and alliance in implementing our market strategy needs to be carefully evaluated against how well partners will carry the value proposition forward, how

'the real issue is how the total surplus in the supply chain is divided between manufacturer, supplier and distributor'

vulnerable we will be if the collaboration or alliance does not work out, and our capabilities in managing partnerships with other companies.

Managing partnerships and collaborations

The signs to look for to judge whether a partnership is going to work include the following [11]:

- *Corporate compatibility* – for a partnership to work, the cultures and business objectives must mesh. The IBM/Microsoft collaboration probably never stood a chance, given the totally different cultures of Bill Gates' irreverent and entrepreneurial software company and IBM's bureaucracy. The alliance died because the partners were both going after the same market – IBM with OS/2, which Microsoft had produced for it, and Microsoft with Windows, which it had produced for itself. Microsoft won.
- *Management style and techniques* – similarities in operating styles help. McDonalds and Coca-Cola share a similar management approach and have an effective and highly integrated partnership. The KLM/Northwest partnership is endangered by Northwest's pursuit of short-term financial gains and a lack of trust between the two organizations.
- *Mutuality* – the partnership is stronger if both sides get benefits not otherwise obtained, and if there is trust and commitment on both sides.
- *Symmetry* – partnerships between 'equals' stand the best chance.

If a partnership-based strategy is to be pursued, then it is also necessary to consider the costs and time involved in managing these issues:

- *Establishing the partnership* – identifying, negotiating with and striking a deal with another organization;
- *Monitoring the partnership* – carefully evaluating the effectiveness and strength of the relationship;
- *Strengthening the partnership* – where necessary investing time and effort in the joint activities needed to improve the effectiveness of the partnership.

So, part of our thinking needs to be given to identifying the collaborations and other relationships that underpin going to market with our value proposition. Perhaps the most critical issues are vulnerability and capability – how fragile is our strategy to a failure in key collaborations, and do we have the capability to manage collaborations where they underpin the market strategy? Negative conclusions here may also drive us back to questioning our market choices and the robustness of the value proposition in the real marketplace.

Co-worker relationships

The underlying argument in Part I of the book was that superior performance comes from customer focus, but superior customer focus comes from the 'part-time marketers' – all the operational employees, service personnel, maintenance workers, functional managers and key decision makers – whose attitudes, beliefs and values impact on the customer. We looked at Avis Europe Ltd and CIGNA Employee Benefits as cases of companies who have achieved remarkable results by taking this issue seriously.

'superior performance comes from customer focus, but superior customer focus comes from the "part-time marketers" '

We will not repeat these arguments here. The task at this stage is to look at our value proposition and to question whether our people can and will deliver the promise to the customer.

Several points are worth adding.

First, do not *assume* that because we have developed a great new market strategy, everyone else in the company is going to agree!

For example, the Automobile Association (AA) in Britain is a 90-year-old organization founded to provide rescue services to motorists, and has positioned itself as the 'fourth emergency service'. Its share of the breakdown rescue service has been eroded by aggressive competitors like Green Flag National Breakdown, who have attacked the AA on price and service. The AA's strategy has been to move progressively into financial services and holidays. In 1995 the unheard-of happened – the AA breakdown service patrolmen balloted for industrial action. The AA's increasing commercialism was completely out-of-line with the service ethic which had attracted the patrolmen to work for the AA. AA patrolmen joined to rescue stranded members – there was strong resentment against selling membership services and insurance [22]. More successful has been the AA Home Assistance service – putting people in touch with high-quality repair firms for household emergencies like broken windows and burst pipes, which seems to exploit the traditional service culture of the AA people [23].

As they used to say on sales training courses – ASSUME is a very dangerous word, because it makes an ASS out of U, and even worse, out of ME!

Second, we need to be *realistic* about our capabilities. The question is: can we deliver this strategy to the customer, with these people, these skills, these traditions, this culture, these processes, these structures and boundaries? The question is *not* (usually): if we started again from scratch, could we deliver the strategy?

For example, Frank Cespedes describes the sort of problems faced:

- When IBM planned to release its System 9370 mainframe, the launch was marked by a squabble between product managers and sales managers – the product managers wanted the computer released quickly, but the sales managers wanted to meet quotas of existing products before the launch (when customers would stop buying until the new product was out). The product managers won. The launch was then plagued by lack of co-operation from sales management and poor product sales.
- At a telecoms firm, a programme of enhanced maintenance and repair services effectively and unwittingly killed the sales of a system upgrade which Sales were launching with a major customer.
- At a packaged goods firm, brand and sales units use different measures of retail distribution. Relationships between the units are plagued by misunderstanding and mistrust because they are using different information systems.

Frank's point is that if we want a seamless process of going to market, then we have to work for it. He has developed the idea of 'concurrent marketing' – the goal is better co-ordination of product, sales and service management, not by vague demands for better 'teamwork', but by carefully developing mechanisms for cross-functional co-operation with clear lines of primary and joint authority, and with new personnel policies that reflect the new priorities in training and career paths [24].

Third, it is easy to underestimate people's capabilities – what they can do if they are given the chance.

For example, one of the most remarkable stories in the US car business of recent years has been the success of Saturn, a subsidiary of General Motors, which has redefined the car buying experience [25]. Saturn's market strategy involved overcoming US buyers' animosity to US cars, by incorporating the owning, buying and shopping experience into owning the car. They have relied on partnership with many collaborators, but none more important than partnership with the customer and with their employees. The company says the Saturn philosophy is one of partnership, but 'We have nothing of greater value than our people ... We believe that demonstrating respect for the uniqueness of every individual builds a team of confident, creative members possessing a high degree of initiative, self-respect and self-discipline' [25]. Indeed, employees are selected for their compatibility with this culture. As we saw earlier, the Saturn 'family' has proved a powerful attraction in the US car market (see p. 72).

However, in most organizations relatively few of our employees and managers are skilled in mind-reading. If we do not discuss, explain, listen, problem-solve and bargain, why would we expect the people in the organization to drive the value proposition for us? More of this when we look at internal marketing (see pp. 592–613).

'why would we expect the people in the organization to drive the value proposition for us?'

However we do it, we need to evaluate our emerging market strategy against the co-worker relationship issue. Our conclusions may even challenge the market choices we have made, and undermine our belief in the value proposition – then we need to do more thinking.

The key relationships

We have looked at relationship marketing and alliances and partnerships as components of our market strategy. But in particular this chapter has asked us to test our market choices and our value proposition very hard against a number of key relationships:

- the relationship with the *customer*, and with different market segments, in terms of the promises tied up in our value proposition and brands and whether we can keep those promises;
- the relationship with *competitors* of different kinds, and in particular whether the competitive differentiation and strategic position we have built will stand up against the level and type of competition we will face;
- the relationship with *collaborators* of various kinds, and the degree to which outsourcing, and partnerships and alliances we may have assumed in developing our market strategy, are actually going to work; and

● the relationship with *co-workers* – the people we rely on inside the company to implement and drive the value proposition.

At each stage we have identified new opportunities – to use relationship marketing, to segment the market by relationship type, to position against competitors, to examine new networking possibilities, and so on. But we have also stressed that our conclusions about these relationships and their impact on the market strategy may well drive us back to re-thinking market choices and re-working the value proposition.

Have We Got A Market Strategy?

	How Are We Doing?						
	Needs more attention						As good as we can get
STRATEGIZING							
● Do we have the mechanisms and processes for management to focus on strategy?	1	2	3	4	5	6	7
● Are we forcing ourselves to look to the future and to confront the changes in our industry?	1	2	3	4	5	6	7
MARKET CHOICES							
● Have we got a view of market definition based on customer needs and customer differences?	1	2	3	4	5	6	7
● Do we have a model of the segmentation of our markets based on customer benefits?	1	2	3	4	5	6	7
● Does our market segmentation link strategy to operations?	1	2	3	4	5	6	7
● Do we know what we are looking for in markets (marketing attractiveness) and in our market position?	1	2	3	4	5	6	7
● Are we avoiding the traps of being stuck in Peripheral Business, Illusion Business or Dead-End Business?	1	2	3	4	5	6	7
● Can we list our priority markets and segments on a page of paper and justify those choices?	1	2	3	4	5	6	7
DEVELOPING THE VALUE PROPOSITION							
● Have we got all we can from mission analysis to link corporate values to market success factors?	1	2	3	4	5	6	7

Figure 6.7   Diagnostic Worksheet 2: Have we got a market strategy?

So, have we got a market strategy?

The issues raised in Chapters 4, 5 and 6 are fundamental. They are not easy. One way of reviewing what you have got so far is the Diagnostic Worksheet 2, shown in Figure 6.7. This provides a way of focusing our thinking back onto the most problematic issues, where we need to do more work.

Really this Diagnostic just takes us back through the Strategic Pathway and asks us to take a view on whether we have really got

• Do we have a thorough understanding of the company's overall corporate strategy and core competencies?		2	3	4	1	6	7
• Can we translate core competencies into differentiating capabilities for this market?	1	2	3	4	5	6	7
• Do we have a foundation for competitive differentiation that will be effective and sustainable?	1	2	3	4	5	6	7
• Do we have a full understanding of our marketing assets and how we can use them to build sustainable competitive advantage in this market?	1	2	3	4	5	6	7
• Do we have strength in branding which we are using as part of our Value Proposition?	1	2	3	4	5	6	7
• Can we write down our Value Proposition on half a page of paper, and does it still look convincing when we do?	1	2	3	4	5	6	7
ASSESSING THE KEY RELATIONSHIPS							
• Can we identify the parties with whom effective relationships are essential to drive the market strategy?	1	2	3	4	5	6	7
• Do we know if relationship marketing offers us leverage?	1	2	3	4	5	6	7
• Do we fully understand what our Value Proposition means to our relationship with the customer and what it will take to deliver the Value Proposition?	1	2	3	4	5	6	7
• Do we fully understand what the market strategy requires of our co-workers?	1	2	3	4	5	6	7
• Are we sure that co-workers can and will deliver what is required to drive the Value Proposition?	1	2	3	4	5	6	7

Figure 6.7 Continued

to grips with the underlying issues – and if not, to go back and think again. Only when we are ticking the scale under 'As Good As We Can Get' in most areas of the Strategic Pathway, can we be reasonably sure that we have put together a coherent market strategy.

However, in most organizations having a strategy is not enough. We have to have a plan as well! For this reason, the next chapter provides a structure for getting from a strategy to a plan.

References

1. Gronroos, Christian (1994), 'From Marketing Mix to Relationship Marketing', *Management Decision*, Vol. 32, No. 2, 4–20.
2. Christopher, Martin A., Adrian Payne and David Ballantyne (1991), *Relationship Marketing*, Oxford: Butterworth-Heinemann.
3. Sheth, Jagdish N. and Atul Parvatiyar (1995), 'The Evolution of Relationship Marketing', *International Business Review*, Vol. 4, No. 4, 397–418.
4. Webster, Frederick (1992), 'The Changing Role of Marketing in the Corporation', *Journal of Marketing*, Vol. 56, October, 1–17.
5. Cravens, David W., Nigel F. Piercy and Shannon H. Shipp (1996), 'New Organizational Focus for Competing in Highly Dynamic Environments: the Network Paradigm', *British Journal of Management*, Vol. 7, No. 3, 203–218.
6. Gummesson, Evert (1990), *The Part-Time Marketer*, Centre for Service Research, Karlstad.
7. Ohmae, Kenichi (1989), 'The Global Logic of Strategic Alliances', *Harvard Business Review*, March/April, 143–154.
8. Clegg, Philip (1956), *A Social and Economic History of Britain 1760–1955*, London: Harrap.
9. Lyons, Teena (1997), 'They're All the Same to Us, Say Bored Shoppers', *Sunday Business*, 16 March.
10. Alderson, Andrew and Paul Nuki (1997), 'Stores Accuse Electrical Groups of Discount Cut-Off', *Sunday Times*, 6 April.
11. Rubython, Tom (1997), 'Turner Threatens to Thwart Murdoch's US Satellite Venture', *Sunday Business*, 30 March.
12. Lambert, Douglas M., Margaret A. Emmelhainz, John T. Gardner (1996), 'So You Think You Want a Partner?', *Marketing Management*, Summer, 25–41.
13. Cravens, David W., Nigel F. Piercy and Shannon H. Shipp (1996), *op. cit.*
14. Massey, Ray (1997), 'Shell Plays its Ace to Clean Up in Card Market', *Daily Mail*, 13 March.
15. Falvey, J. (1993), 'Coming Attractions', *Sales and Marketing Management*, July, 16–21.

16. Cravens, David W., Gordon Greenley, Nigel F. Piercy and Stanley Slater (1997), 'Market-Driven Strategic Management', *Long Range Planning*, Vol. 30, No. 4, 493–506.
17. 'Get Ready for a Brand New Battle', *Marketing Week*, 23 September.
18. Cravens, David W., Shannon H. Shipp and Karen S. Cravens (1993), 'Analysis of Co-operative Interorganizational Relationships, Strategic Alliance Formation, and Strategic Alliance Effectiveness', *Journal of Strategic Marketing*, March, 55–70.
19. Dufek, Don (1997), 'Essential Elements of ECR', American Marketing Association Winter Educators' Conference, St Petersberg, Fl
20. Tomlins, Richard (1996), 'Shares in P&G Slide 4 per cent As Sales Slip', *Financial Times*, 25 October.
21. Mitchell, Alan (1996), 'P&G Slams Inefficient Marketing', *Marketing Week*, 8 November.
22. Harlow, John and Simon Hinde (1995), 'Modernising AA Forces First Strike in 90 Years', *Sunday Times*, 14 May.
23. 'AA Drives Off Cowboy Tradesmen', *Mail on Sunday*, 30 March 1997.
24. Cespedes, Frank V. (1996), 'Beyond Teamwork: How the Wise Can Synchronize', *Marketing Management*, Vol. 5, No. 1, 25–37.
25. Rubel, Chad (1996), 'Partnerships Steer Saturn to a New Marketing Mix', *Marketing News*, 29 January.

CHAPTER 7

Planning marketing:

What do we need to do to get from strategy to a plan?

Introduction

As a market strategy begins to emerge from our evaluation of market choices, the development of a value proposition and definition of a strategic position for our business in its market, and we evaluate the underlying relationships on which the strategy is dependent, then in most organizations we will need to produce a plan.

A lot of people do not like plans, planning or planners. Henry Mintzberg says that strategic planning is not strategic thinking, that the goal of those who promote planning is to reduce managers' power over strategy making, and that real strategic change requires inventing new categories, not just rearranging old ones [1]. He has a point.

' "Strategizing" is the prerequisite'

'Strategizing' is the prerequisite, but the trouble is that organizations like written-down plans as well. The companies I work with do not let you do things unless you can put your great strategic ideas into the sort of plan they recognize. This may be stupid, but it is the way things are.

Mintzberg is right about one thing though – planning is a different activity to developing strategy. Gary Hamel goes further:

> The essential problem in organizations today is a failure to distinguish planning from strategizing. Planning is about programming, not discovering. Planning is for technocrats, not dreamers. Giving planners responsibility for creating strategy is like asking a bricklayer to create Michelangelo's Pietà. [2]

This is stirring stuff, but actually Hamel is wrong. Planning can actually be an incredible source of leverage for creating strategic ideas, building momentum for change and winning people's commitment and enthusiasm for strategic change. (Bricklayers are people too, by the way, and in the building trade probably have some good ideas about strategy, if only we bothered to ask them to tell us.) This is about how we manage the process of planning. However, that is the topic for Chapter 11 – concerned with creating plans that build 'ownership' and get driven through to implementation.

'Planning can actually be an incredible source of leverage for creating strategic ideas'

The goal in this chapter is more modest – we need a structure to articulate our market strategy, to show how we have tested the components of the strategy and to link the strategy to a marketing programme. This conventional view of marketing planning will provide this final stage in defining our Strategic Pathway.

A conventional view of marketing planning

Figure 7.1 provides a conventional model of marketing planning. With minor variations, most flow-chart models of marketing planning look something like this. We can put a little flesh on these bones.

Corporate goals, missions and constraints

Normally, we would expect that the corporate or strategic planning process (or top management) will define for us what we are expected to achieve in the specific product market which our

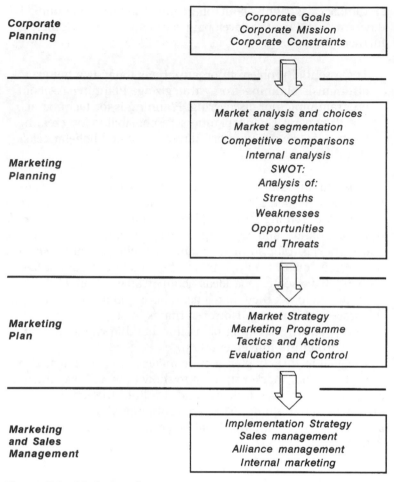

Figure 7.1 Marketing planning

marketing plan is to cover. Ideally, at the start we should have a clear view of our mission, goals and constraints.

Mission

Corporate mission will either specifically cover our product market or will show us how to write a market mission for our specific part of the business (see pp. 179–94 above). More mundane parameters should also be defined at the start: *Customers* – what type, and which, are to be covered by the marketing plan; *Products* – which are to be included in the plan and in our view of the competitive marketplace; *Geographic boundaries* – what are the geographical areas we should include;

and *Strategic Direction* – is this a market where the company wants fast *penetration*, or is prepared to invest for longer-term *development*, or one where we are expected simply to *maintain* the current position, or create a new market position by a *turnaround*, or even one where we are expected to *harvest* what we can get in margins for minimum cost, or to prepare for *divestment?*

In fact, in many practical situations you are likely to find clear guidance here conspicuous by its absence. In the sophisticated multinational branded consumer goods operation and the like – yes, strategic planning will define these things for us. However, in many situations I suspect, and experience suggests, that you will find that strategic/corporate plans either contain nothing other than extended five year budgets, or they simply do not exist. In that case, these parameters have to be generated within the marketing planning process itself.

Actually, if we see the purpose of marketing planning as getting a match between what we have got and what customers want, and then *doing* it – it makes very little difference if we call it Marketing Planning, or Business Planning, or Strategic Planning, or Business Development, or anything we like really! Lack of formal strategic planning may actually be a great opportunity for us*.

Goals

We would also expect to start marketing planning with some idea of what we are expected to achieve in sales, market share, profitability, cash flow and liquidity, portfolio balance, and so on, within a specified time-frame. It also helps, more than a little, if we know the assumptions that have been made in producing those goals – market growth, new product availability, and so on. As with mission, in the sophisticated, high-technology planning framework, the goals are created for us by the strategic planning process. In many real situations, we have to develop our own goals.

Constraints

Perhaps less conventional, but equally important, there is some merit in letting our planners know right from the start what they *cannot* do. We need to know what new assumptions are permitted

---

*We should perhaps remember, though, the old marketing adage: 'there is no such thing as marketing problems, only marketing opportunities – unfortunately some of the opportunities may be insoluble!'

about issues such as: personnel, new products and services, changes to the customer base, organizational structure, marketing strategies, new technology and other critical issues. This is not about being negative, it is about trying to avoid situations where people get excited and produce innovative plans, only to be told about the 'zero head-count growth' policy; the unacceptability of proposed structural changes; the cancellation of new products; or that certain market strategies are incompatible with 'company policy'.

The foundation for our plan is thus what we are expected to achieve, where and with what, and what we are not able to do. That just leaves the problem of how we are going to achieve the things the company wants.

This sounds incredibly obvious and straightforward – but it isn't. Even if we get management to commit themselves to these issues, there is no guarantee they will not change their minds! The world is full of people who think nothing of moving the goal-posts while the game is in progress. But life is like that. The positive side of this is that if missions and goals are *not* written in tablets of stone, we may be able to go back and re-negotiate them when we have seen what we've got and what the market is doing.

This is the corporate context into which the results of our 'strategizing' have to fit – our market choices, value proposition and key relationship strategies.

The strategic marketing audit

The next, and probably largest, stage in our planning process is review of the marketplace and our resources (normally organized around the marketing mix structure). This suggests that we look at the market, product policy, pricing policy, distribution policy and communications policy, and pack our proposals about these things together into an integrated plan. The trouble with boxing things off like this is that most of us close each box when we have finished it, and never open it again. One of the points made by William Giles[3], who actually made these things work for real, is that you have to have the type of *iteration* shown in Figure 7.2. In essence, as we go through the stages of the marketing audit, it is vital that we look back at how the new insights change our view of the earlier stages of the analysis. This provides us with the framework into which to fit our market strategy, and to translate it into a marketing programme.

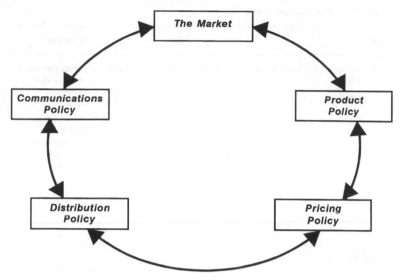

Figure 7.2 Iteration in planning

The market audit

The first, and probably most time-consuming, stage of the strategic audit is the view we take of the marketplace and what makes it work. We have already uncovered the major issues here – market segmentation, competitive differentiation, and so on. What we have to do here is systematically evaluate the position on the most critical market issues. A structure for doing this is shown in Table 7.1.

The product audit

We can then focus specifically on product policy issues, and a simplified structure for this is shown in Table 7.2. It is here that we try to get to grips with how well our products meet customer needs, and what the critical product dimensions are from the customer's point of view.

The pricing audit

Closely related to our product positioning is the issue of price compared to competitors, and the critical issue of *value* as it is perceived by the paying customer. Table 7.3 provides a structure for this stage of our analysis.

Table 7.1 The market audit

Focus	Analyse	Objective
Customer needs and buying factors	Customer priorities in the needs to be met through purchase. Customer group differences	Emphasize customer needs, not products, and the differences between potential segments
Products and customers	Group products by their common need satisfaction characteristics and customers or markets by common characteristics	Create product and customer definitions reflecting the marketplace, not the technology or the internal operations
Key products	Identify the key products for each customer group/market, the ones you *have* to have to be a player in this market	Establish customer group/ market differences in product priorities
Marketing priorities and critical success factors	Evaluation of most important marketing mix element for each customer group/market and the things the 'winners' get right	Establish relative effectiveness of marketing mix variables and competitive requirements
Market segmentation	Product groups and customer types matching	Define customer-related market segments reflecting differences in *customer* needs
Company priorities	Compare each match of product and customer to: – potential competitiveness we could achieve – attractiveness of this business to us	Isolate areas of high and low priority and niche gaps and opportunities in segments, and the match to our goals and capabilities
Market sizing and shares	Use emerging segments to value market and its trend, and shares taken by competitors	Place values on segments to move towards targets
Life cycle and competitive position	Life cycle stage and competitive position in each segment	Prioritize market segments and niches
Competitors	Evaluate: – direct and indirect competition – enterers and leavers – major competitors' characteristics	Identify competitive prospects and our shortfalls
Marketing environment	Evaluate likely impact of broad changes in markets, law, institutions, technology, etc.	Put planning into the broader context of strategic change in the outside world
Market summary	Across the segments, analyse life cycle stage, value, current and required business direction, priority products, marketing mix requirements	Collate market and competitive positioning
Market priorities	Across the segments, analyse our market share and sales projections, chances of success, and priorities	Choose priority market targets
Critical success factors	What *must* be right to achieve customer priorities	Specific action list
Marketing objectives	In priority segments, the key marketing objectives and how they relate to sales and market share	Isolate major marketing goals, compared to corporate objectives

Table 7.2   The product audit

Focus	Analyse	Objective
Competitive performance	In each segment, how well do our products meet customer needs compared to competition?	Identify gaps in matching our products to high priority customer needs
Product dimensions	For the critical products or customer needs, how well do we perform compared to competitors on the most important dimensions?	Concentrate on strategic differentiating characteristics of products, not just the generic product
Product lines	For the critical products or customer needs, where do we stand against market standards, and where are our specific product gaps and deficiencies?	Develop list of shortfalls and actions to remedy

Table 7.3   The pricing audit

Focus	Analyse	Objective
Product pricing	Within each segment, compare our product prices to key competitors, and our price positioning in the segment	Identify product price positioning
Market pricing	Within each segment, compare our product prices to key competitors, across the segments and for the total market	Identify market price positioning and relationship with market share
Price trends	Examine product price index for past and expected future	Identify risers and fallers
Value	Compare perceived quality, price position and market share for our company and key competitors	Break the 'low price' = high sales' perception and look for positioning anomalies
Price levels	For key products, compare our discount structures with key competitors	Compare our strategy with competitors' and track implications for market share

The distribution audit

At this stage we look at the distribution and service patterns in the market, and our performance compared to our competitors. A structure for approaching this task is given in Table 7.4.

Table 7.4 The distribution audit

Focus	Analyse	Objective
Channels	Map all the channels through which products and services reach the customer, and the amount of market served by each. Look at trends	Take broad view of channel system and its changes
Channel services	Identify key service elements of distribution – sales support, technical support, customer service, quality, etc. For each segment, evaluate our service performance against key competitors	Identify gaps in our servicing of the segments
Channel shares	For key competitors, evaluate the proportion of business going through each channel	Compare our channel strategy to competitors
Marketing resources	Divide the market geographically or by customer type, and compare our coverage in manpower, distributors, sales offices, etc. compared to our competitors	Compare our resourcing to competitors' and relationship to the market shares geographically and by customer type
Concentration	Within each segment, see if the 20:80 rule applies to customer numbers and amount of business done	Evaluate implications of concentration for our channel strategy

The marketing communications audit

The goal here is to examine the possibilities and needs for all forms of marketing communications – personal selling, advertising, sales promotion and public relations (see pp. 324–38). We need to examine our positioning in the customer's eyes, and examine the key decision-making units and external influencers who matter, to identify the communications tasks. Messages and media will come out of this. Table 7.5 provides us with a structure for this task.

This is a very sketchy overview of what may be the most revealing and exciting thinking you ever do at the operational

Table 7.5 The marketing communications audit

Focus	Analyse	Objective
Brand/Corporate positioning	Identify customer perceptions of our company and of our key competitors	Identify the broad communications tasks
Decision-making units	With each market segment, model the DMU, identify the roles played by different people, and the relevant messages and media	Isolate DMU targets for communication and message
External influencers	Within each market segment, identify major influence sources and our standing compared to competitors	Isolate influencer targets for communications and messages required
Media	Within each segment, identify available media of communication and compare	Broaden view of communications media
Media performance	Compare our effectiveness in using each medium and expenditure with key competitor	Relate effort to market share and areas for development

level of your company. There is enough here to get started and achieve some major good for your business, but if you want more assistance then go to the marketing planning gurus: William Giles[3], Gordon Greenley[4], Malcolm McDonald[5], Lehmann and Winer[6]. There you will find the worksheets, models and analytical techniques.

'the goal here is to test our ideas about market strategy, to put them into the concrete terms that are understood in the company'

Remember, the goal here is to test our ideas about market strategy, to put them into the concrete terms that are understood in the company, and to look at the reality of going from the market strategy to the operational marketing plan.

Analysis of strengths, weaknesses, opportunities and threats (SWOT)

The conclusions we reach in the marketing audit can be packed into a *SWOT analysis*. In fact, SWOT analysis can be turned into a very dynamic tool for strategy generation and testing, and we will discuss this in more detail shortly (see pp. 282–92 below). For the moment, take SWOT as the structure to evaluate the significance of what we have put into the audit.

The marketing plan

There are many ways of formatting a marketing plan – some simple and some complex. Any of the textbooks mentioned above [3,4,5,6] will give you a format if you need one. What really matters is that you produce a plan which is comprehensible and credible to your intended audience – company cultures differ widely on the requirements for written documents of this kind, and you have to adapt to this if you want to be taken seriously. What matters is that you have covered the key issues:

- a summary of the present position in this market;
- if this is an existing market, a forecast of where we are going in this market if we continue with the current strategy (a *prognosis*);
- our objectives in this market;
- our market strategy – reflecting our key *market choices* – based on our market definition and segmentation, and the market position and attractiveness analysis – our *value proposition* – drawing together our market mission, competitive differentiation and marketing assets – and the *key relationships* to be developed and exploited to drive the strategy;
- the predicted competitive reaction to our strategy;
- our proposed marketing programmes;
- our specific tactics and action plans;
- our financial forecasts.

A framework for addressing these issues is given in Table 7.6. The ultimate in iteration (which really hurts), of course, is that if we get to the last stage and the financial out-turn is *not* what we want, then we go back to our goals, our marketing audit, and so on . . .

Implementation

Conventionally the production of plans is the end of the process – after all, the Action Plan says who should do what. My attitude to this is such that I now urge chief executives to reject out-of-hand, and without right of appeal, *any* plan of *any* kind which does *not* come with a detailed and realistic implementation strategy. It is not enough to produce a great plan and expect other people to go away and make it happen. Implementation is not something we bolt-on at the end of generating strategy – implementation *is* strategy.

This should be where we are very explicit about issues such as the role of sales management in driving the market strategy through to the marketplace, what is needed to manage alliances

Table 7.6 The marketing plan

Focus	Analyse	Objective
The present position and prognosis	Current and historical achievements by segment and what will happen to us in this market if we continue as at present	Provide the context for the plan, and quantify the planning gap (what the new plan will achieve over and above what we would get anyway)
Marketing objectives	Specify the volume, market share and market positioning goals to be achieved, to deliver the corporate objectives set	Translate financial goals into market and customer objectives
Market strategies	Summarize the key strategies across the market and for each segment. Identifying our market choices, our value proposition, and the key relationship aspects of the strategy	Reduce our ideas to a matrix of market strategies by segment
Competitive reactions	Evaluate the likely competitive responses to our most visible strategies	Identify key risks and vulnerabilities, and the need for contingency plans to cope with competitive retaliation
Marketing programmes	Reduce market strategies to marketing programme requirements in products, prices, distribution and service and marketing communications	Identify the programmes needed to make market strategies happen
Tactics and action plans	Break the segment strategies and programmes into specific lists of tactical actions with responsibilities, timing and cash flows	Produce detailed action plans
Evaluation and control	Identify the critical success factors and benchmarks to be monitored to judge progress of the plan, including timing, methods and cost	Specify the marketing control system
Financial forecasts	Evaluate the costs and revenue for each segment strategy and its associated tactics over the lifetime of the plan	Profit and loss accounts by segments, forecasts over the plan period

and partnerships with collaborators and channel members, and the needs for internal marketing to embed the strategy inside the company and make it happen.

My views here are such that we will devote whole chapters to implementation strategy and internal marketing (Chapter 14), and the linking of market strategy to the sales organization (Chapter 13).

For the moment it is enough to note that our marketing plan requires an implementation strategy which details what *organizational changes* are needed to make the plan happen, what *internal barriers* will have to be crossed, what external relationships have to be managed and what the real *costs* of these changes are likely to be.

Executives like techniques that give structure to their ideas. About the best technique available for doing that in planning the way we are going to go to market is *SWOT analysis*.

Make SWOT analysis work*

You should have gathered by now that this is not a 'cook-book' of the latest sophisticated analytical techniques fresh from the university laboratory. The *only* analytical technique I will discuss in detail here is SWOT analysis. In fact, in most cases, if you use SWOT analysis in the way described below, it may well be the *only* technique you need to start changing the way things are, i.e. getting stuff done, instead of producing beautiful plans which just never get implemented. Now this requires that we do not use SWOT analysis to produce the subjective, meaningful, bland, non-operational, comfortable, biased output it normally gives.

What is SWOT analysis about?

As most people will recognize, SWOT analysis is an incredibly simple, but structured, approach to evaluating a company's strategic position when planning, by identifying the company's strengths and weaknesses and comparing these to opportunities and threats in the market. The major attraction of SWOT analysis is that it is familiar and easily understandable by users, and it provides a good structuring device for sorting out ideas about the future and a company's ability to exploit that future.

However, in practice, the use of this tool has generally become sloppy and unfocused – a classic example perhaps of familiarity breeding contempt! The opportunity comes because the fact that SWOT analysis is frequently done extremely badly does not mean it *has* to be the way the technique is used.

---

*The content of this section draws heavily on two articles by William Giles and myself[7,8]. Much of the creative input to this came from William and his 'Marlow Method' of marketing planning.

First, however, it should not be forgotten that the reason SWOT analysis has come to be so widely known (and, we suggest, misused!) is because of its inherent attractions. These are: (a) the technique is simple enough in concept to be immediately and readily accessible to managers – no computer or management scientist is needed; (b) the model can be used without extensive corporate or market information systems – but is flexible enough to incorporate these where appropriate; and (c) SWOT analysis provides us with a device to structure the awkward mixture of quantitative and qualitative information, of familiar and unfamiliar facts, of known and half-known understandings, which characterizes strategic planning.

Experiences with a wide variety of companies and managers suggest that SWOT analysis *can* be made to work, these pay-offs *can* be realized, and real strategic insights *can* be generated and used.

There are a number of very straightforward guidelines to achieve these goals – i.e. we keep the technique because we know how to do it, but we change the rules! The challenge to the reader is to look at how SWOT analysis is used (or neglected) in his/her company's marketing planning and see whether our guidelines can be made to work.

The 'rules' we propose for using SWOT to produce dynamic results are: (a) focused SWOTs; (b) shared vision; (c) customer orientation; (d) environmental analysis; and (e) structured strategy generation.

Focused SWOTs

Experience suggests first, that the more carefully we define the area to be evaluated with a SWOT analysis, the more productive the analysis is likely to be. By focusing on a particular issue, and excluding non-relevant material, we can overcome the bland, meaningless generalizations that executives frequently produce if asked to take a global view of their businesses' strengths and weaknesses.

This definition, which should be *rigorously* and *continuously* enforced, has been made effective in analysing issues as diverse as focusing on: a specific *product market* (with parameters defined); a specific *customer segment* in a market; *product policy* in a given market or segment; *pricing policy* in a particular market; *distribution* systems for particular customer groups; *marketing communications* for different customers and members of a defined decision-making unit; and the study of named *competitors* or groups of similar competitors.

The rule we follow is that attention should first be focused on a critical issue to our planning, rather than being global in perspective – because we can always build up the global picture by putting together our focused analyses, and then it will be a better global picture as well. This is a good practical way of getting to grips with some of the issues raised by market definition and market segmentation that we covered in Chapter 4 (pp. 148–68).

Apart from anything else, the very act of focusing starts to highlight major gaps in knowledge and some of the hidden strategic assumptions that managers make. For instance, some years ago, in a planning session with a retail bank, to break away from the internal view of a particular market segment we asked the planners to undertake SWOT analysis for their major competitors. They came back with detailed (and very good) SWOTs of the other retail banks. We asked: what about the building societies, the insurance companies, the finance companies? They said that these were not 'serious' players in the 'banking market'! We pointed out that the market was for financial services to solve customer problems, and we started to move slowly towards a totally different conception of where the real competition was coming from – people who do better what matters most to the customer, even if they are not professional, prudent bankers. Their view of the market was swamped by the image of one dominant type of competitor. Flushing out this myth was a major break through. Focus and concentration can have many pay-offs.

'Focus and concentration can have many pay-offs'

Shared visions

Because of its apparent simplicity and ease of communication, we have found SWOT analysis to be an excellent vehicle in working with planning teams or groups of executives. There is little or no barrier created through executives having to learn complex analytical techniques (or succumbing to the temptation to leave it to the 'experts').

We have found that the pay-offs from making SWOT the central focus for group or team planning to be numerous: the pooling of ideas and information from a number of sources produces richer results; the SWOT analysis provides a concrete mechanism for expressing team consensus about important issues; and producing a SWOT analysis has the effect of pushing a team towards agreement and flushes out potentially harmful disagreements – indeed, in effect, one can observe managers negotiating the view of the world that the company will adopt for its planning. These potential gains arise primarily from participation of diverse interests in planning (see pp. 447–53 below) – but SWOT analysis provides a mechanism for making participation operational and reaching that potential set of benefits.

'SWOT analysis provides a mechanism for making participation operational'

For example, in the financial services business, another company with which we worked was organized into two semi-autonomous divisions – one serving the retail market and the other the commercial lending market. Undertaking SWOT analysis in joint planning groups proved to be quite literally the first time ever that managers of the two divisions actually found out what their counterparts could do and were doing, and they uncovered many profitable opportunities for collaboration and cross-selling between the divisions – *and* they then did something about them.

Customer orientation

Now we get to the real crunch. The way we can use the SWOT technique in a particularly powerful form is summarized in Figure 7.3.

The first requirement is that in evaluating our strengths and weaknesses we can *only* include those resources or capabilities which would be recognized and valued by the *customer* with whom we are concerned. This helps us to get past the 'motherhood' statements often produced as a list of strengths:

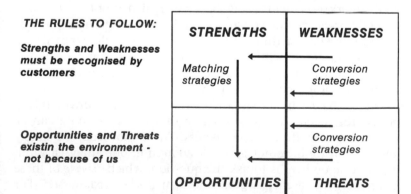

Figure 7.3   Customer-oriented SWOT

service, quality, an established firm, and so on – because we have to define what we believe is *seen* by the customer and is *valued* by him/her.

For example, our 'great private medical scheme' for employees is *not* a strength for these purposes. It is only relevant if we can say that customers would recognize that we treat our employees well, and this in turn has pay-offs in how they deal with customers and the establishment of long-term relationships. Applying this rule is often a considerable discipline on executives, and in the event of disputes which cannot be resolved about what is a strength and what is not, the joy is that we may actually test our claims with a larger pool of our own people, or even with *customers*!

Forcing executives to confront the difference between what *they* think is important and what customers think is important is a substantial contribution of this technique. At the end of the day – however unreasonable, irrational, awkward, intolerant, ignorant or plain foolish the 'experts' think customers to be – it is the customers who buy products, not the 'experts'.

In fact, we are, in a very practical way, forcing users of the technique to identify the critical success factors in their business, their customers' needs, and hence factors influencing customer satisfaction. In one company, for example, what executives told us was their strength of 'technical service excellence' turned out to mean to customers that this was a company that sent out Ph.D.-level engineers to *prove* that products had been abused in use, and that warranties did not apply!

Similarly, in working with a secondary retail bank, the key strength identified by banking executives was 'relationship banking', i.e. the availability of skilled, professionally-qualified branch managers to meet and deal personally with customers. This may be true for affluent, high-income customers, but in fact in the market segments providing critical niches for this company (mainly lower-income consumers and heavy credit users), it was found that the *last* thing such customers normally wanted was frequent meetings with the bank manager. In some ways, the bank's most critical problem was actually to keep the branch managers *away* from the customers!

One problem which regularly emerges is that executives, trying to use the model in this way, claim that the same thing can be listed as a strength *and* a weakness. This is not true – it simply means that we have not gone far enough in our analysis. What we need to do here is to ask the question: which *aspects* of these characteristics are strengths and which are weaknesses? For instance, the commonest 'motherhood' statements might be expanded as shown in Table 7.7.

Table 7.7   Breaking down strengths and weaknesses

'We are an old-established firm'

Strengths	Weaknesses
Stable suppliers for after-sales	Inflexible
Trustworthy	Old-fashioned
Experienced	No innovation

'We are a large supplier'

Strengths	Weaknesses
Comprehensive product range and technical expertise	Bureaucratic
	Offhand with customers
High status/stability reassures customer	No continuity of personal contact

The remaining issue to be addressed is where managers claim that they have a strength (or weakness) which customers do *not* know about and would *not* recognize – but which is too important to leave out of consideration. The easiest way of handling this issue is to include these factors in the list, but to have them boxed-off as 'hidden'. When it comes to the stage of generating strategies, then it is appropriate to consider what would be needed to uncover hidden strengths, if they really are particularly important to the customer and to generating strategies for the future.

Incidentally, for readers who may actually *want* to produce a list of meaningless 'motherhood' statements in their analysis of corporate strengths and weaknesses, we give in Table 7.8 a proforma of standard 'motherhood' statements of corporate strengths, and the reader has only to tick these off in the boxes provided. Our reasoning is that if the SWOT technique is to be used in this pointless and unproductive way, we can at least save time! If that sounds facetious – it is meant to! The point is that *all* the 'motherhood' statements in this table have been given to us by executives in their planning exercises – which is quite an eye-opener.

Environmental analysis

The same discipline is required to view the opportunities and threats in the environment relevant to our point of focus – the specific market, customer, issue, etc. This turns our attention to the lower half of the model in Figure 7.3.

Table 7.8   A checklist of 'motherhood' strengths statements

This checklist shows some of the most meaningless statements executives have given us to describe their companies' strengths, together with our interpretation of their 'hidden meanings'. If the goal of a SWOT analysis is to produce bland, meaningless, non-operational output, the reader can tick off the desired statements (which at least will save some time). Those looking for more useful output from SWOT analysis might prefer to test their own SWOT analysis against this checklist to ensure that they are avoiding such traps.

Strengths	Please tick appropriate boxes	*Hidden meanings*
High quality		We can't think of any real reason why we do business in this market . . .
Low price		That must explain it . . .
Personal service		We still can't . . .
High value to customers		Our products are a bit expensive, but we still sell some
Old-established firm		We must be OK, we've survived so far
Technologically sophisticated		We know more than the customer
Product strengths		Look at the product, never mind the customer.
The 'natural' supplier to this market		We don't know who our competitors are
We are the industry standard		We don't think we have any competition

Here the goal is to list those things in the relevant environment which make it attractive or unattractive to us, and our search for ideas should be as thorough and widely-informed as possible. The major difficulty here is that executives tend to jump the gun and put their strategies and tactics down as opportunities – a classic example of self-fulfilling prophesy!

The way out of this trap is the insistence that opportunities and threats exist *only* in the outside world – the things we propose to do about them are our *strategies*. For example, it may be suggested that price-cutting is an opportunity. This is *not* an opportunity in a SWOT analysis – it is a price tactic which we might adopt. We would *only* accept the desirability of price-cutting if, for example, our size gave us greater cost economies than our competitors, and there was an identified, external market opportunity in terms of there being a price-sensitive segment of the market, or the need to meet a competitor's threatened entry to the market with low prices. The rule is that opportunities exist independently of our policies and actions – the actions we plan are our strategies.

Structured strategy testing and generation

When we are able to complete all four cells of the SWOT matrix, and we have ranked each item in each category in terms of importance, then the matrix acts automatically as a generator and tester of strategies, as shown in Figure 7.3:

- *Matching strategies* – our central focus is on matching our strengths to opportunities in the outside world. Our logic here is that strengths which do not match any known opportunity are of little immediate value (however proud of them we may be), while highly ranked opportunities for which we have no strengths are food for further thought.
- *Conversion strategies* – more difficult is the design of appropriate responses to highly ranked weaknesses and threats. Here the goal is ideally to convert these factors into strengths and opportunities. In some cases this may be relatively straightforward – a weakness in sales coverage may mean adding to the salesforce, a threat from a competitor may be bought-off by collaboration or merger or neutralized by an advertising campaign, but in other cases we may be unable to think sensibly about converting or neutralizing these factors. In the latter case these factors remain the limiting problems in this business and determine how attractive it is to us.
- *Creative strategies* – finally, we have to recognize that going through this analytical process often simply generates new, creative ideas for how to develop the business. Good ideas should never be discarded simply because they are unusual. Whatever recording we are doing, we should have a box especially for creative ideas that may not fit elsewhere in the model.

Iteration

In this way, the SWOT model gives us a mechanism for structuring and categorizing the strategies generated through the SWOT analysis. The final discipline, however, is one of *iteration*. As we identify strategies to

'the SWOT model gives us a mechanism for structuring and categorizing the strategies generated'

SWOT PROFORMA 1 — STRENGTHS AND WEAKNESSES

Market/ Segment/ Issue

Strengths	Rank

Weaknesses	Rank

Figure 7.4 Proforma for customer-oriented SWOT analysis

SWOT PROFORMA 2 — OPPORTUNITIES AND THREATS

Market/ Segment/ Issue

Opportunities	Rank

Threats	Rank

Figure 7.4 Continued

SWOT PROFORMA 3 — STRATEGY GENERATION

Market/ Segment/ Issue

Matching Strategies

Strength	Matching Opportunity	Strategy Required

Conversion Strategies

Weakness/ Threat	Conversion Strategy	Strength/Opportunity Created or Weakness/ Threat Neutralized

Creative Strategy Ideas

Figure 7.4 Continued

match strengths to opportunities, to uncover hidden strengths, to convert weaknesses, and so on, we should always go back and see how the new situation we are building changes the SWOT model and the broad picture we are painting.

Our output is then ready to be entered into the planning process – for programme-building, evaluation, financial appraisal and ultimately for implementation or action planning.

The challenge

The guidelines we have outlined above are incredibly simple to apply, but the disciplines imposed are very severe. We know that this approach is effective, and that it turns the SWOT technique into a dynamic and productive tool for strategic audits and strategy generation. Our challenge to the reader is to use the model and the guidelines on his/her own planning and see what happens! To help, we have designed some documentation to carry out this form of SWOT analysis, and this is given in Figure 7.4.

Used in this way, SWOT analysis gives us a mechanism for putting ideas about our value proposition and key relationships into tangible form and testing them. It is also a good source of new ideas which can enrich the market strategy.

Incidentally, not for the first time, or the last, I lied to you. The planning stage is not just the receptor for our brilliantly conceived market strategy. It is more likely to be where we share the results of our thinking about market strategy with others and find that, in the cold light of day, some of our ideas are not that great. The planning process provides a ready-made structure for homing-in on our strategic assumptions and challenging the most critical. For most of us, this on its own is a tangible step forward.

So, where have we got to?

The goal is that by this stage we have developed a market strategy – we have defined the Strategic Pathway – and we have put those strategic ideas through the sifting process of a strategic marketing audit. The result (we hope) is a customer-focused marketing plan which turns our value proposition into a coherent marketing programme. We should know what we want our company to be about in the market.

However, this is not the end. We turn next to the issues that we have to think about managing in the process of going to market – i.e. to get our market strategy to happen.

References

1. Mintzberg, Henry (1994), 'The Fall and Rise of Strategic Planning', *Harvard Business Review*, January/February, 107–114.
2. Hamel, Gary (1996), 'Strategy as Revolution', *Harvard Business Review*, July/August, 69–82.
3. Giles, William (1989), 'Marketing Planning for Maximum Growth', *Marketing Intelligence and Planning*, Vol. 7, No. 3/4, 1–98.
4. Greenley, Gordon (1986), *The Strategic and Operational Planning of Marketing*, London: McGraw-Hill.
5. McDonald, Malcolm (1995), *Marketing Plans*, Oxford: Butterworth-Heinemann.
6. Lehmann, Donald R. and Russell S. Winer (1988), *Analysis for Marketing Planning*, Plana, Texas: Business Publications Inc.
7. Piercy, Nigel and William Giles (1989), 'Making SWOT Analysis Work', *Marketing Intelligence and Planning*, Vol. 7, No. 5, 5–7.
8. Piercy, Nigel and William Giles (1990), 'Revitalising and Operationalising the SWOT Model in Strategic Planning', *University of Wales Business and Economics Review*, No. 5, 3–10.

Case 4   Allied Dunbar:
Market-led and brand strategy*

The financial services sector in which Allied Dunbar competes has transformed from the 'sleepy industry' of the 1960s into a turbulent and low-growth market characterized by a severe regulatory environment, declining new business figures for many companies, and the continuing threat of competitive invasion by companies from other sectors seeking a share of the savings product market.

Tracing the historical origins of Allied Dunbar brings us to the role of Mark Weinberg, a 'senior statesman' figure in the UK life assurance industry, who came to the UK from South Africa to form Abbey Life in 1961 and Hambro Life in 1970. His third life company, Allied Dunbar, was created by Weinberg in 1971 from Allied, a large unit trust group, and Dunbar, a small private bank, alongside his other insurance companies, Abbey Life and Hambro Life. Weinberg's vision when he created Hambro Life had been to market insurance in a way that was comprehensible to the customer, and the key ideas behind his approach were simplicity and transparency. Hambro Life became Britain's largest unit-linked life insurer. Weinberg left in 1990, together with Allied Dunbar's then Chief Executive Mike Wilson, to establish J. Rothschild Assurance.

Allied Dunbar is now owned by BAT Industries and since 1996, together with Eagle Star, has formed the insurance component of British American Financial Services, alongside Threadneedle, a fund management company. These three operations contributed profits of £370 million in 1995.

From a start of 211 'day one pioneers', Allied Dunbar now employs some 3000 staff at its Swindon head office, and has around 4000 salespeople working as self-employed financial advisers selling and delivering a range of personal financial plans and services, such as life assurance, personal pensions, healthcare insurance and mortgages.

From its earliest days, the marketing and selling strategy of Allied Dunbar was characterized as 'pushy advertising' and 'hard selling', frowned upon by many in the industry, and earning the company the nickname of 'Allied Crowbar'. The company experienced rapid growth until the early 1990s and developed strong functional capabilities in technical expertise, and was run on the rigid hierarchical lines traditional in the

'the marketing and selling strategy of Allied Dunbar was characterized as "pushy advertising" and "hard selling"'

---

* This case study has been prepared by Nigel Piercy, Cardiff Business School, from meetings with company executives, internal company papers and secondary sources.

industry. Some suggest that in this period Allied Dunbar evolved two quite different organizations: head office, characterized by 'benevolent paternalism' and functional expertise and technical excellence; and the self-employed direct salesforce, characterized by aggressive targets and doggedness in selling.

The strategic trauma of the 1990s

A turning point for the company came in the early 1990s. It was at this time that: competition escalated dramatically with new entrants to the market; the regulatory requirements in the financial services industry became progressively harsher and more expensive to meet; the UK's economic recession and high interest rates were having adverse effects on the spending power of consumers for financial services; and consumers were quickly becoming more aware of their choices in financial services and more wary of suppliers, as well as increasingly less willing to commit themselves to long-term savings products. By 1993, industry surveys showed widespread drops in new business figures, with a fall of 5 per cent in annual premium income, an 8.5 per cent reduction in individual annual premium life business, and a 4 per cent drop in personal pensions income.

It was at this time that Allied Dunbar experienced a fall in the growth of new business for the first time in its history. Traditionally, the company had been product- and distributor-led, and found itself with a hierarchical organization, driven by functional experts, not well positioned for strategic change.

Developing a new market strategy

Under the leadership of Chairman George Greener, experienced in the branded consumer goods sector from his time at Mars, Allied Dunbar undertook a radical repositioning in its market strategy based on two central concepts: brand and market-led.

Company research into the market showed that consumers had a low awareness of product offerings and low product knowledge about financial services, in spite of the millions of pounds spent on advertising by life assurance companies. Faced with the difficulties of building brands in the life assurance business, most competitors had focused advertising on name awareness. The problem is that the evidence was that name awareness did not appear to predispose customers to buy the advertiser's products. The conclusion was that the key advertising need for Allied Dunbar was to communicate what the company stood for, rather than just achieving awareness of its name, and to deliver that message to the audience through co-ordinated campaigns involving both above- and below-the-line activities. There was also the critical challenge of aligning what the company stood for with the needs and priorities of customers in the new financial services marketplace of the 1990s.

With a stated goal of developing a top five consumer brand for its life insurance business, in 1992 Allied Dunbar appointed Grey London, an advertising agency, to drive its strategic repositioning through advertising. The advertising strategy was to meet consumer needs for reassurance and trust by persuading people that they could trust Allied Dunbar as a company which offered financial plans that are flexible enough to meet changing needs, emphasizing a much softer image for the company. Allied Dunbar ceased television advertising altogether for nearly two and a half years, returning to the medium in 1994 with an initial spend of some £10 million, and a plan for a £75 million campaign over five years.

The key advertising messages have been 'There may be trouble ahead ...' and 'For the life you don't yet know', and these have been delivered using novel advertising framed by the unique style of actors miming and acting to the sound-track of songs from the 1920s and 1930s, in a style reminiscent of the playwright Dennis Potter. The messages emphasize the unexpected financial problems that occur at home or in the workplace, and partnership with Allied Dunbar to solve these problems, and it does so in a humorous, understated and non-threatening way by telling short human interest stories and relating them to the need for financial planning – the unexpected pregnancy for the middle-aged couple, the executive hearing rumours of redundancies in the wash-room, and so on.

Figure 1 There may be trouble ahead . . .

The company's thinking on the new strategic imperatives is illustrated by the following extract from a letter from Sandy Leitch, Chief Executive, to all Allied Dunbar people in October 1994:

> You hardly need me to tell you that our industry is living through a period of massive and far-reaching change.... Anticipating these changes a year or more ago, we decided that the way to turn them to our advantage, to flourish because of them rather than in spite of them, was to start a process of change in the Company to become a market-led organisation, with a distinctive reputation or 'brand' which would differentiate us from our competitors. This 'market-led' and 'brand' strategy is now gathering momentum – we've already communicated our brand to the marketplace and to all of us, through internal communications.

Part of the company's blueprint for the future is summarized in the wall poster reproduced here as Figure 2. This demonstrates what the strategy of being 'market-led' means to Allied Dunbar, and great internal communications and training efforts have been made to spell out the market reputation or brand identity of the company's new market position, and stress the importance for all Allied Dunbar people of 'living the brand'.

The brand thinking has also become a strategic imperative at a higher level too, in developing a brand portfolio linking the Allied Dunbar brand to Eagle Star and Threadneedle Asset Management brands, as elements of British American Financial Services' portfolio, with each brand differentiated by market position, product offering and channels of distribution. Following that market has also had other implications for Allied Dunbar: the introduction of telephone selling of some services to reflect the customer preferences uncovered by operations like First Direct and Direct Line; the possibility of becoming the first life insurer to launch a credit card and to offer other banking products to customers. (In 1996 the company announced that it would not continue to develop telemarketing within Allied Dunbar, as it was inconsistent with the AD brand position within the BAFS distribution strategy.)

Implementing the market-led and brand strategy

'successful brand repositioning required far more than the advertising spend and the associated literature'

The company's successful brand repositioning required far more than the advertising spend and the associated literature. Allied Dunbar's market-led change rests on a massive investment in internal company change.

The central platform for change is the brand identity and what this requires in the company's responsiveness to its customers. The value proposition details the goal of

Market Led

Becoming Market Led will protect and build Allied Dunbar's competitive advantage, will result in consumers and our clients preferring our products/services and will only be sustainable if there is a mutual reward for all involved parties.

Being Market Led means that we will start with a deep understanding of consumers/clients and their different needs; identify key target markets; develop a brief to meet the needs of those markets; enhance existing, or introduce new products/services that meet those needs; and enhance existing or introduce new channels for their appropriate delivery.

For the life you don't yet know

Figure 2   What does 'Market-Led' mean at Allied Dunbar?

differentiation by developing a brand which holds a very distinctive position in the customer's mind, based on trust and responsiveness.

However, to make those promises come true for customers and employees has entailed large-scale change in organizational structure, investment in training and development for all employees, repositioning marketing and selling in the company; and a major effort to change company-wide processes and systems to deliver value to the customer.

Perhaps most telling is the fact that Allied Dunbar has become a far 'flatter' organization, than the traditional hierarchy with which it started, requiring managers to cope with far broader spans of control. This has been important in developing away from the functional specialisms as leaders of the culture to a more market-focused culture. It has also been significant in creating a greater capacity for flexibility and change, and in taking strategic decisions far lower in the organization.

In working with the Allied Dunbar people to develop their capacity to deliver the new strategy, key approaches have included:

● 'changing the culture' through company-wide 'brand awareness workshops' and measuring the impact through an annual employee attitude survey;

● providing individuals with distance learning materials and workbooks with feedback mechanisms, focused on the brand and the market-led approach, as part of a move from the paternalistic management of the past to a situation where employees take more responsibility for their own performance and development, in the form of a 'personal development contract';

● improving the strategic thinking ability of managers and making stronger links between their activities and the Allied Dunbar strategy through 'strategy and change' workshops;

● introducing a competence-based performance management system, focusing on skills in thinking, innovating, communicating and influencing, goal orientation, showing leadership, and professional ability, linked to annual reviews and the company plan, as well as a 360-degree approach to appraisal;

● closing the gaps between different parts of the organization by combining management development activities and team-based approaches;

● bringing in key outsiders to critical roles in the company to counter the traditional 'financial services' culture.

The results?

Success of the new market strategy was not instant. While the advertising campaign has been admired since the outset and achieved excellent recall and memory scores in market research, there have been some problems, and no immediate upturn in sales and profits.

In March 1996 the *Financial Times* reported that the Chairman, George Greener, had left the company by mutual agreement, leading to a range of senior management changes in the company and the group, in the context of plans to streamline staff numbers in the BAT financial services companies. Greener's legacy, however, was an outstanding level of financial performance in 1996 and excellent prospects for the future. In fact, in 1995 Allied Dunbar's contribution to group profits slipped by more than a quarter, in spite of market share increases in some areas. Even so, in a very difficult market Allied Dunbar passed Sun Life and Standard Life to take third position in the life assurance market behind Prudential and Equitable Life.

However, by the end of 1996 Allied Dunbar had increased profits by 32 per cent, with new business climbing 25 per cent and total premium income growing by 17 per cent. The forecasts of Sandy Leitch, the new Chief Executive of the British American Financial Services umbrella organization, in 1996 were for 20 per cent profit increases for the group over five years, raising new life premiums by 15 per cent and tripling market share in investment business. In addition, the degree change from the 'Allied Crowbar' days of the past is underlined by the company winning the 1996 *Financial Advisor* magazine award for the 'industry's most admired sales force'.

'the degree change from the "Allied Crowbar" days of the past is underlined by the company winning the 1996 Financial Advisor magazine award'

The underlying strategic imperative for Allied Dunbar, and now for the broader British American Financial Services organization, remains the brand. Steve Melcher, Chief Executive, outlines the role of Allied Dunbar in the BAFS multi-brand strategy as reinforcing the proposition of trusted face-to-face financial advice for life assurance, pensions and investment products. He sees the business as being 'the protection markets' where Allied Dunbar dominates by a value-for-money offering backed by a positive claims philosophy: 'We look for ways to pay claims rather than ways in which we can hide behind the small print.'

Work continues to improve direct salesforce productivity and a streamlined sales process, and a programme of redesigning critical processes – point of sales, policy set-up, client servicing and claims processing. The underlying strategy rests on the principle of being market-led and dominating through brand strength within the BAFS framework.

Sources: 'Mark the Midas Man', *Sunday Times*, Rufus Olins, 15 April 1997. 'The Upper Crust Insurance Man', *Daily Telegraph*, 12 April 1997. 'Allied Dunbar Implements Strategic HR Response to New Customer-Driven Markets', *IRS Employment Trends*, October 1995. 'Allied Dunbar In Bid for Lucrative Banks' Territory', *Marketing*, 15 June 1995. 'Adwatch', *Marketing*, 10 March 1994. 'Insurance's Ad Strategy Goes Astray', *Marketing*, 20 January 1994. 'Allied Dunbar Salesforce to Sell Eagle Star Policies', *Marketing Week*, 6 September 1996. 'Companies and Finance', *Financial Times*, 16 July 1996. 'Advalue: the Allied Dunbar Campaign', *Marketing Week*, 24 November 1996. 'Chairman Resigns from BAT Financial Services', *Financial Times*, 9 March 1996.

Questions to consider

1 What differentiating capabilities can be identified in Allied Dunbar's strategy in the 1990s? What are the sources of sustainable competitive advantage?

2 In what ways does the positioning based on the brand differentiate Allied Dunbar from competitors? How does this relate to the multi-brand strategy of BAFS?

3 What are the most important key relationships and collaborations underpinning the Allied Dunbar market strategy?

4 How can a sense of vision be retained in a company like Allied Dunbar in times of turbulent markets and management changes? How do you see the future for Allied Dunbar?

Case 5   IBM*

IBM had sales revenues in excess of $77 billion in 1996 (over seven times those of Microsoft), and is the largest technology company the world has ever seen. The computer giant's dominance in the mainframe marketplace made it one of the corporate success stories of the 1970s and 1980s. However, less well known is IBM's strength in the software business, where even in 1996 it had sales revenues over 50 per cent higher than those of Microsoft.

The dilemma for IBM

IBM's fall from grace as one of the world's most admired companies was both swift and deep. From an all-time high stock-price of $175 7/8 in August 1987 the company's shares tumbled to a level just above $40 by August 1993. Growth in market spending on mainframe computers slowed as network computing emerged, powered by the rapidly growing capabilities of desktop PCs, and smaller, nimbler competitors emerged, eager to sell the benefits and flexibility of PC-based networks. The marketplace disaggregated, rapidly moving from a small number of large companies providing total solution to over 6000 competitors making and marketing a small number of individual products and services.

In this changing IT world, IBM's huge monolithic sales-led approach, focused primarily on total technology solutions, built upon mainframe hardware and software, produced increasingly sluggish sales and profits. The company even reported net losses in 1991, 1992 and 1993. IBM's traditional skills were in R&D, leading to technologically advanced and reliable large-scale hardware and the software, peripherals and services required to run such systems. However, even a hard-nosed, well-informed salesforce, backed by one of the most valuable brand-names in the world, no longer seemed to be the right mix of skills and resources to succeed in the rapidly changing global commercial IT industry. Many analysts questioned the wisdom and ability of IBM to remain a single company providing total solutions, and plans to create 'Baby Blues' by breaking up the company were widely advocated.

'total technology solutions, built upon mainframe hardware and software, produced increasingly sluggish sales and profits'

More problematic than the breadth of IBM's product line, however, was the way in which the company addressed its marketplace. IBM's structure

* This case study has been prepared by Neil A. Morgan, Judge Institute of Management Studies, University of Cambridge, and Garry Veale, IBM (UK).

had grown since the 1960s into a two-dimensional matrix with product groups providing one axis and geographically organized sales divisions the other – as illustrated in Figure 1 below. One effect was that marketing responsibilities were split between:

● *centralized corporate marketing* at head office level, which dealt with IBM global brand management;
● *product-marketing* with a technical emphasis, which was attached to each of the product groups; and
● *geographic marketing*, which drove local campaigns out of each of IBM's sales offices.

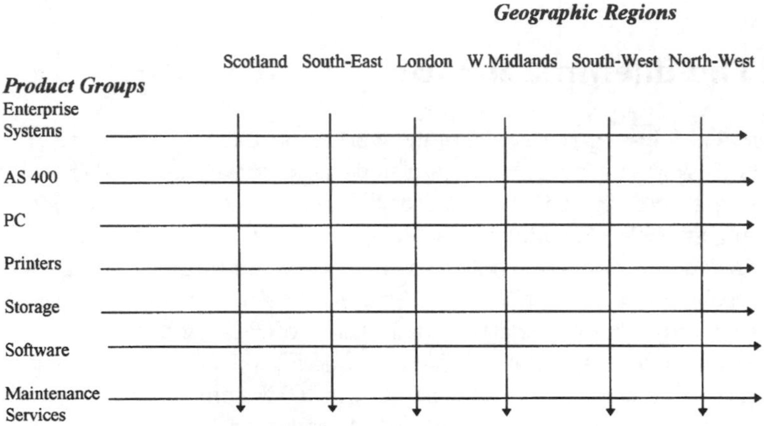

Figure 1   Illustrative representation of IBM's structure in the UK in the 1980s

Customers were therefore dealt with on the basis of where they were, rather than by what they needed, and the IBM view of market segmentation was implicitly built around geography. In a rapidly growing marketplace, with few rivals who could match their product line width and sales coverage, IBM prospered. Sales managers were essentially in the account and relationship management business, with little need or desire to seriously stimulate demand. When growth slowed, numerous smaller product specialists emerged, and industry-based software solution providers began to become more significant value providers, the days of IBM's old structure and implicit market segmentation were numbered.

Responding to market change

Demoralized and disenchanted with defensively seeking to protect existing customer relationships, and the anguished self-examination debating the pros and cons of demerging, IBM went on the attack. Rather than accept the industry pundits' argument that the company was too broadly-based and diversified, and could not hope to compete effectively against smaller, more specialized and nimbler competitors, IBM began to look for ways in which it could exploit its size, product range and service skills to provide total solutions.

In 1991 IBM embarked upon a wholesale restructuring of its organization, beginning with, and driven by its market segmentation approach. Geographic segmentation no longer (and indeed never had) provided a sensible way in which to group customers with similar needs, and therefore provided an inadequate focus for target marketing. Geography certainly failed to provide a mechanism for IBM to create global total solution packages which more closely matched the specific needs of business customers.

'a wholesale restructuring of its organization, beginning with, and driven by its market segmentation approach'

The geographic sales regions as market segments were abandoned, and in the UK a number of the physical locations were scaled down or closed and many of the buildings sold and leased back. The focus for marketing strategy and efforts to stimulate demand moved to newly formed industry solution units (ISUs) focusing on major industrial sectors: banking; insurance; retail; local government; national government; utilities; transport and communications; production and engineering; and oil, pharmaceuticals and chemicals. This is illustrated in Figure 2. Within these ISUs, IBM tried to bring together each of its product groups with a focus on providing solutions to the problems faced by organizations, which were common within each industry.

This change in structure, built upon a new segmentation model, helped to improve IBM's revenue performance by sharpening its market focus and giving clearer sales targets and positioning messages, but initially this was outweighed by the time and budgetary cost of restructuring.

The move to an ISU focus also caused some internal friction, and ultimately power shifts within the companies. Sales region management were no longer the powerhouse roles in the company – this moved to those running the ISUs. In addition, the ISU focus created some tension with the product groups, many of whom had retained some sales support and salesforce capability. The most immediate question, however, concerned the role of the country-level management. In a geographically-based sales organization, country-level management was the obvious and appropriate higher-level management focus. In an industry-based market-ing and sales structure, the role of the country-level management becomes much more difficult to define. The industry-focused ISUs allowed the company to look towards geographic region-level ISU responsibility as a more appropriate second-level management tier. For administrative purposes, IBM had divided up its global operations into: North America; Europe, Middle-East and Africa (EMEA); Asia-Pacific; and Latin America. These global geographic regions began to assume a less administrative and

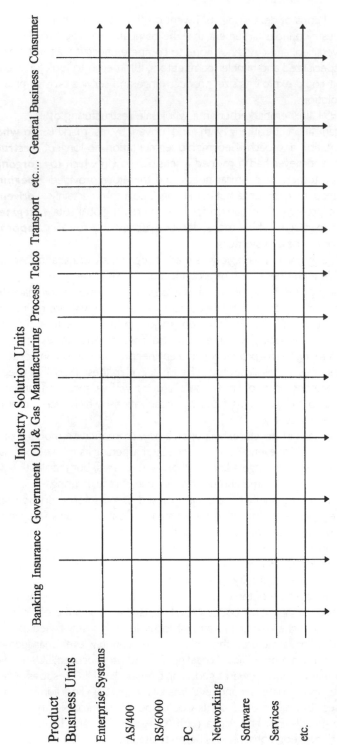

Figure 2 The new IBM segmentation model and organization structure

more management role, becoming the key revenue target and control level as a result of the move to an ISU focus.

Changing structure versus changing behaviour

These structural changes took some time to implement. It took longer to gain the 'mind-set' change required to allow the new structures to deliver on their objective. That goal was to position IBM as the premier IT solution provider to large companies in its chosen target industries.

For many of the salespeople, the differences brought by the new segment structure were not great. If they had looked after one banking customer before, they usually still looked after the same customer. IBM needed more change than this to pull the company back from the brink. In particular, the company required a 'solutions' rather than a 'product' focus – in identifying opportunities, in positioning relative to competitors and in dealing with customers. The new structure was not enough on its own to deliver this.

After allowing some time for the new structure to 'bed down', the company decided to take the bull by the horns. IBM quickly moved away from its traditional focus on short-term revenue and moved towards customer-based measures of market performance. The company introduced new reward and evaluation systems based upon customer satisfaction, market share and profitability. A customer satisfaction index and measurement system was established using both internal and third-party data collection. Customer satisfaction targets for ISUs and individuals were set, and performance monitored and rewarded.

While the general mind-set in the company began to change, the implications of the implicit shift in power within the company caused significant implementation problems. The new ISU focus implied that regions, and even countries, no longer 'owned' customers in the way that they had done in the past. The new segmentation model also caused fears among the product groups that power would move away from them and towards the new ISUs. There were particular fears among the marketing and salespeople within each of the product business units concerning their future in the 'new' IBM.

'the implications of the implicit shift in power within the company caused significant implementation problems'

As a result, there was a long period where co-operation between the new ISUs, which were trying to gain a new focus on customer closeness within their segments, and the 'old hands' in the product business units (PBUs), was not all that it should have been. This was partly driven by an unwillingness to co-operate, but also by the co-ordination problems caused by each ISU trying to tap into knowledge and experience, which was usually in the heads of a relatively small number of people in a large number of PBUs.

Tussles also emerged between the decision-making power and authority of country managers and geographic region heads of the ISUs. For some considerable time it was not very clear where the real decision-making power lay and how the lines of responsibility would be drawn between the old geographic positions and the new ISU positions. This was not helped by countries being the primary units of analysis for expense while geographic regions became the primary unit of analysis for revenue.

A new CEO, Lou Gerstner, arrived from RJR Nabisco in April 1993. Gerstner took stock of the situation for several months, looking both within the company but also, importantly, spending the majority of his time talking with customers about IBM and its position. This was both a useful source of information for the new CEO and symbolically a dynamic message to send to the employees about the mind-set required to turn the company around. (Gerstner continues to spend at least 40 per cent of his time talking with customers and prospective customers.)

Gerstner quickly moved to resolve two issues. First, he announced to the company and the world that IBM was, and would remain, an integrated technology company – it would not be demerging and divesting. Secondly, he stated categorically that what was required to fix IBM's problems was not a complex new corporate strategy, but a simple and well-executed move to a strong customer-needs focus – leading to the development of integrated technology solutions drawing on all of IBM's R&D and product, service and software skills and resources.

Gerstner's third big announcement was that failure to willingly and actively support the changes required to turn the company around could kill the strategy and the company. 'Pushback', as the new CEO described it, would not be tolerated within the company because the company could not afford to tolerate it. With the 'walk the talk' attitude for which he was rapidly becoming known, Gerstner removed several senior-level executives who had been attempting to block what he saw as necessary initiatives. By the end of 1994 some of the benefits of the new segmentation model, the restructuring around it and the accompanying cultural movement to a stronger customer and solution focus started to flow through.

December 1994 marked IBM's first profitable year since 1990. While the company was returning to health by focusing upon the largest customers and prospects within its chosen ISUs, other areas of the business were having a more difficult time. ISUs within each country typically focus upon no more than 20 or 30 of the largest companies within their industry. With such a relatively small number of targets, and a direct sales and marketing staff receiving marketing support from the geographic region level, achieving a strong customer focus is a challenging but 'do-able' task. Outside of the ISUs, things are more problematic.

Smaller customers and prospects, both within and outside IBM's chosen industry targets, are 'owned' by a division of IBM known as 'General Business' (GB). GB is tasked with marketing and co-ordinating all of IBM's hardware, software and service offerings to small and medium-sized business customers (broadly defined as companies with between 200 and 1000 employees). The IBM ISU segmentation model was originally operated by the General Business division. However, the logistics and economics of dealing with 14 industry segments for many thousands of small and medium sized businesses (SMEs), as well as the thousands of SMEs in other industries spread across many regions and countries, have proved problematic in most countries. Given the typically smaller revenue streams per customer in the SME marketplace, dedicating specific 'blue suit' sales teams to each of the 14 industry segments would be uneconomic.

Moving away from the industry focus and trying instead to target larger opportunities with dedicated sales resource is an intuitively reasonable alternative. However, finding cross-industry problems, for which IBM has an available solution, which are large enough in revenue terms to warrant the sales expense, and for which you can find 'triggers' to allow you to target your marketing sufficiently, is a very tall order. Perhaps inevitably, therefore, many of IBM's country-based GB units end up having to make trade-offs between segmentation models based on customer needs, and those driven by the economic realities of the cost of sales using dedicated salesforces and logistical problems caused by the sheer number of customers and prospects in the SME competitive space.

'units end up having to make trade-offs between segmentation models based on customer needs, and those driven by the economic realities'

General Business in the UK has therefore organized itself around an implicit segmentation model using two variables: *customer size* (large, small and very small) and *customer status* (customer or prospect). To some degree, customer size does seem to be associated with some needs and buying pattern differences for many IT products and services, mainly due to the generally higher levels of IT skills and experience. Larger companies within the GB market are more likely to have in-house IT expertise and more formalized IT purchasing routines than small and very small companies. The customer status variable, however, does not reflect any differences in customer needs, but rather the internal belief that existing customers are more likely to buy from IBM than are prospective customers.

These segmentation decisions are driving important new organization structure decisions. Each segment identified required different sales and marketing structures and decisions, with different routes to market, if IBM were to effectively reach customers and prospects in each of the segments. The attractiveness of each segment in terms of the number of potential targets, potential revenue streams per customer and the availability of 'best-of-breed' IBM solutions has led General Business in the UK to build different sales teams, channel structure and target messages and campaigns based upon the five segments identified in Figure 3 below.

The General Business ISU is now one of the largest in revenue terms globally, and it is the fastest growing part of the global IT market in terms of IT spend. It is also the most fragmented part of the market, and the area in which IBM's market share is the lowest of any of the ISUs. The existing segmentation models used in most GB countries, as reflected in their structure, may not provide a sufficient customer needs and solution requirements focus to allow IBM to gain the dominance in GB which they enjoy in their other markets. New segmentation models are constantly being examined – some provide better insights into customer needs, but show no obvious ways of how these segments can be targeted and reached. Others show promise even for targeting and reach, but are so incompatible with IBM's existing sales and marketing processes and systems that they cannot be operationalized without significant structural and system changes.

Market segmentation has played a very significant, and largely unheralded, part in the turnaround at IBM. At the ISU level, the precise segments targeted are constantly evolving and changing, and work because the changes are largely compatible with the newly established systems and processes in the company. In some areas, such as General Business, however, new segmentation models are required and cannot be adopted until new skills and systems in areas such as hybrid channel development and management have been effectively deployed. The company is now smart enough to know that great segmentation approaches are not just about identifying attractive groups of customers with particular needs, but doing so in such a way that targeted offerings and communication can be effectively delivered by the structures, systems and culture that exist inside the organization.

Sources: The Economist, 14 December 1996, pp. 102–3. *Marketing Business*, October 1992, 24–7. *USA Today*, 4 December '1996, 1b and 2b.

Target Size	**Relationship Status**	
	Customer	Prospect
Medium	Key Accounts	"Winback"
Small	Dealer Managed Accounts	"New Business"
Very Small	"Very Small Business"	

Figure 3   General Business (UK) segmentation model

Questions to consider

1 Is market segmentation driven by external market structures or internal organizational structure? What does the IBM experience suggest?

2 What are the most critical implementation problems that IBM faced in embedding a new segmentation model?

3 Is the approach of the General Business ISU more customer-focused than the other industry-based ISUs, or less customer-focused? Does it represent real differences in customer needs, or the limitations of the IBM way of doing business? In what other ways could they segment this business?

4 How does the segmentation and structural change at IBM compare to the model of levels of segmentation? Is there a clear strategic model compared to an operations-level model? Are these compatible?

5 Can market segmentation ever be more than a compromise between how we organize ourselves to do business, and differences in customer needs?

Case 6   Virgin:
The singer or the song?*

There are few days when the British press does not carry stories about some part of the Virgin group, or the exploits of its founder, Richard Branson. Virgin is considered by many to be Europe's most innovative company, and its founder is widely rated as the most 'trustworthy' individual in Britain. The Virgin organization contains a grouping of more than 20 companies, with combined sales of around £1.8 billion and annual profits of some £114 million. The group employs some 12500 people. Virgin is a private company, but if it were quoted on the stock market it would probably gain a place in the FT-SE 100 index. The group has an enormous range of diverse commitments, from the airline and retail businesses, through financial services, to small interests in businesses like the Storm model agency, the Heaven nightclub and various restaurants and hotels. The Virgin group remains very closely identified with its founder – Richard Branson. It is believed that the keyman insurance on Branson's life is for £34 million.

Richard Branson – the Virgin emperor

Aged in his mid-40s, Richard Branson famously does not wear business suits and point-blank refuses to wear a tie – he is more likely to be found dressed in a pink rabbit suit to entertain his employees at staff parties, or prepared for long-distance ballooning, or, to the disgust of Lord King, his protagonist at British Airways, doing business in a baggy jumper. Indeed, recently he was pictured in the national press modelling a wedding gown for the launch of Virgin Brides, to very mixed comments from the public. He has only removed his unbusiness-like beard once – when threatened that it would suffocate him in an oxygen mask on a ballooning trip, and he grew it back immediately afterwards. These characteristics have led to some underestimating him. In fact, he has built a massive business from nothing, and those who have tried to deal roughly with Virgin have found themselves in court and subject to large-scale campaigns to right the wrongs suffered by Branson's company.

---

* This case study has been prepared by Nigel Piercy, Cardiff Business School, from secondary sources. Professor Leyland Pitt, Cardiff Business School, is thanked for valuable comments made on an earlier draft of the case.

Branson has enjoyed spectacular success in his business development, although there have been very public failures as well – bids for TV franchises have failed, the bid for the National Lottery failed, there have been false starts in a number of media ventures, the personal computer venture failed, and the early retail businesses performed poorly in financial terms.

'Branson has enjoyed spectacular success in his business development, although there have been very public failures as well'

Branson's success is said to stem from two attributes which span his enterprises: '*irreverent entrepreneurship*' – the beard and jumpers caricature, but also the willingness to take risks and the insight to ignore industry conventions; and *luck* – no-one would have predicted the spectacular success of Mike Oldfield's 'Tubular Bells' in the 1970s, or even Phil Collins' continued popularity: Branson is notoriously unmusical, he simply signed Oldfield and Collins to the Virgin label because he liked them personally.

The building of the Virgin empire

Understanding the development of the Virgin company is easier if the key points in the development of the Virgin operations from Branson's earliest enterprises are listed:

1968: At 18 Branson launched his first venture, *Student* magazine.

1970: The launch of the Virgin mail order record business.

1973: The Virgin record label takes off with the spectacular success of Mike Oldfield's 'Tubular Bells'.

1977: Virgin Records signs the Sex Pistols, after A&M and EMI had refused the risk.

1981: Phil Collins signs with Virgin Records.

1983: Virgin Vision and Games was formed to market TV, video and computer games software.

1984: Virgin Atlantic airline is launched. The Virgin Music Channel starts.

1986: The non-airline Virgin businesses are floated on the Stock Exchange.

1987: Investment made in BSB satellite TV company. The stake in Music Channel is sold. The publisher W H Allen is purchased.

1988: The small music stores are sold to W H Smith. The BSB stake is sold. Virgin is delisted from the stock market as Branson buys back shares from stockholders, most of whom were small individual investors, because the institutions had never invested in Virgin stock.

1989: Stakes in airline and music businesses are sold to Japanese partners.

1990: Joint venture established for Virgin Megastores in Japan.

1991: Bid for ITV franchises fails. Half the Virgin Megastores are sold to W H Smith. The beginning of the 'dirty tricks' war with British Airways.

1992: Sales of the music business to Thorn-EMI for £580 million. Virgin gains national radio licence in partnership with TV-AM. Joint ventures started with Blockbuster for Megastores in Europe and the USA. Plans for an Express Rail Service are abandoned.

1993: Virgin licenses a Greek airline to fly the Gatwick–Athens route in Virgin colours. Stakes in games businesses are sold.

1994: Virgin Atlantic opens Hong Kong and San Francisco routes. Virgin announces the County Hall hotel development – later abandoned. Virgin's bid for the National Lottery fails. The launch of Virgin Cola, Virgin Vodka and Virgin personal computers.

1995: Start of a partnership agreement between Virgin Atlantic and Delta Airlines. The launch of Virgin Direct personal finance. Virgin acquires a 40 per cent stake in the consortium buying MGM cinemas.

1996: Virgin acquires Euro Belgian Airlines, now renamed Virgin Express. As part of the London and Continental Railways consortium, Virgin wins the Channel Tunnel railway link contract. Virgin Net is launched as a joint venture with CableTel in Internet services. The war with British Airways continues – Branson dedicates £10 million to an advertising campaign to prevent the BA/American Airlines merger. Launch of Virgin Brides, a wedding service and retail business. Virgin begins flights to Johannesburg from Heathrow.

1997: A new record company, provisionally named 'V2', is launched, after Branson is free from 30 month non-competing agreement on sale of original music business. Plans are announced for Virgin jeans to compete with Levi-Strauss, a full Virgin retail banking service, a Virgin express rail link between the City of London and Heathrow Airport, and branded Virgin cosmetics to compete with the Body Shop. Negotiations start with BSB for a TV music channel. The Virgin Group starts operations on the busiest rail network in Britain with fare reductions of nearly 50 per cent for off-peak passengers, with the first refurbished Virgin train named 'Mission Impossible'.

The core Virgin businesses

On the face of things, Virgin is a hopelessly illogical grouping of unrelated businesses – are there really coherent links between airlines, drinks, music, hotels, holidays, airships, balloons, a model agency, clothes, cosmetics, pensions and investment products, and the Channel Tunnel railway? Or, as some commentators suggest, is this a fragile enterprise linked only by the name Virgin and Richard Branson's energy – both of which are stretched to the limit – and a frenetic pace of change?

It could be argued that, in fact, the Virgin projects can be grouped into a number of core businesses:

Music and entertainment

The Virgin music business was the first of Branson's ventures, starting as a mail-order record retailer – named Virgin, says Branson, to reflect his lack of business experience (though the shock to the public was probably also important to him). This led quickly to a record shop on London's Oxford Street and a recording studio. After the Mike Oldfield success, Virgin developed into one of Britain's leading music labels, with acts including Bryan Ferry, Janet Jackson and, eventually, the Rolling Stones. The Virgin name is still attached to the music label, but, as already mentioned, in fact that business was sold to EMI in 1992, for £580 million. Branson is currently getting back into the music business with the 'V2' project. Launched in November 1996, V2 Records is backed by a £50 million investment by Branson's friend and fellow balloonist Rory McCarthy, who has investments in various Virgin joint enterprises.

The residue of the early music business impacts on Virgin in two ways. The record stores led to the Virgin Megastores, challenging the established high street chains, and the sale of the music business has provided the funds for many other ventures – a significant issue to a non-quoted company after a buy-back in the late 1980s – such as the purchase of the MGM cinemas and the European airline forming the new Virgin Express European service.

The retail business had problems by 1987 and the small record stores were sold to WH Smith's Our Price chain in 1987, leaving Virgin with only ten stores, eight of which were Virgin Megastores. Simon Burke, head of Virgin Retail and Virgin Cinemas, reports that the early Virgin retail operations were anarchic – the flagship Oxford Street store actually had a CD factory in the basement (Oxford Street is not a cheap location for a production unit); and another store had leased its best selling space to an electrical retailer, so the store was dominated by white goods, with music in the corners.

'the early Virgin retail operations were anarchic'

Burke's rationalization of the Virgin retail business led to the merger of the British retail operation with Our Price in 1994, to form the Virgin Our Price chain with 320 stores, and becoming the largest entertainment retailer in Britain. Virgin owns only 25 per cent of the retail business, although with W H Smith's financial problems this may change.

The Virgin Megastores have now entered precisely targeted direct marketing campaigns based on 'magalogues', combining targeted product lists with editorial content and mailed directly to key niche markets, backed by direct response advertising in the press. The stores are also attacking the UK book market with the launch of a range of titles aimed at its 'youth' audience. The airline link to Florida has also led to Branson gaining access to Disney theme parks for the Virgin retail stores. Branson has also opened a Virgin Megastore in New York's Times Square.

Burke also manages the Virgin Cinema business, purchased from MGM, with 25 multiplexes and plans to double that number over the next five years. The goal is to 'change the cinema-going experience'. Booking systems have been outsourced to Cap Gemini, Europe's largest computer services group. As well as floor to ceiling screens and digital sound, the higher-priced ticket 'Silver Screen' audience will be able to check their coats into a cloakroom, and be served snacks in their seats. Investment in 1997 runs at around £35 million to establish the UK's largest-ever cinema complex, and to open a chain of 20 new cinemas in three years, as well as expanding the venture overseas. In 1996, profits were £13.5 million, and the company is encouraged by a boom in cinema-going in the UK.

Virgin also operates a national commercial radio station – Virgin 1215 – as well as a London station.

Travel

Virgin Travel makes the bulk of the group's profits – currently around £84 million, or two-thirds of the total – and is the vehicle which carries the Virgin message (and products) throughout the world. This includes the airline Virgin Atlantic, founded in 1984 and Branson's most-prized asset.

It is the airline business that has led Branson into his famous 'war' with British Airlines – triggered by BA's 'dirty tricks' to steal passengers and block Virgin's access to key routes, and continuing with Branson's campaign to stop the BA/American Airlines merger as anti-competitive. In mid-1996 Branson announced that he was dropping all other Virgin business to devote himself totally to the fight – along with a £10 million war chest.

In 12 years the airline has become a very substantial operation – combined turnover of Virgin Atlantic and Express is running at around £1 billion a year, with profits of around £90 million. While continuing to play 'David' to British Airways' 'Goliath', Virgin has become the world's fourth most efficient carrier, and is the 23rd largest airline in the world (in scheduled passenger miles). Indeed, Virgin has reached one sixth the size of the massive British Airways. New international routes have been opened to the USA, the Far East and South Africa, and Virgin Express is offering cheap European flights and threatening to open in the USA, if permitted by regulators. Virgin has differentiated by offering 'first class at business class prices', has innovated many customer services and in-flight 'treats', and makes profits at fares some 50–75 per cent below those of the flag carriers.

Virgin proposes to adopt a similar strategy in the newly-privatized rail travel business in the UK – offering airline services to rail travellers for the first time, including limousine rides to the station, in-travel entertainment, frequent traveller programmes, refurbished trains, higher catering standards and high levels of customer service. This is also the link to the new Channel Tunnel rail connection venture.

Financial services

Virgin Direct has attacked the British financial services industry with a direct marketing operation selling insurance, personal equity plans and personal pensions, with the possibility of mortgages and full personal banking to follow. While disparaged initially by the existing players in the market, Virgin Direct is having a major effect on how financial services are compared and priced in Britain. This market entry was controversial within the Virgin organization, but attracted £400 million in funds in the first 18 months of operation, and has stimulated the high-street banks into seeking partnership with Virgin for new product launches. Following its launch in 1995, by the end of 1996 Virgin Direct had become the 18th largest unit trust provider and the fastest growing. It was also the fourth largest supplier of personal equity plans, with a 7 per cent market share, with 86 000 customers. The Virgin products are cheaper and simpler than traditional offerings. They typically charge a lower management fee (around 1 per cent), and merely track the Stock Exchange index, rather than trying to beat it.

Branded consumer products

In a number of areas Branson has launched consumer products under the Virgin label, which are high-profile, but provide relatively small amounts of income compared to the other businesses.

The Virgin Cola launch has attracted huge publicity. Indeed, Branson still talks about displacing Coke as brand leader and has already carried out market tests prior to launching the Virgin Cola brand in the USA. The Virgin Cola bottle is reminiscent of the classic Coke bottle, but is known as the 'Pammy' because it is said not to mimic the classic Coke bottle shape, but to immortalize Baywatch star Pamela Anderson's curves. In fact, the Virgin product (manufactured by the Canadian own-label specialist Cott, which also produces Sainsbury's Classic Cola) is primarily Tesco's own-label cola, and is stuck at some 3 per cent of the market, with little immediate prospect of further progress against Coke and Pepsi.

The position is similar with Virgin Vodka – the product is produced by William Grant, and the Virgin contribution is effectively a logo and access to the youth market.

Slightly different is the joint venture move with CableTel into making Virgin Net a service supplier for Internet access to be sold through the Virgin

Megastores. The differentiator is easy access to the Web for a £10 per month charge, and a goal of gaining 20 000 subscribers in the first year.

The newest large-scale projects here are the planned entry into the jeans and cosmetics markets with Virgin-branded products. The jeans and casual wear brands will sell through conventional retailers, competing with Levi's, and the former head of Pepe jeans will lead the project. The cosmetics are positioned between the up-market brands and the own-labels of Boots and Body Shop. The cosmetics will sell through specialist outlets staffed by beauty therapists, and the project will be led by managers recruited from The Body Shop. The seriousness of the Virgin cosmetics venture and the target market is shown by the fact that Branson has recruited his sales manager and his two joint managing directors from Anita Roddick's Body Shop, as well as some 20 other Body Shop staff, and located the Cosmetic Co headquarters some 12 miles from The Body Shop head office (which facilitates commuting for at least 23 people at present). Ms Roddick is rumoured to be unamused.

The Virgin jeans project is planned to reach the market in 1998, with a range of other casual wear as well as men's denim, including shoes and accessories, with women's wear to follow. The Virgin cosmetics range of 500 products is to be launched in 1997.

'it is rumoured that Branson is taken with the idea of a fast food chain to challenge McDonalds'

As well as the joint venture moves into jeans and cosmetics as Virgin-branded products, it is rumoured that Branson is taken with the idea of a fast food chain to challenge McDonalds.

Other ventures

Lastly, there are a variety of small ventures which probably reflect Branson's personal interests or his search for fun more than anything else: airships and ballooning, the Heaven nightclub, the Neckar Island resort, the Storm model agency, the exclusive Le Manoir au Quatre Saisons restaurant (a 50 per cent interest with Raymond Blanc costing £2 million), La Residentia hotel in Majorca, the Virgin Brides retail venture, and so on. This list is lengthy. The impact on the total Virgin business is small, though they do bring further publicity, and Branson seems to love them. This said, individually they are significant ventures. For example, the Virgin Brides project is a £5 million joint venture with the American bridal retailer Kleinfeld, as well as being the pet project of a former Virgin Airlines cabin crew member.

Making sense out of chaos?

Is there a strategy?

Branson is quoted as saying: 'Personal experience is the best way of tackling business. I have never read a business book. We often do things and then work out afterwards what the overall strategy was.' Certainly it is difficult to separate the effect of Branson from the Virgin strategy. However, the appearance that he runs the company purely by force of personality may be an exaggeration. The business units in Virgin have a great deal of managerial autonomy, and there are managing directors and finance directors who are not called Branson.

If Branson's strategy can be summarized, it has been to enter areas where Virgin's reputation has a market value which can be used to shake up the market for a small cash outlay. Branson has rarely put large sums into new ventures (the major exceptions being the rail franchise bids, and the acquisitions of Virgin Express and MGM cinemas). For example, of the Virgin Direct financial services operation, Branson says: 'The big insurers are dinosaurs. All they have been able to do is cry that it's unfair. They've been unfair to consumers for hundreds of years.... Enlightened consumers should not have to pay for the privilege of being sold to.'

As a private company, Virgin provides a name and expertise, and frequently looks to partners to provide capital. For example, with the consumer products this almost amounts to the partner organizations paying to use Virgin's name and marketing presence. Virgin has, however, learned that partnerships do not always work out – those with ICL in computers and Norwich Union in financial services did not work and were ended. Branson has also sold businesses to raise funds – the music business, some retail operations, some of the MGM cinemas chain, for example, in classic portfolio management decisions.

Currently Virgin has around ten teams assessing new projects, and the company has, according to Branson, 'targeted about ten industries which we think are fairly large, and fairly complacent, and maybe overcharge quite a lot, and where we think we can do it differently'.

Brad Rosser, a former McKinsey consultant, joined Virgin in 1994 as head of corporate development. His view is that Virgin will invest in a project only if it meets four out of five criteria: the products must be innovative, challenge authority, offer value for money, be of good quality and the market must be growing. Executives at Virgin like to refer to all their products as offering 'first class at business-class prices'.

The structure of the group's management is far removed from the traditional large company hierarchy, with subsidiaries reporting to a holding company. At the centre of the complex web of Virgin operations and holdings, there are a set of family trusts. Few people have an overall view of the whole operation, mainly Branson's relatives and long-term business partners.

Many of Virgin's business partners have been Japanese, and the Japanese class Virgin as the same type of organization as Yamaha and Mitsubishi – a *keiretsu*. *Keiretsu* are families of companies which use their brand names in unconnected business areas – Yamaha makes tennis rackets, musical instruments and motor cycles, Mitsubishi applies its brand to a bank, televisions and motor cars.

In 1996, eight years after buying back Virgin, Branson returned to the stock market. The vehicle was the Victory Corporation, floated on the Alternative Investment Market. Victory will handle the new cosmetics and jeans businesses. Virgin owns 11 per cent of Victory in exchange for the use of the Virgin name, and this is thought to be a sign of Branson's longer-term intention of floating some associates while keeping the parent company private. Victory is a joint venture with Rory McCarthy, a long-term friend of Branson who personally invested £3 million in Victory. The float was not well received by the City, with analysts objecting to Virgin's small financial exposure and the high risk of the new jeans and cosmetics ventures.

Sources: 'Virgin Unveiled', N. Fox and R. Olins, *Sunday Times*, 13 October 1996. 'Branson Takes New Shot at Pop', J. Harlow, *Sunday Times*, 24 March 1996. 'Is Richard Branson Trying to Take Over the World?', *Guardian*, 3 July 1996. 'Likes at Virgin', P. O'Kane, *Irish Times*, 6 September 1996. 'Money-Go-Round', *Daily Telegraph*, 12 October 1996. 'Not Just Mr Nice Guy', I. Griffiths, *Independent on Sunday*, 15 September 1996. 'Party Mood Conceals the Serious Business Success for Virgin', *The Times*, 22 June 1996. 'Virgin Will Bring Airline Standards to Rail Travel', J. Prynn, *The Times*, 30 November 1996. 'Branson Poaches Cosmetic Bodies', *Mail on Sunday*, 9 March 1997.

Questions to consider

1 Is Virgin a prime example of brand extension strategy, or simply a strategic nightmare? Can a brand be extended or stretched too thinly?

2 What is the brand in this company? What happens if Branson quits – or has a balloon or speedboat accident?

3 Can a company this big maintain the role of 'David' to other companies' 'Goliath' in the public mind for much longer? What happens if that image goes?

4 If you had to construct a mission statement for Virgin, what would it say?

5 Why does the City seem to have so little faith in the ability of the Virgin brand to extend to new markets given the evidence?

6 If you look at the market attractiveness criteria pursued by Brad Rosser (the products must be innovative, challenge authority, offer value for money, be of good quality, and the market must be growing), how well do these fit with what Virgin has actually done? Test the criteria against the markets that Virgin has successfully attacked and those where it has failed.

7 What will this organization look like in ten years' time?

8 Can you identify the Strategic Pathway followed by Virgin?

PART III

The *Real* Issues to Manage in Going to Market

CHAPTER 8

Marketing programmes and actions:

But do we *ever* think our marketing through?

Introduction

Parts I and II of the book laid out the basics of market-led strategic change: our goals in working for a better way of managing the process of going to market (Chapter 1); the critical leverage to be gained by going back to the fundamental and unavoidable purposes of creating and managing long-term customer satisfaction in all that we do by building customer focus in our organization (Chapters 2 and 3); and the tools to identify our Strategic Pathway and build an effective market strategy (Chapters 4, 5, 6 and 7). This is the purpose and *content* for managing the process of going to market.

Part III is about the *context* in which we manage the process of going to market – the impact of organization, the market intelligence or 'market sensing' on which decisions are based; the processes of decision making involved in developing plans, budgets and actions in the marketplace in terms of the role of the sales organization in driving market strategy. If we are serious about strategic *change* in how our organizations deal with our customers when they go to market, then by the management of these elements of the organizational context for marketing we can achieve some quite dramatic things, i.e. make the market strategy happen.

This chapter starts us on this track by looking at what market strategy means in the practical terms of doing things in the marketplace. Then, let us get even more *personal* and see how well *we* link our great strategic ideas to actually doing things for customers, in the way we run our own organizations and our marketing.

Marketing programmes

An overview of the link between our market strategy and actually putting things into effect is shown in Figure 8.1. The theory is remarkably clear – as we have seen from our analysis of markets, value propositions and key relationships, we build a market strategy which translates into a marketing programme which leads to a market offering. The market responds – with purchases, payment, recommendations to others and richer customer information (Figure 8.1). What could be simpler or more straightforward?

In fact, as we will see shortly, the translation of our strategy ideas into marketing actions is usually an incredibly weak link in going to market, and we can test this out in our *'the translation of our strategy ideas into marketing actions is usually an incredibly weak link in going to market'* Diagnostic. It is also worth noting that while the structured marketing programme is a convenient mechanism for *us* in planning and organizing marketing, it does not matter one whit to the *customer*. The customer sees only a market offering which he/she evaluates, and probably does not care too much what we go through to produce that market offering. Life is terribly unfair – the reward for neatly and impeccably planning marketing is zero, unless we put together a total package that means value to the paying customer.

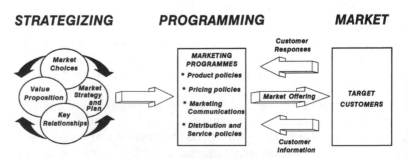

Figure 8.1 Market strategy and marketing programmes

Nonetheless, we will use the conventional model of the structured marketing programme because it is useful in identifying checklists of the issues to be addressed. In fact, this is the area where it is easiest to acquire expertise and assistance – training, consultants, business graduates, workbooks, computer software, and so on. So, it is enough for us to recognize the main issues here, rather than to cover them all in depth. We do, however, need to recognize how technology is radically changing some of these areas of practical marketplace action.

Product policies

The principal issues which are seen as part of product policy can be summarized as:

- Defining the *product itself*, with its 'bundled-in' services, and its purpose and positioning against the competition;
- Selecting an effective *product mix* to service target markets, including groupings into product lines and ranges that make sense to the customer;
- Creating a *branding policy* that will have meaning and identity for the customer (see pp. 215–30), and to represent our competitive positioning and value proposition and provide a management focus (e.g. in the form of brand or product management and planning);
- Developing and launching *new products* to meet emerging customer needs, to fill gaps in our product range, or to replace obsolete products;
- Managing *product deletions*, where products are withdrawn from the market.

These are major issues to any organization, and are likely to go way beyond the 'official' remit of many marketing executives (see Chapter 9 for evidence of this). Nonetheless, they are taken as the foundation of the marketing programme, since other marketing policy areas need to be compatible with the reality of the products and services on offer.

A wealth of conceptual and analytical tools exist to support decision making in this area, which we will not open up here since they are covered in depth in the conventional literature. Examples include: the 'augmented' product model showing the different levels and sources of value which can be offered to the customer (see pp. 194–211); portfolio models to assess the completeness and balance of the product mix; brand management models and planning structures; the product life cycle model, identifying different market conditions and hence effective marketing policies, depending on the stage of life cycle reached; new product development protocols and methods; and product deletion strategies and evaluation techniques.

Pricing policies

The principal issues which make up total pricing policy can be summarized as:

- *Price positioning* in terms of level against competitors and customer expectations (e.g. 'skimming' the market with a high price versus 'penetration' pricing with a low price to gain volume and market share);
- Price *levels and relativities* within the product mix or range and brand choices we are offering, and the margins created;
- Types and forms of price *discounting* in different customer markets;
- Pricing in different customer *markets*: export versus home; direct sales versus transfers to subsidiaries; bidding versus list prices; key accounts versus general market prices.

Generally it must be said that pricing is a 'messy' problem, where we have to balance competing internal interests against uncertain and risky external pressures. Perhaps the easiest way of recognizing and reconciling the problems is the model of iteration in Figure 8.2. This is simply a way of recognizing that we have two big sets of shaping factors: the *marketing environment* in the broadest sense, and *organizational factors* – these set the scene and probably set the real limits within which pricing decisions are made. In fact, pricing is worth a little more attention. In many organizations price is no longer seen as a 'marketing' decision – it is decided higher and elsewhere in the company. This makes price an issue of concern for all managers, not just marketing executives. This was probably one of the first areas where an issue directly impacting on the customer's perception of our value proposition was taken out of the hands of marketing executives in many companies.

From a management viewpoint, the process of making the price decision in practice seems to be one of balancing a range of conflicting pressures and trading them off against each other, until we arrive at a price which we can all live with and which is within the boundaries defined by the marketing environment and the constraints imposed by the organization (Figure 8.2). This is not a scientific model, but seems to be a good representation of

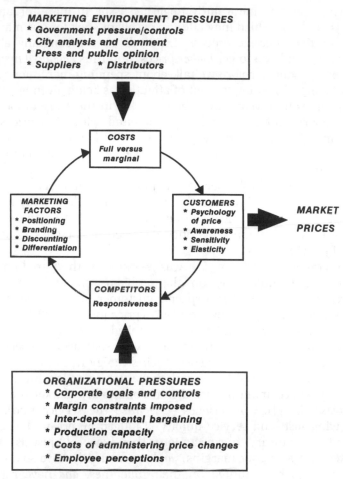

Figure 8.2 The messy pricing problem

what the pricing problem feels like in practice and the balancing act that we have to go through, though there are a number of further points to be made.

The first point is that I am constantly astounded and amazed by the predilection of organizations to charge less for their products and services than customers are prepared to pay. In my view, this is called 'giving money away for nothing'. Normally it rests on our assumptions that our customers are not just *aware* of competitive prices, but also that they are highly *sensitive* to those prices – hence price determines market share. There is a wealth of evidence that in many markets these assumptions are exactly wrong, and that price is far less significant than we think to how much business we do.

This seems to me a fairly neglected issue in many organizations, and one which may offer an excellent start for our market-led strategic change process. Let's talk to the company about what we could do to get *higher* prices, and thus *enhanced margins* for our products, before we talk about spending more money on marketing! For example, a lot of attention is being given by major companies to 'revenue management' [1], in the sense of looking for opportunities to match high demand with high prices (to enhance margins) and lower demand with lower prices (to gain volume) – such as off-peak travel ticket deals, 'happy hours' in bars, and so on.

This is not as far-fetched as it sounds – it is often amazing what you can find when you put the myths to one side and dig a little deeper into the real price/volume relationship. As they say, people don't look for discounts on Concorde tickets or Porsches. Consider the following cases.

A couple of years ago I was working with a well-known computer manufacturer on the problems of developing new marketing strategies for a specific customer market. The executives involved believed that you *had* to price just below IBM, or you would sell nothing. This credo was applied across the board to all their products: the computers (or boxes), software, and services. In fact, by the time we finished, their strategy was to *increase* the price of their boxes – because they wanted to be less involved in what was becoming a price-driven commodity market – and to *increase* the price of services – because the service market is growing fast, and service quality is judged by price. The result was that, contrary to expectations, they have sold just as many boxes (but at higher margins), *and* consequently have sold more software to be mounted on their machines, *and* have rapidly expanded the services business – indeed, they now earn more revenue from services than selling computers and software.

Shortly afterwards I did some similar work on strategic marketing planning with a small retail banking company. The target segments they wanted were the conventional banker's 'ideal' market targets – the high net worth individual, the high-income individual, the high potential earner, and so on. However, they lacked the image or branch network of the big retail banks, and were thrown back on the conclusion that they *had* to compete on price. This is a dangerous conclusion in any business, but perhaps more so in financial services than most. The point is, however, that the amazing thing we found on examining their customer base was that their most profitable type of customer was both highly brand loyal and largely insensitive to price. Their most profitable customer was not the high net worth or high-income customer – it was secretaries and clerical workers on modest incomes. These consumers apparently prefer a non-glamorous bank, but more significantly: they never use management time, indeed probably never even see a manager; they overdraw every quarter and so always pay bank charges; they would rather use a cash machine outside than a bank clerk inside the bank; and if they borrow they do so on a credit card, at a phenomenally high interest rate.

However, note two things: price is one of the many factors taken into account by the customer; and in neither of these cases was that the message the company wanted to hear – the computer company loved its computers and the bank wanted to act like NatWest. Nonetheless, these cases emphasize that we neglect the realities of pricing at our peril.

Indeed, one very old game which I still play with some companies, to open up the pricing issue, is that of asking executives to make a snap decision on what they think would improve their bottom line most – a 10 per cent increase in sales, a 10 per cent reduction in costs, or a 10 per cent increase in price? Most executives opt for volume growth or cost-cutting to improve profitability. In fact, however you work the figures the picture will almost inevitably be that price increases give more profit leverage than cost-cutting or selling more. If you try this, you will probably find that the sceptics' response is that this assumes that you can increase price by 10 per cent without losing sales. This brings us back to the real question: *Why not?*

For example, if this intrigues you, consider whether any of the following routes to obtaining higher prices may be applicable to your company in one of its markets:

'routes to obtaining higher prices may be applicable to your company'

- Is the strength of customer relationship built by the salesforce enough to negotiate higher prices or to build margin protection clauses into contracts?
- Does our value proposition give us enough competitive differentiation so that we can get a premium price higher than our competitors?
- Does our segmentation of the market show some types of buyers who are less sensitive to price and where our added value would justify a higher price to the customer?
- Would multiple branding of the product open several price positions in the market instead of just one?
- As we bring new products and new marketing methods to the market, does this give opportunities to skim the market?

Secondly, in most markets the bargain basement is a bad place to be. Few companies can sustain the very low price position, unless they have a massive cost advantage over their competitors. For example, one of the success stories of the 1980s was the Scottish clothing stores What Everyone Wants. They were the subject of the joke that a shoplifter went on a day-long stealing spree at WEW and, burdened by his haul, took a taxi home, only to find that the value of his swag was less than the taxi fare. WEW did spectacularly well with rock-bottom clothes prices to meet the needs of the low-income customer. By 1997, however, WEW was in deep trouble and looking to sell off its stores. Plans now centre on transforming WEW into a more upmarket discounter as The Store. However, climbing out of the bargain basement is difficult.

Thirdly, price wars are dangerous and highly contagious. Analysis of the result of price wars in a wide range of industries – computers, mobile phones, air travel, DIY, champagne, electrical goods, cigarettes, newspapers, sports shoes, food retailing, perfume – shows remarkably similar results: margins decline, the weakest companies crash and the product becomes a commodity sold on price only [2]. The pressures to play this game are numerous:

- Customers may no longer equate low price with low quality as markets become more discerning;
- Retailers throughout the world *love* discount sales to shift stock and have some fun;
- Over-capacity in an industry is a severe temptation to start price-cutting;
- Price may look like a good way for the weaker brands to undermine the brand leader;
- Predatory pricing (undercutting competitors to squeeze them out of the business) may be the only response to competition we can think of;
- It makes us look good to everyone if we can say we are reducing prices to increase value to customers.

The harsh reality is that price wars are only likely to be good for you if: customers are highly responsive to prices; your competitors cannot or will not just match your price cuts to restore the status quo in market share; and ultimately you are the lowest-cost producer and can sustain low prices longer than the rest. Otherwise we should think very carefully before being too aggressive on price.

The last point I would make before leaving pricing is that all too often, because they do not have sole control of the pricing decision, marketing executives do not regard price as a marketing variable (they may say they do, because they have read the right books, but they don't really). It may be that price is decided high in the organization, not by the marketing executives. It may be that there are multiple interests to satisfy if we want to change price (see Figure 8.2). On the other hand, it may just be that we are surrounded by *myths* about what prices the market will bear and what they will not and the real relationship between price and value.

These factors define the problems of creating and implementing a new pricing policy – they do not change the fact that price is a marketing variable because it is one of the things that matter to customers (although perhaps not always in the way that we assume and expect).

The challenge is simple: 'Price is how we tell the customer how good we are'. So, how good are we telling our customers that we are?

In case this sounds hopelessly exaggerated, consider the following example. In the US Marriot hotel chain, in some of the hotels there is a 'Concierge Floor'. The price of a room on the Concierge Floor is about $220 compared to about $140 for an ordinary room. For this difference the customer gets: a Concierge lift giving an appearance of security (which is an illusion, since all floors are accessible by stairway) but a reality of exclusivity; their 'own' reception desk and staff; 'free' continental breakfasts and coffee; and a room which differs markedly from the standard room in that it contains a bowl of boiled sweets and a TV in the bathroom, but is *identical* in virtually every other respect. You may not be impressed by this, but in my view a 60 per cent price differential buys an awful lot of melon slices, coffee and boiled sweets, and the rest is extra margin.

We keep coming back to the simple fact that if you offer customers something they value they will pay you for it, and they do not care what it costs you to provide it.

Now, let's take pricing policy as a marketing variable and challenge some of the myths!

'let's take pricing policy as a marketing variable and challenge some of the myths!'

Marketing communications

Probably the most visible and 'glamorous' aspects of the marketing programme are in the area of marketing communications. However, the key point to make is that however exciting and creative, this is about linking our product and price offer to our customers and nothing else. Creative awards and advertising agency hype notwithstanding, the management problems are: deciding objectives for the communications programme; integrating the different forms of communication (getting the ad agency and the salesforce doing things even vaguely compatible would be a start in the right direction in many cases); and evaluating, in mundane terms like value for money, what we are actually getting for our spend on communications (not easy, incidentally, but not impossible).

The communications methods open to us in delivering marketing to the customer can be classified as:

- *Advertising* – using mass media like TV, radio, press, outdoor and transport media to reach large audiences, and also more specialized vehicles such as direct mail, exhibitions, trade publications, the Internet, etc., but also including the communications role of product packaging, point-of-sale displays, sales literature, etc. and electronic media (see pp. 336–38);
- *Personal selling* – face-to-face representation by seller to buyer, plus the supporting materials for presentation, display, etc.;
- *Sales promotion* – events with short-term objectives, often sharing the same media as advertising, e.g. price cuts, customer competitions and incentives, distributor incentives, 'special offers', collectables, etc.;
- *Public relations* – a label greatly abused in practice, but intended to refer to the creation and maintenance of corporate images relevant to different audiences.

Broadly, in each of these areas the principal issues to be addressed can be summarized as follows:

- Deciding on the *role* of each form of communications in delivering the market strategy to the marketplace, i.e. the target customer. These roles may be quite different, e.g. advertising to the consumer backed by sales efforts aimed at the distributor, but should be compatible.
- Setting *objectives* for each form of communication which represent achieving the role we want it to play. These objectives will have to be set in very different terms. For advertising, objectives may be about altering customer awareness, or changing customer belief about a product. For personal selling, objectives traditionally are more likely to be sales revenue, market coverage and cost-based, although increasingly they are being set in terms of customer relationships (see Chapter 13). For sales promotion, objectives are likely to be related to specific events, e.g. repeat purchases motivated by collectables, trial rates for new products gained through sampling or special offers, and the like.

- Managing the communications *process*. In advertising and sales promotion, this is likely to be about handling relations with external agencies, budgeting, and evaluating the success of the spend against objectives. In personal selling, this opens up the area of recruitment and selection, training, organization and allocation, remuneration, and evaluation of the field salesforce.
- The *integration* of communications activities. This is not just in deciding what role they should all play, but actually arranging it – comparing the messages delivered by salespeople to the positioning our advertising is trying to gain, balancing the attractions of short-term gains from a price cut or special deal with the long-term position we are trying to build for a brand, or simply co-ordinating ad campaigns, sales promotions and sales calls. The goal is what some executives describe simply as getting everyone 'singing from the same song sheet', and it is not easy. For example, consider the equation: 'Fantastically effective reduction in stocks held in the channel as a result of continuous replenishment and customer partnering by the salesforce' plus 'amazingly effective sales promotion campaign launched by the product manager and the advertising agency' equals massive stockouts and unhappy customers.

It may not be very glamorous, but that is about all managers need to know about marketing communications – it is just a means to an end. However, a number of issues behind this are worth bearing in mind.

Most of us are dependent on an advertising agency for creative and media work. This is one of the key relationships we described in Chapter 6. Agency relationships have frequently been problematic [3], but building a relationship of trust and understanding may be an important source of competitive advantage, which should not be underestimated [4].

The question of co-ordinating marketing communications has been championed by Don E. Schultz and his 'Integrated Marketing Communications' model [5]. His point is simple – you get the maximum value for money if all your communications come together for the customer in the marketplace to deliver the important message in a consistent and coherent way. However, what he also tells us about in practice is the disintegration of marketing communications, reflecting battles over 'turf' and budget and reward systems that work against integration. He tells us about marketing people working with ad agencies to do one thing, while the sales organization is working with channel members to do something

'you get the maximum value for money if all your communications come together for the customer in the marketplace to deliver the important message'

else, and it all sounds terribly familiar. Our value proposition is the vehicle for integrating communications for the elusive 'one sight, one sound' or the 'seamless stream of communication' – so let's just do it that way.

We also have to be realistic enough to recognize that the traditional media of advertising – TV, newspapers, and so on – are rapidly becoming channels of distribution in their own right, in the form of off-page selling and direct-response TV advertising. This just helps confuse things further, but then who said life was going to be straightforward? And these are highly important developments for some companies.

Distribution and service policies

Perhaps the 'Cinderella' of marketing for too long was the channels and logistics systems that actually get our products and services into the hands of the paying customer. The problem is that in many instances the control of distribution is located with the operations area or specialist distribution management, not with marketing. The trouble with this is that the customer probably does not care too much how we organize it, the customer is typically unreasonable and selfish enough to think that the following is really what distribution is about:

- Is the product/service available in the outlet *I* want to use, when *I* want to buy it?
- How long do I have to *wait* to get delivery of the product and how *sure* am I that it will get here on time?
- Can I get spare parts, maintenance and after-sales service *quickly* and *reliably*, and do I *believe* the promises made about spares and maintenance?

In other words, the distribution system, however sophisticated, is about simple service to the customer – and that is why it matters to marketing. The principal *marketing* issues to be addressed in distribution are thus about channels on the one hand, and logistics on the other:

- Selecting, motivating and controlling distributors and outlets, although this may sound a trifle optimistic when we look at the realities of retailer and distributor concentration and power in some markets;
- Providing the promise and reality of the delivery and services that the customer wants, through our transportation arrangements, our stockholding and the location of our warehousing in the marketplace.

A couple of points should be made before we move on. In many situations, it can be said that our great products and the excellent value they represent, together with our smart advertising and high-quality selling to the trade, can fall very flat simply because the customer cannot lay hands on the product in the store, or get delivery in any sensible time, or we let him/her down because our delivery and service promises are broken. This is like jumping the queue in a Glasgow pub – you can *do* it, but probably only *once*!

Strategically, the problem is to get our delivery and service lined up with the other elements of marketing, in the market offering made *to* the customer, as it is perceived *by* the customer. This sounds obvious and straightforward, but experience suggests that in practice it is not. One of the problems in separating transportation, warehousing, stocking, maintenance and other service issues from marketing is that these people want to do things *their* way, not the *customer's* way.

Tom Peters[6] tells the story of a senior technical manager in a multinational who, to this day, forbids his staff to buy technical equipment from a particular supplier (though it is a superb company that supplies superb products). The reason is that some ten years earlier when the manager was a departmental executive he bought an instrument from the company and had a small sub-component problem. The supplier sent highly-trained engineers to 'prove' that the sub-component had been abused, so that warranties did not apply, and later did not return 'phone calls, was offensive in correspondence, and so on. The result is the manager's standing order not to buy from that company again. He says: 'I know it's emotional, I know it's irrational, but it's *my money*'. The point I make is not that treating customers shabbily will lose you business – we should know that because it is obvious. The real point is that ten years ago, *somewhere* in that instrument supplier, *someone* thought that cracking down on warranty claims was a fine way to save some money and to build a better bottom line – and she/he was probably rewarded by the organization for doing it.

Again and again you find companies doing things which 'make sense' to them (and they can 'prove' it), but which destroy the long-term value of their brands and the market offering as it is perceived by the customer. The underlying moral is that providing customers with the service levels and types we need in making up the market offering to that customer is likely to cause our transport, warehousing, maintenance and service people to do their jobs worse in *their* terms. This is what the real fight is about.

However, it would also be silly to proceed past distribution and communication in marketing without recognizing that the Internet and the World Wide Web of electronic communications has crept up on us as a new form of interactive selling, advertising and distribution and service.

Internet marketing

We are only just beginning to see the first glimpses of what the Internet may mean to conventional marketing communications and channels of distribution, let alone the whole new way of doing business which it offers in some industries. The chances are that none of us will remain unaffected by this for long.

Although it is well-known to most 12-year olds, let us get some of the terminology out of the way.

- *Internet* – a computer link-up crossing the world which is the 'international network of networks' and which no-one owns or controls;
- *World Wide Web* – a multimedia (text, sound and graphics) subset of the Internet which allows easy viewing and exchange of data;
- *Web Site* – a location on the Web which can be accessed by computer users and which displays one or more Web pages.

The Internet is an amazing and pervasive thing with many implications for how we do business. This said, we need to be realistic. We have come a long way since the 1970s when, as Clifford Longley remarks, the Internet was the answer to a question nobody was asking, and 'not even the wildest visionary was wondering how to use his telephone, at his own expense, to fill his computer screen with an advert for Coca-Cola'. Nonetheless, by 1997 only 800 000 homes in the UK have any kind of Internet access, and there are more things like nerd chat pages with 'Hi there, I'm Dave. I'm into country and western and Airfix. . . .' messages than serious electronic commerce [7]. John Dvorak, a leading US computer analyst, dismissed the Internet as 'an overhyped plaything destined to disappoint all but the most masochistic technofreaks' and his mantra is 'Web, schmeb!' [8]

'the impact of the Internet on marketing is already being felt, but you ain't seen nothing yet'

That is now. The future impact is a different question, however. In fact, the impact of the Internet on marketing is already being felt, but you ain't seen nothing yet. Consider the following.

Internet advertising

At its very simplest, the Web provides a new advertising medium. For example, most large companies now have their own Web sites to visit. However, it is an advertising medium with some interesting characteristics. The basic costs of a Web site are about the same regardless of the size of the company – there is little economy of scale, although some users do spend a fortune. All Web sites are international. Small businesses can now afford to advertise internationally. Foreign business can advertise here at low cost. The economics are radically different from those of conventional media. For example, consider the text of current IBM advertising:

Open a shop in every city in the world? That takes millions of pounds worth of resources, doesn't it? . . . we can help you open for business in every city around the globe (at least every city the Internet reaches) for a down-to-earth price. How in the world can we do that? With a powerful IBM solution that lets millions of Internet users find, see and buy your products without leaving their chairs. It's like having shops without paying rent . . . .'

The implications are not just important for consumer goods and multinational corporations either. J & H Bunn is a fertilizer company based in Great Yarmouth. Their problem is that farmers (their customers) do not work 9 to 5. The Internet provides farmers with e-mail and ordering facilities 24 hours a day. A modest application? J & H Bunn spent only £1,000 developing a Web site which has generated literally thousands of sales leads and promotes the point of contact for 24-hour ordering. Dial-A-Basket is a small company in St Albans selling gift baskets. Its Web site has gained electronic orders from places as diverse as Europe, Latin America, New Zealand and the USA, for an absurdly small financial outlay. *That* is how drastic the change in the economics is.

Internet shopping

In 1996 Tesco launched the trial of the first on-line superstore for grocery shopping on the Internet, while both Tesco and Sainsbury have been offering wine and flower delivery services via the Web site 'CompuServe Barclay Square mall' for some time. Safeway is looking to extend its self-scanning systems to customers' homes. Boots the Chemists is piloting its first 'virtual branch' for home shopping in 1997. The number of on-line households is expected to reach 1 million by 2000, with a spend of £1.25 billion. It is likely that 'virtual shops' and 'virtual malls' will expand both in this type of consumer marketing and also in business-to-business markets.

Internet revolution

The Internet is likely to do a lot more than provide an advertising medium and an extension to home shopping. It can and will create new businesses, new markets and new ways of doing business.

For instance, the law is not traditionally seen as a high-technology profession. But Davis & Co has become the first City law firm to structure itself around teleworking and electronic communications to offer clients a 24-hour, seven day service in what is effectively a 'hollow' organization. Global Internetwork is set to reduce the cost of international phone calls by two-thirds by offering a phone service via the Internet, and traditional telecoms firms seem at a loss as to how to respond (they might consider reducing their prices – just a thought).

'many traditional barriers between service businesses are disintegrating, because basically they all process transactions'

In fact, more generally, many traditional barriers between service businesses are disintegrating, because basically they all process transactions. Take banks – they used to be defined by branch networks, but these are closing. If a bank just processes payments, why do you need a bank? Quote: 'Give me a piece of the transaction business and the banks are history' (Bill Gates, Microsoft, 1996) [9]. On the other hand, Nationwide Building Society is actually talking to retailers about partnership to sell groceries from building society branches – not holding stock, just processing orders – though with no takers at present. Add to this, at the other end of the scale, small businesses operating from home computers offering new specialized services globally, and no market is likely to remain untouched.

Now consider the related issue of marketing information.

Marketing information

The information issue in managing marketing is one of the most critical we face, yet possibly the hardest on which to put a handle. In our approach to 'making sense' of theory (pp. 138–40), we said that the information function was concerned with intelligence about the marketplace, to create information flows for planning and for control, using the tools of marketing research to build marketing information systems.

We also said there is nothing particularly wrong with looking at marketing information in this way and at this level, other than the fact that it wholly misses the point about the real role of information in marketing and the potential leverage it provides for market-led strategic change. There is a more significant agenda to be opened than one concerned with the tools and technology of information. This is concerned with the fact that marketing information is not just facts and figures, it is about the 'creation of meaning' or 'market sensing'. Now this may sound very high-blown and esoteric. It is not. It is about the basics of figuring out a few central issues concerning markets: what do we actually *know*; what are the key *assumptions* we make about the outside world – customers, competitors, environmental change, and so on; who *shapes* and *controls* this model of the world that we assume to be true, and on which we base our decisions; and what are the opportunities for *re-shaping* and *re-defining* this model of the world to change how people think about the customer and to change what they think are the most important things to the business? In other words, what leverage does *managing* marketing information offer us in managing market-led strategic change?

But information has another significance in the process of going to market that we should note here.

As we saw in Figure 8.1, the parallel to every exchange of goods and money (every transaction) is an exchange of information. The ownership of the transaction and the information it produces is a major source of competitive advantage as direct marketing and database marketing become significant in more and more of our markets.

In fact, it was as long ago as 1982 that I wrote about the 'macro marketing information system' emerging as a competitive factor resulting from new technology facilitating the formation of electronic links between manufacturers, retailers and consumers. I pointed out at this time that whoever controlled the database would control the channel of distribution and much more besides [10,11,12,13]. That analysis of retailer information strategies is worth re-visiting. At the time no-one listened – more nonsense from ivory tower academics! That macro marketing information system is now a reality, and it is controlled by retailers, with many strategic consequences (e.g. see pp. 259–62 above). Well, sorry about this – but I told you so! Don't say you weren't warned! But what of the impacts on marketing?

Database and direct marketing

The customer databases built by retailer and airline loyalty programmes, by direct marketing of financial services, by direct response TV advertising by firms like Daewoo and Heinz, are the route to realizing 'one-to-one marketing' – what Don Peppers calls 'mass customization' or individual deals for every buyer (at least in theory). The early manifestations we are seeing now are important, but perhaps not quite so revolutionary:

- Sainsbury is experimenting with individual catalogues of grocery products from which the customer can order, and collect the order when it has been compiled by the customer's personal shopper, while several supermarket chains offer the facility to shop from the home or workplace by phone, fax or computer.
- American Express uses its customer database to tailor offers (such as a special sale at Harrods or an airline deal) to small groups of customers, based on their spending patterns.
- Procter and Gamble use database marketing for Pampers nappies – individualized birthday cards to babies and reminder letters to parents to move up to the next size, and so on.
- Nestlé, the Swiss food firm, has 80 000 members for the Casa Buitoni club, increasing purchases of pasta products by a promotional newsletter and recipes.
- In the USA, Procter and Gamble has been experimenting with direct marketing of its range of household products – detergents, toothpaste, toilet paper. Using its database, the pilot scheme makes contact with the consumer to supply these products direct to the home. The consumer gets the convenience of home delivery and a good price for bulky essential purchases, and the company gets to take that consumer out of the competitive marketplace, at least for a while.

These are all extremely novel and exciting developments, even if they fall a bit short of the 'mass customization' model – at least as yet. However, this area is changing fast and needs watching.

Marketing intentions versus market realities

We have covered a lot of ground in attempting to clarify what the substance of going to market is about. Now we reach the stage of testing out which bits matter most to the individual or organization, as part of clarifying what needs to go on our personal agendas for creating market-led strategic change.

The pursuit of market-led strategic change suggests that we are seeking something new. We tried in Chapters 2 and 3 to focus on the satisfaction of customers as the central issue (in Diagnostic 1). Now the issue is whether we have got our marketing 'act' together or not.

Getting the marketing act together

One of the major practical problems we face in dealing with this lengthy, overlapping, conflicting, uncertain, messy, and complicated set of issues which make up market strategies, marketing programmes and plans, is packing the whole thing together, i.e. creating the 'market offering' that matters to the customer (Figure 8.1). It seems inherent in the nature of the issues we are managing that all too often it goes wrong because we do not succeed in doing this effectively – where effectiveness is judged by the customer, not by ourselves.

'this lengthy, overlapping, conflicting, uncertain, messy, and complicated set of issues which make up market strategies, marketing programmes and plans'

We may start with grandiose ideas about our missions and our competitive positioning, and how we can achieve these through differentiation and advertising strategy, and the like. However, what matters is the reality of what this turns into in the marketplace (i.e. what the customer receives, perceives and consequently evaluates).

This is about what some have taken as the difference between 'intended' and 'realized' strategies. Now there is a theoretical argument surrounding this distinction [14], but for present purposes we are dealing with something really very simple:

- *Intended Strategy or Strategic Intent* – what *we* think or want the business to be about in the marketplace;
- *Perceived Strategy or Strategic Reality* – what the business is *actually* about in the marketplace, as perceived by the people who run the business, and ultimately as perceived by the target customer (the ones we have *lost*, as well as the ones we have gained, incidentally).

Before we set about changing the way we do things, one of the things we should really sort out is where we are now. The purpose of Diagnostic 3 (Figure 8.3) is to force us to do just this.

Company:	Market/Segment/Customer Type:

Strategy:

Completed by:	Time Period:

OPERATIONAL MARKETING POLICIES	STRATEGIC INTENT	STRATEGIC REALITY	STRATEGIC GAP
Products and Services			
Pricing and Value			

Communications
 	
  - Selling
  - Advertising
  - Promotion			

Distribution
 	
  - Channels
  - Logistics
  - Service			

STRATEGIC POSITIONING			

Conclusions/Implications/Actions

Figure 8.3 Diagnostic Worksheet 3 – Have we got our marketing act together?

Goals of Diagnostic 3

The overall aim of this Diagnostic is to evaluate our performance in translating our market strategies into realities in the marketplace. It is positioned here as an instrument we can use to evaluate our present position, before building new strategies and plans. (However, we can also use the same framework as a mechanism for evaluating our success in changing things as well.)

More specifically, at the present stage, Diagnostic 3 tries to evaluate the gap which may exist between Strategic Intent (what *we* think the business is seen to be doing in the marketplace) and Strategic Reality (what the people who run the business and the customer tell us the business is *really* about in the marketplace). This gap is evaluated in Diagnostic 3 in each of the following areas of the marketing programme and in our Strategic Positioning:

- Our *products and services*, in terms of such issues as quality compared to competitors, fullness of range, image and brand identity compared to alternatives, design attributes, functional features and 'extras', reliability of services, and so on;
- Our *pricing and value*, in terms of the real position in price level against competitors and alternatives (prices that customers are quoted and pay rather than published list prices), and how we are seen in 'value for money' compared to competitors;
- Our *communications*, in terms of the quality and role of our selling efforts and our coverage of the market, the image and awareness created by advertising, the effectiveness of our promotions, and so on, all as compared to our competitors;
- Our *distribution*, in terms of the availability of the product in the marketplace (at the time, in the form, in the place that the customer wants it), the quality of the service provided in terms of waiting time, service provision, maintenance, and so on;
- Our *strategic positioning*, in terms of the stage of the life cycle our product has reached, the strength of our market position, our success in achieving a differentiation in the customer's eyes, and what we have achieved in customer satisfaction.

On most of these issues we are not looking for sophisticated, research-based quantification to start with — qualitative input in the form of two or three bullet points in each box of the diagnostic is often enough to achieve what we need. More sophisticated inputs can be developed later, if the exercise is paying off for us.

Instructions for completing Diagnostic 3

As with all the diagnostics in the book, the aim is to reduce issues to a few simple and unambiguous points, which is in itself a painful but useful discipline. The way to complete Diagnostic 3 is as follows.

Company

To avoid ambiguity, specify which part of the operation is being covered. This may be the whole company, part of the operation, or even a single brand, depending on how productive the diagnostic is for us.

Market/Segment/Customer type

Again, we should be clear about whether we want to look at the whole market, or just one segment or customer type. The diagnostic can be used at any of these levels, but we should be consistent, throughout completing it, in what part of the marketplace we have in mind.

Strategy

Within the parameters we have just defined, we should put a label on our overall strategy for this company or brand, in this market, during this time period, which describes what we wanted to achieve.

Completed by

This requires a little further discussion in considering how to use the diagnostic most productively, but for the moment we will assume that we are completing the diagnostic ourselves, and are willing to put our own names to it!

Time period

We should be clear about whether this is an historical analysis (and if so, how far back we want to go), or just the current period, or planning for the future, and so on.

Strategic intent

We should complete this column first. This is where we describe, in no more than two or three bullet points for each box, what our intended strategy was for each of the elements of the marketing programme (see the *Goals of Diagnostic 3*, pp. 342–43, for a view of the issues which should be addressed and questioned in each area of the marketing programme). The underlying question here is: 'For our strategy to be real, what would each part of the marketing programme have to achieve?'

Finally, we need to summarize where we wanted our operation to be in terms of the strategic position we intended to take and where we intended to be in a differentiated position compared to our competitors. Again, the question is: 'For our marketing strategy to work, where should we be on strategic positioning?'

Strategic Reality

The next stage is the real killer! Go back through each of the issues you have addressed above – the marketing programme and the strategic positioning that your strategy required – and now ask: What have we *actually* got, what is the *reality?*

Strategic Gap

The third column simply asks us to specify, in two or three bullet points, what the difference is between our Strategic Intent on each of the issues and the Strategic Reality we see in the marketplace, and *why* the differences exist. Normally, there are certain conclusions we can reach, which should be noted. But the real fun has not started yet!

Using Diagnostic 3

Now we can get on to the really interesting issues – whose views go into the diagnostic, and how do we interpret what we find?

Whose views go into the Diagnostic?

There are a number of issues here, although practicality suggests that not all will be open to us all the time. The most significant of these issues relates to *whose* view of the Strategic Reality we should take on board:

- To start with, there is no doubt that we are likely to get some useful insights into how well our strategies are translated into reality by completing the analysis *ourselves*, as objectively as possible, and focusing on the strategic gaps which we identify. At the very least, this forces us to confront what we already know, by putting it into a new structure. This is useful, but we can make it a lot more useful.
- We can ask our *staff* in the field, our *sales and service* people, our *technical* departments, in the company what they believe to be the Strategic Reality, i.e. let us see what the people who are in touch with the market day-to-day tell us about the reality.
- There is, of course, only one logical conclusion we can reach – which is that ideally we ask our *customers* and our *distributors* what is the Strategic Reality that they perceive in our marketing programme and our strategic positioning. This can be turned into an expensive and sophisticated market research exercise, or it can be much simpler. The point is that the real answer to whether we have got our marketing act together or not can only

come from one source – the paying customer. We may have to make do with second-best – distributors, salespeople, outside experts – but all they are really doing is giving us their views about what matters to the end paying customer.

There may well be practical difficulties in doing this, but the further you progress down this list of participants in the analysis, the better the results are going to be. With each new set of inputs to understanding the Strategic Reality as it is perceived by others, we are going to collect new strategic gaps and further ideas for what conclusions we should reach.

There is also a variation which may be useful in applying this diagnostic. We assumed above that our view of Strategic Intent was both correct and, by implication, fully understood. If we are not completely comfortable with this, we can also test the Strategic Intent column as well by asking the same people what the Strategic Intent was as they understand it, in delivering the strategy to the market. This may well lead us to incorporate in our conclusions quite simply that Strategic Gaps exist because the key players – like salespeople, service staff, distributors, and so on – did not *know* what was required of them in making the strategy happen. In fact, American researchers have suggested that if you really talk to service and distribution employees about their work priorities, it is clear that their *real* mission in most cases is simply to stay out of trouble, i.e. which customers can we ignore and give poor service to, without getting pain from the company? Now compare that to the marketing plan!

More on this theme will follow in Chapter 14, when we consider the role of internal marketing strategy.

Interpreting the findings

As with all the diagnostics in the book, the most important stage is to stand back from the boxes we have completed and see what conclusions we can draw and, where appropriate, the implications for action. The types of issue which this diagnostic throws up are:

'How serious are the gaps between what we think the strategy is and what the perceived reality is?'

- How serious are the gaps between what we think the strategy is and what the perceived reality is?
- Why do these Strategic Gaps exist, what could be done to move the reality closer to the intent, would this be possible and would it pay?
- Are some of the Strategic Gaps realistically impossible to close, is our strategy hopelessly out of line with our resources and capabilities?

- Where, in formulating strategies and planning marketing programmes, do we confront the Strategic Reality as it is described to us by the salesforce, the distributors, the customer?
- Is the problem one of reformulating the strategy (i.e. moving the intent closer to the reality) or managerial action (i.e. moving the reality closer to the intent)?

I have yet to do this with a company where we concluded that there were no important Strategic Gaps. If done thoroughly, this piece of analysis can achieve two major things for us: first, it uncovers how well we translate our market strategies into integrated operational programmes; and secondly, it forces us to look not just at our goals and creative ideas, but at what the operational personnel and the paying customers tell us it really looks like from their point of view. The results can be both revealing and insightful in their own right, but can also push us towards asking how we can actually go about changing and adapting to the realities of the match between our company's capabilities and what matters most in the marketplace.

More specifically, the output from this analysis is likely to fall into the following categories, which can be handled differently, and the implications of which are examined separately in the next parts of the book:

- Strategic Gaps because there are too many internal barriers to make the Strategic Intent real – consider the organization questions in Chapter 9.
- Strategic Gaps because line management do not accept the validity of the Strategic Intent – consider the issue of market understanding in Chapter 10.
- Strategic Gaps because the Strategic Intent is out of line with corporate capabilities, or they represent aspirations not shared by the people who actually run the business – consider the planning process in Chapter 11.
- Strategic Gaps because the marketing programme is not resourced in line with the Strategic Intent – consider the budgeting problem in Chapter 12.
- Strategic Gaps because the marketing and sales organizations are poorly integrated – look at Chapter 13 for some views on this and some tools to close the gap.
- Strategic Gaps because, when plans and Strategic Intents were conceived, we did not take the implementation issue seriously – see Chapter 14 on implementation strategy and strategic internal marketing.

Our progress so far towards market-led strategic change

With our goals revealed in Chapter 1, and our orientation towards customer focus and long-term customer satisfaction laid out in Chapters 2 and 3, the purpose of Part II of the book was to set out the major issues of market strategy that we need to incorporate in our thinking.

In Part III, we have started by trying to simplify things down to three aspects of the process of going to market: market strategy, marketing programmes and information (see pp. 138–40). The simplifying structure gives us a framework in which to fit and locate all the ideas and theories, advice, training, prescription and advocacy, and techniques available in marketing.

Market Strategy was seen to be about a set of complicated and messy issues: market choices, the value proposition and the key relationships underpinning the strategy. Inevitably what we found was that the most difficult and uncertain issues are the ones that matter most, because they define what we really have to offer to the customer.

Marketing Programmes were defined as the packing together of elements of product policies, pricing policies, marketing communications and distribution and service policies. Each of these policy areas breaks down into a number of sub-components, each with its own technical literature and specialist expertise. For our purposes, however, what matters here is defining a market offering to the customer, which emphasizes the things that matter most to that customer.

The final area we opened up was *Marketing Information*. We postponed detailed consideration of this issue for the moment, because it is particularly significant to the theme of market-led strategic change and merits its own chapter. We did, however, dwell for a while on the emergence of Internet marketing and database marketing out of this.

Lastly, having unpacked a diverse set of issues, we got personal and focused on how well *we* actually put these together to create something of value for the customer – strategic intent versus strategic reality in how we go to market and our positioning in the market. Hopefully, *Diagnostic 3 – Have we got our marketing act together?* will have brought us back to the ground with a bump, after the heady stuff of strategizing!

If we have got anything by now, it is probably a set of issues about changing the way in which our company manages its process of going to market – possibly quite a worrying list in some cases. The next stage is to deal with what we can *do* about that set

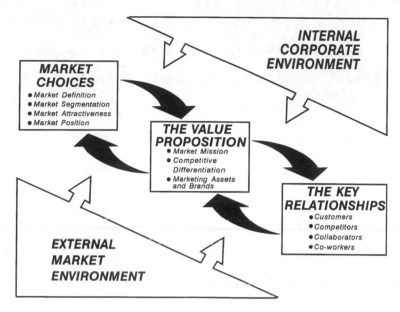

Figure 8.4   The strategic pathway

of issues, and that is the task of the remainder of Part III of the book, where we examine the key elements of the context for managing the process of going to market, and where we get into issues of planning implementation strategy and internal marketing. In short, as shown in Figure 8.4, we have defined the Strategic Pathway, but for it to become a reality we need to put it into the context of both the external market environment (how we understand the market) and the internal corporate environment (the structures and processes inside the company). The Strategic Pathway must pass through both of these.

References

1. Cross, Robert (1997), *Hard-Core Tactics for Market Domination*, London: Orion Business Books.
2. Smith, David and Matthew Lynn (1993), 'Price Wars', *Sunday Times*, 26 September.
3. Bentley, Stephanie (1996), 'Ad Effectiveness: Measures of Strength', *Marketing Week*, 1 November.
4. Simms, Jane (1996), 'Managing the Primal Scream', *Marketing Business*, September, 38–40.
5. Schultz, Don E. (1993), *Integrated Marketing Communications*, Chicago: NTC Books.

6. Peters, Tom (1989), *Thriving on Chaos – Handbook for a Management Revolution*, London: Pan Books.
7. 'Encyclopaedia, Yellow Pages, or Kook's Refuge' (1997), *Daily Telegraph*, 13 March.
8. Donath, Bob (1997), 'No 'Web, Schmeb' for Business Marketers', *Marketing News*, 14 April.
9. Gosling, Paul (1996), 'Baked Beans and Bacon from a Hole in the Wall', *Independent on Sunday,* 10 November.
10. Piercy, Nigel (1982), *Retail Marketing: The Missing Link*, Research Studies in Business and Finance, UWIST, 1982/24.
11. Piercy, Nigel (1983), 'Retailer Information Power: The Channel Marketing Information System', *Marketing Intelligence and Planning*, Vol. 1, No. 1, 40–55.
12. Piercy, Nigel (1984), 'Retailer Marketing – Informational Strategies', *European Journal of Marketing*, Vol. 17, No. 6, 5–15.
13. Piercy, Nigel (1984), 'Developing Marketing Information Systems for the 1980s and Beyond – A British Perspective', *Journal of International Marketing and Marketing Research*, Vol. 9, No. 3, 111–132.
14. Mintzberg, Henry (1988), 'Opening Up the Definition of Strategy', in J. B. Quinn, H. Mintzberg and R. M. James, *The Strategy Process*, London: Prentice-Hall.

CHAPTER 9

Organization for marketing:

Do we organize to make it happen – or don't we, and what happens next?

Introduction

We turn, in this chapter, to the issue of organization for marketing, and whether or not we really *do* organize to make marketing happen. However, the question here is really twofold: what strategic gaps do we create for ourselves simply by the way we organize for marketing, but also how are we going to have to think about organizing marketing for the new market strategies and particularly the collaboration and partnership-based relationships which are becoming critical to driving these strategies?

First, we will look at where we are with marketing departments and then at the new ideas developing about how we will organize marketing for the future.

So, what's the beef about organization for marketing?

Experiences with a variety of organizations suggest that one of the things that goes wrong with how we go to market in UK companies is that we simply do not organize ourselves properly to make it happen. Indeed,

'one of the things that goes wrong with how we go to market in UK companies is that we simply do not organize ourselves properly'

it seems that in some cases we organize to make it virtually impossible for it to happen effectively! And that is before we even think about how the process of going to market will fit the new types of organization which are emerging fast (see pp. 251–63).

The theory is about methods for fine-tuning conventional marketing organizations, such as: the best ways of running brand and market manager systems; where most productively to use a matrix structure to cope with complex combinations of diverse products and markets; how best to develop segment or sector management specializations, and so on. This is fine, until you do research into how companies really organize for marketing.

This task was difficult, because the first thing I found was that in a large number of companies there were *no* structures or systems whatsoever for implementing marketing. In many others, marketing structures were weak token gestures with no real chance of changing anything. This was astonishing, but we have now looked at a number of sectors – manufacturing, retailing, financial services, professional services – and broadly the same conclusions are reached. We have to conclude that, generally speaking, companies do *not* organize to make marketing happen in any real way – even if they *think* and *say* that they do.

Now, the first reaction of many executives to this is simply that if companies do *not* organize for marketing, then they *should*, and that is the end of the matter. The problem is that it may not be quite that simple in the real world – if a company has organized marketing *out* of the powerful decision-making bodies, then there may be some impediment to getting it organized *in*. In a rational, reasonable world, organizing to make marketing more effective would be a technical or administrative issue, central to the rational management of the process of going to market. However, in the world in which most of us have to live, it may be that rational, formal organization for marketing is not where we *start*, it is where we *finish*. It may even be that the conventional marketing organization is finished anyway, for the reasons we set out in Chapter 1. Whatever view we take on that question, it may well be that in practical terms the routes to market-led strategic change are more likely to be through changing how people look at the market (the 'market sensing' issue in Chapter 10) and the processes we go through to make major strategic decisions about market strategy (planning and budgeting marketing considered in Chapters 11 and 12), and how we drive market strategy through to the salesforce (Chapter 13).

Quite simply, starting by reorganizing marketing may achieve very little other than disruption. (Although, this said, in some extreme cases, turning an organization's marketing strategy around may involve 'breaking the mould' and using restructuring to shake the company by the scruff of the neck – more of this later.) Generally, we should be a bit sceptical about going after reorganization instead of having, and being committed to, a customer-led market strategy.

What worries me about starting with organization is that it may have been a token response to the problem of matching what we do to what the customer values most, rather than real commitment, and that is why the Marketing Department is in disgrace. Superficial restructuring and the creation of job titles never was good enough to achieve real market-led strategic change. Certainly some companies do actually regularly reorganize as a *substitute* for having a market strategy – they work hard, they feel good, but all too often they achieve nothing other than disruption. Indeed, some reorganization fanatics cause even more substantial harm by actually making life even *more* difficult for the paying customer than it was to begin with – I have in mind the kind of constant organizational restructuring which results in: breaking customer relationships by moving salespeople around; pestering customers with frequent announcements about our internal organizational arrangements; leaving the customer uncertain about even who to contact and how to place an order, and generally feeling unloved and unwanted. This is not smart.

In one case, for instance, I worked with a high-technology company which was trying to cope with the effects of the latest annual restructuring of its business. One of its main competitive strengths had always been that it specialized its marketing and selling efforts, by the customer's industrial sector. This meant that as a customer you formed relationships with particular specialist salespeople, service engineers, advisers/consultants and account executives who *knew* your industry (because most of them had worked in it at some time). From the customer's point of view, this counts for quite a lot, with large, risky investments in high-technology equipment. Also, the products were 'badged' for your industry; advertising and promotions were targeted at you; and so on. However, this type of organization is 'old-fashioned', and the company decided to have Business Units specializing in product groups (because the products were high-technology and needed specialist attention). This arrangement looked infinitely better when drawn as a neat set of matrices on the organization chart, and the company was very proud of what it had done. However, as a customer you were now expected not just to form a completely new set of working relationships, but to form them with product specialists who knew nothing about your type of business. This may sound trivial and insignificant. The result for the supplier, in the sector we examined, was a new business market share dropping from 65 per cent to 30 per cent in the space of 12 months. Now let's talk about what is trivial and insignificant!

There are a number of things we need to do in this chapter. We want to provide a basis for evaluating what type of marketing organization we actually have at present, but also to put this in the context of a fuller view of why and how organization matters in market-led strategic change and the radical new agenda which is emerging. In particular, we need to get past the mythology of marketing organization and get to grips with the reality, and put a handle on what this means for our own organizations. If nothing else, we should be able to study how we have currently organized marketing to recognize the barriers, obstacles and hurdles faced in making marketing happen. However, do not be surprised if you end up joining me in the conclusion that the days of the fully-integrated Marketing Department are probably over (if they ever existed outside the pages of the textbook), and the real challenge we are facing is how to manage the process of going to market in new types of organization, without Marketing Departments.

But does organizing marketing really matter?

Agreed, the paying customer is probably not that interested in how we choose to organize marketing, or not, as the case may be (although, as we saw above, they may well care about the effects on them). Agreed, people who are really committed to market-led goals will probably achieve them by hook or by crook, whatever the personnel people put on the organization chart or in the procedures manual. But organization matters for a number of reasons, not least because it defines the 'Monday morning' reality that our marketing executives experience, and routinely have to cope with, in trying to get things done. Consider the following 'Monday morning' reality pictures*. These are all composites put together from a variety of sources, but just consider for a moment which sounds most like *your* company.

'it defines the "Monday morning" reality that our marketing executives experience, and routinely have to cope with, in trying to get things done'

---

* These scenarios come from simply asking a large number of marketing executives to describe what their typical Monday morning is like in the Marketing Department in their companies. The names are fictitious for obvious reasons, and the situations are composites – but the feeling is real.

Monday Morning in Company A

Fiona Stewart, Marketing Manager, arrives at her small cubicle office, in a corner of the order processing room. Most of the available space in the office is occupied by product package dummies, printers' proofs of sales brochures, artists' layout boards and models of point-of-sale displays. It is 9.30 and she finds taped to her chair, by the secretary she shares with the Purchasing Manager and the Office Supervisor, a list of phone calls to be made. The calls are urgent – the printer has major problems with the new sales brochures and wants to change the layout, which means Fiona will have to obtain permission for the changes from her boss, Roy Burgess the Sales Director, and then arrange for some new typesetting, and then get back to the printer. The Regional Sales Managers are calling to complain about delays in the arrival of the new retail point-of-sale displays, and Fiona has to sort out the supplier and negotiate a new deadline for the promotion campaign (she knows this will have to be explained and defended to Roy, who will not be pleased). The local university is doing a 'free' piece of market research for Fiona, but needs authorization for £25 travelling expenses for the student researchers, which will have to be authorized by the Finance Director and countersigned by Roy (who is not the world's greatest fan of market research, and will object that the annual Sales and Marketing Plan is already written, so why bother?).

The chance of Fiona off-loading any of this work is zero, because her one-and-only Marketing Executive, James Blackwell, is out with the salesforce attempting to find out why the new salesperson report cards are not being completed properly. Fiona knows that the real reason is that the Regional Sales Managers think that the report cards are a waste of precious selling time, and are highly suspicious of what will happen to the information anyway. This, however, is not an explanation acceptable to Roy, who persuaded the Board to invest £25,000 in a proprietary sales reporting system. Roy selected James to undertake this job because he believes that James will have to join the salesforce soon anyway, to develop his career, and might as well gain some field experience now.

Fiona makes a cup of instant coffee from the kettle in the corner, but smiles briefly when she sees a direct mail advertisement in her in-tray for a short course on strategic marketing. This reminds her that Roy is presenting his Sales and Marketing Plan to the Board on Wednesday, so she can expect a series of urgent requests from him for extra information, figure-checking and proof-reading. She reflects that at least this means she may get to see the plan, but then the phone rings . . .

Monday Morning in Company B

Frank Hurst has progressed in Company B from Technical Sales Manager to National Sales Manager, and now Marketing Director. His Monday is carefully scheduled by his secretary, because the rest of the week will be taken up by making sales visits with the new salespeople in the field, and a day with the Board of a national key account to pitch for the next year's business. Today, however, is mainly devoted to clearing up the aftermath of last Friday's presentation of next year's Strategic Plan to the annual sales conference.

Frank is aware that the sales managers and area representatives are unhappy with the targets for the next year, and about the lack of consultation with them when the plan was formulated. Unfortunately, this has coincided with the Transport Manager's decision to remove car phones from company vehicles of all staff below senior management grades and the Personnel Director's launch of a new company-wide Job Evaluation Programme. Memos of complaint from the sales managers are already on Frank's desk. Frank's problem is to defend the Strategic Plan, in which he really played little part himself and in which he secretly has little faith, while heading off the impending crisis on salesforce terms and conditions of employment. The major fear is that he will lose some of his key sales staff to the competition, which will disrupt his sales plan, strengthen the competition, and also create major problems in recruitment and training, which is a nightmare in the company's specialized technical field.

His first task for the day is to make a case to the Managing Director for the reinstatement of the car phones for sales staff, to delay the application of Job Evaluation to the salesforce, and to set up a series of regional meetings with the salesforce. Frank has built enough slack into his operating budget so that, if need be, he can run a salesperson incentive campaign to overcome some of the immediate problems of sinking morale, but he knows that this is an 'elastoplast' solution. However, 'right now', he tells himself, 'elastoplast is better than bleeding to death!' Funnily enough, he has just received the same direct mailshot as Fiona. He frowns and throws the leaflet unread and crumpled into his wastebin with some irritation, before starting his first memo to the Transport Manager.

Monday Morning in Company C

Michael Lucas is 27 years old and an MBA, and he worked previously as a Product Manager and then Group Product

Manager for a national branded goods manufacturer, after brief experience with a management consulting firm. Last year he joined Company C as Marketing Manager. Michael was away from the office the previous week, attending a five-day course on strategic marketing. This is, strangely enough, the same course being offered to Fiona and Frank, but as a regular customer for such programmes Michael went on an earlier running of the programme. He is delighted to see that the computer software he ordered to apply the new strategy screening matrix covered in the course is already sitting next to his personal computer. His secretarial work is handled by Viv Croxford, the Managing Director's PA. Michael had initially been worried about the arrangement, but has found Viv delighted to produce his reports because it gives her the chance to use the graphics package on her word processor and the new colour printer which Michael has purchased.

In the centre of Michael's empty desk is a typed note from Viv to let him know that 'JBC', the Managing Director, would like a word about the Marketing Plan. This is no problem since JBC's office is opposite Michael's, and they frequently chat informally over coffee about the development of the business, long-term market changes and new ways of doing things in the company.

Michael's week is clearly structured in his personal organizer: he has two days' work on the computer to reconcile the figures in the five-year plan and to design the appropriate visual displays for JBC to present to the Board next month; he has one day to catch up on the reports and journal articles in his in-tray and to meet a lecturer from the local university business school to discuss new developments in computerized 'expert systems' for allocating salesforce resources; and one day to prepare his presentation to the national salesforce.

The only dark spot on the horizon is that on Friday he has to attend and make a presentation on the Marketing Plan at the sales conference, and he anticipates a rough ride. He has not yet recovered from his first meeting with the National Sales Manager, who took him, in his very first week with Company C, to meet a major client in the North East of England. The client and the National Sales Manager spent two hours badgering Michael into conceding a new discount structure. Afterwards, in a local pub, while the client ordered pints of beer for himself and the National Sales Manager, he looked at Michael, laughed and said: 'And how about you, bonny lad, a Snowball?' Michael no longer wears baggy Armani suits, or carries his Gucci document case with shoulder-strap on trips into the field. Michael arranges lunch with JBC, and turns to his computer and the long-term sales forecasts with considerable relish.

Monday Morning in Company D

Geoff Kearsley is 45, an engineering graduate, and has spent 20 years in sales and marketing management, prior to obtaining his present post as Sales and Marketing Director at Company D. His department has more than 100 staff, covering sales, sales support, product planning, advertising and promotion, marketing research and planning, order processing, and exporting. It is a busy time of year, because in four weeks' time the Marketing Plan must be presented to the Board, and then Geoff leaves for a three-week trip, meeting distributors in Europe and the Middle East, to investigate the feasibility of establishing sales subsidiaries as joint ventures.

His Monday diary consists of a set of meetings with small gaps in between. First, the Sales Manager needs to see him to discuss shortlisting candidates for two senior vacancies in the Sales Support section. However, the bulk of the morning will be devoted to the monthly Interdepartmental Executive Committee. The IEC agenda looks innocuous, but Geoff suspects that there is to be a renewed campaign to relocate order processing from Marketing to Accounting. He also has a series of problems to do with the pricing discretion given to salespeople, which the Internal Audit Committee wants to reduce effectively to zero, and the lack of tight liaison between his order processing system and the despatch of goods by the warehouse (controlled by Operations).

The afternoon starts with a meeting with the section heads in Marketing to discuss progress with the annual Marketing Plan, and a meeting with the Managing Director to discuss the company's current advertising spend and the new 'value-for-money' campaign in the company. Geoff has also to evaluate and authorize a pile of price adjustment forms on his desk, and a request for a non-standard product for a major customer, which he anticipates will go down like a lead balloon with Operations. At the back of his mind is the worry that he needs to stay up-to-date with the gossip about the new restructuring plan being formulated by the Personnel Department. He too opens the same direct mailshot for the course on strategic marketing, and decides to send one of the new Product Planners, who is junior enough to be spared from the office. It is time for his first meeting of the day.

'we should look at some of the pressures towards "short-termism", inertia, navel-gazing, "not invented here", and complete lack of customer orientation that we create for ourselves'

So what – we all have problems?

Just consider those Monday mornings again. Before we make new demands on our executives, perhaps we should look at some of the pressures towards 'short-termism', inertia, navel-gazing, 'not invented here', and complete lack of customer orientation that we create for ourselves, simply by how we organize marketing. In fact, perversely, if that is the best we can do in trying to organize the process of going to market, perhaps we should start again, because most of what we have got so far does not look like an effective way to create and drive market strategies.

Why else does marketing organization matter?

Even if you are not impressed by the scenarios above, there are a number of other reasons why organization, as the 'hidden face' of marketing, matters quite a lot.

Strategy and structure

The conventional logic is that the organization structures we adopt follow the strategies we are trying to implement. There is a wrinkle to be added to this, which is that in the short term we may have to adapt our plans and strategies to the capabilities of the existing organization structure, but more of this later. For the moment, let us accept that, in the longer term at least, our structure follows our strategy.

This suggests one other issue straight away – if our organization for marketing is weak, driven by short-term problems, essentially tactical, isolated from strategic decision making, and wholly lacking a customer-led market mission, then what does this tell us about our market strategy? Think about that one, for a moment or two!

A more conventional view was shown by the 1995 announcement by Ford of the biggest restructuring in modern corporate history [1]. This was described by a Ford executive to a Harvard Business School audience as 'the mother of all re-engineerings'! The effect was to integrate the company's American and European subsidiaries, as part of the globalization strategy in the Ford 2000 programme, to bring new models to the showroom faster and at lower cost than the competition, and the restructuring is an essential part of implementing that Ford strategy in the marketplace. Enthusiasts for restructuring as the answer to all our problems should note that by 1997 the Ford 2000 programme was blamed for the company's losses in car making and the loss of market share to GM and Chrysler, and the Chairman's job is on the line.

Strategy as structure

One of the major points we made earlier was that competitive differentiation is a central part of market strategy – as part of the value proposition to our customers. One of the most important lessons we have learned about competitive differentiation is that at the end of the day it is not so much about what we *say* – advertising, selling, promotion, packaging – as far as the customer is concerned, it is also about what we *do*. One of the critical things in what we *do*, from the customer's viewpoint, is whether we organize to do well the things that matter to the customer. As in many complex marketing issues, Theodore Levitt of Harvard Business School summarizes this more succinctly than most:

> The way a company manages its marketing can become the most powerful form of differentiation. Indeed, that may be how some companies in the same industry differ most from one another . . . It is not simply the heavy advertising or the clever packaging that accounts for the pre-eminence of so many General Foods and Procter and Gamble products. Nor is it their superior generic products that explain the successes of IBM, Xerox, ITT and Texas Instruments. Their real distinction lies in how they manage – especially in the cases of P & G, General Foods, IBM and Xerox, in how they manage marketing [2].

If we look at how we have chosen to organize for marketing, then we may get to grips with two things: how the customer sees us handling things that matter to him/her; and the opportunities for being distinctively better in handling those things than our competitors (and, by implication, the missed opportunities for so doing).

For example, in 1993 IDV (the group marketing the J & B whiskey, Smirnoff, Bailey's and Cinzano drinks brands) described its restructuring as a key part of its marketing strategy. The market strategy rests on brand development, establishing premium brands, and innovation. The restructuring involved regrouping the company's 150 brands into categories, such as local or national, regional, international and development brands, to gain greater focus on the customer for each brand category [3].

Structure and the market

Ultimately, the only logic for organizing anything is how we see the market – the things we organize show what we think is important; the way we divide things up shows how we categorize customers and which we see as most important; and so on. The way in which the marketing operation is organized reveals a great deal about what we believe to be important and what we believe to be unimportant, and how we believe the marketing works. Where marketing is a peripheral, tactical part of the company, this reveals the real attitudes towards customers, and the real importance attached to customer satisfaction, far more accurately than what we say.

Many recent reorganizations in companies have been motivated by the pressure to build enhanced customer and market focus through the marketing structure. In 1993, Philips Consumer Electronics reorganized its marketing to integrate sales and marketing, as a counter to the product specialization built by its traditional product management structure. By 1996, Philips was reorganizing again to split the unified sales and marketing director post 'to sharpen the relationship between the brand and its consumers' [4]. Market signals are sometimes ambiguous!

Structure and information

In a self-fulfilling prophesy, our organizational structure represents how we look at our markets and make sense of them, and at the same time it shows how information is collected and how it flows. Structure and information are two sides of the same issue, and we will discuss this further in Chapter 10.

Structure and power

If nothing else, structure gives us a snapshot of who is powerful and who has influence in an organization. Where a Marketing Department is small, controls few resources or important decisions, is not represented on the key decision-making units and committees, executives in it are paid less or graded lower, and so on, then again we can draw our own conclusions about attitudes towards customers, and how the role of marketing is seen by those who make the real decisions in the company.

'structure gives us a snapshot of who is powerful and who has influence in an organization'

For example, in 1994 IBM revealed its plans for restructuring its worldwide marketing and sales organization – moving from geographical-based structures to an industry focus. This was part of Lou Gerstner's search not just for efficiency but more for cultural change at IBM and to transform IBM account executives 'from order-takers to business advisers'. The new structure has account executives bypassing the geographical branch managers who had previously controlled their careers, to report to industry group heads. The hidden agenda was one of eroding the traditional power of IBM's geographically-based sales chiefs – many of the new industry heads have been appointed from outside the company and have not come up through the traditional IBM salesforce route – to build greater customer focus [5].

These hidden, but highly significant, dimensions of organization are very revealing of the inner workings of a company and the real opportunities and barriers to creating market-led strategic change.

Now, I would be the last one to suggest that simply creating Marketing Departments or hiring new marketing specialists will change anything of much significance – we are trying to put a handle here on the 'substance' of marketing, not the 'trappings'. Indeed, what you have sometimes seen in the past has been the expanding Marketing Department as top management's cop-out – we hire the 'marketing experts' to take care of everything about customers, with the express objective that *we* can then forget about customers and get back to doing things the way we always have!

However, this said, a good starting point in getting to grips with the real context for making marketing decisions and implementing them is to look at how our marketing organization stacks up against that which is normally assumed.

The mythological corporate marketing organization

With varying degrees of explicitness, most textbooks, as well as training and development courses in marketing, assume that marketing is organized in a particular way. The logic for how marketing issues are evaluated, for applying techniques of marketing analysis, for building marketing plans and strategies, all rests on this model of how marketing is organized (or if it isn't, how it *should* be). In fact, as we will see (pp. 378–85), this view is increasingly out-of-date anyway. The characteristics of this textbook model of the marketing organization can be summarized as follows:

● *A marketing department* – it is assumed that there is one, and that it will be formally organized and resourced around the market entities that matter most – geographical areas, customer types, product groups, specialized marketing functions, and so on;

- *A Chief Marketing Executive* (CME) – it is assumed that there is one – not only this, it is assumed that s/he will be a powerful figure in the company, controlling significant resources and managing the customer interface;
- *Integration of marketing functions* – this view of the CME further implies that all the 'customer-impinging' activities will be integrated by the Marketing Department, so they can be welded into a consistent total offering to the customer, and this is reinforced by the marketing programme structure as the basis for planning and managing marketing. The CME is assumed to control not simply advertising and selling, but also product policy, pricing, distribution, and so on;
- *Powerful* – it follows from all the above that the CME will be recognized as a powerful figure in the company, controlling many critical resources and activities;
- *The voice of the market in the company* – by controlling the company interface with the customer and the distributor, by collecting information on marketing performance and market change, the CME and the Marketing Department provide corporate decision makers with guidance in lining up company resources to achieve what the customer values; and
- *Structure follows strategy* – besides, since we all believe in the 'marketing concept' (don't we? – because we all say we do), then it follows logically that to implement marketing we will naturally organize marketing along the lines above.

Now the model of the marketing organization described above is very conveniently assumed to be true, so that we can move on to the more interesting things, like strategy and planning systems. There is only one small problem with this. Outside the relatively small number of blue-chip, fast-moving consumer goods, normally multinational, companies, this model of the marketing world is no more than *mythology*, and increasingly in the blue-chip companies it is *history*.

'this model of the marketing world is no more than mythology, and increasingly in the blue-chip companies it is history'

The world that marketing executives from the majority of organizations tell us about is nothing like this mythology – see the 'Monday morning' scenarios described earlier (pp. 355–58).

So, that is the *mythology* of marketing organization – now let me tell you about the *reality* of marketing organization that we found when we went and looked at how UK companies actually 'do' marketing.

The reality of corporate marketing organization

The 'Monday morning' scenarios given earlier sum up a lot of the reality of corporate marketing as it has been described to us by a variety of different marketing executives, but we have some harder evidence than this. We conducted a research study of marketing organization in the UK manufacturing sector [6]*. This study involved manufacturing companies, or strategic business units, with between 100 and 1200 employees. So the study excludes small companies (where obviously you would expect the organization of marketing to be pretty rudimentary), but also excludes the very large organizations. We initially contacted 600 companies, and got information from roughly 300.

Marketing Departments?

In around half the companies (55 per cent in fact) studying the marketing organization was actually very easy indeed. It was easy because there was nothing to study – they did not have anything even vaguely approximating to a marketing organization or department. This was a somewhat startling finding.

Now in some cases we might conclude that this is probably something of a gap in the corporate line-up. But, in fact, in quite a few of the companies where we looked at *why* there was no Marketing Department, the reasons given were plausible:

- Some had purely Sales Departments, with no involvement in other aspects of the marketing process, and saw no need for this in their 'type of business'.
- In some cases, the companies concerned were essentially sub-contract manufacturing units, rather than normal trading companies – private-label suppliers to the major retail chains, automotive component suppliers to the motor manufacturers, and the like. In these firms, in effect, they operate as manufacturing units for a totally separate marketing organization owned and operated further down the channel.
- In other cases, we were told that the Chief Executive 'did' the marketing. Now there are two ways of looking at this: either

---

* This part of the chapter is based on studies of manufacturing organizations, but we have done similar studies in the retail and financial services industries [7,8].

the CEO 'does' the marketing, along with the other critical things like arranging the office cleaning, hiring the night-watchman, designing the company letterhead, and so on; or maybe marketing is *so* central that only the CEO can effectively negotiate with customers, make significant product and price decisions, and so on. You decide.

A variant on the above was that a part-time marketing consultant, or advertising agency, or other third party, was said to 'do our marketing'. I would in no way wish to denigrate the work of specialist agencies or consultants. However, this sounds like a massive cop-out – i.e. the agency 'does' the marketing, which means that we don't have to worry about it, or change anything, and we can get on with running the business the way we always have! That may sound unkind, and in some cases it may be unfair. But, as excuses go for avoiding the pain of changing the way things are done, it's not a bad one.

Nonetheless, it is astounding that, in what we believe to be a reasonably representative sample of the heart of British manu-facturing industry, about half do not have a Marketing Depart-ment or a Chief Marketing Executive.

This is not to say that having a Marketing Department is a 'good' thing and not having one is a 'bad' thing – far from it, because life is rarely that simple. It does mean that the conditions assumed as 'normal' in how we have all been trained in marketing simply do not exist in many companies, and that is a major cause for concern.

A Chief Marketing Executive with clout?

Turning to the companies with a CME, it became clear that if you exclude the salesforce half these departments have fewer than five people in them (including the CME). Marketing Departments, we find, are typically very *small* in head-count in these companies.

Integration of marketing functions?

In those companies which did have at least some kind of marketing organization, the first thing we tried to establish was what they did. What are these Marketing Departments actually responsible for? The astonishing conclusion was that about half these Marketing Departments had formal responsibility only for advertising and market research. Only about one in six had any serious integration of even a very partial listing of 'marketing' responsibilities. In fact, we found that in large numbers of the companies 'marketing' areas such sales, distribution, customer service, exporting and trade marketing *did* exist, *were* formally organized, but were organizationally *separated* from the Marketing Department and the Chief Marketing Executive.

Indeed, one interesting insight was gained by looking at marketing 'critical success factors' as perceived by executives. Basically, the more important the critical success factor was thought to be, the less likely it was to be handled by the Marketing Department! (This observation is underlined by the fact that studies in 1997 reveal that, as more and more companies recognize the critical importance of customer service, they tend to take this responsibility away from marketing.)

This amazed us, so we decided to dig a bit deeper. Being naive and gullible, perhaps we were being fooled by the question of 'formal responsibility'. We all know that formal organization charts can be misleading as guides to reality, so perhaps we need to get to grips with what they *do*, not just what they are formally responsible for. We turned therefore to look instead at the important decisions where the Chief Marketing Executive, and hence the Marketing Departments, had some decision-making involvement.

What do Marketing Departments actually do?

We took a fairly lengthy list of 'marketing' responsibilities and asked whether the Chief Marketing Executive played any role in such decisions, and, if so, *how much* of a role? In fact, there seemed to be five broad areas of involvement of Marketing Departments: *selling, product policy, marketing services, corporate strategy,* and *physical distribution.* Now, this is a little closer to the conventional view of what marketing is about, but the results do not mean that *all* CMEs are responsible for *all* these areas, simply that these are how responsibilities fall into groups. So we dug a little further into this somewhat messy, but nonetheless real, picture of what Marketing Departments *do* in these companies.

Different types of Marketing Department?

It was clear that the responsibility factors above were not shared equally by all the CMEs and Marketing Departments in the study, so we took each company's scores on the responsibility factors, and grouped the companies according to their scores. The result is shown in Figure 9.1.

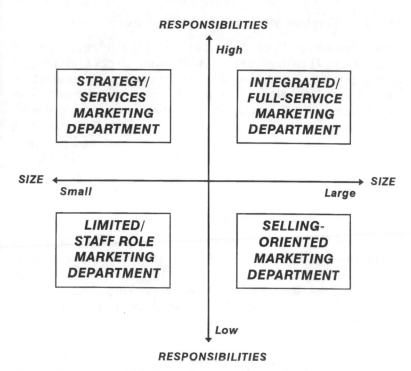

RESPONSIBILITIES

High

STRATEGY/
SERVICES
MARKETING
DEPARTMENT

INTEGRATED/
FULL-SERVICE
MARKETING
DEPARTMENT

SIZE ←——————————————→ SIZE
Small   Large

LIMITED/
STAFF ROLE
MARKETING
DEPARTMENT

SELLING-
ORIENTED
MARKETING
DEPARTMENT

Low

RESPONSIBILITIES

Figure 9.1 Types of marketing department

What we found was that, in terms of responsibilities (shared as well as formally 'owned'), we could identify four quite different types of Marketing Department, each making up roughly one-quarter of the sample. It is quite interesting to see how these Marketing Departments differ.

Integrated/Full-Service Marketing Departments

These were the closest we found to the 'textbook' model, and they represent a relatively high degree of integration of marketing functions and personnel. These organizational units had high scores on *all* the responsibility factors, so they control or influence the major marketing decisions, and they are large units in terms of head-count in the company. Make no mistake, these departments have 'clout' – they have a high *power* ranking in their companies. However, they account for only one in four of the Marketing Departments in the study and one in eight of the companies researched (because don't forget, half had no Marketing Department at all).

Strategy/Services Marketing Departments

These Marketing Departments represent a much lower degree of integration. Their high responsibility rating comes from product policy, marketing services and corporate strategy, not from selling or physical distribution. They are also much smaller units – in some cases only two or three people. However, they are powerful. This power comes not from involvement in the line marketing activities, but from being close to strategic issues and planning, and thus close to top management. Small, non-integrated units, but high-powered with 'clout' and influence.

Selling-Oriented Marketing Departments

These are large departments in manpower, but score far less in terms of integration and have relatively low scores in the strategic areas – corporate strategy, product policy, and so on. They are dominated by the selling responsibility. They are, however, generally relatively powerful in perceived rank within the business.

Limited/Staff-Role Marketing Departments

These are small departments, with the lowest scores on all the responsibility factors, and are mainly involved with staff services such as market research and sales promotion. They are not powerful. Indeed, they seem largely peripheral to the main business of the company – token gestures towards the marketing concept.

We have by now shown this model to, and used it with, several hundred executives and almost as many different companies, and with few exceptions most executives have recognized *'describe what it is* the situations described as relating to their own *like to work in* companies. Indeed, one of the exercises we have used *such a department* with executives is to ask them to judge which type of *– what are the* Marketing Department they have in their companies *problems, the* and to describe what it is like to work in such a *barriers, and so* department – what are the problems, the barriers, and *on?'* so on? The responses from executives to such questions are interesting, even if the executives may be accused of exaggeration in some instances! Responses fall into the following pattern:

- *What is it like working in a Strategy/Services Marketing Department?* – The most common complaint here is (and I quote one executive, for whose sentiments I take no responsibility): 'the meat-heads in the field, who just won't listen, who can't think past today, and don't understand what we are trying to do with the business!' Less emotionally, people describe the problems of being isolated from the field operation, the problems of communication with the sales and distribution operations, and the lack of line authority over people in the field. People also describe being uncomfortable with reliance on only informal influence and advocacy, and on top management sponsors, for the credibility and acceptance of the sophisticated marketing strategies and plans they produce.

- *What is it like working in a Selling-Oriented Marketing Department?* – The real answer is, just the same as working in a Sales Department, because there is a lurking suspicion that these are repackaged, relabclled Sales operations, rather than Marketing Departments as such. One executive (for whose articulations I also disclaim responsibility, but include for balance) suggested somewhat forcibly to me that the real problem he faced was 'the MBA fairies at head office, who have never met a customer or done a deal in their lives, and should get their hands dirty before they try and tell us about marketing strategy!' You will understand that people get a bit heated about issues such as these. What people describe is an isolation from centralized decision making, and a lack of involvement or consultation about major strategic marketing decisions. They describe how intelligence from the field is apparently ignored, and their problem is to 'sell volume, not quality'. People describe the domination of short-term, urgent issues over longer-term marketing questions. These executives describe company views of marketing as purely high-pressure selling, razzmatazz and hype and lavish executive entertainment expenses.
- *What is it like working in a Limited/Staff-Role Marketing Department?* – People in this situation gain sympathy from most audiences as the great unloved of the marketing community. These are the purveyors of sales brochures, the organizers of sales promotions and sales conferences, the doers of market research (which is almost always ignored by decision makers), the progress-chasers. People here describe their role as the marketing 'gofers', as being peripheral and powerless at the edge of things – isolated both from the field and strategic levels. The only problem is that every so often someone turns round and holds you responsible for declining sales and market share, poor strategic positioning or the like because you *are* the Marketing Department, aren't you?
- *What is it like working in an Integrated/Full-Service Marketing Department?* – Maybe marketing executives are just natural whingers, but any expectation that executives from this type of

marketing organization will be evidencing smug smiles and happy dispositions compared to their less fortunate peers is quickly dashed. Executives here describe the effects of bureaucracy – committees to co-ordinate the disparate parts of the marketing operation; interdepartmental committees about budget, production issues, staffing and training, etc., memos and reports, and jurisdiction disputes, and so on. They describe interdepartmental conflict – with finance, with operations, with corporate planning. They describe the intervention of top management and interdepartmental committees in 'marketing' issues like advertising and promotion – where everyone is an 'expert'. They describe having token control of resources, where allocation decisions are really made by others. They describe the pressure to 'disintegrate' marketing in the perpetual 'empire-building' game in their organizations.

Problems in our marketing organizations

If we put together these various pieces of evidence, what emerges is a list of fundamental things that seem to have gone wrong in how we organize for marketing. There is no sign that newer organizational forms for marketing solve these problems, and there is some suspicion that they make them worse! Even with what we have found so far, we can ask ourselves the following questions: is this *really* the way to effective implementation of market strategies? (see Chapter 1) is this *really* how we are going to achieve the focus on customers and customer satisfaction in the companies that we said we wanted? (see Chapters 2 and 3); is this *really* how we are going to pack together our strategies and marketing programmes to create a distinctive differentiated total offering to the customer? (see Chapters 4 to 7); or is this where some of the worst Strategic Gaps come from? (see Chapter 8). Just consider what we are really saying about how companies organize for marketing.

Isolation of strategy from operations

In many of the real situations we find, companies have developed marketing organizations, apparently designed purposefully and specifically to drive an impenetrable wedge between strategies and operations in marketing. It is really quite simple – the more our organizational arrangements divorce strategies and plans from operations, the greater and the more difficult are the integration problems we face. Have a look at the gaps between Strategic Intent and Strategic Reality that we found in Diagnostic 3 (pp. 340–47), and consider how many are the direct or indirect result of how we have chosen to organize for marketing.

Reactive, short-term marketing

Given the choice between thinking long-term and going for short-term results in income, and demonstrably solving urgent operational problems, most of us will probably plump for the latter most of the time – it is easier, more comfortable, more familiar, it is what we are good at, and in many of the organizational situations we have described above it is apparently what the company seems to *want* us to do. If you organize, manage, evaluate and reward marketing to solve short-term problems (promotions to counter sales declines, 'jollies' to keep a major account sweet, new sales literature to cheer up the salesforce, and so on), and to react in panic to competitive and economic threats which you did not see coming – then you can hardly be surprised if this is what you get.

No direction or mission

It follows from the last two points that by separating strategic marketing issues from the operational level of doing things, with the resulting dangers of short-termism and reactive marketing, we may well have organizationally created for ourselves a headless monster stumbling from crisis to crisis. If that is how you are running your marketing, then the achievement of a strategic direction, or the drive of a customer-oriented mission, is likely to be just a little bit elusive.

No market leadership in strategy

In many of the real marketing organizations we have studied, those wonderful visionary concepts of the Marketing Department as the voice of the customer in the corridors of power, the constant provider of the discipline of the marketplace, are simply cloud-cuckoo-land. If you organize marketing around sales brochures or short-term selling operations, or keep the marketing organization weak and peripheral, then you have already made your choice about marketing's voice in long-term strategy. The question is: did you mean to make that choice; and, indeed, did you realize you had made it?

Weak implementation of marketing

If you follow the conventional logic, how you organize something is how you implement what you are trying to do. For reasons not unrelated to those above, if you look at how companies actually organize for marketing, it is not a bad indicator of just how serious they are about actually making it happen – or not, as the case may be.

Lack of resourcing

One of the other indications of not really being too serious about marketing is not resourcing it – in the full sense of providing the management time, the head-count, the financial budgets, the space and freedom, and everything else that is needed to do things. I have actually got a bit tough on this one, and would like to make rather more of the point in considering planning and budgeting (pp. 472–74).

For the moment you may say: 'But budgeting has not got anything to do with organization – please let us deal with one thing at a time.' Unfortunately, resource allocation has *everything* to do with organization, not least because organization represents *power*. When you think about it, this is really quite clear if we think about the inner workings of companies:

Resources	*Link to organization*
People	Departmental head-count
	Staff grading and salaries
	Growth/decline in staffing
Money, space, time, equipment, overheads	Formal budgets
	Getting on the agenda
	Membership of relevant committees
	'Ownership' of the spend

To take the limiting case, if your marketing executives have to fight to the death for every small resource item they want, make extensive cases to different committees for small expenditures, build extensive cases for all personnel changes, and wait in the queue behind all the other more established departments – your marketing organization is weak, burdened with resource hassle, and you are likely to see the effect in terms of what actually gets done.

'to do your job well in the customer's terms you are going to have to persuade other people in the company to do their jobs less well in their terms'

Conflict with other departments

It was pointed out some thirty years ago, by Philip Kotler, that one of the problems with being a conscientious marketing executive is that to do your job well in the *customer's* terms you are going to have to persuade other people in the company to do their jobs less well in *their* terms, for example:

Marketing wants	to get:	which causes	to do less well in:
Product variants	Segment specialization	Production	Controlling operations costs
Many price lists	Exploit customer differences in price sensitivity	Finance	Controlling admin costs and unit revenue
Instant delivery of products and spares	Customer satisfaction and competitive advantage	Transport and Ware-housing	Scheduling delivery vehicles and controlling stock levels
Customer-care trained staff at point-of-sale	Customer perceptions of care and service	Personnel	Training costs and standardization of training across the company

The result of differences in perspective and departmental goals and objectives is *conflict* – hidden or open, but conflict nonetheless. When all the time-consuming rational debating, the bargaining and negotiation and the horse-trading is done, there is only one way of resolving conflict, and that is by the use of *power*. Quite simply, weak, non-powerful Marketing Departments lose the internal battles. The trouble is, it may be the most important battles they lose, because things like managing for customer satisfaction and making market strategies work are the *most* likely to cause discomfort elsewhere in the organization.

Strategy follows structure

What we have seen and been told about by executives all too often can be described as the exact reverse of the rational, conventional logic. Far from the strategies chosen leading to the adoption of appropriate organizational structures to implement marketing, we see the existing structures (because of what they stand for) as a prime determinant of what goals and strategies are actually adopted by a company. This may sound perverse, unless you dig a little deeper and ask what organizational structure *really* represents. When you get past the 'rational' explanations, structure is about:

- *Power* – the organization chart is a snapshot of who runs the organization (and who doesn't);
- *Inertia and the status quo* – because structure tells us about who runs things, it also tells us what are the vested interests in the present position, and it is not hard then to figure out what they are likely to buy in terms of strategic change (and what they won't);
- *Status* – issues of organizational level and position, relative departmental size, recognition in key memberships of decision-making committees, and so on, are about status or perceived power and sponsorship (or the lack of it);
- *Culture* – or simply 'the way we do things here' is partly shown by organization positions and the 'share of voice' that different parties have in making important decisions (or the lack of it);
- *Information* – information is the other dimension of organizational structure, because structure shows us how the information flows – or perhaps yet more revealing, what information does *not* flow. As we will see in the next chapter, this tells us much about what the company believes and takes notice of (and what it ignores).

In these terms, then, how you organize for marketing starts to look quite significant. The next issue is: if we have got the marketing organization wrong in terms of the things we need to change to become market-led, what do we do about it?

The rational response to the conclusion that our marketing organization is out of line with our strategic intent is that we should reorganize marketing. No, seriously, it is! In many practical company situations, it must be said, this is simply not likely to be on the agenda for the foreseeable future.

However, to be fair, in some organizations it *is* on the agenda, for two reasons. First, there are signs that many companies are now increasingly desperate to put a handle on their marketing, and they may be more receptive than ever before to reorganizing their marketing as part of this. Secondly, there may be hidden benefits in the process of reorganizing which give more leverage for market-led strategic change than does the actual reorganization you end up doing. For many years, I was a believer in first deciding what you wanted to do and only then deciding how best to organize to do it. More recently, I have concluded that, in some cases at least, the barriers to doing things rationally are so immense – the culture, the history, the vested interests, the resistance to change, and so on – that it may be that you actually have to *start* by reorganizing just to break the stranglehold of the status quo. I have laid out a methodology for approaching reorganization in marketing in a technical book [9].

Marketing with no organization – or with the 'wrong' organization

Either because we cannot do anything about it, or because we think it is not the most urgent issue in marketing, we may face a future of driving market-led strategic change in a company with no supporting marketing organization or, even more difficult, with the 'wrong' or inappropriate marketing organization. This may sound defeatist, but experience suggests that it is a practical reality.

'we may face a future of driving market-led strategic change in a company with no supporting marketing organization'

In fact, such situations are far from hopeless anyway, because to really put a handle on marketing to achieve things we have to get involved with two further organizational issues, even if we do have the opportunity to reorganize marketing. These issues provide the rest of the organizational context for marketing. These issues are:

- *Information* – i.e. how an organization understands and hence reacts to its environment (i.e. the customer); and
- *Process* – i.e. the how, where and who of decision making processes relating to market strategies and market programmes, the partnership between marketing and sales, and the implementation of customer-led strategies in the marketplace.

In situations where we have to persevere without the benefit of the textbook marketing organization, these are our primary levers on the way things are done, as they matter to the customer.

Even if we have the chance to introduce or redesign the marketing organization, this needs to be done in conjunction with issues of information and process anyway. Indeed, in some ways the way we formally organize marketing will probably *always* be out of line with our marketing strategies, because strategies develop and change faster than structure, as we fight to match our offering to the customer's priorities. This is not, however, an excuse for giving up on the organizational issues in managing marketing – they matter!

However, as we will see, the reality is increasingly that we have to forget about Marketing Departments and look at what new types of structure we need to focus on customers, to develop new strategies, to deliver the service that matters, to integrate, to collaborate, to manage partnerships, and to manage change.

So, what type of marketing organization have we got?

So far in this chapter we have said, first, that we organize marketing matters for some really quite important reasons: it creates the corporate realities that our marketing executives have to confront daily; it is about effectively implementing our market strategies (or not, as the case may be); it is about competitive differentiation and how we reflect the structure of the market into our operations; and it is about who calls the shots in putting marketing into effect. Certainly the paying customer is unlikely to care very much about the intricacies and niceties of our organizational design – but s/he *will* care about what that design means in things like: forming relationships with sales and service individuals; responsiveness and flexibility of the company to customer demands; the quality of service and customer care achieved; performance in delivering value compared to what our competitors can do; and so on. So, it matters.

We have a problem here, however. That problem is the mythology of corporate marketing organization as it is propounded by marketing textbooks and consultants, and, more importantly, as it is *assumed* by most people who tell us how to do marketing. We have seen that for many, perhaps most, marketing executives in the real world the organizational situation is light years away from that conveniently assumed by the textbook.

'That problem is the mythology of corporate marketing organization as it is propounded by marketing textbooks and consultants'

Having thrown our hands up in horror at the unfairness of life, now is the moment to get more personal and to evaluate what type of Marketing

Department we have in our *own* organization. We can then start to question what barriers this provides to our goals of market-led strategic change.

What type of marketing organization have we got?

In fact, we can use the model in Figure 9.1 to allow us to take a better view of what type of Marketing Department we really have in our company, by positioning ourselves on this model. The specific things on which we can evaluate and benchmark our present position are as follows:

- whether we *have* a Marketing Department in anything but name only;
- the *size* of the Marketing Department compared to other departments in the company;
- the *participation* of the Marketing Department and the Chief Marketing Executive in the key marketing and strategic decisions of the company.

There are a variety of ways in which we can use these comparisons to evaluate whether we have an appropriate structure, what the internal organizational barriers to the marketing may be, and different views of how marketing should operate in our company. The sort of issues we should try to address are:

- Has the analysis let us put a handle on the actual issues and the *real* (possibly well-hidden) problems of making marketing happen in this company? Review the material in this chapter to see what conclusions we can draw about the real obstacles and barriers inside the company to market-led strategic change.
- How well does the reality of our marketing organization stand up to managing customer satisfaction, as described in Chapter 3? How many of the gaps and shortcomings of our performance (as measured by Diagnostic 3) are explained by the inadequacies of how we organize for marketing? What can we realistically do about this?
- How close is the reality of what we have found in our marketing organization to what we assumed to be the case. How does this change our view of our strategic capabilities and how good we are at marketing? Review this and take the conclusions found to building implementation strategies (Chapter 14).
- How clear is the role and mission of the Marketing Department in our business? Do different people have different ideas about

what marketing is doing and what it should be doing in the company – both inside the Marketing Department and elsewhere in the company? Review this and consider the conclusions in terms of the internal marketing strategy (see Chapter 14).

- There are no rights and wrongs in organizational structuring, but how well does the reality of our marketing organization match the Strategic Intent we identified in Diagnostic 3 (pp. 340–47)? Are some of the gaps between Strategic Intent and Strategic Reality explained by how we organize for marketing? Review this in the light of how we can close the gap between Strategic Intent and Strategic Reality – see Chapter 11 on customer-oriented planning process (pp. 444–62).

- Is the reality of our marketing organization suitable, capable and appropriate for the market strategies we want to drive through for the future? Revisit this issue when you have considered the market strategies described in Diagnostic 3 together with the development of new plans for the future (Diagnostic 2). It may be that the only conclusion we can reach is that we need to redesign our marketing organization to drive our market strategies through. On the other hand, the only practical conclusion may be that we have to face up to 'marketing without organization' because organizational redesign is not an option available to us – in this case we may need to think of influencing strategic choices and then implementation through working on marketing information issues (Chapter 10) and the key decision-making process (Chapters 11 and 12) rather than directly through reorganizing marketing.

No simple diagnosis of this kind is going to tell us everything we need to know, but it is a start in confronting some of the barriers to market-led strategic change which are hidden inside the company's structure. The conclusions we reach should be carried forward to our implementation strategies and action plans (Chapter 14).

And what's worse is – if you think that is complicated, you haven't seen anything yet!

The issue of the type of Marketing Department is still important in many companies, along with the questions about its effectiveness in driving market strategy. One of the implications of the developing focus on the process of going to market instead of conventional organizational structures is that the future is even more complicated. In fact, the question is rapidly changing to: '*What* Marketing Department – where has it gone?'

What Marketing Department?

There is vocal opinion which suggests that the traditional Marketing Department is a thing of the past, as Market Strategy moves to a relationship focus instead of transaction, and that centralized marketing organizations are 'dinosaurs' [10,11]. Popular commentators say that top management considers marketing departments to be 'a millstone around an organization's neck' [12] and that 'marketing departments are in top management's sights' [13]. Others point to the business process re-engineering technique being applied to marketing [14], with the resulting demise of traditional ways of organizing around processes such as order generation and order fulfilment.

'the traditional Marketing Department is a thing of the past, as market strategy moves to a relationship focus instead of transaction'

For example, in 1993 the Unilever-owned toiletries company Elida Gibbs (now Elida Fabergé) radically revised its marketing structures. In effect, the company divided the traditional Brand Manager's job into three and abolished the job of 'Marketing Director'. A process perspective suggested that their marketing was partly operations and partly the development of new initiatives. Instead of forcing these processes to fit with established functional boundaries, they were separated. The company separated day-to-day operating and tactical marketing from longer-term issues of brand development, creating three centres of expertise: one for the consumer/brand, one for the category and one for the retailer/customer. Category managers bridge the gap with Sales as well as taking over operational marketing to the retailer, and report into Sales. The former Sales Director is now Customer Development Director and the former Marketing Director is Brand Development Director. The Brand Manager's job for the big brands divides into two responsibilities: consumer-directed communications is one job, and innovation management is another.

Similar developments are apparent in other consumer goods companies such as Procter and Gamble, Colgate Palmolive and Heinz, particularly in the adoption of category management (see pp. 259–60).

Indeed, category management is just one part of the move towards 'trade marketing', through which suppliers and retailers 'co-market'. The role of its traditional Marketing Department has been in decline in this type of channel for some years now.

At the end of the day – if there is a better way of going to market than having a traditional Marketing Department, then they will disappear.

Process in going to market

At a time when channels of distribution have become more complex and demanding; buyers are increasingly cynical; data-base marketing is pushing towards micro-segmentation, the predicted pressures for change in how companies go to market are:

- *Breaking hierarchies* – the speed and flexibility we need comes from reducing the number of organizational levels and numbers of employees, creating smaller business units and empowering line management to manage key business processes.
- *Self-managing teams* – the critical changes in how we respond to customers will be managed by groups with complementary skills, in the form of high-performance multifunctional teams to achieve the fast, precise and flexible execution of programmes, possibly organized around market segments and categories, and possibly temporary in duration, like a task force.
- *Re-engineering* – critical organizational processes will be radically restructured to reduce cost and increase spend and flexibility, and to increase responsiveness to customers.
- *Transnational organizations* – competing globally requires more complex structures and new skills to manage in networks and alliances.
- *Learning organizations* – organizations will require the continual upgrading of skills and the corporate knowledge base, leading to the adding of value for customers through knowledge feedback, to create competitive advantage through enhanced capabilities.
- *Account management* – achieving customer focus may require new structural mechanisms built around key accounts [16].

'much emphasis is being placed on the role of teams that cross functional boundaries to deliver value to the customer, or "pan-company marketing"'

Currently, much emphasis is being placed on the role of teams that cross functional boundaries to deliver value to the customer, or 'pan-company marketing'. This raises many questions over the need for the traditional Marketing Department. To that, add the new scenario created by going to market through networks of partners held in place by strategic alliances (see pp. 251–63). Some of the most dramatic effects are being seen in the sales organization, and we will open this up in Chapter 13. For the moment, the point is that new ways of going to market means a new way of organizing for marketing.

New ways of going to market

Fred Webster's view is that as the focus of marketing changes from transactions to relationships, and then increasingly to managing strategic alliances among independent organizations, there will be blurring in traditional external boundaries between the firm and its market environment, which will be paralleled by less distinct boundaries between functions inside the organizations. His key conclusions are:

- At the corporate level, in the network organization the role of marketing will be to help design and manage strategic partnerships with suppliers and technology partners.
- At the business level, the key task facing marketing managers will be deciding which marketing functions and activities are to be purchased, which are to be performed by strategic partners, and which (if any) are to be performed internally.
- At the operating level, there will be more emphasis on relationships with customers and less on customer manipulation and persuasion, and this may lead to dominance by the sales organization [17].

A more detailed view of how alliances and partnerships may affect the role of the marketing organization is provided by Ravi Achrol [18]. He proposes two innovative marketing organizational forms: the marketing exchange company and the marketing coalition company, as shown in Figure 9.2. Both the models are of organizations acting as hubs of complex networks of functionally specialized firms, where emphasis is on managing transorganizational boundary-spanning.

The *marketing exchange company* is compared to a brokerage or marketing information-based clearing-house, where the strategic core is a worldwide network of marketing offices and information centres – the 'marketing information network company'. Prototypes for this organizational form are the 'hollow corporation' (where manufacturing and other operational functions are devolved to external suppliers, and only marketing remains) and

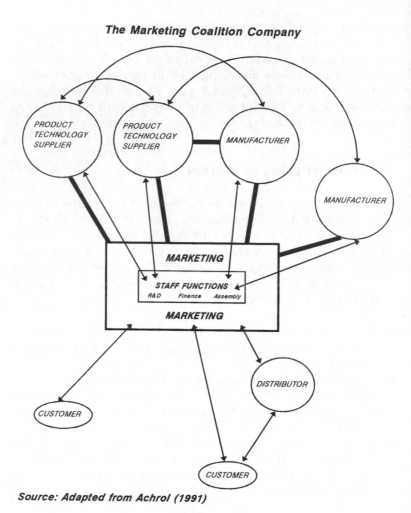

Source: Adapted from Achrol (1991)

Figure 9.2 (a) Marketing companies and networks

the great Japanese trading houses. Indeed, reflection suggests many similarities between Achrol's marketing exchange company and the powerful wholesalers of the nineteenth century stimulating the entire marketing chain.

The *marketing coalition company*, on the other hand, is conceived as the co-ordinating centre of a network of strategic alliances – the marketing exchange company is a quasi-market, whereas the marketing coalition company is a quasi-organization. Achrol argues that this organization reflects certain key environmental changes: the trend towards a smaller in-house manufactured product component; growing recognition of the need for a climate of innovation; and the rapid growth in strategic alliances.

The Marketing Exchange Company

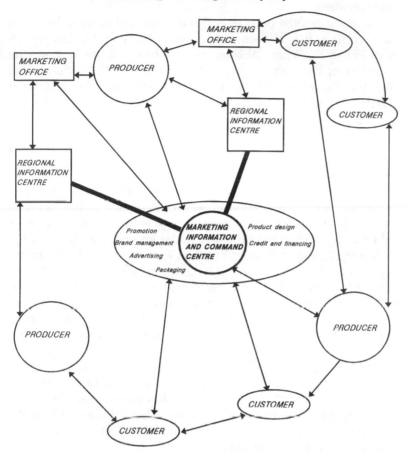

Source: Adapted from Achrol (1991)

Figure 9.2   (b) Marketing companies and networks

The critical distinction made by Achrol is that the marketing exchange company is the organizing hub for market information and complex exchanges, while the marketing coalition company is the hub for organizing a division of functions among an alliance of specialist firms. The link is that both are transorganizational entities and both have one central function – marketing. It is also argued that the critical managerial focus will shift from organizing internal systems to organizing boundary-spanning processes. Organizational issues will thus be less about internal structure and departmental boundaries and more about 'alternatives or substitutes for organization': establishing productive norms of behaviour rather than hierarchical control; and developing a 'quasi-judicial system' of management.

We discussed the issue of collaborations and partnerships as a key relationship element of market strategy in Chapter 6 (pp. 251–63). What Webster and Achrol tell us is how the development of such strategies will impact on the location and organization of marketing. It is a long way from the traditional textbook model of a Marketing Department.

But realistically?

This is exciting stuff – new ways of going to market with new structures and processes, and so on. In reality, at the moment much of this remains no more than a few high-profile examples of new approaches to marketing and a lot of crystal ball-gazing. It is nonetheless very worrying that, for example, a 1996 survey by the Chartered Institute of Marketing concluded that, notwith-standing TQM, BPR and globalization, the widely reported upheaval in marketing organization and structure does not seem to have happened for most companies. And as we saw earlier, some companies are trying new ways of reorganizing marketing and then going back to what they started with. Look back to the new challenges we identified in Chapter 1 (pp. 13–22), and see how unsettling you find the prospect of continued corporate complacency and clinging to the models of the past. There is a compelling case that we need to do some hard thinking about the best ways to organize how to go to market effectively, and to do this sooner rather than later.

So, if this is the future, let's get ready for it. However, the objective is going to market effectively with a customer-focused market strategy, not spending our lives designing organizations.

A changing management agenda

The organizational issue is important in managing the process of going to market, and the ways organizations organize are increasingly diverse. The issues to consider are:

● First, let's evaluate what we have got now, in terms of the problems we have created for ourselves in implementing our market strategy – start with the Strategic Gaps and how we overcome them.

- However, we should be open to the conclusion that there may be better ways for our company to go to market than with a traditional Marketing Department. Some companies believe that re-engineering marketing is the way ahead (e.g. Elida Fabergé).
- Some companies believe that the process of going to market is managed better by multifunctional teams which cross functional boundaries and even organizational boundaries by including suppliers, distributors and customers in these teams.
- If market strategy is based on networking through alliances and partnerships, this raises a major question for the location and management of marketing. Webster and Achrol offer some guidance on what this may look like – but the reality is that we do not actually know how it will work. We know that network organizations are *not* the answer to all companies' problems. We know that different networks operate very differently (see pp. 252–58).

'If market strategy is based on networking through alliances and partnerships, this raises a major question for the location and management of marketing'

But how marketing will operate in the network organization remains to be seen. For those who need to pursue this question further, some preliminary ideas can be found in Piercy and Cravens [19].

So, does the organizational dimension of marketing matter, or does it matter?

The purposes we went after in this chapter were: to underline the hidden significance to customer-led market performance of how marketing is organized; to look at the gap between the mythology we have always assumed about the way marketing is organized and the reality that marketing executives experience; and then to evaluate what type of Marketing Department we have in our own organizations and how things are changing. This leads us directly into issues of information and decision-making processes as the other critical elements of the real organizational setting in which we have to make marketing happen. The context we have to cope with is a radical corporate re-think of the best ways to organize how we go to market.

References

1. Lorenz, Andrew (1995), 'Ford Drives to Win World Leadership', *Sunday Times*, 1 January.
2. Levitt, Theodore (1984), 'Marketing Success Through Differentiation – of Anything', *Harvard Business Review*, January/February, 83–91.
3. Stewart, Allyson L. (1994), 'Some Global Firms Rearrange International Markets in Their Favor', *Marketing News*, 11 April.
4. Mitchell, Alan (1996), 'Stemming the Sea-Change', *Marketing Business*, November, 24–27.
5. Ziegler, Bart (1994), 'IBM Plans to Revamp Sales Structure to Focus on Industries Not Geography', *The Wall Street Journal*, 6 May.
6. Piercy, Nigel (1986), 'The Role and Function of the Chief Marketing Executive and the Marketing Department', *Journal of Marketing Management*, Vol. 1, No. 3, 265–290.
7. Piercy, Nigel (1989), 'The Role of the Marketing Department in UK Retailing Organizations', *International Journal of Retailing*, Vol. 4, No. 2, 46–65.
8. Piercy, Nigel and Neil Morgan (1989), 'Marketing Organization in the UK Financial Services Industry', *International Journal of Bank Marketing*, Vol. 7, No. 4, 3–10.
9. Piercy, Nigel (1985), *Marketing Organization: An Analysis of Information Processing, Power and Politics*, London: Allen and Unwin.
10. Webster, Frederick (1992), ' The Changing Role of Marketing in the Corporation', *Journal of Marketing*, Winter, 1–17.
11. Goetsch, Hal (1984), 'Centralized Marketing is Still OK', *Marketing News*, 26 September.
12. Brady, John and Ian Davis (1993), 'Marketing's Mid-Life Crisis', *McKinsey Quarterly*, Summer.
13. Mitchell, Alan (1993), 'Transformation of Marketing', *Marketing Business*, November, 9–14.
14. Mitchell, Alan (1996), *op. cit.*
15. Mitchell, Alan (1997), 'Brand New Model', *Marketing Business*, February, 44–49.
16. Piercy, Nigel F. and David W. Cravens (1995), 'Marketing Organization and Management', in M. J. Baker (ed.), *The Companion Encyclopaedia of Marketing*, London: Routledge.
17. Webster, Frederick (1992), *op. cit.*
18. Achrol, Ravi S. (1991), 'The Evolution of the Marketing Organization: New Focus for Turbulent Environments', *Journal of Marketing*, October, 77–93.
19. Piercy, Nigel F. and David W. Cravens (1995), 'The Network Paradigm and the Marketing Organization: Developing a New Marketing Agenda', *European Journal of Marketing*, Vol. 29, No. 3, 7–34.

CHAPTER 10

Information and intelligence for marketing:

From market research to market sensing

Introduction

Of all the marketing areas in which I have worked with companies, I have no hesitation in saying that marketing information is the most difficult, because it is the area which is most surrounded by misconceptions and misunderstanding. It is the area where it is easiest to convince ourselves that the answer to all our problems is to do more market research, or collect more information and store it on a computer database – i.e. make a token gesture and ignore what really matters, so that we can get on with doing things the way we have always done them. It is the area of marketing which sounds most academic, esoteric and theoretical (for which read: impractical, vague and useless in the real world). It is the part of marketing which is most easily and most defensibly 'delegated' to junior executives – after all, 'real managers' are too expensive and important to spend time digging up market information and processing it – the trouble is that the expensive managers then take no notice of what the information says.

This is a great pity. Experience suggests that the marketing information area is more significant than we normally think, and for different reasons. I would say that it is the single area where you can make the

'the marketing information area is more significant than we normally think, and for different reasons'

greatest and most significant difference to market strategies, marketing programmes and customer satisfaction. Information offers us this leverage because it is not really about doing surveys and collecting facts and figures, or building computerized databases – these are just the trappings, the incidentals. Marketing information is about how we understand, think about, and deal with the environment, i.e. the customer, the partner and the competitor. This is why information gives leverage – if you can influence how decision makers and operational staff *think* about the marketplace, then you have a good chance of influencing what they *do*.

From market research to market sensing

For these reasons, we are not going to discuss all the conventional technology of marketing information – marketing accountancy techniques, marketing research methods and things like questionnaires and sample design, sources of information, or building mathematical models and integrated marketing information systems. All that can come later if you need it.

This book is for managers. Managers do not design questionnaires, collect data, build models, and so on (or they should not). Those are jobs for market researchers and technicians. What managers have to do is to *understand* – to understand the customer, the distribution systems, the partners in an alliance, the competitors, and the big changes in the marketplace that can make us rich or put us out of business.

This chapter is not about marketing research, it is about *market sensing* – how those of us inside the company understand and react to the marketplace and the way it is changing. This is actually a more difficult issue than market research techniques, but it is more important too.

Does market sensing make any difference? Well, it seems to. Consider the following cases:

● *Encyclopaedia Britannica* was first published in Edinburgh more than 200 years ago. By 1990, Encyclopaedia Britannica's sales in the USA had reached $650 million, with profits of $40 million. However, during the early 1990s CD-ROM technology gained acceptance in the consumer market for encyclopaedias, especially in the key US market. The management of Encyclopaedia Britannica did not respond to this threat – in spite of the fact that they had CD-ROM technology in one of the company's divisions. Management simply did not *believe* that CD-ROM technology could undermine their traditional market. The company's marketing advantage in the USA was a 2300-person direct salesforce, each earning a commission of $300 on the sale of a $1,500 encyclopaedia. In fact, by the early 1990s the competitors' CD-ROM packages were available to 7 million US households, with computers with CD drives, at prices ranging from $99 to $395. By 1994, Encyclopaedia Britannica's US sales had declined so far that the salesforce was halved in size, and the company was in serious financial trouble. To compete against CD-ROM competition would have required the company to change both its product and its direct selling strategy. Management simply did not believe that they had to change. An extreme example of faulty market sensing [1].

- *Waterford Wedgwood plc*, the Irish manufacturer of crystal and china, entered the 1990s with declining sales and growing competition from low-cost crystal makers in Eastern Europe. A key market is the US premium crystal market (items over $25), where there are 120 competing suppliers. Waterford's management believed there was an opportunity in the market for cheaper crystal products. This was not just a 'hunch' – management's belief in the existence of price-conscious buyers who would be willing to pay a high but 'sensible' price for crystal products was tested and confirmed by focus groups conducted in three countries and 30 hours of taped interviews with consumers. Waterford designed the Marquis brand products to be different enough from traditional Waterford (in price and design) to avoid weakening the equity of the main brand, but to still gain from the Waterford brand identity. For example, a long stem wine glass from Waterford is around $50, while the Marquis equivalent is $30. Marquis Crystal by Waterford was launched in 1990 – the first new Waterford brand for 200 years. By 1994 Waterford's sales were up by around 30 per cent and share of the US premium crystal segment was up by 7 per cent to 34 per cent, based on inspired market sensing [2].

- *Motorola* is a $22-billion high-tech global enterprise that started as a six-person firm making and selling battery eliminators (wires to plug battery-powered radios into mains electricity). The Motorola case has been described many times because of the distinctive leadership and culture of innovation. However, another characteristic has been the constant search for new ideas and what they call 'sensing opportunity'. From the battery eliminator business, the company moved into the expanding market for radios themselves and then televisions, and then into the diodes and transistors that underpin the embryonic worldwide electronics business. What they call 'sensing opportunity' is a form of market sensing that has driven the spectacular growth of the company, when it could have simply coasted in existing markets [3].

These examples illustrate market sensing, or market understanding by managers, not sophisticated marketing research or technology-driven marketing information systems. If you want another illustration of the difference between market sensing and market research, consider the statements in Table 10.1: The Silly Things We Say.

Table 10.1   The silly things we say*

What did they say?	Who said that?
'I think there's a world market for maybe five computers'	Thomas Watson, Chairman, IBM, 1943
'Computers in the future will weigh more than 1.5 tons'	*Popular Marketing*, 1949
'I have travelled the length and breadth of this country and talked with the best people, and I can assure you that data processing is a fad that won't last out the year'	Business books editor, Prentice-Hall, 1959
'There is no reason why anyone would want to have a computer in their home'	Ken Olson, Chairman, DEC, 1977
'Who the hell wants to hear actors talk?	H. M Warner, Warner Bros, 1927
'A cookie store is a bad idea. Besides, the market research says that America likes crispy cookies, not soft and chewy cookies like you make'.	Response to Debbie Fields' idea for the Mrs Fields Cookies business.
'We don't like their sound and guitar music is on the way out'	Decca Recording Company, rejecting the Beatles
'No'	Response to Steve Jobbs, founder of Apple Computers, when he attempted to interest Atari in his new computer.
'We don't need you. You haven't got through college yet'	Response to Steve Jobbs, founder of Apple Computers, when he attempted to interest Hewlett-Packard in his new computer
'640K ought to be enough for anyone'	Bill Gates, Microsoft, 1981

* Adapted from Lloyd, C. (1995), 'Towards the One-and-a-half-Ton Computer', *Sunday Times*, 12 November

Some of these statements look amusing, with the benefit of 20:20 hindsight. This is not the point. The point is that every one of those wholly wrong-headed statements could probably have been 'proved' to be correct at the time by extensive (and expensive) market research. It is just as true that Encyclopaedia Britannica could probably have commissioned market research in the 1980s to 'prove' that CD-ROM was a fad that would not affect the published encyclopaedia business and Waterford could have run surveys to demonstrate that a lower-priced brand would destroy the premium crystal market in the USA.

Conventional marketing research is actually very limited in what it can really do – see the Myths of marketing information below. It is also used and badly abused in many situations, and at the heart of the problem is that we have been brought up in traditional marketing to expect far too much from marketing research:

- We expect market research to give us new ideas for products and services and to tell us which is the best advertising – but innovation is not democratic, so if one person in a thousand has a great idea, why do we bury it as '0.001 per cent of the sample said . . .' or, more likely, ignore it as 'other responses'? The advertising legend in the USA, George Lois, goes further. He says that doing research is about being careful and 'Being careful guarantees sameness and mediocrity' [3]. He says his two best campaigns were the Braniff airlines 'If You've Got It, Flaunt It' ads of 20 years ago, and the 1990s poster campaign for the then unknown clothing designer Tommy Hilfiger, which listed the few 'great designers for men' as: R _ _ _ _ L _ _ _ _ _, P _ _ _ C _ _ _ _ _, C _ _ _ _ _ K _ _ _ _, and T _ _ _ _ H _ _ _ _*. These campaigns infuriated company lawyers, market researchers and competitors, and were outstanding successes for the companies concerned. The 'big idea' is not a votable issue – surveys of opinion about them are meaningless.
- We want to know things – so we ask people questions and call it market research. Why do we believe that people know, or will tell us the things we want to know? Scientific market research techniques have become much more sophisticated in the past 20 years, but still fail to produce the result of national elections, unless they are already a foregone conclusion. Those same sophisticated techniques were used to test the taste of Coca-Cola's 'new Coke' on 190 000 people prior to launch. The taste test results were positive. The product failed miserably.

---

* Yes, OK, it took me a while too. They are: Ralph Lauren, Pierre Cardin, Calvin Klein and Tommy Hilfiger.

People do not buy the product for its taste – new Coke just was not 'cool'. Bob Worcester of the MORI research agency says: 'Ten per cent of people believe ICI makes bicycles. You show them a list of products like paints and fertilisers, throw in bicycles as a dummy, and one in ten will tick it' [4]. Fifty years ago, a US academic surveyed Americans' attitudes towards the Metallic Metals Act – 38 per cent said it should be passed. There was no such thing as the Metallic Metals Act.

'market research gives us the answers we want because it studies the segment of the market that gives the "right result"'

- How often is it true that market research gives us the answers we want because it studies the segment of the market that gives the 'right result'? Of course most existing customers say they are satisfied – why should they own up to being stupid and buying the wrong product; of course most existing customers say they are happy – do you want them to wear a sign saying 'I am stupid'?; what about the customers who left or never tried us? Marketing databases, like those created from the retailer loyalty schemes, are wonderful – but what about consumers who do not join the scheme, or only visit the store infrequently – are they of no interest, because profiling them by recency, frequency and monetary value will tell you they do not matter (so do they starve to death, or shop elsewhere?) [5].
- When Disney transferred its Disneyland format to Europe – EuroDisney near Paris – the company lost $921 million in the first year. The decision to enter the European market was well-supported by research: figures showed the growing number of European visitors to the US theme parks. In the conventional Disney way, the location was based on modelling population figures – 17 million people live within a two-hour drive of the Paris site, and 109 million within a six-hour drive, which are much better figures than the US parks show. The figures were encouraging, but the launch of EuroDisney was an expensive lesson in the importance of market understanding, not market research. The company ignored the failure of amusement parks in France, it dismissed anti-Disney demonstrations, as insignificant, and it ignored the fact that European holiday patterns are completely different from those in the USA – people in Europe have longer holidays and spend less on each. Myopia also led the company to ban alcohol from its park – you try telling the French they cannot drink wine at lunchtime and see what happens! Excellent research that ignores the things that really matter (because no-one asks the right questions) reinforces company myopia and costs a lot of money to put right.
- Research can provide you with the perfect justification for ignoring new market opportunities. Initial evaluations of tofu,

organic tomatoes and alfalfa sprouts as food suggested they were for weirdos only. Organic food is one of the fastest growing categories in the fresh food sector. The future is not best predicted by opinion polls.

You probably think this is just a petulant tirade against market researchers. Well, try the following test on your own company.

The elephant in the market

When a family suffers a trauma, such as incest or alcoholism, it often refuses to acknowledge it – a syndrome known to therapists as 'the elephant in the living room' – which everyone steps around and pretends is not there [7]. Well, maybe we should think about the elephant in the market, or maybe the elephant in the company. When you look at the things that are studied by our market analysts and researchers, published by our research agencies and reported in our marketing information systems – are they really the things that matter to managers in under-standing the market (or are they the things that we always measure because they are easiest to measure)?

Try this in your own company. Figure 10.1 suggests that any question of information differs in two respects: *importance* and *urgency*. Different types of research question are then:

● *Priorities* – important and urgent questions that need speedy answers to support management decision making. Issues like quality performance and brand performance would probably fall here – they are core issues for most of us and if things go wrong we need to react.

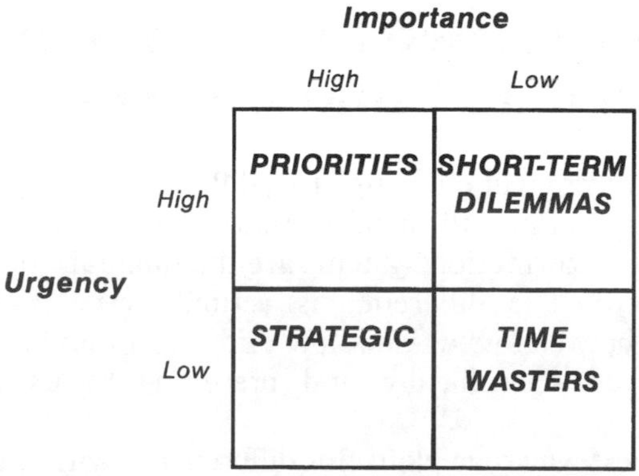

	Importance	
	High	Low
High	PRIORITIES	SHORT-TERM DILEMMAS
Low	STRATEGIC	TIME WASTERS

(Urgency labelling "High" and "Low" on the left axis; "Urgency" as vertical axis label)

Figure 10.1 Strategic and non-strategic marketing information

- *Time Wasters* – questions that do not really matter, they may be 'nice to know', but that is all. These should be ignored.
- *Short-Term Dilemmas* – urgent but unimportant questions that should be resolved by a judgement call, not extensive study. Dwight Reskey of Pepsi-Co calls these 'the curse of the brand manager' – issues such as the colour of the package, the typeface for the logo, Reskey describes these as the 'tyranny of the in-box. People busy themselves with lots of tiny, immediate projects, winning momentary job satisfaction while avoiding bigger issues that are important to their business' [8].
- *Strategic* – questions that may not be important to the day-to-day running of the business, but are critical to long-term direction. This might include questions like: 'Are there limits to our growth potential in this market, and what are they?'

The challenge is simply this – look at what happens in your company and see where the efforts and resources go. How much of our information is truly strategic (i.e. vital to the long-term direction of the business) and how much goes on Short-Term Dilemmas and Time Wasters? You may be depressed by the conclusion – typically 1–10 per cent of the effort goes into the Strategic area which generates 90–99 per cent of the value.

If we are to improve on this, let's consider a few fundamental issues:

- the difference between market research and market sensing;
- the mythology surrounding the information issue in marketing;
- the underlying role of information in market strategy;
- managing the process of market sensing.

The difference between market research and market sensing?

Many managers will challenge this difference – they would, they have been trained to believe that precise information and immaculate information systems are the hallmark of professional management. The difference is actually very real. It is the difference between what we know and understand and what can be measured scientifically and presented to us in research reports.

The easiest way to explain this difference is with Murphy's Law – the principle that if something can go wrong, it will. Many of the predictions of Murphy's Law have been denied by scientific, rational research. What we *know* is that Murphy's Law is right and the scientific researchers are wrong. Consider the following examples from the fascinating research of Robert Matthews (9), which actually demonstrate this:

Murphy's Law predicts:	*Scientific research says:*	*The reality is:*
When your breakfast toast falls on the floor, it will land face down if it can	Experiments show that if toast is tossed in the air a large number of times, it will land face down only half the time, as probability theory would predict	Few of us toss our breakfast toast in the air – it normally slides off the plate because you are reading the paper. When this happens, the toast will land face down most of the time, and this can be proved
If your queue in the bank or supermarket can be beaten by the neighbouring one, it will be	The mathematics of queues indicate that those in the bank or super-market are subject to random delays, and on average will tend to move at the same rate. Therefore all queues have the same chance of finishing first	When you are in a queue you are not interested in averages, you just want to be out fastest. If there are, for example, three queues of the same length, the chances are only 1 in 3 that your queue will suffer fewer delays than the others – two-thirds of the time the other queues will do better and will finish before us
If a place can be in an incon-venient part of a map, it will be (i.e. the edges or the crease down the middle of the road atlas you are trying to read while driving)	The random distribution of destinations means that only in a small number of cases will a particular destination lie on the edge or in the centre	If the width of the 'Murphy Zone' on the map is just one-tenth the total width of the map, that zone accounts for half the total area of the map. Any destination has a better than 50:50 chance of ending up in an awkward place

This leads to three points of comment about research and management:

- If something is true and you know it to be true, having someone measure it and write you a report about it does not make it any more or less true – it simply stops you doing something about it, while you wait for the research to be done.

'The real challenge is not making market research more sophisticated, it is trying to ensure that the things that managers "know" and "understand" are the right things'

- Most research is crude and arbitrary in the assumptions it makes – this reflects technology and budgets, not competence – and measuring the wrong things badly is not an inspiring description of what we should use to make decisions.
- The real challenge is not making market research more sophisticated, it is trying to ensure that the things that managers 'know' and 'understand' are the right things and they are well understood. As we will see shortly, this is actually something we can work on. It also leads to identifying the important information needs and the role that market research can usefully play.

Myths of marketing information

At the risk of seeming perverse, perhaps we can build up to the issue of what marketing sensing is really about by flushing out some of the myths about marketing information which stand in the way of effective market sensing. Most of these myths are to do with our needs for information, and how we use it when we have got it.

Myth 1 – We need more marketing information

There seems to be a built-in presumption in the minds of many market researchers and computer analysts that if you give managers more information they will make better decisions. Much of this presumption rests on the 'scientific' model of decision making. Perhaps the clearest manifestation of this at the moment is 'database marketing' – where we aim to build a bank of information containing everything it is possible to know about our customers. However, to be fair, managers are also party to this conspiracy – the research evidence is that *however* much information they already have, when faced with a decision managers will demand *more* information.

Perhaps the greatest danger is that we simply create 'information overload' for our executives, such that they cannot cope with all the information we direct at them. The result is that instead of helping managers to understand the marketplace, we overwhelm them with facts, figures, reports, and so on. If anyone says they need more information – try asking them why.

'the greatest danger is that we simply create "information overload" for our executives'

Myth 2 – We need marketing information faster

One of the joys of listening to the disciples of technology and 'database marketing' is to observe their simple pleasure in how quickly they can get results on their desks – with scanning at the retail electronic point-of-sale, we can monitor sales and cash flow by the hour! This is impressive technology, but raises a couple of minor questions such as:

- So what? What are you going to *do* with the information when you have got it? (*Probably sit around waiting for some more.*)
- What did you *used* to do with your time, instead of watching hourly results? (*Run the business, perhaps?*)

Certainly, one of the major uncertainties we all face is due to the fact that much of the information we get is out-of-date by the time we get it. No quarrel with that. But let's not be silly about this! More to the point are questions about what information we *need*, how *complete* it is, and what we *use* it for, than simple technology-driven speed of delivery.

Myth 3 – If we try hard enough, we can know everything

There is a seductive notion that if we just invest enough in market research, if we can just get enough computing power, if we can just crunch enough numbers, then we will know *everything* there is to know about this market – and then we cannot get it wrong.

There are a couple of problems here. The largest is the simple, unavoidable fact that you can *never* have the most important information because it does not exist when you need it. With the biggest market research budget in the world and the greatest computer, the most crucial uncertainties remain.

One way of looking at this is shown in Figure 10.2. This suggests that as we move from issues of marketing operations

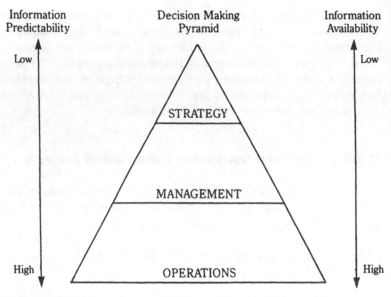

Figure 10.2 Information availability and the marketing problem

(e.g. stock control, order progressing, service scheduling, and the like) to issues of marketing management (sales force planning and control, budgets against expenses, advertising coverage, and so on) to issues of market strategy (mission, segmentation, competition, differentiation, positioning), then two things happen: the *availability* of the information we really want is less and less, as is the *quality* of what information is available.

On the things that matter most, we cannot reduce uncertainty to zero or anything like it. Anyway, this is why going to market is fun, and why some people do it better than others.

Myth 4 – We know what marketing information we want

Surely no-one still believes that managers know what information they want? Consider the following story:

Picture the scene: A Royal Navy warship is proceeding across the ocean, when its radar detects a stationary vessel directly in its path, some miles distant. The Captain is informed, and immediately radios the message: 'You are on a collision course with me, please steer 10 points South immediately'. Within minutes he receives the reply: 'You are on a collision course with me, alter course 10 points North immediately'.

Somewhat rattled by such insubordination, the Captain radios: 'I am a large vessel on urgent business, please steer 10 points South immediately'. The reply comes back: 'My business is also important, change *your* course immediately'. The Captain is now an interesting shade of purple, his fingers are twitching over the missile launch controls, collision is imminent, and he radios the message: 'I am one of Her Majesty's frigates, with nuclear arms, proceeding on Royal Navy business. You will steer South 10 points *now!*' There is a short delay before the reply, which reads: 'I am a lighthouse, I suggest *you* steer 10 points North now!' *The moral*: Believing you have all the facts you need is risky, even if you have a nuclear missile with you.

Strangely enough, in expecting managers to know (and thus to be able to tell us) what information they need, we are on a loser in most cases. If you ask managers what information they want, you are likely to get one of three responses (only one of which is absolutely frank, and that one doesn't help us much):

- Exactly *what I get now* (because I am right, and who the hell are you to suggest I am not);
- *Everything* (because then I will be all-powerful and rule the world); or
- *Don't know* (please help me).

Going back to Figure 10.2, what is even worse is that as we move to the most important decisions, the predictability of information *needs* approaches zero. The real truth is that we can only decide what we need to know when we can *model* our decisions. The idea that we model the decisions and then we know what our information needs are comes directly from the notion that making decisions is 'scientific'. In this scenario: we know with certainty and can quantify our single, paramount goal; we can identify and isolate all the options open to us; the goal implies the quantitative criterion of choice; we input full information to work out the pay-off for each option; we apply our criterion to make an optimal choice. What could be simpler, and what better way to identify precisely our information needs?

In the real world, however, a few things get in the way: fuzzy, unclear, qualitative and multiple goals; the inability to identify all the options which exist; lack of information availability; and often the impossibility anyway of separating and isolating one decision from all the rest. That is why we cannot give simple answers about what information we want.

The truth is that we actually know relatively little about how managers make decisions faced with unresolvable uncertainties, and we should at least avoid some of the sillier assumptions that people make.

Myth 5 – We know why we want the information

This brings us back to the fairy-tale of scientific decision making. Obviously we want information to make better decisions between the options open to us, to monitor performance, and so on. This sounds sensible, but it does not tie up very well with the role information actually seems to play in organizations.

Two learned and prestigious American researchers [10] have examined the way managers use information in organizations and found that generally: much of the information collected has little *relevance* to decisions; information is frequently collected *after* the decision has been made; much of the information requested is subsequently ignored; regardless of how much information is available, *more* is requested; managers complain about the *inadequacy* of their organization's information resources, while ignoring what information is actually available to them; and the relevance of information requests is less conspicuous than their *insistence*.

These researchers concluded of this 'information perversity' that 'It is possible, on considering these phenomena, to conclude that organizations are systematically stupid'. Equally, they note that it may just be that we have a very limited understanding of why and how managers use information.

'we have a very limited understanding of why and how managers use information'

Certainly, the evidence is that managers search for marketing information for all sorts of reasons, including the following: to *justify* decisions already made; to provide managers with *reassurance* about decisions made; to *signal* to all concerned that something matters and that we are being 'rational' about it; to build *consensus* about something, so that we all think about it in the same way; to provide a 'collective memory'; to *delay* decisions and 'take the heat off'; to *prevent* decisions being made (until the research is completed); to *reconcile* diverse viewpoints about an issue; to *ritualistically* recognize a problem area, even though we know there is nothing we can do about it; to provide the basis for *negotiation* about the issue; to provide *conciliation* between diverse viewpoints in an executive group; to establish *'ownership'* of a particular issue or set of issues; to gain influence; or to build personal *'secret' files* of our own on important issues for the future. These reasons for obtaining and using marketing information have precious little to do with the 'scientific' model of the rational decision maker.

However, there is something we should bear in mind about this. We have *no basis whatsoever* for assuming that there is anything wrong about this use of information. The simple truth is that we do not know enough about how organizations actually work to dismiss or condemn such information practices. Indeed, some people would say that these are the *most* important and valuable functions of information in organizations, because they provide decision makers with the comfort, reassurance and influence they need to make decisions and to get their jobs done.

Myth 6 – Well, we know what we don't need to know

Perhaps the fastest way to understanding the culture and dogma of an organization is to look at its information resources. However, don't just look at what information they collect – look at the information they choose *not* to collect; look at the information they *discard*; look at the information they receive but *discredit* and refuse to believe. Then you will start to put a handle on that organization's dogma, stereotypes and the critical strategic assumptions they make about the world, and thus about what works and what doesn't.

If that sounds a bit brutal – then try asking anyone who has ever been a junior market analyst, business analyst, financial analyst or anything similar, about how they used to do reports and analyses when they joined the company, but they always seemed to get it 'wrong', and had to do it again until they got it 'right'. (Where 'wrong' means 'not what we expected you to tell us', and 'right' means 'what we expected you would tell us'!)

An even more dramatic example. A short while ago I was working with a group of executives from a large firm in the computer industry, who faced the task of building a new market position in a specific key account. One of the basic techniques we used was SWOT analysis (enumerating our strengths and weaknesses and the opportunities and threats in the market – see pp. 282–92 above for a full description). The group did a SWOT analysis of their own current position, and the results were depressing – they saw the market as dominated by IBM and could find no way around this. We tried another tack – we said: 'Go away and pretend that you are the competitors and do the SWOT from their point of view, because their threats and weaknesses define our opportunities'. This they did. They came back several hours later with a SWOT analysis of IBM's view of the market and they were pleased – they could actually see some chinks in the IBM armour. We then said: 'Great, now what about the other competitors?' They said: 'Well, we didn't do a SWOT for them, we don't know anything about them, and besides, they are not *real* players!' This 'not real players' category, incidentally, included a few 'minor' companies like DEC, Honeywell and the Japanese. That is not the real point, however. The real point is that the story shows how to go from being number 2 in a market to number 5 in the space of three years, because you did not take the competitors seriously enough to collect information about them. That is the real point.

I like to discuss cases like this with managers by asking them if they will accept that ultimately all organizations, including their own, behave like the 'Ravenous Bugblatter Beast of Traal' from Douglas Adams' book, *The Hitch-Hiker's Guide to the Galaxy.* Readers may recall that the Ravenous Bugblatter Beast of Traal is

'we assume that because we cannot see our competitors, they cannot see us'
'a mindbogglingly stupid animal, it assumes that if you can't see it, it can't see you – daft as a brush, but very very ravenous'. The parallel is, of course, that we assume that because we cannot see our competitors, they cannot see us, which gets us back to organizations like the computer company described above.

Myth 7 – We measure what matters

One way to turn a blind eye to all the points above is to adopt the view that we have done OK so far, so we must be doing it right – i.e. we research and evaluate what matters, so let's talk about something else.

The evidence is, however, that what most of us measure is not what matters but what is *easiest to measure.*

Now there are two sides to this as well. The first is that we *literally* measure what is the cheapest and easiest problem to measure; for example, sales, not customer satisfaction; marketing costs, not the value of marketing assets; established competitors, not new ones; and so on. This is one thing we can, and should, challenge.

At a deeper level, however, secondly, we measure what the culture of the organization *tells* us it is easiest to measure and what matters (usually because that's what we've always done, and it suits us just fine, thank you). That is more difficult to deal with, but needs challenging as well.

My all-time favourite (and true) story of looking the wrong way comes from the days when I worked in retailing. Our Head Office team was convinced that a particular manager's stock deficits could only be explained by fraud. They checked the goods-in at the back door, stock control, and cash-in at the checkouts. But everything balanced perfectly – the store was being run beautifully, apart from the fact that every so often they seemed to lose an entire lorry-load of produce. The team sat and watched the checkouts for days, but could never find a discrepancy between till rolls and cash received. They had just about given up, when someone finally had the sense to *count* the checkouts – there were 11 instead of the ten for which they had books (ten for the company and one for the manager). It is a very easy assumption to make! It is the things we don't think we need to know that catch us out time and time again.

Or consider the following account published in the *Sunday Times* in 1996, describing events at the Bloemfontein Pelanomi hospital:

> every Friday over a period of months a couple of years ago, hospital staff found the patient occupying a certain bed in intensive care lying dead with no apparent cause. At first it seemed coincidental. Then doctors feared a 'killer disease'. Deaths continued. Finally, a nurse noticed the Friday cleaning lady doing her weekly chores. This maid would enter the ward, unplug the life-support systems beside the bed, plug in her floor polisher, clean the ward and once again plug in the patient, leaving no trace of the cause of the patient's death. How many died in the South African Floor Polisher Massacre?

None of us can ever afford to believe that we have all the relevant facts and can ignore new, unexpected information!

Myth 8 – We know what we know

There are two issues here, depending on where you put the emphasis in the name of this eighth myth. We know what we *know* – all too often it would seem that we have a very limited view of what is actually available in the company, and who knows what. We can make progress by finding the internal experts and the undisseminated information, and conversely the blockages to information flows. Alternatively, we *know* what we know – do we really, or do we just accept what we are told?

Myth 9 – We know who decides what we know

Sounds reasonable, but let's just think that one through. If you consider some of the hidden effects of formalized information systems, you come up with factors like these:

- *Constrained data sets* – We cannot have information on everything. This selectivity in the information system determines what we know (and, in large part, what we don't).
- *Skewed data sets* – The selectivity in what data we collect comes from the biases and prejudices of the systems designer, easy information availability and the designer's understanding of the problems we face.
- *Static data sets* – Information systems become self-perpetuating and reinforcing, so we are stuck with the selectivity and biases.

'there is ample evidence that once information systems are formalized people become far more "careful" about the data they put in, and what they communicate'

On a less technical note, there is ample evidence that once information systems are formalized people become far more 'careful' about the data they put in, and what they communicate. There is more to it than this though. Consider the following situation.

A market analyst in a high-technology company needed to get data on advertising spend divided by product group, as part of a programme of evaluating the absorption of marketing costs by different products, markets and channels. This was a surprising but real information gap. The strategy was clear – to approach the Advertising Manager for the necessary data on advertising and sales expenses by product. The result was that the Advertising Manager was very difficult to get to see, hostile and very unhelpful. The information provided after much discussion was: incomplete, contained only budgeted figures, not expenditure, was not split by product, and contained many 'mistakes' and 'errors'. There appeared to be something of a barrier. As the market analyst said at the time: 'They always say 'Smile, it could be worse', so I smiled and it got worse'. She concluded that the fact that no-one (including the Accounting Department) had *any* figures on advertising and promotional spending, other than in gross, total budget terms, might well be because the Advertising Manager did not *want* anyone to know. It started to become clear that there was significant 'slack' or discretionary spend built into the Advertising Manager's budget, which he had no intention of uncovering. Conversations with management accountants and the corporate planning unit showed that they too were well aware of the problem, but they did not know what to do either.

The only strategy open seemed to be to persuade the Marketing Director to *order* the Advertising Manager to provide the information. The persuasion was easy, because the Marketing Director had already given this 'order' numerous times, with no effect whatsoever. Not wholly insignificant was the fact that the Advertising Manager, though relatively junior in the hierarchy, was: a long-term employee who had been around since the business started, had been to school with the Managing Director, and regularly socialized with the MD because their children were the same age, played at the same tennis club, and so on. The market analyst concluded that the only way forward was to get the information indirectly, or to remove the need for the information, at least for the time being. Besides, the MD and Advertising Manager would soon be retiring. . . .

Now, let's ask the question again – do you *really* know who makes the hidden choices which determine how your organization understands the outside world?

Myth 10 – Well, we know what it means

Charles Hardy recounts the story of the Peruvian Indians in South America who suffered at the hands of Spanish invaders. The point of the story is that the Indians saw the sails of the Spanish ships on the horizon but believed this must be some new phenomenon of the weather, and did nothing to prepare to defend themselves against the Spanish invasion.

The question is: how often are companies wrong-footed in the marketplace simply because they ignore important information for the reason that it is inconsistent with managers' past experience?

Even worse, if we buy research to tell us only the things that are consistent with our past experiences, confirm our existing conclusions and validate a 'no change needed' strategy. Impossible?

Not impossible, according to studies by the Center for Strategic Research in Boston [10]. They found widespread beliefs among major users of market research that market research was biased and distorted to confirm views rather than to challenge them. They concluded: 'Market research is a very wonderful thing. It can support or deny any premise or allegation or lack thereof that you want' [11].

From myths to reality

Now some of these myths about marketing information are just silly, because they represent a lack of understanding of what is feasible and what is not. However, in other ways, dispelling some of these myths is useful, because it moves us closer to the reality of information in the organizational setting – the 'hidden face' of marketing information.

The hidden face of marketing information

Let us stop thinking about what information in organizations is *supposed* to be, and ask ourselves what marketing information is *really* about. One way of opening up this question is to recognize at least three levels at which we need to understand the marketing information function:

- the *rational* level – marketing information is about objective research and developing information systems to give us facts and figures;
- the level of *power* in the organization – marketing information is about the 'ownership' of information, controlling access and interpretation, and all that this implies; and
- the *political* level – marketing information is about filtering, omission and manipulation to exert influence.

What we have considered so far is mainly the first of these levels, but the 'hidden face' of marketing information is about the second and third levels.

The point is that the rational view of marketing information is important and has value to us in what we are trying to achieve – but it is only the surface of many of the real problems that we face. What marketing information is *really* about is creating a picture of the world that the company faces. This picture is highly imperfect, because it results from all the mechanisms through which we filter the world to simplify it and make sense of it. This picture means we know and understand the world only at several removes. This picture is the one that determines what we produce and how much, who we employ and how many, and how much finance we need and what type. This, in turn, means various things:

- The company view of the marketplace is not neutral – it is important to everyone in the company;
- Controlling the picture that the company has means that someone fixes the frame of reference for all the discussions and

decisions which are made in the company – and it is likely that there will be competition to perform this function;

- No-one knows the reality of what is happening in the marketplace – it would be too large a job to take in all the information available and some information is never available, so we have to 'guesstimate' anyway, and most of us are not constantly in the marketplace to see what is happening (or if we are in the field, we do not see enough of what is happening);

- We all have no choice but to know the world through the information system, and, in the case of the market, through the Marketing Information System – whether this has been formalized or not;

- He who controls the company's picture of the marketplace controls a lot more besides.

> *'No-one knows the reality of what is happening in the marketplace – it would be too large a job to take in all the information available and some information is never available'*

What we are describing here as 'controlling the picture' is discussed by real academics as 'environmental enactment' and the 'creation of meaning' by the part of an organization which acts as 'gatekeeper' to absorb critical uncertainties. This sounds very heavy, and it is. However, the practical significance is immense. Let us consider a case example to make it a bit more real, and to check whether what we are describing here is something you should find out about in your own company.

Consider the case of *negotiating* market definitions and sales forecasts. The rational economic analyst will tell us that defining market size and forecasting sales is a complex statistical process. In other words, market size and sales forecasts are issues of *fact* and *statistical* prediction, and *objectivity*. Well, this was not how it seemed in working with a sales management team from a major computer company a little while ago. Consider this case in a little more detail.

Negotiating market definition and sales forecasts: a case example

The background

The 'hidden agenda' created by the Marketing Director in a computer company was to gain acceptance and commitment from the Southern regional sales team to the following:

- defining the market for computer services as far broader than just the repair of the 'boxes' as they break down in the field, and to work on the sale of 'insurance' deals to the customer;

- countering the prevailing 'company wisdom' that the market for maintenance and service would dramatically reduce as the newer technologies spread through the market;
- accepting that growth in this services segment of the market over five years would be from £70 million to £300 million per year.

The team

This was led by Keith (a Liverpool lad made good – with a very forceful personality), whose brief was to represent to the team the Marketing Director's views. The team consisted of a small number of 'bullish', street-wise Sales Branch Managers (mainly Glaswegian Ed and Cockney Kevin, who were experienced in the business and committed to the status quo), as well as Mark, an ex-public school music-lover, given to violent outbursts, and with no history of commitment to the Southern Region, or to the services business, and Paul, a Business Planner – quiet, thorough, reluctant to openly assert himself, but gaining sway in the group by virtue of taking on the planning tasks they did not relish and thus gaining the aura of the 'expert'). One extra player was Roy, a Central Services market researcher who had been briefed by Paul to give an evening presentation on worldwide MR data on the services market, to try and encourage the team to be more adventurous in their view of their own market.

Market definition

The group initially saw the services market as currently worth £80 million, of which their existing mainframe maintenance business segment was some £70 million. They had been 'sold', from outside the group, the concept of a user life cycle of service needs (from isolating computer needs, through systems design, to purchase and then the need for upgrading and replacing equipment) – this they had labelled the 'cradle to grave' or 'womb to tomb' strategy.

However, in spite of this, their current firm and unmovable stance was that the business they were already in constituted the bulk of the market. The hidden agenda was to commit them to the view that this was not the case and that over the five-year planning period maintenance would be a relatively small part of the total computer services market.

The counters to this pressure which had already emerged were that: (a) there was no hard evidence available to them about the growth in the market; (b) they had currently very little technical expertise to offer in such markets as business or IT consultancy;

and (c) the margins on other services were currently much lower than those on maintenance services (and they believed this was the way it had to be).

They were, however, moving in the direction where they would have to accept that they were in only one relatively low-growth segment of the services market – and were trapped to some extent by the Sales Managers' case that the company could not look for growth in the maintenance services market because it was adversely affected by the impact of more efficient new technology which makes computers less prone to breakdown.

Market research

The MR presentation provided a lot of conflicting evidence about the worldwide computer services market size, the competitors and the impact of technology, forecast over the next five years.

This conflict provided the opportunity for individuals to choose those pieces of evidence which suited the position they wished to hold – which they duly did. The data sources were suspect enough that they could easily 'rubbish' the pieces of information which did not fit their existing view of the world.

Market forecasting

The team was asked to examine in detail the future that they saw for the maintenance services segment – i.e. the area in which they were currently experienced and 'expert'. (Note that the existing company view, encapsulated in the written Strategic Plan for the UK, was that there would be a limited degree of growth in the market over the five-year period.) This Strategic Plan was held and quoted by Paul, the Business Planner, and supported by the Sales Managers, who were not required by this plan to show any significant growth in services sales – only as more mainframes were sold were there to be more services sales, and the sales of mainframes were to grow at only 10 per cent a year (with a declining services requirement because of the improved technology).

There was strong entrenched resistance in the group to undertaking this exercise, because of the dangers and 'discomfort' they perceived in revealing unwelcome views. Events unfolded in the following way:

- The team initially refused to undertake the exercise of market forecasting because it was too complex, and because it had been done before by others and built into the statistical market models used for the Strategic Plan.

- The group were persuaded instead, with the advocacy of Keith, to enumerate the factors that would impact on the services market in the five years. This was done, and it was suggested that these factors should then be fed into the model to see what their implications were – this was to be controlled by Paul (whose goal seemed to be to ensure that the forecasts for the market remained unchanged).

- However, as the discussion proceeded, the volatile Mark took the floor and led the group through their brainstorming outputs, to arrive at a smaller list of some 12 factors, which would impact on the volume of business, the revenue it would generate and the margins on services.

- This was a threat which led Ed to wait until the coffee break, when the meeting room was empty, and then to fill the overhead projector screen with figures showing that there would be *no* growth in the services market, and that only if Central Sales could increase the sales of mainframe computers by 50 per cent per year would there be the required growth in services sales. (This was, by definition, 'impossible'.) His colleagues were bemused by these figures, until it became apparent that he had applied the factors reducing service requirements to *all* sales and the whole market, not just the new technology component of incremental sales.

- Discussion reverted to Mark's 12 factors, and it was possible to give signs to these indicating their effect on the market growth rate. This then provided the basis for proceeding. Interestingly, it emerged that when it was inevitable that the team would have to accept the revision of the company model forecasts, that nobody knew which assumptions and which factors had been included in the model – they only knew that they liked the answer it gave.

The case is illustrative of some of the 'real' issues in market definition and sales forecasting, such as:

- the political sensitivity of market definition and forecasts;
- the entrenched position taken by those with interests which may be affected by forecasts, e.g. the Sales Managers and the Business Planner;
- the use of information selectively to make cases;
- resistance to examining issues which are threatening – i.e. if they are taken off the agenda, then the status quo prevails;
- the power of the group/team decision-making forum in undermining the strength of entrenched positions.

What is described above is a process of *negotiating* the picture of the world that managers are prepared to accept. It has little to do with subtle statistical technique. It has a lot to do with market sensing.

Market sensing*

The difference between market sensing and conventional market research or information systems is that our focus is on managers' *understanding* of the market. Understanding is not the same as information. It is about developing new ways of looking at the outside world, to improve the way in which we develop our market strategies and deliver our marketing programmes. This is a process which we can *manage* for greater effectiveness in most companies. This is not something to be taken lightly.

What we are building up to is no less than a challenge to the organization's culture. This perhaps suggests the enormity of what we are talking about – there are no quick and easy ways of changing corporate culture in any of its forms.

However, challenging the status quo is always fun. One of my favourite stories on this comes from the operations research literature of World War II. Researchers made a film of the military drill used by soldiers to load and fire the big guns, looking for ways of improving efficiency. They found that in slow motion the film showed that at the end of the drill, just before firing the gun, two soldiers who played no other role stood to attention behind the gun. No-one could explain what this was for, but assumed it was essential because that was how it was *always* done. Finally a World War I veteran looked at the film and said: 'Ah, yes, of course . . . they used to hold the horses to stop them bolting!'

The way we see things here

The underlying problem is that *telling* people what their problems are, and, by implication, to get their act together, has proved to be a singularly ineffective approach to winning people's commitment and ach-

'telling people what their problems are, and, by implication, to get their act together, has proved to be a singularly ineffective approach'

---

* This section leans heavily on Nigel F. Piercy and Nikala Lane (1996), 'Marketing Implementation: Building and Sustaining A Real Market Understanding', *Journal of Marketing Practice: Applied Marketing Science*, Vol. 2, No. 3, 15–28.

ieving effective strategy implementation. This is for a number of reasons.

First, corporate culture may be such a barrier that they simply do not believe us. Culture has been defined in many ways, but a useful definition is 'the way we see things here'. This includes the process of selecting the information we accept and reject, the issues we monitor and those we ignore, and all the assumptions we make inside the organization about the outside world – what works in this market and what does not, who the competitors are and how they respond to competitive challenges, what matters to customers, how the market is changing or not changing, and so on. The underlying point is that people in organizations develop simplified models, which become their shared understanding of the world. The problem arises when that shared understanding becomes out-dated and inflexible, and yet we still cling to it – and, after all, we must be right because everyone around us agrees.

Secondly, 'telling' people what their problems are is unlikely to gain their 'ownership' of those problems – communication effectiveness demands that we recognize the importance of employee and manager perceptions of events and the strength of two-way communication to identify problems in those perceptions. Quite simply, it is naive to expect attempts at one-way communication to change people's minds about things.

Thirdly, it is too easy to be simplistic in assuming that we know how managers search for information and use it when they have it for decision making. There is abundant evidence to suggest that the information search and use in organizations is complex and reflects many needs other than making better decisions.

Changing the way we see things here

It follows that a critical precursor to strategy implementation and change is that the people who have to change in a company see the need and reasons for change, But just telling them does not seem to work.

This suggests the need for an approach to improving the understanding that managers and specialists have of their markets, which uncovers the problems to be solved and identifies the new challenges to be met, but which involves 'finding out' what matters, not just being told. In this situation the role of the marketing planner or analyst becomes one of managing the *process* of market sensing, not simply the provision of information and conclusions. The approach described below is a simple method of achieving some of these things.

A structure for market sensing

The approach discussed here is simple and accessible to managers. The goal is simply to provide a structure for executives and planners to articulate what they know about changes outside the company, and to identify the most critical gaps in that knowledge.

There are two stages. First, the framework in Figure 10.3 provides a mechanism for capturing information. We need to specify at the top the Environment to be evaluated and the Dimension of the environment to be analysed on this particular sheet (see comments below on how to manage these choices for maximum effect). The time-frame (normally three to five years) and the market in question also should be specified.

The task then is to brainstorm the events in the chosen part of the company's environment which might take place or which are currently developing. The most important events are listed on the form (and also mnemonic codes for ease of reference). However, the framework also requires that we identify specific effects on the company if this event takes place. If we cannot do this, the event is too broad and should be defined more narrowly, or it is unimportant to our analysis. For example, events like 'Single European Market' or 'change of government' are normally too broad. If the impact of an event includes some good things and some bad things, we should separate these and look at the event as two issues for ease of analysis. Then we need to do two further things: assess the current view of the *probability* of the event happening (initially a subjective 'guesstimate' which we may want to test and evaluate further), and the *likely effect* of the event on the business if it does happen (the suggested scale runs from 1 = Disaster to 7 = Ideal, and again this is something on which we may want to take an initial view, which can be refined at a later stage). We can complete as many of these forms as we need to build a full view of the most important aspects of the environment as they impact on the company.

Secondly, the events (or their codes) are then entered on the model in Figure 10.4 – positioned by the scores we have placed on the probability of each event occurring and the effect of the event if it does occur. The broad categories of event are categorized into:

- *Utopia* – events with a very good effect which are very likely to occur;
- *Field of dreams* – events which are highly desirable but seem unlikely to happen the way things are at the moment;
- *Danger* - events which are very threatening to the company and which are very likely to happen;

Environment:		Time-Frame:		
Dimension:		Market:		

Events	Specific Impacts			Probability*
				Effect**
1.				
Code:				
2.				
Code:				
3.				
Code:				
4.				
Code:				
5.				
Code:				
6.				
Code:				

* Probability: Hi, Medium, or Lo; or 0-100%
**Effect: 1=Disaster; 2=Very Bad; 3=Bad; 4=Neutral; 5=Good; 6=Very Good; 7=Ideal

Figure 10.3 A framework for market sensing

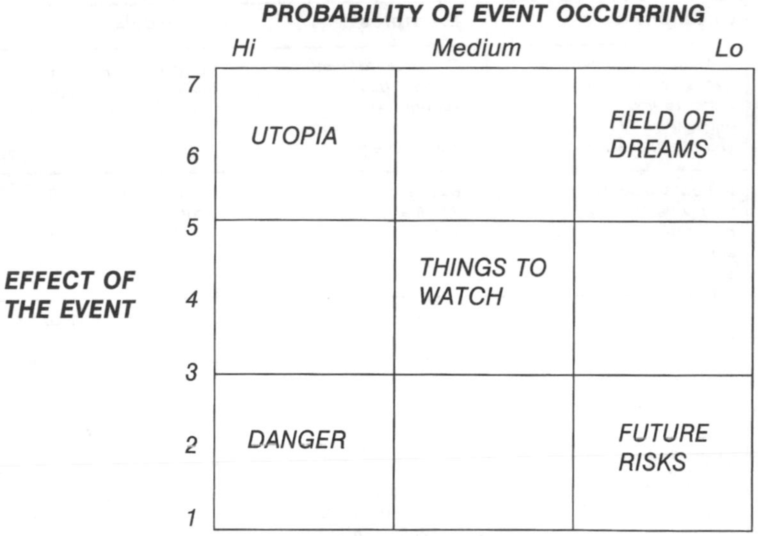

PROBABILITY OF EVENT OCCURRING

	Hi	Medium	Lo
7			
	UTOPIA		FIELD OF DREAMS
6			
5			
		THINGS TO WATCH	
4			
3			
	DANGER		FUTURE RISKS
2			
1			

EFFECT OF THE EVENT (rows 7 through 1)

Figure 10.4 A model for market sensing

- *Future risks* – undesirable events which seem unlikely to happen but which we may want to monitor in case they become more likely; and
- *Things to watch* – where we do not see the probability as very high and the impact is relatively neutral but where monitoring is needed in case either of these changes.

What we now have is a model of the outside world, which we can use for testing the robustness of proposed market strategies, identifying information gaps and evaluating market attractiveness. However, making this truly effective is far more about how the process of market sensing is *managed*, rather than just filling in forms and building models.

'What we now have is a model of the outside world, which we can use for testing the robustness of proposed market strategies'

Managing the market sensing process

The methodology described above is very simple to implement. It is accessible and provides a structure for the information and intelligence in the company, and captures a picture of the outside world as it is currently understood in the company. This is, however, only a starting point in achieving our goal of building and sharing real market understanding so that it impacts on strategic decisions and implementation. There are a number of key issues to be addressed in managing this process, which are summarized as a checklist in Figure 10.5 and discussed below.

Questions	Examples	Goals
1. What environment needs addressing better to improve our market understanding and our market strategies?	Business, Market Competitive, Technological, Legal, International Environments	FOCUS on the area where our assumptions are weakest
2. How should we subdivide the environment to analyse it more effectively?	Business Environment: Political, Economic, Social and Technological	FOCUS on the most critical aspects of the chosen environment
3. How should we interpret the impact of changes we identify in the environment?	Impact on customer/ supplier relationship. Impact on market size and share.	LINK TO PLANNING: by confronting the importance of change to our strategies.
4. Who should interpret the picture built and what are the critical questions they should address?	Planning team to specify in writing: how we are exploiting the good things and defending against the bad things in our strategies, and how we are monitoring the most critical issues.	LINK TO PLANNING: by challenging conventional views about strategies and information needs.
5. How do we link our new market understanding to decision making?	Plans must state explicitly how they reflect changes in the most critical aspects of the environment.	LINK TO PLANNING: by demanding that issues are addressed and not ignored.
6. What information should be provided?	Published studies, reports, corporate intelligence, etc.	ENRICH THE PROCESS: by stimulating thinking.
7. Who should be consulted/involved?	Planning team, cross-functional representatives, line managers, suppliers, customers, outside experts.	ENRICH THE PROCESS: by bringing more viewpoints to bear to challenge conventional assumptions.

Figure 10.5 Checklist for managing market sensing

The first two points relate to how to focus thinking to the maximum advantage, the next three are concerned with linking market sensing to planning, and the last points address the issue of how to enrich the sensing process.

Choosing the environment

The first issue is what approach to the outside world is potentially most needed to confront change and influence behaviour in the company. For example, the basic framework described above has been used to evaluate the business environment, the market environment; the competitive environment; the technological environment, the legal environment; and, the international environment, in different companies and to deal with different types of problems.

For example, in one clothing company we used the most general version of the model (the business environment), and the model produced by executives was 'Utopian' in the extreme – i.e. every event they could identify in the environment around their business fell into the Utopia cell of the model shown in Figure 10.4. This suggests that managers believe they know everything and everything is certain. When asked if they had considered re-naming the company the 'Smug Corporation', the executives said things like: 'You have to understand, we do not have competitors, only imitators'. When the scanning was re-focused onto the competitive environment, their views started to change quite dramatically.

Sub-dividing the environment to focus attention

The second point of focus is how to sub-divide the environment to ensure that people address the most important aspects and highlight the gaps in understanding that are most critical.

For example, with one high-technology company which was led by R&D and driven by scientific innovation in product, one glaring omission in management thinking was about competition – as evidenced by recent new product failures and as claimed by the company's Marketing Manager (who felt he was largely ignored). This problem was approached by asking teams of managers associated with new product projects to specifically address the competitive environment in their planning. This was sub-divided into: *Direct Competition* (i.e. other companies in the same industry producing the same type of product); *Customer Competition* (i.e. the tendency in key markets for customers to develop their own materials and to substitute this for product purchase); and *Generic Competition* (i.e. different technologies capable of serving the same customer needs). This has become a permanent and essential part of the company's new product planning, because their views on market positioning have changed dramatically, developing, for example, into deals with key customers to help them produce their own products and collaborations with companies outside the industry to use the newer technologies becoming available to meet customer needs.

Identifying the impact of environmental changes

If events that happen outside are of any importance, it is because they influence something that matters to the company. There is advantage therefore in addressing, at the earliest stage, what these impacts may be. For example, in viewing the market environment, we could ask for each event to be analysed in terms of its impact on customer/supplier relationships, or with the competitive environment, the impact of each event on our market share. The aim is to encourage thinking to be very specific to the company and its goals.

Interpreting the model of the environment for strategy building

Probably the most important issue is how we interpret the model of the environment which has been built. Here there are three questions to stress and demand attention. Given that the model is a picture of the things happening outside which we regard as most important to the survival and prosperity of the company, then we should demand responses to the following questions:

- We have identified the changes in this market which are potentially very advantageous for our performance in this market, and which are likely to happen (Utopia in the model) – the question is: *where, explicitly and realistically, are we exploiting those factors in our market strategies?*
- We have also identified the changes in this market which are potentially major threats, and which are also likely to happen (Danger in the model) – the question is: *where, explicitly and realistically, are we defending against these changes in our market strategies?*
- If it has been done properly, the model we have produced shows the things that are most important to our position in this market – the question is: *are we monitoring and evaluating these factors in our marketing information system?*

It is amazing how often executives have to admit that their plans and strategies do not address the real changes in the marketplace where they intend to operate – this is the moment when new thinking about strategies may become possible for the first time, because managers are confronted with their own logic. Even more surprising are situations where managers are forced to admit that their information systems do not focus on the things that really matter to their performance – the systems report the figures and statistics that are easiest to report and that have always been reported.

'It is amazing how often executives have to admit that their plans and strategies do not address the real changes in the marketplace where they intend to operate'

For example, precisely this situation was found in work with a wholesaling company. The company essentially has a sophisticated telephone marketing system, selling specialized wooden furniture to schools and homes and training centres for the disabled. In undertaking a view of the business environment at a boardroom level, one conclusion reached was that just about the most significant factor for profitability was merger and acquisition activity in the furniture manufacturing sector, which led to increased pressure on the wholesaler's margin. The point is that nowhere in the company was there any monitoring or evaluation of this merger activity – every time, a new merger came as a big surprise. Managers objected that it was not possible to have advance information on mergers and acquisitions. They are quite right. However, few such events take place without gossip at the exhibitions and trade events and without comments in the trade press and so on. The data may be soft, but maybe that is more use to the Board than sitting back and waiting to be surprised again. People often suggest it is an exaggeration, but it seems all too often the case that we do not watch the things that really matter because the information does not fit the computerized information system.

There is also another type of question that can be raised concerning our model of the environment:

- Are there things we can do to *reduce uncertainties* about important issues, to improve the power of the model?
- Are there things we can do to *change* the position of events in the model?

An initial response to the first of these questions may be negative. This is not always necessarily true. For example, in work with a company targeting the water industry in the build-up to privatization, one major unknown at the time was the form that privatization would take, which was a barrier to developing market strategies. Clearly the government is unlikely to provide such information ahead of time – but it was possible to go to a specialized agency in contact with senior civil servants and politicians and to get a pretty good idea of the plans, which is what the company did.

To some, the second question may appear even more out-landish – how can a company change the environment? Clearly in the general sense it cannot. However, the point of making the whole exercise focused bears fruit here. If, for example, the largest issue in the 'Danger' area is competitive entry with a new product, then maybe the strategy to pursue is one of collaboration.

This is an area where creative thinking may become possible, as we ease people away from the status quo represented by corporate culture. For instance, in the USA, Hershey, the chocolate company, came very close to persuading the federal authorities to alter the date of the change to daylight saving time to November, instead of it being in October. The reason is because parents do not like their small children making 'trick or treat' visits to houses after dark – an extra hour of daylight on 31 October (Halloween) is worth several million dollars worth of extra chocolate sales in the USA. The company failed in this attempt, but it remains surprising how creative thinking may be about 'unchangeable' events in the environment, given the chance.

Linking market sensing to plans

If the benefits of this approach are to be realized, the conclusions reached by understanding the environment that matters should be linked to the decisions made about market strategies. This may take no more than agreement that strategic market plans must state explicitly how they reflect changes in the most critical aspects of the environment.

Providing information as a stimulus to thinking

Another decision requiring careful thought is what information should be provided to the executive and planning teams scanning the environment, through written reports, presentation by outside experts, and so on. The key to handling this seems to be not to overload people with new information but to provide enough that is new to help people break the mould. Certainly, it is disastrous at any point to suggest to people that they are wasting their time because everything has been done before by 'Corporate Intelligence' or 'Market Research' departments. The aim here is to enrich the sensing process, not truncate it.

Who should be consulted and involved?

Perhaps the most actionable lever for enriching the sensing process is consultation and participation. The argument is clear: it is that consultation with managers and employees and their participation is critical to determining their responses to market developments. This follows the principle that giving discretion to managers and empowering them to find solutions and innovations is a powerful lever for strategic change which should not be underestimated.

Clearly, the marketing analyst can use the framework provided here to undertake an appraisal of the market environment as an individual exercise, but this is unlikely to impact on the problems we set out to solve, and ignores a major opportunity to build consensus on the need and direction for change. The issues to consider in managing participation in this type of exercise are:

- *A team* – If we want 'ownership' and commitment, we need to involve the key players in implementation in the analytical stage of planning, for how else can we get a 'buy-in' to new strategic directions?
- *Cross-functional representation* – One of the most powerful levers for change in major corporations is the use of the powerful and informed cross-functional team which pools specialized expertise around a focused problem. At the simplest level, it may be that people from Operations and R&D can contribute useful insights into market change. At a deeper level, if we expect co-operation and support across departments for market strategy implementation, it makes sense to have them involved and consulted in the process.
- *Line and staff specialists* – Similarly, managers from line roles and staff roles may bring very different insights and sources of intelligence to the table, and challenge conventional ways of addressing the market. There is also the question of gaining credibility and 'buy-in' from line management as a foundation for effective implementation of resulting strategies.
- *Outsiders* – In some situations it may be possible to gain from the involvement of outsiders, who bring new information and understanding of the markets we are appraising. This might include suppliers, customers, or experts from the relevant research institutes and universities.
- *Culture shakers* – It is sometimes good to include company 'non-conformists' to shake some of our conventional beliefs and assumptions. In looking at how people fit into corporate cultures, Vijay Sathe[12] suggests the categories in Figure 10.6. How many of our market sensing group are Mavericks or Rebels, who will look at things in a new way, for which we can learn new insights?

  'It is sometimes good to include company "non-conformists" to shake some of our conventional beliefs and assumptions'

- *Unhardening the categories* – Alan Kantrow[13] suggests that all humans suffer not just from hardening of the arteries but also 'hardening of the categories – the traditional ways in which we look at information in the company – and we risk becoming 'prisoners of our categories'. Part of our task is to break down the information we have into different categories to see what we learn – new market definitions, different types of customer segment, different ways of comparing ourselves to our competitors, different ways of grouping customer priorities, and so on. Remember the (alleged)

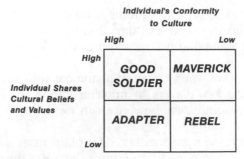

Figure 10.6 Cultural conformity and non-conformity

quotation from US President Ronald Reagan: 'It is not interpreting the future that is difficult, the problem is predicting the past'.

It may not be possible to exploit all these sources of influence over the creation of market understanding in all cases, and it may not be necessary to do so. The principal points are summarized in Figure 10.5 as a checklist for consideration in managing the process of building and sharing market understanding with managers.

The point of this is very simple – the tools for building and refining market understanding have to be placed in the hands of the line managers and technical specialists upon whom we depend for the effective implementation of market strategies. How can we expect people to commit to something when they do not see the reason for it?

These market sensing procedures have been developed to work with line managers and planning teams to enrich and enhance their understanding of the most critical aspects of their markets, to use this as the basis for developing market strategies of which they may take 'ownership' and drive through to effective implementation, with all that is implied in terms of organizational change and disruption to the status quo.

The approach described is accessible and easily applied, though it may achieve these characteristics at the expense of sophistication and rigour – the professional analysts and researchers can probably produce a more thorough and certainly a more sophisticated picture of the world – but then we are back where we started and it remains *their* picture of the world, not the manager's. The logic is one of sacrificing some sophistication to win commitment, which provides an argument for justifying the approach to managers who may reject the technique on the grounds that others have already done this work – Corporate Intelligence or Market Research.

A note of caution

However, a word of warning! These are fundamental issues not to be taken lightly – there are risks as well as opportunities.

For the most part, people in organizations do not cling to the familiar way just out of perversity or bloody-mindedness (although there are exceptions to this!), but because it is a way of getting on with the things that we think matter. When we start to tamper with the flow and use of marketing information, we have to run the risk of *reducing* performance in the short term. For example, we can compare the opportunities and risks like this:

The problem	The opportunities	The risks
There is a too limited flow of customer and market information to managers	Increase the flow and amount of information to put more important issues on the agenda	Information overload
Key managers have adopted a simplified model of what works in the market and what matters to customers, which is invalid	Force managers to confront and cope with a different view of the world, and to track the implications for marketing strategies	Abandoning the accepted and assumed model of the world creates confusion, uncertainty and self-doubt which 'freezes' decision makers
We ignore the impact of major changes in the marketing environment	Develop new sensing approaches that change our view of what is happening out there, and how we need to change our strategies	We make managers so fearful and intimidated by the speed and complexity of change in the outside world, that they cannot make decisions – they just sit and watch the outside world in bemused wonderment

continued

The problem	The opportunities	The risks
Strong group consensus in our decision making, which means they will not look at new information or new ways of doing things	Operate on the inertia and 'group think' by redesigning group memberships and the 'ownership' of critical information types	We create resistance to change, conflict between groups, internal competition and in-fighting

People do not adopt simplification mechanisms, group consensus, a false sense of stability, and so on, for the hell of it. These are mechanisms which allow us to make sense of things (however arbitrarily and inflexibly) and to get on with things (like making decisions and doing the work). We may *have* to change some of these things to get a new strategic direction – but slowly and with care!

Market intelligence

One of the things people say when they are introduced to market sensing is that you still need information to build the picture – so we are straight back to the conventional marketing research reports, and nothing is new. This is a fair point. However, while we may use marketing research reports in building a new picture of the market and a better understanding, it seems more likely that the most valuable inputs will be messy, qualitative, subjective and incomplete market intelligence than neat research reports.

Indeed, many companies now have in-company intelligence units to co-ordinate and disseminate soft data and improve shared corporate knowledge [14]. If the issue is, for example, competitors' promotional activities, knowing what they are doing and responding is what matters, not having it written in a report with full statistics and graphics. The goal is to know something that your competitor does not, or, if we all have the same information, to use it more effectively than the competitor.

Intelligence is about knowing things. For example, when the Southwestern Bell Telephone Co. in the USA heard rumours about new competitors entering the telephone market with special packages for home renters, they were able to counter this quickly by a programme of appointing apartment complex managers as Southwestern Bell sales agents. Similarly, feedback

that new independent 'micro' phone companies appealed particularly to younger telephone renters led Southwestern to move
resources into product offers and promotions based on college
companies[15]. This is about spotting patterns of change in the
market and using that understanding to respond, not complex
market research projects.

The issue of competitive intelligence is not new. As long ago as
1981, *Business Week* published *The Business Intelligence Beehive*,
describing how Japanese companies had set up surveillance posts
through the heartland of the US computer industry in Silicon
Valley in California, to monitor US technology development by
hiring American software experts. Competitive intelligence sources run all the way from readily available 'open sources' (like press
clippings, government records, trade shows, industry reports) to
observation of competitors' activities and interviews with competitors' suppliers, customers, former employees, present employees, and so on. This is not particularly sophisticated. Yet in 1995 a
US survey was still able to divide US companies into:

- *Intelligence Ostriches* – who did not use intelligence gathering,
  and did not believe that their competitors gathered intelligence
  about them; compared to
- *Intelligence Eagles* – who know that these competitors are
  watching their every move, and do the same in return[16].

You might like to raise the issue of which category your company
falls into.

The point is that while intelligence may be no more than a
press cutting, a chat with a competitor's employee at a meal, a
note from a salesperson about a rumoured new product coming
out, compared to the beautifully-produced marketing research
report complete with statistics and graphics – if our goal is
understanding, then it is probably a better source[17].

It may be a bit brutal for European taste, but Figure 10.7
shows the American view of the sources of competitive intelligence that can be exploited in market sensing. It is certainly food
for thought for most of us.

So, where have we got to?

The role of information is critical in market-led strategic change
for two reasons: it shows us the challenges in the market to which
we have to respond, and it builds an understanding and
commitment to change.

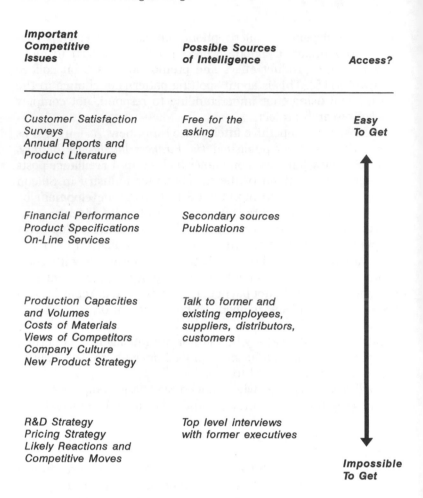

Important Competitive Issues	Possible Sources of Intelligence	Access?
Customer Satisfaction Surveys Annual Reports and Product Literature	Free for the asking	Easy To Get
Financial Performance Product Specifications On-Line Services	Secondary sources Publications	
Production Capacities and Volumes Costs of Materials Views of Competitors Company Culture New Product Strategy	Talk to former and existing employees, suppliers, distributors, customers	
R&D Strategy Pricing Strategy Likely Reactions and Competitive Moves	Top level interviews with former executives	Impossible To Get

Figure 10.7   Sources of competitive intelligence

'Our focus is on market understanding not marketing research techniques and marketing information systems'

Our approach here is not conventional. Our focus is on market understanding not marketing research techniques and marketing information systems*. Our goal is to improve our market sensing, not our information technology, and we explained why and unpacked a set of myths about marketing information and the 'hidden face' of marketing information in organizations.

---

* If notwithstanding, you still want to read more about marketing research techniques and marketing information systems, then you can find a review in Piercy and Evans [18].

However, the major contribution here is a tried and tested model of market sensing to improve how we understand the marketplace and to share that understanding inside the company. This is a powerful technique, and it is one that can be *managed* to re-shape how people inside the company understand customers, competitors and change outside the company.

The importance of getting better in this area is twofold: to achieve better understanding for our market strategizing and marketing programmes, and to build understanding and commitment to change. This is the real challenge in the marketing information, not research techniques and information systems – they can come later.

So far, then, we have unpacked two major areas in the real context for marketing: organization and information. Now we turn to the third: *processes* of planning and budgeting the process of going to market.

References

1. Samuels, Gary (1994), 'CD-ROM's First Big Victory', *Forbes*, 28 February.
2. Valente, Judith (1994), 'A New Brand Restores Sparkle to Waterford', *Wall Street Journal*, 10 November.
3. Flatow, Peter J (1996), 'Managing Change: Learning From Motorola', *Marketing News*, 1 July.
4. Lamons, Bob (1996), 'Research Won't Yield the Big Idea', *Marketing News*, 18 November.
5. Bowen, David (1996), 'There's No Safety in Numbers', *Independent on Sunday*, 20 October.
6. Reed, David (1997), 'Information', *Marketing Business*, March, 56.
7. Harris, Robert (1996), 'Our Dance Around the D-Word', *Sunday Times*, 4 August.
8. Murphy, Ian P. (1997), 'Urgency of Strategic Research', *Marketing News*, 6 January.
9. Matthews, Robert (1997), 'Murphy Really Does Sock It To Us', *Daily Telegraph*, 2 April.
10. Feldman, Martha S. and James G. March (1981), 'Information in Organizations as Signal and Symbol', *Administrative Science Quarterly*, Vol. 26, 171–186.
11. 'Respondents Assail the Quality of Research' (1995), *Marketing News*, 8 May.
12. Sathe, Vijay (1988), *Culture and Related Corporate Realities*, Homewood, Illinois: Irwin.
13. Kantrow, Alan (1989), *The Constraints of Corporate Tradition*, New York: Harper and Row.
14. Stewart, Thomas A. (1995), 'Getting Real About Brainpower', *Fortune*, 27 November.

15. Long, Pat (1995), 'Turning Intelligence Into Smart Marketing', *Marketing News*, 27 March.
16. Shermach, Kelly (1995), 'Much Talk, Little Action on Competitor Intelligence', *Marketing News*, 28 August.
17. Button, Kate (1994), 'Spies Like Us', *Marketing Business*, March, 7–9.
18. Piercy, Nigel F. and Martin Evans (1994), 'Developing Marketing Information Systems', in M. J. Baker (ed.), *The Marketing Book*, 3rd ed., Oxford: Butterworth-Heinemann.

CHAPTER 11

Marketing planning process

How do we create plans with *'ownership'* to make things happen?

Introduction

We looked earlier (Chapter 7) at marketing planning as the framework into which we fit our market strategy, to test it and to communicate it. The aim of this chapter is to look at the planning process as a powerful source of leverage for working on achieving market-led strategic change, and actually making market strategy and marketing programmes *happen*. This implies that we need to look at planning in a rather different light.

'the planning process as a powerful source of leverage for working on achieving market-led strategic change'

Many authorities, in textbooks and in training courses, discuss the process of planning as an orderly sequence of steps, in applying rational-analytical techniques to developing market strategies and marketing programmes (see pp. 271–82 for just such a model). Their attention is focused on techniques of analysis, of ever-increasing sophistication in the models we use, and outputs of carefully constructed strategic and operational marketing plans, produced to standardized formats with carefully balanced figure-work.

Issues such as corporate culture, management style, information flows, organizational structures, participation, and the like, are treated either as facilitating mechanisms or as mere context, to be set aside as trivial compared to the real business of complex analysis and plan-writing. This approach completely misses the main point. The underlying truth is that these issues are not mere context, they *are* the process.

The *process* of planning is significant because the way we design and manage the process will have a direct impact on what goes into the plan and, even more to the point, whether anything useful ever *happens* as the result of planning. Apart from anything else, it is one of the few chances we have to do something constructive to move the company's culture closer to our market strategy rather than vice versa. Indeed, it is becoming clear that what a managed planning process offers us is a mechanism to put a handle on organizational development, because planning process is another form of organizational 'learning' and adaptation (see pp. 69–81). Our goal here is to guide that organizational development and learning towards our market-led goals.

This is a vital point to grasp, because it leads us to a management agenda which *really* matters – *managing* the planning process to get the *results* we want in the customer market. The trouble is that it is precisely this agenda which is normally totally *ignored*.

My firm belief is that the most important and productive thing to focus on in planning is not the techniques and formal methods, it is quite simply commitment and 'ownership'. It is a hard life. There are no real rewards for beautifully designed planning systems incorporating the latest computerized models. The rewards come from getting our marketing act together and getting people *excited* and *motivated* enough to drive the market strategy and *do* the things that matter to customers in the marketplace. That is, after all, the only source of real rewards.

Professional planners often object to this view of things. This is understandable – these people love their computer spreadsheets, their planning manuals, their analytical techniques, their 'expert systems' and all the other trappings of formal planning systems. In truth, there is nothing wrong with these things – as long as we remember at all times that the goal is to deliver effective market strategies to the paying customer, not just to produce clever plans which never happen. The credo of market-led strategic change should be that we will *not* tolerate the SPOTS syndrome here (*Strategic Plan On The Shelf*)!

We can work up to confronting the real issues in marketing planning in the following way. We looked at the conventional view of what marketing planning is supposed to look like in Chapter 7. We kept this simple. Having got that out of the way, we can turn here to the question of why it doesn't seem to work quite like that in the real world. This helps us to build up the agenda to be addressed in *managing* planning to create and achieve market-led strategic change. Finally, we can get personal, and Diagnostic 4 gives us a basis for evaluating how well our own planning process works, to see where we should start with these new approaches.

So what goes wrong with planning?

On the face of things, planning seems to offer us just what we have always said we wanted – a way to pursue market-led strategic change, to get our marketing act together, and to give the customer what s/he most values. This is, indeed, the potential. What is equally apparent is that there seem to be a few barriers in the way of realizing that potential.

For a start, the studies by researchers like Gordon Greenley [1, 2] and Malcolm McDonald [3] in the UK and others in Europe [4] suggest that all is not well with the practice of marketing planning. These studies reveal that: managers see planning as a failure; planning has been fully adopted by very few British and European companies anyway; many so-called plans have little or no strategic content and are little more than financial budgets; there are many managerial objections to doing planning; and it is widely in 'disrepute' with managers. On a far less systematic basis than these studies, over the last couple of years we have been testing out some of these problems with the companies and managers with which we work. What we have found makes interesting reading.

The benefits of planning

If you look at the sorts of problems that managers describe in their lives – coping with too many different products and markets, missed opportunities, wasted selling efforts, lack of co-ordination in marketing and sales or integration with production and other departments, plans which are budgets, not strategic, lack of focus and mission, no sensitivity to customer requirements, and so on – then planning should be a gift from heaven, because it helps us sort out just these problems.

So, we trot happily in to see the managers and tell them about what plans can do for them and the hidden benefits of a systematic planning process. However, when we do this, rather than going down on their knees in eternal gratitude, the reaction of managers to the idea of planning seems more associated with comments like:

- We never needed it *before*, so why do we need it *now?*
- Planning takes too much *time* and it *kills* initiative!
- Plans are *inflexible, inaccurate,* and nobody *uses* them anyway!
- Planning is a meaningless, pointless *ritual!*

In fact, much of our current understanding of the real problems of effectively implementing and operating strategic planning in organizations comes from the responses made by groups of executives in planning workshops and the like to two wholly naive questions that we have asked: 'What do you want your planning process to achieve for your company?'; and 'What goes wrong with marketing planning in your company?'

' *"What do you want your planning process to achieve for your company?"* '

So, what do you want from planning?

Broadly, the answers from managers to this simple question are as follows:

- *A good plan* – Perhaps a largely predictable response, but one which generally refers to plans which are achievable, action-able and capable of being implemented, rather than to technical, analytical sophistication.
- *The creation of teams and the 'ownership' of output* – There is a recurring comment that plans which are not 'owned' by teams of executives are unlikely to gain implementation, even if they are formally approved and accepted by the company. There is widespread concern that planning should achieve commit-ment among executives to 'making it happen', even if this is at the expense of rigour, sophistication and innovation in the planning process itself. Various executives suggested to us in different ways that 'second-rate plans which *happen* are better than first-rate plans which sit on the shelf'.
- *Developing a continuous process* – While executives typically do not want to spend more time planning, they *do* want planning to operate continuously, and not to be a 'once-a-year ritual'. We found some disillusionment with planning, paradoxically not just because it consumes managerial time and resources which could otherwise be devoted to 'running the business', but because planning does not become *part* of 'running the business'.

- *Identifying real information needs* – In situations varying from executives experiencing what amounts to technology-led information overload to those where little real market information existed, executives saw an advantage of planning as a way of isolating and identifying their *real* information needs.
- *Understanding strategy and shaking dogma* – Executives often found the concept of market strategy unfamiliar and uncomfortable, but, more appositely, quite frequently do not understand what their own company's market strategies *are*, let alone their rationale, and suggested that they had what amounts to culturally-based 'dogma' rather than genuine market strategies for the future. Contrary to any expectation that executives want planning to reinforce the existing culture, we were often told that this was a problem, and executives wanted to find ways of shaking and testing the beliefs and values of their culture. This was expressed by one manager as being able to 'think the unthinkable' and even allowed to 'say the unsayable', without the ceiling falling in, when developing and planning new market strategies.

'executives wanted to find ways of shaking and testing the beliefs and values of their culture'

So, on the face of things anyway, managers seem to want quite surprisingly reasonable things from planning. This leads directly to our second naive question.

So, why don't you just do it?*

Perhaps the most outstanding characteristic of the responses to our second question, about what goes wrong with planning in practice, was that on no occasion that we have recorded did executives complain to us of the lack of either formal planning techniques, computerized models or statistical information systems. The perceived gap is not scientific planning methodology. Rather, the planning pitfalls executives perceive appear to be in the following areas:

- *Analysis instead of planning* – Executives have told us frequently that they see planning as bogged down with analytical techniques and models which are far removed from the reality

---

* One manager showed me a rubber stamp he keeps on his desk, which prints the message 'JFDI'. This politely translates into 'Just Flipping Do It', which he stamps onto bureaucratic memos and executive excuses for inaction. I too now have one of these stamps. It doesn't make people do things, but it is very satisfying.

they perceive, and which do not lead to actionable plans. We spend our time building models, not making plans that someone can take away and *do*.

- *Information instead of decision* – In similar vein, executives have described planning disintegrating into constant demands for more and better information. Some are cynical enough to suggest that the reason for this is that it is easier than making decisions. This too is associated with considerable difficulty in producing an actionable plan from the planning process.

- *Incrementalism* – At its simplest, executives have described to us many situations where the primary determinant of a plan is quite simply the previous plan, or at least the previous budget. The planning task then degenerates into negotiating and arguing about minor departures from the previous year, rather than creating new strategies.

- *Vested interests rule* – Executives suggest that the powerful in the company exert undue influence over plans, to protect budgets and head-counts, to build empires, and so on. Many manifestations of this were cited: refusal by key players to participate in planning, followed by a rejection of plans by those same players on the grounds of lack of consultation; blockages in the availability of important internal information to planners; side-tracking disputes about jurisdiction and minor company rules and policies; outright, dogged argument against anything which changes the status quo; 'politicking', bargaining and 'horse-trading' outside planning meetings to divert plans from going in unwelcome directions; and so on.

- *Organizational 'mind-set'* – Many executives have suggested that conventional planning processes are, by definition, inward-looking and bounded by 'the way we do things here'. So they never produce anything new.

- *Resistance to change* – Some executives have suggested that strategic change emanating from the marketing department is seen as threatening – or even 'unreasonable' – and is often successfully resisted by other departments and organizational interest groups.

- *No 'ownership' or commitment* – It seems that in many cases plans are produced (often by staff planners) and accepted, but, in the absence of 'champions' determined to make them work, nothing ever happens as a result of the planning effort. Plans produced by central planners like 'rabbits out of a hat' seem to do little other than irritate line managers.

- *No resourcing* – executives have pointed out many resource-related pitfalls: the simple refusal by management to provide resources; the rejection of plans, with the comment that they are unrealistic because it should have been known all along that resources would not be released; and perhaps the most threatening outcome being approval and acceptance by management of the plan, but rejection of the accompanying resource request (see pp. 472–78 below).

- *No implementation* – We have received bitter complaints about situations where planning absorbed resources and management time, and even created excitement and support for change, but led to nothing more than a report on a shelf, which was never effectively actioned.
- *Diminishing effort and interest* – Largely as a result of lack of resourcing and implementation, executives point out that if planning is to be no more than an annual ritual, and managers perceive this, then it is hardly surprising that efforts and interest diminish over time. It becomes a self-fulfilling prophesy that planning is a waste of time.

Now, these pitfalls may not be true of how planning works in *your* organization. This is not the point for the moment (we will come to that issue later!). The point is that if you look at what managers say they *want* from planning, and the reasons why it goes *wrong* – there is almost no mention of wanting more sophisticated planning techniques and systems.

Now, the trouble with this is that what we really know a lot about is the techniques and the systems. If you look at the conventional marketing planning textbooks, planning manuals, briefcase planning systems, consultancy advice, management training and all the rest of it – they are obsessed with model-building and computer systems, and analytical techniques. In contrast to this, what managers seem to be telling us is that we are all missing the point about what really matters in making planning effective as far as they and their companies are concerned.

So, we have started to re-think how we work on planning with companies, and have developed an approach which is about *managing* the planning *process*, not just the techniques of planning.

Managing all the dimensions of planning

A multidimensional model of planning

The way we present planning process to companies now is summarized in Figure 11.1. We suggest that there are at least three dimensions of the planning process, and if we are in any

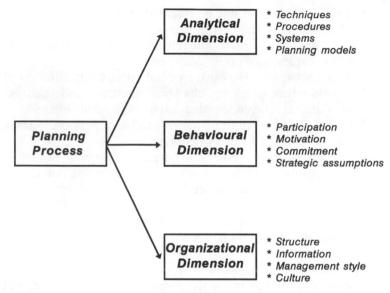

Figure 11.1 A multidimensional model of marketing planning process

way serious about *managing* planning then we have to address all three of these process dimensions.

Analytical planning dimension

There is no doubt that to produce effective plans we need the tools for the job – the *techniques* to analyse our problems and opportunities and identify the solutions and strategies; the formal *procedures* and systems to organize our planning and make it part of running the business; a *structure* for our planning to make it comprehensive and manageable; *iteration* to make our planning dynamic and thorough; and a *written plan* as the output capturing our ideas and strategies as a basis for communicating them.

I have no quarrel with this element of the planning process, with but two provisos. *First proviso*: let us not delude ourselves that this is *all* that planning is about, because then we end up believing that if we can just formalize planning enough and train people in more sophisticated techniques of planning (or perhaps hire 'professional planners' who have this expertise already), then we will improve our performance. There is abundant evidence that it is not enough.

Second proviso: let us be wary of the trap of creating a planning bureaucracy that actually gets in the way of *doing* things. At the risk of being repetitive, it must be said again that there are no brownie points in the real world for smart, clever, formal plans, until and unless they lead us to effective action in the customer market – which we have already said amounts to no more than being best at what matters most to that customer. Indeed, some of the most exciting and effective planning exercises I have run with managers have been conducted wholly outside their companies' formal, sophisticated, inflexible, inward-looking but legitimate planning systems (see pp. 454–59 below). At the end of the day, a bunch of dedicated people who care about a problem enough to generate a strategy, and then to go away and *do* it, cuts more ice in the real world.

However, we do have a couple of problems here. To begin with, it is the analytical dimension of planning that we know a lot about – we can train people in financial investment appraisal, the Boston matrix, Porter's structural analysis, PIMS analysis, Business Position Assessment and other similar models, marketing research techniques, spreadsheets and databases and all the other paraphernalia; we can design planning schedules and systems; we can write company planning manuals, and so on. We know a lot about these things. The only trouble is that it can all be pointless (and sometimes positively harmful) unless we also sort out the problems that people have in doing planning, and the real attitude of the organization towards the planning.

Behavioural planning dimension

Process means *how* we do things as well as *what* we do. How we do things leads us straight to the problems that our *people* have in building and using marketing plans. The type of issues we have to sort out here have very little to do with formal planning techniques – *managerial perceptions* of planning and the uncertainties they are expected to confront in planning; *participation* levels and types in the planning groups and teams, and managers' attitudes towards this; the hidden *strategic assumptions* that managers make (and believe) about what the company can and should do, and what drives the market; the *motivation* (or otherwise) to make planning effective; the *commitment* to strategic change, or the preference for the status quo; and the '*ownership*' by individuals of the problem of making things happen, without which it is unlikely that too much will ever happen as a result of planning.

The sad truth is that we know that these things matter, but most of us ignore them when we set-up and try to manage our marketing planning. You can test that one out for your own organization with Diagnostic 4, at the end of the chapter.

'we know that these things matter, but most of us ignore them when we set-up and try to manage our marketing planning'

Organizational planning dimension

Ultimately, all of this has to be seen in the context of the organization itself – the *organizational structure*, with all that this means in terms of formal responsibilities, vested interests and power to get things done or stop things happening; the *information* issue, and the problems of access and control of information, the inadequacies, the politics; the *culture* of the organization – 'the way we do things here', and all the sub-cultures in different parts of the organization; the *management signals* that tell us about the real attitudes and beliefs of management rather than the lip-service (and if we persist in telling line managers that planning is the number one top priority, but could they do it on Sundays, please, because we are not going to give them any other time or resources, then the signal about real priorities is patently obvious, and we should not be surprised if managers understand it, even if we don't); the existence and direction of *mission and vision* in how the organization is run; and the *hidden norms and values* that really determine what people do in the organization.

We may not know too much about managing people in planning, but we know even less about matching formal planning to organizational attributes of this kind.

The conclusion to which I am drawn by examining the literature of planning, by analysing how we train executives in planning, and most of all by studying the practices that I have observed in companies, is that we know *most* about what matters *least* in planning (the analytical techniques and formal systems), and we know *least* about what matters *most* (the behavioural and organizational dimensions), and that we have not even recognized yet the underlying problem of managing these dimensions of planning to give a *consistent*, managed planning process.

Some research evidence

Although it is very crude stuff, we have done some research recently to try and substantiate the existence and significance of these hidden dimensions of the planning process. The research was carried out among approximately 200 medium and large UK companies – companies where there is some form of planning (so you would expect them to be above averagely effective in getting the planning act together).

A technical write-up is available elsewhere [5], but the basic question we sought to answer was: 'What predicts the credibility and utilization of marketing plans?' So, the issue is whether we produce plans that people believe in, and use, to run the business. The predictors of plan credibility and utilization that we found in the study were: (a) the formalization of planning and learning of planning techniques; (b) a factor called 'planning thoroughness'; (c) the avoidance of behavioural planning problems; and (d) positive signals from the organizational environment. It is probably worth considering each of these a bit further.

Formalization and planning techniques

It was not what we were trying to prove, but nonetheless the degree to which planning was formally organized and documented, and the more analytical techniques were brought to bear, the higher the credibility and use of the plan (particularly the credibility, incidentally). Actually, this does make sense if you look at what people mean by keeping planning 'informal' – we don't really do *any* planning; we do things the way we have always done them; planning is for chief executives behind closed doors, not the riff-raff out in the field; we pretend to plan, but never let it get in the way of ad hoc, short-term reactions to events as they happen day-to-day; and so on.

'Planning thoroughness'

This factor was to do with three things: whether planning drew on experience and knowledge from all parts of the organization (or the degree to which it did); whether the planning activity was seen to be adequately resourced in time and money; and whether people believed that good planning performance was rewarded in the same way that good operational performance was. So this is really about consultation/participation, and the signals sent by the company to say whether planning is important (or not).

Avoidance of behavioural planning problems

We used a large number of attitude and belief measurements to identify a number of behavioural planning problems at the individual level:

- *Planning recalcitrance* – characterized by people believing that planning was a bore and a ritual, and that it was disorganized, with executives mainly picking on the weaknesses in plans and being easily side-tracked into short-term operational issues.
- *Fear of uncertainty in planning* – Executives are seen to resist long-term commitments and to be uncomfortable with long-range forecasting, and so emphasize the present, not the

future. People resist learning and change, and desperately seek a 'rational' decision-making technique that will make the decisions for them and take the discomfort away.
- *Political interests* – People see planning as dominated by the vested interests in the company, leading to planning becoming bidding and bargaining for resources, with information sharing precluded and much 'padding' in forecasts and estimates.
- *Planning avoidance* – People are seen to 'go through the motions' in planning, to give compliance, not commitment, so nothing gets challenged because planning is about avoiding responsibility for doing anything.

It must be said, when we have presented this material to managers in company workshops, it is normally the behavioural planning problems which start the heads nodding in agreement and the accusing fingers pointing!

Organizational signals

This was a measure of a number of factors to do with the company's attitude towards strategic planning, towards marketing and the customer philosophy of management (or lack of it), as perceived by the people who do the planning.

These would seem to be the things that are associated with marketing plans that are credible and actually used. Where this has led us is towards a somewhat different agenda to be addressed in managing planning.

The real management agenda

If we are at all serious about putting a handle on the planning process, so that we can use it to unleash our company's potential for market-led strategic change, the real agenda to be addressed has at least four parts: (a) techniques and formalization; (b) the behavioural issues in planning; (c) the organizational issues in planning; and (d) the consistency between all these issues.

Techniques and formalization

It is clear that if we want plans to be credible (the first stage in getting them implemented), we need to provide a formal system and the appropriate techniques. This seems to be for two reasons: it shows people we are serious about planning how we go to market; and it gives executives the tools to do the job. This is necessary but not sufficient, however.

Behavioural issues

The critical issues here are the *managerial perceptions* of the planning process, with all that this means in terms of their *motivation* to make planning work effectively and their *commitment* to planning. The variables to be managed here are *training* for the planning job, designing *participation* from a motivational and political viewpoint, and what *signals* the organization sends about planning.

Organizational issues

The critical question is the degree to which the organization is seen to be, and believed to be, *supportive* of the planning effort. Part of the way into this is the *example* set by senior management, the *resourcing* of planning and the *rewards* of all kinds for good performance in planning. Ultimately, these things are important, as they impact on *planning credibility* in the organization and reflect the surrounding issues of culture, organizational structure and information systems, and so on.

Consistency

While just recognizing the questions above is a great step forward, we also have to think about how we manage the planning process dimensions consistently with each other. We do not know enough about this to make generalizations; it is one you will have to test out for yourself – Diagnostic 4 may help here.

To get to grips with what this may mean, consider some of the conclusions reached by William Giles [6]. He suggested that if we look at what companies achieve in their planning in terms of the sophistication of strategies and plans on the one hand and the ownership and implementation of strategies on the other hand, we get the picture shown in Figure 11.2, with four scenarios:

- *Cavaliers – low ownership and weak strategy.* Planning is an annual ritual for the satisfaction of senior management. The documentation is often thick and glossy, full of internal budgets and lengthy 'to do' lists that demonstrate frenetic activity. The whole process may even be delegated to a junior member of staff and rubber stamped by senior management later.
- *Pundits – good planning but low ownership.* Many organizations inadvertently end up here. Planning is done by experts and not shared by those who will eventually implement the plans. Specialist planning departments are recruited to do the job that really belongs to line management. Strategic decisions

become the prerogative of the planners. The plan appears to bear little resemblance to the cut and thrust of real life. It is hard to judge its strategic quality, since it is never really put to the test of implementation.

● *Missionaries – ownership high and strategy improving.* The organization is really beginning to move in the right direction. Irrespective of the strength of the strategy, implementation is in full swing. The entire organization knows where it is heading. However, few organizations reach this stage because their preoccupation with improving strategy leads them inevitably towards the ivory tower of the 'Pundits'. 'Missionaries' are in a transient stage. Once ownership has taken root, it is far easier to improve strategy sophistication subsequently without impairing implementation. 'Missionaries' are only a short step from the 'Leaders' position.

● *Leaders – strategy sophisticated and ownership high.* This is where all companies would like to believe they are positioned. In reality, few are. These companies are typified by sustainable market strategies that are well understood by the implementers who have played their part in fashioning them. Departmental and functional boundaries have broken down. People work together in interdepartmental teams that focus firmly on the customer for the good of the entire organization. These organizations are exerting significant influence on their customers and competitors [6].

If the position of your company on this model is undesirable, then we are back to the question: how do we change? William

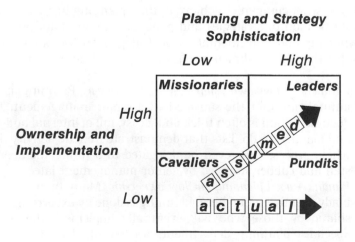

Figure 11.2 Sophistication versus ownership

Giles argued that all organizations start as 'Cavaliers', and in the quest for improvement the natural progression for most companies has been to invest more in the quality and sophistication of planning. This has been accompanied by the assumption that the organization will automatically become a 'Leader'. In reality, organizations move further down the 'Pundits' cul-de-sac, since nothing like the same energy is devoted to ownership issues. The result is the difference between assumed and actual progress shown in Figure 11.2.

William Giles made four observations, which are worth noting:

- *Better planning does not automatically lead to better implementation.* Increasing investment in sophistication without an equal investment in ownership makes planning an ivory tower activity. The planners become 'Pundits', and implementation fails.
- *Over-sophistication hinders ownership.* Once a 'Pundit', additional investment in technical expertise is unlikely to turn an organization into a 'Leader'. The behavioural investment that increases ownership is different from the technical expertise that increases sophistication.

> *'The behavioural investment that increases ownership is different from the technical expertise that increases sophistication'*

- *Ownership makes implementation work irrespective of strategy.* An organization can only reach the 'Missionary' stage after a significant human investment in behaviour and attitudes of its people. This will be effective if a level of strategy sophistication has not previously been achieved. If it has, it may be necessary to reinvent strategy in order to nurture ownership.

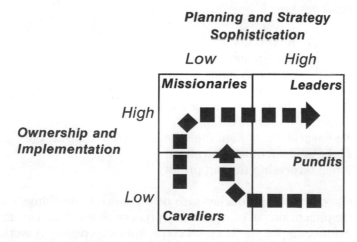

Figure 11.3   Routes to planning effectiveness

- *Sophistication follows ownership and implementation.* Virtually the only route to becoming a 'Leader' is by being a 'Missionary' first and concentrating on sophistication in the later stages of development. This sometimes means that senior management has to conceal its pride while the transition takes place.

The conclusion suggested by Giles [6] is that getting out of the Pundits box may actually mean giving up some planning sophistication and concentrating on winning ownership first. Then sophistication can be regained with the support of the people involved – see Figure 11.3. We will see shortly that this can be achieved in several ways.

Now, this is a highly demanding and complex managerial agenda, and we may quite simply not be able to do it all at once. That is fine – let's pick off the problems one at a time.

So what can we actually do?

Certainly, when we work on these issues with companies, one of the reactions of managers to the agenda of issues to be addressed in managing planning is that even if they agree with our conclusions, they don't know where to start. This is perfectly reasonable – as we have said, it is a very demanding and lengthy agenda. However, there are a number of ways into the problem of managing the planning process, which we can take singly or as a group according to our priorities. These development approaches are:

- Manage the process
- The tools for the job
- Chunking by champions
- Manage participation
- Building effective planning teams
- Facilitate the process
- Be illogical, turn planning upside-down and inside-out
- Make implementation strategic
- Make ownership the top priority

These practical approaches give us a chance to do things on all three dimensions of our planning process, to see if we can make it work better for us. They all come from experience in working with companies on these issues.

Manage the process

If planning is the way your company gets from strategy to programmes of action – and it is for most of us – then the planning process deserves serious management attention to design it and run it to achieve the things we want. There are many criticisms of planning (see pp. 431–32 and pp. 433–36 above). These criticisms are undoubtedly true for many company planning systems. They are not, however, the unavoidable characteristics of planning. They are the characteristics of *bad* planning. They are the characteristics of *badly managed* planning.

We have talked a lot about 'ownership' – winning the hearts and minds of the people in the company to get their commitment to implementation of market strategies. There is an ownership issue here as well – ownership of the job of managing the planning process.

This is becoming both more difficult and more important, as the responsibility for generating and planning market strategy becomes a pan-company issue, not just something that is done by a marketing department.

The observation is simple – if you look at companies where planning really is turning strategizing into operational programmes of action, it is because someone is driving the planning process to achieve this effect (and often without any resources or formal authority to do it).

The tools for the job

If planning is to do what we want, we need to make sure that you give the people involved appropriate tools and techniques for planning. Re-read the comments above about planning sophistication (pp. 441–44) and consider again the meaning of the word 'appropriate'. You do not need state-of-the-art technology to do a basic job of turning market strategy into practical action. We have already given you more tools than you probably need:

'You do not need state-of-the-art technology to do a basic job of turning market strategy into practical action'

- structures for analysing customer markets and segments and making choices (pp. 147–76);
- tools for working on market mission and competitive positioning (pp. 179–232);
- methods for analysing relationship issues (pp. 237–67);
- checklists of key issues and plan format (pp. 276–81);

- a customer-oriented SWOT to sift and test strategy ideas (pp. 282–92);
- a methodology for managing the market sensing process (pp. 411–24).

If you make those tools work for you and share them with participants in planning, you will probably be way ahead of most of your competitors in actually getting the important stuff done.

Chunking by champions

One thing we have found in some companies is the tendency to prefer administrative neatness in the company to getting things done in the market. There is a strong danger that by trying to make our planning process all-encompassing, closely integrated with financial and strategic planning, and a 'perfect' system with all the feedback loops covered, and so on, we simply create for ourselves a hopeless bureaucracy.

So, there are two things we can try, almost irrespective of the rest of our formalized planning.

First, let's not start out by trying to solve the problems of the whole universe in a single plan. Let's postpone ruling the world for the moment and focus on one self-contained area of the business. It may be: a vertical market in which we want to develop a stronger position; a market segment which has been ignored; a type of customer with whom we are losing out; a new product market; a weak product area; a perennial problem area; or whatever. Let's talk about developing a free-standing plan and market strategy for this area of focus, and see how we get on. This is what has been called 'chunking' [7].

Secondly, let's find some people who *really* care about this part of the business. It does not matter whether we talk about 'champions' [7], 'monomaniacs with a mission' [8], 'change-masters' [9], 'mavericks' or 'rebels' [10], 'fixers' [11], or 'marketing subversives' [12]. We know who they are (or if we don't, we should). They are the people in our organizations who will make things happen – possibly in spite of company policy, lack of resourcing, absence of authority and formal responsibility, and 'insurmountable' barriers to implementation.

'let's point the champions at the problem, give them the tools and let them make it happen for us'

It may be 'riding the back of a tiger' (the words of a Managing Director in a company where we did this, not mine), it may be uncomfortable for top managers and staff planners, it may be disruptive, but if things are stuck – let's point the champions at the problem, give them the tools and let them make it happen for us.

For example, in one sophisticated, high-technology company with which we worked over several years, the formal planning system is a professional planner's dream. The company is multinational, so has planning at: head office (the big global strategies); geographic zones (e.g. Europe and UK); national level (e.g. UK); business level (product-based divisions); and business units and functions (a matrix structure within each product division). By use of great computer power and the employment of several hundred full-time planners, they integrate and co-ordinate the business through formal planning of impressive complexity and sophistication. There is only one minor problem with this – the real business is just ticking over, and is wide open to attack as and when the competition feel like it. It is only a start, but they have made some positive steps forward just by forming teams of people who *care* about a particular market (people from all over the company, irrespective of function or seniority) and pointing them at a vertical user market, with the instruction: 'Create a new strategy for this market, and then do it'. Now, this does not fit in well with the formal planning system. What it has done is to regain lost market share in some customer markets that matter a lot to this company.

It may be messy, but does that really matter?

A couple of points of caution: if you do it, you had better *mean* it; and it involves your *best* people, it is not a dumping ground for the lemons that no-one else wants. Management control comes from how we define the strategic issues and the priorities we place on them; after that it is over to the people who get things done. It is a powerful tool to be used carefully, but it is one we can pick up as we need it.

Manage participation

Let's talk more generally about *who* should do the planning. Let's talk about *participation* in planning. Now, participation is one of those things that has had a very bad press over the years. The general impression seems to be that participation is some sort of a managerial cop-out: we cannot control people so we have to 'share' decisions (with gritted teeth, and when no other choice is apparent); we stick people with the problems we cannot solve (because that will teach them that life at the top is not as easy as they thought); or we do it to pay lip-service to 'industrial democracy' and justice and fairness, and so on.

This all misses the main point. That point is that participation is one of the few issues on which we can exert a *direct* influence to shape up the planning process and the plans that it produces.

It is also a route to unleashing the vast reservoir of human ingenuity and resourcefulness that we normally prefer to ignore or, worse, we 'police' out of the organization. If we agree that 'ownership' is what really matters in planning, then we have to open up the planning process to those who we want to implement the plan, and who have something at stake.

In particular, I have no patience whatever with the objection that all participation does is 'waste' time by letting people 'rediscover the wheel'. The easy answer to that is 'No problem, because if *they* discover it, it is *their* wheel, not ours, and *they* will make it roll!'

In fact, you may have no choice anyway. We have seen that in many companies multi-functional teams and partnership-based collaborations are operating across traditional functional, and even organizational, boundaries. The process of going to market with a customer-focused market strategy and an effective implementation programme is bigger than any department, and many companies now manage that process, not departmental plans. Maybe the real skills in planning how we go to market are about how we involve people and help to make teams productive?

So, let's talk about managing participation purposefully to achieve. Some of the issues to consider are outlined below.

- *Build effective teams for planning* – If we want participation to work, we should *design* teams for a purpose. In fact, we know quite a lot about the roles people can play in teams, and broadly what adds to and what detracts from the effectiveness of a team (see the next section for more details).
- *Functional interests* – If our goal is to have people in production, operations, sales, finance or other functions 'buy- in' to plans, then just maybe they would respond to being involved in the planning? There is also the point that our plan may actually be better if we include in our thinking the way all the specialist functions see the problem.
- *Discipline interests* – As well as market planners and market researchers, should we involve line managers, and should we have financial analysts or R & D experts, and so on?
- *Political mix* – Should we represent the political, influential and powerful – because they have the power and influence we need on our side if the plan is going to happen?
- *Fixers and champions* – What emphasis in team composition do we place on people who care about the problem, and people who get things done in our company?
- *Culture carriers* – How do we include, and to what extent do we include, those who know 'the way we do things here', because

that is the constraint on whether the plan gets accepted and implemented?

- *Genuine participation* – How do we achieve genuine participation in making important choices and getting things done? This is not: a token gesture towards consultation which nobody really believes in; manipulating groups of people to do what we want by rigging the agenda; getting people together in a room so that you can tell them what to do; 'management meddling' in the detail to make some participants make the 'right' decision. In some companies, this is a serious struggle which should not be underestimated.

If participation is a problematic issue in your company, then some of the points below about teams and changing the shape of the planning process may be useful.

Building effective planning teams

There is little doubt that effective teams offer enormous power to get things done. Teams are an incredible mechanism to gain advantages like:

- getting across traditional *departmental boundaries* to focus on the processes that matter – such as the process of going to market rather than marketing and operations departmental plans;
- bridging traditional *organizational boundaries* – between members of a group, between seller and buyer, between seller and distributor;
- building real *communication* links between the people who can get things done;
- developing *commitment and ownership* among the people who have to do things if our market strategy is going to become a reality;
- becoming *self-directed* and self-managed groups who drive the process.

The potential gains from the power of teams are phenomenal. Anyone who has worked in a team-based environment will also tell you about the incredible *pain* of working through and with teams!

For example, some organizations have a culture of top-down management control, and people simply are not prepared for the idea of self-directed teams making decisions for themselves. Ian

Ferguson [13] of CIGNA describes the early stages of their team-based operations as characterized by:

- *Chaos* – nothing is defined, roles are unclear, nobody knows quite what to do, people are uncomfortable, arguments and rows start;
- *Conflict* – disagreements abound, there is no consensus about how to operate;
- *False teams* – things are quicker, and it looks like you have a real team, but you don't because there is no real commitment to getting the job done, and conflict and chaos are just under the surface.

In fact, Ferguson says you probably have to go through these stages before you can get to a real team.

In some cases you really do have to recognize that simply writing down names on a sheet of paper does not create a team, just a list.

It is almost a career-damaging insult these days, but some people do not have natural aptitudes for team working – they are not 'good team players' – which is not helped by the usual lack of provision of skills training in group-based decision making. Some people are dedicated non-participants – look at the participation games listed in Table 11.1, and see if you can honestly deny that these happen!

Table 11.1 Games played in teams

The devices used by team members to avoid making any contribution:

- *The Grand Silence* – the ideal game to avoid doing anything, but difficult to sustain indefinitely.
- *The Monologue* – this involves a lengthy statement of opinion by the team leader or the facilitator. This may be brought about by the Grand Silence, or, failing this, by the '*What do you think?*' ploy. Some team leaders thoroughly enjoy this.
- *The Hobby Horse* – confused by the inexperienced with the *Monologue*, and once under way they are very similar. However, this game requires finding out what the target feels passionately about, which may involve making an effort, which is a breach of the whole spirit of game-playing.
- *I Know, But I'm Not Going to Say* – a game only for the skilful, who communicate only through raised eyebrows and facial expressions. A beginner attempting this game is likely to encounter the unpleasantness of:
- *Uproar* – noisy banter and argument, sometimes accompanied by personal accusations and threats, providing the chance to pay off old scores while still not contributing to the team's work.
- *Martyrdom* – when all else fails, then a martyr is elected for the meeting who is expected to do all the work. Successful players sometimes institutionalize this into a permanent martyr called the team secretary.

If you think this is wrong and the teams you have formed are working fine – try the diagnosis in Table 11.2, and see how the people in the teams feel about this way of working. At least this may give you a better idea of the problems that have to be solved.

Table 11.2 Diagnosing teams*

Questions for team members	True	More true than false	Neither true nor false	More false than true	False
1. We really do not know why we are a team	1	2	3	4	5
2. We are all 'too different' to work together as an effective unit	1	2	3	4	5
3. We are all good at our own jobs, but we do not know how to use them to help the team.	1	2	3	4	5
4. Our meetings are endless, ineffective and dominated by a few people	1	2	3	4	5
5. Trying to reach consensus is impossible – we cannot agree on anything important	1	2	3	4	5
6. The frequent friction among some team members is affecting the rest of us	1	2	3	4	5
7. We are not skilled at managing ourselves as a team – attempts at constructive criticisms usually end up in hurt feelings	1	2	3	4	5
8. We feel isolated from other departments and the rest of the organization	1	2	3	4	5
9. Our team really does not get much done	1	2	3	4	5

* Source: Adapted from Kuehn, Bill (1996), *Nine Traits of Highly Successful Teams*, CareerTrack International

Carelessly constructed teams can be a nightmare for all concerned – a clash of personalities and value systems can be wholly counter-productive. Sal Divita [14] advises watching for the following characteristics of team members as a guide to whether the team will work:

- *Bullies* – whose main satisfaction comes from putting the others down;
- *Challengers* – only interested in what is in it for them;
- *In-Betweeners* – unable to take a position on anything;
- *Traditionalists* – committed to maintaining the status quo;
- *Synthesizers* - driven by the need to make continuous and constant improvements in things.

The dominant values and personalities then predict what will happen: Traditionalists will produce a plan not much different to the present situation; Challengers will produce a positive plan as long as there is something in it for themselves; In-Betweeners will produce a plan reflecting what they believe management prefers; and Synthesizers will come up with a giant leap forward that no-one else in the company is likely to accept [14]. None of these are likely to be the outcomes we want.

The way through this seems to be how well we design teams (see below) and how well we support them (next section).

Designing teams

'If we want participation to work we should design teams for a purpose'

If we want participation to work we should design teams for a purpose. In fact, we know quite a lot about the roles people can play in teams, and broadly what adds to and what detracts from the effectiveness of a team.

What we can try to do is get to the creativity in any group of people, by focusing on the different contributions we want from different team members, and what we want a team leader to do. We need to recognize not just *task roles* (expertise to get the job done, to provide the purpose), but also *maintenance roles* (keeping the group cohesive, to provide the basis of co-operation). The task roles we need may include: *the Initiator* – starts things off, possibly the team leader; *the Clarifier* – interprets and gets things specific; the *Information Provider* – gives expertise, research or knowledge; *the Questioner* – confronts the basic issues for the group; and *the Summarizer* – pulls things together for the group. On the other hand, *maintenance roles* may include: *the Supporter* – gives emotional support to contributors; *the Joker* – provides humour, light relief, release of tension; the *Experience Sharer* – uses personal feelings, experiences to open things up; and the *Process Observer* – stands back and helps free up blockages in progress. We need to recognize the importance of both types of role, and we can look at our planning teams in this light.

Identifying these roles suggests the analytical framework in Figure 11.4. This identifies the scenarios of:

- *Full Team* – a good balance of task roles to get the work done and maintenance roles to keep the group together;
- *Ineffective Team* – dominated by maintenance roles; everyone has a wonderful time, but they do not get the job done;
- *Non-Cohesive Team* – dominated by task expertise, but with no social fabric to hold the group together as a working unit;
- *No Team At All* – a group with no relevant task roles and little cohesion, which is likely to produce no results and turn people off.

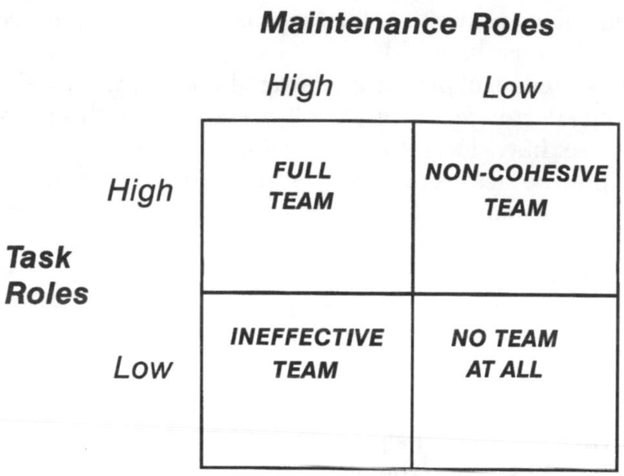

Maintenance Roles

	High	Low
High	FULL TEAM	NON-COHESIVE TEAM
Low	INEFFECTIVE TEAM	NO TEAM AT ALL

Task Roles

Figure 11.4 Balancing roles in team design

The classic research of Dr R. Meredith Belbin [15] tells us more about the characteristics of unsuccessful teams. It is not that they have poor morale or lack of conflict, but unsuccessful teams: lack 'clever' people; parallel the shortcomings of the corporate culture from which they are drawn; have ineffective combinations of roles; have team-role clashes, overlaps or voids; and allocate manpower to roles badly. The Belbin work suggests that successful teams have the following characteristics: (a) team members can make two types of contribution: technical or professional expertise *and* by taking a team role; (b) each team needs a balance of functional roles and team roles, the ideal mix depending on the team's goals and tasks; (c) team effectiveness is greater when members recognize and adjust to the relative strengths in the group, both in technical expertise and ability to engage in specific team roles; (d) personal qualities fit members for some team roles better than others; and (e) a team can use its technical abilities to the best only when it has the needed range of team roles to enhance efficient teamwork.

However, this leaves the question of how we can support and manage teams to achieve results.

Facilitate the process

If planning involves participation and cross-functional teams and line managers from different disciplines, we can probably do better than just telling them to get on with it, and when can we see that plan, please? (A fair approximation of some company practice, it must be said.)

If the outcome of planning matters to us, we will need to invest time and effort in *facilitating* the process. Indeed, this is one of the things we have learnt from Business Process Re-engineering programmes – teams of managers need help to get things done.

CIGNA Employee Benefits is an example of a remarkable company turnaround based on a team-based approach to management of customer service. Ian Ferguson of CIGNA talks about what they had to learn in that company about the skills and processes of facilitating teams [16]. He discusses facilitation skills as:

- *Directing the team* – helping a team to accomplish specific tasks to reach goals, but knowing that the amount of direction has to be varied and must not challenge the team's ownership of the process and its outcomes;
- *Supporting the team* – building an environment where people can speak their minds and take appropriate risks, because they are confident they will be listened to;
- *Managing differences* – building the ability for the team to deal effectively with disputes and disagreements;
- *Role modelling* – providing an example of how to behave in teamwork – being open, listening and being listened to. Ferguson calls good facilitation 'the art of nudging' [16].

CIGNA invested heavily in building process facilitation skills in consensus decision making and handling difficult team members; and coaching facilitators as well as the cross-functional teams.

Whether facilitation involves re-skilling people inside the company or using outside support, the experience of those companies which built participative team-based processes that work is that you just have to invest in providing facilitation.

Be illogical, turn planning upside-down and inside-out*

We can improve the management of the planning process – we can challenge assumptions, we can 'chunk', and we can manage participation and team-based working – but what can we do about the process itself?

---

* This section draws heavily on an article by William Giles and myself [17], and again William takes credit for much of the originality.

The 'logical' sequence of planning

We looked at a conventional sequence of the activities adopted in planning in Figure 7.1. The underlying logic is one of sound, quantified mission and goal definition, followed by appraisal of capabilities and environments, leading to the setting of marketing objectives and the choice of market strategies and tactics. Our problem is that it seems that many conventional writers and consultants on planning actually believe that real planning follows such an orderly and rational sequence of goal-setting, analysis and decision making.

Indeed, the apparent rationality of such structures cannot be denied. What could be more seductively reasonable than to decide what we want to achieve *before* deciding what we are going to do? In spite of this logic, we wish to suggest that this is a model of a strategic or marketing *plan*, not a planning *process* – quite simply, it focuses on what we want to produce and not *how* we produce it. It does not adequately or validly represent the human and organizational realities that we and others have experienced in the practice of planning.

An alternative model of the strategic planning process

An 'illogical' view of the planning process, which differs from the rational, sequential model in a number of important respects, is shown in Figure 11.5.

This model has been created and reinforced by working with many groups of managers facing the prospect of producing strategic plans for their businesses.

For example, at the start of a planning exercise with a financial services company, the view expressed by one senior manager was: 'We know right *now* what needs to be done . . . So, why don't we write the plan now, in five minutes, and we can have some great lunches instead of planning meetings for the next six months!' This offer was extremely tempting, but was rejected (honestly, it was). However, reflection suggested that the manager actually had a good point – that group of line managers *did* have an extensive agenda of tactical issues to be resolved to make their business more effective, and, what is more, those tactical issues had very real implications for what strategies could sensibly be laid down for the business. The seeds of the approach described in our 'illogical' model lie in a variety of such experiences with managers. It must be said that apart from anything else, with a truculent group of senior managers like these, there was really no other way to proceed anyway!

This process of building a 'pencil sketch' of the marketing plan based on 'known' realities and constraints, which can then be

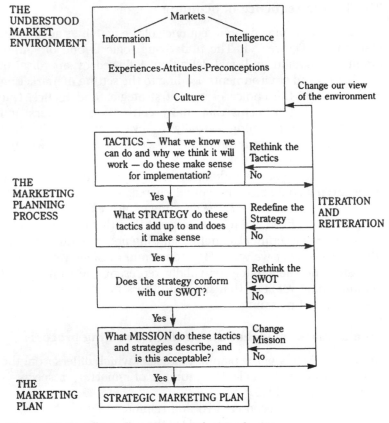

Figure 11.5 'Illogical' strategic marketing planning

tested and refined and rewritten, has since been encapsulated in the 'Marlow Method' of structured iterative planning by William Giles[18], which is described by him elsewhere. But let's unpack this model a bit more and see just how 'illogical' it really is.

The 'understood environment'

'we take the current understanding of the environment held by a company as a fundamental shaping force on managers' perceptions of the market'

First, we take the current understanding of the environment held by a company as a fundamental shaping force on managers' perceptions of the market and what actions are possible and potentially effective. The suggestion here is that information and intelligence from the market environment is 'understood' through a filter constructed from past experiences, attitudes and predispositions, and the culture which tells managers what to give attention to and what to ignore. This perception of the world is highly imperfect, subjective and biased, but represents *reality* to the people concerned. It is impossible to ignore or avoid this influence on executives' perceptions, and we take it as implicitly the initial base-point in planning.

The conventional model carries the inherent risk that it will force managers unwittingly to freeze their most critical, and probably their weakest, assumptions as 'tablets of stone' in order to proceed 'logically' through the process. Our view is that this is something to be avoided at all costs, since it removes any possibility of new strategic insights being generated – see our discussion of market sensing (pp. 38–96 above).

The 'understood environment' almost inevitably is associated by managers with a host of tactical proposals based on both current policies and known inadequacies of current implementation of marketing and business strategies. This set of practical ideas about what needs doing in the marketplace tends then to be structured into a set of strategies through a process of rationalization. These tactics-driven strategies can then be tested against the traditional SWOT analysis and fixed to some concept of a market mission which can then be tested in turn against managerial aspirations.

Iteration and planning

Clearly the success of the 'illogical' model depends almost wholly on the existence of a process of *iteration* in planning, as shown in Figure 11.5. It is vital that planners move backwards and forwards in the planning system, to test the implications of each new analysis or piece of information on analyses already completed, and to consider their importance for what has yet to be done. Without the painful 'crawling-over' the data and the interpretation, the approach we discuss will founder. We suspect this is actually true of *all* approaches to planning anyway, but it is particularly the case with what we describe here.

Planning and information

We should recognize yet again the interdependence of planning and information, or 'market sensing', as we have called it. By starting with the 'known environment' and issues of tactics and implementation familiar and urgent for managers, it is possible to *manage* a process of incremental discovery of new insights and new views of the world. We suggest this to be a more effective route to incrementally changing the 'dominant reality' or organizational 'mind-set' than swamping executives with new information which they cannot process and which is likely to be avoided (since acceptance would be too great a challenge to the individual's understanding of how the business works).

Behavioural planning constraints

We discussed earlier the emergence of behavioural planning problems (see pp. 439–40). The effect of such factors may be at least partially reduced by allowing planners to focus on what is familiar and relatively certain, and allowing *them* to 'drive' the planning process rather than having it imposed on them. Given the reality of how managers actually do their jobs, there are advantages in starting with the detail of implementation and tactics to gain commitment and involvement, and working back from this to the development of strategic directions.

Planning horizons and continuity

One of the risks of 'rational' strategic planning is that it separates strategy from running the business. Strategic planning is seen as an unavoidable burden imposed on managers, which is merely an irrelevant distraction from the real job of running the business. We suggest that starting with the problem and opportunities which are closer to the day-to-day managerial reality offers a greater chance of integrating tactics with strategy, and ultimately strategy with tactics.

Planning and change

Strategic planning means change in organizations in order to implement the strategies adopted. It is broadly recognized that change of this kind is likely to meet with resistance – some quite above-board, and some hidden in the culture and the power structure of the organization. Getting a reasonable 'fit' between strategies and cultures is widely recognized as essential to gaining successful implementation.

Our view has become that a planning process which achieves internal consistency, support from internal coalitions, resourcing from management and commitment at the delivery level is frequently as effective as we can expect any planning process to be. In particular, we see this as having advantages over conventional, outward-looking, mission-oriented planning which formulates strategies that the company is not capable of putting into effect.

This is, incidentally, quite different from what some call 'bottom-up' planning. There we just give the whole problem to line managers and ask them to solve it for us.

Another step forward?

One step we can make towards our goal of market-led strategic change is just to challenge the pervasive conventional sequential model of strategic planning. A structured, but iterative, planning process of the type described in Figure 11.5 may offer substantial advantages.

The issues for the manager to consider include the following:

- Understand what is really happening in the construction of your marketing plans. In particular, is the process conventional or environment- or tactics-driven?
- Consider the 'understood environment' that planners adopt and its implications for strategies produced.
- Examine the information demanded and used by planners, and how this impacts on the strategies and plans produced.
- Evaluate the behavioural planning problems in your planning process, and the degree to which the process you use makes these worse.
- Study the link between your strategic plans and how the business operation is managed day-to-day. Can the process be changed to improve this integration?
- Look at how strategic planning is impacting on the culture of your organization. Can the planning process be managed so as to avoid conflict but achieve incremental changes in culture?

The real issue to be confronted here is not one of increasingly sophisticated planning models and techniques, nor is it about the more rigorous 'policing' of formal planning systems. The issue is one of facing up to the realities of how executives work and think about their business and taking this as the entry-point to strategic planning. Diagnostic 4 (Figure 11.6), may help in homing-in on these issues in your own organization.

Make implementation strategic

We will not go into detail here, because implementation strategy is the topic of Chapter 14. However, for the moment, note that implementation rates a chapter of its own for two significant reasons.

Company:	Completed by:

The part of Marketing Planning on which we are focusing:

QUESTIONS ABOUT YOUR MARKETING PLANNING

	Completely False	More False Than True	More True Than False	Completely True
1. We produce a *written* Marketing Plan	1	2	3	4
2. Our Marketing Plan is produced *annually*	1	2	3	4
3. Our Marketing Planning activity is part of the *formal* planning system in the company	1	2	3	4
4. Our Marketing Plan starts with written *objectives*	1	2	3	4
5. Our Marketing Planning involves an *audit* of the company's strengths and weaknesses	1	2	3	4
6. Our Marketing Planning involves an *audit* of the opportunities and threats we face in the environment	1	2	3	4
7. Our Marketing Plan covers *three to five years*, not just the next 12 months	1	2	3	4
8. Our Marketing Plan includes the plan for *all elements* of marketing i.e. products, prices, distribution and communications; operations and sourcing; and personnel and financing requirements	1	2	3	4
9. Our Marketing Plan includes far more than just sales targets and cost budgets	1	2	3	4
10. Our Marketing Plan includes *financial* estimates (revenue, cost, and profits) of the outcomes of our strategies	1	2	3	4
11. Our Marketing Plan is presented to *top management*	1	2	3	4

Figure 11.6 Diagnostic Worksheet 4 – Evaluating our marketing planning process

	Completely False	More False Than True	More True Than False	Completely True
12. Our Marketing Plan involves substantial inputs from *other functional departments* — finance, production, personnel, etc.	1	2	3	4
13. Our Marketing Planning involves *all senior managers* in our marketing/sales organization	1	2	3	4
14. Our Marketing Planning uses *experience and knowledge* from all levels and parts of the organization	1	2	3	4
15. We give Marketing Planning *adequate time and resources*	1	2	3	4
16. Good management performance in Marketing Planning earns the same *rewards* as good operational performance	1	2	3	4
17. Marketing Planning is certainly not seen by managers as a *meaningless ritual*	1	2	3	4
18. In our Marketing Planning managers are rarely uncomfortable or ineffective in thinking and planning about the long-term future	1	2	3	4
19. It would be unusual for our Marketing Planning to become just a *struggle for resources* — budget, head-count, and so on	1	2	3	4
20. Managers are *committed* to Marketing Planning and could not be said to just 'go through the motions'	1	2	3	4
21. Our Marketing Plan details *responsibilities* and the *timing* of actions to be taken	1	2	3	4
22. Our Marketing Plan is the basis for the *allocation of resources* throughout the period it covers	1	2	3	4
23. Our Marketing Plan provides the basis for *evaluation and control*	1	2	3	4
24. Our Marketing Plan could never be said to just *sit on the shelf* — unloved and unread — because it is constantly in use	1	2	3	4
25. Our Marketing Plan is seen as one of the *most valuable documents* we have in the company	1	2	3	4

Figure 11.6   Continued

MARKETING PLANNING PROFILE

1. Written plan	1	2	3	4	FORMALIZATION OF
2. Annual plan	1	2	3	4	MARKETING PLANNING
3. Formal	1	2	3	4	IN THE COMPANY
4. Objectives	1	2	3	4	
5. Internal audit	1	2	3	4	FULLNESS OF
6. External audit	1	2	3	4	MARKETING PLANNING
7. Long-term	1	2	3	4	
8. Integrated plans	1	2	3	4	
9. More than budget	1	2	3	4	
10. Financial plans	1	2	3	4	
11. Top management	1	2	3	4	MANAGEMENT
12. Departments	1	2	3	4	INVOLVEMENT IN
13. Senior Management	1	2	3	4	MARKETING PLANNING
14. Participation	1	2	3	4	MARKETING PLANNING
15. Resourcing planning	1	2	3	4	THOROUGHNESS
16. Planning rewarded	1	2	3	4	
17. Planning recalcitrance	1	2	3	4	BEHAVIOURAL
18. Fear of uncertainty	1	2	3	4	PLANNING PROBLEMS
19. Political interests	1	2	3	4	
20. Planning avoidance	1	2	3	4	
21. Responsibilities	1	2	3	4	USE OF THE
22. Resources	1	2	3	4	MARKETING PLAN
23. Control	1	2	3	4	
24. Used	1	2	3	4	
25. Useful	1	2	3	4	

Conclusions/Implications/Actions:

Figure 11.6 Continued

First, implementation is not something different, it is not what we send the troops away to do when we have done the clever strategic bit for them. Implementation *is* strategy. Any plan which does not spell out in realistic detail precisely how the strategy is going to be implemented should be returned to sender. It is as simple as that.

One step we can take therefore is to make it clear to all concerned that we expect market strategies to be directly connected to an implementation strategy, or we will not even look at them.

Secondly, it is no use looking at implementation as some kind of bolt-on accessory that we consider after the main part of the plan has been written. Implementation is *reality*.

Implementation problems, costs and opportunities should be part of our earliest thinking, because they tell us which market strategies are worth working up for the plan, and which are no-hopers (however much market research and clever analysis we do) because they cannot be *done*.

Another step forward we can take is to insist that implementation issues are considered in the planning, not after the plan is written, when people are committed to the plan. If we are serious about making plans happen, we need to think about how we get the support and commitment we need from the people who actually run the business from top management down to the point of sale. Another step towards our goal may be to incorporate an internal marketing plan into our conventional external planning.

Make 'ownership' the top priority

We have argued throughout that what matters at the end of the day is whether our planning produces the 'ownership' and with people's commitment to make the plan happen. These are fragile and intangible issues.

At least one step forward would be to make it clear to all planning teams that while we will obviously look at their figures and projections, their strategies and tactics, we will also demand, as a prerequisite for accepting any plan, evidence that there is a champion who is determined to make it happen.

'we will also demand, as a prerequisite for accepting any plan, evidence that there is a champion who is determined to make it happen'

People have funny ideas about 'ownership' and commitment. Some time ago I was in a meeting with senior management from an engineering company concerning a project they wanted us to do with one of the company's subsidiaries. My view, which I stated openly, was that unless a key player in the subsidiary was keen enough on the project, and had enough commitment to it, and would take 'ownership' of the problem of making it work, then we were all wasting our time. Their response was: 'Well, we'll *tell* them to do it!' I said: 'You will *tell* them to be committed?' and they said: 'Yes!' As they say, I made my excuses and left.

The point of the story is that you cannot demand and legislate for commitment, you cannot police it. You *can* work for it, and hope to unleash its potential.

The silly thing is that we all 'know' a lot about commitment, because we have all read the books and gone on the training courses about it. We all agree that the chances of gaining commitment improve as we move up the spectrum of management action in the following way:

- *Education*
- Two-way *communication*
- *Participative* decision making
- *Support* in the face of barriers
- *Negotiating* and bargaining
- *Manipulation*
- *Coercion*

We all agree that education, communication and participation achieve long-term commitment to our goals, while manipulation and coercion do not. We all feel good about this. Then we go back to the office and we *tell* the people what to do, and if they don't do it, then we fix the bastards. We 'get' them through evaluation or reward systems. Alternatively, we create company 'policies'. I have long since come to define company 'policies' as the rules and regulations we create to police the 3 per cent of our employees who work badly (and who don't change what they do because of 'policies'), at the cost of upsetting the 97 per cent of the people who were working properly in the first place (and may not be any more). Coercion and manipulation are easier, faster and it is what we know best. The trouble is, it doesn't work.

So, when we look at a plan, let's ask some questions about enthusiasm, fun, pride, irrational emotional faith, belief, idiosyncratic determination, stubborn support, bloody-mindedness, commitment and 'ownership', as a prerequisite. What is more, let's behave and act as though these things matter too, and that we value 'ownership' as equal to, or even above, sophistication in planning.

Perhaps the neatest way of putting this issue in a nutshell comes from ever-succinct William Giles:

'If it was possible for an entire organisation to sing the same song from the same song sheet and face in the same direction at the same time it would be a powerful force. If that song was good, the direction true, and the timing right, it would be a very serious threat to competitors' [19].

What sort of planning have we got?

The main point made in this chapter is that the way we manage our planning process is one of the most powerful sources of leverage we have in market-led strategic change. We have highlighted the real management agenda in managing the planning process, and looked at a set of tools we can use to work on that agenda. However, before we start on this path, we should try to find out where we are at the moment in terms of how our marketing planning works. This is the purpose of Diagnostic 4.

Goals of Diagnostic 4

The overall aim of this diagnostic is to evaluate a number of key elements of our planning, to give us a view of where we should start and where we can start in putting a handle on the problem of managing the process to achieve the things we want – plans which focus on the customer, and people who are committed and 'own' the task of making the plan happen.

More specifically, the diagnostic asks us 25 questions about our marketing planning, to get to grips with the following issues:

- The *formalization* of our planning, in terms of whether we have written plans produced annually as part of the company's formal planning system, giving us clear written objectives (Questions 1 to 4);
- The *fullness* of our planning, in terms of what our analysis covers, the length of the planning period and the incorporation of strategies, programmes and financial analysis (Questions 5 to 10);
- The *management involvement* in planning, reflecting feedback and input from top management, other functional areas and senior marketing/sales managers (Questions 11 to 13);
- The *thoroughness* of our planning, in terms of taking expertise and knowledge from throughout the company (i.e. genuine participation) and resourcing and rewarding planning work (Questions 14 to 16);

- The avoidance of *behavioural planning problems*, which we summarized earlier as planning recalcitrance, fear of uncertainty, political interests and planning avoidance (Questions 17 to 20);
- The *use* of the marketing plan, in terms of assigning responsibilities, allocating resources, evaluation and control, active use and credibility (Questions 21 to 25).

Instructions for completing Diagnostic 4

As always, the aim is to keep the exercise as simple and unambiguous as possible – what matters is the results and our interpretation of them. This diagnostic is largely self-explanatory, but the following should make the logic clear.

Company

We may want to do this separately for different parts of our organization, so specify which you are going to focus on here.

Completed by

This needs further comment, but here we just specify whose views are represented. For the moment, let us assume we do it ourselves.

The part of planning on which we are focusing

In some organizations there may be several levels to planning – corporate, divisional, operating unit, and so on. We should specify which of these we are looking at. In other organizations, marketing planning (as we have described it here) may go by another name (Business Plan, Business Development Plan, Strategic Plan, Sales Promotion Plan, or whatever). If so, we should be clear about which part of our company's planning we are examining.

The questions

The diagnostic asks us to consider 25 short statements about planning and to decide how true each statement is about our planning. For this we use a simple 4-point scale running from 'Completely False' to 'Completely True'.

Planning profile

When all the statements have been scored, we then take the scores forward and enter them on the profile. The profile is completed by joining up the scores with a continuous downward line. This gives us a picture of the main attributes of our planning process.

Conclusions/Implications

Our interpretation of the picture built up should lead to specific conclusions and implications, and the identification of actions needed.

Using Diagnostic 4

Now we can turn to the really interesting questions: who should complete the diagnostic, and how should we interpret the findings?

Who completes the diagnostic?

There are a number of options here which should be considered.

- The profile provides us with a framework for summarizing *our* views of how well our planning process stands up to the challenges posed in this chapter. This is interesting, may help in deciding where we start in revitalizing our planning, and provides a benchmark. We can, however, make it a lot more revealing.
- We can ask our *Chief Executive* to complete the diagnostic, and we can ask the *other departments*, and see how our benchmark stands up to what they think our planning is doing for the company – and what they think it should be doing.
- Most fun of all, however, is to ask our own people – the *managers and executives* who play some role in the planning process, and who are expected to take some notice of what the plan says. Now *that* may bring us down to earth with a bump!

A couple of years ago I was asked to spend a day running a workshop on planning for a particular company. The participants were the Business Development Director (who had formal responsibility for their version of market planning) and his line and regional managers (who had to do the planning and use the plan). As it happened, I gave them an earlier version of Diagnostic 4, as an example of the type of issue they might want to look at in developing their planning system. The Director said: 'We'll fill it in now!' I suggested that this was not the best idea in the world, but he insisted. He was the client. So we all filled it in. The Director's response was a model of its kind. He told us that just about everything was perfect in their market planning – it was completely formalized and integrated, with all available analysis being incorporated, it was the top priority for all senior managers, totally participative, and produced the single most valuable document that ever existed in the company. Well, perhaps he was right. However, this was not what his line managers said. We spent the rest of the day confronting the differences between the Director's view of how planning worked in the company and the rather different perceptions of the line executives who had to do the real planning and put the plans into action. The day was bloody, but effective in getting to the real problems.

This diagnostic works quite well in isolating these differences in the perceptions of planning inside the company. Experience suggests, however, the need for a little sensitivity in how we use it!

Interpreting the findings

'Where are the most serious gaps in our planning process as we have now profiled it?'

If we use this diagnostic seriously and rigorously, then it can help us to home in on the following issues, to see where we need to start in getting to grips with managing the planning process.

- Where are the most serious *gaps* in our planning process as we have now profiled it? Do these relate to the techniques or methods we use (in formalization and fullness)? Do they really relate to the signals the organization sends that tell managers the real attitudes to planning (management involvement and planning 'thoroughness')? Or is the underlying problem the attitude of the manager involved in the planning process (behavioural problems)? Perhaps the real test of how seriously things are going wrong is whether the plan is ever actually used in running the business (use of the marketing plan).
- We should compare the profile of our planning to our earlier analysis to see if we can now find better insights into the problems we identified here, and if working on the planning process offers us a new way of solving the problems we found earlier. If we are not taking the *customer satisfaction* issue

seriously (Diagnostic 1), can we address this by incorporating it into the issues we address in the planning process (e.g. through customer-oriented SWOT analysis)? If our problem is getting to strategize rather than run the day-to-day business and to address the real market strategy issues (Diagnostic 2), can we get to grips with this by how we manage the planning process? If we found big gaps between our *strategic intent* and the *strategic reality* (Diagnostic 3), can we do something about this by the way we manage our planning process (e.g. think about 'illogical planning' and the participation issue)? If we found that our problems in getting market strategies to happen related to our lack of formal *marketing organization* or to shortcomings in our *information* and intelligence (market sensing), are there opportunities for influencing the way things are done through the planning process – in reallocating responsibilities, confronting new intelligence, incorporating the market sensing framework as part of the process, and so on?

- We should contrast the views of other groups, particularly line management, with the benchmark provided by our own judgements, or those of the Chief Executive, because then we can home-in on the things that matter to the people who actually *do* the planning, and those we expect to *use* the plan at the end of the day.

The point of our interpretation of this diagnostic is to decide which parts of the management agenda for managing the planning process are most urgent for us, and which are most accessible to us. This leads us into asking how the problems and goals of market-led strategic change can be addressed by influencing and re-shaping the process rather than the plan.

So, where have we got to?

This is probably one of the most important chapters in the book, because it offers a route to getting some real leverage for our goal of market-led strategic change.

We started off with a reasonably conventional view of market planning process in Chapter 7. But, for reasons which should now be obvious, we restricted ourselves to the basic issues that matter rather than getting involved in complex models and techniques. The thinking is that getting the basics right is a step forward for most of us. The approach to planning offered here is operational and accessible for *any* organization.

However, the evidence is that all is not well in the practice of planning. Time and time again it goes wrong or never gets past producing simple sales budgets. If we want to unleash the potential for creating and implementing market-led strategic change in planning – then we have to manage the *process*, not just the techniques. This opens up a new management agenda recognizing the need to formalize planning and to give people the tools to do the job, but also the behavioural problems and organizational issues in managing a planning process – and trying to manage those dimensions of process compatibly and consistently with each other.

This is a rough and tough agenda. We may not be able to address the whole agenda straight away. So, we have offered a list of things you can try, based on our experiences with a variety of companies: actively *manage* the process; provide people with accessible and appropriate *tools*; don't go for holistic and integrated systems that look good – pick the problems that matter most and aim the *champions* at them; manage the *participation* issue purposefully to achieve momentum for change; *turn planning inside-out* and see if we can get some *real* involvement from the people who actually run the business; build *effective teams* and *facilitate* the team-based process; make the *implementation* a strategic issue, not something we worry about after we have got the marketing plan in place; and look for '*ownership*' and commitment in plans, not just rational logic, and make people believe that this is the top priority.

That is not a nice neat package, but they are all things that have proved their worth in the real world – i.e. they *can* work in the right hands.

Finally, to get us started we looked at Diagnostic 4 as a way of focusing on the deficiencies of our own current planning process. This tells us where to start and which tools to use first.

Now, let's talk about whether we can get the resources to do the things that matter to our customers.

References

1. Greenley, Gordon (1983), 'Where Marketing Planning Fails', *Long Range Planning*, Vol. 16, No. 1, 106–115.
2. Greenley, Gordon (1988), 'Managerial Perceptions of Marketing Planning', *Journal of Management Studies*, Vol. 25, No. 6, 575–601.
3. McDonald, Malcolm (1994), *Marketing Plans*, London: Heinemann.
4. Verhage, Branislaw and Eric Waarts (1988), 'Marketing Planning for Improved Performance: A Comparative Analysis', *International Marketing Review*, Summer, 20–30.

5. Piercy, Nigel and Neil Morgan (1994), 'The Marketing Planning Process: Behavioral Problems Compared to Analytical Techniques in Explaining Marketing Planning Credibility', *Journal of Business Research*, Vol. 29, 167–178.
6. Giles, William (1990), *Making Strategy Work*, Marlow, Bucks: Strategic Marketing Development Unit.
7. Peters, Tom and Nancy Austin (1986), *Passion for Excellence*, New York: Harper and Row.
8. Drucker, Peter F. (1979), *Adventures of a Bystander*, New York: Harper and Row.
9. Kanter, Rosabeth Moss (1983), *The Change Masters – Corporate Entrepreneurs At Work*, London: Unwin.
10. Sathe, Vijay (1988), *Culture and Related Corporate Realities*, Homewood, Illinois: Irwin.
11. Peters, Tom and Nancy Austin (1986), *op. cit.*
12. Bonoma, Tom (1986), 'Marketing Subversives', *Harvard Business Review*, November/December, 113–118.
13. Ferguson, Ian (1994), 'Re-engineering from Top to Bottom', *Banking and Financial Training*, March, 7–12.
14. Divita, Sal (1996), 'Being a Team Player Is Essential To Your Career', *Marketing News*, 9 September.
15. Belbin, R. Meredith (1981), *Management Teams – Why They Succeed or Fail*, London: Heinemann.
16. Ferguson, Ian (1994), *op. cit.*
17. Piercy, Nigel and William Giles (1989), 'The Logic of Being Illogical in Strategic Marketing Planning', *Journal of Marketing Management*, Vol. 5, No. 1, 19–31.
18. Giles, William (1988), 'Marketing Planning for Maximum Growth', in M. J. Thomas (ed.), *The Marketing Handbook*, Aldershot: Gower.
19. Giles, William (1990), *Marketing Kinetics*, Marlow: Strategic Marketing Development Unit.

CHAPTER 12

Budgeting for marketing:

How do we *resource* marketing to make it happen?

Introduction

In the previous chapter we dealt with planning market strategies and marketing programmes as a *process* – one which we can manage to create and reinforce market-led strategic change. There is a second area of process that we have to consider, which is directly linked to planning. This is the process of *budgeting*, or *resource allocation* for marketing.

Now if you look at the conventional textbook on marketing, you will find that budgeting is treated as a very minor issue – a technical exercise of computation to calculate the optimum marketing spend. This is fairly tedious stuff, and accordingly we delegate it and computerize it at the first opportunity. This is not a strategic question.

Well, if you talk to marketing executives about budgeting and resource allocation, they normally have a somewhat different view. They talk about issues like these:

- The *'hassle factor'* – the sheer difficulty and inordinate amount of time it takes to get resources, in terms of the papers to be written, the committees to be attended, the bargaining to be done, to get even minor amounts of resource;

'the sheer difficulty and inordinate amount of time it takes to get resources'

- The absolute *refusal* of some organizations to provide resources for anything called 'marketing', let alone something like 'the process of going to market' (yes, I do mean it, even in this day and age);
- The *conflict* over marketing expenditure with accountants and general management;
- The *lack of control* by marketing executives over resource allocation and actually spending the money;
- The *struggle for jurisdiction* over marketing expenditures;
- The dead-weight of *historical views* over how much should be spent on marketing;
- The imposition of *rigid control measures* that link marketing spend to sales, with the interesting effect that when times get hard and we lose sales and market share, we automatically spend *less* on marketing at precisely that moment when we need to spend *more*;
- The pressure to prove the value of marketing to meet the criterion of *accountability*, which grew up in the recession of the early 1990s;
- The growth of a corporate ethos of being lean, downsizing and '*doing more for less*';
- As the process of going to market becomes a *pan-company responsibility*, the strength of the marketing budget centre diminishes and responsibility for expenditure becomes unclear;
- *Outside interests* drive the company's expenditure in marketing, instead of the market strategy – distributors dictate margins and demand co-marketing deals; suppliers demand partnership and influence over marketing resource use; collaboration strategies eat into marketing resources for internal co-ordination needs.

This is just a little different to the neat set of budgeting techniques that we are given by the textbook, but this is the reality that our marketing executives experience. Now, let's talk about marketing budgeting for real! But there are a couple of basic points to be made before we get started.

Planning and budgeting

There can surely be few things more futile and damaging than to get people excited about new plans and innovative market strategies, and then to refuse to resource these plans and strategies.

No – that does *not* mean we expect everything that the marketing department wants to be resourced without question. All we are asking is that the ground rules are clear from the start, and that they are applied consistently.

I will admit that budgeting is one of the things that I am prepared to get nasty about. My advice to those who produce market strategy proposals and plans now is to include contingencies. What this means is that when you go to top management and show them all the great things they can have (sales, market share, customer satisfaction, profit), which is what they said they wanted, and then you show them what it will cost – the two things are *directly* and *explicitly* linked. We have to deliver the message – you cannot have the bag of sweeties without paying the penny (sorry, but life is like that). If you only want to pay a halfpenny, then you get half the sweeties (or perhaps less).

It sounds silly, but expecting market strategy to happen without resourcing it is not very smart. However, if you stand back and look at what happens in companies, all too often this seems to be exactly what management expects. Sometimes it seems to work too – real champions for the customer cause may well make it happen regardless. This said, if a company does not have a 'marketing budget', will not resource the market strategies it has asked for, and generally makes life difficult on resources – this is a pretty clear signal about real attitudes towards the marketing process and ultimately towards customers.

Budgeting is not boring

Far from being the province of accountants, counting the beans, and producing, with the precision and exactness for which their profession is well-known, statements of variance against budgets and sales targets, budgeting is about something of critical importance – how do we get the resources we need to get our act together and then to go away and do the things that matter to customers? Put like this, budgeting is an issue of strategic importance, of considerable relevance to whether we make market-led strategic change happen, and one where we also need to get our act together. It is not about mechanical bean-counting.

It is also true that the expenditure on activities like advertising and sales promotion can be headline news for larger companies – attracting both City attention and the trade press to alert competitors to what we are doing.

For example, in the USA, transparency and disclosure means that newspapers like *USA Today* publish 'Pitch and Profit' figures detailing marketing costs and profits across the whole range of consumer-packaged grocery products. Even the consumer knows what companies are making on a box of cereal or a can of soft drink. (And with the profit and marketing cost accounting for 69.6 per cent of a soft drink and 69.3 per cent of a pack of breakfast cereal, there is consequently much public pressure for price reductions [1].)

The UK has not quite reached that stage yet, but the days when marketing expenditures were 'confidential' are rapidly disappearing.

What is the marketing budget?

This is a very easy question to answer in some companies, because there is *no* marketing budget. This in itself is also a very clear signal about a company's real priorities and attitudes towards customers.

Strictly speaking, the term 'marketing budget' should refer to all the direct and overhead costs associated with the marketing function in a company – or, in the 're-engineered' company, the costs of the process of going to market. The marketing budget in companies seldom means this.

The problem is that accountants face considerable technical difficulties in allocating 'marketing' costs to products anyway, and frequently do not bother – in effect, they treat marketing as a type of overhead expense. This is related to the philosophy of cutting marketing expenditure when sales go down – along with the other 'overheads', like the canteen, secretarial support, maintenance and a few other non-essentials, like training. This leads to the next problem as well.

In any case, we have seen that 'marketing' itself means very different things in different companies. Normally we would not expect to be held responsible for things we do not control, so if we have no control over order processing, or transport, or even things like selling costs and distributor commission, then we would not normally expect to have budgetary control for these items exerted over us. Even accountants agree to this principle.

In fact, there is some evidence of exactly the reverse happening in some companies – the marketing budget is made up of costs over which the marketing department has little or no jurisdiction.

'the marketing budget is made up of costs over which the marketing department has little or no jurisdiction'

For instance, in one industrial chemicals company the newly-appointed Marketing Director faced a major barrier in obtaining even modest sums for the new promotional campaigns which were central to his plans. On the face of things, the company's view seemed hardly surprising – the marketing budget already accounted for some 5 per cent of sales, which is high for an industrial company. However, the reality was that more than 95 per cent of that budget consisted of two items: commission paid to distributors, and the costs of the order processing office. Distributor commission rates were set by the Finance Director, and order processing is a fixed cost of being in the business. The accounts showed a massive marketing budget which was unlikely to be increased, while the discretionary spending open to the Marketing Director was close to zero.

Incidentally, this type of situation is not restricted to the unsophisticated company. One of the interesting observations of the blue-chip fast-moving consumer goods is that, where marketing and advertising expenditure is truly massive, marketing executives may have the least *real* control over the size of the spend or its allocation between products and markets. In these companies it seems that because marketing expenditure is *so* large, and *so* visible, marketing budgeting is an issue for the Board, not the Marketing Department.

However, in the present setting, we are most interested in the control of the level of marketing expenditure, rather than the accounting system and its peculiarities. For our present purposes, the 'marketing budget' refers to those items of expenditure and other resources that we need the company to commit in order to implement our plans and strategies. Issues of technical accounting principles in deciding what goes in what budget can be left to one side for the moment.

It should also be noted that our interest is the *resources* we need, not just financial budgets. Obviously, in many cases we need money. But the real resource backing we need may mean other things as well – people, space, computer time, management time, training and development of skills, and so on. This is the real resource issue – what we need to make market strategies and plans *happen*.

You cannot prove anything

Probably the source of most of the problems in getting resources for marketing is the fact that at the end of the day there is one critical uncertainty – we can never *prove* that particular marketing expenditures have achieved particular results, and we can never *prove* that the budget we are requesting will achieve exactly what we are predicting. We are back to the 'Black Box' called the market shown in Figure 12.1. We can measure *inputs* to the Black Box (advertising, salesperson time, promotion, discounts and so on) and we can measure *outputs* (sales, market share, cash flow, profits and the like). What we can never do in any practical way is say what inputs create what outputs or when.

'we can never **prove** *that the budget we are requesting will achieve exactly what we are predicting'*

My academic colleagues will object to this, and produce complex mathematical computerized models that analyse hundreds of years of past results and make allowances for cumulative and lagged effects, and all the rest of it. I repeat that at the practical level, when you are standing in the boardroom pitching for a marketing budget, you cannot *prove* anything. I know of no practical way around this central and critical uncertainty.

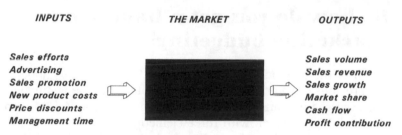

INPUTS	THE MARKET	OUTPUTS
Sales efforts		Sales volume
Advertising		Sales revenue
Sales promotion		Sales growth
New product costs		Market share
Price discounts		Cash flow
Management time		Profit contribution

Figure 12.1   The market as a black box

This remains with us whether we are trying to defend existing budgets against cost-cutting, or trying to obtain new resources to implement a new marketing strategy. You can run, but you can't hide – you cannot prove what you need:

We say . . .	They say . . .
We spent 2 per cent of sales last year and hit the target	But it was a great product and the market was growing, so you would have hit the target anyway
We need a £100K advertising spend for the new product	How do you know it won't sell anyway, and in any case that gives us a ridiculously high % of sales?

We say . . .	They say . . .
To make the plan work, we require a budget for promotion	Well, we never needed one before, and we've done OK so far
If we double the marketing spend we can increase profitability	you're not serious, are you?

and so it goes on . . .

That is why marketing budgeting is never really just the application of textbook budget-setting techniques.

So how do you get a handle on marketing budgeting?

Much of the groundwork on marketing budgeting was done in the previous chapter when we looked at planning. Budgeting is a process issue too, and the same general points apply. So this is a much shorter chapter, with three elements to it.

First, we will look briefly at the conventional view of marketing budgeting. Secondly, we will turn to the reality of how marketing budgeting processes actually operate in organizations. Thirdly, we will use these realities to see where we need to focus attention.

The conventional view of marketing budgeting

Just like planning, the *process* of marketing budgeting has three dimensions (analytical, behavioural and organizational – see pp. 435–38). Just like planning, virtually all the attention has been focused on the analytical techniques, rather than the bits of the process that matter most to results. However, let's start with a quick look at these analytical techniques.

Most experts approach this in one of two ways: either prescribing what budget-setting techniques we *should* use in marketing; or describing what techniques managers *actually* use.

Prescriptive approaches to marketing budgeting

The prescriptive wisdom of the experts offers us the following tools for setting marketing budgets.

Economic analysis

Economic theorists give us the principle of *marginality* – we should go on spending on marketing until the marginal income from the marginal unit of expenditure is equal to its cost, because until that point income exceeds expenditure, and because this is how to maximize profits. Now that is really good practical stuff that we can all take away and use!

Management science models

Econometrics offers us a wide variety of mathematical models to determine the optimum marketing and advertising spend. Some of the models available are very elegant, with complex calculations to balance many influences on effectiveness. However, as is often said, there is only one problem with management science models – managers never use them. In fact, when they do, they probably use them for the 'wrong' reasons, but we will get on to that issue shortly.

Corporate budgeting approaches

Faced with the critical uncertainty about the sales response to marketing efforts, the managerial literature offers a number of ways of trying to sort things out so we can get things done. These approaches include *programme budgeting*, *output budgeting*, and the *'objective and task'* model. Of these the most commonly prescribed (and claimed by managers to be in use) is the 'objective and task' model.

The 'objective and task' approach seems to solve the problem for us by taking away the uncertainties and organizing things logically:

- Translate corporate goals into marketing *objectives* (e.g. our corporate goal of 10 per cent growth in product sales revenue requires a 50 per cent growth in customer awareness, 20 per cent growth in trial of the product and 2 per cent growth in distribution coverage).
- Define the *tasks* required to achieve these marketing objectives (e.g. media advertising to achieve awareness, sampling to achieve product trial and trade promotions to gain distribution coverage).

- *Cost out* these tasks (how much advertising, sampling and promotion will be needed, and the expenditure required).
- The sum of these costs is the *marketing budget* for the product.
- Repeat this for each product and market in the marketing plan to get the total marketing budget.

Now that is nice and straightforward. Of course, all we have really done is build a gloss of logic and methodology to hide the real guessing about how we turn corporate goals into marketing objectives in the first place, how much we need of each marketing activity to achieve the objectives, and so on.

Strategic budgeting guidelines

In 1982 the Cahners Publishing Company published a set of marketing budgeting guidelines. These were produced by The Strategic Planning Institute using the PIMS database. Fifteen years on, those guidelines still look good, and are still way ahead of conventional corporate budgeting rules. The Cahners guidelines can be summarized:

- *Market share is important.* The higher your market share, the more you should spend to protect it. (High market share is not an excuse to reduce investment because you have 'won'.)
- *New products.* New products require higher advertising and marketing expenditure than established products. If your plan involves introducing several new products, you cannot do it with the same '% to sales' figure that keeps existing products going.
- *Growth markets.* Markets or segments growing more than 10 per cent a year will require a higher-than-average advertising and marketing spend. You cannot keep up with fast-growing markets by spending the same '% to sales' that you spend in slower growth markets.
- *Plant capacity utilisation.* If you are operating at less than 65 per cent of capacity, you should consider increasing advertising and marketing expenditure.
- *Prices.* Products with low unit prices require higher advertising and marketing support than products with high unit prices. Premium priced products and heavily discounted products should get more advertising and marketing support than products with average prices.
- *Customer spending percentage.* Products that account for less than 5 per cent of a customer's annual purchases need more advertising support than those accounting for a high percentage of the customer's purchases.

- *Quality.* Higher quality products generally require higher advertising and marketing expenditure. Quality does *not* sell itself.
- *Product lines.* Companies with broad product lines should budget more than companies with narrow product lines (there is less economy of scale).
- *Product standardization.* Standard, off-the-shelf products need higher advertising and marketing expenditure than custom, made-to-order products [2].

These principles are based on analysis of the PIMS data covering the performance of many companies. They are intuitively reasonable. Which of us could say that we follow them? Which of us does not have a Finance Director who would rubbish every one?

Judgmental budgeting models

Perhaps the last resort of those who despair of ever sorting out the budgeting issue in marketing is to lay down guidelines or go for 'me-too' budgeting. Guidelines are normally 'percentage-of-sales' ratios or 'unit rates'. 'Me-too' budgeting looks at what our competitors do – the 'pooled wisdom' approach. This is tantamount to saying that we don't know what we are doing, but we will assume our competitors do, and copy them. What is even better is that you can spend literally thousands of pounds getting the information to copy them. Logically, these guidelines are a nonsense. They do, however, simplify the problem so that we can deal with it and get on.

Sequential models

Those who like to play safe pack all these approaches together so that we do each calculation in turn and keep going until we get to a figure that we like.

There are really two objections to the prevailing wisdom about how we *should* budget for marketing. One objection is *technical* – these models do nothing to overcome the central 'Black Box' uncertainty about the marketplace, they obscure it and hide it away. In any case, they often demand information and resources we do not have. The other objection is *organizational* – anyone who believes that you set budgets and get them by plugging-in models of this kind (sophisticated and mathematical, or crude and judgemental) can surely never have participated in a real budgeting decision in a real organization and seen what really goes on?

'anyone who believes that you set budgets and get them by plugging-in models of this kind (sophisticated and mathematical, or crude and judgemental) can surely never have participated in a real budgeting decision'

Descriptive approaches to understanding marketing budgeting

We get a bit closer to the reality if we look at the somewhat sparse evidence about how budgeting actually happens and what managers tell us it is like.

Precedent

Again and again, it has been shown that the best possible predictor of this year's marketing budget is last year's marketing budget (plus or minus a bit depending on inflation and company profitability). We may not like it, but it happens to be true. (It is also not as bad as it sounds, because the alternative of 'zero-base budgeting' usually sets the scene for a massive, time-consuming, political bun-fight.)

Incrementalism

It follows that most of the management attention focuses not on total budgets, but on the changes we want to make to what is set by precedent. This means we take the £1 million as read, and fight about the extra £10,000.

Calculation models

When managers are asked directly what methods they use to set marketing budgeting, they tell us about: *rules-of-thumb*, like percentages-to-sales (last year's sales in the unsophisticated company, and next year's forecast sales in the 'state-of-the-art' sophisticated marketing company); *affordability* – we spend what we can 'afford'; maintaining a share of *industry spend*; maintaining *parity* with the competition; and the '*objective and task*' approach. What this really tells us is that people recognize that the problem of getting the 'right' budget is so complex that we cannot solve it, so we use a simplification device. We know it gives the 'wrong' answer, but we *have* to make decisions and get on with things.

Experiential

As a result of the crude budgeting techniques we use, we take a 'suck it and see' approach, i.e. try it and see what happens, then try something else.

Negotiation

Perhaps the most significant point here is that budgets are not really calculated, they are bargained and negotiated. And bargaining and negotiation is about influence and control (or the lack of those things).

The reality of the budgeting process

The conventional view of marketing budgeting is concerned with analytical techniques, varying from complex simulation models to simple 'percentage-of-sales' approaches. To be fair, these methods all have their place. But let's talk about some of the cruder realities of what it takes to get our marketing strategies resourced, and why we sometimes don't. To get started on the search for reality, consider the case of the Worldwide Computer Corporation.

Worldwide Computer Corporation

WCC is a long-established computer manufacturer based in the UK, but operating worldwide. In view of its size and the diversity of its customers, WCC is organized into a number of 'business centres', each of which is concerned with a single area of business – either a customer type, a geographic area, or a specialized product application.

One of these business centres is concerned with meeting the specialized needs of a single customer – International Tele-communications Ltd (ITL). The customer concerned is one of the largest international organizations in the world, based in the international telecommunications business. The 1985 sales turnover of this WCC business centre was £30 million representing approximately 14 per cent of the UK market (i.e. ITL's expenditure in the UK on computer products and services).

The business centre did not have any formal budget in 1985 for advertising or sales promotion, but the 'operating expenses' of the business centre amounted to approximately £1 million. This figure includes the costs of sales personnel in contact with various parts of the customer organization, in-house service personnel providing a pre- and post-sales service and advisory function, and a small amount of expenditure on sales literature and public relations events (e.g. Wimbledon tickets, golf matches, theatre outings and the like) to facilitate contacts with the customer.

The marketplace activities of the business centre were organized around sales teams, each specializing in a different computer type or set of applications. In addition, there was one executive responsible for organizing sales promotions for all the sales teams. The business centre was, in 1985, for the first time carrying out a formal market planning process, which involved the senior management team in devising a five-year plan.

The goal of the planning exercise was to develop strategies to turn the business centre into a £100 million turnover business by 1990. Although this involved more than tripling the size of the WCC business centre, this represented only 25 per cent of the estimated 1990 market at ITL (i.e. the UK spend). Although the planning gap facing the WCC managers seemed considerable, a laborious process of defining user segments in the market was carried out. This changed the picture dramatically, from one of a single customer whose need was for computers, to six user-oriented segments with different needs, which could be met by different combinations of products and services. As a consequence, it was possible to define various marketing targets for information and persuasion at a variety of locations in ITL, and to plan very distinct mixes of activities to attach each segment.

The starting point was the 1986 position, where sales to ITL were £30 million, divided between hardware (40 per cent), software (40 per cent) and services (20 per cent). The company's estimates of the gross margins, i.e. cost of goods sold before the operating expenses of the business centre (marketing costs), were: hardware 20 per cent, software 50 per cent, services 60 per cent. The new market plan involved a large increase in the personal selling effort, and sales promotion and advertising targeted in the chosen market segments. The out-turn in 1991 was estimated sales (at 1985 prices) of £100 million, divided between hardware (10 per cent), software (40 per cent) and services (50 per cent), and gross margins were assumed to be constant. However, to achieve this result required that the marketing spend should increase from £1 million in 1985 to £6 million in 1991.

The dilemma facing the business centre managers was how this budget requirement could be justified to senior management – i.e. can a sixfold increase in the marketing budget be justified to grow the business from £30 million to £100 million sales turnover, given that it increases profitability of the business centre as well?

The problem?

Now at this point some companies would be jumping up and down with excitement and building action plans. This was not the position in WCC. The business unit managers pointed to sales growth and enhanced profitability resulting from an increased marketing budget. Company management took the stand that to increase 'operating expenses' from 3 per cent of sales to 6 per cent of sales was against 'company policy', particularly since this involved increasing the expenditure sixfold. The culture of this company was adamantly opposed to such levels of marketing expenditure, regardless of the effect on growth and profitability. There is *no* rational analytical technique that resolves the issue.

The result?

Bargaining and negotiation started, but led to complete deadlock. The chief executive started the search for a buyer of the business unit – prime among the potential purchasers being ITL. When 'rational' approaches are deadlocked, the man with the power makes the decision, and it may not be the decision you wanted.

The moral?

Now let's talk about what budgeting is really about.

Real marketing budgeting processes

If you ask managers about the marketing budgeting process, you get a very different view to that in the textbook. They do not tell us about methods of calculation, they tell us bluntly about who actually *runs* budgeting in their companies. They tell us about bottom-up budgeting* and top-down budgeting.

In fact, research by the Marketing Communications Research Centre at Cranfield [3] identified a number of variations:

'If you ask managers about the marketing budgeting process, you get a very different view to that in the textbook'

---

* Personally I dislike this term. This is because many years ago I worked for a man who claimed to have been Sales Director for the launch of the first roll-on deodorant in the UK. The story is that the product was imported from the USA and marketed with the American packaging and user instructions. The product had to be withdrawn from the market after only a few months. The American package included the instruction on the glass tube of deodorant 'Push Up Bottom'. Unfortunately some UK consumers had done precisely this, and not only did it do nothing for their personal freshness but it was quite painful! The story is probably apocryphal, but I doubt that you will use the term 'bottom-up budgeting' in the same way ever again!

- *Bottom-up budgeting* is where initiative lies at the product management level and resource demands are pushed up through the organization – this is rarely found now;
- *Bottom-up/Top-down budgeting* involves more negotiation and involvement of other departments, but initiative remains at the product level; and
- *Top-down/Bottom-up budgeting* involves far greater control by top management over marketing budgets, and changes the basis for negotiation.

To these variations, I would add one of my own from my work in this area:

- *Top-down budgeting* – the man at the top says how much you get, and there is no room for negotiation [4].

These pragmatic views of what the marketing budgeting process is like in practice differ according to: where the *initiative* lies for marketing resource demands; who *runs, controls* and *influences* the resource-claiming process for marketing; the amount and type of *negotiation* involved; and who is involved and *participates* in marketing budgeting – what level of management, what other departments, what interdepartmental committees, and so on. This leads to quite an interesting question.

What really determines marketing budgets?

If we forget about budgeting techniques for the moment, then the evidence suggests that the resources we actually see companies putting behind marketing are determined by the nature of the budgeting process and the context in which it operates.

Marketing budgets are influenced and determined by factors like the following:

- *Power* – the power of the marketing function (if there is one) relative to other players in the organization, in terms of organizational structures, participation in important decisions, and status;
- *Strategic contingencies* – just how important and critical a company believes its market problems and its customers are;
- *Process control* – who sets the rules and the agenda for the budgeting process, which interests participate in the budgeting

decisions, who chooses the 'rational' techniques to be used in calculating marketing budgets;
- *Political influence* – who controls the information and exerts control over what people think;
- *Bargaining and advocacy* – how good people are at building cases and doing deals to get resources;
- *Corporate culture* – the acceptability or otherwise of resource claims for marketing in the historical frame of reference of 'the way we do things here'.

This is not the place to unpack academic research about these different issues [4]. It *is* the place to say that these are the issues to be addressed in managing the marketing budgeting process.

The real management agenda

The conclusion I put forward is very similar to the one we reached when examining the planning process: putting a handle on a process like marketing budgeting does not involve learning cleverer analytical techniques, it involves getting to grips with the messy realities of the behavioural and organizational dimensions of the process. This is the real management agenda for marketing budgeting.

If you see marketing budgeting as a major blockage to making marketing happen in your company and achieving market-led strategic change, then consider the following points:

- Making sense of the budget and resource issues is easiest in the context of the specific problems we have uncovered in analysing our marketing performance and context in the earlier parts of the book; and strategic planning is a vehicle for capturing and articulating these problems. So weld marketing planning and marketing budgeting together.
- Figuring out why we have resourcing problems and what we may be able to do about them involves getting a handle on the *process* and its context – who runs the marketing budgeting in our company and who influences what happens? This may be painful, but it is more productive than building analytical models and getting hurt when they are ignored.
- Bear in mind that there are few things more politically explosive in organizations than resource allocation. Careers and corporate empires hang on these issues. Some marketing resource problems we

'Figuring out why we have resourcing problems and what we may be able to do about them involves getting a handle on the process and its context'

will never solve. Others we may be able to do something about. In both cases we can carry these issues forward to our implementation strategy.

However, it is important, in looking at our marketing budgeting, that we do not see this as something important in its own right. We should link our conclusions here to the other stages of our analysis of where our marketing goes wrong and what we need to do to get the act together:

- Are the problems in getting customer satisfaction taken seriously related to marketing resource problems (Diagnostic 1), and will the measurement of customer satisfaction help us in getting marketing resourced?
- To what extent are the problems we face in building a coherent market strategy related to resource allocation problems (Diagnostic 2)?
- To what extent do the strategic gaps (Diagnostic 3) exist because marketing is not adequately resourced, and should this be part of our budgeting argument?
- Are resource-related problems linked to how our marketing is organized or the shortcomings in our market sensing that should alert us to the need for marketing expenditures and the operation of our planning process?
- Is the way to change the 'dominant reality' of what we should invest in marketing through market strategizing and market sensing, and participation in the planning process, rather than conflict on budgeting itself?
- What problems here do we carry forward to our implementation strategy?

Our progress so far

Budgeting for marketing is frequently a highly problematic area for executives, and the new realities for companies mean that it is likely to stay that way or get worse. We have tried here to put a handle on the organizational realities of getting marketing resourced, as well as looking at budget-setting techniques. The important point is that we should see marketing budgeting as a *process*, and as a process which is inseparable from the planning process. The underlying truth is that all too often marketing seems to happen *in spite of* the attitude of companies towards budgets and head-counts. If we are serious about market-led strategic change, then we cannot escape the conclusion that it comes with a price-tag.

This leads us to the last process-related area of the context for market-led strategic change – the link between marketing and sales management.

References

1. 'Cereal Makers Not the Only Ones Milking Profits', (1996), *USA Today*, 13 June.
2. Lamons, Bob (1995), 'How to Set Politically Correct Budgets', *Marketing News*, 4 December.
3. Marketing Communications Research Centre (1981), *Setting and Allocating the Communications Budget*, Cranfield, Beds: Cranfield School of Management.
4. Piercy, Nigel (1986), *Marketing Budgeting – A Political and Organisational Model*, Beckenham: Croom Helm.

CHAPTER 13

Managing the sales organization:

Driving market-led strategy into selling operations

Introduction

After the heady stuff of customer focus, market segmentation, value propositions, branding strategy and competitive differentiation, and relationship management, and the powerful tools of market sensing and strategic in building market-led strategic change, turning attention to the sales organization may bring the reader down with a bit of a bump. Tough.

The days when we could see the salesforce as the 'order-takers' out in the field, who have nothing to do with market strategy, have gone. In fact, they probably never existed outside the fevered imaginations of some marketing executives who believed that strategies sold products. In the real world, salespeople sell products and marketing departments are being disbanded.

The reasons for turning to the selling operation as a further source of leverage for achieving market-led strategic change are numerous.

First, many companies have discovered the hard way that the implementation of market strategies may depend critically on winning the support of the salesforce. Evaluating Strategic Gaps (Diagnostic 3) often uncovers a weakness of precisely this kind.

'The days when we could see the salesforce as the "order-takers" out in the field, who have nothing to do with market strategy, have gone'

At its simplest, market strategies that are not planned in the light of the reality faced by salespeople in the field will probably fail. Better news is that the salesforce may provide the major source of competitive differentiation and relationship management that can be exploited in our market strategy. In either case, the salesforce link is a common weakness in getting the act together around customer-focused strategies. It does not have to be. Indeed, as we will see shortly, some companies actually see marketing and sales personnel as a *team*. And a very effective team it can be.

Secondly, it is becoming increasingly apparent that the effective salesperson plays a strategic role in managing customer relationships, not simply a tactical one. For instance, recent research in the USA[1] shows, in a wide variety of industries, that the salesperson has a major influence on the buyer's motivation to continue the supplier relationship, and thus on the long-term sales from that customer. In addition to this direct effect, salespeople exert a strong *indirect* effect on the customer relationship influencing the perceived reliability of the supplier and the perceived value of supplier services which differentiate that supplier from others. This describes a strategic sales role with responsibility for managing the customer relationship which lies at the heart of most market strategies, with a far greater role in co-ordinating other internal functions to deliver 'seamless service' to the customer.

Thirdly, salesforces are *very* expensive. Clearly it depends on what type of selling you mean – order-takers cost less than order-makers; and most sales organizations include different levels of seniority and reward. However, estimates suggest that the average cost of a salesperson on the road in the UK is currently around £45,000. This is an average – so the range around it should be remembered. Also, the figure is probably an under-estimate anyway. And this figure tells us nothing about all the other inputs to the face-to-face sales process – technical customer visits, service personnel, managers, chief executive visits to customers, and so on.

In industrial marketing companies it is not unusual for the salesforce budget to be three-quarters of the total marketing and promotional spend. If you look at the number of sales calls you are likely to get for your average of £45,000, and the number of sales calls that may be needed to make a sale, you can only draw one conclusion: salesforces are incredibly expensive.

Fourthly, partly as a result of these costs, a lot of corporate attention is being given to increasing salesforce effectiveness and productivity. This brings us back to the importance of linking market strategy to selling operations, if we are serious about

'we want a creative, powerful and long-term synergy between marketing and sales'

market-led strategic change. In fact, we do not just want better links, we want a creative, powerful and long-term *synergy* between marketing and sales built around an integrated process of going to market. As we will see, this is not impossible – the best organizations already do it.

However, this is not the place to get involved in the technical and operational aspects of the sales manager's job – we could not wish to trespass across departmental jurisdictions. However, the pursuit of market-led strategic change should be facilitated by examining the following issues:

- linking market strategy to the sales organization and vice versa;
- confronting the new challenges facing the selling operation in current markets;
- looking at international benchmarks of sales organization excellence; and
- thinking hard about what we *know* and what we can *do* about the underlying sources of sales organization effectiveness.

We conclude with a diagnostic worksheet to evaluate our own selling operations.

I said earlier that our interest in the selling operation from the point of market-led strategic change was not about interfering in how salespeople and sales managers do their jobs. Sorry – I lied. Of course it is!

At the very least, the goal of this chapter is to provide the basis for a dialogue between marketing and sales personnel and departments. If this dialogue is as productive as it should be, then maybe we can make some progress towards building the team that can drive market strategy through the company and into the marketplace. Our attention focuses here on what has proved for many companies the single biggest barrier to this implementation of market strategies and usually the most ignored resource for building those strategies – the salesforce.

Linking market strategy to the sales organization

It is quite amazing how often we find that managers present a market strategy and plan, and have no answer to the question: 'What does the salesforce have to do to get that right, and can they do it?' A starting point is to sit down and summarize the market strategy we have produced for a particular market or product or segment or customer, and just to ask what *does* this salesforce have to do and *how* can they do it if the strategy is to become real. This is so obvious that no-one ever seems to bother to do it. Ideally, this is something done with people from the salesforce. A simple format is shown in Table 13.1. What we are

Table 13.1   Do we know what the marketing strategy means for the salesforce?

Elements of market strategy	Market strategy	Requirement from salesforce in implementation
Market definition		
Market attractiveness		
Market position		
Market segmentation		
Market mission		
Competitive differentiation		
Marketing assets and brands		
Customer relationships		
Collaborator relationships		
Co-worker relationships		
Competitor relationships		

likely to find is that for a strategy to be implemented we *need* the salesforce to commit to it.

Certainly, as suggested earlier, we need to recognize that the salesperson's role is becoming a strategic one, not a tactical one. Relationship *marketing* means in reality that we have to develop relationship *selling*, and the manager of the real customer relationship is more likely to be the salesperson than the business planner.

The reality of relationship-based strategies is that building the customer relationship that provides the competitive advantage we described in Chapter 3 depends not least on our skills in developing effective relationships *inside* the organization. These may be collaborative relationships with human resource managers or with operations or with partners in a network – but they are also critical in linking sales to the other participants in the process of going to market (including, but not only, the marketing department).

In fact, it is probably true that unless we get the sales relationship right the relationship marketing strategy will fail, and relationship marketing will be just another fad of the 1990s that never worked out.

Much of the leverage we need to drive relationship-based, customer-focused market strategies comes from including the salesforce as an integral part of the implementation process. This requires a team-based approach.

We could make a start, though, by saying that any market strategy that does not clearly show the role of the salesforce in implementation has not been finished and we refuse to look at it.

The consequences of not managing the sales linkage effectively have been seen all too often:

- At Lantech, salespeople achieved high customer satisfaction at the expense of profitability by overcoming long lead times from the factory (resulting from ineffective sales forecasting by marketing) through the simple expedient of ordering machines from the factory 'on spec', and only finding a customer for the machine when it was nearly ready to leave the factory. This 'beat the system' and kept customers happy – but at great cost to the company in changing machine options and specifications in the factory at the very last minute.
- Some companies have been surprised, when they started to evaluate salespeople on customer satisfaction, that salespeople can be very skilful in winning 'brownie points' from customers in satisfaction questionnaires by making all sorts of product and price concessions that would not otherwise have been

made. This is a long way removed from the goal of having customer satisfaction drive profits – indeed, it is probably the reverse – but the questionnaire results look good!

- If our salespeople are rewarded mainly by individual commission or bonuses, why would we expect them to devote time to team-based selling or non-selling duties?
- If salespeople are evaluated and rewarded on the basis of sales volume, then it is unlikely that they will be relationship-oriented – why should they be? Performance appraisal has to be designed to reflect the goals and behaviour that will drive the market strategy. A rare academic quotation is actually useful here:

> This . . . is not to say that all organizational behaviour is determined by formal rewards and punishments. Certainly it is true that in the absence of formal reinforcement some soldiers will be patriotic, some presidents will be ecology minded, and some orphanage directors will care about children. The point, however, is that in such cases the rewarder is not causing the behavior desired but is only a fortunate bystander. For an organization to act upon its members, the formal reward system should positively reinforce desired behavior, not constitute an obstacle to be overcome
> 'On the Folly of Rewarding A, While Hoping for B', Steven Kerr, *Academy of Management Journal.*

Apart from the obvious idea that all executives should spend some time in the field with the salesforce – participating and conducting, not just observing, and in the toughest part of the market, not just the showcases – sometimes what we learn from the salesforce can actually create new market strategies.

'sometimes what we learn from the salesforce can actually create new market strategies'

For example, Enterprise Rent-A-Car is one of the largest car rental firms in the USA, with 300 000 cars and $3 billion in annual revenue. It started as a car leasing business in a Cadillac dealership in 1957. Enterprise got into short-term rental in 1964 in response to a customer request to a sales office for a temporary replacement car, not a long-term lease, while his own car was being repaired. As a result, the salesforce started to call on insurance companies and repair garages to prospect for temporary replacement deals. (Incidentally, then and now they took doughnuts with them, because salespeople know what it takes to be popular!) The salespeople found that insurance offices and garages *hated* making car rental arrangements for customers –

because it was extra unpaid work and they then had to give the customer a lift to the rental company. Enterprise provided both services and has built a billion-dollar rental business with 25 years' uninterrupted profitability. A market-led strategy – created by the salesforce, based on customer service (and doughnuts).

We need to build a team-based partnership between sales and the other parts of the company with a stake in the process of going to market – customer service, accounts and billing, operations and stockholding, logistics, and marketing. But we need to do it now, because the world of customers and competitors is changing fast. In some companies it is already happening – at Elida Fabergé traditional brand management has disappeared, to be replaced by category management which merges the interests of the company's salesforce with brand marketing strategy around the major retail customers.

The new challenges facing the sales organization

The modern marketplace in which most of us have to survive is imposing enormous pressures on competitiveness through such factors as global sourcing by major customers and reductions in supplier bases, low economic growth in many countries, and new sources of overseas competition emerging in many product markets. In case that does not sound like much of a challenge, have a look at the supplier reduction figures for major US companies in Table 13.2 and think again. Other pressures come from the goal in many companies to be 'leaner' and to look for savings in the large costs represented by the salesforce.

The result of such pressures has been aggressive efforts by major organizations such as Ingersoll-Rand, Hewlett Packard and General Electric to counteract escalating sales costs and declining salesforce productivity through such mechanisms as account management, lead generation systems, computer-assisted sales programmes, telemarketing and systems contracts. At the same time, multinational organizations like Colgate-Palmolive, Compaq Computer, IBM, Procter and Gamble, Xerox and Kraft are among those undertaking major restructuring of sales organizations to improve effectiveness and competitiveness.

Selling organizations are being forced to. adapt. Sometimes screaming and kicking, but adapting nonetheless. For example,

Table 13.2   Reducing supplier bases*

	Number of suppliers before reduction programmes	Number of suppliers after reduction programmes	% change
Xerox	5,000	500	−90%
Motorola	10,000	3,000	−70%
Digital Equipment	9,000	3,000	−67%
General Motors	10,000	5,500	−45%
Ford Motors	1,800	1,000	−44%
Texas Instruments	22,000	14,000	−36%
Rainbird	520	380	−27%
Allied-Signal Aerospace	7,500	6,000	−20%

*Source: Emshwiller, John R. (1991), 'Suppliers Struggle to Improve Quality as Big Firms Slash Their Vendor Roles', *Wall Street Journal*, 16 August

one US study of sales managers in major companies [2] suggests that the pressures for change in sales organizations, which are shared by many of our companies, come from the following factors:

- a growing emphasis on customer-oriented selling, which requires more varied types of salespeople of greater sophistication;
- the need for greater flexibility and faster decision making, which requires structural change to get away from slow bureaucratic organizations;
- wider corporate restructuring, which removes many of the traditional barriers between manufacturing, sales, logistics and customers;
- budget restrictions causing greater scrutiny of the sales process for effectiveness and profit contribution; and
- the need to organize salesforces to serve different market segments which demand different selling approaches, managerial structures and compensation systems.

The danger signs that we are not making the right changes in selling include: too many customers lost to competitors; high salesperson turnover, particularly losing key people to the competition; negative feedback from customers; delays in delivery through poor communication and condition; and large differences in salesperson productivity, where the best are performing well but drag behind them a 'tail' of low performers.

'The danger signs that we are not making the right changes in selling'

Even by the end of the 1980s it was clear that the traditional role of the salesforce was changing to respond to market demands. In 1988, the Learning International Organization identified seven new selling strategies:

1 *Differentiating similar products and services* – salespeople have to build on the advantages in their products and services.
2 *Building business solutions* – selling a package of products and services to solve complex customer problems, not selling single products or services.
3 *Selling to more educated buyers* – buyers are better-informed and more knowledgeable, changing the role of the seller.
4 *Consultative selling* – the salesperson role becomes one of identifying customer needs and developing acceptable solutions.
5 *Team selling* – as customer needs and products become more complex, selling requires a team approach.
6 *Knowing the customer's business* – selling depends on in-depth knowledge of the customer's business and building enduring relationships.
7 *Adding value by service* – providing service as part of the selling process to create and retain customers.

For example, recent research into success in winning bids for major contracts[3] suggests that the top five success factors are: leadership from very senior departmental managers; creating a team spirit; leadership from the board of directors; including team members with specialist product/service knowledge; and giving team members clear instructions on how to handle the bid. Many organizations are re-thinking the sales process and the customer relationship, and some see the fundamental changes in the way suggested in Figure 13.1.

Further confirmation of how the world facing the sales organization has changed is the 1996 findings of The H. R. Challey Group, who have studied customer views of what they require from their vendors' salespeople. What major business customers in the USA demand is that vendors meet their business needs:

- to focus on the things they do best and 'outsource' the rest – but without adding overhead costs in closely supervising suppliers;
- to know the customer's business well enough to create products and services that they would not have been able to design and create themselves; and
- to give proof in hard evidence that the supplier has added value in excess of price.

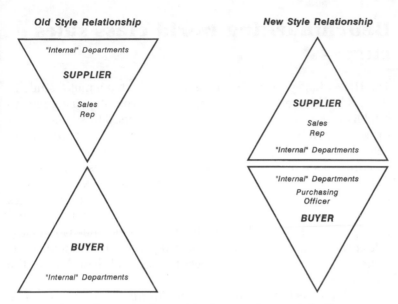

Figure 13.1 Changing relationships between buyers and sellers

To evaluate a seller's potential to meet these needs, corporate customers judged salesforces on the following factors:

1 Managing our satisfaction personally
2 Understanding our business
3 Recommending products and applications expertly
4 Providing technical and training support
5 Acting as a customer advocate
6 Solving logistical and political problems
7 Finding innovative solutions to our needs.

The research suggested that, as far as corporate customers were concerned, only salesforces which excel at these seven factors could adequately fill the customer's basic business needs. The findings regarding how the best salesforces address this is the subject of the next section of the chapter.

For the moment, though, we have seen that sales organizations are under great pressure in many companies. This is no time for 'ivory tower' marketing executives to start whining about their market strategies and the salesforce 'barrier'. It *is* the time to talk in terms of a partnership to drive the important market-led strategies on which we all rely.

'This is no time for "ivory tower" marketing executives to start whining about their market strategies and the salesforce "barrier"'

Benchmarking world class sales success*

The H. R. Challey Group has recently conducted a major study in the USA [4], interviewing over 1 000 corporate customers to establish what they want from sellers. They used this information to identify a group of selling organizations that customers believed to be the 'best' or 'world class' because they excelled at meeting customers' basic business needs. These world-class selling organizations included companies like AT&T Consumer Products, Exxon Chemical, IBM and Xerox. These companies were 'benchmarked' to identify the critical success factors and their standards of sales excellence – how the world-class salesforces manage customer satisfaction, understand their customers' business and deliver the critical benefits to the customer.

The findings of this study make one thing very clear – in some very important ways market-led strategic change can be *driven* by sales organizations. There are vital lessons here that we have to manage the sales process as part of creating and implementing market strategies.

The Challey report identifies some general points about world-class sales organizations and eight specific benchmarks for sales organization excellence. These findings give us some very specific insights and an agenda for managing the selling process.

General findings about world-class excellence

'The overriding philosophy of the best salesforces is stated most simply as: "Be the outsource of preference"'

The overriding philosophy of the best salesforces is stated most simply as: 'Be the outsource of preference'. Their basic priority is to add value to the customer's business. The route to this is:

- identify and measure the business needs of industrial customers;
- develop the added services to surround products to guarantee the customers' business improvement; and
- measure again, both for management control as well as proof for customers that their business was improved.

---

* This section leans heavily on the report: *Benchmarks for World Class Sales Success*, The H. R. Challey Group, Ohio, 1996.

This is underpinned by a changing culture – focusing on benefit or business results, not products, and on utility and ease of use, not price and delivery. Adding value to the customer's business involves driving *market mission* through the *sales process*. For example:

In office products:	'We're not an office products company or a supplies company; we are your purchasing department'; 'We are not forms, we are information flow'
For AT&T:	'We are not telephones; we are communications'
For IBM:	'We are not computers, or even information; we are decision analysts in problem-solving'
In engineering:	'We are not motors or parts; we are manufacturing improvement'
For Exxon and DuPont:	'We are not chemicals; we are improved manufacturing processes'

For some of the companies, achieving this focus has involved major structural and organizational change – no-one suggests it is easy. The conclusion, however, is vitally important: 'Our top sellers are changing from peddlers to relationship managers, from order-takers to consultants'.

'Our top sellers are changing from peddlers to relationship managers, from order-takers to consultants'

These top-class selling organizations share certain key characteristics which give the benchmark processes for world class sales excellence.

Benchmark processes for sales excellence

Cutting across diverse products, channels of distribution and customer types, the eight sales benchmark processes found in the Challey study were:

- Establishing a customer-driven sales culture
- Market segmentation
- Recruiting and selecting salespeople
- Training and development
- Compensation and incentive

- Sales service and support systems
- Customer feedback
- Information technology

Although the Challey findings are based on very large US organizations, they are important to us for two main reasons: they tell us how our competitors are shaping up the sales process; and they can give us useful insights into how we can improve our own selling operations and the implementation of our market strategies.

Benchmark 1 – Establishing a customer-driven sales culture

'In the world-class sales organizations, customer satisfaction is the most important success driver, and the salesforce is the critical customer representative in the company'

In the world-class sales organizations, customer satisfaction is the most important success driver, and the salesforce is the critical customer representative in the company, not just the traditional order processor, generator of leads or closer of deals. In these companies, customer satisfaction measures are used to prove value to the customer, to justify price, to compare against competitors, as well as determine salesperson rewards. But these satisfaction measures are not just the traditional 'soft' measures, but 'hard' criteria, such as money saved, cycle time reduction, or profit improvements.

The processes used by these companies in 'building a customer culture' are of three main types:

- *Making an exclusive career out of sales* – developing a sales career structure that recognizes that sales requires specialized skills; customers vary in size and complexity, so need different salesperson coverage; and several sales specialities are needed to satisfy customers.
- *Decentralizing profit and loss responsibility closer to the customer* – to improve speed of response to customer requests, to have less frequently needed services available from the centre, but, most important, to allow sales units to adapt and tailor to customer needs at the point of contact.
- *High-level customer contact* – making customer contact or sales a high-rank position on the corporate ladder, and/or requiring top levels of management to have some sales responsibilities, which both signals the priority of customer contact and allows relationships to be built at all levels in the customer's organization.

Benchmark 2 – Market segmentation

In the world-class sales organizations, market segmentation is taken through to selling operations when customers or customer groups require specialized added-value – products have to be tailored to different industries, and different sales, service or distribution processes must be established for different industries. The options found in these companies are:

- Segmenting by customer industry;
- Segmenting by size of customer;
- Segmenting by product or service offered;
- Segmenting by geography;
- Segmenting by prospect (new business develop-
  ment) versus customer (existing customer penetra-
  tion) – involving salespeople acting as 'hunters' or
  'farmers' to exploit their different selling skills.

'as products and customers become more specialized and adding value becomes more vital, market segmentation becomes more critical'

Changing organizational arrangements for new market segments has been disruptive for some companies, but as products and customers become more specialized and adding value becomes more vital, market segmentation becomes more critical.

Benchmark 3 – Recruiting and selecting salespeople

There is widespread recognition in these companies that recruitment and selection can be the two most critical steps in building a successful salesforce and avoiding many sales management problems. The strategy is to match salesperson skills, focus and motivation to the needs of the customer. Methods of achieving this include careful attention to:

- *Systematic internal sourcing* – taking people into the salesforce from any part of the organization if their skills are appropriate, and particularly to fill more senior selling roles.
- *Careful and systematic external sourcing* – particularly for entry-level or more junior roles in the sales organization.

Benchmark 4 – Training and development

As customers demand more added value and more knowledge-able salespeople, training and development becomes a continual process for all sales personnel – the experienced and the new. The excellent sales companies' training and development for sales-people is characterized by:

- *Content training* – covering products and applications, sellers' operations and systems, individual behavioural skills, customer and market information, customer-based business methods and practices and general business management, based on the selling role.
- *Allocating clear responsibility for training* – whether to training specialists, sales managers or individual salespeople for self-development.
- *Defining clear structures for training* – whether formal or informal.
- *Recognition of coaching* – the sales manager's coaching role is not replaced by formal training.

Benchmark 5 – Compensation

The compensation systems used by top-class sales companies reflect their business strategies, and the intended role of the salesperson in that strategy. The factors reflected in the choice of mix of compensation between fixed and variable were: mutual profitability (of customer and seller); consumer satisfaction (measured specifically enough to track individual customers and salespeople); the level of expertise and breadth of skill of the salesperson; the contribution to the sales team; and sales volume.

The main compensation options found in the companies were:

- *Mainly fixed compensation* – to promote long-term customer relationships, not just transactions.
- *Fixed plus variable compensation* – to balance long-term customer relationships and individual transactions.
- *Mainly variable compensation* – to manage mainly shorter-term objectives.

All three approaches were found in the world-class sales organizations. The choice about whether to include variable compensation was associated with essentially tactical roles (i.e. short term or transaction-based), but where all critical selling factors are within the salesperson's control. In this situation, variable compensation motivates the person to generate transactions.

Benchmark 6 – Independent sales service and support systems

The days of the 'lone wolf' salesperson selling individual products and services have gone. Top salesforces define their businesses as 'seamless integration' of all the benefits they offer – including quality production, just-in-time delivery, new product development, engineering support, responsive service and financial improvements, all tailored to fit individual customer needs. The preferred method is team selling.

'The days of the "lone wolf" salesperson selling individual products and services have gone'

Central to the relationship-oriented role of their salespeople, the top sales organizations provide customer service, administrative support and technical support from a group of specialists. Depending on the circumstances, this involves:

- *Service and support direct to the customer* – where the salesperson covers many customers, then services are more likely to go direct to the customer. This includes: product or application expertise, transaction convenience (e.g. order entry, transport, stock adjustments) and business function expertise (e.g. financial or legal support). The key is extending the partnership with the customer back into the internal functions of the seller's organization.
- *Service and support to the salesperson* – where salespeople have fewer customer accounts, administrative, technical and problem resolution support is channelled to the salesperson.

In both cases, customer service is operated in partnership with the salesforce to build and maintain customer relationships.

Benchmark 7 – Direct customer feedback

The top sales organizations demonstrate a belief that customers must be positioned as the drivers of strategy. Direct customer feedback measuring customer satisfaction is found in five forms in the best sales organizations:

- *Evaluation of transactions* – including pre-sale needs analysis (how well business solutions are developed for the customer), post-sale service evaluation (whether or not customer expectations were met) and formal proof of benefit to the customer (e.g. documenting shipping performance reports, and customer cost savings).
- *Evaluation of the total customer relationship* – including feedback shared within the organization to improve processes, feedback

shared with the customer to reinforce the relationship, and objective criteria for performance-linked rewards.
- *Independent data collection* – third party customer satisfaction surveys are the norm.
- *Internal data collection* – when customer contacts are high-level, more personal ways of evaluating customer input are more usual.
- *Customer councils* – many of the excellent companies are using customer councils to bring together existing customers to collect feedback and deepen the company relationship.

Benchmark 8 – Information technology

The complex selling process requires and gets IT support in the top sales organizations. This includes:

- *IT benefits to the customer* – providing quick response in the areas that are critical to customers.
- *IT benefits to the salesperson* – providing fast access to all information needed to service the customer.
- *IT benefits to management* – providing performance measurement to support decisions to improve the customer/organization interaction.

These signs of sales organization excellence and the benchmarks they provide give us some vital insights into how things have changed in the modern salesforce. The next stage is to move closer to what we can evaluate in our own organizations to develop our marketing strategic capabilities in the salesforce.

The hidden secrets of sales organization effectiveness*

Of course, the Challey benchmarks become more useful if we ask: 'How do you get there?', rather than just looking at what the best world-class sales organizations have already achieved.

Consider the following research findings, and see what further insights they may offer into what is actually required to drive

---

* This section draws heavily from Nigel F. Piercy, David W. Cravens and Neil A. Morgan (1997), 'Sources of Effectiveness in Business-to-Business Sales Organizations', *Journal of Marketing Practice: Applied Marketing Science*, Vol. 3, No. 1, 43–69.

customer-focused and relationship marketing strategies through to the salesforce. These new customer
imperatives and benchmarks suggest that among the
most critical questions facing executives are: what
skills, structures and policies lead to effective salesforces, and how can these lessons be applied? In fact,
to address these types of questions, an international
team of business school researchers has been conduct-
ing a series of country-specific studies of salesforce effectiveness,
using a detailed analytical methodology which has been developed and refined over a number of years. Some of the most
important results of the British element of the international
research programme are discussed below. This research offers
some unique insights into the minds, attitudes and management
processes of sales managers in Britain, which are highly relevant
to achieving market-led strategic change.

'what skills, structures and policies lead to effective salesforces, and how can these lessons be applied?'

In these studies we consider more effective sales organizations
to be those that display higher sales, market share, profitability
and customer satisfaction, compared to their competitors and
compared to their own corporate objectives. Overall, we suggest
that the following are the critically important factors in
understanding sales effectiveness in the most effective sales
organizations:

- They have a salesforce compensation strategy which balances
  fixed salary with an incentive element.
- Their salespeople share a number of similar and important
  success characteristics.
- Their salespeople perform exceptionally well on a number of
  critical dimensions – the drivers of salesforce effectiveness.
- They focus throughout on building long-term customer
  relationships.
- Their field sales managers play a critical role as coaches rather
  than commanders.
- They are 'right-sized' and soundly organized at the sales unit
  level.

There are no magic answers or 'quick-fixes' to achieve sales
organization effectiveness, but the more effective sales organizations we have studied consistently apply the factors above and
achieve dramatically superior performance in the marketplace.
There are important lessons that can be learned from this. This
logic is summarized in Figure 13.2. The results of our study spell
out a challenging action agenda to be addressed in improving salesforce effectiveness, which our experience suggests may lead to very
different approaches to sales management in British companies.

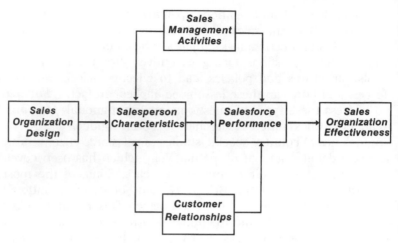

Figure 13.2 Sources of sales organization effectiveness

Identifying effective sales organizations

The British survey includes data from a large number of field sales managers, representing organizations operating in a wide range of selling environments. The measures of effectiveness used were sales volume, market share, profitability and customer satisfaction results. Achievements were rated against the major competitor during the past two years, and against the sales units' own objectives in these areas. The rankings given in each of these areas were combined to give an overall index of sales organization effectiveness.

The sales organizations were placed into two categories, on the basis of the overall effectiveness index, to create a higher effectiveness group and a lower effectiveness group. Our intent was not to suggest that the lower effectiveness group is performing *poorly* – the division is made to learn more about the factors that impact on effectiveness by comparing the stronger and weaker performers in the group of companies studied.

The differences between the groups are dramatic in the extreme. The higher effectiveness group are substantially and significantly better on all the criteria, both compared to competition and in achievements compared to objectives. The size of the difference in performance was startling, and underlines the importance of our central question: What explains the difference between higher and lower sales organization effectiveness? What enables the more effective sales organizations to perform better than their key competitors and their assigned objectives?

Conventional measures of sales performance

At first sight it might be expected that such radical differences in sales organization effectiveness would be explained by conventional productivity measures.

First, we should ask whether the most effective organizations are simply those in the most attractive industries – but in fact both groups are in industries experiencing equally low growth or decline. For the overwhelming majority of companies in the study, their industries were growing less than 5 per cent a year or were declining. However, the higher effectiveness companies *are* doing markedly better in growing sales faster than the industry growth rate.

However, it is striking that on the many conventional measures there are no significant differences between the lower and higher effectiveness groups in terms of issues such as: the size of the sales unit; accounts per salesperson; new customer sales or number of sales calls/week. In fact, the higher effectiveness organizations actually sell substantially *less* per salesperson, have a significantly higher expense level and spend more time in purely selling activities rather than support, training and the like. But, of course, the high effectiveness companies are growing their sales faster than their markets are growing, and their effectiveness compared to competitors and objectives is vastly superior. These are the sales organizations from which we can learn the hallmarks of sales organization effectiveness. We need to probe deeper into what drives effectiveness.

To understand the underlying characteristics of the more effective sales organization we examine: (1) sales force compensation approaches; (2) the characteristics of successful salespeople; (3) the drivers of salesforce performance; (4) the role of the sales manager; and, (5) the impact of sales organization issues on sales organization effectiveness.

Salesforce compensation

It may be that part of the difference in sales organization effectiveness is explained by differences in how salespeople are compensated and most particularly the proportion of incentive or bonus payment included in the total compensation package. In fact, the average salary percentage was 87 per cent in the lower effectiveness group and 80 per cent in the higher effectiveness group, but of more interest is that very few British companies pay less than 50 per cent salary, and a significant number pay 100 per cent salary.

The comparison between the high and low effectiveness groups suggests a difference of *balance* between fixed and variable compensation, rather than an absolute difference. A large proportion of the most effective organizations pay salaries in the 75–95 per cent range, while far more of the less effective companies pay salaries in the 95–100 per cent range.

It seems that incentive payment is a significant influence on sales effectiveness, but is associated with compensation packages where salaries represent 75–95 per cent of total pay – not less and not more. This is an interesting benchmark and puts a new perspective on the debate about the merits of fixed salary versus incentive-based pay. By basing a relatively high portion of total compensation on salary, sales management is better able to guide salesperson activities and priorities. But by also offering an opportunity for incentive compensation, management encourages (and rewards) superior performance.

Characteristics of successful salespeople

'even clearer difference between higher and lower effectiveness sales organizations lies in the salesperson's attitudes and behaviour'

A further and even clearer difference between higher and lower effectiveness sales organizations lies in the salesperson's attitudes and behaviour.

Higher effectiveness is connected with superior salesperson *motivation*. Where salespeople are better motivated in terms of getting a sense of accomplishment from their work, feeling a sense of personal growth and development, where they are stimulated, challenged, imaginative and creative in their work – then sales organization effectiveness is markedly higher. Having a *customer orientation* among salespeople is also strongly linked to sales organization effectiveness. Where salespeople focus on customer needs, adapt selling approaches to customer requirements, possess good selling skills and product/service knowledge, and base selling strategy on customer needs – then sales organization effectiveness is significantly higher.

Alongside issues of individual motivation and customer orientation, consider the impact of *team orientation*. Where salespeople are willing to accept direction and reviews from the manager and to co-operate as part of a sales team – then sales organization effectiveness is higher.

Lastly, *sales support orientation* also distinguishes between higher and lower sales effectiveness. Where salespeople spend time in sales call planning, non-selling activities and sales support activities – then again sales organization effectiveness is higher. These characteristics describe the functioning of a co-ordinated sale unit, rather than 'lone wolf' salespeople each pursuing their own objectives rather than those of the organization.

These factors are much 'softer' than traditional approaches to sales management, which emphasize compensation and sales expense and productivity measurement as the basis for direction and control, but our findings describe powerfully some key differences between higher and lower sales organization effectiveness. As characteristics of salespeople that relate to effectiveness, these factors offer useful benchmarks. However, they lead us next to consider whether salespeople with these characteristics also display high performance.

The drivers of salesforce performance

Our findings regarding salesforce performance were concerned with three areas: *outcome* performance, *selling* performance, and *non-selling* performance (behavioural performance). These factors also uncover highly important hidden differences between the higher and lower effectiveness sales organizations, which are hidden in the internal processes of the company, rather than openly displayed in their sales productivity measurements.

First, consider the difference between outcome performance, or achieving goals, in the higher and lower effectiveness organizations. The higher effectiveness salesforces are those where salespeople obtain a high market share as well as high sales revenue, and beat sales targets and objectives, but also emphasize sales of high margin products and sales to major accounts and new product/service sales. The differences here were substantial and important. These issues provide good benchmarks for executives to appraise the results of their own sales units and to position them against the higher effectiveness groups in our research.

While high performance in outcomes can be linked to selling activities, the differences we found between the higher and lower effectiveness sales organizations concerning *sales presentation* and *technical knowledge* performance are quite small. However, really major differences lie in the performance of non-selling activities. In the areas of performance we have identified as salesperson adaptiveness, teamwork, sales planning and sales support, we see major and highly significant differences between the higher and lower effectiveness sales organizations.

The issue of *adaptiveness* in selling suggests that the higher effectiveness sales organizations are those where salespeople are flexible and experiment with the selling approaches they use, and adapt and vary their selling styles between different customers and different selling situations. It is worth executives considering whether the capacity for adaptiveness of this kind is included in salesperson appraisal and development in their organizations, and how their sales units would compare with the best on these benchmarks.

Turning to the question of *teamwork*, in the higher effectiveness salesforces salespeople are rated highly in successful team selling and in building working relationships with other employees to close sales and to solve customer problems and meet service requirements. This raises the important issues for executives concerning whether these activities are fostered and developed in their own sales organizations, and how they compare with the higher effectiveness sales operations in our research.

In a similar way, the more effective salesforces in our study were significantly ahead of the rest in *sales planning* activities. Where salespeople were rated highly in their performance on planning sales calls, customer sales strategies and account coverage, as well as daily activities – then the effectiveness of the sales organization is higher. These are important practical benchmarks for the development and appraisal of salespeople in activities and behaviour which relate significantly to effectiveness.

Lastly, and perhaps even more significant, the higher effectiveness sales organizations are those where salespeople perform well in *sales support* activities of various kinds. Where salespeople are rated highly in providing aftersales service, checking on product delivery, handling customer complaints, following up on customer product use and troubleshooting on customer application problems, as well as identifying new product/service ideas from customer experience – then the effectiveness of the sales organization is higher. This provides further benchmarks for appraising sales performance leverage, and the challenge to executives is again to compare their own sales units with the most effective salesforces in our research.

'the sales organizations which are consistently outstripping their competition and beating their own objectives are those where salespeople display superior performance in adaptiveness, teamwork, sales planning and sales support'

The dominant conclusion is that the sales organizations which are consistently outstripping their competition and beating their own objectives are those where salespeople display superior performance in adaptiveness, teamwork, sales planning and sales support. It is on these 'softer' factors that the gap between the higher and lower effectiveness salesforces really opens up. The more effective organizations do score better in the important selling performance areas of sales presentation and technical knowledge, but these differences are far less significant. These findings raise important questions about whether sales training and salesperson appraisal in our companies are focusing on the factors that really drive effectiveness.

The role of the sales manager

Another highly important question to address is: what do field sales managers *do* in the most effective sales organizations, to achieve the superior salesperson behaviour and sales organization results they obtain?

In the research study, sales managers answered a number of questions about their work, and these activities are grouped into monitoring, directing, evaluating and rewarding activities. Managers were also asked how much effort they devoted to coaching salespeople and communicating with them. The comparisons between more and less effective sales organizations show dramatic differences in the extent to which the sales manager performs these activities in the most effective sales organizations, compared to the lower effectiveness group. What we see very clearly in the more effective sales organizations is the sales manager functioning as a coach rather than scorekeeper or controller.

Sales manager *monitoring* activities distinguish the most effective sales organizations. Importantly, this is not simply about spending time in the field with salespeople. Monitoring in the effective sales organizations is far more about observing selling performance and reviewing call reports with salespeople and making joint calls with them, as well as watching travel costs and expenses, and the credit terms given to customers. These monitoring activities help the sales manager to more effectively coach and develop the sales team. These factors provide some insightful benchmarks for considering how our own sales managers monitor salespeople, and how they compare with the most effective sales organizations in the research study.

Even more dramatic are differences in the form of sales manager *directing* in the most effective sales organizations. In the effective sales organizations sales managers place great emphasis on helping salespeople to develop their potential, in actively participating in on-the-job training, in coaching sessions and discussions of performance evaluations with salespeople, as well as providing rewards for good results. Direction in the most effective sales organizations is very different from the 'command and control' approach popular in many of the traditional approaches to sales manager training and development. These are notable benchmarks for examining how our sales managers direct salespeople, and how this compares to the really effective sales organizations.

There are also important differences in how sales managers *evaluate* salespeople in the more effective sales organizations. The distinctive differences between high and low effectiveness sales organizations are in the emphasis on evaluating the professional development of salespeople and the quality of their sales presentations, as well as appraising their sales results, sales calls and profit contribution. The balance between these approaches to management evaluation of salespeople contains important insights into the working of the most effective sales organizations. While managers in both the more and less effective sales organizations perform these evaluation activities, the former do so to a greater extent.

Other important characteristics of the most effective sales organizations are found by examining how sales managers approach the *rewarding* of salespeople. The big difference in the more effective sales organizations centres on the efforts made by sales managers to provide performance feedback and to compensate salespeople on the basis of the *quality* of their sales activities, using more non-financial incentives but still linking rewards to achievements. Less dramatically, sales managers in the more effective sales organizations use incentive compensation linked to sales results, and reward salespeople for the quantity of sales activities, but the differences here are smaller. These factors provide a useful framework for examining how a company's salesperson reward mechanisms operate, and how they are perceived to work by salespeople and sales managers.

The activities of field sales managers in the most effective sales organizations are characterized by two important differences: in the more effective sales organizations, field sales managers are more active in all areas of control studied, rather than falling back on traditional compensation controls to manage the salesforce; and the balance of their activities in monitoring, directing, evaluating and rewarding salespeople is quite different. They place more emphasis on observing sales performance and reviewing call reports; they emphasize coaching and helping salespeople to develop their potential; they evaluate sales results but also their salespeople's professional development; and they provide more performance feedback and emphasize the quality of sales activities as well as simply the quantity of activities.

'these issues provide a powerful set of benchmarks to compare a company's sales management practices with those in the most effective sales organizations'

It is these sales management activities which distinguish the most effective sales organizations. It is also the extent to which these activities are performed which underpins the superior salesperson performance and sales results achieved in the most effective sales organizations. We suggest that these issues provide a powerful set of benchmarks to compare a company's sales management practices with those in the most effective sales organizations. The findings also have major implications for recruiting, training and developing sales managers to achieve high effectiveness – the orientation and skills of a coach are different from those of a command and control manager.

The design of the sales organization

Our study findings indicate that high effectiveness and superior results are not just associated with sales management practices, but also with the soundness of the structures and selling effort allocations made at the sales unit and sales territory level. While management practices are linked to guiding and focusing salesperson performance, how well we organize sales is related to whether we give salespeople the opportunity to perform well.

Our research examined the satisfaction of field sales managers with a variety of issues in sales territory, design and operation, and these results provide a further source of insight into the underlying characteristics of the most effective sales organizations.

In the most effective sales organizations managers saw little need to change the number of salespeople employed, whereas this was significantly different in the less effective sales organizations. Overall, sales managers in the more effective organizations had much sounder territory organization, and this is also a distinguishing characteristic of effectiveness.

These findings show that in the less effective sales organizations managers are significantly less satisfied with the sales productivity and call numbers made in their sales territories. The less effective sales organizations are also characterized by problems relating to the lack of equivalence of workload across sales territories, the number of accounts and especially the number of large accounts in different sales territories, as well as the market potential in territories and the associated questions of territory geographical size and travel costs. It is apparent that the most effective sales organizations score higher satisfaction on all these dimensions of territory design. We conclude that effectiveness is not just related to management activities, but also to the soundness of the sales territory design and allocation of sales efforts and costs that result from effective sales territory design.

These issues also provide useful benchmarks for evaluating the strengths and weaknesses of sales territory design, and for executives to make comparisons with the most effective sales organizations in our research.

'effectiveness is not just related to management activities, but also to the soundness of the sales territory design and allocation of sales efforts'

Conclusions from the sales effectiveness research

In our search for the hallmarks of effective sales organizations, we have made a number of proposals which challenge managers to examine the performance of their own sales organizations, but, more importantly, to judge whether they are focusing on the factors that really drive sales effectiveness. We showed that the differences in effectiveness between sales organizations are dramatic: in beating the competition and company objectives in sales, market share, profitability and customer satisfaction. There is nothing marginal about the differences between companies in sales organization effectiveness – the gap is massive.

But when we look for explanations of effectiveness differences in conventional measures of salesforce size and productivity, the figures show little of significance. However, we can see that the effective sales organizations are growing and prospering in difficult industries, and the others are not. The real differences between the most effective and the least effective sales organiza-tions come when we examine the salesforce *compensation strategy,* the characteristics of *successful salespeople* and the underlying *drivers of salesforce performance*. Arising out of these comparisons, we conclude that effective sales organizations focus throughout on developing and fostering *customer relationships*. Finally, we note the critical *sales manager role*, and the '*right sizing*' and effective design of the sales organization.

1   Salesforce compensation strategy

The most effective sales organizations display an balance between the motivating effect of incentive payments and the security provided by fixed salary. Importantly, they do not pay wholly by fixed salary, nor do they allow incentive payments to dominate and possibly distract efforts from important non-selling activities. They mainly pay fixed salaries in the range of 75–95 per cent of total compensation. Payment systems that consist of fixed salary (e.g. more than 95 per cent of total compensation) are found mainly in less effective sales organizations.

2   The characteristics of successful salespeople

In the most effective sales organizations, salespeople are rated higher in their *motivation*, in terms of the sense of personal achievement they get from their work and the enthusiasm they display, but also they outperform salespeople in less effective organizations in their *customer orientation* their *team orientation*, and their *sales support orientation*. These findings highlight several important questions about the recruiting, training and developing of effective salespeople.

3 The drivers of salesforce performance

We saw that in the most effective sales organizations the salesforce performs significantly better in gaining market share, focusing on selling high margin products and on major accounts for long-term business, and exceeding sales targets and objectives. However, of greatest interest are the activities or behaviour that underpin these excellent outcomes in the effective sales organizations. Traditionally sales management has focused on developing selling skills. We found that the effective sales organizations were rated better in performance on selling capabilities like sales presentation and technical knowledge, but not to a significant level. These are necessary, but not sufficient to generate superior results. The major drivers of salesforce performance that characterize the most effective sales organizations come from *adaptiveness* in selling, *teamwork*, *sales planning* and *sales support* activities. These findings establish benchmarks for executives, and raise important questions regarding where to focus managerial attention and development efforts to build a more effective sales organization.

4 Customer relationships

Cutting across these findings in each of the areas above is the focus of the most effective sales organizations on building and sustaining long-term customer relationships. Effective sales organizations outperform the less effective in achieving customer satisfaction. Effective organizations pay enough incentive compensation to motivate salespeople, but not so much that customer interests are lost through the pursuit of commission above all else. Effective salespeople are customer-oriented. Effective salesforces adapt their selling to customer characteristics, work in teams to handle customer problems and provide customer service, plan sales strategy around customers and provide support to customers in checking on performance and responding to complaints. The focus on activities that develop productive long-term customer relationships characterizes the most effective sales organizations and underpins their dramatically superior results. Indeed, sales executives in the study made the point strongly that this was the most important area in which to focus efforts for improvements in sales organization effectiveness in the future.

'the focus of the most effective sales organizations on building and sustaining long-term customer relationships'

5 The sales manager role

'in the most effective sales organizations the sales manager is more a coach and communicator than a commander and scorekeeper'

Our research shows that in the most effective sales organizations the sales manager is more a coach and communicator than a commander and scorekeeper. In the effective sales organizations: *monitoring* is really about observing sales performance, reviewing call reports and watching salesperson day-to-day activities; *directing* is associated largely with helping salespeople to develop their potential, coaching and training; *evaluating* is more associated with appraising salesperson professional development and the quality of sales presentations, as well as judging sales results; and *rewarding* is associated with providing regular feedback and rewards (often non-financial) linked to results (frequently the quality of work, not just the quantity).

These findings suggest a very different role for the sales manager in the effective sales organization. This critical management position combines the role of coach, communicator and facilitator with the more traditional functions of keeping score and allocating financial rewards. In effective sales organizations the field sales manager participates in field sales activities and provides a role model, and goes far beyond the traditional command and control model of sales management.

Such insights are highly significant to examining the role of sales managers in our own companies and reacting to the implications for sales manager recruitment, training and development and appraisal, particularly in balancing the need for 'people' skills and team skills with capabilities in sales techniques and product/service knowledge.

6 'Right-sizing' and organizational design

It is also clear from our research that the most effective sales organizations are associated with management confidence that effectiveness cannot be increased by adding further salespeople to sales units, and a high level of satisfaction with the design of sales territories and the allocation of resources to territories. Success here impacts on the retention of sales staff, as well as their performance and satisfaction. This area is problematic – in a period of widespread corporate downsizing and restructuring, sales staffing levels and allocations may suffer. Our findings suggest that this should be a high priority in recovering sales effectiveness after large-scale organizational changes.

These findings also provide significant benchmarks for appraising the salesforce size and allocations and territory design in our own companies, since superior positions on these issues are highly associated with sales organization effectiveness.

There are no 'quick-fixes' or panacea in the important search for sales organization effectiveness. However, what our research offers is a clear and tested set of benchmarks which distinguish the most effective sales organizations from others, grouped into the six hallmarks of sales organization effectiveness we have discussed, and these provide the basis for the worksheets at the end of this chapter (Diagnostic 5) (Figure 13.3).

We have emphasized throughout that there is a clear challenge to the manager to appraise his/her company's sales operations using our hallmarks as the basis for this audit. The data we have provided allow comparisons to be made with the most effective sales organizations we found in our research. We suggest that many insights can be generated from an audit of this kind, and it is likely that the results may challenge many company beliefs about how best to recruit, train and develop salespeople and sales managers, and manage sales efforts.

However, experience suggests that while we have identified a set of factors that managers must address to boost sales organization effectiveness, acting on these lessons may mean facing new problems. We have found that the more effective sales organizations focus on developing and maintaining long-term customer relationships through teamwork, adaptiveness and customer support in the sales organization. This result is consistent with the current emphasis on relationship marketing strategy. However, achieving that focus requires attention to structural and 'people' issues by sales management.

'the more effective sales organizations focus on developing and maintaining long-term customer relationships through teamwork, adaptiveness and customer support in the sales organization'

The goal of structural decisions is to provide salespeople with high-performance situations to exploit – for example, through having a 'right-sized' salesforce, effective territory design, focused selling teams and appropriate spans of control for sales managers. Poor sales management decisions in these areas can establish unnecessary and avoidable performance hurdles. These issues must be addressed alongside the 'people' decisions that aim to develop successful salespeople, capable of winning in the marketplace. These 'people' decisions are critically concerned with compensation strategy, having salespeople with the desired success characteristics, and focusing appropriate types of management attention on the underlying drivers of salesforce performance. This is the route to high effectiveness in the sales organization, based on long-term customer relationships.

However, relationship-oriented selling and team-based sales may require very different skills and capabilities from those of the

Sales unit/group:	Completed by:	Time: Date:

Part 1: Evaluating Sales Organization Effectiveness

Compared to our major competitor how well has this sales unit performed in the following areas in the year:	Much Worse						Much Better
Sales volume achieved	1	2	3	4	5	6	7
Market share achieved	1	2	3	4	5	6	7
Profitability							
Customer satisfaction	1	2	3	4	5	6	7

Compared to the objectives set for this sales unit, how well has this sales unit performed in the following areas in the last year:	Much Worse						Much Better
Sales volume achieved	1	2	3	4	5	6	7
Market share achieved	1	2	3	4	5	6	7
Profitability	1	2	3	4	5	6	7
Customer satisfaction	1	2	3	4	5	6	7

Comments/Implications:

Part 2: Evaluating Salesperson Characteristics

To what extent do the salespeople in this sales unit:

	Needs Improvement						Outstanding
Motivation							
1. Obtain a sense of accomplishment from their work.	1	2	3	4	5	6	7
2. Feel a sense of personal growth and development in their work.	1	2	3	4	5	6	7

Figure 13.3 Diagnostic Worksheet 5 – Evaluating our own sales organization

3. Get a feeling of stimulation and a sense of challenging involvement in their work.	1	2	3	4	5	6	7
4. Have a high level of respect from their supervisors	1	2	3	4	5	6	7
5. Have respect from fellow workers	1	2	3	4	5	6	7
6. Have a sense of being creative and imaginative in their work	1	2	3	4	5	6	7
7. Get a sense of loyal association with the company	1	2	3	4	5	6	7
8. Feel a sense of being innovative in their work	1	2	3	4	5	6	7
Customer Orientation							
9. Focus on satisfying customer needs	1	2	3	4	5	6	7
10. Customise their selling approaches to individual	1	2	3	4	5	6	7
11. Possess expert selling skills	1	2	3	4	5	6	7
12. Possess extensive product/service knowledge	1	2	3	4	5	6	7
13. Study customer needs to guide selling strategy	1	2	3	4	5	6	7
Team Orientation							
14. Are willing to accept direction from line manager	1	2	3	4	5	6	7
15. Co-operate a part of a sales teams	1	2	3	4	5	6	7
16. Accept the line manager's authority	1	2	3	4	5	6	7
17. Welcome performance reviews	1	2	3	4	5	6	7
Sales Support Orientation							
18. Spend substantial time planning sales calls	1	2	3	4	5	6	7
19. Perform non-selling activities effectively	1	2	3	4	5	6	7
20. Perform sales support activities effectively	1	2	3	4	5	6	7

Comments/Implications

Figure 13.3 (*Continued*)

Part 3: Evaluating Salesforce Performance

How well are the salespeople in this sales unit performing in these areas:

	Needs Improvement						Outstanding
OUTCOME PERFORMANCE							
1. Producing a high market share	1	2	3	4	5	6	7
2. Making sales of those products with the highest profit margin	1	2	3	4	5	6	7
3. Generating a good level of sales revenue.	1	2	3	4	5	6	7
4. Quickly generating sales of new company products and services	1	2	3	4	5	6	7
5. Identifying and selling to major accounts.	1	2	3	4	5	6	7
6. Producing sales or contracts with long-term profitability	1	2	3	4	5	6	7
7. Exceeding all sales targets and objectives during the year.	1	2	3	4	5	6	7
BEHAVIOURAL PERFORMANCE							
Sales Presentation							
8. Listening attentively to identify and understand the real concerns of customers	1	2	3	4	5	6	7
9. Convincing customers that they understand their unique problems and concerns	1	2	3	4	5	6	7
10. Using established contacts to develop new customers	1	2	3	4	5	6	7
11. Communicate their sales presentations clearly and concisely	1	2	3	4	5	6	7
12. Work out solutions to a customer's questions and objections	1	2	3	4	5	6	7
Technical Knowledge							
13. Knowing the design and specification of company products/services	1	2	3	4	5	6	7
14. Knowing the applications of company products/services	1	2	3	4	5	6	7
15. Keeping abreast of the company's production and technological developments	1	2	3	4	5	6	7
Adaptiveness							
16. Experimenting with different sales approaches	1	2	3	4	5	6	7
17. Being flexible in the selling approaches used	1	2	3	4	5	6	7

Figure 13.3   (*Continued*)

18. Adapting selling approaches from one customer to another	1	2	3	4	5	6	7
19. Varying sales style from situation to situation	1	2	3	4	5	6	7
Teamwork							
20. Generating considerable sales volume fro team sales (sales made jointly by two or more salespeople)	1	2	3	4	5	6	7
21. Building strong working relationships with other people in the company.	1	2	3	4	5	6	7
22. Working closely with non-sales employees to close sales	1	2	3	4	5	6	7
23. Co-ordinating with other company employees to handle post-sales problems and service	1	2	3	4	5	6	7
24. Discussing selling strategies with people from various departments.	1	2	3	4	5	6	7
Planning							
25. Planning each sales call	1	2	3	4	5	6	7
26. Planning sales strategies for each customer	1	2	3	4	5	6	7
27. Planning coverage of assigned territory/customer coverage	1	2	3	4	5	6	7
28. Planning daily activities	1	2	3	4	5	6	7
Support							
29. Providing after-sales service	1	2	3	4	5	6	7
30. Checking on product delivery	1	2	3	4	5	6	7
31. Handling customer complaints	1	2	3	4	5	6	7
32. Following-up on product use	1	2	3	4	5	6	7
33. Troubleshooting on application problems	1	2	3	4	5	6	7
34. Analysing product use experience to identify new product/service ideas	1	2	3	4	5	6	7

Comments/Implications

Figure 13.3 (*Continued*)

Part 4: Evaluating Sales Management Activities

To what extent do the sales manager(s) in this unit:

	Not at all						To a great extent
Monitoring Activities							
1. Spend time with salespeople in the field	1	2	3	4	5	6	7
2. Make joint sales calls with salespeople	1	2	3	4	5	6	7
3. Regularly review call reports from salespeople	1	2	3	4	5	6	7
4. Monitor the day-to-day activities of salespeople	1	2	3	4	5	6	7
5. Observe the performance of salespeople in the field	1	2	3	4	5	6	7
6. Pay attention to the extent which salespeopl in the field	1	2	3	4	5	6	7
7. Closely watch salespeoples' expenses	1	2	3	4	5	6	7
8. Pay attention to the credit terms that salespeople quote customers.	1	2	3	4	5	6	7
Directing Activities							
9. Encourage salespeople to increase their sales results by rewarding them for their achievements	1	2	3	4	5	6	7
10. Actively participate in training salespeople on the job	1	2	3	4	5	6	7
11. Regularly spend time coaching salespeople	1	2	3	4	5	6	7
12. Discuss performance evaluations with salespeople	1	2	3	4	5	6	7
13. Help salespeople develop their potential	1	2	3	4	5	6	7
Evaluating Activities							
14. Evaluate the number of sales calls made by salespeople	1	2	3	4	5	6	7
15. Evaluate the profit contribution made by each salesperson	1	2	3	4	5	6	7
16. Evaluate the quality of the sales presentations made by salespeople	1	2	3	4	5	6	7
17. Evaluate the professional development of salespeople	1	2	3	4	5	6	7
Rewarding Activities							
18. Provide performance feedback to salespeople on a regular basis	1	2	3	4	5	6	7
19. Compensate salespeople on the basis of the quality of their sales activities	1	2	3	4	5	6	7
20. Use incentive compensation as a major means for motivating salespeople	1	2	3	4	5	6	7

Figure 13.3 *(Continued)*

21. Make incentive payment judgements based on the sales results achieved by salespeople	1	2	3	4	5	6	7
22. Reward salespeople based on their results.	1	2	3	4	5	6	7
23. Use non-financial incentives to reward salespeople for their results.	1	2	3	4	5	6	7
24. Compensate salespeople based on the quantity of their sales activities	1	2	3	4	5	6	7

Comments/Implications

Part 5: Evaluating Sales Territory Design

How satisfactory is the design of the territories assigned to salespeople in this sales unit on the following issues

	Very unsatisfactory						Very satsifactory
1. The number of accounts in each territory	1	2	3	4	5	6	7
2. The number of large accounts in each territory	1	2	3	4	5	6	7
3. The sales productivity in each territory	1	2	3	4	5	6	7
4. The geographic size of each territory	1	2	3	4	5	6	7
5. The number of sales calls made in each territory	1	2	3	4	5	6	7
6. The amount of travel required in each territory	1	2	3	4	5	6	7
7. The market potential in each territory	1	2	3	4	5	6	7
8. The number of territories in the sales unit	1	2	3	4	5	6	7
9. The assignment of salespeople to territories	1	2	3	4	5	6	7
10. The equivalence in workload across territories	1	2	3	4	5	6	7
11. The overall design of territories	1	2	3	4	5	6	7

Comments/Implications:

Figure 13.3 (*Continued*)

stereotypical 'lone wolf' salesperson of the past. In the same way, behaviour-based control by sales managers requires a different set of skills from those of the 'command and control' model of field sales management.

Sales training and development will have to emphasize team building, conflict resolution, interpersonal skills and other capabilities relevant to the drivers of salesforce performance and to developing the needed success characteristics in salespeople. This will require time and money. It may not always succeed – the truly individualistic 'lone wolf' salesperson may not easily be converted into an effective team player. Nonetheless, the findings of our research into the characteristics of the more effective sales organizations point the direction in which many firms will have to move over the next several years to develop truly effective sales organizations.

Looking at our own sales organization effectiveness

The items studied to draw conclusions about the sources of sales organization effectiveness can be used as benchmarks against which to examine our own selling operations.

Let me stress from the outset that this is not a weapon with which to beat up sales managers and the members of the salesforce. It is a device to uncover the underlying drivers of performance in the sales organization, to evaluate the fit with market strategy and to identify the areas that can be improved for that fit between strategy and sales. This is about building a partnership between marketing and sales – not scoring points or paying off old scores. It is more about listening and giving help across the marketing/sales barrier than about control and coercion.

This diagnostic is designed to be used at the field sales unit level, and it works best there. It may be completed by the field sales manager, or s/he may nominate an outsider, such as the manager of another field unit. One way or another, though, we need to get the input of the salespeople as well – possibly in their reactions to the unit or branch manager's views or possibly in completing the diagnostic themselves and comparing their views, to those of the sales manager.

The output from the diagnostic can be used in several ways:

● We can use it as the basis for discussion with salespeople in the unit concerned to get their views on how the effectiveness of the unit can be developed and improved.

- We can use the results as a way of comparing the effectiveness of different sales units in the company, to identify the most effective and to see what we can learn from them to improve things in the less effective units.
- We can use the diagnostic regularly as a way of tracking change in how sales are managed at the field unit or branch level, to see what works and to find new areas for improvement.
- But most important, the diagnostic is a way of evaluating how well the sales organization is driving marketing strategy through to the marketplace.

As with the research results in the previous section of the chapter, the different points of the diagnostic can produce different types of insight:

- Part 1 looks at effectiveness in achievements in sales volume, market share, profitability and customer satisfaction against the competition and against company goals. There is no point in trying to impress by exaggerating achievements or trying to make a point by underestimating achievements – the figure can always be validated anyway. We should look both at the *level* of achievement by the sales unit and also the *problems* – is market share or customer satisfaction being 'bought' at the expense of profitability, or vice versa?
- Part 2 looks at the motivation, customer orientation, team orientation and sales support orientation displayed by salespeople in the unit or branch.
- Part 3 gets into the detail of the sales unit's performance – both outcome performance, as traditionally measured and also behavioural performance in selling.
- Part 4 turns to the activities of the field sales manager in terms of monitoring, directing, evaluating and rewarding activities.
- Part 5 looks at how robust is the design of the sales territory, and identifies areas which may need improvement.

At each stage the diagnostic asks us to comment on the evaluations made and to identify the implications for how we could improve effectiveness in each sales unit or branch. In assessing the implications of our evaluations, attention should be given to the following types of issues:

- Are there unmet training and development needs to work on the motivation of salespeople, and to help them develop greater skills in customer orientation, team orientation and sales support orientation? (Conclusions here may not be what you expect. In one company in the building trade we were surprised to find that, contrary to company expectations, it was the older, more experienced salespeople who had aptitudes for customer orientation, sales support and team work. The younger, less experienced salespeople were driven by price-cutting and individual sales achievements. The reason: younger salespeople had only experienced selling in a severe economic recession, while the older salespeople had a longer-term view. The lesson: be prepared to listen and learn when you talk to the people who bring in the company's revenue!)

● Do we need to review how we go about recruiting salespeople in terms of what we look for, and how we introduce new people to the selling operation?

'do we give people incentives to produce anything other than sales outcomes?'

● In comparing outcome and behavioural perform-ance, do we give people incentives to produce anything other than sales outcomes? If the com-pany does not value behavioural performance by salespeople beyond lip-service, then why should we expect salespeople to excel in these areas?

● In looking at how sales managers spend their time, do they have the aptitude and freedom to be coaches and communicators, or are they pushed into a command and control way of operating? What does this tell us about the training and development needs of sales managers, and what we should look for in promoting and recruiting to this critical role?

● How well have territory designs and coverage of the market stood up in an era of corporate downsizing and structural change?

● How well positioned is the salesforce to implement market strategies? What does this tell us about the priorities in managing the sales organization, and the realities that need to be reflected in market strategies?

Where does that leave us with the salesforce?

'the need to build a partnership between sales and the other owners of the company's process of going to market (including the marketing department, but also others as well)'

The goal of this chapter was to underline the need to build a partnership between sales and the other owners of the company's process of going to market (including the marketing department, but also others as well), to gain the more effective implementation of market strategies. We saw that the consequences of failing to build this link are serious – many strategic gaps and implementation failures can be traced to market strategies disappearing into a black hole somewhere between the office and the sales organization. Addressing this link is urgent and important – the goal is partnership to drive market-led strategic change.

We put this goal into the context of the challenges facing sales organizations to change in response to customer demands and company pressures for increased productivity. This was reinforced by studying the H. R. Challey Group benchmarks for world-class sales success.

We then turned to research evidence about the sources of effectiveness in British sales organizations, and the diagnostic worksheet for in-company use, based on the research findings.

This is the basis for building market-led strategic change in partnership with the sales organization – the challenge is to put it into effect.

References

1. Biong, Harald and Fred Selnes (1996), *The Strategic Role of the Salesperson in Established Buyer-Seller Relationships*, Marketing Science Institute Report.
2. The H. R. Challey Group (1991), *New Benchmarks for World Class Sales Success*, Ohio: The H. R. Challey Group.
3. Bartram, Peter (1997), 'Bidding Tricks', *Marketing Business*, January.
4. The H. R. Challey Group (1996), *The Customer Selected World Class Sales Executive Report*, Ohio: The H. R. Challey Group.
5. Piercy, Nigel F., David W. Cravens and Neil A. Morgan (1997), 'Sources of Effectiveness in Business-to-Business Sales Organizations', *Journal of Marketing Practice: Applied Marketing Science*, Vol. 3, No. 1, 43–69.

Consider what it is like to buy a new car. We travel to the distributorship
for the car we like – usually in an unpleasant part of town.

As we enter the showroom a salesperson attaches to us, and *stays* with
us. He (normally) will make the effort to separate us – the female partner
is sidelined, while sales pressure is applied to the male partner. We explain
what we want – this is a waste of time because the salesperson clearly is
not interested in what we think, only in closing the deal and selling as many
add-ons to the product as possible.

By now we are talking about the car the salesperson wants to sell, not
the one we came in to see. Of course, we have to make our minds up
quickly, for there are many others who want 'our car' – usually not in
evidence in the showroom, or probably outside the salesperson's
imagination.

Our objections to the vehicle being sold are systematically and skilfully
overcome; our attempts to negotiate on price lead to a meeting with
a senior salesperson who is even ruder and more aggressive than the
first and who squashes our pathetic attempts to get a good discount on
the list price.

Our attempts to get a good trade-in price on our current
'Our attempts to get
a good trade-in price
on our current car
are met with barely
disguised derision'
car are met with barely disguised derision, and we are
grudgingly offered a trade-in value several hundred pounds
lower than the list price, because of the numerous faults
instantly discovered in our vehicle and the 'impossibility' for
the dealer of selling it on.

Finally, we sign the contract, and commit ourselves to the
expenditure. Somehow our salesperson loses interest at about this point,
and we end up with a clerical worker, who explains about the two-month
waiting list for the new car, and the £800 charge for number plates and
delivery (which is mandatory because we are not allowed to supply our
own number plates or collect the car from the manufacturer's plant even
if we want to), and the charge for the extras we agreed to, and the cost
of the road fund licence, and so it goes on.

---

* This case study has been prepared by Nigel Piercy, Cardiff Business School, from
secondary sources, with input from Mr Patrick Farrell, Marketing Director,
Daewoo Cars, and Ms Rachel Hushon, Account Executive, Duckworth, Finn,
Grubb, Waters. Professor Leyland Pitt made valuable comments to improve an
earlier draft of the case. The Daewoo advertisements are reproduced by kind
permission of Daewoo and Duckworth, Finn, Grubb, Waters.

When we finally get the vehicle it has faults, so we take it back. Now we deal with the 'service' people, whose main aim is to 'prove' that there is nothing wrong with the car, and if there is, it is our fault, and 'no', we cannot have a lift to work while they look at it...

The evidence from countless customer surveys suggests that this is what it feels like buying a car (whatever people in the trade say) – and customers hate it. It is not like this at all if you buy from Daewoo.

Daewoo is a South Korean corporation which has entered the UK car market with a highly successful launch – selling 35 000 vehicles in less than two years – which is continuing to change many of the basic rules of how car companies compete and how they deal with their customers. Following its market entry in 1995, by mid-1996 Daewoo announced an investment of £700 million in setting up a car factory in Britain. The new plant is expected to be preceded by large-scale investment by Daewoo in design, development and marketing and sales.

Daewoo was a name unfamiliar in the UK until the mid-1990s – although owners of Nokia mobile phones and Nike trainers were already customers of Daewoo companies. Starting as a textile company in 1967, Daewoo's product range is vast – including aircraft, banking, shipbuilding, petrochemicals, textiles, construction, heavy industry, computing and automotive manufacture. For example, Daewoo produces wing assemblies for British Aerospace, Lockheed and Boeing.

Initially, in preparing for the car launch, the company promoted itself in Britain as 'the biggest car company you've never heard of'. In fact, businesses now owned by Daewoo have produced cars for some 60 years and it has 11 car plants in nine different countries, but Daewoo was blocked from operating in the European car market until 1992 by a joint-venture agreement with General Motors. Daewoo is Korea's second biggest car maker and the world's 33rd largest business group. In common with other Pacific-Rim country corporations, Daewoo has an aggressive plan for expansion and globalization.

Patrick Farrell, recruited from Rover as Marketing Director, came from a background in market research and advertising, and joined Daewoo when it was effectively a 'virtual car company'. Farrell drove the pre-launch publicity to establish the Daewoo presence, and a market strategy that involved taking control of the distribution chain by dealing direct with customers – eliminating dealers from the channel. Farrell's unique selling proposition for Daewoo was to be the most customer-focused brand in the car market. This thinking was based on a large-scale market research programme analysing car buyers' attitudes, and a highly effective creative partnership with Duckworth Finn.

Daewoo launched its car operations in the UK market on 1 April 1995, on the back of a £150 million investment and an award-winning £11 million advertising campaign produced by Duckworth, Finn, Grubb, Waters. Examples of Daewoo's brand proposition to customers are shown in Figure 1 – one of the launch messages from 1995, and an example of the 1997

Figure 1 Daewoo advertising

campaign. Right from the start, Daewoo told consumers that there were no commission-earning salespeople and no distributors, and that is why the value of the car was so high. In short, Daewoo's market positioning is based on an innovative packaging of benefits and services around the car, a totally new approach to distribution and the customer's purchasing experience, and an emphasis on customer service.

Daewoo set an ambitious target of achieving a 1 per cent share of the UK new car market by the end of 1997, but performance has greatly exceeded this target. In fact, the company sold 10 000 vehicles in the first six months of the campaign and achieved a 0.9 per cent share of the market in eight months from launch. Daewoo's launch was the most successful new marque launch ever in the UK market, beating Proton's record of ten years' standing and becoming the 27th largest car firm in the UK, ahead of companies like Chrysler and Subaru (and, perhaps more importantly, ahead of Hyundai, the market leader in the Korean home market). In spite of some industry scepticism, achieving 1 per cent of the UK car market can be put into context as follows:

Brand	Years in the UK market	Market share
Volvo	38 years	1.7%
Mazda	25 years	1.2%
Hyundai	14 years	0.9%
Proton	7 years	0.5%
Kia	5 years	0.2%

The market

The UK car market is fiercely competitive, is experiencing little growth and has over-supply from local production and strong import brands with more than 40 competing firms. However, standards of customer service are low in many areas. For example, Patrick Farrell, Daewoo's Marketing Director, writes in 1996 that 'the direct response campaign we ran in January this year generated more than 125 000 responses and more than 50,000 stories of recent maltreatment by the motor trade, many of which were almost beyond belief ... a significant proportion of the trade still lags behind the standards set by retailers in other industries'.

Pre-launch research by Daewoo with 200 000 motorists found that traditional motor dealers did not make customers feel welcome. Some 63 per cent of motorists found car showrooms to be intimidating places, a similar proportion believed that the salesman usually 'wins' and 86 per cent said they would be prepared to travel up to 50 miles for a better buying experience, and people generally disliked haggling over prices and the whole purchase experience in the traditional dealer's showroom.

'traditional motor dealers did not make customers feel welcome'

There is some basis for this mistrust on the part of car buyers. Recent surveys show that on a £12,000–£13,000 new car, the customer who haggles can get a price reduction of up to £1,600, while the customer who does not haggle pays the list price for the same car. In both cases, the unwary are likely to pay over the odds for the financing deal as well.

Similarly, research from the agency Foote, Cone and Belding suggests that women car buyers (who account for more than one third of new car purchases) feel particularly intimidated and patronized by traditional car dealers and salespeople, as well as insulted by conventional 'toys for boys' car advertising.

In spite of these signs of market opportunity, the company recognized that launching a new brand in the mature UK car market was going to be hard. Nissan and Toyota succeeded in market entry by building better cars, but the other larger players have already largely closed the quality gap. Companies like Lada attacked the market with low prices and corresponding status. Mid-market launches by Hyundai and Proton, adopting conventional market strategies, had failed to achieve what Daewoo wanted – 1 per cent of the market within three years. Brainstorming sessions by Daewoo's UK management, culminating in summer 1994 at the Tylney Hotel near Daewoo's Rickmansworth headquarters, have effectively rewritten the 'rule-book' for the motor trade in Britain.

The company's market position does not rest on product quality, low price, a 'life-style'-based brand image or any conventional platform. It is based on customer service and value in the customer's terms. Delivering these promises is based on direct selling, not conventional car distributorships, and highly innovative advertising to build and sustain the image of value and customer service.

The Daewoo market strategy

The Daewoo *product strategy* is far from sensational in itself. Designs appear old-fashioned, and are, in fact, based on old General Motors models. In fact, Daewoo's entry-level car, the Nexia, was the previous model of the Vauxhall Astra (though coming into the market at a price £2,000 below the basic Astra), and was sold in other parts of the GM world as the Opel Kadette, or the Pontiac Le Mans. However, a first difference is that from launch Daewoo delivered the car without the 'traditional' hidden extras: the car is delivered without charge, with number plates, a year's tax and a full tank of petrol. (These charges have traditionally meant an additional charge to the customer of £400–600 on top of the list price.) Perhaps most significant of all to the budget-conscious consumer, nervous about running costs as well as purchase price, the sticker price of the Daewoo car includes three years free' servicing, covering everything except the tyres. This alone breaks the fundamental rules of how business is done in this market. Then add to this the fact that the Daewoo vehicle also has a three-year/60 000-mile warranty, three years' AA breakdown cover, security registration and a mobile phone, with no additional charges. Also the vehicle will be collected for servicing and a courtesy car will always be provided, with no additional charge to the owner, and possibly the bewilderment of competitors is quite understandable. (In fact, new Daewoo models, including a supermini, executive and 'people carrier' vehicles, are to be launched.) Further industry confusion was created when Daewoo added three years fully comprehensive insurance to the package for the 1997 campaign. Indeed, dated mechanicals or not, it is the first time in history that a car company has made a 'Buy One, Get One Free' offer – the first 1000 buyers in April 1995 were promised a replacement N-registration car* in August that year.

In *pricing*, the new car buyer's nightmare that someone else will buy the same car at the same time for a better price does not exist for Daewoo buyers. Daewoo operates a fixed price strategy with no haggling. However, the Daewoo value strategy in services and product benefits is outstanding. The trade dislikes this approach, but customers appear to prefer it and to choose fixed prices rather than endure the stress of bargaining.

'the new car buyer's nightmare that someone else will buy the same car at the same time for a better price does not exist for Daewoo buyers'

The main source of competitive differentiation for Daewoo cars is not the product offer or the price deal, but the way in which the cars are sold and distributed.

The buying experience for the Daewoo customer has been described as 'a car browsing environment with the hassle factor removed', where customers are welcomed, given 'permission' to explore, and left alone by staff unless help is requested. A company executive said at the time of launch: 'Customers will be treated as if they are in Harrods ... They will receive the utmost courtesy and attention when they require it. There will be no sales pressure, just perfection in attention to detail ... Our philosophy is not short-term gain, but long-term customer satisfaction ... We will demonstrate honesty openly and will make car buying a delightful experience.' The Daewoo strategy for delivering those promises is revolutionary.

First, Daewoo has side-stepped the traditional distribution channel and does not employ a franchised dealer network. Distribution is through a wholly-owned network of 'Motor Shows', i.e. roomy, friendly car shops mostly in retail park locations, and smaller 'Car Centres'. The company view is that dealing direct strips out a profit tier of 30–35 per cent of the

---

* In the British car market, new registration prefix letters start in August each year, so the prefix letter makes the age of the vehicle clear to all, and impacts directly on the trade-in price.

price of the vehicle. This saving is reinforced by the use of flexible employment terms, for example zero-hours contracts for distribution staff (paid only when needed for work). Daewoo's launch goals were: high coverage of the country, total control of the sales operation, and lowest possible risk to capital. Direct distribution and partnerships achieve these goals, but also side-step the costs for the manufacturer of promoting vehicles to distributors and the inefficiencies of independent car distributorships with no economies of scale in their operations.

Secondly, the Daewoo distribution outlets are blatantly designed to react directly to specific points of customer dissatisfaction with traditional car dealers. There are no traditionally aggressive car showroom sales-people chasing commission – Daewoo's salespeople are paid salaries and are not allowed to approach a visitor to the store unless invited. Touch-screen computers allow prospective buyers to investigate choices and finance options (not competing for the computer with their children, who have their own touch-screen computers to design their own cars in the supervised crèche and playroom area). The aisles are wide enough to accommodate a double buggy, and the floors are soft enough so that high heels do not clip and draw attention. A coffee bar provides the facility to sit and think. Test drives can be arranged to and from the home, not the showroom, and refunds/exchanges can be made in the first month by the buyer who remains unsure about his/her purchase.

Daewoo's strategy also recognizes that there are three important elements to the car business: new car sales, service support, and used car sales. Because each of these has very different requirements, Daewoo has 'unbundled' them. New car purchases are made infrequently, and for most consumers are a major investment – buyers do not look at new cars often, but when they do they will travel some distance to see the cars they want to see. Daewoo relies on a small number of flagship sites to pull in buyers to see the cars, reducing investment in the network. Used car sales are important, but are fitted into the network wherever this does not detract from market positioning of the new cars. The major problem is servicing, where the market requirements are almost opposite to those for new car showrooms – there need to be many sites because customers do not want to travel far for service and repair, but they need to be small because of operational efficiencies in servicing modern cars. The strategy here is based on partnership.

Servicing and maintenance for Daewoo cars is provided through a collaborative deal with Halfords, the motoring superstore chain owned by Boots, and visited by 30 million people a year. Thirty of Halfords superstores will include Daewoo car salesrooms by the end of 1996, and all 136 branches will provide service for Daewoo cars – early in 1997 the Halfords outlets were already providing 20 per cent of Daewoo's retail sales volume. Halfords does not earn commission for car sales – its income comes from service and repair and increased customer traffic. The Halfords mechanics are Daewoo-trained, and

Daewoo staff will be present in the Halfords stores to ensure that staff receive the customer service promised. Unsurprisingly, Halfords customers with other brands of car now find Daewoo literature discreetly placed in their vehicles when they are collected from servicing or repair.

More recently, in 1996 Daewoo has started a joint venture with the supermarket group Sainsbury's Savacentre group, to locate Daewoo showrooms at Savacentre's food and clothing sites. The pilot outlet at Colney sold 200 cars within its first 12 months of operation.

The resulting Daewoo network has three tiers designed around customer needs:

- the *Daewoo Motor Shows*, the flagship new car sales outlets based on retail parks, with high levels of traffic and large catchment areas;
- the *Daewoo Car Centres*, smaller to gain market coverage and providing some servicing as well as new and used car sales; and
- the *Daewoo Support Centres*, which concentrate on servicing, based at Halfords sites, but which have also proved successful in selling vehicles and developing into additional showrooms.

Driving the launch was the Daewoo *branding and advertising* strategy. Daewoo faced the twin problems of the company's credibility as an import brand with no customer awareness in Britain and customer cynicism about motor trade promises of customer service. With a mix of direct response advertising – to actually listen to customers in the 'Daewoo Dialogue' – TV and press spots using the types of messages in the ads shown in the case, Daewoo took prompted awareness of the brand from 4 per cent in September 1994 to 50 per cent by the end of December that year, and customer perceptions of a new customer focus were growing. Indeed, in the launch, Daewoo's advertising awareness by November 1995 was 77 per cent on the back of an £11 million spend, compared to the highest-spending car firm's 64 per cent from a £64 million spend. The 'four pillars' of the brand proposition developed by Duckworth, Finn, Grubb, Waters with Daewoo were:

- *Direct* – treating customers differently;
- *Hassle-free* – clear communication with the company for customers, and no sales pressure and haggling;
- *Peace of mind* – the features that worry customers, and are traditionally expensive 'extras', are permanently available with every Daewoo (and Daewoo stays in touch with the buyer throughout purchase and use in the 'Daewoo Contact Wheel' with members of the 'Daewoo family'); and
- *Courtesy* – by openly respecting customer needs and preferences throughout the purchase and use process.

Industry reactions

'industry views were that the Daewoo strategy would not work'

As the extent of Daewoo's impact on the market has become apparent, the reactions of competitors have evolved along the following lines. Initially, industry views were that the Daewoo strategy would not work – after-sales service would be too expensive to fund, customers would reject the lack of independent franchised dealers, and independent servicing would not work. Initial industry surprise and scepticism about Daewoo's strategy developed into criticisms of the company for being too aggressive and arrogant, accompanied by rumours in the motor press that car buyers would lose because trade-in prices would be depressed (perhaps deliberately devalued by dealers). One industry analyst commented: 'Daewoo – huh, that's 'Lada with Attitude'!' Most recently, Daewoo has been subject to a variety of 'dirty tricks' and attacks: being banned from one local motor show and threatened with exclusion from others as a response to the Daewoo advertising campaign, and attempts to discourage national newspapers from running Daewoo advertisements. Daewoo was forced to withdraw advertising that exposed 'overcharging' by dealers and underlining a 35 per cent price advantage for Daewoo over rival cars. In Scotland complaints to the national trade association led to the withdrawal of Daewoo ads showing a car being sliced by an electric saw with the caption 'The dealer's slice ...'.

Competitors' denial has evolved into bewilderment and now hostility, but with little sign of a coherent strategic response. This may be because Daewoo is in the process of smashing an industry structure which has developed largely unchanged over 100 years. Certainly by mid-1996, Volkswagen and Rover followed Saab in scrapping hidden 'delivery charges' and incorporating these into list prices – one of the Daewoo strategies which competitors had criticized from the outset. By 1997, industry analysts were saying that conventional franchised dealers were doomed to disappear – having lost control of service, parts, and finance and insurance, they will next lose control of the provision of the vehicle. Currently, car dealers in Britain hold £1.25 billion of surplus inventory – they have what is not selling in abundant supply. By mid-1997, Rover announced a 25 per cent reduction in its dealer network, and Ford was looking at the same kind of overhaul.

The future?

Daewoo's spectacular launch strategy has earned a number of prizes and accolades for the company and its Marketing Director, Patrick Farrell. By mid-1997, Daewoo had been rated number 4 in the top car makers' list in a customer satisfaction survey by BBC TV's *Top Gear* programme and the US motor industry analysts J. D. Powers – this achievement should be put into the context that Daewoo is a new supplier with little product innovation in the market. Currently, the company's customer satisfaction scores are running at 3.8 on a 4-point scale. However, there is no sense of complacency at Daewoo – executives know that this is only the beginning. Early in 1997, Farrell says: 'In a sense we are still in launch mode ... This year the marketing effort will focus on growing the number of retail outlets, launching a new range of cars, and injecting some 'emotion' into what is currently a very rational brand proposition.'

'the company's customer satisfaction scores are running at 3.8 on a 4-point scale'

It remains to be seen what strategic responses will emerge from the other 42 car manufacturers operating in the UK, and how the distribution channels for cars will further develop.

Sources: 'Adding Drive to the Weekly Shop', *Professional Engineering*, 19 June 1996. 'A Driving Force', Jane Simms, *Marketing Business*, February 1997. 'British Cars Limp into the Lada League', *Daily Mail*, 10 April 1997. 'Buy a Car, Get One Free', *The Times*, 1 April 1995. 'Car Dealers Must Adapt Or Die', *Sunday Business*, 13 April 1997. 'Daewoo Plans Flexible Contracts', *Financial Times*, 29 August 1996. Daewoo Overtakes Other Importers', *Financial Times*, 7 September 1995. 'Daewoo Pronounces Death of the Salesman', *Observer*, 9 April 1995. 'Daewoo to Sell Through Halfords', *Independent*, 28 November 1995. 'Daewoo to Set Up its Own Car Supermarkets', *Financial Times*, 11 October 1994. 'Dealer System is Collapsing', *Motortrader*, 24 February 1997. 'How a Car Buyer Can Go from 0 to £1600 in Eight Minutes', *Daily Mail*, 8 April 1997. 'Fantasy Fleet', *Business Age*, 1 October 1995. Halfords Open Doors to Daewoo', *Financial Times*, 28 November 1995. 'How to Woo the Daewoo Way', *Guardian*, 2 May 1995. 'Koreans Drive Hard for Market Share', *Independent on Sunday*, 16 July 1995. 'Koreans Offer a Crèche Course in Customer Care', *Daily Mail*, 11 October 1994. 'Sacred Cows', Patrick Farrell, *Marketing Business*, May 1996. Westward Ho for Korean Car Makers', *Observer*, 3 December 1995.

Questions to consider

1 The dilemma facing the motor industry is: how can we respond positively and effectively to the competitive challenge from Daewoo? How can they?

2 Is it possible to trace the Strategic Pathway that Daewoo has designed for itself, through its various stages?

3 Of the innovations associated with the Daewoo launch, which have been the most effective in achieving market share? What has Daewoo 'sensed' about this market that has been ignored by the established firms?

4 There is little in the Daewoo market research findings that has not been known for years – why have the established car firms failed to innovate in a customer-focused way?

5 What will Daewoo have to do to sustain its market performance – how many of its competitive advantages are likely to be enduring?

6 If Daewoo can attack an industry as competitive as the car sector through a value and customer service strategy – what other sectors may be open to an entry of this kind (insurance? travel?)?

7 What are the brand extension possibilities for Daewoo associated with the successful launch of the cars?

Case 8   Trolleywars

Competitive rivalry and strategic positioning in the British supermarket industry*

The battle for market leadership

The competitive pattern of the British supermarket sector through the 1980s and early 1990s was dominated by J. Sainsbury plc, more than 120 years old and in the sixth generation of founding family management. Sainsbury was positioned on its strength in product and store quality and customer service, and had achieved the status of a British 'institution'. Sainsbury had led the way for the increasingly sophisticated British grocery consumer to exotic new foods and an innovative range of high-quality wines and household products, and pioneered superstores and high-quality own-label products. Sainsbury was market leader in every sense.

The second competitor was Tesco. Tesco had grown as a downmarket discount retailer, whose origins were in the market stalls of the East End of London and growth through early self-service stores in London and Essex. By the 1960s Tesco was one of Britain's fastest growing companies, and the company started to drop its cheap and dowdy downmarket image and attacked the middle of the market. However, in the early 1990s Tesco was wrong-footed by the economic recession – the company was behind Sainsbury in quality, service and market reputation, and its market share was under attack in a value-oriented market by price discounters like Aldi.

Behind the main players were smaller competitors like Safeway, Asda and Kwik Save – each potentially threatening, but each with its own problems in the 1980s and early 1990s.

The structure of the old grocery market and the strategic positioning of the main players changed – some say changed for ever – in 1995.

The day in 1995 that Sainsbury finally lost market leadership in the British supermarket sector was headline news in many national newspapers. Comments were made about the 'end of an era' in Britain, particularly since Sainsbury lost its market share leadership to Tesco, its traditional rival with its 'pile it high, sell it cheap' background. The trauma was not so much the loss of a few market share points, but genuine loss of market *leadership* – in quality, innovation, customer service

'The trauma was not so much the loss of a few market share points, but genuine loss of market leadership'

---

* This case study has been prepared by Nigel Piercy, Cardiff Business School, from secondary sources and executive discussions.

and the ability to change in line with customers' requirements. (Indeed, in the 1970s and early 1980s Tesco led on market share, but was never recognized as 'market leader'.) Nonetheless, this was the time when reality caught up with reputation.

The loss of leadership in market share for Sainsbury resulted from a steady erosion of the lead over Tesco: in 1994 Tesco took 12.9 per cent of the market compared to Sainsbury's 13 per cent, and by 1995 Tesco had reached 14.4 per cent against Sainsbury's 12.9 per cent. Sainsbury has lost share primarily to Tesco, but also to Asda and Safeway. The resulting picture of market shares in 1996 is shown in Table 1.

Table 1   1996 market shares in UK grocery market

	%
Tesco	15.3
J. Sainsbury	11.8
Savacentre	0.9
Asda	7.8
Safeway	7.8
Co-op (Food)	5.8
Kwick-Save	4.0
Somerfield	3.6
Others	43.0

Source: *Verdict on Grocers and Supermarkets* 1997

The financial performance of Sainsbury has also deteriorated dramatically in this period. In 1993–96, Sainsbury shares slumped more than 30 per cent from 579p to 404p, underperforming against the FT-SE index by 48 per cent and the supermarket sector by 28 per cent. The Sainsbury family own some 40 per cent of the company, and in the 1992–96 period some £1.2 billion has been wiped off the value of its holdings. This decline has not been stopped by further profit warnings by the company to the City.

By 1996, Tesco's rate of sales growth was three times faster than Sainsbury's, and by 1997 forecasts suggest that Tesco had become a significantly bigger profit earner than Sainsbury. In 1997 Tesco continued to increase profit levels, while Sainsbury and Safeway both issued profit warnings to the City, and Tesco sales were almost a third higher than Sainsbury's. Analysts did not believe that Sainsbury could ever regain market leadership. This is reflected in the relative performance of their shares – compared to the rest of the retail sector, Tesco clearly outperforms Sainsbury by a wide margin, and in 1996 Tesco share value equalled Sainsbury's for the first time. The signs in 1997 were that Sainsbury had no effective strategy to recover the position and the gap achieved by Tesco was increasing.

The challengers

The major players in the supermarket industry remain: J. Sainsbury, Tesco, Asda, Safeway, Somerfield and Kwik Save. These are very different kinds of organizations, and have adopted market strategies which have in some instances led to direct conflict.

J. Sainsbury plc

Sainsbury remains 40 per cent in family ownership, and David Sainsbury, who became chairman and chief executive in 1992, represented the sixth generation of family leadership (see Table 2). The erosion of market position has coincided with David Sainsbury's tenure – indeed, in 1996 some City analysts said he had only kept his job by virtue of his family name – but the underlying sources of the problems go back further.

Table 2   The Sainsbury chain – keeping it in the family

	Born	Appointed	Relationship to previous chairman
John James	1884	1869	Founder
John Benjamin	1871	1928	Son
Alan	1902	1956	Son
Robert	1906	1967	Brother
John	1927	1969	Nephew
David	1940	1992	Cousin

Source: 'Counter Attack', *Sunday Times*, 14 January 1996

Sainsbury's market success was based on bringing to the market new food and wine assortments, including its strong own-label products – at times reaching 60 per cent of the product assortment on sale in Sainsbury stores – merchandised as high-quality products in well-designed stores, surrounded with a higher level of customer service than competitors. This strategy was associated mainly with the leadership and vision of John Sainsbury.

Lord (John) Sainsbury was an autocrat, feared throughout the organization, but widely respected as 'a man with a gut instinct for the grocery business'. Lord Sainsbury's management style rested on rigid lines of command, with power concentrated in the hands of a small family-dominated group at the centre of the company. The Sainsbury culture was seen from outside as smug and arrogant, cautious and conservative, secretive, and with considerable animosity between Sainsbury and its suppliers. These structures and this culture drove an effective strategy through the 1970s and 1980s, but they are not well-suited to managing change and being responsive to market developments.

David Sainsbury is reported to be a shy and cerebral man with many interests outside business. His focus of attention, on assuming the chairmanship, was on expansion into the USA with successful purchases of Shaws and Food Giant (since proving problematic and time-consuming) and in diversification, rather than the core UK grocery business. His preference is for a more consensual manage-

'the extremely nice David Sainsbury took over with this loose management style, and everything ground to a halt'

ment style, consulting with people about decisions, in a company which has no experience of working in this way. A senior executive with a rival chain is quoted in 1997: 'Lord Sainsbury ran an incredibly tight ship. The staff were used to being barked at, and then the extremely nice David Sainsbury took over with this loose management style, and everything ground to a halt.'

Executives report that staff morale has hit rock-bottom – the chairman wants the culture to change in a very traditional company, but managers see two previous chairmen – John and Robert – still at head office, looking over David's shoulder. Reports indicate that low morale is leading to an unusually large number of specialist buyers leaving to join competitors.

Meanwhile, outsiders criticize Sainsbury's for 'resting on its laurels' and sticking to old strategies at a time of fierce and innovative competition from Tesco, Asda and Safeway, who have been more responsive and flexible in keeping up with market changes.

The largest example of the Sainsbury company's inability to respond to market change and competitive pressure is the loyalty card strategy. In 1994, as part of its renewed marketing efforts, Tesco launched a loyalty card programme – the Tesco Clubcard. The Sainsbury chairman's response was to rubbish this ploy as 'electronic Green Shield stamps' and effectively declare business as usual. (This was in spite of the major success of the Spend and Save loyalty card in Sainsbury's DIY company, Homebase.) The Tesco Clubcard was a major success from launch – by the end of 1996 there were 9 million Clubcard members who shared £58 million worth of vouchers and coupons.

Sainsbury's response was confused and unclear as the Tesco success unfolded. By the end of 1995 Sainsbury announced, after conflicting statements, its own loyalty card launch. However, much competitive ground had been lost, and the signs are that Sainsbury's lack of initiative, and final 'me-too' response, has not recovered the ground lost. Indeed, analysts suggest that much of the profit fall in Sainsbury's 1996 performance is blamed on the costs of coming too late to market with the

Reward loyalty card – in January 1997 the City saw a £60 million profit reduction as largely the result of the costs of the Reward card scheme.

The Sainsbury response to loss of market leadership and continued fierce competition has been sluggish and piecemeal, and analysts suggest that company management has yet to develop a strategy of recovery. The chairman's explanation, that decline was because 'we haven't communicated well', confused many in the City, but is regarded by industry specialists as symptomatic of the lack of strategic direction in the company. One industry insider commented of David Sainsbury's performance that 'once he got the top job, he was a bit like a rabbit in the headlights'.

The most immediate response to loss of market leadership at Sainsbury was internal restructuring. The chairman/chief executive role was split to create two joint chief executives; with one of these posts being filled by Dino Adriano from heading the successful Homebase DIY chain to run the British supermarket business. A new marketing director was hired –

'The most immediate response to loss of market leadership at Sainsbury was internal restructuring'

Kevin McCarten, with a track record at P&G, Woolworth and Superdrug – although it has been suggested that he is being blocked in his change strategies by the Sainsbury 'old guard'. The company has announced a number of customer service initiatives – e.g. home delivery, a free breakdown rescue service for consumers shopping at its stores, checkout bag-packers – but has done little to promote them, or to target its large advertising spend at winning customers back from Tesco and Safeway.

The major strategic platform promised by the company is a series of price-cutting campaigns – although there have been suggestions that 'buying' sales growth at the expense of profit may not be sustainable for long. While some smaller rivals may be vulnerable to price-cutting, Tesco has publicly stated that it will match any Sainsbury price cuts. Sainsbury is also pursuing the acquisition of smaller rivals to 'buy' additional market share, as opposed to improving the effectiveness of its core business.

Critics also point out the need to slaughter several 'sacred cows' at Sainsbury. The dogged determination to maintain the private-label business – around 50 per cent of its product lines in-store – conflicts with the strength of leading food brands and reduces customer brand choice compared to Tesco. The unwillingness to try new store formats – like Tesco's successful smaller in-city Metro stores – has to change.

Most recently, Sainsbury has attempted to regain this initiative by announcing the Sainsbury Bank, to lead the way in supermarket-based financial services. Critics suggest this strategy fails to address the problems in the core grocery business, and will bring problems of its own – not least because banks are highly unpopular with customers when they say 'no' to loans, account applications, and other services, and when they increase charges. Some critics also draw attention to Sainsbury's history of strained supplier relationships as a suspect basis for an alliance with a financial services company.

Nonetheless, early in 1997 the Sainsbury Bank opened in 244 stores, underwritten by a £30 million investment by the company, as a start to going national during 1997. The Sainsbury Bank represents an alliance with the Bank of Scotland, and will offer Visa credit cards (where use earns Reward loyalty points) and an instant access savings account. Personal loan, mortgage and insurance products are planned. Kevin McCarten is talking of a target of half a million customers in the first year of operation. Initial City reactions are highly favourable, judging the Sainsbury banking products to be flexible, convenient and highly competitive compared to conventional banks.

Tesco

Tesco was founded by Jack Cohen (later Sir John) from his food trading in the post-War East End of London, and the business was associated from its earliest growth with high-volume, low-price retailing with limited service and quality in merchandising – encapsulated in Cohen's 'pile it high, sell it cheap' slogan. Tesco currently operates 545 stores (including the Wm Low stores purchased in 1994).

The strategic turnaround of this business is largely associated with the leadership of Ian (now Lord) MacLaurin. An engineering apprentice, MacLaurin was hired in 1958 by Cohen personally, apparently because of his cricketing prowess. MacLaurin became the protégé of Arthur Thrush, Retail Director, and became chairman in 1973 – fighting an early and highly significant boardroom battle to start a new image for Tesco by abandoning the downmarket Green Shield trading stamps collectables, which had been the major Tesco marketing ploy of the 1960s. MacLaurin as chairman was partnered with David Malpas as Managing Director – credited by many as the 'brains' underpinning MacLaurin's strong leadership.

MacLaurin's strategy in the 1980s was founded on opening new stores in out-of-town locations, with much higher levels of quality and value. The substantial change in the Tesco organization to implement this strategy is associated with MacLaurin's autocratic management style.

Although the company's aggressive price-cutting had caused some problems in the 1980s, the major challenge was in the early 1990s. Having moved the operation progressively into the middle of the market, Tesco was wrong-footed by the economic recession of the early 1990s. Tesco's market share was under attack from price discounters like Aldi, while it still had not caught up with Sainsbury in non-price competitiveness.

'Tesco was wrong-footed by the economic recession of the early 1990s'

The bad times of 1992 led to a series of internal changes and marketing initiatives. MacLaurin abandoned his role as 'retail dictator' and gave much freedom to Terry Leahy, a marketing man put into the succession line for chief executive, who drove a number of critical marketing programmes:

- introduction of a 'value line' that matched or undercut the discounters in commodity items, while maintaining its margins on most of the range;
- establishing smaller in-city Tesco Metro stores, to reflect the reaction by some customers against out-of-town superstores;
- the launch of the Clubcard loyalty programme, which doubled the company's sales growth;
- an effective challenge to high-street chains in the sale of newspapers, magazines and books;
- adopting the newest technological innovations at the point of sale, such as consumer operated scanning;
- a 1996 customer care programme creating 4500 new jobs in Tesco stores, including customer assistants in blue waistcoats to pack bags, unload trolleys, fetch forgotten items and replace damaged goods;
- experiments with all-night opening in key locations.

In 1997 Tesco was in the headlines again for its conflict with the manufacturers of branded designer goods, which Tesco had started to stock and sell at discounted prices. Brands sold witout the manufacturer's 'permission' (and sourced from third parties) included Levi 501 blue jeans, as well as Chanel, Christian Dior and Clarins perfumes and cosmetics.

MacLaurin and Malpas retire in 1997, and leave a legacy of market strength, focus on customer responsiveness and competitive strengths from market leadership. Tesco is rated highly as a company able to produce and implement new initiatives.

Part of the legacy is from the purchase of AB Foods' 109 supermarkets in Ireland, as well as international expansion into the potentially lucrative Eastern Europe marketplace.

The new chief executive is Terry Leahy, who is renowned for his devotion to customer-driven policies and is credited with the recovery from the 1992 downturn when the group had moved upmarket while its customers were suffering from the recession – he drove the Value Lines strategy that rescued the situation and pioneered the loyalty card programme.

Asda

As third player in the market, Asda has no aspiration to market share leadership, but under the leadership of Archie Norman the company has established a strong and highly differentiated position in the market.

Norman joined Yorkshire-based Asda in 1991 on the basis of experience as a McKinsey consultant and five years as a finance director at Kingfisher, the owner of Woolworths and Comet. The prospects at Asda did not look good – many of the stores were in poor condition, and the company had debts of £1 billion and needed a further injection of £700 million to survive.

During the 1980s Asda had lost touch with its roots as a northern-based discounter. In trying to simulate the success strategies of Sainsbury and Tesco, the company had allowed its good-value image to erode and alienated its traditional customer base, without appealing to a new base. Asda had also acquired 60 stores from Gateway in 1989 in an attempt to expand from its northern base, and gained massive debts. In fact, by 1995 Norman had brought in a profit of £246 million, tripling profits in three years, with a net cash flow of £4.2 million, leading share price up from 27p to 102p, and Asda is established as Britain's third largest grocer.

Part of Norman's strategy has been to change the Asda culture to reinforce the 'good-value ethos'. Although a man who criticizes the 'cult of the personality' in business, Norman has been described in the trade as 'the Gazza of food retailing, he is constantly playing to the crowd'.

'His management style has been characterized by an ethos of austerity'

His management style has been characterized by an ethos of austerity – expensive company cars have disappeared; head office executives are sent to stores to pack bags at checkouts on the busiest days at Christmas; the executive box at York Races has gone. The reason for abandoning perks was said in the company annual report to be because they 'carry a sense of status and hierarchy antipathetic to the corporate culture'. The new management style also involves: 'red hats' – headquarters staff who need time to think can put on a red baseball cap, which means no-one will speak to them for two hours; 'listening groups' held weekly in 200 stores as a forum for ideas and complaints; and asking staff to select a product and creatively promote it, to win the keys to a red Jaguar for a month.

When Norman arrived at Asda, he started his 'Day Zero' turnaround strategy. The centre of the strategy is to present Asda to the customer as the most competitive discounter among the top four supermarket chains. The implementation of this strategy by Norman has been described variously as 'outspoken', 'slightly wacky' and 'playful', and the process of embedding ground-breaking standards of customer service has included such tactics as:

- 'pet stops' in-store for families to leave animals while they shop;
- 'brolly patrols', where shop assistants escort customers to their cars with umbrellas to protect them from the rain;
- in-store events like 'singles nights' and 'fancy dress days' – with the first couple to marry as a result of an Asda 'singles night' offered the opportunity to have the wedding ceremony in the store and the reception in the store cafeteria;
- checkouts with red carpets for big-spending customers.

This is all part of what Marketing Director, Michael Fleming, described as a strategy of bringing 'theatre and life' into supermarket retailing.

Norman has pursued his position as the leading discounter by a series of attacks on price-fixing arrangements. Going after discounting opportunities in pharmaceuticals, toiletries and books that break free of price-fixing, Norman has reinforced his own strategic position and also focused price-cutting onto far higher margin products than staple commodity groceries. Asda has gained enormous publicity for these moves, and Norman has been portrayed as a 'pioneering shopper's champion'. In fact, Norman has not always succeeded in getting around price-fixing – for example, in vitamin products where the manufacturers obtained injunctions to maintain resale prices. While Asda, like Sainsbury, held back from a loyalty card, Norman aggressively counter-attacked Tesco's Clubcard by telling customers that Asda would honour the Tesco money-off coupons sent to Clubcard holders, and advertises that Asda's prices are lower 'every day'. In 1996 Asda announced plans for its own loyalty card – interestingly and somewhat cheekily named 'Clubcard', the same as Tesco's established loyalty card   and the move towards offering financial services to card holders.

With the recovery phase completed, Asda is now fighting to maintain the momentum of success – 'Operation Break-out'. The strategic options for British retailers are basically the same for all players: expand overseas; increase non-food product lines; and acquire other retail businesses in Britain. Norman is joining the other major players in pursuing higher margin non-food areas like clothes and electrical goods. At Asda the basis for expansion in clothing is the 'George' range – designed by, and named for, George Davies, the creator of Next. Norman has set an ambitious target of making the George brand the second largest clothing brand in Britain, after Marks & Spencer. He continues to pursue the high-margin, over-the-counter medicine market and the possibility of discounting here if price-fixing agreements can be abolished. Asda plans to become the first supermarket to open book stores to compete directly with traditional book retailers, and, along with Boots, is investigating the possibility of locating doctors and other healthcare services on store premises. Norman has acquisition plans within the UK, but is first upgrading existing stores to increase the range of fresh foods and trying to recreate a market-stall atmosphere in restyled butchery, bakery and delicatessen departments.

'Asda is now fighting to maintain the momentum of success'

Early in 1997 Asda launched 'Value Cannonball', a price campaign led by the message that, unlike rival loyalty schemes, savings for customers at Asda are immediate, and to fight off the effect of Kwik Save's new own-label range. City reactions are cautious, based on fears that Asda's margins are levelling off and cost pressures mounting.

Norman is now looking to his personal political ambitions by standing for Parliament, retaining the chairman's role but with Allan Leighton, formerly Marketing Director at Mars, in position as his successor.

Safeway

Although one of the largest retail chains in the USA, the British Safeway chain, acquired by Argyll in 1987, is in fourth place, and, with Asda, very much second division to Tesco and Sainsbury. The Argyll Group (now known as the Safeway Group) purchase of the Safeway and Presto stores led to the conversion of the larger Presto stores to the Safeway brand and the sale of the Lo-Cost discount stores to the Co-operative Retail Services, while the smaller Presto stores were sold to the Spar voluntary group. The Presto brand is maintained in Scotland and the north-east of England.

Safeway's market position has rested on a very large advertising campaign with the prize-winning 'Look Who's Talking Now' television advertisements dubbing adult voices and conversations into the mouths of small children in-store. These ads have achieved extremely high consumer awareness scores. This campaign is associated with Safeway's determination to become more customer oriented. In 1995 Safeway's advertising spend was £39 million (compared to £26 million by the market leader, Tesco, £40 million by second-placed Sainsbury and £16 million by Asda in third place in the market). Underpinning this, there have been major investments to upgrade stores and improve service quality, and also major restructuring as part of the 1993 'Safeway 2000' review. This review led to the formation of task forces, reporting to Board level and supported by external consultants.

'This campaign is associated with Safeway's determination to become more customer oriented'

A critical process was the development of the 'Safeway customer proposition' and the central customer promise that Safeway is concerned with 'Lightening the Load'. The Safeway re-positioning since 1994 is based on brand and service – executives freely admit that while they follow market prices, they do not claim to be a price leader, although they reject Sainsbury's claim that there is as much as a 4 per cent price difference.

The brand message in the advertising campaign is that Safeway will do everything to make the shopping trip easier – for example, by the roving teams of 'Queue Busters' used to home in on queues at checkouts and counters; and simply by having more staff on the shopfloor to handle customer queries and customer service.

The implementation of the brand strategy also rests on a campaign concerned with 'Getting the Basics Right Every Time' at store level. The strategy has involved developing the product range to have broader appeal – research in the Safeway 2000 project found that the company was perceived as strong with single people and pre-family couples but not in the family shopping market. While the 'Safeway Savers' is a value-oriented positioning, major efforts were also made to improve the range of customer services offered in-store and upgrade store layout and design. An 'ABC' loyalty card followed in response to Tesco's Clubcard launch. Much of the development has been based on customer feedback – for example, the company maintains a 'family connections' panel of 1500 consumers to discuss perceptions of Safeway and developing service needs.

Recently, Safeway has turned to a process of internal 're-energizing' in the form of the M.A.D (Make a Difference) campaign – focusing on the customer proposition and having all employees and managers think about the working styles and practices needed to support the company's strategy. Some 8 000 managers have already been sent on one-day workshops run by an external agency to support this process.

Behind the re-positioning of Safeway has been the closure of unprofitable stores, and some 3000 job cuts. However, by 1996 the company was planning the opening of the large stores, and the creation of 5000 new jobs, in line with improving profitability and market share.

Gateway/Somerfield

In 1994 Gateway undertook a radical re-branding, moving its stores progressively from the 'shabby' Gateway image to the more upmarket Somerfield brand.

The origins of the Somerfield brand illustrate the problems that have been confronted by David Simons on joining the company as chief executive in 1993 – at the company's all-time low, when its debt had reached £1.3 billion.

The company started in 1964 as a chain of the early self-service stores founded by Frank Dee, who opened 70 stores under his own name. By 1970 those stores had become part of Linford Holdings. In 1977 Linford Holdings bought Gateway, a 14-unit chain named for 'Bristol – Gateway to the West'. By the end of 1977, there were more than 100 stores around the country operating as Gateway. In 1983 the Frank Dee stores were brought under the Gateway brand, and Linford Holdings was renamed the Dee Corporation. For the next few years the Dee Corporation expanded through a series of mergers and acquisitions, gaining ownership of Keymarkets, Lennons, International Stores, Fine Fare and Carrefour Hypermarkets. In 1988 the Dee Corporation was renamed the Gateway Corporation.

A major turning point came in 1989, when Isosceles bought Gateway for £2.1 billion, and sold 60 of the larger stores to Asda. In 1990 the first Somerfield store was opened, trading alongside the Gateway stores, but with a greater emphasis on fresh food.

However, by 1992 it was necessary for Isosceles to ask its banks for a halt to repayment of its £1.3 billion debt, to avoid bankruptcy and to refinance. In 1993 David Simons joined the company as chief executive, when an operating company – Somerfield Holdings – was formed to separate the store business from the debt held by the parent company Isosceles. Simons quickly launched the Price Check campaign – a deep price-cut strategy taking up to 15 per cent off major brand prices – which triggered a price war driving prices down across the whole grocery sector, and turned a 15 per cent sales decline for Gateway to 11 per cent growth.

By 1994 the decision had been made to phase out the now somewhat tarnished Gateway brand name and replace it with Somerfield stores and a cheaper chain called Food Giant. Sales and profit recovery continued – sales of £3.05 billion in 1994 and £3.14 billion in 1995. By 1996 operating margins had increased from 1.75 per cent to 2.65 per cent and a market flotation was announced. After a painful seven years, the City judged that the company had turned the corner.

'there are analysts who see the high street image of the stores as shabby and downmarket'

Nonetheless, there are analysts who see the high street image of the stores as shabby and downmarket. The company has come through a period in which the competition had invested heavily in customer loyalty, while Somerfield had to rely on existing customers – leading to lost market share.

The company has demonstrated strength in low price marketing – its 1990s price-cutting campaign took market share back to 7 per cent from the low of 3 per cent. The capabilities for customer service improvement and quality-based strategies seem more limited – not least because the company's trading margins are around 3 per cent compared to the sector average of 7 per cent.

While the Somerfield image change has worked – the supermarkets have a strong emphasis on fresh food – by 1996 the rate of change of stores from the Gateway brand to Somerfield was running at 100 per year. The total chain consisted of 610: 275 Somerfields, 28 Food Giants and 307 Gateways.

The Somerfield operation is also differentiated by its high-street-based, compared to the increasingly criticized out-of-town, developments of its major competitors.

Kwik Save

Kwik Save holds around 4 per cent of the market – slightly ahead of Somerfield. Kwik Save's strategy has been to occupy a distinct niche position in the market – it has concentrated on supplying quality brands at heavily discounted prices. The strategy has been wholly focused on price. Store quality and services are low, the stores are dark, and have old-fashioned turnstile entrances and unfriendly staff – but the major brands are cheap.

'Store quality and services are low, the stores are dark, and have old-fashioned turnstile entrances and unfriendly staff – but the major brands are cheap'

Analysts suggest that Kwik Save is in the 'Dark Ages' in many areas – its supply chain management is rudimentary, with store deliveries two or three times a week instead of daily like its competitors; for this reason, stockouts are frequent, shown by gaps on the shelves; there is no prospect of a loyalty card because the company's systems and IT are not sophisticated enough to handle it; for the same reason, customers cannot use Switch debit cards on the Kwik Save checkouts.

The company hit the financial headlines in November 1996. Kwik Save's profits up to August 1996 had fallen 40 per cent, from £125 million to £80 million, as a result of competitive pressures from the larger supermarket chains on the one hand, and sharply targeted, focused overseas discounters like Aldi and Netto on the other. The superstores have stolen Kwik Save's price advantage, while the aggressive continental discounters are trying to steal their customers too. Shares slumped from a year's high of 612p to 300p.

Kwik Save retained its prominent position in the financial press by announcing the results of a £4 million strategic review conducted by Anderson Consulting. The highlight of the review was the proposal to close 107 loss-making stores, shedding some 2000 jobs, although the seriousness of the redundancies is reduced by the existing high staff turnover. The 1996 accounts have an exceptional charge of £87½ million to cover store closures and redundancy costs, removing most of the year's profit earning. Some analysts have suggested that up to 300 stores will have to close eventually.

The Anderson consultants recommended a strategy of 'New Generation Kwik Save', involving a new range of own-label products, more fresh and convenience foods and longer opening hours. Industry experts comment that all those things are already available in the superstores, so where is the potential competitive advantage? The opportunity to imitate Asda's strategy does not exist, because Asda had large stores and a residual value-for-money image, and Kwik Save has neither of these. Speculation continues that Kwik Save may be taken over by a competitor from Britain or overseas.

The prospects for the future

By early 1997, analysts were suggesting that the 'Big Four' – Tesco, Sainsbury, Asda and Safeway – were looking strong, at the expense of the 'also-rans', like Kwik Save. The impact of buying power and marketing technique has been felt very directly on market shares. Specialists suggest that the end result must be consolidation among the 'also-rans' and the exit of one or more of the foreign discounters who have entered the UK market. City analysts have suggested that market saturation is looming – the growth in new stores is faster than sales growth in the market – suggesting that further 'shake-out' is inevitable. Although fraught with competition law problems, the City expects to see the larger chains acquiring some of the smaller ones.

Early in 1997 analysts were forecasting the inevitable onset of the most severe price war among the major supermarket groups for 15 years – an influential retail consultant reported that both Sainsbury and Tesco were considering major price-cutting moves. The forecast was based on the possibility of Sainsbury pursuing a price-cut strategy to win back market share – and to be seen to be doing something positive competitively – but every price cut being equalled or exceeded by Tesco.

Sources: 'Argyll Reaps Harvest of More Aggressive Marketing Campaign', *Financial Times*, 30 November 1995. 'City Loses its Taste for Sainsbury's', *Sunday Business*, 5 May 1996. 'Counter Attack', *Sunday Times*, 14 January 1996. 'Food for Thought', *Marketing Business*, March 1995. 'Good Food Earns Less at Sagging Sainsbury', *Daily Mail*, 25 January 1997. 'Kwik Save to Close 107 Stores', *Daily Telegraph*, 8 November 1996. 'Nimble Rivals for Squeeze on Sainsbury', *Daily Mail*, 2 November 1995. 'Norman Conquest', *Sunday Times*, 29 October 1995. 'One Glorious Innings, Now for the Big Test', *Independent on Sunday*, 26 January 1997. 'Safeway Closes 17 Stores' *Financial Times*, 5 April 1995. 'Somerfield Hopes to Float from Gateway to Success', *Sunday Business*, 5 May 1996. 'Supermarkets and Superstores', Keynotes 1996 Market Report. 'Supermarkets Prepare for Price War', *Daily Telegraph*, 27 January 1997.

Questions to consider

1 How can Sainsbury's recover their market position – or is the situation unrecoverable? Can the company ever again be the real market leader? What would this take?

2 How would you describe the strategic position of each of the main competitors in the supermarket sector? How does this picture now differ from five years ago?

3 Is price war the inevitable competitive outcome in this sector? Does price-cutting pay off if you are in this type of business?

4 How can Sainsbury have made the huge error of allowing Tesco to consolidate a strengthening market position with the Tesco Clubcard, and not fight back for so long?

5 If you do a SWOT analysis for each of the competitors, does it indicate whether the companies can sustain their present positions or whether further change is likely?

6 What are the major environmental trends over the last five years on this market to which the companies have had to adapt? Why have some companies succeeded in making that re-positioning, while others have not?

7 What are the likely environmental trends for the next five years, and how well positioned are these companies to adapt to these new issues? How different is the competitive structure likely to be after another five years?

BA's tenth anniversary in the private sector

In 1997 British Airways celebrated its tenth anniversary as a company outside the public sector by offering £5,400 tickets on Concorde to New York for £10 each. The offer brought some 30 *million* attempted phone call responses.

From the bad old days to success

BA was privatized in 1987. At this time the business was variously described by analysts as 'a state-owned shambles' which was 'fat, inefficient and complacent'. The organization was showing some of the highest losses in the airline business and was highly 'consumer-unfriendly' – indeed, it had a worldwide reputation for poor customer service. The company's well-known disdain for its customers led some to suggest that BA stood for 'Bloody Awful'! Looking back in 1995, Mike Street, BA's Customer Services Director, said in the *Financial Times* that 'In the early 1980s, British Airways was a disgrace. We were on the floor. We were bankrupt, financially and emotionally. The word 'customer' wasn't in our dictionary.' Indeed, when Saatchi's launched the slogan 'The World's Favourite Airline' for the newly-privatized BA, it was widely regarded as something of a joke.

'The company's well-known disdain for its customers led some to suggest that BA stood for "Bloody Awful"!'

After a decade in the private sector, BA is the world's most profitable airline, having dislodged Singapore Airlines from that position in 1996. The company is a global player in airline communications; it has won awards as one of the most respected companies in Europe – in terms of customer satisfaction, employee empowerment, core competences and innovation. The company's advertising and marketing campaigns have won numbers of awards for creativity and innovation, and these achievements span an era of worldwide global recession, when competitors in the industry were

---

* This case study has been prepared from secondary sources by Nigel Piercy, Cardiff Business School.

suffering badly. BA enjoys a dominant share of flight slots at Heathrow, Europe's most important international airport; it dominates the UK domestic flight market, and has operating costs significantly lower than its major international rivals.

There are a variety of interesting factors underlying this remarkable turnaround, but also some major questions about what the company can do to sustain its performance over the next decade.

Leadership

One of the most significant factors in the BA turnaround has been the management leadership taking the business from privatization into its first decade as a fully commercial organization. At privatization, the Chairman was Lord John King, with Sir Colin Marshall as CEO. These managers brought great vision to the enterprise and an aggressive and determined management style. Lord King retired as Chairman in 1993, to be replaced in that position by Marshall, and the CEO post has now passed, in 1996, to Robert Ayling, previously Marketing and Operations Director, and latterly Managing Director. The change in performance and culture at BA can be traced in large part to the leadership and commitment by these managers and other members of the senior management team. The strategic decisions made by these managers are key to understanding the turnaround of BA. Indeed, evaluating what the future holds for BA rests largely on Ayling's strategy statements.

A strategy of service-driven profit

Colin Marshall is widely credited with 'reinventing' BA, in his role as CEO and later Chairman. Initially he was responsible for reducing staffing levels from 60 000 to 36 000, and for abandoning unprofitable routes and selling under-used assets to raise cash.

It was also Marshall who recognized early on that the future airline industry was likely to consist of a very small number of very large airlines. He placed great emphasis on globalizing the business, primarily through establishing alliances and partnerships in the USA, Australia and Europe, to overcome gaps in BA's coverage of routes as well as to access the lucrative but highly protected US domestic market. It was also through the early 1990s that King and Marshall led a revolution in BA focused on three issues: to improve the product; to improve customer perception of BA; and to improve profitability.

'a revolution in BA focused on three issues: to improve the product; to improve customer perception of BA; and to improve profitability'

The methods used to drive the service-driven quality strategy included the use of Total Quality Management, applying benchmarking against the best companies in the world to undertake widespread Business Process Re-engineering, and continues in scenario planning to cope with the future.

Perhaps the most distinctive aspects of the BA strategy are seen in: the advertising and promotional campaigns; constant upgrades to the product on offer; the new approach to customer relationships and customer loyalty; the attention to staff morale and training and development; and aggressive responses to competition in fare-cutting and promotional campaigns.

The *advertising* spend has been massive, currently running at around £40 million – making BA one of the largest advertisers in the world. The early campaigns with Saatchi's launched the slogan 'The World's Favourite Airline', and this has been followed over the years with a succession of award-winning creative campaigns used internationally. BA has also been highly active in below-the-line communications, particularly in exploiting its customer database to target the profitable business class and first class passengers.

The advertising strategy is linked to product strategy, most particularly in the strong and highly innovatory *branding* which has been established by BA. Branding is both for the company name itself and also for the different ticket segments, such as Club Europe for business class travellers.

The *product* itself has been subject to constant improvement, largely in response to passenger feedback. At the end of 1995, for example, Robert Ayling announced a spend of £80 million over two years to pamper passengers with the ultimate in in-flight entertainment, promising that 'We're going to have problems getting passengers off the aircraft at the end of their journey'. Improvements include the provision of 'beds' in first class, as in the days of the 1940s, improved seating, interactive media on board, as well as innovations in check-in arrangements to reduce queuing time and 'hassle' for the passenger. BA operates a 'queue combining' system, with check-in staff working their way along queues to save time at the desk, and innovative automatic barcoded luggage label printers and automatic ticketing for domestic flights – and this in an industry where operations traditionally was concerned only with the aircraft's well-being, not the passenger's. BA looks to be on the way to becoming one of the most 'wired' companies in the UK – with the effect of achieving self-service, ticketless check-in on major US flights for passengers with hand baggage by mid-1996. A recently announced marketing partnership with The Body Shop will offer the retailer's skin and body care services to BA passengers in airport lounges.

Much of the product improvement, however, is traced less to the hardware of passenger comfort than to the building of a customer service culture among BA staff. There have been a succession of highly effective company-wide programmes for staff training and development to build customer focus: Customers First, Putting People First, A Day in the Life, To Be the Best, and Winning for Customers. Even by 1996, the company was still responding to customer perceptions – the Breakthrough programme has been initiated by BA's customer service training to address customer views that flight attendants were humourless and distant. In 1995, the company launched a £500 million customer service programme called

Insight, to address shortcomings in BA's service and style found in customer research. And this is in a company where in 1991 the Customer Relations Department took an average of more than 12 weeks to respond to customer correspondence and lost 60 per cent of customer calls on any one day. Management acting as the champion for the customer led, in the space of four years, to a doubling of the retention rate of complaining customers to 80 per cent. Indeed, rather than just trying to reduce complaints, BA has developed an IT-supported service recovery system to retain customers and to reward employees who can uncover hidden problems.

The importance of employee commitment in the strategy of service-driven profit is shown also in the quarterly employee opinion polls undertaken at BA.

British Airways was one of the pioneers of marketing based on *customer loyalty*. It was the first European airline to launch a frequent-flyer programme, and now operates an Executive Club segmenting passengers into three categories according to their importance to the company. This is tied to the innovation of the Air Miles loyalty programme, the largest loyalty scheme in the UK.

Underpinning this is the *marketplace performance unit*, which tracks some 350 measures of performance – aircraft cleanliness, punctuality, technical defects in the aircraft, customer opinions on check-in performance, the time it takes to get a reservation agent on the phone, customer satisfaction with in-flights and ground services, and so on.

These strategies have been put in place at a time of great financial pressure and the need for cost-saving throughout the business – they were not luxuries added to the costs, they were the route to enhanced profitability.

The Virgin trauma

The first signs that all might not be well with BA came with its strained relationship with Virgin Atlantic, or, more precisely, its founder, Richard Branson. Branson is perhaps the most dynamic entrepreneur in Western Europe, and has endured the best part of a decade of competitive and personal attacks from BA. It is rumoured that Lord King detested Branson from the outset, perhaps because of his refusal to wear a suit and tie.

It seems that the global customer service-based strategy at BA was just falling into place when Virgin happened. Virgin Atlantic was a very small operator, opening up the transatlantic routes with a highly differentiated offering based on the Virgin branding in consumer goods and music.

'BA staff were instructed to "inhibit" Branson's "ability to compete"'

Subsequent lawsuits have uncovered an aggressive and robust response from BA to this competitor which on occasion went outside the law. BA staff were instructed to 'inhibit' Branson's 'ability to compete', both by personal attack in the press and a variety of 'dirty tricks'. These centred mainly on a 'passenger poaching' strategy. BA sales teams, known as 'hunters', would approach business class passengers booked on Virgin and offer them upgraded seats to transfer to BA. While aggressive, this is not illegal. Unfortunately there are suggestions that BA hunters also hacked into Virgin's booking systems to identify target passengers, and may on occasion have suggested that Virgin flights were cancelled or full to encourage passengers to swap airlines. If true, then this is illegal. After initially dismissing Branson's claims as a publicity stunt, in 1993 BA admitted in court that its employees had waged a campaign to discredit both Branson and his airline, and paid £610,000 in damages plus legal fees to settle Branson's libel action, and made a public apology. Further financial settlements were made in 1996, and further cases are outstanding between Virgin and BA in the USA.

Following Lord King's retirement, widely suggested to have been precipitated by the Virgin case, Marshall agreed a truce with Branson. By January 1996, Branson was accusing BA of further 'dirty tricks' evidenced by sworn statements from passengers, and threatening further legal action in the USA and Europe.

The antipathy is not wholly one-sided. Branson has taken BA to the European Commission, accusing BA of breaching EC anti-trust rules by using its dominant market position to exclude smaller competitors. In 1996 Branson also announced that he had spent $1.5 million out of $15 million budgeted for advertising and lobbying in the USA to kill the proposed BA and American Airlines alliance. The Chairman of BA is said to be less than amused at the 'No Way BA/AA' sticker on the tail of one of Branson's aircraft.

In 1996 Branson was not only committing large resources to blocking BA's alliance with American Airlines, but also starting a campaign against the extension of the relationship with Japan Air Lines.

The war between BA and Virgin looks set to continue.

The signs of trouble ahead

There are already signs that the continuing Virgin dispute has damaged employee morale at BA. Generally, the City was concerned to see downturns in the employee opinion survey results at BA in 1994. These results showed criticisms of the company's operations and a feeling that there had been no response to earlier employee suggestions for change. The company promised a change in management style and more modern offices. However, it was reported in December 1995 that in new employee surveys a large proportion of BA staff believed that they were not treated with 'honesty and respect' and only one in two felt that their departments were well managed. The company suggested that the survey showed that 'fierce loyalty to the airline is coupled with frustration'. By 1996, BA was said to face a 'summer of mounting staff discontent' over cost-cutting exercises and divisions rumoured to be planned for hiving-off.

It was also reported in 1995 that BA's customer approval ratings, which had risen sharply in the early years after privatization, had started to tail off. At the same time, the City started to raise substantial doubts about the company's long-term strategy, particularly in the context of the equity stakes taken by BA in partners. Analysts suggested by the end of 1994 that BA would struggle to sustain profit growth and that the plans for a 'global airline' were flawed.

'The clear advantage enjoyed by BA is no longer so evident'

Generally, there is some sign that the competitors have caught up with BA, in the customer service area particularly. The clear advantage enjoyed by BA is no longer so evident. The erosion of BA's competitive advantage was traced by one analyst to the following factors:

Cost cutting

From 1991 to 1994 BA cut £580 million from its cost base, with further cost-cut targets in view, but this raises the question of whether cost-cutting can be sustained in the longer term at this level, with reducing quality and service.

Alliances

The poor performance of some partner organizations casts doubt on BA's alliance strategy, since if the equity stakes taken do not produce profits it becomes hard to see how BA can achieve its global carrier goal – indeed, in mid-1994 only Qantas, among BA's overseas partners, was making a profit.

Competition

All airlines are cutting costs and improving service, and while BA still leads, the gap is closing.

Price-cutting

As competitors cut costs, they will be able to reduce fares to win market share, and fare-cutting retaliation by BA will reduce profitability.

More recently, an influential analysis in *The Economist* has suggested that there are four major areas of uncertainty over BA's future. The most immediate cause of uncertainty for BA came from the $1 billion lawsuit from Branson's Virgin Atlantic in the US courts. Apart from the financial implications of this and the other actions brought by Virgin, the reputation of BA has suffered, and the image of BA as 'a squeaky-clean friend to the consumer' is changing to that of 'an anxious, over-bearing giant trying to squash a feisty little rival'.

Other problems in the USA stem from the stake taken in USAir to gain access to the American north-east, from which two-thirds of transatlantic passengers depart. USAir has continued to make substantial losses, in spite of a major cost-cutting exercise. USAir also suffered two major crashes, which further depressed its bookings. The latest proposal for an alliance with American Air has also become embroiled in anti-trust regulations, and the collapse of the USAir partnership – the reaction of USAir to the mid-1996 announcement of the BA/American Airlines alliance was legal action against BA for breach of contract and monopolistic behaviour, to end its code-sharing and frequent-flyer programmes with BA, and the demand that BA sell its stake and remove its directors from USAir's board. BA announced the sale of its USAir stake at the end of 1996. However, USAir and the other US airlines continue to lobby against the BA/American Airlines alliance. In 1997 nine airlines, led by United in the USA and Lufthansa in Germany, formed an alliance to counter the threat in BA's proposed deal with American Airlines. The group includes Air Canada, Scandinavian Airlines, Thai International, Varig, All-Nippon Airlines, South African Airways and British Midland. The alliance is preparing to launch its own brand name and combined service, ahead of the BA/AA merger.

Meanwhile, it is believed that BA is looking to develop cross-marketing and promotion with American to bridge the gap between the end of the USAir deal and the approval by regulators of the alliance with American Air. The company risks a major loss of profit if it continues without some US-based collaboration in place.

The alliance with Australia's Qantas airline was entered into to give BA access to the fast-growing Asian market, also ran into problems with regulators, who attempted to prevent the integration of flights in South Asia.

Closer to home there is threat to the competitive advantage which BA gains from having Heathrow as its home port. BA already has two-thirds of the available flight slots and is unlikely to get more. Heathrow is severely over-crowded, and long-haul passengers are being lost to Frankfurt and Amsterdam, both offering superior ground facilities. However, the biggest threat to BA's 'Fortress Heathrow' comes from the possibility of an 'open-skies' deal between Britain and the USA, which would allow US airlines to run services beyond Heathrow. 'Open skies' are unlikely to happen in the near future, but pressure from the USA continues. More immediately, Heathrow represents a very high-cost base for the company.

'there is threat to the competitive advantage which BA gains from having Heathrow as its home port'

Also in the UK, BA's attempts to extend their cost cutting into the commissions earned by travel agents and credit-card charges has met with much resistance.

The British Airways response to new market conditions

The response to these changing conditions is the responsibility of Robert Ayling, made Managing Director in 1993 and who took over as Chief Executive in January 1996, following the surprise resignation of Sir Colin Marshall. Ayling stressed the importance of continuity in management: 'The danger in any sort of succession is that there is a discontinuity, and when the company is a brand such as ours, continuity in the management of that brand is essential.'

Ayling sees the major threats as deregulation, lower fares and more aggressive competition, and is putting into effect radical changes in the BA organization, including shedding a further 5000 jobs, and taking £1 billion out of the cost base by 2000, starting with a thinning of the senior management group from 25 to 11 to streamline decision making.

Ayling's stated aim is to make BA the best-managed company in Britain by 2000, and to make the customers 'absolute king'.

His initial attack has been on BA's 'meetings culture' and bureaucracy, and to substitute initiative for meetings – he was recently quoted as saying: 'If people would communicate properly with each other, they wouldn't need the bloody meetings.' To counter the tendency to cling to hierarchy and 'deference' to authority, he has launched the 'Leadership 2000' campaign, with the goal of evaluating all functions carried out by headquarters staff and identifying those which would be better done by managers who deal directly with customers. Mid-level managers are to take far more responsibility for running their parts of the business and far greater control of staffing issues. Managers are to have measurable performance targets based on customers' perceptions of service shown by customer research. The running of Leadership 2000 has been put in the hands of a group of line managers from different parts of the company, taken out of their jobs to work full-time on the project.

Ayling also believes that while under Marshall's leadership the company focused on improving marketing and customer consciousness, with more intense competition, BA's internal focus must change from achieving service quality to controlling the cost of quality. He suggests that the airline's progress in improving its attention to customers has not been matched by the elimination of inefficient working practices. However, by the end of 1996 it was clear that BA was facing increasing fuel costs and that improving service standards was pushing up staff numbers and salary rates.

Ayling also has a goal of extending BA's global reach to enable it to look after its customers' needs on a worldwide basis, leading to the code-sharing agreement with American Airlines in June 1996, and the purchase of France's Air Liberté in February 1997, after a bidding battle with other airlines. He is committed to the view that future competition will not be between individual airlines but between competing networks.

Current speculation concerns BA as a 'virtual airline'. Ayling's moves to transform BA into a company that focuses on transporting passengers and cargo may lead ultimately to a company that only needs to have its own pilots, cabin crew and brand marketing – everything else (e.g. aircraft, engineers, catering and computing) can be contracted from outside. Ayling's moves to franchise the BA brand to smaller airlines flying BA colours is seen as the start of the 'virtual airline', along with the plans to hive off the large engineering divisions, following the sale of the BA engine overhaul business to General Electric in 1992. Franchising and outsourcing provide great leverage on cost structures, but also carry new risks – poor performance by a franchisee impacts on the BA brand in the customer's eyes.

'Current speculation concerns BA as a "virtual airline"'

Early in 1997, BA was rumoured to be about to enter partnership with Eagle Star to build the new financial services division, with jointly-branded insurance products. Rumours also continue of controversial investments and collaborations with cut-price airlines and tour operator airlines.

Sources: 'Ayling Aims to Keep BA's Leading Edge', Andrew Lorenz, *Sunday Times*, 5 November 1995. 'BA in New Dirty Tricks Claims', John Harlow, *Sunday Times*, 6 March 1994. 'BA Revamps Service with £500M Plan', *Marketing Week*, 22 September 1995. 'BA Staff Feeling "A Bit Let Down"', *Daily Telegraph*, 12 December 1995. 'BA Stood for "Bloody Awful"', Charles Gurassa, *Across the Board*, January 1995. 'British Airways Sets Streamlining Goals for 2000', John D. Morocco, *Aviation Week & Space Technology*, 23 September 1996. 'Championing the Customer', Charles R. Weiser, *Harvard Business Review*, November/December 1995. 'Going to the Polls: BA's Quarterly Opinion Surveys', *IRS Employment Review*, May 1996. 'Managers of Transformation', Bernard C. Reimann, *Planning Review*, May/June 1993. 'Richard Branson's Air Strike', Wendy Zellner, *Business Week*, 14 October 1996. 'The Obstacles in BA's Flight Path', *Marketing Week*, 5 August 1996. 'Virgin Alleges New BA "Tricks"', John Harlow, *Sunday Times*, 8 January 1995. 'We are Flying into Turbulence', *Economist*, 4 March 1995.

Questions to consider

1 Is being the 'world's favourite airline' compatible with being the world's largest airline?

2 What are BA's core competencies?

3 What are the strategic gains in becoming a 'virtual airline', and what are the weaknesses of this strategy?

4 Is there a way that BA can 'make peace' with Virgin? Does it need to?

5 Does an involvement in financial services make sense in strategic terms for BA?

6 Is 'open skies' over Heathrow a reasonable price to pay for the alliance with American Air?

PART IV

Making Market Strategy Happen

CHAPTER 14

Implementing market strategies and the role of strategic internal marketing:

Turning market strategies and plans into effective marketing action

Our progress towards market-led strategic change

By this stage we should have accumulated a fairly lengthy list of new things to try, and things to put right, in how our organization goes to market. To reach this point we have gone through a process of testing the *customer-focus and content* of our market strategy in Parts I and II and the *organizational context* for our process of going to market in Part III. We will see in a moment how we can fit these things together.

The issue now is quite simple – *implementation*, or making it happen, for our companies and for our customers, in the real world. In an ideal world, of course, there would be no need for a chapter on implementation. It would be redundant because:

- our market strategy would be driven by our customer focus and obsession with responding to customer needs in a completely customer-focused organization;
- our market choices, value proposition and relationship strategies would bring our differentiating capabilities to bear on those customer needs, and we would learn more to continuously improve;

- our market sensing and planning would be participative and culture-shaping in turning the market strategy into effective programmes of action; and
- our sales and marketing would be a completely integrated process built around customer relationships.

Oh, if only . . .

If that is what it is like in your company, then you do not need what follows here. However, if that is what you believe, you are probably wrong. Most of us are not working in companies like that, and for us implementation is worth a lot more attention.

'some would go as far as to say that implementation is strategy'

In fact, the implementation issue cannot be avoided. Indeed, some would go as far as to say that implementation *is* strategy – on the grounds that without a systematic management approach to the execution of plans and strategies they simply will not happen, and so remain ideas which never become strategy in any real sense. Others suggest that implementation is *different* from strategy – it is the difficult part; they argue that finding out what a company needs to do in its markets is easy; it is putting new things into effect that is difficult. Whichever view is taken, to ignore implementation when we look at market strategy is to ignore an important part of the reality which executives face.

There is no need, however, to make implementation issues complex or abstract – this defeats the object. Our focus is quite simply described as 'making strategy work', and identifying the things that are needed to get from the plans to the action. There is a problem, however. While executives and organizations have become increasingly aware of theories of market strategy and the technical tools of market analysis and strategic market planning, there has been much less attention given to the processes involved in executing plans and strategies. The result has been described by one authority as executives being 'strategy-sophisticated' but 'implementation-bound', and this seems to be a familiar situation in many companies. In short, we need to do far better in responding to the executive's question: 'We know what marketing *is*, but how do we *do* it?'

The urgency of this topic is underlined by the frequent failure of plans, and the strategies they represent, to reach the marketplace and achieve the results promised. The underlying problem is that in most situations market strategies have to survive in a corporate and organizational environment which may provide fundamental barriers to successful change.

The approach we have developed to work on this has two elements: building implementation strategies for our market strategies, and turning these into internal marketing programmes to match our external marketing programmes.

Actually it is a big leap forward for many companies just to recognize implementation as a serious issue anyway. But even when we do, it becomes clear that all too often we lack the practical tools and techniques for getting the act together and creating an implementation strategy. Well, things are changing. This is a gap which we can now try to fill. Implementation is the new focus, and we are learning fast.

However, do not be misled. This is no pushover and we have no easy answers. Marketing implementation is *different* from what we have looked at so far, and in many situations it is infinitely more *difficult* than creating clever market strategies and impeccable marketing plans. It is also potentially *dangerous* to the champions of change, personally and to their companies' performance, if we get it wrong. However, it also *matters* more as well.

The goal of this chapter is to open up the implementation issue. We can build up to this in the following way. To start with we can look at why we have implementation problems at all and the problems we face in getting people to put the implementation question on the management agenda in the first place. Then we can look at the sources of the barriers to getting market strategies to work as they are perceived by executives.

The end-product, to which we are progressing, is the early identification and evaluation of the implementation problems facing our plans and strategies, and the identification of the strategies needed to overcome those barriers. This feeds into the operational techniques of internal marketing.

The reaction of some executives when we talk about internal marketing is that they have enough problems already in dealing with the external market, without getting involved in all this stuff.

On the other hand, Tom Farmer, founder and chief executive of the successful UK car exhaust and tyre company, Kwik Fit plc, describes the development of his business in the following terms. He refers inevitably to his corporate advertising message 'You can't get better than a Kwik Fit fitter' and suggests: 'Now people leave school wanting to become Kwik Fit fitters, and women dream of falling in love with one!' This led Farmer to perhaps his most revealing statement: 'In any business there are two types of customer – *internal* customers and *external* customers' – one is the person with the sick motor car, but the other is the person who has to crawl underneath the wet, dirty, rusty, unpleasant vehicle and fix it. The business depends on both types of customer. This is not sentimentality – Farmer started with one shop in

Edinburgh in 1971 and now runs a £418 million public company with almost 1000 outlets.

This stacks up well against our experiences in working with executives from a wide range of manufacturing and services businesses, as well as public sector bodies in healthcare, museums and the like. We have been struck forcibly and repeatedly by one major barrier to putting strategies and plans into effect. That barrier is provided by the people, the systems and procedures, the departments and the managers whose commitment and partici- pation are needed to implement strategies effectively, i.e. the *internal customers* for our plans and strategies.

For instance, Thomas Masiello[1] has concluded from his research in the USA that in the range of different industries he studied, typically:

'most employees do not see how their jobs have anything to do with customers or customer needs'

- most functional areas do not understand the concept of being driven by customer needs, and if market plans exist they are not told about what is in them or what they mean;
- consequently, most employees do not see how their jobs have anything to do with customers or customer needs;
- most functional areas do not really understand the roles of the other functions in the company, so they have no basis for co-operation; and
- most functional areas have little or no meaningful input to the market direction of the company (this includes people like customer service engineers, R&D executives, and so on).

So, maybe we need to do something about the internal customers of all kinds to get our act together with the external customer.

The trouble is that the conventional training and development of executives, quite reasonably, has focused on the *external* environment of customers, competitors and markets, and the matching of corporate resources to marketplace targets. The argument we now present to executives is that, while analysing markets and developing strategies to earn a living in the external marketplace remain, quite appropriately, our central focus, it is frequently not enough on its own to achieve the implementation of market strategies.

In addition to developing marketing programmes aimed at the external marketplace, to achieve the organizational change that is essential to make those strategies work, there is a need to carry out substantially the same process for the *internal marketplace* within our companies.

The silly thing is that it seems that the reality in many organizations is that there is an explicit assumption that plans and strategies will 'sell' themselves to those in the company whose support and commitment are vital. When made explicit in this way, this is just as naive as making similar assumptions that, if they are good enough, our products will 'sell themselves' to external customers.

We have frequently been surprised that those same executives who have been trained and developed to cope with behavioural problems – like 'irrational' behaviour by consumers and buyers, or the problems of managing power and conflict in the distribution channel, the need to communicate to buyers through a mix of communications vehicles and media, and trying to outguess competitors – have taken so long to arrive at the conclusion that these same issues have to be coped with *inside* the company. The paradox is that we dismiss the 'better mousetrap' syndrome for our external markets, but adopt exactly this approach in expecting managers and operatives, whose support we need, to make a 'beaten path' to the planner's office.

In particular, we now insist that it is not acceptable or reasonable for managers to adopt a 'don't blame me' attitude as a response to organizational barriers to strategic change and to the 'irrational' behaviour of those who hold different views about the desirability of that change. Real commitment to improving the process of going to market *must* involve a managerial duty of creating the conditions necessary to permit strategic change to happen.

Implementation versus strategy

Traditionally, implementation has been regarded as what follows after new market strategies have been created, plans have been written and approval has been obtained, and what remains is simply a matter of telling people what to do and waiting for the results to happen. If we think about implementation at all, then we see it as the logistics of getting things organized:

- We focus on developing the organizational arrangements needed for the new strategy – allocating responsibilities across departments and units, and maybe creating new organizational structures where necessary;

- We allocate resources in the form of budgets and head-count to support the activities underpinning the strategy to the appropriate parts of the organization;
- We produce 'action lists' and 'action plans' and do presentations to tell people the way things are going to be done; and
- We develop control systems to monitor outcome performance in sales, market share, profit, and so on, to evaluate the success of the strategy and to take remedial action if things are not turning out how we wanted them.

'it is illogical to plan strategies that are not firmly rooted in the organization's capabilities'

There are some very substantial problems in approaching implementation in this way. First, it is illogical to plan strategies that are not firmly rooted in the organization's capabilities, and yet we seem to set up planning systems to do precisely this. Secondly, organizational structure and resource allocation are important, but on their own they are very weak, and usually very slow, approaches to the organizational change inherent in many new market strategies. Thirdly, outcomes like sales, market share and profit are what we want to achieve, but the driver of these outcomes is likely to be the behaviour of people in the organization who impact on what the customer receives in service and quality, which suggests we should focus on the behaviour, not just the outcomes.

Organizational processes which treat implementation as an after thought, when the real work of generating innovative strategies and writing strategic plans has been done, are counter-productive for a number of reasons. The 'dichotomy' between strategy formulation and implementation that exists in many organizations is fraught with dangers:

- It ignores or underestimates the potential link between market strategy and a company's unique implementation capabilities and weaknesses – strategies should logically exploit the things we are good at doing and avoid dependence on the things that our competitors do better.
- More generally, it risks ignoring the competitive advantage which may be achieved by identifying and exploiting the organization's core capabilities and competencies in each market, by reflecting the views of the 'professional planner' in the corporate ivory tower, not the understanding of those who are working in the marketplace concerned.
- It encourages a weak linkage between strategy plans and operating plans – strategies which cut across operating plans

and budgets and do not fit departmental plans are likely to be ignored and under-valued inside the organization.

- It ignores the hidden but often highly significant 'inner workings' of the organization – the culture and how it shapes people's behaviour; boundaries between functions, regions and organizational interest groups which may provide barriers to communication and co-operation; and the role of the powerful and influential in the organization.
- It may prevent a company from ever exploiting 'time-based' market strategies, or from realizing first-mover or pioneer advantages in a market – traditional approaches to implementation are too slow and cumbersome to support fast change in market strategy. For example, in markets where the most important competitive advantage comes from the company's ability to execute effectively a succession of appropriate, but increasingly short-lived strategic initiatives (for example, as Canon has done in bringing new computer equipment to market), traditional approaches to planning and strategy and implementation provide an insurmountable barrier to market success.
- It ignores the practical problems of understanding the real capabilities and practical problems faced, as a company moves into operating through a network of collaborations and strategic alliances with other companies.

If we separate strategy from implementation in how we run things, then we create problems for ourselves. Traditional approaches do little to overcome these self-induced barriers to change. Quite simply, we need better ways of integrating strategy and implementation.

In fact, we need to dig even deeper. There are many examples of market strategies that fail [2], not because they are weak strategies, but because they fail other tests. David Jobber suggests the underlying reasons are:

- they do not fit with an organization's culture, and the people do not support them and make them effective;
- they are not supported by key management players, perhaps because they involve unwelcome change or because they compete with other projects for resources;
- they do not fit existing planning and budgeting systems, and so 'fall into the cracks' and fail to become formally recognized in the company or to get the resources they need;
- they do not sit well on the existing organization structure of departments and units, so are neglected or given only lip-service, and fail through lack of ownership.

'These are the types of barriers that drive us to look more closely at the implementation issue in transforming the process of going to market'

These types of problem are unlikely to be solved through management advocacy, presentations, internal communications to *tell* people the way things should be done, or management sabre-rattling. They are unlikely to be overcome by tighter control systems and budgeting, or reorganization. These are the types of barriers that drive us to look more closely at the implementation issue in transforming the process of going to market.

So, what is the beef about implementation?

How *can* implementation be seen as an afterthought by so many companies? Many of us have concluded that the market strategy which looks good, makes managers feel good, but has no effect whatever on the realities of running the business and changing its direction, is a harmful and expensive waste of time. In fact, as shown above, the real problem is not just strategizing and planning, it is *implementation*.

The underlying danger is that we constantly underestimate the degree and type of change that will have to happen if our plans and strategies are to succeed. It is not enough to talk about organizing things and producing action lists on their own – we have to put a handle on the deep-seated, strategic change in our organization that we need for the market strategy to *happen*. This is the real implementation beef.

In fact, marketing implementation failures often occur for a number of very simple reasons, even if actually *solving* implementation problems is seldom easy. At least if we can see where implementation goes wrong we can make a start. It comes down to issues like the following:

- *Separation of planning from management.* If we organize, staff, operate and organizationally separate planning and the strategy process from line management of the business, we create a fundamental divide which may be difficult to bridge. Planning which is perceived as something different from running the business is unlikely to succeed. Imposing grandiose market strategies on line management is unproductive, ineffective and even destructive. The routes around this problem may be: job rotation – we do not have professional staff planners, we take executives out of line management for a period to work on marketing planning; or more simply managed participation, as discussed in Chapter 11 – we involve line management directly in strategizing and planning (see pp. 447–54). Admittedly, participation of line executives is expensive in cost, time, the conflicts to be confronted and, not least, in terms of top management stress – but if we are serious about making market strategy work, that may be the price we have to pay.

- *Hopeless optimism.* Perhaps because of the isolation and separation of staff planners from running the business, all too many of the plans we see are so far removed from practical reality that it is probably just as well that they never get to the implementation stage. We certainly need vision, but not fiction. This is why we proposed in Chapter 11 the radical approach of turning the whole planning process upside-down and inside-out (see pp. 454–59). Whilst this may not be the solution in all situations, it can do two things: it can provide an antidote to the more extreme lunacies of the ivory-tower strategic planner and analyst; and it can tell line managers that what they are doing is important and has long-term implications.

- *Implementation is recognized too late.* Possibly also as a result of planners' isolation from the operation, and the sheer excitement of identifying and researching new strategies, we often never face up to the implementation issue until it is too late. Examining implementation issues *after* we have already committed ourselves and everyone else to what we are going to do is ineffective for two reasons: first, we end up with the strategic plans which *cannot* realistically be implemented with the resources, people, capabilities and systems that we actually have; and then we persist stubbornly with strategies which make sense economically only because we have totally ignored the real organizational change and implementation costs. Implementation realities need to be an integral part of our planning, not something we think about afterwards.

- *Denial of implementation problems.* Perhaps partly as a result of the previous point, some planners (and some top managers) deny the existence of barriers, obstacles and hurdles in implementing strategic plans – 'if this is the way we *say* it is going to be, then this is the way it is *going* to be!' Sabre-rattling statements by top management make them feel good, and make the planner's life a lot easier, because s/he has been *told* there is no such thing as an implementation problem, so clearly there isn't one! Unfortunately, life is rarely quite this simple. All our evidence suggests that many of the most significant implementation barriers are covert, and become more covert but not less problematic when they are driven underground by macho top management posturing. We ignore such issues at our peril.

- *Implementation bolted on at the end.* It seems likely that many of the problems we have observed, as outlined above, are created, or at least worsened, because we still see implementation in many planning systems as something bolted on at the end of the planning, when the 'real' work has been done, just to tidy up the loose ends. This is *exactly* the wrong way to see implementation! In some ways this reflects the attitude that producing plans is clever, while going away and putting them into effect is an inferior activity to be left to others. If that sounds exaggerated, just look at who gets the 'brownie points' in *your* organization's career paths – the planners or the doers? Implementation is effective only when it is clearly *integrated* with the rest of the strategy process and *before* the plan is finalized.
- *Implementation is a black box.* Lastly, we find cases where senior managers over-react, and when the signal is sent by the organization that a market strategy will be 'difficult' to implement we dump it immediately before we get burnt fingers. We have found that often when implementation barriers are carefully and explicitly broken down into sources and types of obstacles, into key players for and against, alongside each of our key strategy items, two things can be achieved. First, some of the barriers actually disappear – they were just the myths and stereotypes of the corporate culture. Secondly, once we flush out the real implementation issues explicitly and in detail, we may be able to construct implementation strategies to cope with the problems and to get the strategy to happen. At the very least, we end up with an explicit and detailed case for changing a strategy that will be too expensive to implement. At best, we create an implementation strategy that matches each major element of the plan. We will look at this issue in detail in this chapter.

These are some of the underlying problems we have found when companies have trouble with making their plans happen. Perhaps the most basic point is that we have to learn to cope with the fact that a lot of the time our formal structures, processes and ways of doing things will be out of line with the needs of the marketplace, and accept that messy and unorthodox things that work are better than neat systems that don't.

'market strategies and marketing plans which do not confront implementation realities contain the seeds of their own failure'

Let's get to grips with the fact that market strategies and marketing plans which do not confront implementation realities contain the seeds of their own failure – so let's not be surprised when they fail. Let's do something about it instead!

But we don't have a problem (So kindly take your smart ideas and get lost!)

Perhaps the most basic reason why market-led strategic change and hence the implementation issue are completely ignored by companies is quite simply that they do not believe that they *have* a problem, or that they need to *change* anything, or even if they do think things are going wrong they will not change – until it is too late. Table 14.1 illustrates just such an approach to avoiding change, revealed by *Yes, Prime Minister*. Does it sound familiar?

Table 14.1   The four-stage approach to avoid change just because something has happened*

Stage	What we say is . . .
1	There may be something happening . . . but we don't need to do anything.
2	There really is something happening . . . but we should do nothing.
3	There really is something major happening . . . but there is nothing we can do.
4	Something major has definitely happened . . . we probably could have done something, but it's too late now!

* Source: The Foreign Office Standard Approach, *Yes, Prime Minister* [3]

Let us assume that we have agreed that some things need changing in the way your organization goes to market – because if you have used the instruments provided here, it is unlikely you will have concluded that all is 100 per cent perfect in your company's process of going to market. What we are suggesting is that organizations (and, indeed, different parts of the same organization) differ dramatically in two important respects:

- the perception that there is a problem in our organization which should be taken seriously (or, conversely, that there isn't really a problem at all); and
- the willingness to try something new to solve the problem (or, on the other hand, the lack of willingness so to do).

We can put this together to produce the picture shown in Figure 14.1.

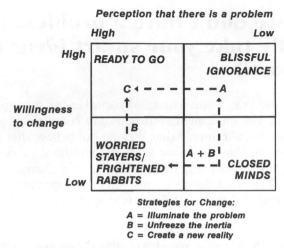

Figure 14.1   Recognizing the problem and preparing for change

So, a first step in getting to grips with the marketing implementation issue is to ask where we are currently on this model. Which of the following best describes the situation in our company, department or unit?

- *Closed Minds* – We do not accept that we have any kind of problem in the market that could not be solved by a new brochure, the salespeople working harder, or sending our junior staff on training courses. Therefore, why *should* we change? And, anyway, we're not *going* to change! The Closed Minds can be mightily frustrating. One Chief Executive has assured me that he was so frustrated in his attempts to build customer responsiveness in a bureaucratic and slow-moving company that he sneaked in at the weekend and put on every office wall a copy of the 'Kill the Snake' sign shown in Table 14.2. He says it did not change much, but it irritated the bureaucrats, and that made him feel better!
- *Worried Stayers* – Yes, we *know* we've got problems, yes, we *know* we are under threat, but if we just stick to doing things our way it's bound to come right in the end, isn't it? Besides, it's cheaper. (This is similar to waiting for a bus that never turns up, and refusing to budge from the bus stop, because we are convinced it is at that precise moment that the bus will arrive.)
- *Frightened Rabbits* – OK, we've got some problems, but please keep extremely quiet about it, because the trick is to keep still in the middle of the road and concentrate very hard on staring at those headlights coming towards us . . .

Table 14.2   The snake

IF YOU SEE A SNAKE . . .

1. Do not write me a memo about it.
2. Do not commission a consultant's report to identify the snake's characteristics.
3. Do not form a committee to review the 'snake situation' and to adjudicate on departmental snake responsibilities.
4. Do not apply to Human Resources to appoint a Manager of Snake Affairs.
5. Do not go home pretending that you have not noticed the snake.

KILL THE SNAKE!

(then say sorry to whoever owned the snake, and explain that it has gone a bit limp).

- *Blissful Ignorance* – We are always open to new ideas and thoroughly enjoy talking about them, but we don't think *we* need them, because *we've* got it right already, so 'if it ain't broke, don't fix it!'
- *Ready to Go* – Yes, we've got a problem in the market, and yes, we want to solve it. Give us the tools and we will find the resources, commitment and money to use them and make it happen. It is important, though, that this should be measured and planned change, not panic and the 'headless chicken' scenario. We should avoid what has been called by cynical commentators on government policy the 'Politicians' Syllogism', i.e. *Step One*: We must do something. *Step Two*: This is something. *Step Three*: Therefore we must do this.' [3].

Now, that sounds harsh. How could it be that we have problems in the market and we do not ever see them? Quite easily, if you look at our analysis of the market sensing issue! But there is more to it than this.

Tom Bonoma and Bruce Clark [4] have made some progress on this issue with their 'Marketing Performance Assessment' framework. To start with, they point out the following basics:

- Satisfaction with market performance depends on what management *expected* in the first place. Jubilation or despair depends not just on the actual results achieved, but on the psychological distance between what was thought achievable and what was achieved. If we expect poor results and get mediocre ones, we may be highly delighted. This has, of course, nothing to do with the potential we might have achieved.
- How much marketing effort we have to make to get a given result depends on our skills and our structures. As a

consequence, we may get good results with minimal effort, or bad results with massive effort, depending on the match between what we have got and what the market needs. This complicates further seeing whether we have got a marketing problem, or if one is on the way.

- Our results depend on the environment – market trends, competitive action, and so on. Our results may look good because of external factors totally outside our control – we may even do well *in spite* of our marketing competence (or, strictly, our lack of it), if we are in the right place at the right time. Of course, relying on such good fortune continuing carries a bit of a risk.

The point is that seeing how good or bad our marketing performance is may be far from straightforward.

Now, consider the different strategies for market-led strategic change that are implied (as in Figure 14.1):

- *A: Illuminate the problem* – The goal is to change the perception that 'we don't have a problem', or to move from 'Blissful Ignorance' to 'Ready To Go'.
- *B: Unfreeze the inertia* – The goal is to increase the willingness of the organization to do something about the problem, or to move from 'Worried Stayer/Frightened Rabbit' to 'Ready To Go'.
- *A + B: Illuminate the problem and/or unfreeze the inertia* – The goal is to open the 'Closed Minds'. This is the most problematic situation of all. Perhaps the most difficult choice here is where do you start – can you do both things at the same time and move straight to 'Ready To Go', or do you work on one thing at a time and go through the 'Blissful Ignorance' or 'Frightened Rabbit' stage on the way? That choice will depend on prevailing conditions.
- *C: Create a new reality* – The goal is to build a programme of market-led strategic change and drive it through to implementation.

'why are there implementation problems anyway?' However, the underlying question we have yet to tackle is: why are there implementation problems anyway?

So, why doesn't it work?

Before we jump to conclusions about where things need changing (or in anticipating future difficulties), let's just consider how planning and strategy building goes wrong. Figure 14.2, adapted from Tom Bonoma [5], is a good starting point.

Strategy

Appropriate   Inappropriate

	Appropriate	Inappropriate
Good	**Success**	**Roulette**
Bad	**Trouble**	**Failure**

Execution Skills *(Good / Bad)*

Figure 14.2 Diagnosing the marketing problem

The strategy versus the implementation skills

This suggests that the trouble with diagnosing for implementation problems is that you have to think about the strategy (which may be appropriate or inappropriate) as well as execution skills (which may be good or bad) to try to decide what is going wrong. The possible situations to consider are:

- *Success* – If we have a sound strategy, matched by good implementation skills, then we would reasonably expect success in meeting our targets for growth, share, profits, and so on – as long as our expectations in setting these targets were realistic.
- *Trouble* – We may conclude that the strategy is good – it is the right thing to do – but our skills and capabilities for implementing it are poor. The strength of the strategy may never become apparent, because we are bad at putting it into effect. This is, of course, what we normally assume to be the explanation when things go wrong – after all, it is obvious that our *great* plans and strategies go wrong only because of the incompetence of line management in the field!
- *Roulette* – This is a gamble, because we rely on excellence in our implementation skills and capabilities to drive a weak strategy. This gives us time to improve the strategy. Otherwise we end up in the failure box.
- *Failure* – A weak strategy and poor implementation skills. This is hard to diagnose, because the weakness of the strategy is hidden by the implementation failure. The danger is that we invest more and more to improve the execution of an inappropriate strategy.

This may sound an obvious analysis to do before we act on implementation failures – if so, why do so few of us actually think it through like this?

However, it does get more complicated if we allow for the fact that life is inherently unfair – things change. Notwithstanding our wise words about matching strategy to our differentiating capabilities (see pp. 194–211), the unavoidable consequence of market-led strategic change is that you may have to re-position to survive in a market, in ways which require new capabilities, and the inevitable consequence of real markets is that strategies do not stay appropriate for ever. The implementation issue may change because of the degree of *stretch* we are asking from people in the company.

For example, consider the model in Figure 14.3, which raises the question of whether we need 'strategies for stretch or more of the same.' The judgement we make here is likely to be highly indicative of the type of implementation barriers we face and the approaches needed to develop an effective implementation strategy.

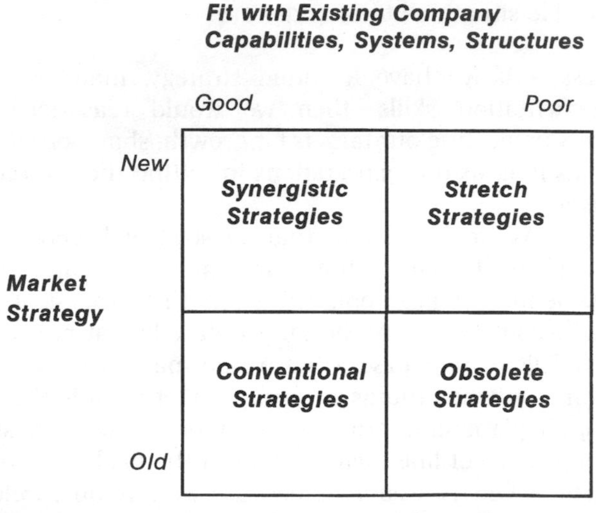

**Fit with Existing Company
Capabilities, Systems, Structures**

Figure 14.3 Strategies for stretch or more of the same?

Where our market strategy is essentially a continuation of the type of approach we usually take – i.e. *Conventional strategies* – it follows that there is probably going to be a good fit with the company's capabilities, and relatively few new implementation problems. An example of this type of strategy from the retail sector is the development of growth from increased market share through sales promotion, new product launches, price positioning, and so on. The implementation tasks here are probably mainly concerned with action planning, resource allocation, internal communications and the day-to-day leadership skills of line management.

On the other hand, look at the case of *Synergistic strategies*. This is where we have developed new market strategies to achieve the things we need in the external market, but they are designed around existing company capabilities and systems. We may be doing new things – but they are the things we know how to do and have the resources to do. An example from the retail sector is the move of major players like Sainsbury and Tesco into petrol retailing and financial services – entry into totally different product markets, but based on customer franchise and retailing skills. Implementation strategy may be about no more than resource acquisition, action planning and internal communications, so that managers know what the new strategies are.

What is more worrying is where our plans and strategies are relatively conventional for the company, but have a poor fit with company capabilities, systems and structures – critical people have left, we have been left behind by the competition, or perhaps the market has changed in its requirements. Then we are left attempting to drive *Obsolete strategies*, which are familiar but no longer appropriate to the company. A classic example was the determination of Encyclopaedia Britannica to continue selling books through direct selling, when the market was moving to CD-ROM for this type of publication (see pp. 388–89). The problems then are surviving the short term with what we have got, but as quickly as possible developing new strategies to cope with new realities.

This leads to the case of *Stretch strategies* – the new things we need to do to perform in the external marketplace, but which are unfamiliar and currently do not fit well with the company's capabilities and systems. An example of this type of strategy is provided by the move of computer companies from selling technology to relationship-based marketing of solutions to customer problems, involving huge changes in culture and priorities. These strategies may be the only route to marketplace success – but only if we can execute them effectively. In this situation, we may need to think not just about what we have to do to develop organizational learning and changing internal systems and structures to implement the strategy, but also about what we have to do to develop a programme of organizational change, and ultimately how we manage the processes of strategy building to win commitment and support for new strategies.

However, before jumping to easy conclusions about why things go wrong – let's test our great strategies and how we handled them first.

Testing out the strategy versus blaming the salesperson

Before we can expect our market strategies to achieve anything, we need people to know about, to understand, to believe in, to accept, and then to do them. This applies both to top management, whose support we need, right down to field people, whose actions and commitment we depend on.

'How many of the plans and strategies that never "happen" are really no more than vague, grandiose management aspirations'

Some of the basic questions we should ask are set out in Figure 14.4. *First*, if we have not produced a *coherent* and *complete* strategy which is linked to tactics and actions, we can hardly be surprised if nothing happens as a result of it. How many of the plans and strategies that never 'happen' are really no more than vague, grandiose management aspirations and ego-trips, or, at the other extreme, are no more than projected financial budgets?

Secondly, if we produce brilliant ivory-tower plans which, realistically, are impossible for this company, with this management, at this time, can we really expect any more than lip-service (and that only if we are lucky)? Here again, Tom Bonoma[5] has outlined some of the common scenarios we create for ourselves:

- *Management by assumption* – We assume 'someone' will get the nitty-gritty work done, so in reality 'no-one' does.
- *Structural contradictions* – We create strategies that our systems and structures *cannot* deliver.

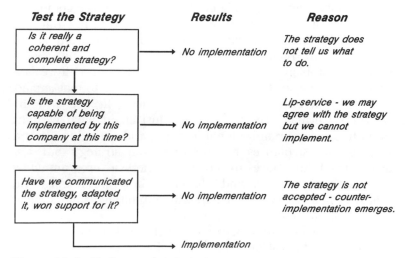

Figure 14.4 Testing market strategies

- *Empty promises marketing* – We build programmes which rely on abilities and resources that we have not got and cannot get.
- *Bunny marketing* – We have no clear strategy, so we create a profusion of plans instead. (The analogy is the man with lots of rabbits who needed an ox, but no matter how much he bred rabbits, he never seemed to end up with an ox.)

Thirdly, if we are not prepared to make the effort to communicate and to win support (adapting our plans if need be), non-acceptance and counter-implementation must surely follow, rather than 'ownership' and commitment.

Indeed, some would say that one of the outstanding skills of middle management is *counter-implementation* – dogged, pervasive, determined and effective efforts to ensure that something will *not* happen. If that sounds exaggerated, consider the 'D's of counter-implementation, and see how many you recognize in your company:

- *Deflecting goals* – We say to the planner: 'what you want (A) is just a little bit too 'ambitious', so let's go after something a little bit more modest instead (B)' (where, of course, B is not even vaguely related to A).
- *Diverting resources* – The money and the people and the time are suddenly absorbed in 'urgent' work elsewhere (with profuse apologies) but never to return.
- *Dissipating energies* – If enough hassle and aggravation are created, you can wear most people down eventually.
- *Delaying decision* – If you can put things off long enough, they may leave or just lose interest and forget about it, or it may just be too late.
- *Destroying credibility* – Rumour, innuendo and even the right sort of praise can make anyone suspicious about a new plan and its sponsors. Consider for a moment the instructions in the excellent *Yes, Prime Minister* [3] for rubbishing someone or something threatening, by offering support: *Stage One*: Express absolute support. *Stage Two*: List all the praiseworthy features, especially those which make the person unsuitable for the job, or the project impossible to accept. *Stage Three*: Continue to praise these qualities to the point where they become positive vices. *Stage Four*: Mention the bad points by defending and excusing them.
- *Deflating excitement* – If the problem is that people are getting excited about a new strategy and are in danger of making it happen, then make them feel bad about it, and take the fun out of it – that should slow them down.

- *Depth charge* – If all else fails, outright conflict and attack may work, particularly if they don't see it coming until it is too late – maybe because you 'forgot' to ask them to the meeting that matters.

However, the real point is that if you ignore people by not listening to them and not actively working for their support – do not be surprised if they turn on you. Let's just think that one through before we blame the salesperson for our failed plans and strategies.

What about execution?

With all this said, however well-developed and researched are our market strategies, and however carefully we evaluate implementation issues and build implementation strategies, one critical resource we should absolutely not ignore is the ability of our line managers to put plans into effect – their *execution skills*. Quite simply, however much strategy we talk and however many plans we write, in reality, the way the strategy implementation process is managed at the interpersonal level is likely to be a critical determinant of implementation success. In fact, in many cases it is true that managers' personal skills of leadership and action may have to *substitute* for having the right structures and administrative policies – because external markets change faster than companies can respond with their formal systems.

'the way the strategy implementation process is managed at the interpersonal level is likely to be a critical determinant of implementation success'

One way of looking at managerial execution skills is as follows:

- *Interacting skills* – this refers to how a manager behaves and influences the behaviour of those around him/her, and includes leadership by example and setting the standards by providing a role model, as well as bargaining and negotiating and using power to get the right things to happen. In most organizations, the managers who have superior interacting skills are well-known for their bias for action and getting things done.
- *Allocating skills* – this is about how a manager sets the agenda for others by budgeting time, money and people around the highest priorities to achieve implementation, even if this is at the expense of 'fair play' and administrative 'neatness'. In some

cases this may even involve 'cheating' the system to get things done and reward those who perform – even if this is not formally approved behaviour.

- *Monitoring skills* – this refers to how the manager develops and uses feedback mechanisms that focus on the critical issues for success, rather than just the information provided by the company's information systems. This may involve face-to-face discussions, participation in key tasks and coaching, rather than score-keeping and awarding penalties.
- *Organizing skills* – in the sense not of designing formal organizational arrangements, but of networking and arranging and fixing things to achieve the right kind of action [5].

The importance of these issues is that managers' execution skills represent a hidden but vital resource for strategy implementation. This is a resource we need to consider when we look at the internal market and ask questions like: what are we really good at doing here, and who do we need on our side to make the strategy happen?

However, with all this said, our strategies *may* fail because they are put into effect badly. At one level, this may be relatively straightforward – the skills needed are not available, things are done badly, and so on. This can happen to any company – you think you are close to the customer, you train people, you set up systems and processes, and it is all rendered obsolete because the market changes. One level of the execution problem is that a great gap opens up between what we do and what the market wants, while we are looking the other way. The remedy here is simple – close the gap.

However, at a deeper and more worrying level, a company may have learned routines for implementing strategies which are flawed and ineffective – but, in spite of the flaws, we continue with the routine. This is what Chris Argyris calls 'designed error' [6]. The problem is that we not only have to find out what is wrong with the implementation process, but also why we continued unaware that it was wrong, or why, when we knew it was wrong we still did nothing about it, i.e. the defensive routines that people have to protect themselves from the discomfort and disruption of having to change.

The real execution or implementation barrier is not gaps in skills, or even recalcitrant attitudes and change-resisting behaviour from line managers and operatives. The real barrier is those defensive routines and the 'designed error' that they protect from challenge. If we are to get to grips with an implementation *strategy*, then we have to confront these issues.

Building implementation strategies

The approach here is described in more detail in articles by myself and Ken Peattie[7,8] looking at how successful implementors really do it, in a variety of different companies. The sorts of issues with which we need to grapple hinge around questions like these:

- *Basic objectives* – what do we need to make the market strategy work, what resources are necessary, who controls those resources;
- *Problems* – what are the most critical elements, who controls them, will they co-operate with us, will they respond with delays, resistance, and so on; how will we cope with these tactics;
- *Games* – what counter-implementation games are people likely to play;
- *Delays* – how much delay should we build into the plan, how much negotiation is going to be needed; and
- *Fixing the game* – what senior management help can we expect, who can we use as a political 'fixer', can we build coalitions that will help us, what do we have to do to establish a 'contract for change' with key players in the organization?

The underlying goal is to anticipate implementation barriers as early as possible, to allow us to steer a path between ignoring such problems, or seeing them as totally intractable. The logic is of four stages in developing implementation strategies, and of iteration backwards and forwards between those four stages to build a complete picture in the way shown in Figure 14.5. The

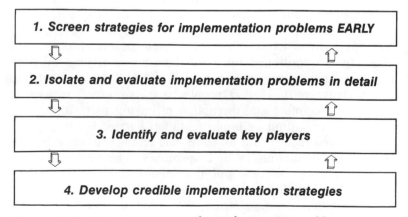

Figure 14.5 Screening strategies for implementation problems

output is either movement forward in terms of generating an implementation strategy, or feedback to the planning process indicating that some barriers cannot be overcome and the relevant strategies are likely to fail if not adapted in some significant way. (It should be borne in mind, though, that 'significant' adaptation of strategies to make them more easily implemented may come down to no more than 're-labelling' the strategies.) The four stages are as follows.

Screening strategies for implementation problems

At the earliest stage possible, we screen the strategy possibilities we have identified for implementation barriers, in terms of the acceptability of each key strategy to the company. In particular, note that the *earlier* this issue is faced, the less wasteful the planning process will be, for two reasons: first, if there is an absolute barrier, and a strategy is not capable of being implemented, it can be abandoned or 'shelved' before it has used up too much time and effort; however, secondly, if we identify problem areas early enough, we can devote more time to solving them. Implementation barriers may be fundamental cultural mismatches, but are often down-to-earth factors such as obtaining a budget or head-count – where company policies forbid increased expenditure, or recruitment, or expenditure on something like advertising may simply be seen as 'wasteful' by the corporate culture.

'Implementation barriers may be fundamental cultural mismatches'

As shown in Figure 14.6, we can sift our strategies through a matrix to identify the following categories. The '*Losers*' should probably be discarded. More discussion is usually generated about '*Low Risk/Low Pay-off*' and '*Push Over*' strategies, on the grounds that if they are acceptable to the company then possibly they should be more central to the strategic plan. However, it is the '*Conflicts*' that we are likely to want to focus on, because these are high in priority but low in acceptability.

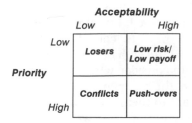

Figure 14.6 Priority and acceptability of a strategy item

Isolating and evaluating implementation problems

Now that we have isolated those strategies which, on first sight, are high priority *and* low acceptability, these can be analysed further. We can examine the forces surrounding the implementation of these key strategies facing implementation barriers, and try to see the balance between opposing and favourable forces and the likely impact of the various factors identified. It is not unusual, for instance, to find that some of the reasons 'why not' for a strategy, which are apparently 'insoluble', when tested are not as overpowering as we first thought.

While generally the picture which emerges from isolating problems should give us an overview of all those significant factors of different kinds in the company which relate to getting our strategy implemented, and which are most important, we will probably need to refine and reconsider this overview in two ways. First, we can evaluate the key players in our implementation problems. And, secondly, we can ask what else would have to happen to move the issues, to see if this changes the picture.

Evaluating key players in implementation

First, if our thinking has produced little insight into what is likely to prevent things happening, or what we have to do to make them happen, we may not have got to the heart of the problem – so we may have to be a lot more specific about the people, the departments, the committees, and so on, that we have to cope with.

Broadly, the categories into which our key players will fall are as shown below in Figure 14.7 and discussed as follows.:

- *Influential Supporters* – With these key players the goal is to utilize and reinforce this source of support for what we are trying to achieve. We will be concerned to ensure that these key players stay on our side, and remain involved in the decision with which we are concerned.
- *Influential Opposition* – These are the key players who are influential and involved, but almost inevitably will oppose our plans. First, we have to consider whether their influence is great enough to outweigh our supporters (or vice versa). If it is, we may want to consider whether there are strategies we can employ to win their support – perhaps by doing 'deals' on things important to them, or by negotiating, or by 'selling' our ideas to them. Alternatively, we may want to consider what may be done to reduce the influence of intractable opponents.

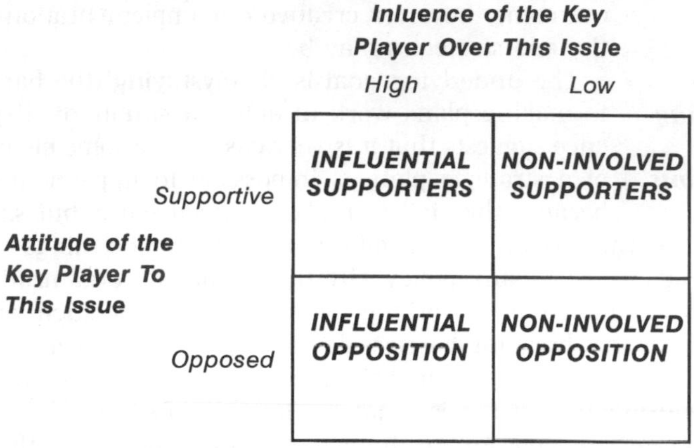

Inluence of the Key
Player Over This Issue

	High	Low

		High	Low
Supportive		INFLUENTIAL SUPPORTERS	NON-INVOLVED SUPPORTERS
Opposed		INFLUENTIAL OPPOSITION	NON-INVOLVED OPPOSITION

Attitude of the
Key Player To
This Issue

Figure 14.7 Key player matrix

We may consider how these key players might be eased out of the decision-making unit – by the action of a senior player who is on our side, or, perhaps more surreptitiously, by removing them from the circulation list, or influencing the agenda for the decision-making unit!

- *Non-Involved Supporters* – With these key actors, who are not influential in the decision but who support our goals and plans, the main possibility to consider is what may be done by us or them to increase their influence – the reverse of the tactics above for Influential Oppisition!
- *Non-Involved Opposition* – These are the parties providing unhelpful 'noise' in the system, but since they are not directly influential we may not see these as a major threat. However, if it seems likely that their influence will increase or they provide support for Involved Opposition, then we may need to allow for this extra problem and consider the appropriate stance to take.

The final stage involves packing all the problems and their possible solutions together, to see if we can succeed in generating an implementation strategy.

Developing implementation strategies

By going through the implementation issues in this detailed way, we hope to turn apparently intractable, unbeatable barriers into things which may be moved, at least a little. Naturally, in taking this approach we have to accept that some things cannot be

'The underlying goal is "de-mystifying" the barriers to making plans work in different situations'

overcome, however creative our implementation tactics and strategies may be.

The underlying goal is 'de-mystifying' the barriers to making plans work in different situations. Experience suggests that it is very easy to see some elements of a strategic plan as impossible to implement, not because they fail to make financial sense, but simply because they are innovative, different to how 'we do things here', are against 'company policy', fly in the face of 'organizational myths', and so on. Working with planners on such issues suggests that breaking barriers down into their constituent parts and addressing them at this level frequently leads to the conclusion that strategies may be feasible after all, if we can integrate an appropriate implementation strategy with our strategic plans, and if we are prepared to look into the organizational realities of how things happen in our companies. The experience of one company with this approach is illustrated in the Lion Machines Ltd case study (pp. 628–34).

So far, we have an approach to open the closed minds by illuminating the problems and unfreezing the inertia. First, we test our strategies for their adequacy and then we break down implementation barriers into their smallest components and see what we can do about them. We do this early, systematically, and iterate between the strategy and the barrier. Then, we can either say that a strategy should be abandoned, or that we know what to do to make it work. We can then use an internal marketing framework to put implementation strategy into effect.

Strategic internal marketing

What we are now calling 'strategic internal marketing' has the goal of developing a type of marketing programme aimed at the internal marketplace in the company that *parallels* and *matches* the marketing programme aimed at the external marketplace of customers and competitors.

This model comes from the simple observation we have made that the implementation of external market strategies implies changes of various kinds within organizations – in the allocation of resources, in the culture of 'how we do things here', and even in the organizational structures needed to deliver our market strategies effectively to our customer segments. Such changes may not be welcomed by those most directly affected.

Internal marketing seems to be coming of age as a way of coping with this type of strategic change – in 1997 research by Marketing Forum found that nearly 80 per cent of their delegates came from organizations committed to communication with employees, and, for companies with a total marketing budget of more than £20 million, three-quarters have a dedicated internal marketing budget.

'Internal marketing seems to be coming of age as a way of coping with this type of strategic change'

In practical terms, the attraction of internal marketing is that exactly those same techniques of analysis and communication which are used for the external marketplace can be adapted and used to market our plans and strategies to important targets within the company. Indeed, one of the major attractions of talking about 'internal marketing' instead of culture change, implementation, and so on, is that we know how to *do* it. The goals of the internal marketing plan are taken directly from the implementation requirements for the external marketing plan, and the objectives to be pursued. Depending on the particular circumstances, this process might include:

- gaining the support of key decision makers for our plans – and all that those plans imply in terms of the need to acquire personnel and financial resources, possibly in conflict with established company 'policies', and to get what we need from other functions, like operations and finance departments;
- changing the attitudes and behaviour of employees and managers, who are working at the key interfaces with customers and distributors, to those required to make plans work effectively;
- winning commitment to making the plan work and 'ownership' of the key problem-solving tasks from those units and individuals in the firm whose working support is needed; and
- ultimately managing incremental changes in the culture from 'the way we always do things' to 'the way we need to do things to be successful' and to make the market strategy work.

In short, *that* is why we may need an internal marketing strategy. Now let's go into more detail about what it is.

But what is 'internal marketing' anyway?

Internal marketing is not my invention, and the term is somewhat ambiguous, reflecting the views of different people who have used the technique in different settings. This is clearer if you look at the sources of internal marketing.

Service marketing and quality

The original and most extensive use of internal marketing was in improving the quality of service at the point of sale in services businesses like banking, leisure, retailing, and so on – the so-called 'moment of truth' for the services marketer. Some call this 'selling the staff', because the 'product' promoted is the person's job as a creator of customer service and value. Now, I have nothing against efforts to introduce a bit of customer care into the retail store or the bank – a tad less offensiveness and arrogance in dealing with paying customers is all to the good. However, all too often these internal marketing programmes are, in practice, essentially tactical and restricted to the operational level of the organization.

In fact, there is a substantial theoretical underpinning for this form of internal marketing, which comes mainly from the 'Nordic School of Services', and the pioneering work of people like Evert Gummesson[9] and Christian Gronroos[10].

Indeed, in all fairness to advocates of this form of internal marketing, there is a lesson here for us all if we believe that our carefully prepared market strategies are let down by the quality of implementation at the point of sale. It is apparent and obvious that marketplace success is frequently largely dependent on employees who are far removed from the excitement of creating market strategies – service engineers, customer services departments, production and finance personnel dealing with customers, field sales personnel, and so on. These are all people called 'part-time marketers' by Evert Gummesson[11] – they impact directly and significantly on customer relationships, but are not part of any formal marketing organization, nor are they typically within our direct control. Indeed, one of the advantages of thinking about the process of going to market instead of conventional marketing is that it should help us to identify who are the important 'part-time marketers' who participate in the process just as much as marketing people do.

'marketplace success is frequently largely dependent on employees who are far removed from the excitement of creating market strategies'

Indeed, recent US research for example, suggests that we should all think more carefully about the impact of organizational communications on employees – as 'advertising's second audience'[12]. The chances are that employees are more aware and more influenced by our advertising than are our customers, so we should use that productively to deliver messages to employees.

Some companies take this very seriously, to good effect. Think of the Day's Inn TV advertising in the USA which says 'Thank you for staying with us' – to the *staff*, not just the guests. Then ask yourself when you last said that to the people in your company who handle customers! (Really this is about recognizing that we don't get people's commitment just because they work for us – we have to work hard to win their 'hearts and minds' if we want commitment instead of just compliance.)

An interesting case of where this can lead is Kinko's Copiers. This is a US company which positions itself as 'the world's branch office' – it offers 24–hour facilities for photocopying, computer services, audio-visual production, video-conferencing and Internet access, and post office services. In fact, the company started as a single rented Xerox machine in an old hamburger stand in California and has expanded to locations throughout the USA, and is growing in Europe and the Far East. The founder, Paul Orfalea, has understood throughout how important office services are to his customers – high-quality production and reliable despatch of documents may mean survival or death to a small business; a curriculum vitae is not just a photocopying job, it is the prospect of employment for the customer who comes in off the street. However, Orfalea is also adamant about something else, for he says and means: 'If you never take care of your co-workers, you won't be able to take care of your customers. . . . The attitude of our workers is our *biggest* competitive advantage.' [13] This belief is central to how he has successfully differentiated and owned this simple service business. Anyone can open a copy shop – but it won't be a Kinko's.

At the same time, we are learning that, while there is no one 'right' strategy in a given product market situation, there are good and bad ways of *delivering* market strategies which determine whether they succeed or fail. The critical issue is *consistency* between strategies, tactics and implementation actions. This suggests that real culture change is a central part of the process of going to market effectively. At its simplest, the disgruntled employee produces the disgruntled customer, and then we all have problems. Tom Bonoma has hit this nail right on the head: 'treat your employees like customers, for your customers will get treated like employees' [15]. Given how appallingly badly so many of us treat our employees, the real enormity of the task becomes apparent! Internal marketing focusing on customer service and quality strategies can help here.

' "treat your employees like customers, for your customers will get treated like employees" '

Internal communications

The largest growth in this area has been investment in internal communications programmes of various kinds – where 'communication' is understood as telling our employees what is going on, and delivering messages which support the business strategy. Conventionally, where it happens at all, it tends to be a responsibility of the Human Resources Department [16]. This is a start, but there is a danger that we may miss an important point: communication is a two-way process – we are supposed to listen as well as tell people things.

Perhaps the most visible sign of commitment to internal communications to win employee commitment to strategies of customer service is the huge investments made by companies like British Airways, Sainsbury and Safeway, to build programmes that justify management changes to employees and explain the background to things like media stories about the company [17]. Indeed, BT has actually formally merged internal communications with public relations.

Obviously, it is good if employees know when the 'special offers' are and deliver against our value proposition promises at the point of sale. It is even better if they actually feel they are being treated as trusted insiders by the company.

The manifestations are mundane: company newsletters, conferences, training, video-conferencing, satellite TV transmissions, interactive video, e-mail, and so on. The trouble is, most of this is about instructing and informing people, rather than winning their real involvement and participation.

This may be why internal communications go wrong. Peter Bell of the Added Value Internal Communications Consultancy discusses the emergence of in-company barriers to internal communications 'that halt or distort the flow of information, whether they take the form of misunderstandings and misconceptions, hidden agendas and internal politicking, or even myths' [17].

Even more telling about how we may miss the point is the view of Chris Argyris of Harvard Business School [18]. Argyris says that many internal communications strategies are misconceived to the point of being counter-productive. He cites the case of a chief executive who was determined to improve his company's performance in innovation and time to market, and formed special task forces to work on this issue. The task forces found that every new idea in the company was subjected to 275 separate checks. By redesigning channels of internal communication, 200 of these checks were eliminated, which dramatically

'many internal communications strategies are misconceived to the point of being counter-productive'

reduced the time to get a new idea to market. A success story? Not according to Argyris. He says the chief executive *failed*, because at no stage did he ask the really unsettling questions like: 'How long have you known that we have had an excessive number of barriers to innovation?' or 'What is it that prevented you from questioning these practices?'

This highlights a fundamental problem in some internal communications programmes – they become about telling and persuading, not listening. This is internal *selling*, not internal *marketing*.

What is really encouraging, though, is that we can see that many of our current success stories – companies like Avis, CIGNA and British Airways – *are* actually going to enormous efforts to *listen* to their employees' feedback, and to react positively to it, to improve the value they deliver to their customers. We see Asda's 'Tell Archie Campaign' to encourage staff to make comments and suggestions direct to the chief executive, and we see in-store terminals at Safeways to collect staff suggestions. It can be done, and it seems more effective in changing attitudes and building commitment than sending out more company newsletters.

Innovation management

Closer to what we have in mind here as internal marketing strategy is the use of the internal marketing framework to place, and gain use of, innovations like computers and electronic communications in the IT field. These applications use tools of market analysis and planning to cope with and avoid resistance to change. The argument here is that people in an organization are customers for our ideas and innovations. This encourages us to:

- look at customer needs – even in hierarchical companies, people are not robots waiting to be told what to do, so making the effort to understand their needs increases the likely effectiveness of innovation;
- delivering the goods – the needs of customers tell us what matters most to them;
- raising unrealistic expectations – is as dangerous with internal customers as it is with external customers [14].

Corporate positioning

Others talk of internal marketing in terms of creating aware-ness, understanding of, and co-operation with, functions, departments or processes inside the company. This is about creating an image, and just letting people know we are there and what we do. This may be of particular significance, for example, to gaining influence for the non-integrated marketing department (see pp. 370–75), in the absence of formal power or 'clout' in the company, or of sharing the idea that we are all involved in managing the process of going to market, rather than it being what marketing executives do. This form of internal marketing is also becoming more significant as formal marketing organizations disappear in some companies and are replaced by new organizational arrangements such as process-based teams, network collaborations, and so on. The need to explain who does what and how things operate becomes more important, not less.

Internal markets instead of external markets

'The terms "internal market" and "internal marketing" have also been applied to internal relationships between different parts of the same organization'

The terms 'internal market' and 'internal marketing' have also been applied to internal relationships between different parts of the same organization – making them suppliers and customers as a way of improving the focus on efficiency and value. This is common in total quality management programmes, and in wider applications such as the reform of the UK National Health Service.

This can lead to some interesting issues. For example, work with the R&D division of a major brewery suggested that the internal customer issues were really about the type and degree of dependence between the internal supplier (in this case the provider of R&D solutions to process problems in the brewery) and the internal customer (here the production and sales units of the brewery) – which in turn reflects the freedom of either internal supplier or customer to deal with third parties outside the company. (And where third party collaborations *had* to be handled via the R&D Division, we counted this as the same as them supplying their own expertise.) The model we produced is shown in Figure 14.8. This suggests that internal market relationships could include:

- *Independence* – Both parties can deal directly with outsiders, suggesting the need for conventional competitive marketing and purchasing strategies inside the company (including the 'hostage-taking' possibility for the brewery's R&D Division to make it harder and less desirable for units to buy R&D expertise externally).

INTERNAL CUSTOMER
Can we buy outside
as well as inside
the company?

		Yes	No
INTERNAL SUPPLIER Can we sell outside as well as inside the company?	**Yes**	**INDEPENDENCE** *Competitive marketing and purchasing strategies*	**CUSTOMER DEPENDENCE** *Internal buying by the customer*
	No	**SUPPLIER DEPENDENCE** *Internal marketing by the supplier*	**CONVENTIONAL COMPANY LINKS** *Internal transfers*

Figure 14.8 Internal/external customer relationships

- *Customer dependence* – The internal customer has little freedom of choice and acts as an internal buyer to R&D, and may have to compete with outsiders for R&D resources and attention (indeed, in this situation the internal customer may have to look at internal marketing to 'sell' their problems to R&D).
- *Supplier dependence* – R&D is in competition with outside suppliers for the internal customer's business and needs to actively market inside the company to get that business.
- *Conventional company links* – Both parties are constrained to behave like conventional organizational departments, and effectiveness is probably best enhanced by working on internal relationships for collaboration and partnership.

It was interesting in the brewery that managers in R&D could identify all these possible relationships with different units in the company. They had never previously taken the idea of customers seriously, and this approach gave that a start in segmenting their internal customer market, and developing better ways to handle relationships with different types of customer.

The other interesting lessons learned in the brewery case were: not only do some technologists not understand marketing, they do not *want* to understand it; there is a real need for professional specialists inside organizations to acquire the awareness and skills needed for customer relationship building.

It can all go horribly wrong, however. For example, one health insurance company recently moved to a huge new office block, with an expensive, state-of-the-art catering facility built next to the office block in the company's new 'park'. Concerned with issues of efficiency in the internal market, management pressured the catering manager to 'sell' the new restaurant and catering facilities to employees, and proposed to evaluate his success by restaurant usage rates by employees. As an entrepreneurial sort of fellow, he toured the new offices (his marketplace), and quickly arranged for the removal of all kettles, coffee machines, soft drink machines, snack facilities and microwaves and toasters with which employees had equipped themselves, and then pressured departmental managers to enforce company rules about employees not eating or drinking at their work stations. The result is a high usage figure for the catering facility – employees have nowhere else to get food or drinks. Management are delighted. However, they now have to deal with a bunch of very unhappy employees who are getting meaner by the day and are liable to lynch the catering manager some day soon (a serious risk, in fact, since the company is in Texas).

There are some interesting issues here which may be relevant to our companies, but there is another dimension to internal marketing as well.

Strategic internal marketing (SIM)

Finally, there is the use of SIM as the parallel to our external market strategy and marketing programme, which aims at winning the support, co-operation and commitment we need inside the company if our external market strategies

'The key issue here is the organizational and cultural change needed to make marketing happen'

are to work. This is the view of internal marketing we are mainly taking here, although it is informed by the other types of internal marketing, which have a longer history. The key issue here is the organizational and cultural change needed to make marketing happen.

What does strategic internal marketing look like?

We know why we need it and where it comes from – but what does it involve? The logic here is really quite straightforward.

The structure of SIM

A structure for an internal marketing programme, as we have used it with companies, is summarized in Figure 14.9. The easiest way to make practical progress with *internal* marketing, and to

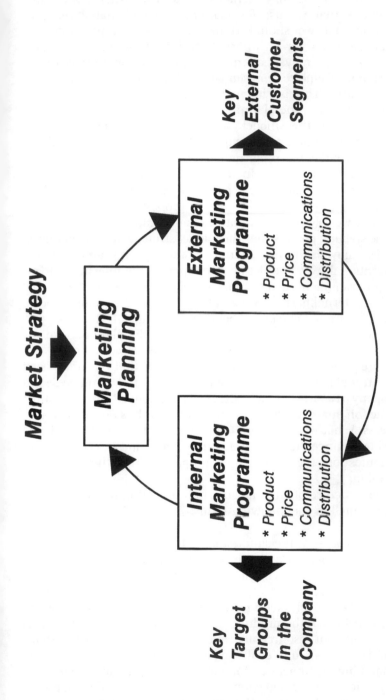

Figure 14.9   Internal and external marketing

establish what it may achieve, is to use exactly the same structures that we use for planning *external* marketing. This suggests that we should think in terms of integrating the elements needed for an internal marketing mix or programme, based on our analysis of the opportunities and threats in the internal marketplace represented by the company with which we are working. This is shown in Figure 14.9 as a formal and legitimate part of the planning process.

In fact, in this model we take the internal marketing programme not only as an *output* of the planning process and the external marketing programme, but also as an *input* – i.e. constraints and barriers in the internal marketplace should be considered and analysed as a part of the planning process at both strategic and tactical levels. For our proposals to make sense in practice, we rely on this iterative relationship.

The starting point is that the market strategy and the planning process may define an external marketing programme in the conventional way, and, less conventionally, the internal marketing programme needed to make it happen. However, it may well be that internal barriers suggest to executives that some external strategies are not capable of being implemented in the time-scale concerned, and we have to feed back into the planning process the message that some adjustments are needed.

More positively, however, it is equally true that our analysis of the internal market may suggest new opportunities and neglected company resources which should be exploited, which in turn impact on our external marketing plan and thus on the planning process. What we are trying to make explicit for executives is the need to balance the impact of both internal and external market attributes on the strategic assumptions that they make in planning.

The structure of such an internal marketing programme can be presented in the following terms:

- *The product* – At the simplest level, the 'product' consists of the market strategies and the marketing plan in which they are written up. What is implied, however, is that the product to be 'sold' is those values, attitudes and behaviours that are needed to make the marketing plan work effectively. These hidden dimensions of the product may range from increased budgets and different resource allocations, to changed control systems and criteria used to evaluate performance, to changed ways of handling customers at the point of sale. At the extreme, the product is the person's job – as it is redefined and reshaped by the market strategy. We may be able to identify positive 'product benefits' – ways in which the market strategy will make people's working lives more enjoyable. There may also be negatives – changes that people will not like, which brings us to price.

- *The price* – The price element of the internal marketing mix is not *our* costs, it is concerned with what we are asking our internal customers to 'pay', when they buy-in to the product and the marketing plan. This may include the sacrifice of other projects which compete for resources with our plan, but, more fundamentally, the personal psychological cost of adopting different key values, and changing **'what we are asking our internal customers to "pay", when they buy-in to the product and the marketing plan'**
  the way jobs are done, and asking managers to step outside their 'comfort zones' with new methods of operation. The price to be paid by different parts of the internal marketplace, if the marketing plan is to be implemented successfully, should not be ignored as a major source of barriers and obstacles of varying degrees of difficulty.
- *Communications* – The most tangible aspect of the internal marketing programme is the communications media and the messages used to inform and persuade, and to work on the attitudes of the key personnel in the internal marketplace. This includes not only written communications – such as plan summaries and reports – but also face-to-face presentations to individuals and groups who are important to the success of the plan. Broadly, we should remember that to assume that simply 'telling' people will get them on our side is likely to be as naive inside the company as it is outside. We suggest it is important to consider the full range of communications possibilities and associated goals, as we would with external customers, and we should not forget to budget the time and financial costs which may be associated with these activities. In reality, just letting people know what we are trying to do would be a step forward for most of us! At the simplest level, the purpose of our internal marketing communication may be served by a video presentation explaining things, or a roadshow taking the message out to the regions and the distributors. But real communication is two-way – we listen, we adapt, we focus on our audience's problems and needs (see pp. 594–97 above).
- *Distribution* – The distribution channels element of the mix is concerned with the physical and socio-technical venues at which we have to deliver our product and its communications – meetings, committees, training sessions for managers and staff, seminars, workshops, written reports, informal communications, social occasions, and so on. Ultimately, however, the real distribution channel is human resource management, and in the lining-up of recruitment training, evaluation and

reward systems behind marketing strategies, so that the culture of the company becomes the real distribution channel for internal marketing strategies. In fact, Dave Ulrich [19] makes some radical points about this, which are worth confronting. He says that if we really want complete *customer commitment* from our external customers, through interdependent, shared values and shared strategies – then we should give our customers a major role in our:
- staff recruitment and selection decisions;
- staff promotion and development decisions;
- staff appraisal, from setting the standards to measuring the performance;
- staff reward systems, both financial and non-financial;
- organizational design strategies; and
- internal communications programmes.

Now that is *really* using our human resource management systems as the internal marketing channel. That is *really* taking the internal and external customer issue to its logical conclusion. The companies taking this seriously and trying it in the USA are minor players like General Electric, Marriott, Borg-Warner, DEC, Ford Motor Company, Hewlett-Packard, Honeywell, and some even less significant organizations! Just try thinking about that for a minute or two. Then, let's talk to our HRM people about our joint interests (see back to pp. 97–98 above).

'let's talk to our HRM people about our joint interests'

However, in an era of downsizing and dumbsizing, one of the questions managers ask is often: but how can you use internal marketing when you are telling people that their departments are closing and their jobs are going? I had trouble with this until I looked around and saw that this is exactly what the best companies are capable of doing. For example:

- Kate Owen, a senior manager at the British Petroleum Group, describes how in the period from the late 1980s to the mid-1990s that major company slimmed from 120 000 employees to around 60 000. In the 1980s, BP had eleven businesses, ranging from a computer company to a minerals business to a cooked meats and animal foods business. By 1995, they had three businesses: BP Exploration to find the oil and gas, BP Oil which refines and markets the fuel, and BP Chemicals. She does not say that these changes were easy or free from pain – far from it. She does describe moving from a bureaucratic, complex organization, with 89 standing committees and a huge head office, to a vastly leaner business. She describes the struggle to change the values of the people in the organization, to give them power, and to have them accept radical change in structure and process. She also describes how executives actively participated in the planning and execution of strategies that led to the removal of their own jobs from the company. There were many financial safeguards for managers in this position, which is one of the costs of change, but nonetheless people worked with management to remove their own jobs, and that is simply amazing.

- A different approach has been developed by Jim Meadows at AT&T, as it has gone through a period of massive restructuring and change. Instead of simple downsizing and removing executives whose jobs and departments were redundant, Meadows developed a 'talent pool' called Resource Link. The AT&T argument is that it made more sense to retain strong performing people, whose jobs were being shed, and lease them out within the business where their skills were needed. The Resource Link is widely used, and is now half volunteers. There are more ways than one of marketing the closure of a department or job [20].

Internal market research

It also follows that we can use our market research techniques inside the company to get to grips with who has to change, in what way, how much, and what the patterns are, in our internal marketplace.

Finally, as with the external marketing programme, we should not neglect the importance of measuring results wherever possible. This may be in terms of such criteria as people's attitudes towards the market strategy and their commitment to putting it into practice, or customer perceptions of our success in delivering our promises to them – or, perhaps more appositely, our lack of success as presented by complaints and so on.

Internal marketing targets

Again, in exact parallel with the conventional external marketing plan, our internal marketing programmes should be directed at chosen targets or segments within the market. The choice of key targets for the internal marketing programme should be derived directly from the goals of the external marketing programme and the types of organizational and human change needed to implement market strategies. The internal marketplace may be segmented at the simplest level by the job roles and functions played by groups of people, e.g. top management, other departments, and marketing and sales staff.

Alternatively, we might look beyond job characteristics to the key sources of support and resistance to the external marketing plan which are anticipated, to identify targets for reinforcement, or for persuasion and negotiation. Perhaps at the deepest level we might choose our targets on the basis of the individual's attitudes towards the external market and customers, and the key values that we need communicated to external customers, together with people's career goals.

For instance, one approach used successfully in internal marketing of IT has been to apply the diffusion of innovation models, widely recognized in conventional consumer research. The idea here is to identify and specifically target the 'opinion leaders' in the company (regardless of rank or functional specialization), because if they can be persuaded to change, the rest will gradually follow.

The hidden face of Strategic Internal Marketing

In fact, as well as giving us a model for analysing internal marketing needs, we can go further because this structure also provides a practical route to get to grips with what we have referred to as the 'corporate environment' for market strategy.

The model in Figure 14.10 suggests that to get to grips with the 'corporate environment', when we get to a company we may start by asking about the techniques, the systems and so on, but behind this the really important questions are: 'Who *runs* the organization?' and 'Who has *influence* in this organization?'

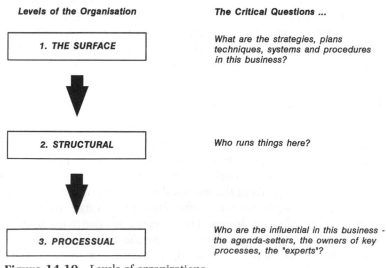

Figure 14.10 Levels of organizations

On this basis, we have developed a crude analytical device used to encourage managers to go beyond the superficial aspects of how their organizations work in planning internal marketing, to distinguish between a level of *systems* analysis, which is primarily about techniques and systems, and the level of *structure* and *process* analysis, in the way suggested by Figure 14.11. This can have the effect of widening the debate from simply the presentation of the plan to the company to the more difficult and covert issues of power and culture in companies in the way shown.

Figure 14.11 Levels of internal marketing

At the rational level, for example, the 'product' is the marketing plan or strategy, but the additional dimensions suggested are the implied changes in culture and environmental perceptions, and the status of others in the company, while at the most covert level the 'product' implies the existence or threat of changes in the individual's role or job design which are needed to implement the marketing strategy. Similarly, the 'price' people are asked to 'pay' starts simply as the alternative opportunities given up, but at deeper levels involves the status and loss of control they may feel, and the psychological adjustment to strategic change required of others in the company.

We have found that managers are far more comfortable using the term 'internal marketing' to focus attention on the elements of the corporate environment inside the company that need to be changed in order to implement marketing plans, and that this terminology provides an acceptable and legitimate framework for unpacking the issues in the company. It may sound tacky, but it works!

But does it work?

'internal marketing has something to offer in achieving the sorts of strategic change we want'

An easy question to ask, but a difficult one to answer. Certainly, the case evidence suggests that internal marketing has something to offer in achieving the sorts of strategic change we want. Consider the following examples drawn from our work with different types of organizations.

A museum

Perhaps some of the simplest examples of the real barriers to implementing customer-focused market strategies come from the public sector, where the marketing concept is still regarded as innovative. In one case, for instance, the new marketing director of a public sector museum was trying to implement a strategy of converting an open-air museum site into a historical 'theme park'.

While apparently broadly supported by the organization (i.e. lip-service is paid), there were substantial barriers slowing down and reducing effective implementation. One such barrier was the operating personnel and the traditional culture of the museum. Quite simply, personnel were being asked to abandon their training as custodians and protectors of exhibits, and to become entertainers in costume who encouraged the 'customer' to handle and use exhibits. There was a major difficulty for employees in achieving the transition from 'policeman' to 'entertainer'.

More covertly, at a deeper cultural level, the senior managers of the organization have some considerable distaste for commercialization of their traditional 'business' by their political masters. Accordingly, they must give open support for obvious reasons, but real commitment is less easily obtained.

This pervasive attitude impacts on allocations of budget, manpower and the priorities imposed by the organization. It is these issues which provide the real agenda for this senior marketing executive – not the problems of generating a creative and innovative market strategy and plan for the museum.

We have found similar problems in other public service organizations faced with imperatives to become 'market oriented' and 'commercial. The internal attitudes and potential resistance to income-generating activities from managers and operatives from the 'public service' tradition – hidden behind approving lip-service to marketing concepts – pose the most serious (but the most covert and difficult) barrier to actually implementing the new market strategies being devised by executives in such organizations.

A corporate bank

Another case example involves one of the secondary banks in the UK. The bank consists of a large retail branch network, backed by a number of small specialist units at the London centre. One of these units is Corporate Banking, servicing mainly multinational company headquarters in the City of London. The plan developed by this unit created a new market strategy of servicing medium and large-sized corporate customers in all areas covered by the retail branch network (currently in the retail branch managers' remit), with the goal of a substantial increase in market share in the corporate market for the group.

On the face of things, the internal marketing needs were to inform branch managers of the new strategy, and to use this to reduce the pressure from the network for more staff to cover the corporate market. Branch managers were required to provide sales leads and market intelligence to the centre. Admittedly, branches would lose potential income, but they had never succeeded in realizing much of that potential anyway.

However, at the political level, an apparently rational strategy was deeply tied up with the power struggle within the organization – in terms of the centralization of control of the branches, the clash of cultures between technical City-based bankers and banking 'salespeople' in the field, and indeed ultimately the actual survival of the corporate banking unit. The real 'price' to be paid by branch managers was more than potential loss of income – it was far more to do with a loss of autonomy for the branch manager in the local area, and a down-grading in status to an operator of 'commodity' consumer and small business banking.

The internal marketing strategy evolved has proved far more problematic than the external strategy. The key elements were written and spoken sponsorship from the chief executive – epitomized by a short memo to all branch managers, reading: 'The train is now leaving the station. You are either on it or . . .' – as well as joint planning between branch managers and corporate banking executives to gain some participation and communication between the branch managers and the corporate banking executives. This has been reinforced by operating on the evaluation/reward system to offer the branch manager some financial gain from assisting the corporate executive to exploit 'his' area, and greater rotation of staff between the branches and the centre.

Progress continues, but the company has paid a substantial price for the new corporate banking strategy, in time spent on winning branch managers round, and in increased managerial staff turnover at the branch level. It would be wrong to suggest that internal marketing offers easy answers to the problems of implementing market-led change. What is shown is the additional insight which can be generated, leading to an agenda of implementation issues at various levels. It should be said also that the case demonstrates vividly that the external strategy and its direct costs may be only the tip of the iceberg compared with the efforts and costs required to create change through an internal marketing strategy.

A financial services organization

In a medium-sized financial services organization, the central strategy, designed by the central Marketing Department and championed by the new General Manager, was 'cross-selling' between two divisions: the retail banks, and the finance company. The concept was that since the banks and the finance company shared the same geographical areas, it would make sense for the bank to refer commercial loan business to the finance company, and for the finance company to push its commercial customers into banking with the group. Indeed, it was such an obvious strategy that the new General Manager could not understand why it had not already happened.

At a wholly rational level, this strategy was the product, and the price was the commission sacrificed by managers in referring business across divisions rather than selling more of their own products. Distribution and communication was by written plan, presentation at sales conferences, and so on. The effect in Year 1 of the new strategy was zero results in cross-selling.

Of course, if you dig deeper, as we had to, the product is really not just cross-selling, it is a changing role for the branch manager and increased control at the centre.

The most intractable issues were the hidden political and cultural barriers represented by the costs to managers of collaborating closely with divisional counterparts historically perceived, at best, as competitors – cultural barriers made worse by differences in ethnic and educational background and professional training between the divisions. The approach taken here hinged on the formation of joint planning and problem-solving teams, and the redesign of the management information system to allow clear measurement of the implementation and success of the new strategy.

Progress with implementing the cross-selling strategy continues in this company – with some remaining conflicts and breakdowns. Success is difficult to evaluate, but recent discussions with branch managers suggest awareness of what they themselves describe as a change in the 'culture' of their company, and quite tangible operational changes in how the two operating divisions work together. Cross-selling is now happening in a significant way.

In one sense, this is a success story – they now *do* cross-selling. But if you look at the real cost to the business of getting cross-selling to happen – the strategy is an unmitigated disaster. At current levels, it will take about 20 years for the margins earned through cross-selling to pay back the cost of the joint planning team exercise, let alone the staff turnover they created on the way. In these terms, the strategy is an abject failure.

One of the lessons we have learned is that if you plan your internal marketing strategy *at the same time* as your external market strategy, your financial evaluation may actually mean something, because it will include the *real* costs of implementation. You may well reject a market strategy when you see the 'hidden' costs of implementation.

So, does it work?

It is impossible to say conclusively. The case evidence suggests that it helps, but it is difficult to generalize. But where companies do make the internal marketing effort, it seems to have a good effect, and many more companies are now formalizing it in the search for effective implementation of market strategies that 'stretch' their companies. There are some cases that suggest that internal marketing may be the ideal vehicle to build the collaboration between market management and human resource management that we discussed earlier (see pp. 97–98). So, there may be value in adding an internal marketing structure to our market-led strategic change – because the evidence is that currently most of us simply don't bother.

'internal marketing may be the ideal vehicle to build the collaboration between market management and human resource management'

How do we plan internal marketing?

The real joy of internal marketing strategies and programmes is that we can *directly* translate our external marketing policies, using *precisely* the same tools and techniques, and even present the plan in the same format:

- *Internal market strategy* – asks us to work out, in broad terms, an internal market strategy that is needed to gain the successful implementation of an external market strategy. It is here that we need to confront the real implications of our external market strategy for the internal customer – the decision makers, managers, operatives and others without whose support, co-operation and commitment the external strategy will fail. This is the most critical question in the whole internal marketing exercise. It should not be skimped. It may be worth consulting the people directly concerned – doing internal market research. It is certainly worth incorporating some diversity of opinion. As we learn more, we can come back and redraft and rethink our conclusions here. It is here that we should take a view of what it is likely to cost us to achieve these things and consider the deadline for achieving them to implement the external marketing strategy on time.

- *Internal market segmentation* – is about identifying the targets in the internal marketplace around which we can build internal marketing programmes, which are different in what we have to achieve and how we are going to do it. This may not be straightforward, but is the route to real insights into the internal market problem, and effectiveness in how we cope with that problem. The most obvious way of identifying internal segments may be by role or function, or location, and this may be sufficient. It might be more productive, however, to think of who are the innovators and opinion leaders who will influence others. We might approach this more directly in terms of the role that different people will play in implementing the external strategy and the problems they may face in this, or simply how much different people will have to change to get the external strategy to work.

- *Internal marketing programmes* – specify what internal marketing programmes will be needed in each internal market segment to achieve the objectives we have set. In each area we need to collect our thoughts about the rational issues but also the human and cultural issues. To us, the product may be a great new marketing plan that we need to inform people about (internal marketing communications), through formal presentations (internal marketing distribution), adjusting commission and evaluation systems if need be (internal marketing price). To the internal customer, the same plan may be about disruption and threat (product), loss of initiative and status (price), imposed without consultation by management (communication), and rigorously 'policed' through coercion (distribution). If internal marketing is about anything, it is about confronting and coping with this conflict. It is this confrontation which will drive us away from thinking about internal marketing as writing customer care brochures and doing great plan presentations, towards coping with the human and organizational realities of what strategic change takes and costs. This is also the stage to take a look at the cost implications of what we now see to be necessary in our internal marketing: does the internal marketing cost mean that the external market strategy is no longer attractive? Do we have to account for internal marketing cost which is more than we expected, but bearable? Do we have to change the external strategy to reduce the internal marketing cost? Are there cheaper ways of achieving the critical internal marketing goals?

- *Internal marketing evaluation* – what we can measure to see if we are getting there, ideally quantified and objective – reduced customer complaint rates, or higher customer satisfaction scores. This may be ambitious, and we should not abandon important objectives because they are difficult to evaluate – we may have to settle for a subjective or qualitative evaluation, which is better than nothing.

The logic is simple – we can use our familiar and established marketing techniques to package and work on our problems *inside* the company. Strategic internal marketing directly parallels our external market strategy, and it is a route to achieving implementation of those external strategies. It is no more than a means to an end, but one which gives us important tools in the right circumstances.

So, where have we got to?

The point to which we have been building throughout this discourse on market-led strategic change – building a customer-focused organization, defining our Strategic Pathway and managing the organizational context for the process of going to market and sales – is implementation. This chapter has tried to pull our thoughts together around the simple notion that the only thing that matters in all this is what we actually deliver to a paying customer.

In fact, when we focus on implementation of our market strategies, we can separate out a long-term and a short-term issue. The short-term issue is what has mainly occupied us so far – getting things to happen *now*. The longer-term issue is about how we manage things to *avoid* the implementation problems we have considered here.

What this means is that there is a need to consider both process management and execution skills in implementation. The difference is that managing the strategy process has the goal of integrating implementation and change issues with the market strategy, with the goal of avoiding the emergence of implementation barriers. On the other hand, execution skills are concerned with how to manage a way through the change problems and barriers which stand in the way of market strategy. While these are different approaches, they are not mutually exclusive, and in most practical situations we will need to give attention to both.

The reasons for this are suggested in Figure 14.12. The four implementation scenarios suggested are as follows:

- *Weak Implementation*, where the management of process and execution skills is inappropriate to drive a market strategy;
- *Management-driven Implementation*, where the emphasis is on leadership and control by management to put a strategy into effect and to overcome problems which may exist;
- *Implementation-driven Strategy*, where the emphasis is on exploiting the capabilities of the existing organization and adapting strategies to 'fit' with this reality; and
- *Integrated Strategy and Implementation*, which achieves implementation by both managing key processes and applying management execution skills.

The 'Weak Implementation' scenario is largely based on managers assuming that once plans and strategies are written, people will go away and make them happen. Some managers make these assumptions implicitly in how they approach things, and then get upset when their edicts and commands are not put into effect or are implemented half-heartedly or haphazardly. Any market strategy that matters to an organization deserves to have implementation taken more seriously than this.

'Any market strategy that matters to an organization deserves to have implementation taken more seriously'

The 'Management-Driven Implementation' scenario is probably closest to the traditional view of how

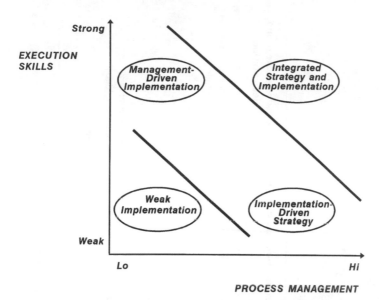

Figure 14.12 Execution skills versus process management in marketing implementation

things should be managed. The emphasis is on line management to take charge, to overcome obstacles, to lead, to coerce and to make things happen – it relies on high-quality management execution skills to overcome implementation barriers. It is fast to put into practice and may achieve change in the short term, but it lacks longer-term effectiveness in sustaining change.

The 'Implementation-Driven Strategy' scenario is where the focus of market strategies is dominated by exploiting existing capabilities and skills in the organization, mainly by adapting market strategies to 'fit' with the organization's existing competences. This is also fast to be put into effect, and will keep implementation costs low. It is weaker in achieving strategic change because the emphasis is on exploiting what we already have, not developing new capabilities – this is fine until the point when our capabilities do not provide what the market wants, i.e. our strategy becomes out-dated by market change.

The 'Integrated Strategy and Implementation' scenario is the ideal to which we aspire. Implementation is not an issue, because it is fully integrated with the market strategy, and we are not forced to cling to existing skills and processes, because part of developing strategy is developing the appropriate processes, structures, skills and capabilities to drive the strategy. It is slower to achieve and expensive, and in the short term not outstandingly

'The "Integrated Strategy and Implementation" scenario is the ideal to which we aspire'

Table 14.3 Implementation scenarios

	Weak Implementation	Management-driven implementation	Implementation-driven strategy	Integrated strategy and implementation
Characteristics	Ignore implementation	Focus on the management of execution and behaviour	Focus on exploiting the capabilities of the existing organization and matching them with new strategies	Building implementation and strategy together
Timing	N/A	Fast	Fast	Slow
Cost of implementation strategy	None	Medium	Low	High
Ability to manage strategic change	None	Short-term: high Long-term: low	Short-term: low Long-term: low	Short-term: low Long-term: high
Implementation effectiveness	None	Medium	High	High

effective. It is probably the only route to long-term sustained strategic change. It is also the scenario we understand least well, and find rarely in practice. We will assume, however, that this is the situation to which we aspire.

The characteristics of these different implementation scenarios are summarized in Table 14.3. A good question for the executive to raise at this point is: which of these scenarios sounds most like how we do things in our company, and how can we improve the way we do things?

With that broader challenge laid down, it only remains to overview the managerial agenda for market-led strategic change in Chapter 15.

References

1. Masiello, Thomas (1988), 'Developing Market Responsiveness Through-out Your Company', *Industrial Marketing Management*, Vol. 17, 85–93.
2. Jobber, David (1996), 'Theory Without Practice', *Marketing Business*, February, 51.
3. Lynn, Jonathan and Jay Anthony (1987), *Yes Prime Minister, Volume II*, London: BBC Books.
4. Bonoma, Thomas V. and Bruce Clark (1990), 'Assessing Marketing Performance', in T. V. Bonoma and T. J. Kosnik, *Marketing Management: Text and Cases*, Homewood, Illinois: Irwin.
5. Bonoma, Thomas V. (1985), *The Marketing Edge: Making Strategies Work*, New York: Free Press.
6. Argyris, Chris (1985), *Strategy, Change, and Defensive Routines*, New York: Harper and Row.
7. Piercy, Nigel and Kenneth J. Peattie (1988), 'Matching Marketing Strategies to Corporate Culture: The Parcel and the Wall', *Journal of General Management*, Vol. 13, No. 4, 33–44.
8. Piercy, Nigel (1989), 'Diagnosing and Solving Implementation Problems in Strategic Planning', *Journal of General Management*, Vol. 15, No. 1, 19–38.
9. Gummesson, Evert (1988), *Marketing – A Long Term Interactive Relationship*, Gothenburg: Anderson Sandberg Dheen Ltd.
10. Gronroos, Christian (1983), *Strategic Marketing and Management in the Service Sector*, Cambridge, Mass.: Marketing Science Institute.
11. Gummesson, Evert (1990), *The Part-Time Marketer*, University of Karlstad, Research Report 90:3.
12. Gilly, May C. and Mary Wolfinbarger (1996), *Advertising's Second Audience: Employee Reactions to Organizational Communications*, Cambridge, Mass.: Marketing Science Institute.
13. Rubel, Chad (1996), 'Treating Co-workers Right is the Key to Kinko's Success', *Marketing News*, 29 January.

14. Divita, Sal (1996), 'Colleagues are Customers, Market to Them', *Marketing News*, 21 October.
15. Bonoma, Thomas V. (1990), 'Employees Can Free the 'Hostages'', *Marketing News*, 19 March, 14–15.
16. Mitchell, Alan (1994), 'The People Factor', *Marketing Business*, October, 24–28.
17. Mitchell, Alan (1994), 'The Message Not The Media', *Marketing Business*, November, 21–24.
18. Mitchell, Alan (1994), 'The Revolution Within', *Marketing Business*, January, 22–25.
19. Ulrich, Dave (1989), 'Tie the Corporate Knot: Gaining Complete Customer Commitment', *Sloan Management Review*, Summer, 19–27.
20. Coles, Margaret (1996), 'Avoid the Axe on the Talent Pool', *Sunday Times*, 8 December.

CHAPTER 15

An agenda for market-led strategic change

What are our *real* problems in the process of going to market?

Introduction

This book is about transforming the company's process of going to market*. The route to this is by becoming *market-led*, and by managing the difficult, messy and uncomfortable process of *strategic change* which this implies for organizations.

A lot of ground has been covered in unpacking the issues central to achieving this market-led strategic change. The role of this chapter is to take a brief overview of the groundwork and to home-in on the real problems that we have in our companies.

We said at the outset that this was a book for the person who wants to change the way the company goes to market, and who

---

* I took a very strong line in Chapter 1 suggesting that conventional marketing was finished and that we had to refocus our thinking onto the process of going to market as something more fundamental than having a marketing department or function. I stand by that. However, talking this through with executives suggests a caveat. There is no reason why a conventional marketing department should not be a central part of running the process of going to market, as long as it crosses internal boundaries to deliver value to the customer. In fact, you can argue that this is what marketing was always supposed to do. However, I still think we had our chance and we blew it – companies no longer have faith in conventional marketing, and we need to find new ways of doing things.

will champion that change and drive it through the company. This is not a simple task. Much of what we have considered here is about building an effective agenda for change – an agenda which probably has both open and hidden levels!

This agenda is our central focus if we are to take the challenge of market-led strategic change seriously.

So what are the real problems?

'the real problems for virtually all organizations are incredibly obvious and straight-forward'

At the simplest level, the entire logic of this book is based on the observation that the *real* problems for virtually all organizations are incredibly obvious and straightforward. The real problems are not about the lack of sophisticated skills and techniques. They are about the following obvious and basic issues:

- Recognizing and accepting that traditional marketing is no longer the way forward – to cope with the challenges facing the company now we have to focus on the *process of going to market* and get better at co-ordinating and managing that process;
- The attitude of our company (its culture and values, the behaviour of managers and employees) and how it results in our treatment of the paying customer – not what we *say* but what we *do*;
- The massive power for competitiveness and innovation which comes from something as simple as *listening to the customer* and getting better at doing the things that matter most to the customer;
- The problems of building and sustaining *customer focus* in organizations which would rather focus on internal needs than customer priorities;
- *De-mystifying and clarifying* our *market strategy* – distinguishing between creative strategizing and formal planning; making clear choices about market and segment targets; applying our differentiating capabilities to define our value proposition to the customer; and identifying the key relationships we will have to manage to deliver that promise;
- Turning the strategy into a structured and coherent *marketing or market plan*;
- *Getting the marketing act together* – so that the fine words in the market strategy and the plan turn into the real delivery of the value proposition to the customer;

- *organizing* ourselves to make it easier to go to market, not creating barriers and obstacles, in companies that have weak marketing organizations or no marketing organization, and where new hollow and alliance-based organizations are emerging;
- Managing key *processes* like planning and resource allocation to build 'ownership', commitment and action – because our people are determined to make things happen;
- *Market sensing* to build real management understanding of the market, not market research to build piles of reports, and to challenge our assumptions, not confirm them;
- Building partnership between Sales and the other owners of the process of going to market (including marketing departments where they are still around, but much more besides), to drive market strategy through to the customer relationship;
- Taking the issue of *implementation* and the *organizational change* it creates seriously enough that we plan it, resource it and make it part of our strategic thinking in the first place, and using internal communications and internal marketing as ways to manage market strategy in the new environment we face;
- Learning from the *experiences* of other companies in how you deal with these issues for real.

In fact, it may be worth underlining the process perspective – in Chapter 1 we said that the issue was not marketing, it was the process of going to market; and in Chapters 11 and 12 we talked about process as a multidimensional issue. We can put these two things together in the way shown in Figure 15.1, to provide a checklist.

Looking at the whole process which creates a market offering is much broader than looking at 'marketing' in the conventional sense – it involves everyone in the company and it crosses traditional departmental boundaries and even organizational boundaries to focus our attention firmly on what the customer gets that creates value for that customer and differentiates us from the competition.

But process is about more than analysis, strategizing and plan-writing, it also has a behavioural and organizational dimension. While the analytical dimension is concerned with building customer focus and a market strategy that is linked directly to marketing programmes, the behavioural dimension is concerned with the people issues in the process, and the organizational dimension is concerned with the real context in which the process operates.

The behavioural dimension is concerned with things like the real attitudes that people show towards customers and customer

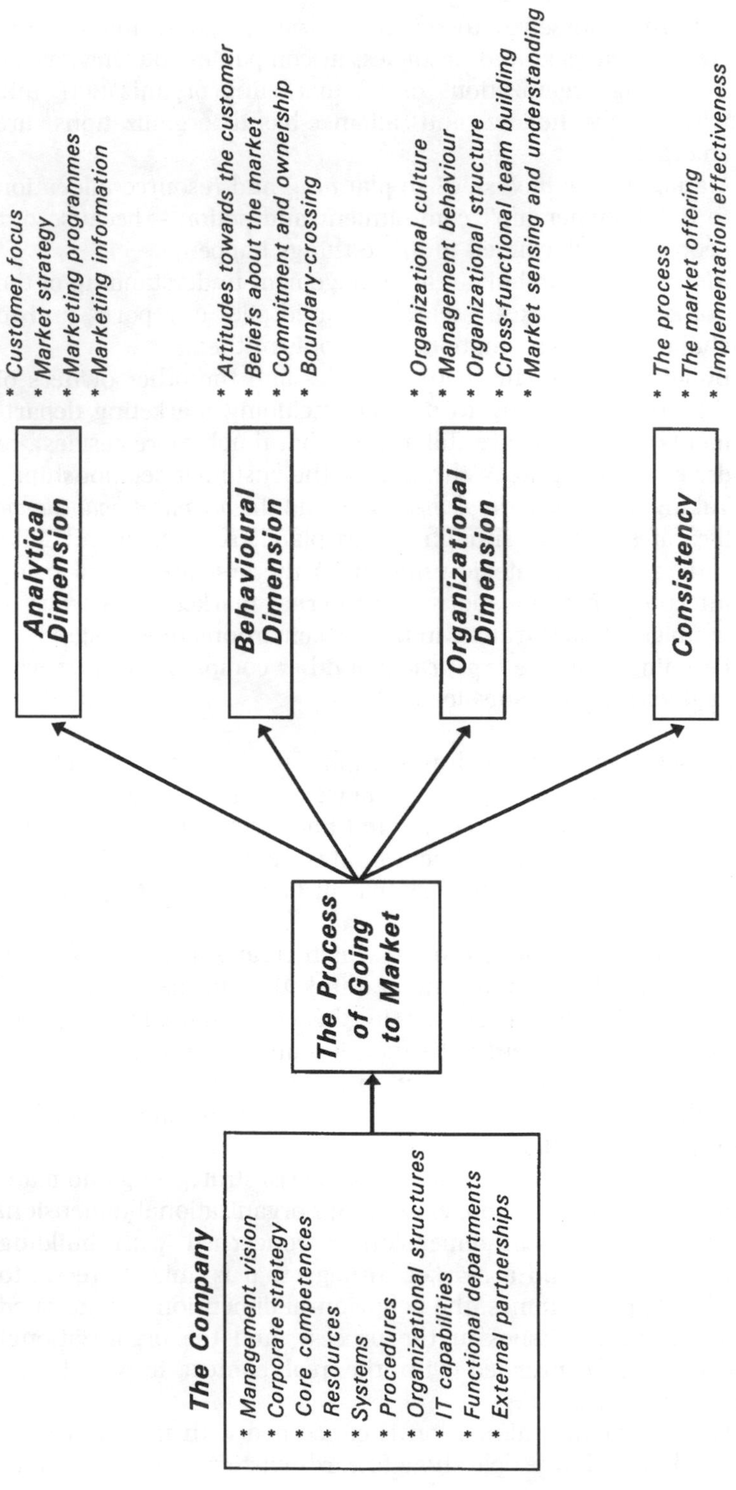

The Company

* Management vision
* Corporate strategy
* Core competences
* Resources
* Systems
* Procedures
* Organizational structures
* IT capabilities
* Functional departments
* External partnerships

The Process of Going to Market

Analytical Dimension

* Customer focus
* Market strategy
* Marketing programmes
* Marketing information

Behavioural Dimension

* Attitudes towards the customer
* Beliefs about the market
* Commitment and ownership
* Boundary-crossing

Organizational Dimension

* Organizational culture
* Management behaviour
* Organizational structure
* Cross-functional team building
* Market sensing and understanding

Consistency

* The process
* The market offering
* Implementation effectiveness

Figure 15.1 The process of going to market

service, and their underlying beliefs about what matters in the market; their commitment to customers and their ownership of the problem of making market strategies effective; as well as their ability and willingness to cross traditional boundaries to get things to happen. The organizational dimension is concerned with the culture of the organization and the leadership and role model provided by managers, as well as organizational structures that reinforce traditional arrangements as opposed to cross-functional team-building, and, underpinning all this, the way the organization understands the market.

The consistency dimension is concerned with managing the process of going to market so as to deliver the market offering to the customer, and is concerned with implementation effectiveness. This is the real test – does the market offering live up to the promises we have made? Or does our value proposition offer customer value and service which people do not believe in, and which the organization cannot deliver?

Listing the real issues is as simple as that – but doing something about them is not. The diagnostics and worksheets should help. This brings us back to the point of Market-Led Strategic Change. Let's just remind ourselves of what that means.

Market-Led . . .

The logic we have pursued is that if you cut through the corporate trappings to the real substance – there is only one thing that links and integrates everything and gives a purpose to everything, and that is the customer. Being market-led means putting the customer at the top of the management agenda, and using that as the focus for how we manage the organization and achieve our corporate objectives. It is about interpreting customer demands and needs to the key players inside the organization and changing their priorities. It is about the integration of all company activities and investments around what matters most to our survival – the customer for what we do. This is not about being reactive and drifting helplessly with the vagaries of the randomly changing marketplace. Far from it. It is about purposefully focusing on the customer and aiming our resources at being best at what matters most to our customer.

We have the tools to achieve this – the customer-focused organization, market strategies, marketing programmes and market sensing. We all too often do not *use* them very effectively, but they are there.

'It is about purposefully focusing on the customer and aiming our resources at being best at what matters most to our customer'

. . . Strategic Change

The sad truth is that, for most of us, tackling these underlying basic problems is not about fine-tuning and marginally improving tactical and technical marketing performance. It is about deep-seated, fundamental strategic change in our organizations. It is about changing cultures, challenging the *status quo*, breaking the inertia, coping with obstacles and resistance to change, changing the distribution of power and how management controls the operation. It is about a few trivial issues like that!

The point is that just because strategic change is difficult, it does not mean we ignore it – we have to create it and manage it. When all is said and done, *nothing* is impossible.

Anyway, it has frequently amazed me in working on strategic planning with diverse organizations to see unconventional, way-out strategic ideas initially dismissed out-of-hand by the prevailing wisdom – only to see those same strategic ideas successfully implemented later, because someone cared enough to make it happen. *Nothing* is impossible. It may be difficult. It may be costly. It is *not* impossible.

Market-Led Strategic Change

So, MLSC has two components. The first – being market-led – is about the up-front content, focus and integration of our market offering to become better at doing the things that matter to the paying customer. The second – strategic change – is about coping with the revolution created by being market-led. Now, let's consider the real management agenda.

The real management agenda for market-led strategic change

Creating the momentum for strategic change starts with isolating and defining the strategic issues, i.e. establishing the agenda to be addressed. That is the real control that management exerts over the organization.

An outline, or checklist, for focusing management attention on MLSC, and packing together the material we have covered in the book, looks like this:

What to change	● The process of going to market, not marketing (Chapter 1) ● Company-wide ownership of the process of going to market (Chapter 1) ● Our attitude towards customers (Chapter 2) ● The focus of the whole organization on customers (Chapter 3)
Routes to change	● Strategizing (Chapter 4) ● Re-thinking market choices (Chapter 4) ● Developing and testing the value proposition to our customers (Chapter 5) ● Managing the key relationships that underpin the market strategy (Chapter 6) ● Developing a coherent plan out of the strategizing, – not *vice versa* (Chapter 7) ● Turning strategy into programmes of action (Chapter 8)
How to change	● Confronting the organizational realities (Chapter 9) ● Market sensing to develop new ways of understanding the outside world (Chapter 10) ● Managing the key processes of planning and budgeting to build ownership and action (Chapters 11 and 12) ● Partnership with sales (Chapter 13) ● Developing implementation and internal marketing strategies to manage change (Chapter 14)

How you choose to approach this agenda will depend on your circumstances and the most urgent issues for your company. In the right situation, the MLSC structure can be turned into a company-wide programme. The agenda can be integrated into an existing management training and development programme, leading to training and development work for our key executives. It can be addressed as part of organizational development, leading to changes in our structure, systems and procedures. It may simply be the agenda for the next Board meeting or a Director's workshop. In other situations, we may have to pick the issues off, one at a time, using whatever resources and support we can get. The important thing is to get started.

This MLSC agenda follows the structure of the book, and it can be followed in this order, or the highest priority issues ranked first. However, there is the question of getting started to consider first.

But where do we start?

In times of turbulence and change, we need to think very seriously about what we need to do to help managers cope. When we look at our programmes of change, one test is to ask: 'What are we doing to help and support our managers to do the following things?':

- to understand the 'big picture', not just day-to-day running-the-business decisions;
- to identify the alternatives open to us;
- to learn from best practice in leading companies everywhere, including competitor and partner organizations;
- to make sense of the future and the role managers have to play in shaping that future;
- to build networks of information that cut across traditional boundaries and reinforce our learning; and
- to answer the manager's top three questions*

One very nice summary of the options here is provided by William Band [1], a Canadian McKinsey consultant. In the same way that we have done here, Band argues that the greatest barriers to success in the struggle for a customer focus came from organizational structures and processes, and employee attitudes and beliefs – so, he says, the way we manage organizations and people will have to change. In the same way that Tom Bonoma talks about 'marketing subversives' [2] who take advantage of 'loose' money, people and time, to make marketing work, in spite of the company's policies and procedures, Band talks about *'where you start depends on how fast change is needed and where the leadership comes from'* marketing's 'organizational revolutionaries' attacking the status quo with planned change strategies (and allies in human resource management – see pp. 96–97 above). Band argues that where you start depends on how *fast* change is needed and where the *leadership* comes from, and he identifies the following options:

- *Annexation* – start with the part of the organization that is most willing to change and has the greatest chance of success, and add extra 'chunks' later;
- *Perestroika* – where top management leads the change process, dragging the organization behind, screaming and kicking;

---

* The manager's top three questions are always the same, they are: (1) What about me? (2) What about me? and (3) What about me?

- *Guerrilla Campaign* – a bottom-up, hidden, selective exploitation of opportunities for change as they occur;
- *Palace Coup* – those who want change take control.

It may be somewhat unoriginal and trite (and why break the habit of a lifetime now), but the following seems to be a wholly appropriate thought with which to end this book:

> Somewhere in the African jungle this morning a gazelle will wake up. The gazelle knows it must run faster than the slowest lion, otherwise it will die. Somewhere else in the jungle a lion wakes up. The lion knows it must run faster than the slowest gazelle, otherwise it will starve. The moral is whoever you are, wherever you are, you better wake up and start running . . ..

References

1. Band, William (1989), 'A New Type of Office Politics Spurs Desired Cultural Change', *Marketing News*, 3 July, 10.
2. Bonoma, Thomas V. (1986), 'Marketing Subversives', *Harvard Business Review*, November/December, 113–118.

Case 10 Lion Machines Ltd

Lion Machines Ltd is the UK division of a multinational manufacturer of materials handling and management systems products. Financial performance has been variable, and during the late 1980s there was a steady shedding of staff, although current manpower is still of the order of 10 000 employees in the UK and Europe.

The business had been through a number of phases of reorganization and restructuring in the 1970s and 1980s, and had now arrived at a form of matrix. Production, Research and Development, Marketing and other service functions were operated centrally as resources for the whole group, while a number of large Business Units have been established, each to focus planning and delivery (together with after-sales service and selling of materials handling consultancy) on a major industrial sector. Direct selling was organized in a number of geographic regions, reporting jointly to the Business Units and to Marketing at head office.

Lion Ltd is, and always has been, a technology-driven company. Most of the senior positions are filled by engineers, or 'tekkies', and the role of Sales, and latterly Marketing, has been seen as the disposal of the high-technology products coming out of R&D. The company has struggled for some years with the notion of being 'customer oriented'. Nonetheless, the company continues to sneer at the 'second-rate' products and to despise the mere 'marketing muscle' of their most successful competitors, in comparison to their own technological excellence.

'The company has struggled for some years with the notion of being "customer oriented"'

The current Chief Executive is Robert Small. Mr Small is a Lion technology man through and through, having started with the company in the mid-1960s in a junior role, and then through a series of general management roles, reaching the post of CEO in 1987.

Jim Patterson

Jim Patterson is a Sales Manager in the Central Sales Group. He is in his early fifties, and has been with Lion for some 15 years. He started his career as a computer technician, progressing to become a systems analyst and programmer, before moving to Lion in a technical sales function. Jim is well-known in the company for his many 'hobby-horses', although it is recognized that he has often been proved correct in his forecasts of trouble developing for the company. Jim has been in the company long enough that he is respected, and is on first-name terms with many of the main board directors, including the current Chief Executive, and Ken Snode, the Production Director.

It is also true that Jim is widely known and revered throughout the Sales and Marketing functions within Lion, having survived many of the various reorganizations in recent years. For example, this is not least because he is reputed to have been responsible for almost losing a major nationalized industry account in the 1970s. The story is that when he made a routine call on the company's operations manager to check on progress with an installation, the operations manager said: 'Good, I'm glad you're here ... did you know your f&$%*!* machine has gone down again?!', to which Jim is said to have replied: 'No, but if you hum it, I'll try to join in!' Fortunately, unlike most of his profession, the operations manager had a sense of humour!

Jim is currently of the opinion that Lion has made a serious strategic error in this same nationalized industry.

A neglected market

The industrial sector in question is a relatively small market. It is the UK water industry.

At one time, Lion had a share of water industry spend on this type of machinery and systems which was of the order of 60 per cent of the total available. This was achieved by a specialized sales team, covering only the water industry, selling a set of customized products designed specifically for the water industry. However, at the time that the Business Units were set up, this specialized effort was disbanded, and the water industry was taken over by the new Public Utilities Business Unit. This Business Unit's resources were spread over all public utilities and nationalized industries, and every one of these was massive in comparison to the water industry.

The Business Unit manager's case was that the other public utilities and the major nationalized industries were far larger, and the spend was expected to be vast, both in a spending spree prior to denationalization, and then in attempts at rationalization after privatization. Because the water industry was relatively small; late in the queue for privatization; and Lion already had a dominant market share – resources were diverted away from this sector towards others.

The Business Unit was headed up by Michael Price, who had been involved in the internal reorganization task force which had created the current Business Unit focus of the organization. This role as General Manager of the Business Unit was seen within the organization as something of a reward for his efforts in that task force.

Mike Price himself had thought that he would be given control of the manufacturing or engineering industries Business Units and was a little disappointed with the job of General Manager, Public Industry Business Unit, and this was also quite widely known in the company. These other two Business Units were much bigger and more prestigious than the one for public industry, and had enjoyed considerable growth since being set up. Each of the Business Units also had a business planning manager, whose role was to guide the strategy of each unit. In the Public Industry Unit this role was filled by ex-accountant Steven Martin who, while extremely good at analytical planning, did not enjoy a good working relationship with Mike Price.

The disbanding of the specialist water industry team and its integration into the Public Industry Business Unit had not gone unnoticed by customers, and there was some hostility towards Lion and its products among water industry engineering managers for what was seen as 'abandoning' the water industry customer. There was some feeling among customers that Lion products were, in fact, no better than those of competitors, and if there was to be no specialized product range and support services offered by Lion to the water industry, then it might be safer to buy from the larger US firms with all their international strengths in engineering and R&D across the board.

'*there was some hostility towards Lion and its products among water industry engineering managers*'

At the time of this case, in the late 1980s, the Lion share of water industry spend had sunk to 25 per cent of the market, and there was no sign that it would be maintained at even this level. Jim Patterson had written a number of reports on this situation to his line superiors and to the Marketing Department, both predicting the fall in market share and explaining the reasons.

A champion for the water industry

The response to Jim's reports had been overwhelming apathy from both Sales and Marketing, and outright hostility from the Public Industry Business Unit. The Business Unit argued forcefully that it was hard enough to get resources for the public sector anyway, compared to the more 'fashionable' areas of manufacturing and engineering, and that to fragment efforts would be disastrous. There was also little enthusiasm in Production for customizing products for the water industry, in spite of the fact that customization may mean no more than how the products are 'badged', and the formatting of the computer software that controls the more sophisticated machines and systems.

As a result of the realization by Robert Small that there might in fact be a significant problem, and his wish to placate Jim Patterson, the stage had been reached where Jim had been offered the chance to step out of his line sales role for one year, with safeguarded salary and commission, if he was prepared to create and champion a strategy to retrieve the Lion position in the water industry. Jim's interpretation of this was that he was being told to 'put up, or shut up!' He accepted this brief.

This meant that he had to create a strategy to take market share back to 50 per cent in three years (which appeared to be reasonable, given the effects of privatization plans on the industry). Jim accepted this offer, knowing that success would probably gain him a promotion for his last years with the company (he is planning to retire at 55). His other top management 'sponsor' is George Watson, the main board Sales Director, who shares some of his concerns, and is a 'buddy' from way back.

A plan of campaign

To start with, Jim had a small formal allocation of resources – he was allocated funds to hire two industry specialists as 'consultants', although this was at the expense of the Business Unit, since the company operates a 'zero head-count growth' policy which is absolute. These posts have been filled by two former water industry managers – one from an engineering department and another from a technical laboratory/research department.

Jim also knows that there are one or two senior sales personnel in Lion who have retained informal links with the water industry (indeed, hence the residual 25 per cent market share). For example, there is Frank Livingstone in the North-West, who has retained a major share of his local water industry business. Also there is Tom Evans in Wales, who has actually captured his local water business from the competition, in spite of Lion's new policies, largely on the back of the very strong relationships he had built with customer engineering departments. In addition, there are a number of more junior salespeople in the Central Sales Region who have technically got responsibility for the water industry, but along with the other utilities. Lastly, there are also some product specialists who have interests in relevant products, where Jim believes there would be some personal interest in developing custom products for the water industry.

He knew that to succeed, his strategy would have to be accepted by both the Business Unit board and the Product Group board (mainly technical specialists liaising between Sales/Marketing, R&D and production) before it could be presented to the main board. The main product group that will be affected by Jim Patterson's proposals is headed by Rob Hall, a former Production Control manager. In this more general role Rob Hall is somewhat frustrated by the 'support' role that the product groups are expected to play for the Business Unit. Indeed, prior to the Business Unit's introduction a few years earlier, the product groups had been the focus of business activity and responsibility. Rob Hall knew Jim Patterson quite well, having worked in the same product group in the late 1970s, and he always admired Jim's ability to get business in 'tough' times.

What Jim needed was to map out the process by which he can achieve the goals, identify the barriers and package his strategy within the company.

Developing a marketing implementation and change strategy

Jim was able to persuade Frank Livingstone, Tom Evans and the junior salespeople from Central Sales to join him as a water industry task force, together with Phil Jenkins (a product specialist nominated by Rob Hall).

They spent several months, meeting intermittently, in getting to grips with the water industry problem and generating what they believed to be the key problems to be confronted in regaining market share. This amounted to a strategy of market specialization, under the copy title of 'The Lion Roars in Water'.

The most critical issue, they believed, was the 'badging' of products for the water industry, followed by the specialized sales efforts and customized control software for water industry applications. However, it was clear that these strategies were unacceptable in several parts of the company.

'it was clear that these strategies were unacceptable in several parts of the company'

In discussing the critical customer need for badged products, after much debate the team decided that the major obstacles to the strategy were the General Manager of the Business Unit (who saw their strategy as fragmenting and challenging his own responsibilities), the Production argument that customized products lose economies of scale in production, and the Marketing view of the market as Public Industry – to be taken as a whole, not split into segments. The forces on their side were the Chief Executive's personal interest in the project and the precedent it might set for revitalizing other parts of the Lion operation, the growing recognition in the company that the water industry issue was a legitimate and serious problem, even if it did cut across the new organizational structure, as well as the existence of the task force itself and its growing informal network of interested parties in the company. Jim had been contacted by a variety of people in Lion who had previously serviced the water industry customers and who retained their loyalty to these customers – many regarded Lion's current positioning as a mistake.

The task force spent a considerable amount of time debating how to drive their emerging strategy through the Lion structure, and what would be needed to make what had seemed a total impossibility more attainable. On the way, they found that they discarded many potential barriers to badged products as illusory and unimportant (for example, everyone believed badging was expensive – if you cost it out, it is very cheap, the real problem is that people don't want to do it). In truth, as they realized, when badging was rejected as a strategy along with other aspects of customer specialization – no-one had ever pushed the question 'Why not?'

Clearly the major asset was the public interest of the Chief Executive, but against this was the opposition of Mike Price in the Business Unit and Ken Snode, the Production Director. They concluded that there was little they could do to win these players' support.

Similarly, they sought ways of bringing Watson, the Sales Director and Rob Hall from the Product Group closer to the decision making unit, by inviting them to meetings and keeping them informed of progress. Gradually, they evolved a strategy for implementing their new marketing policies for the water industry sector.

For the most serious opposition, they reasoned that the tactics were to use the Chief Executive's support as a lever, and to 'soften up' the opposition with customer feedback, salesperson reports, market research, and so on. Similarly, they wanted to change the position of Marketing, by presenting them with the water strategy as part of the solution to *their* problem of putting market issues higher on the agenda than technical ones – the continuing 'Marketing Versus Tekkies' argument in the company. They also saw the need for more internal communications focusing on the water industry strategy to keep people informed and supportive.

The task force slowly developed the 'Lion Roars in Water' strategy, both as an external market strategy but also with a parallel implementation strategy for the marketing plan. They knew that simply writing a plan for the water industry would mean that all progress would cease after its presentation, and they held back from the formal reporting stage until they felt more confident in support for the strategy inside the company. Their approach to what they called their 'internal marketing' involved a variety of activities.

What they really wanted was the 'breaking-out' of the water industry from the public utilities sector, as a specialist niche. However, the Business Unit retained strong objections to fragmenting the market and its own size relative to the other Business Units, Production objected to customizing products, and Marketing/Sales preferred to avoid external market segmentation by industry sector. Jim led the task force members through a variety of what he called 'softening-up' activities before their plan presentation:

- 'lobbying' senior managers prior to announcing the new water strategy, to negotiate support and sponsorship, in personal meetings and at social occasions;
- spreading word through the 'grapevine' that the market specialization strategy had found favour with top management;
- stressing that the success of the water industry strategy could be a precedent for similar team-based approaches to solving other problems in the company;
- emphasizing to Marketing the importance of the water industry strategy in putting marketing and customer issues higher on the agenda than technology issues;
- expanding the membership of the original team to represent the other interests – particularly field sales;
- arranging seminars on technology issues for water industry managers, with the goal not of informing customers about Lion, but of exposing company technical management directly to customer views about Lion Ltd. (It is rumoured but not proven that Jim suggested to some of the customers what they might say to Lion senior management at these events);
- involving Business Unit and Marketing/Sales managers in 'social/PR' events with water industry managers, again to expose those managers

to the (helpfully forthright) customer comments about the withdrawal of Lion's specialized offers to the water industry; and
● running a small trade magazine advertising campaign at a very modest cost, with the theme 'The Lion Roars in Water', and copying full-colour off-prints to managers throughout the company.

In fact, their success was mixed. They got the badged products and customized software for the water industry, and the company agreed to a specialized advertising campaign using the strategy name. However, they did not succeed in separating water from the other public industries, and it remains under the control of the Business Unit. Water remains a 'poor relation' market sector in the Business Unit. Nonetheless, it is recognized in the company that Jim Patterson and his team did get enough of what they wanted to claw back a substantial market share for Lion in the water industry in time for the anticipated growth in customer spending, which was, after all, the point of the whole thing.

Jim Patterson returned to a sales management position at the end of the year, at an enhanced grade, and retired from the company two years later. He now works as a freelance consultant. The task force has been disbanded, and the members have gone back to other roles in Lion. In recent years, Lion's position in the water industry has weakened.

Questions to consider

1 What were the most serious implementation barriers faced by the task force and the new strategy for the water industry?

2 Can you trace the development of the implementation strategy elements that were important to the task force?

3 What forms of internal marketing were used, and at what level did these operate?

4 Could you have done better in developing and driving the market strategy? What would this have involved?

5 Was it worth the effort to go to this much trouble for a part of the market which is so small compared to the other sectors?

6 How could the momentum have been sustained by Lion to retain its improved position in the water industry?

The OPUS Process

The OPUS Process was developed in Sweden by Erik Juhlin in the late 1970s. Many companies, he discovered, carried out large and expensive market research projects but did little or nothing with the results, so he developed a process to ensure that, when market research was carried out, the project leads to implementation of change. I hat was in 1979, and shortly afterwards he was joined by Peter Winiger from Switzerland, since when the OPUS Process has developed continuously. OPUS practitioners now operate in nine countries in Western Europe and North America.

The OPUS Process is designed to develop and implement an agenda for achievable change, through researching customer views and involving staff. OPUS projects fall into three main categories: (a) product and service improvements where the customers are external; (b) product and service improvements for internal customers; and (c) projects where people inside an organization work together to identify and then overcome obstacles to the achievement of their own objectives.

> **'The OPUS Process is designed to develop and implement an agenda for achievable change, through researching customer views and involving staff'**

The OPUS analytical process, illustrated in the Otis and Nokia case studies, consists of four phases: the *qualitative research* phase, which uses Painstorming Groups, a kind of focus group; the *quantitative research* phase, which uses the OPUS Box Interview, an innovative survey instrument; the *action phase*, which takes the survey results and decides what actions will be taken to address the survey findings; and the *implementation phase*, where client staff take responsibility for carrying through agreed actions.

As with any management consulting project, the first step must be to find a *project sponsor* who will champion and pay for the project. Clearly, such a sponsor will have his or her own clear ideas about what must be achieved – but the OPUS Process is based on the shared understanding of the participants, so it is important that the sponsor is willing to discuss the objective with them. Of course, he will always have the last say but, in our experience, other people almost always contribute, at least by enriching general understanding of what achieving the objective will mean in practice.

---

* This case study has been prepared by Noel Austin, The OPUS Partnership.

An *OPUS Team* – which is a form of steering group – comprises what is sometimes referred to as a 'diagonal slice' through the organization. It should include senior and middle managers, supervisors and members of the workforce and members of all the functional groups or departments involved in managing and delivering the service under review. Under some circumstances, such as projects carried out for public service organizations, it may also include external stakeholders. The purpose of this is to ensure that there is always someone in the OPUS Team who understands every aspect of service delivery, a cross-section of the people responsible for managing service delivery, and senior managers who are able to take decisions to allocate resources and change policies. They must understand that they will play a central role in the project and that their attendance will be required at three meetings of the OPUS Team.

OPUS Team Meeting 1 starts with introductions and decisions on its rules of behaviour – on the basis that more progress will be made if destructive behaviours are outlawed. The OPUS Process is explained, and team members discuss and finalize the project. The meeting explores what 'a customer' or 'a client' means. Customers may be organizations or individuals, they may be large or small and, if individuals, they may take a range of different job roles.

In carrying out a project of this nature it is important to consider all possible forms of market segmentation before carrying out a survey – once the data have been collected it is impossible to rework them to take account of additional segmentation criteria. Age, location, geography, length of service, gender, socio-economic group may all be ways of segmenting the marketplace. Team members brainstorm possible criteria and then choose those that they consider to be most relevant.

The Team then discusses the number, composition, timing and location of Painstorming Groups. A *Painstorming Group* is a kind of focus group – the reason for the name will become apparent below – and a typical project includes two or three Painstorming Groups.

Armed with the list of topics produced in the first OPUS team meeting and the lists of names and addresses generated by Team members, the facilitators plan and recruit the Painstorming Groups. Taking a major topic at a time, participants are asked to state the problems they have had with the product or service that is the focus of the project. They are reminded that these problems should be based on experience, not on surmise, and that it is by solving their problems that our client will improve service. Both large and small problems are relevant – a small problem experienced by many customers could be as important overall as a large problem experienced by a few. These problems are expressed at the lowest level – sometimes a problem stated by a participant can be 'decomposed' into two or more problems. Continuous probing ensures that we have a clear understanding of each problem. Typically, each group runs for between one and a half and two and a half hours.

After the meetings, the tapes are analysed and prepared for the second OPUS Team meeting. Typically, each Painstorming Group generates 200–250 discrete problems after duplicates have been eliminated. Analysing the Painstorming Group and wording the statements are key activities in the OPUS Process. The things that people say have to be understood in the context of how the discussion was running at the time and then re-expressed in terms which make each statement free-standing, devoid of context. We then cluster the problems into the major topics identified by the OPUS Team at its first meeting.

The purpose of *OPUS Team Meeting 2* is to review the results of the Painstorming Groups and to commission the quantitative phase of the project. We read the problems one at a time and invite Team members to decide whether or not they should be considered for inclusion in the quantitative phase. Legitimate reasons for discarding problems include: the problem is outside the scope of the current study – it is noted and passed to the client manager with responsibility for the area in question; the problem is a consequence of legislation and therefore inescapable; the solution to the problem would be in conflict with corporate policy; it is effectively a duplicate of another problem. No problem is discarded merely because Team members think it is trivial or an admission of fault. The task of the Team is then to reduce the number of problems to about 150 by eliminating effective duplicates. These 150 problems will then form the basis of the quantitative survey.

> **'No problem is discarded merely because Team members think it is trivial or an admission of fault'**

We also develop a list of need statements, derived from the problem statements, which encompass the unsatisfied needs of the target population. These are modified as appropriate and then agreed.

The OPUS Team agrees the method of distribution of the *OPUS Box Interviews** which comprise the quantitative phase of the project. We strongly urge that client staff should distribute them. This engages more

---

* The OPUS Interview Box is a lightweight, formed plastic box with four compartments and an outer envelope to carry the client's message to recipients. When assembled it contains a pack of about 150 slips of paper, on each of which is printed one of the problem statements agreed by OPUS Team Meeting 2. It also contains the Quality Barometer, a small questionnaire that asks for demographic information as agreed by the OPUS Team, and asks respondents to score the agreed needs as to their importance and the level of performance achieved by the client. The Quality Barometer sometimes also asks respondents to assess the levels of performance of our client's major competitors. The assembled boxes are despatched in a cardboard mailing sleeve with an addressed, prepaid return label. Completing a Box Interview takes about 20 minutes, during which time the recipient completes the Quality Barometer and sorts the problem slips into the compartments. The left-most compartment is marked 'this is a very important problem for me' and the right-most 'this is not a problem for me or I have no opinion'. The completed boxes are mailed to The OPUS Partnership for processing.

client staff in the project and increases their commitment to the outcome. We sometimes recommend that Box Interviews also be distributed to staff for completion, to allow us to compare the views of customers with staff perceptions of those same issues.

Within a couple of days of despatch to the company, boxes begin to return – under normal circumstances about 85–90 per cent of boxes are returned if they were distributed by hand and perhaps 70–75 per cent when posted to recipients. After an interval of about four weeks, during which we collect and analyse the data, we are ready for OPUS Team Meeting 3.

The results of the box interviews take several forms:

- A list of the problems in decreasing order of importance. This is valuable because, if the population as a whole has a particular problem with our client's offering, he would be well advised to do something about it. Less obviously, if our client is already using resources to solve problems that appear at the bottom of the list, he can reallocate those resources to a more important task without having a significant impact on his customers.
- A list of the needs in decreasing order of importance, with a graphical presentation of the performance levels for each need. This shows which of the important needs should be the focus of management action.
- A list of the 30 most important problems related to the needs in decreasing order of importance. This is the report that provides our client with his agenda for action – the problems that most concern customers are those that relate to their most important unsatisfied need. Only when this need has been satisfied will they become concerned about problems relating to lower ranked needs.
- Comparisons between the views of members of market segments. These are important because they enable our client to see whether particular problems relate to segments of his market and to assess whether, if a particular action is taken, customers in a particular segment will see this as beneficial.
- Comparisons between the views of customers and the views of staff. This analysis is valuable for assessing how close staff are to customers and what training needs they have. Unsurprisingly, the further removed staff are from customer contact, the less well they understand the customer's view. Directors are almost always the worst informed.

OPUS Team Meeting 3 is the point at which the OPUS Process becomes a change driver. We present the key results to the Team and facilitate a discussion of what the results mean. The problems are then clustered into groups, each of which suggests a coherent programme of action, and the team divides into syndicates to discuss what to do about each one.

By the end of the meeting, a detailed Action Plan will emerge, consisting of three different types of action:

- *Quick fixes*: some problems have straightforward and easily implemented solutions. These are valuable because customers can see early action on the basis of the views they expressed, and OPUS team members make a rapid transition from a steering group to an action team.
- *Projects*: some problems have clear solutions that involve board-level decisions and/or the allocation of significant resources. A team member undertakes to propose the action programme to the relevant decision maker.
- *Creative phase*: some problems will be understood, but will not have a clear solution. Under these circumstances a different kind of project may be established, consisting of creative processes which, together with the use of the OPUS Box Interview to prioritize solutions, generate and select solutions for implementation.

We have a range of tools and techniques to use in *implementation* of the action plans. These include project planning and management techniques and a range of internal and external communications tools. As a result of their membership of the OPUS Team, client staff take charge of the implementation process and accept a high level of accountability for its success. The Otis plc and Nokia Mobile phones case studies illustrate the OPUS approach to managing market-led strategic change.

Otis plc

Otis plc is the UK operating subsidiary of the renowned global company that specializes in building, installing, maintaining and refurbishing lifts and escalators. At the end of the UK's 1980s boom, there was a collapse in the number of new building starts and major refurbishments, and a corresponding collapse in the demand for new lifts and escalators. This led to substantial reductions in the numbers of engineers and fitters employed by the industry, and some of the redundant staff started their own businesses, providing maintenance and refurbishment services at lower prices than those offered by the major companies in the industry.

At this time, Otis, in common with the other major suppliers, began to place increased emphasis on its service business as a source of both turnover and profit across the whole European market. The company initiated 'Service 2000', a project whose objective was to improve the quality of the service offering, to be launched to customers in 1996. However, in 1993 increased competition from the large number of small service providers, combined with easier market access for other European majors, was already resulting in loss of market share. It was clear to Bill Evans, Director of Sales and Marketing for the UK and Ireland, that early action must be taken to halt and reverse this trend. At about this time, The OPUS Partnership was commissioned to work with Otis to achieve this objective using the OPUS Process.

The objective of the project was to increase the loyalty of service customers, by developing a detailed understanding of the views of service customers and hence to develop and implement a strategy to improve service quality, as a way of stopping and reversing attrition rates.

At the time of this project, Otis was organized into 13 regions covering the whole of the UK and Eire. The OPUS Team consisted of 20 people from across the UK, forming the preferred 'diagonal slice' of the organization. It included the project sponsor, Bill Evans, Director of Sales and Marketing, the Director of Quality, the Director of London Region and a variety of managers and staff drawn from across the company, together with Roy Gaynor and Noel Austin of The OPUS Partnership.

At OPUS Team Meeting 1, after introductions and agreement of the rules of behaviour for the Team, we presented the OPUS Process. Team members then discussed and commented on the project objective and agreed that it was a key objective for Otis, and it was not modified. The meeting then explored what 'an Otis service customer' meant. Customers could be organizations or individuals, they could be large or small and, if individuals, they could take a range of different job roles. This led to a discussion of possible ways of segmenting the service marketplace, and eventually to voting on those segmentation parameters which were most important. Segmentation could be by:

- the type of building (e.g. apartment block, education, office, and so on);
- the building ownership (private, trust, public);
- the geographic sales region;
- the customer role (e.g. consultant, facilities manager, agent, owner);
- the number of lifts in the building.

The team then discussed the number and composition of Painstorming Groups. The OPUS Team felt that there were unlikely to be conflicts between members of different interest groups and decided that two Painstorming Groups should be held in London. There was no reason to believe that customers in different parts of the UK and Eire would have different problems – though, of course, the priorities they attached to them might be. So participants would be drawn from a range of different types of building and ownership, job roles and sizes of organization in the Home Counties.

Finally, the OPUS Team brainstormed and prioritized the range of topics that it wished to be investigated during the rest of the project. These included: the quality of the engineering maintenance service; communication with supervisors and management; contractual arrangements; and problems specific to particular types of customer.

Armed with the list of topics produced in the first OPUS Team Meeting, and lists of names and addresses generated by Team members, the facilitators planned and recruited the Painstorming Groups. These were arranged to take place at lunchtime at the Grosvenor House Hotel in central London about two weeks after participants had been contacted.

Six or eight people took part in each Group session. Taking a major topic at a time, we asked participants to state the problems they had with lift maintenance, first in general and then with the service provided by Otis. Each group ran for about two hours and was audio-recorded. We were already becoming aware of the differences in view between large and small customers and the public and private sector, but because of the structure of the OPUS Process we were able to wait until the quantitative phase to draw our conclusions about this.

We then prepared for the second OPUS Team Meeting. Between them the Painstorming Groups generated about 350 discrete problems after duplicates had been eliminated. We clustered them into the major topics identified by the OPUS Team and printed them on OHP foils for presentation to the team.

After reminding team members of what had happened to date, we read the problems one at a time and invited them to decide whether or not each problem should be considered for inclusion in the quantitative phase. Some problems were discarded for the usual reasons.

A number of the identified problems were a consequence of the age of installed equipment; the immediate reaction of Team members to these was, 'Well – what do you expect? It's old technology'. After further consideration they realized that, since there were a large number of customers with older equipment, these problems might affect a significant proportion of their customer base and could be among the reasons for loss of market share. It was also agreed that every problem statement would refer to 'our contractor' rather than to Otis or one of its competitors, as this would allow us to identify industry-wide problems that Otis could then solve to secure competitive advantage.

'this would allow us to identify industry-wide problems that Otis could then solve to secure competitive advantage'

We then presented the need statements, which were modified as appropriate and then agreed. Respondents would be asked, on the Quality Barometer, to score the performance both of Otis and of its key competitors against the unsatisfied needs. We also finalized the segmentation questions to be shown on the Quality Barometer.

The OPUS Team agreed the method of distribution of the OPUS Box Interviews which comprised the quantitative phase of the project. It was agreed that 420 boxes would be distributed to customers; about 30 boxes would be freighted to each region, and managers and staff would personally distribute the boxes to chosen individuals in their customer base.

It was also agreed that 108 boxes would be distributed to staff for completion, permitting a comparison between the views of customers and staff perceptions of those views.

By the cut-off date, some 248 customer boxes (59 per cent) and 80 staff boxes (74 per cent) had been returned and were included in the results. It was noticeable that return rates varied by region. After an interval of about ten days for data collection, analysis and preparation, the results were presented to OPUS Team Meeting 3.

Studying the high-ranked problems and needs, the team came to several key conclusions. First, there were significant differences between the views of large customers, who would pay a high price for lifts which never broke down and so would pay for preventive maintenance, and small customers, for whom cost was a major issue and who preferred to pay for repairs rather than preventive maintenance. Secondly, there were several groups of problems, which included health and safety issues, such as lift floor levels being out and indicator lamps not working; contract conditions and pricing; and communication with local engineering supervision and management. Thirdly, there were significant differences between the views of customers and staff perceptions of their views. Unsurprisingly, field staff had a better understanding of customers than office based supervisors and managers.

In the *Action* phase, Otis retained responsibility for large service customers, whose key requirements were reliability and preventive maintenance. The company developed a range of new service contracts for these customers, where the emphasis was on continuity of operation rather than rapid response to breakdown.

Small service customers, whose key requirements were low cost and a responsive repair service, became a different and separate responsibility of Evans Lifts.

Otis also developed a range of add-on products designed to improve the performance and reliability of installed equipment. One such was a servo-mechanism which enabled older lifts to align floor levels correctly.

Over the following 18 months Otis implemented a comprehensive action plan based on the results of the project, and began to see additional sales and profits arising from the new service contracts and enhancement products. However, even so, the improvements were less than Bill Evans believed to be possible. He suspected that one of the reasons was that members of the salesforce perceived obstacles to increased sales, which were the result of their experiences over the previous few years, when market conditions had been very tough. A further OPUS project identified and dealt with these obstacles.

In an interview in 1996, Bill Evans said: 'We wanted to know how best to shape our maintenance service – a major part of our business. Of course, we had lots of information and our own ideas, and already had many key initiatives in place. What we really needed was detailed knowledge of our customers' views and the reasons they would keep coming to Otis ... the facts come from our customers and the ideas come from us. What the facilitator does is guide us through a really effective process to our own conclusions, decisions and actions. It's

'What we really needed was detailed knowledge of our customers' views and the reasons they would keep coming to Otis'

phenomenal: we're 67 per cent up on last year. If we hadn't done what we did, we'd not be where we are today.'

Nokia Mobile Phones

Nokia Mobile Phones (UK) Ltd is the UK operating company of Nokia, the worldwide Finnish telecommunications manufacturing group and host to one of the group's largest research and development facilities. From a small start, Nokia had grown to be one of the largest suppliers of mobile phones and telecommunications equipment in the world. This had resulted in rapid growth of the R&D function and its consequent expansion from its original building in Camberley, Surrey into two additional buildings housing a total of 450 staff, most of whom were R&D engineers.

At the time of this case study Nokia had already begun planning for a move to a single, integrated R&D facility on a greenfield site near Camberley. The company's Facilities Department provided most support services, including facilities management, telecommunications and security, but excluding IT and personnel, and was actively involved in planning the design and operation of the new building.

Anne Johnson, Facilities Manager, had observed the problems experienced by some of Nokia's competitors, whose growth had outstripped their ability to manage it, and had resolved that the Department would support growth in demand by increased effectiveness rather than by linear growth. However, it was sometimes criticized by its customers for a lack of responsiveness to new requirements and changing patterns of demand. Anne therefore called upon the services of The OPUS Partnership to help the Department to improve its existing service to customers and to collect information about the services and facilities that these customers would expect in the new building.

'it was sometimes criticized by its customers for a lack of responsiveness to new requirements and changing patterns of demand'

The Objective of the project was to identify the needs of internal customers and current perceptions of service levels and to use an improved understanding of these needs to improve service quality, and to ensure that services in the new building would meet customer expectations.

The Facilities Department consisted of about 15 staff, and the OPUS Team involved managers and staff at all levels. It totalled about 12 people, including Anne Johnson, her two assistant managers and members of the transport, mail room, telecommunications, reception and security functions, together with Noel Austin of The OPUS Partnership.

Because the Facilities Department was small and well integrated, introductions at OPUS Team Meeting 1 were brief, and we spent a little while agreeing rules of behaviour. There was no disagreement either about the objective of the project or about the need for it, and the meeting soon moved on to a discussion of the Department's customers. These were everyone in the three Camberley buildings and also in an outpost in Bracknell, some nine miles away. These customers could be classified or segmented in a number of different ways, including: job role (e.g. manager, secretary, engineer); location; time with the company; and management level.

We then discussed the number and composition of Painstorming Groups. Team members were confident that it would be easy to recruit a dozen or so people from the four buildings for each of two Groups and that these would be enough to meet the needs of the project. They undertook to recruit participants and make arrangements for the sessions, which would be held in a conference room in one of the Camberley buildings.

Lastly, the team brainstormed a list of topics for discussion by the Painstorming Groups. These included a wide range of subjects, including: car parking, catering, security, telecomms, travel arrangements and physical working conditions.

The Painstorming Groups took place about two weeks after participants were recruited. There was no difficulty in getting the discussion going, although in each case there were people who, because of their problem-solving culture, found it easier to discuss solutions than problems. Each meeting lasted for $3\frac{1}{2}$ hours – exceptionally long by our normal standards, although experience shows that internal Groups tend to last longer than external ones. Our subsequent analysis revealed a total of 620 discrete problems – again exceptional. We prepared them for presentation to the OPUS Team by grouping under the topic headings agreed at the previous Team meeting, and deduced an underlying need for each coherent set of problems.

At OPUS Team Meeting 2 some of the problems were identified as relating to a particular situation (window locks in a particular building) or to a particular person's hobby-horse. Some of these were allowed to remain, as it was not clear to what extent these problems were shared by others, who took a lower profile in commenting on them. However, after some two hours of discussion the number of problem statements had been reduced to about 320, still double the number needed for the quantitative stage of the project. The Team decided that Anne Johnson and Noel Austin should be delegated to complete the task.

We then presented the need statements, which were debated, modified as appropriate and agreed, and finalized the segmentation questions for the Quality Barometer. It was agreed that every member of Nokia Mobile Phones staff at the four sites would receive a Box Interview.

The OPUS Partnership assembled 420 Interview Boxes and delivered them to the Facilities Department. Within two or three days all 420 boxes had been handed out and had begun to return to a central collection point in each building. When the cut-off date arrived, some 392 customer boxes (93 per cent) and 18 staff boxes (60 per cent) had been returned and were included in the results.

After data collection and processing, the results were presented to OPUS Team Meeting 3. Significant groups of high-ranked problems related to: internal communications, both electronic and paper; and health and safety issues. However, a study of the segment comparisons revealed differences between the views of the occupants of different buildings, lengths of service and job role. The Team identified that the top 31 problems overall encompassed the top 10 problems of every segment, and took the decision to institute an action programme to solve all of them over a few months.

The OPUS Team decided that, if it was to secure the support of the Department's customers for the actions it wished to take, it should publish: a summary of the results to every customer; its action plan; and regular reports on the progress made and revisions to plan if necessary. The Team therefore decided to publish a Departmental newsletter to communicate with its customers.

Actions taken in response to the high-ranked problems included:

- installation of air conditioning in buildings where there were complaints about excessive temperatures in summer;
- increased security patrols in car parks;
- increased frequency of fire drills;
- updated internal telephone directories;
- a newsletter to inform staff about progress with the new building.

The large number of problems solved led to recognition by the Department's internal customers of a widespread and substantial improvement in the service they received from the Department, despite continued growth and the disruption caused by the occupation of a further building. Plans for the new building are now well advanced, and its layout and operation have been influenced by the knowledge gained from this project.

Interviewed recently, Anne Johnson said: 'When deciding to undertake an internal customer service audit our first consideration was to find a method that would encourage our customers to respond by making it simple and interesting to use. We also wanted to sort the results in many different ways to respond to individual customer groups' needs. OPUS is ideal for this purpose. The process was really enjoyable and motivating for our people on the OPUS Team whilst being fun and quick to complete for our customers.'

Questions to consider

1 Why does a process-based approach seem to lead to better implementation of change?

2 What are the parallels and links between the OPUS model and internal marketing?

3 What are the problems for external consultants or change agents in being involved but not taking ownership of the problems? How can these be overcome?

4 What lesson can be learned from the OPUS Process that can be applied generally to implementation problems?

5 What does the Nokia case tell us about the needs for internal suppliers to take marketing seriously? Why would the external customer care?

6 What does the Otis case suggest about the problems of faulty market sensing and how to overcome them?

In 1884 the first Swallows clothing stores were established in a Victorian marketplace. Ownership of the firm passed from father to son for two generations, spanning two World Wars. In 1974 the company had 19 stores, most of which were located in traditional indoor marketplaces. Since 1974, the company has experienced a period of sustained growth. The number of stores operating has increased rapidly, and most established stores were extensively modernized, with many relocated from market outlets to larger and more modern units. In 1991 Swallows acquired 40 additional stores from a competitor, which are maintained as separate outlets administered from the company's central offices.

The growth in the number and size of Swallows Stores has resulted in expansion beyond traditional boundaries, with most new branches being opened in the South East of England and the Midlands. Presently the Group runs 142 Swallows Stores and 58 other branches, and has plans to open many more. One consequence of the increase in company size has been the relocation of central administration. The Head Office was first located above the company's (then) flagship store. Growth forced a move to separate offices, until 1996 when ever-increasing demands on Head Office led to a move of administration to a Central Office and the creation of a distribution centre on the old site.

The need for market orientation

The recession of the early 1990s had a considerable impact on the company – for the very first time the company was forced to make employees redundant. Fortunately the company fared much better than its main competitors from 1993 onwards, to the extent that the management of the company instigated a large expansion scheme which saw considerable growth in the South East of England and the Midlands. However, despite this recovery it was becoming increasingly obvious that all was not well with Swallows Stores. First, an expensive and high-profile promotional campaign did nothing to overcome a marked reduction in

---

* This case study has been prepared by Lloyd C. Harris, Cardiff Business School, on the basis of company visits and executive interviews. The company name has been changed to preserve confidentiality at the request of company executives.

'a poor winter fashion collection followed by a disastrous summer collection saw sales and profits falling well below expectations by the mid-1990s'

sales, and then the cutbacks of the early 1990s led to reduced product quality and increased expenses. Finally, a poor winter fashion collection followed by a disastrous summer collection saw sales and profits falling well below expectations by the mid-1990s.

Top management at Swallows recognized the problem at a relatively early stage. Considerable debate and analysis eventually led the directors of the company to attribute poor performance not to market conditions, but to an ever-reducing level of customer focus and market orientation. Consequently, the company attempted to reverse its paternalistic tendencies of internal promotion, and appointed new senior managers from outside the company to key positions, as a way of revitalizing the customer and market orientation of the company. More importantly, the key shareholders of the company publicly committed themselves to the need for market-led change. Unsurprisingly, the 'new blood' of Swallows faced considerable difficulties in developing and modernizing what was then a traditional and product/sales-oriented culture. Briefly, the barriers they encountered fell into two principal categories:

- Problems of traditional company assumptions and beliefs; and
- Barriers of structure, systems and strategy.

Traditional company assumptions and beliefs

The barriers from common assumptions and widely held company beliefs centred on six main issues:

- employee distrust of other employees who are 'outspoken';
- the belief that 'traditional' management is most appropriate during high growth periods;
- an assumption that store managers should be autocratic;
- a strong 'blame' culture;
- a commitment to growth rather than customer focus; and
- internal company politics.

Employee distrust of other employees who are 'outspoken'

Executives say that Swallows highly values junior employees who are heard to 'speak their minds', and within branches, Sales Assistants who speak freely to their superiors are considered 'valuable assets'. Managers believe that Managers' Assistants who offer opinions are viewed as 'full of potential – store management material'. However, in contrast to these management beliefs, employees seem to distrust and isolate employees who are viewed as 'outspoken'. Indeed, 'outspoken' for employees of Swallows means a person who challenges employees of a higher rank or who questions the actions or procedures of the company.

Cases of outspoken employees are well known. For example, a manager reports that recently at Central Support a new buyer 'lasted about two weeks before she was sacked' due to 'not fitting in', that is, challenging existing systems and structures. Similar cases are also evident at branch level, with Store Managers aware of past cases of dismissals for 'inappropriate behaviour'. The culture of Swallows is characterized by a strong belief in obedience, adherence to existing philosophies and methods, and motivated by a belief that 'speaking out' is inappropriate and disloyal.

Traditional management is most appropriate during high growth periods

Employees of Swallows hold widely shared views on the nature of their job roles. Consistently across all functions and for most hierarchical layers, employees view their job as 'fire-fighting' or 'reactionary'. Most employees consider reactive decisions to be more appropriate than proactive planning. The over-emphasis on reactive management has been recognized by certain senior Central Support Managers. However, the majority of Central Support middle-management employees consider that pressure for a more proactive stance is unrealistic because of environmental conditions.

Store managers should be autocratic

The general belief in reactive management is related to employee opinions of management styles. Particularly at branch level, employees are dismissive of consultative, or 'bureaucratic', managers or supervisors. Employees regard autocratic management from Store Managers and Central Support Managers as legitimate and proper. Indeed, employees actually seem to prefer orders rather than consultation, as they want to be told what to do, not asked their views, because 'that's the manager's job'.

A strong 'blame' culture

Discussions in the company suggest strongly that employees of Swallows tend to avoid responsibility for errors if at all possible, preferring to pass the blame to others. While employees take great care not to become 'outspoken', the organization structure and 'hands-on' top management style allows most employees to avoid taking full responsibility for actions or mistakes and to attribute errors or poor decisions to other departments or groups. At store level, branches 'blame' Central Support departments for problems, while Central Support employees tend to pass the blame to the branches. In contrast to theories of empowerment and ownership, at Swallows people compete highly effectively to avoid responsibility and ownership. Employees at Swallows generally perceive problems as somebody's *fault* rather than as an issue which needs to be addressed. The possible causes of such defensive beliefs within the

'employees of Swallows tend to avoid responsibility for errors if at all possible'

branches is probably linked to Store Managers' antipathy to Central Support management 'interference' and the belief that their authority and control techniques are poor.

A commitment to growth rather than customer focus

Employees at Swallows seemed to have fairly consistent shared views about the priorities which the organization should pursue. At the branch level, employees expressed views that they considered the main objective of the organization to be the acquisition of profit. Employees consistently held the view that company profits were only obtained via the timely and accurate supply of products to the shopfloor. Moreover, such profits were only desirable for one reason – the rapid growth of the company. However, while long-serving employees in particular considered that these should be the chief priorities of the company, it seemed that employees with wider retail experience considered that such objectives were over-emphasized by middle-management. Employees with wider experience often hold the view that other priorities should also be considered by the company. These other objectives primarily centred on a greater emphasis on staff rewards (not necessarily financial rewards), with a significant number of employees considering customer satisfaction to be an under-emphasized priority. Such responses were common from employees with wider retail experience outside Swallows and rare among long-serving employees.

The views of branch-level employees are also shared by employees at the Central Support office. However, while long-serving and more recent employees shared similar views to their branch-level counterparts, many Central Support employees added a further priority for Swallows. Briefly, many Central Support employees considered the gaining of profit for growth to be driven by the underlying objective of top management to float the company 'in the next few years'. Store employees generally considered profit to be the main priority to achieve growth, while Central Support employees considered that the overall objective was to gain profit to allow growth to enable company stock-market flotation.

Company politics

With the exception of Store Managers, store-level employees seemed unaware of, or at least not involved in, company political behaviour. However, Store Managers and Central Support employees divided into two distinct political camps. The first political group mainly comprises recently employed Central Support employees and employees with wider retail experience outside the company. This group considers the company to be too internally focused and in need of radical change. Thus, the first political grouping of employees views the development of customer orientation as crucial to future success. Moreover, this set of employees is confident of overcoming less customer oriented employees and developing positive customer orientation growth.

'This group considers the company to be too internally focused and in need of radical change'

The second political grouping is far less focused on customer orientation. This second political camp consists mainly of long-serving employees at Central Support, middle-management, or established larger branches, championed by a small (but vocal) number of top management. This political group is by far the larger of the two and has tended to be the more vociferous, even though few top managers agree. Such employees consider that the company should promote people internally and leave company-wide problems to Central Support.

Barriers from structure, strategy and systems

The barriers linked to company structure, strategy formulation/implementation and organizational systems showed six key constraints on market orientation:

- Organizational structure;
- Weak training and appraisal systems;
- Autocratic 'communication';
- Reward based on profit (not customer satisfaction);
- Insufficient strategic marketing planning; and
- Poor company image of marketing and a powerless marketing department.

Organisational structure

The Group operates with a Central Support Office and with the distribution function centrally handled from a distribution centre. These two central offices jointly serve the needs of 200 stores and branches. Employees at the Central Support offices are divided into functional groups, each headed by a General Manager who in turn reports to the Board of Directors. Branches are divided into geographical and trading name groups and are managed by an overall Area Manager. Branches are supervised by a Store Manager, a Manager's Assistant and a supervisor, with varying numbers of Sales Assistants. However, despite the above 'official' company structure, employees at Central Support and at the branches have developed a clearly defined unofficial hierarchy. Store Managers are aware that stores are viewed in hierarchical rather than geographical terms, and often describe their future career moves in terms of moves from smaller to larger stores and then to area management.

Weak training and appraisal systems

The training and appraisal systems of Swallows are noticeably geared towards the branch level. Store-level employees are supposed to be appraised every six months, but the majority of Store Managers do not consider such appraisals 'worthwhile or feasible'. The principal means of training shopfloor employees centres on a method of open learning labelled 'Know It All!'. All store-level employees are given a 'Know It All' folder on induction which contains a number of chapters relating to 'company best policy'. Employees are 'encouraged' to read chapters or sections of chapters, complete simple exercises and return the completed work sheets to their Store Manager. However, they are 'encouraged' to do this during unpaid hours or off-store and receive no financial or non-financial reward for doing so. This may explain the largely negative shopfloor attitude towards training. Consequently, branch-level employees are mostly 'trained' for their role through on-the-job experience and by other members of staff who pass on knowledge about job roles. Employees are also negative about the incompleteness of the 'Know It All' folder. At present employees have been supplied with two chapters, on merchandising and customer care, and have been waiting for 'two or three years' for the remaining 'seven or eight'.

The training of Store Managers is considered by the Store Managers to be 'infrequent', 'sporadic' or 'haphazard', with the opportunity for training 'dependent on whether you talk to the Area Manager at the right time' rather than upon real training needs. Similarly, Central Support employees view training as something which they 'have to initiate' and which is done 'infrequently'. Central Support Managers are not formally appraised in any way.

Autocratic 'communication'

Communication from Central Support to branches occurs in a number of different ways. Employees receive communications through a voice-mail system, a weekly newsletter, the periodic company newspaper or, less frequently, direct telephone communications. Store Managers are also likely to receive information through regional meetings held approximately quarterly, while Store Managers and Managers' Assistants are invited to attend company-wide conferences which are held two or three times per year. What is distinctive about Swallows' communication systems is that such methods are used primarily as a means of sending and clarifying directives rather than for two-way communication. Indeed, many Central Support departments have no formalized system for branch-level feedback.

Reward based on profit

Rewards are considered by employees to be purely financial, with few non-financial rewards. The majority of branch employees are paid an

'Rewards are considered by employees to be purely financial, with few non-financial rewards'

hourly rate which is the company standard (with extra payments for London-based employees), while Central Support employees are generally salaried. In addition to basic pay, branch employees can earn extra money for Sunday work and Bank Holiday opening. However, the main ways in which the company rewards employees is through a bonus scheme based on performance and through performance related pay (PRP). The majority of branch employees (including Store Managers) are confused as to the precise methods of calculating bonus or PRP and are unsure as to which employees are eligible (for example, part-time or full-time). Consequently, employees believe that such rewards are not necessarily designed for the benefit of employees. Employees' views on employee rewards rarely refer to non-financial rewards, such as praise. (Although some long-serving Central Support employees believe that they were rewarded for company loyalty by informal guarantees of a job for life.)

Insufficient strategic marketing planning

Interviews with long serving employees and document analysis led to the identification of a number of past company strategies. First, approximately ten years ago the growth of the number of branches was slowed in order for the company to implement a strategy of computerization and technological improvement. This strategy centred on the development of what was then one of the first EPOS systems in the United Kingdom. Since that date the principal strategic objective of Swallows has been the continuous growth of branches, with all other strategies either subservient to this objective or developing as a consequence of the growth objective. A number of tactics have been developed to aid the growth of the company, specifically improvements in the quality of merchandise, attempts at line concentration, product image improvement via the removal of the company name from garments, a streamlining of the business through technological improvements, and a phase of staff redundancies.

Past strategy development was limited to two abortive attempts at strategic planning which collapsed within a matter of months, and the most recent effort, which was in the very early stages of initiation. Strategies which emerged were informal and mostly oral, with no traceable written document of intent, strategy or tactics. A mission statement was produced for the company by the then General Manager of Personnel. The statement is widely seen to be a statement of best policy towards employees rather than a serious attempt at corporate mission.

Through discussions with long serving employees and document analysis it was also possible to identify the past activities which Swallows employees considered to be 'marketing'. The past activities of the central marketing function were heavily concentrated on in-store activity, such as point-of-sale material, store layout and promotional equipment. Point-of-sale promotion was viewed as the primary task of marketing. The presentation of products was also considered part of the remit of the marketing function, which decided hanger, label, ticket and any other printed devices which communicated image. The marketing function was also responsible for external promotional activities. This included local newspaper, radio and television advertising, often linked to some variation of sales promotion.

'*Employees are far from complimentary about the success of past marketing efforts*'

Poor image of the marketing department

Employees are far from complimentary about the success of past marketing efforts. Employees of all levels are united in agreeing that past external promotional campaigns have been unsuccessful. A television campaign featuring a well-known TV comedian is the subject of much criticism. The television, radio and poster campaign was a much talked of subject in the months running up to the start of the promotion and marketing managers were quick to capitalize on their newly found prominence.

Unfortunately the company had overestimated the potential of the promotion, leading to company-wide high-performance expectations. Despite early evidence, the conflicting messages of the promotion were confusing present customers and deterring potential customers. Managers reacted by intensifying the campaign. Eventually, sales dropped at such a rapid rate that top management stopped the campaign and many of the marketers responsible left the company. The result of this and other smaller-scale disasters is a general mistrust of *any* marketing indicatives, to the point where some Store Managers discreetly argue for the closure of the Marketing Department and the delegation of in-store promotions to Store Managers.

The future for Swallows?

The case of Swallows Stores Ltd highlights a number of common barriers to the development of a market-led company. The case illustrates that what employees believe and, more importantly, assume sets the boundaries of their behaviour and actions. Employees of Swallows distrusted other employees who were 'outspoken' because they challenged the organizational 'mind-set' and imbalance deeply held beliefs and assumptions. This is also apparent in employee attitudes towards Store Managers. Traditional and autocratic management is valued because it is a comfortable style for all concerned; managers give orders and employees unquestioningly obey. This issue is linked to the strong 'blame' culture of the company wherein employees avoid responsibility and ownership, preferring to attribute fault rather than solve problems. The problems of the company are compounded in a commitment to growth that frequently overrides a focus on customer needs and which has led to the formation of politically active groups.

The barriers of traditional company assumptions and beliefs are manifested in structural, systemic and strategic obstacles. Swallows is structured in a way which is geared towards rapid growth and not customer-friendliness. Similarly, a market-led focus is not apparent in systems which reward for store sales, not customer satisfaction, and training and appraisal systems which are incomplete and unrealistic. These problems are probably compounded by an insufficient emphasis on long-term considerations; issues which are apparent in weak strategy development and a much maligned Marketing Department. In summary, traditional employee beliefs and assumptions are manifested in company systems, structures and strategies which combine to impede the potential for market-led change.

Questions to consider

1 If the company is committed to building and sustaining a higher degree of market orientation or customer focus, how can they deal with the internal cultural barriers to this change?

2 To what extent are the company's problems the result of mixed messages being sent by management to employees?

3 How can a marketing department in this type of situation establish a useful and productive role for itself?

4 Is it possible to fit this company's problems into an internal marketing framework and to use this to develop ideas about how to manage the change that the company seems to want? Do the 'levels' of internal marketing become important?

5 Is customer focus (or market orientation) part of this company's market strategy – or is it an afterthought? Why do they want it? What happens if they do not get it?

6 How could the company revise its processes and systems to improve the customer focus it achieves?

7 Is this company one where a move from outcome-based to behaviour-based management would be effective?

INDEX